Forensic Management
of Sexual Offenders

PERSPECTIVES IN SEXUALITY
Behavior, Research, and Therapy

Series Editor: RICHARD GREEN

University of Cambridge
Cambridge, England, United Kingdom and
Gender Identity Clinic
Charing Cross Hospital
London, England, United Kingdom

Forensic Management of Sexual Offenders

Robert Alan Prentky, Ph.D.
Justice Resource Institute
Bridgewater, Massachusetts

and

Ann Wolbert Burgess, D.N.Sc.
University of Pennsylvania
Philadelphia, Pennsylvania

Kluwer Academic / Plenum Publishers
New York, Boston, Dordrecht, London, Moscow

Library of Congress Cataloging-in-Publication Data

Prentky, R. A.
    Forensic management of sexual offenders/Robert Alan Prentky and Ann Wolbert
Burgess.
        p. cm. —(Perspectives in sexuality)
    Includes bibliographical references and index.
    ISBN 0-306-46278-8
    1. Sex crimes. 2. Sex crimes—Investigation. 3. Sexology—Research. 4. Forensic
sciences. I. Burgess, Ann Wolbert. II. Title. III. Series.
HV6556 .P74 2000
616.85'83—dc21
                                                                                                00-029631

ISBN 0-306-46278-8

©2000 Kluwer Academic/Plenum Publishers
233 Spring Street, New York, N.Y. 10013

http://www.wkap.nl/

10 9 8 7 6 5 4 3 2 1

A C.I.P. record for this book is available from the Library of Congress.

Printed in the United States of America

Preface

Over the past several decades the seeming escalation of crimes involving sexually deviant, coercive, and aggressive behavior has become an increasingly serious problem, manifested in costs to both victims and society at large. The long-term psychological impact of sexual assault on adult and child victims has been documented numerous times. The costs incurred by society include a network of medical and psychological services provided to aid victim recovery, the investigation, trial, and incarceration of offenders—often in segregated units or special facilities—and the invisible but tangible blanket of fear that forces potential victims to schedule normal daily activities around issues of safety. Despite the gravity of the problem, there has been a paucity of empirical research directed at the etiology, course, remediation, and management of sexually deviant and coercive behavior. In treating these disorders and in making crucial decisions about how to manage these offenders, clinicians have been forced to rely on their personal experience. Such experience by its nature is unsystematic and lacks the validation that empirical research provides.

The lack of sound empirical data addressing the problem is certainly noteworthy, though not surprising. The paucity of research in this area may well be attributable to historical scientific timidity about most aspects of sexual behavior. In 1922 Dr. Robert L. Dickinson, writing in the *Journal of the American Medical Association*, stated that "in view of the pervicacious gonadal urge in human beings, it is not a little curious that science develops its sole timidity about the pivotal point of the physiology of sex" (Henderson, 1981, p. 6). Indeed, Dickinson's observation would apply to most, if not all, aspects of sexuality.

Perhaps the most well-known study of "sexual deviation" was that by the neuropsychiatrist Richard von Krafft-Ebing. Although he was a prolific writer on many aspects of psychiatry, Krafft-Ebing is best remembered for his textbook, *Psychopathia Sexualis*, a study of over 200 forensic case histories. He wrote in the Preface to the first edition of that book, "The object of this treatise is merely to record the various psychopathological manifestations of sexual life in man and to reduce them to their lawful condition." Krafft-Ebing received severe criticism, if not censure, for the book. In 1893, the *British Medical Journal* remarked, "Better if it had been written entirely in Latin, and thus veiling in the decent obscurity of a dead language" (p. xl). Krafft-Ebing must have anticipated the furor his book would arouse. He resigned his professorship at Strasbourg and founded the Sanatorium Mariagrun, near Graz, Austria, where he lived in seclusion during the 1880s. When professional and public outcry diminished, Krafft-Ebing was called by the University of Vienna to assume the highest academic post by taking over Meynert's clinic and teaching activities. Apparently immune to criticism over his highly controversial book, Krafft-Ebing revised *Psychopathia Sexualis* through the 12th edition.

Roughly 100 years after Krafft-Ebing's death, we have replaced Victorian reserve with a post-Modern sexual revival, characterized by explicit and widespread use of sexuality in media, entertainment, advertising, and marketing. This apparent "renaissance" in sexuality has *not*, however, translated into an equivalent renaissance in empiricism. Since sex remains fundamentally tawdry, it remains off-limits for scholarly inquiry. As recently as 1989, the task of gathering epidemiological data in the fight against AIDS was mired in Congressional controversy.

Perhaps even more than other areas of sexuality, human sexual aggression has long been in the shadow, discredited as a subject of respectable scientific inquiry or reserved for ideological sparring. With the exception of some excellent infrahuman research, there has been, until recently, precious little empirical work done on sexually coercive and aggressive behavior. The past two decades, however, have witnessed major scholarly contributions to this field and the exponential growth of the Association for the Treatment of Sexual Abusers, a fledgling organization in 1987 that now has more than 1500 members, sponsors an annual international research and training conference that attracts over 1200 participants, and publishes its own research journal.

In this book we review and discuss the major advances that have taken place over the past 20 years in the management of human sexual aggression. This book is, first and foremost, a forensic volume, intended to reflect what we know and don't know about the most effective management of sexual offenders. In so doing, we also attempt to tackle major controversies and obstacles that we face. It is our principal goal to separate supposition from fact and myth from reality. By employing an empirical litmus test, we hope to identify what is known, what are sound, empirically based hunches, what is mere speculation, and what probably lies in the realm of mythology. To reduce somewhat the scope of this undertaking, we have focused on those aspects of the problem that have the most immediate and urgent impact on society: the legal disposition and management of sex offenders. Although the greater problem of sexual coercion and violence is a social problem, indeed perhaps a public health crisis, the most immediate need is to assist the virtual army of specialists who attend to every facet of the management of known sex offenders. It is for those specialists—clinicians, forensic examiners, attorneys, judges, investigators, parole agents, probation officers, policy- and lawmakers, and social scientists—that we wrote this book.

The book presents a dual perspective, that of a forensic psychologist and a forensic nurse. Our colleagueship began in the early 1980s at a National Institute of Mental Health conference on the treatment of sex offenders. That meeting led to our collaborative work over the past two decades. Combined, our work with sexual offenders spans more than 50 years. The roots of this volume originated at a National Academy of Sciences Panel on Understanding and Control of Violence. The commissioned report on sexual violence (by

R.A.P.) led to a collaborative effort to revise and redirect the core of the report around the central theme of management. It is our singular mission to assist the field through cautious, prudent analysis of what is known, and judicious recommendations, guided by empirical data. The speed with which this field is evolving is at once exhilarating and daunting, leaving us with the necessary admonition that relatively little of what we share with our readers today may apply tomorrow.

Acknowledgments

There are numerous individuals to whom I (R.A.P.) owe a very considerable debt of gratitude, most notably the many colleagues who have been my mentors over the years and the deep generosity of the federal agencies (the National Institute of Justice and the National Institute of Mental Health) that have supported our research over the past 20 years. Dick Laymon and Christy Visher, both of NIJ, and Jim Breiling (NIMH) have guided and shepherded our research projects for over two decades. Their confidence and support have been unwavering.

In particular, I would like to thank my research colleague of two decades, Ray Knight, for his unrelenting devotion to empiricism and his infusion of science into a deeply flagging field. Ray and I enjoyed the most dedicated and talented research team that any empiricist could hope for. Although the research staff are far too great in number to list, I would be remiss if I failed to mention two old-timers, Alison Martino and David Cerce, who have been stoically gathering and coding data nonstop for the past 22 years. I have treasured a very special collegial relationship over the years with Enny Cramer, Tim Foley, Don Grubin, Bert Harris, Roy Hazelwood, Marty Kafka, Austin Lee, Nathaniel Pallone, Sue Righthand, Theo Seghorn, and, of course, my coauthor Ann. Theo, who surely is one of the most unheralded pioneers of this field, has been a wise and loyal friend and advisor, as well as the magnet that drew me into this field. A very dear friend, the late Fay Honey Knopp, provided me with strength and inspiration during the hardest of times.

There are many others who, in the course of preparing this book, helped to locate and supply much needed articles. We would like to thank, in particular, Lloyd Sinclair, Asher Pacht, Robert Miller, Kim English, Steve Hart, and Roxanne Lieb. We would also like to thank Karl Hanson, Steve Hart, Vern Quinsey, Douglas Epperson, and David Thornton for permitting us to include their risk assessment scales in the Appendix of this book. We also wish to acknowledge with gratitude the Colorado Division of Criminal Justice and the U.S. Bureau of Justice Assistance (D97–DB–15A–694) for permitting the reproduction of Colorado's Sexual Predator Risk Assessment Screening Instrument.

We would like to extend a very special thanks to Assistant Attorney General Laurie Robinson of the U.S. Department of Justice and her Special Counsel Marlene Beckman for the courage and the wisdom to bring to fruition the Center for Sex Offender Management, and to Mimi Carter of the Center for Effective Public Policy and Project Director of CSOM, for her tireless energy and enthusiasm that has made CSOM the first major interdisciplinary, federally initiated and funded undertaking to stem the tide of sexual violence. To the best of our knowledge, the federal government has never before undertaken a project of such scope, magnitude, and potential benefit.

We would like to acknowledge, with thanks, the American Psychological Association for permitting the reproduction of text and tables from two of our earlier articles (*Journal of Consulting and Clinical Psychology* [1997, *65*, 141–149] and *Journal of Abnormal Psychology* [1969, *74*, 249–255]). We are grateful to Kluwer Academic/Plenum Publishers for permitting reproduction of material from articles appearing in *Sexual Abuse: A Journal of Research and Treatment* (1997, *9*(4), 335–347) and *Law and Human Behavior* (1997, *21*, 635–659), and to *Criminal Behaviour and Mental Health* for permitting reproduction of text appearing in *CB&MH* (1993, *3*, 381–392).

Finally, it is with all my love that I (R.A.P.) dedicate this book to my wife Jackie and our children Michael, Jeffrey, and Samara.

Contents

CHAPTER 1

Incidence and Prevalence

Perhaps one the murkiest and most contentious questions concerns the frequency of sexual violence. More than any other type of criminal conduct, sexual offenses, in their extraordinary diversity, are likely to fade into the unfathomable abyss of human experience, never to be known by the criminal justice system. The innumerable problems that plague investigators who have estimated the frequency (or incidence) of rape and child molestation were reviewed by Quinsey (1986). Essentially, those same problems remain unsolved today.

To begin with, the terms *prevalence* and *incidence* are often confused or used interchangeably. Incidence, which refers to the number of behaviors of a particular type, may, at the present time, be more reliable than prevalence, which refers to the proportion of people who engage in the particular behavior. Incidence is a simple frequency and should provide a larger predictive target and be less sensitive to underreporting. Other problems include the lack of precision in the specification of the domain of criminal behaviors being estimated, sampling biases, definitional ambiguities, and the variety of sources used for data acquisition. Although these methodological problems plague incidence estimates in most areas of criminal conduct, sexual crimes seem to be especially affected. Sexual offenses, for instance, are not as behaviorally "clean" as nonsexual crimes such as robbery, burglary, auto theft, or assault and battery. That is, sexual assaults often include nonsexual offenses (e.g., kidnap, breaking and entering, robbery, simple assault), as well as a variety of different sexual offenses. The charges resulting from such a string of criminal acts will differ from one district attorney's office to another, and the resulting conviction may be for a "lesser" offense that is *non*sexual (e.g., pleading out to simple assault). Given all of these "constraints" imposed by the vagaries of the legal system, it is not the least surprising that incidence/prevalence estimates are remarkably "soft" (i.e., wide variations between estimates and wide ranges within estimates).

UNDERREPORTING

One of the most serious impediments to estimating incidence and/or prevalence is underreporting. The March 1985 BJS Bulletin noted that

In the course of twice-a-year interviews conducted with more than 125,000 people each year in the National Crime Survey, only about 100 cases of rape or attempted rape are reported. When the sample is compared to the size of the general population, it is estimated that *each reported incident represents about 1,200 rapes or rape attempts that took place across the country.* (p. 1)

The National Crime Survey estimated that during the 10-year period from 1973 to 1982, there were about 1.5 million rapes or attempted rapes in the United States (Bureau of Justice Statistics [BJS], 1985), yielding an estimated annual rate of 150,000.

Although the magnitude of the problem of underreporting differs considerably according to the victim age and gender, we can offer reasonable hypotheses about where the problem is greatest. Underreporting tends to be greater when offenses are committed:

- Against boys than against girls
- Against teenagers than against children
- Against teenage boys than against teenage girls
- Against known victims than against strangers (for both children and adults)
- Against adult men than against adult women

In addition, the lower the violence, the higher the underreporting, particularly with adult victims.

ESTIMATED FREQUENCY OF SEXUAL ASSAULT OF ADULT WOMAN

The study by Koss, Gidycz, and Wisniewski (1987), based on a self-report question-naire administered to 6159 students enrolled in 32 colleges and universities across the United States, revealed that, of the responding women, 15.4% reported being raped, 12.1% reported an attempted rape, and another 11.9% reported some form of sexual coercion. Of the responding men, 25.1% reported involvement in some form of sexual aggression. The victimization rate of 38 per 1000 from this study indicated that 38 out of every 1000 women reported being raped during the preceding 6 months (using the FBI's narrower definition of rape, which is restricted to forced or attempted vaginal intercourse). The perpetration rate of 9 per 1000 from this study indicated that 9 out of every 1000 men reported that they raped a woman during the preceding 6 months. Koss et al. (1987) noted that the rape victimization rate of 38 per 1000 was 10–15 times higher than the rates that are based on data from the National Crime Survey. Koss (1990) noted that ''the most important conclusion, however, is that *all* of the studies document levels of violence that far outdistance official estimates. They suggest a scourge, if not an epidemic, of violence against women in the United States'' (p. 375). Gavey (1991) replicated the findings of Koss et al. (1987) in New Zealand. Gavey administered Koss' Sexual Experiences Survey to 347 female and 176 male under-graduates. Over half of the women (51.6%) reported some type of sexual victimization and one-quarter (25.3%) reported rape or attempted rape.

Johnson (1980) did a prevalence study using life-table analysis. Based on age-specific rape rates from the National Crime Surveys in 1972 on 250,000 people in 13 cities, he estimated the probability that a woman would be the victim of sexual violence during her lifetime. He concluded that ''nationally, a conservative estimate is that, under current conditions, 20–30% of girls now under twelve years old will suffer a violent sexual attack during the remainder of their lives'' (p. 145). Russell (1984) sought to replicate this finding using age-specific rape rates derived from her survey of 930 women in San Francisco in 1978. Unlike the NCS data, which are based on subjects who are 12 years of age or older, Russell's data included experiences at any time during the subject's life. Nevertheless, her finding of a 26% probabilty that a woman will be raped at some point in her life is quite comparable to Johnson's report. Herman (1981) reviewed the findings of five retrospective surveys of sexual abuse in female children. Based on interviews with a combined sample of over 5000 adult women, Herman found that 20 to 33% reported some form of sexual victimization by an adult male during childhood. Even the original Kinsey studies of 40 years ago, based on interviews with over 4000 women in the United States, revealed that 24% had experienced sexual advances by a man over the age of 15 and at least 5 years older than themselves when they were under 14 years of age (West, 1981).

A national probability sample of 2008 people in Canada revealed that 54% of the women and 31% of the men had experienced unwanted sexual advances at some point in their lives (Badgley, 1984). Of those women who reported an unwanted sexual advance, 22% defined the "advance" as an assault or attempted assault. The equivalent figure for the men was 15%. These figures are all the more noteworthy given that Canada has a relatively low sexual assault rate compared to the United States (Quinsey, 1984).

Overall, the National Victim Center and Crime Victims Research and Treatment Center reported in 1992 that 13% of all adult American women have been the victim of forcible rape at some time in their lives (NVC/CVRTC, 1992). The NVC/CVRTC Report estimated that there were 683,000 forcible rapes during 1992, which translated to about 1871 rapes per day. The American Psychological Association's Task Force on Male Violence Against Women concluded that "between 14% and 25% of adult women have endured rape according to its legal definition" (Goodman, Koss, Fitzgerald, Russo, & Keita, 1993, p. 1055). Goodman et al. (1993) remarked that "perhaps the most startling theme to emerge from these articles is the extraordinarily high prevalence of male violence against women," (p. 1055). Senator Joseph Biden (1993) observed that

> If the leading newspapers were to announce tomorrow a new disease that, over the past year, had afflicted from 3 to 4 million citizens, few would fail to appreciate the seriousness of the illness. Yet, when it comes to the 3 to 4 million women who are victimized by violence each year, the alarms ring softly. (p. 1059)

Although numerous methodological problems clearly preclude any definitive conclusions (see Koss, 1993a,b), a diverse cross-section of studies spanning several decades suggest that approximately 25% of adult women have experienced some form of sexual victimization and somewhere between 10 and 15% of women have been raped.

Hidden Rape and Social Acquaintance Rape

Although hidden rape and social acquaintance rape are operationally distinct, they are often discussed in the same context. Hidden rape refers simply to sexual assaults that were never reported to the police or to a rape crisis center. Social acquaintance rape (or "date" rape) refers to an initially consenting social encounter that eventuates in a sexual assault. Since social acquaintance rape is much more likely to go unreported than stranger rape, there is substantial overlap between the two.

In her well-known study of rape on college campuses, Koss (1988; Koss et al., 1987) administered a self-report questionnaire to a sample of 6159 students enrolled in 32 colleges and universities throughout the United States. In brief, 15.4% of the women reported that they had experienced, and 4.4% of the men reported that they had perpetrated, since the age of 14, an act that qualified as rape. Based on her findings, Koss estimated that the victimization rate for women was 38/1000, which is 10–15 times higher than the rates based on the annual National Crime Survey (Bureau of Justice Statistics, 1984). The NCS rates were 3.9/1000 for women aged 16–19 and 2.5/1000 for women aged 20–24. The self-reported rape rate by the men, which is undoubtedly conservative, is 9/1000. Even this rate, however, is 2–3 times higher than NCS estimates of the high risk of rape for women between the ages of 16 and 24. These figures reflect, of course, victimization rates only among college students.

A small sample of 71 self-disclosed date rapists at a university suggested to Kanin (1984) that date rape is an "extraordinarily under-reported offense." Despite the fact that his sample was markedly *unrepresentative*, consisting only of those men who volunteered, Kanin nevertheless found that the self-reported rape rate was three times higher than the "official" rape rate of the local community in which the university was located. Rapoport and Burkhart (1984) examined a sample of 201 male university students, finding that 15% of the students reported raping at least once or twice and 12% reported physically restraining a woman during a sexual encounter. A total of 28% of the students reported using a "directly coercive method" at least once and only 39% of the students denied any coercive sexual involvement. Rapoport and Burkhart (1984) found that two scales on the California Personality Inventory (Re & So) predicted the amount of sexually coercive behavior. Low scores on these two scales suggest immaturity, irresponsibility, and a lack of social conscience. Struckman-Johnson (1988) found that 22% of a sample of 355 university women reported having been raped on a date, while 10% of a sample of 268 university men reported that they had forced sex on a date at least once.

Although several studies have looked at the personality correlates of date rapists (e.g., Kanin, 1985; Koss & Dinero, 1988; Koss, Leonard, Beezley, & Oros, 1985; Rapoport & Burkhart, 1984) and attributions of responsibility for date rape (Collier & Resick, 1987; Kanekar & Vaz, 1983; Mazelan, 1980), the *major* contribution of the studies on hidden rape and date rape is to underscore the prevalence of rape and the apparent size of the gap between *official* and *real* victimization rates. There is no reliable evidence to suggest that the "date rapist" constitutes a taxonomically homogeneous group and should thus be considered as a unique subtype. Although several writers have identified subtypes with profiles that match some of the hypothesized features of the date rapist (e.g., the "double-standard" rapist of Gebhard, Gagnon, Pomeroy, & Christenson, 1965, and the "masculine identity conflict" rapist of Rada, 1978b), Knight and Prentky (1990) have maintained that a variety of different subtypes of rapists, similar only in that they all have low levels of expressive aggression, could commit "date" or social acquaintance rapes.

Intimate Violence

Intimate violence may be defined as violence between individuals who have an intimate relationship (spouses and former spouses, boyfriends, girlfriends, and former boyfriends and girlfriends). Greenfeld (1998) reported that in 1996 there were 1800 homicides of intimates. Approximately 75% of the victims were female. The incidence of lethal violence appears to have dropped over the preceding 20 years, from 3000 victims of intimate murder in 1976. In general, murder of an intimate accounts for about 10% of the murders nationwide in a given year. The number of known victims of nonlethal violence is around 1 million per year. Again, there appears to be a decline, from 1.1 million in 1993 to an estimated 840,000 victims in 1996. Overall, about 85% of the victims of intimate violence are female. These estimates come from National Crime Victimization Survey data, and include a range of crimes involving interpersonal violence (robbery, rape, sexual assault, simple assault, aggravated assault, murder).

ESTIMATED FREQUENCY OF SEXUAL ASSAULT OF CHILDREN

If the problems inherent in estimating the frequency of rape are sufficiently daunting, the problems of estimating the frequency of child molestation are even greater. Most of the problems mentioned with regard to rape seem to be magnified when it comes to child molestation.

The assumption that sexual crimes against children and teenagers are drastically underreported is now accepted as a virtual truism. One of the strongest sources of evidence for this assumption comes from offenders themselves, who report vastly more victims than they have been convicted of.

Perhaps the most dramatic self-report data on victimization rates *from offenders* come from the research of Abel and his colleagues (Abel & Rouleau, 1990; Abel et al., 1987). Abel et al. (1987) recruited 561 subjects through a variety of sources (e.g., health care workers, media advertising, presentations at meetings). The subjects were given a lengthy structured clinical interview covering standard demographic information as well as a history of deviant sexual behavior. The 561 subjects reported a total of 291,737 "paraphiliac acts" committed against 195,407 victims. The five most frequently reported paraphiliac acts all involved criminal conduct: (1) nonincestuous child molestation with a female victim (224 of the 561 subjects reported 5197 acts against 4435 victims); (2) nonincestuous child molestation with a male victim (153 of the 561 subjects reported 43,100 acts against 22,981 victims); (3) incest with a female victim (159 of the 561 subjects reported 12,927 acts against 286 victims); (4) incest with a male victim (44 of the 561 subjects reported 2741 acts against 75 victims); rape (126 of the 561 subjects reported 907 acts against 882 victims). The remaining 16 categories included a wide range of paraphilias, which may or may not have involved coercion. The first five categories included a total of 64,872 acts. The total number of subjects and victims involved cannot be determined since the categories are overlapping (i.e., many subjects reported multiple paraphilias and hence were recorded in multiple categories). As Chappell (1989) pointed out, it is impossible to determine how representative these offenders are compared to all of the nonincarcerated or unidentified sex offenders in the population.

Fromuth, Burkhart, and Jones (1991) examined the "hidden child molestation" of adolescents by asking 582 college men to fill out a questionnaire. Only 3% of the sample acknowledged that they had sexually abused a child, prompting the authors to offer a host of possible reasons for this presumed underestimate. Briere and Runtz (1989) found that 21% of their college students reported some degree of sexual attraction to children and 7% revealed some inclination to have sex with a child if they could be assured immunity from prosecution. The 7% figure might have come very close to the 3% figure reported by

Fromuth et al. (1991) if Briere and Runtz had asked whether the subjects had in fact molested a child. Based on data averaged from two telephone surveys, Finkelhor and Lewis (1988) estimated that 10% of the adult men admitted to sexually abusing a child.

Rather than relying on the questionable veracity of adults' reports of highly socially disapproved behavior, Finkelhor and Dziuba-Leatherman (1994a) conducted a national telephone survey of 2000 children between the ages of 10 and 16. Sexual abuse involving physical contact was reported by 3.2% of the girls and 0.6% of the boys, revealing "levels of child victimization that far exceed those reported in official government victimization statistics" (Finkelhor & Dziuba-Leatherman, 1994a, p. 415). The rape rate, for instance, was about 5 times higher than the estimate of 0.1% reported in the National Crime Survey. Finkelhor and Dziuba-Leatherman (1994b) concluded that, "one reality, not widely recog-nized, is that children are more prone to victimization than adults are" (p. 173). One example offered is the rape rate, which is 1.60 per 1000 for adolescents (ages 12–19) and 0.50 per 1000 for adults. The overall rate for sexual abuse among children and teenagers (ages 0–17) in 1991 was 6.3 per 1000, a threefold increase since 1986 when the equivalent rate was determined to be 2.1 (Finkelhor & Dziuba-Leatherman, 1994b).

Finkelhor (1994) surveyed the estimates of child sexual abuse in 21 countries, includ-ing the United States and Canada. All studies reported rates of abuse that were quite com-parable to the rates in North America, ranging from 7 to 36% for women and 3 to 29% for men. In general, females are abused 1½ to 3 times more frequently than males. Given the aforementioned methodological problems that compromise the accuracy of frequency estimates of child sexual abuse, the ranges provided in these recent studies, particularly the studies employing national probability samples, are probably our "best guesses" at this time.

The National Survey of Adolescents (NSA) conducted telephone interviews with 4023 male and female adolescents and parents or guardians (Kilpatrick & Saunders, 1997). Extrapolating from the NSA sample to the national population of adolescents, Kilpatrick and Saunders (1997) concluded that of the 22.3 million adolescents (ages 12–17) in the United States, roughly 1.8 million have been the victim of a serious sexual assault, 3.9 million have been the victim of a serious physical assault, and almost 9 million have witnessed violence.

Holmes and Slap (1998) examined the prevalence of sexual abuse of boys by identifing 166 studies representing 149 samples of sexually abused children. Prevalence estimates varied enormously, from 4% to 76%, depending on how sexual abuse was defined and the type of sample studied. Boys at highest risk for sexual abuse were: (1) non-Caucasian, (2) 12 years old or younger, (3) of low socioeconomic status, and (4) not living with their father. The perpetrators were likely to be known to the victims but unrelated. The abuse most often occurred outside of the victim's home, involved penetration, and multiple assaults. Holmes and Slap (1998) concluded that "sexual abuse of boys appears to be common, under-reported, underrecognized, and undertreated. Negative sequelae are highly prevalent and may contribute to the evolution from young victim to older perpetrator" (p. 1860).

NIS FINDINGS

The National Incidence Study of Child Abuse and Neglect (NIS) is a Congressionally mandated task assigned to the National Center on Child Abuse and Neglect (NCCAN).

NCCAN conducted NIS-1 in 1979 and 1980, and the findings were published in 1981. NCCAN conducted NIS-2 in 1986 and 1987, and the findings were published in 1988. NCCAN conducted NIS-3 in 1993 and 1994, and the findings were published in 1996. One of the principal objectives of NIS-3 was to examine changes in incidence estimates from NIS-1 and NIS-2.

The NIS studies attempted to assess more accurately the scope of child abuse and neglect by including *all* cases known to professionals, not just those cases that were officially recognized by the system. NIS data are collected from child protective service workers, law enforcement records, juvenile probation records, hospitals, schools, day-care agencies, mental health and public health workers, and social service agencies. The NIS-3 study included data on 50,729 cases.

Overall, NIS-3 found that 1.6 million children were victims of maltreatment (rate of 23.1 per 1000 children under the age of 18). Of these children, 743,200 were victims of physical, sexual, or emotional abuse (rate of 11.1 per 1000 children) and 879,000 were victims of neglect (rate of 13.1 per 1000 children). According to NIS-3 findings, there were 217,700 victims of sexual abuse, with a rate of 3.2 per 1000 children. This rate is, of course, about one-half that reported by Finkelhor and Dziuba-Leatherman (1994b). Although girls were sexually abused about three times more often than boys, boys were at greater risk of serious injury than girls.

NCVS FINDINGS

The National Crime Victimization Survey (NCVS) was started by the Bureau of Justice Statistics of the Office of Justice Programs (Department of Justice) in 1972 to complement the FBI's Uniform Crime Report. The NCVS gathers reports from a nationally representative sample of 100,000 respondents in 50,000 households. Respondents, aged 12 or older, are asked about any crimes that they experienced, whether or not the crime was known to the criminal justice system. The most recent summary of NCVS findings was reported by Greenfeld in a February 1997 Bureau of Justice Statistics pamphlet entitled "Sex Offenses and Offenders" (NCJ-163392).

The number of rapes and sexual assaults reported by respondents (aged 12 or older) in 1995 was approximately 355,000, with about 90% of the victims being female. During that same year, the number of forcible rapes reported to the police throughout the country was 97,460, about one-fourth the number reported to the NCVS researchers (Greenfeld, 1997). Approximately 90% of rapes and sexual assaults were perpetrated by a single offender. In almost three-fourths of the assaults (73.5%), the victims were known to the perpetrators (i.e., nonstrangers).

SEXUAL HOMICIDE

Although sexual homicide remains the highest profile crime by media standards, it continues to represent a miniscule percentage of the homicide rate. Between 1976 and 1994 there were (estimated) 405,089 murders in the United States (Greenfeld, 1997). Of these murders, the circumstances surrounding the murder was known in 317,925 cases (78.5%).

Of these 317,925 murders, 4807 (1.5%) were classified as sexual homicides. If we examine the number of sexual homicides only within the past decade, the proportion has declined to less than 1% (Greenfield, 1997). Thus, in any given year there are approximately 20,000 homicides in the United States, and, of that number, 200–300 will be classifiable as sexual murders.

Of those who commit sexual homicide, 95% are male, 58% are Caucasian and 40% are African-American. Unlike nonlethal sexual assaults, in cases of sexual homicide the victim is more likely to be a stranger (approximately 40% of the time, compared with about 25% of the time with nonlethal sexual assault). The victim–offender relationship changes, however, when the victim is a child. Of the 405,000 murders between 1976 and 1994, about 11% (37,000) were of children. When young children are murdered, the killer is most often a member of the child's family. When older (adolescent) children are murdered, the killer is more likely to be an acquaintance or unknown to the victim.

Between 1976 and 1994, approximately 37,000 children were murdered (Greenfield, 1996). The victim–killer relationship in child homicide varies according to the age of the victim. Young children are more likely to have been murdered by a family member, while teenagers are more likely to have been murdered by an acquaintance or a stranger (Green-feld, 1996). Overall, about 20% of child murders are committed by family members, and another 20% of child murders are committed by another child (Greenfield, 1996).

NIBRS

As Greenfield (1997) noted, the new National Incident-Based Reporting System is the "next generation" of data on criminal offenses. NIBRS will replace the antequated 70-year old Unified Crime Reports (UCR) that collected aggregate data on eight categories of crimes. Rather than restricting itself to these eight "index" crimes, the NIBRS will gather data on 57 types of crimes. Unlike both the UCR and NCVS, which categorized sexual assault into two groups (UCR: Forcible Rape and Sex Offenses; NCVS: Rape and Sexual Assault), NIBRS classifies sexual assault into six categories: Forcible Rape, Statutory Rape, Forcible Sodomy, Sexual Assault, Forcible Fondling, and Incest. In a pilot phase of the NIBRS, the first three NIBRS-participating states (Alabama, North Dakota, and South Carolina) have already submitted their data to the Bureau of Justice Statistics.

In Conclusion

Although it is not possible to measure with precision the magnitude of the problem, it is reasonable and defensible to conclude that approximately 1 million children, teenagers, and adults are victims of sexual assault each year. It is all too apparent that, as Senator Biden (1993) noted, any medical condition of comparable gravity and scope would elicit a rapid and concerted response.

CHAPTER 2

Victim Impact

Over the past several decades our awareness of the magnitude and the impact of sexual victimization has increased considerably. Sexual abuse has become an acute problem, manifested in ever-increasing costs to society as well as to its victims. The costs incurred by society include medical and psychological services to aid victim recovery, the apprehension and disposition of offenders, and the invisible climate of fear that makes safety a paramount consideration in scheduling normal daily activities. In addition to the monetary costs associated with sexual abuse (see Prentky & Burgess, 1990), the impact of such abuse on its victims has been well documented.

RAPE AND SEXUAL ASSAULT

Empirical research on sexual violence against women and children is a relatively young and fragmented field. The reemergence of the women's movement in the late 1960s and early 1970s helped to focus attention on the plight of the rape victim, and the establishment of the National Center on the Prevention and Control of Rape in the mid-1970s provided governmental support and a funding mechanism for research. The closing of the Center in the late 1980s left a void for funding until 1994, when Congress directed the National Research Council to develop a research agenda to increase understanding and control of violence against women, focusing primarily on prevention, education, social and legal strategies, including consideration of the needs of underserved populations.

The consequences of rape and sexual assault are broader than the specific traumatic impact it has on victims. Families, spouses, and friends may well be affected. Society suffers economically, both in the use of resources and in the loss of productivity related to fear and injury. Research has brought an increased understanding of the impact of trauma, in general, and of interpersonal violence, in particular. Rape and sexual assault are associated with a host of short- and long-term problems, including physical injury and illness, psychological symptoms, economic costs, and death. It is important to recognize at the outset that part of what is known about the consequences to victims comes from studies of

9

people who were seeking help. Such victims may *not* be representative of all victims. These victims may have suffered more severe trauma than victims who did not seek help, thus biasing the results toward the most severe cases. The opposite is also possible, that victims who have come forward have suffered less fear and damage to their self-esteem and therefore the worst cases remain hidden. Victims who agree to participate in research may come from very different social, ethnic, and economic backgrounds than those who do not participate. Finally, researchers do not always have the understanding or resources to reach subgroups of victims who may either be at high risk for violence or face special challenges in recovery (Crowell & Burgess, 1996). The impact of sexual assault on victims may, nevertheless, be summarized in two major areas: impact from rape and sexual assault in adulthood and impact from sexual abuse in childhood and adolescence.

IMPACT FROM RAPE AND SEXUAL ASSAULT IN ADULTHOOD

Physical Consequences

Surveys of adult females have found that women believe that in a "typical" rape there is a high risk of physical injury and possibly death (Gordon & Riger, 1989; Warr, 1985). The data indicate, however, that between one-half and two-thirds of rape victims sustain no physical injuries (Beebe, 1991; Kilpatrick, Edmunds, & Seymour, 1992; Koss, Woodruff, & Koss, 1991); and only about 4% sustain serious physical injuries (Kilpatrick et al., 1992). Genital injuries are more likely in elderly victims (Muram, Miller, & Cutler, 1992). Very few homicides are associated with rape. In 1993, for instance, only 106 of the 5278 female homicide victims were reported to have been raped (Federal Bureau of Investigation, 1993). Even though serious physical injury is relatively rare, the fear of serious injury or death during rape remains very real.

Rape can also result in transmission of a sexually transmitted disease (STD) to the victim, or in pregnancy. STD infection has been found in up to 43% of rape victims (Jenny et al., 1990), with most studies reporting STD infection rates between approximately 5 and 15% depending on diseases screened for and type of test used (Beebe, 1991; Lacey, 1990; Murphy, 1990). The rate of transmission of human immunodeficiency virus (HIV) related to rape is unknown (Koss et al., 1994) but is of concern to a sizable proportion of rape victims (Baker, Burgess, Davis, & Brickman, 1990). Approximately 5% of rapes result in pregnancy (Beebe, 1991; Koss et al., 1991).

Rape has health effects beyond the emergency period. Self-report and interview-administered symptom checklists routinely reveal that victims of rape or sexual assault experienced more symptoms of physical and psychological ill health than nonvictimized women (Golding, 1994; Kimerling and Calhoun, 1994; Koss et al., 1991; Waigant, Wallace, Phelps, & Miller, 1990). Sexual assault victims, compared with nonvictimized women, were more likely to report both medically explained (30% versus 16%) and medically unexplained symptoms (11% versus 5%). Consequently, rape and sexual assault victims also seek more medical care than nonvictims. In a longitudinal study, rape victims seeking care at a rape crisis center were initially similar to matched nonvictims in their self-reported physician visits, but at 4 months and 1 year after the rapes they were seeking care more frequently (Kimerling & Calhoun, 1994).

A number of long-lasting symptoms and illnesses have been associated with sexual victimization, including chronic pelvic pain, premenstrual syndrome, gastrointestinal disorders, and a variety of chronic pain disorders, including headaches, back pain, and facial pain (for reviews, see Dunn & Gilchrist, 1993; Hendricks-Matthews, 1993; Koss & Heslet, 1992). Persons with serious drug-related problems and high-risk sexual behaviors were also characterized by an elevated prevalence of sexual victimization (Paone, Chavkin, Willets, Friedman, & Des Jarlais, 1992).

Psychological Consequences

Victims of rape and sexual assault exhibit a variety of psychological symptoms that are similar to those of victims of other types of trauma, such as war and natural disaster. Following a trauma, many victims experience shock, denial, disbelief, fear, confusion, and withdrawal (Burgess & Holmstrom, 1974b; Herman, 1992; van der Kolk, 1994). Women who have sustained sexual or physical assault have been found to disproportionately suffer from depression, thoughts of suicide, and suicide attempts (Herman, 1992; Hilberman, 1980; Hilberman & Munson, 1978; Kilpatrick et al., 1985).

A large empirical literature documents the psychological symptoms experienced in the aftermath of rape (for reviews see Frieze, Hymer, & Greenberg, 1987; Lurigio & Resick, 1990; McCann, Sakheim, & Abrahamson, 1988; Resick, 1987, 1990; Roth & Lebowitz, 1988). Rape, with the exception of marital rape, is more likely than partner violence to be an isolated incident, which creates a somewhat different course of recovery. For many victims, postrape distress peaks approximately 3 weeks after the assault, continues at a high level for the next month, and by 2 to 3 months postassault recovery has begun (Davidson & Foa, 1991; Rothbaum, Foa, Riggs, Murdock, & Walsh, 1992). Many differences between rape victims and nonvictimized women disappear after 3 months, with the exception of continued reports of fear, self-esteem problems, and sexual problems, which may persist for up to 18 months or longer (Resick, 1987). Approximately 25% of women continue to have problems for several years (Hanson, 1990).

There are few reliable predictors of positive readjustment among rape survivors (Hanson, 1990; Lurigio & Resick, 1990). In general, those assaulted at a younger age are more distressed than those who were raped in adulthood (Burnam et al., 1988). Some research suggested that Asian- and Mexican-American women have more difficult recoveries than do other women (Ruch & Leon, 1983; Ruch, Gartnell, Armedeo, & Coyne, 1991; Williams & Holmes, 1981). Victims of these ethnic backgrounds, as well as Moslem women, face cultures in which intense, irremediable shame is linked to rape. Recent direct comparisons, however, have revealed no ethnic differences in the psychological impact of rape as measured by self-report and interview-assessed prevalence of mental disorders among Hispanic, African-American, and white women (Burnam et al., 1988; Wyatt, 1992).

The actual violence of an assault may be less important in predicting a woman's response than the perceived threat (Kilpatrick, Saunders, Veronen, Best, & Von, 1987). Indeed, the fear that one will be injured or killed is equally as common among women who are raped by husbands and dates as among women who are raped by strangers (Kilpatrick et al., 1992). Likewise, acquaintance rapes are equally devastating to the victim as stranger rapes, as revealed by standard measures of psychopathology (Katz, 1991; Koss, Dinero, Seibel, & Wisniewski, 1988). However, women who know their offender are much less likely to report the rapes to police or to seek victim assistance services (Golding, Siegel, Sorenson, Burnam, & Stein, 1989; Stewart et al., 1987). The impact of rape may be moderated by social support (Ruch & Chandler, 1983; Sales, Baum, & Shore, 1984). Unsupportive behavior, by significant others in particular, predicts poorer social adjustment (Davis, Taylor, & Bench, 1995), and proceeding with prosecution appears to prolong recovery (Sales et al., 1984).

One way of systematizing some of the psychological symptoms evidenced by victims is the diagnostic construct of posttraumatic stress disorder (PTSD) (Burge, 1989; Kemp, Rawlings, & Green, 1991). This construct has been used to understand a range of psychological responses to traumatic experiences, from natural disasters and military combat to rape and other forms of criminal assault (Davidson & Foa, 1993; Figley, 1985; Herman, 1992; von der Kolk, 1987). On the basis of clinical and empirical inquiries, a growing number of clinicians now suggest that PTSD may be the most accurate diagnosis for many survivors of interpersonal and family violence (Browne, 1992; Bryer, Nelson, Miller, & Krol, 1987; Burge, 1989; Davidson & Foa, 1991; Dutton, 1992; Gondolf, 1990; Herman, 1986, 1992; Kemp et al., 1991; Koss, 1990; Koss & Harvey, 1991; van der Kolk, 1987; Walker, 1991, 1992).

Twenty-five years ago, Burgess and Holmstrom (1974b) coined the term *rape trauma syndrome* to describe the psychological aftermath of rape. Today, many assaulted women, like other victims of trauma, receive diagnoses of PTSD. A very large proportion of rape victims (94%) who are evaluated at crisis centers and emergency rooms meet the criteria for PTSD within the first few weeks after an assault, and about half (46%) evidence symptoms of PTSD 3 months later (Rothbaum et al., 1992). Rape and sexual assault are more likely to lead to PTSD than other traumatic events affecting civilians, including robbery, the tragic death of friends or family, and natural disasters (Norris, 1992).

Rape and sexual assault affect seriously young youth. In a national study of young adolescents, aged 10 to 16 years, more than one-third reported having been victims of sexual or physical assaults. This group revealed significantly more psychological distress, including sadness and symptoms of PTSD, even after controlling for other variables that predict similar outcomes (Boney-McCoy & Finkelhor, 1995). Although this study did not report outcomes separately for girls and boys, the authors concluded that sexual assault in particular posed a very significant risk factor to the mental health of adolescents.

Consequences to Family and Friends

Rape and sexual assault may also affect other family members and friends, making them into secondary victims. Davis et al. (1995) found that rape, attempted rape, and aggravated assault of women all had negative psychological consequences on their friends, family members, and romantic partners, regardless of the victim's level of distress. Female friends and family members were more affected than male friends and family members, particularly with regard to increased fear of violent crime. Some rape victims also experienced sexual dysfunction and difficulties with interpersonal relationships, both of which can have negative effects on their family relationships. Sexual dysfunction may be long lasting. Burgess and Holmstrom (1979a) found, for example, that 30% of rape victims reported that their sexual functioning had not returned to normal for as long as 6 years after the assault.

Impact from Sexual Assault in Childhood and Adolescence

As Finkelhor and Asdigian (1996) noted, "Youth are the most victimization-prone segment of the population" (p. 3). Indeed, over half of all victims of sexual assault known to the criminal justice system are under the age of 18 (Langan & Harlow, 1994). Since many sexual crimes perpetrated against youth, particularly against adolescents, go unreported, the category of young victims surely represents a substantial proportion of the total number of sexual assault victims.

Research on the aftermath of childhood sexual abuse suggests a wide range of symptoms related to a variety of psychological disorders (Neumann, Houskamp, Pollock, & Briere, 1996). Although there is a large and growing literature on the proximal (short-term) effects of child sexual abuse, most studies have focused on distal (long-term) effects (i.e., samples of adults who were sexually abused as children and who are now the subject of an outcome study to determine the long-term effects of the abuse).

The primary *proximal* effects of sexual abuse are:

- *Anxiety/Phobic Reactions* and *Posttraumatic Stress Disorder* (PTSD) (Kilpatrick & Saunders, 1997; Kiser, Ackerman, et al., 1988; McLeer et al., 1988; Porter, Block, & Sgroi, 1982)
- *Dissociation/Multiple Personality Disorder* (MPD) (Braun & Sachs, 1985; Kluft, 1985; Liner, 1989)
- *Depression/Poor Self-Esteem* (Cavaiola & Schiff, 1988; Friedrich et al., 1986; Livingston, 1987; Sansonnet-Hayden, Haley, Marriage, & Fine, 1987; Sgroi, 1982)
- *Sexually Inappropriate and Promiscuous Behavior* (Friedrich, 1988; Friedrich & Reams, 1987; Goodwin, 1985; Sgroi, 1982; Yates, 1982)

The primary *distal* effects of childhood sexual abuse are:

- *Dissociation/MPD* and *PTSD* (Anderson, Yasenik, & Ross, 1993; Bagley, 1991; Briere & Runtz, 1990a, 1993; Chu, Dill, & McCormack, 1990; Coons, 1986; Lindberg & Distad, 1985; Nash, Hylsey, Sexton, Harralson, & Lambert, 1993; Ross, Anderson, Heber, & Norton, 1990; Ross et al., 1991; Ross, Norton, & Wozney, 1989; Rowan, Foy, Rodriguez, & Ryan, 1994; Schultz, Braun, & Kluft, 1989; Swett & Halpert, 1993; Winfield, George, Swartz, & Blazer, 1990; Wolfe, Sas, & Wekerle, 1994)
- *Serious Psychopathology* (e.g., Borderline Personality Disorder) (Alexander, 1993; Anderson et al., 1993; Briere & Zaidi, 1989; Brown & Anderson, 1991; Bryer et al., 1987; Gold, 1986; Gross, Doerr, Caldirola, Guzinski, & Ripley, 1980–1981; Herman, Perry, & van der Kolk, 1989; Nash et al., 1993; Ogata et al., 1990; Stone, 1990; Swett & Halpert, 1993; Westen, Ludolph, Misle, Ruffins, & Block, 1990; Winfield et al., 1990)
- *Eating Disorders* (Bulik, Sullivan, & Rorty, 1989; Coons, Bowman, Pellow, & Schneider, 1989; Goldfarb, 1987; Hall, Tice, Beresford, Wolley, & Hall, 1989; Moeller, Bachmann, & Moeller, 1993; Palmer, Oppenheimer, Dignon, Chaloner, & Howells, 1990; Schecter, Schwartz, & Greenfield, 1987)
- *Alcohol and Drug Abuse* (Anderson et al., 1993; Briere & Zaidi, 1989; Brown & Anderson, 1991; Moeller et al., 1993; Peters, 1988; Pribor & Dinwiddie, 1992; Stein, Golding, Siegel, Burnam, & Sorenson, 1988; Winfield et al., 1990)

- *Depression and Suicidality* (Anderson et al., 1993; Bagley, 1991; Briere & Zaidi, 1989; Brown & Anderson, 1991; Elliott & Briere, 1992; Gold, 1986; Moeller et al., 1993; Pribor & Dinwiddie, 1992; Stein et al., 1988; Winfield et al., 1990)
- *Revictimization* (e.g., Briere & Runtz, 1988; Jackson, Calhoun, Amick, Maddever, & Habif, 1990; Kendall-Tackett & Simon, 1988; Moeller et al., 1993; Wyatt, 1992)
- *Prostitution/Promiscuous Behavior* (Bagley, 1991; Burgess, Hartman, & McCormack, 1987; James & Meyerding, 1977; Silbert & Pines, 1981; Widom & Ames, 1994)
- *Victimization of Others* (e.g., Groth, 1979; Rivera & Widom, 1990; Seghorn et al., 1987; Widom, 1989; Widom & Ames, 1994)

Relatively few studies have focused on the short-term sequelae of sexual abuse in samples of children, and those that have usually focus on the children that have been identified as victims through contact with a social service agency or through the court system. Although family histories often are collected, the empirical spotlight focuses almost exclusively on the index child. The literature on short-term outcomes of identified victims clearly suggests a wide range of responses to the abuse, from no apparent symptoms to mild symptomatology (situation-specific anxiety or phobic reactions, depression, delays in the acquisition of normal developmental skills, especially social and interpersonal skills), moderate symptomatology (anxiety or phobic reactions and possibly some signs of PTSD, sexually inappropriate acting out and sexualized aggression, depression, impaired self-esteem), and severe symptomatology (in addition to the above, clear signs and symptoms of PTSD and Dissociation, and, in the most extreme cases, MPD). The multiplicity and complexity of outcomes of childhood sexual abuse are attributable not only to the nature of the abuse but also to a host of other concurrent experiences, both positive and negative, that the victim is exposed to.

The primary proximal effects of sexual abuse include anxiety and phobic reactions and PTSD (Kilpatrick & Saunders, 1997; Kiser et al., 1988; McLeer, Deblinger, Atkins, Foa, & Ralphe, 1988), Dissociation (Kluft, 1985; Liner, 1989), depression and poor self-esteem (Cavaiola & Schiff, 1988; Friedrich, Urquiza, & Beilke, 1986) and sexually inappropriate and hypersexual behaviors (Friedrich, 1988; Sgroi, 1982) have been implicated as symptoms of abuse.

In contrast to the very early studies on the effects of sexual contact between children and adults that suggested such contact was not harmful (Bender & Blau, 1937; Bender & Grugett, 1952), more recent studies have suggested the opposite. A meta-analytic study of the long-term effects of child sexual abuse included 38 studies, aggregating 2774 women who reported a victimization history and 8388 women who reported no such history (Neumann et al., 1996). Neumann et al. (1996) found that depression, suicidality, anger, anxiety, revictimization, self-mutilation, sexual problems, abuse of substances, impaired self-concept, interpersonal problems, obsessive-compulsive symptoms, somatization, dissociation and symptoms of posttraumatic stress *were all significantly associated with sexual abuse.*

Overview of Childhood Sexual Victimization

As noted, most studies have focused on long-term or *adult* outcomes. Relatively few studies have focused on the short-term sequelae of sexual abuse in samples of children, and those that have, usually focus on the children that have been identified as victims through contact with a social service agency or through the court system. Although family histories often are collected, the empirical spotlight focuses almost exclusively on the identified victim of abuse. The literature on short-term outcomes of identified victims clearly suggests a wide range of responses to the abuse, from no apparent symptoms to *mild symptomatology* (situation-specific anxiety or phobic reactions, depression, delays in the acquisition of normal developmental skills, especially social and interpersonal skills), *moderate symptomatology* (debilitating anxiety or phobic reactions and possibly some signs of PTSD, sexually inappropriate acting out and sexualized aggression, acute depression, markedly impaired self-esteem, and *severe symptomatology* (in addition to the above, clear signs and symptoms of PTSD and Dissociation, and *in the most extreme cases*, MPD). The multiplicity and complexity of outcomes of childhood sexual abuse are attributable not only to the severity of the abuse but also to a host of other concurrent experiences, both positive and negative, that the victim is exposed to.

A unique and interesting study by Pithers, Gray, Busconi, and Houchens (1998) examined the taxonomic complexity of problematic sexual behavior in childhood by examining a sample of 127 6- to 12-year-olds who were exhibiting such problematic behaviors. Most of these children (109, 86%) had themselves been sexually abused. Using standard cluster analytic procedures, the investigators found five distinct subtypes of children with sexual behavior problems: (1) Sexually Aggressive (more likely male, more likely diagnosed as ADHD or Conduct Disorder, more likely to use aggression and to penetrate victims), (2) Nonsymptomatic (more likely female, fewest number of psychiatric disorders, fewest number of victims, force and penetration rare), (3) Highly Traumatized (males and females equally represented, highest number of psychiatric diagnoses, including PTSD, extensive histories of abuse and second highest for sexual abuse of others, though penetration is rare), (4) Rule Breaker (more likely female, aggression present though penetration is rare, highest number of extended families with an additional sexual abuser, longest latency between own abuse and onset of problematic sexual behavior), and (5) Abuse Reactive (more likely male, high number of psychiatric disorders, high level of abuse, highest number of sexually abusive acts against others, shortest latency between own abuse and problematic sexual behavior).

Pithers et al. (1998) found that "across all of the child types, attachment between parents and children was profoundly insecure" (p. 404), noting that "insecure attachment of parents and children may be a potent intervening variable that could explain the link between child maltreatment and adolescent delinquency and adult criminality, including sexual offenses" (p. 404).

Recapitulation Hypothesis

A commonly reported clinical and theoretical explanation for the origin of sexually aggressive behavior, particularly behavior with an early onset, is "recapitulation," the notion that you will repeat history or do what was done to you (Finkelhor et al., 1986; Kempe & Kempe, 1984; Lanyon, 1986; Rogers & Terry, 1984). It is reasonable to conclude that this hypothesis went from being a silver bullet, to a tarnished bullet, to a complex bullet. Although the cycle of violence is neither inevitable nor inexorable (Garland & Dougher, 1990; Kaufman & Zigler, 1987; Widom, 1989), there is ample speculation and some empirical evidence that sexual violence may, at the very least, *increase the risk* for subsequent sexual violence (e.g., Becker, Kaplan, Cunningham-Rathner, & Kavoussi,

1986; Condy, Templer, Brown & Veaco, 1987; Fehrenbach, Smith, Monastersky, & Deisher, 1986; Friedrich & Luecke, 1988; Gebhard et al., 1965; Longo, 1982; Prentky & Burgess, 1991; Prentky, Knight, Sims-Knight, et al., 1989; Seghorn, Prentky & Boucher, 1987; Tingle, Barnard, Robbins, Newman, & Hutchinson, 1986). Increasing the risk implies the interplay of other factors that may aggravate or mitigate risk. When we fail to take into consideration the nature of the sexual abuse as well as these other factors, the overall signal for sexual abuse is weak. In a report from the U.S. General Accounting Office on the Cycle of Sexual Abuse, prepared for the Subcommittee on Crime of the Committee on the Judiciary (U.S. House of Representatives), 25 studies were reviewed (23 of which were retrospective) (General Accounting Office, 1996a). The report concluded that

> Overall, the retrospective studies, prospective studies, and research reviews indicated
> that the experience of childhood sexual victimization is quite likely neither a necessary
> nor a sufficient cause of adult sexual offending. The two prospective studies concluded
> that the majority of victims of sexual abuse during childhood did not become sex
> offenders as adults.... In addition, the majority of the retrospective studies concluded
> that most adult sex offenders against children did not report that they were sexually
> victimized as children. (GAO, 1996a, p. 3)

The GAO (1996a) report went on to conclude that

> Further research would be necessary to determine what kinds of experiences magnify
> the likelihood that sexually victimized children will become adult sexual offenders
> against children and, alternatively, what kinds of experiences help prevent victimized
> children from becoming adult sexual offenders against children. (p. 13)

Although research in this area clearly is needed, sufficient work has been done to offer reasonable speculations. Prentky and Burgess (1991) hypothesized, for instance, that protracted sexual abuse that is intrusive and/or violent is importantly related to the development of sexually deviant and aggressive fantasies, and may well increase the risk of sexually aggressive behavior. Moreover, we found that the coincident association of sexual abuse and caregiver instability substantially increased the likelihood of sexual violence in adulthood (Prentky, Knight, Sims-Knight, et al., 1989). Of adult sex offenders who apparently experienced *no* caregiver instability or sexual abuse, 22.6% still evidenced a high degree of sexual aggression in adulthood (Prentky, Knight, Sims-Knight, 1989). Among those who experienced caregiver instability *or* sexual abuse, 51.4% evidenced a high degree of sexual aggression in adulthood. Among those who experienced *both* caregiver instability *and* sexual abuse, 87.5% evidenced a high degree of sexual aggression in adulthood.

Overall, the literature does permit some general speculation about "morbidity" factors (factors that hypothetically make childhood sexual abuse worse, i.e., more morbid, hence increasing the severity of the effects:

- Age of onset
- Relationship to offender
- Duration of abuse
- Invasiveness/violence

Morbidity Factors

As may be apparent, childhood sexual abuse varies enormously in its short- and long-term effects. Clearly, not all experiences of sexual abuse in childhood and adolescence have equivalent impact. Indeed, we can identify the most important morbidity factors (i.e., factors hypothesized to increase the severity of the effects of abuse). Generally speaking, (1) the earlier the age of onset, (2) the closer the relationship between the victim and the perpetrator, (3) the longer the abuse lasts, and (4) the more invasive and/or violent the abuse is, the more serious and long-lasting is the impact. The only one of these four morbidity factors that may be questionable is the relationship of the victim to the perpetrator. The rationale for this morbidity factor is that the closer the relationship between victim and perpetrator, the greater the sense of betrayal and loss of trust. What makes this factor questionable is that it may be confounded with the duration of the abuse (i.e., stranger abuse is most often a single, isolated assault, whereas abuse perpetrated by familial members or extended family members may go on for years).

These morbidity factors must be added to a complex equation that includes other critical factors, such as availability of supportive caregivers, the timely provision of therapy, and the premorbid ego-strength of the victim. Moreover, sexual abuse within the family is rarely an "isolated" event in an otherwise happy, healthy, nurturant family. There may well be other forms of caregiver dysfunction, such as neglect, emotional abuse, and physical abuse, that magnify, or in some indiscernible ways modify, the effects of the sexual abuse. Each form of abuse has the same morbidity factors associated with it:

	Age of onset	Duration	Severity	Relation to offender
Physical abuse	✓	✓	✓	✓
Sexual abuse	✓	✓	✓	✓
Emotional/psychological abuse	✓	✓	✓	✓
Neglect	✓	✓	✓	✓

Thus, in our clinical work we must not draw immediate assumptions about impact (e.g., automatically assuming that someone will evidence symptoms of PTSD) without first acquiring as much detailed information as possible about the abuse and, of course, without examining results of appropriate assessment tools. The following list summarizes the complex issues determining the outcome of abuse:

- How composites of abusive experiences interact
- The age of onset and the duration of the abuse
- The severity and invasiveness of the abuse
- The stability of caregivers through childhood and adolescence
- The presence (and role) of nonabusive adults
- The quality of out-of-home and institutional placements
- Peer influences and the quality of peer role models

Traumatic Amnesia

The processes by which the mind deals with protracted trauma, particularly in cases where the trauma is profound and the individual cannot escape or avoid it, are well known. In their wonderful book on the subject, Fay Honey Knopp and Anna Rose Benson (1996) stated that

> increases in the complexity and prevalence of complex PTSD symptomology are specifically related to the experience of early interpersonal trauma, with both longer

duration (the period of time during which the trauma is repeated) and younger age of the victim at the initial onset of the trauma associated with increased psychopathology in the adult survivor. Persistent and prolonged childhood trauma is related to the presence of a large variety of elaborate and interrelated posttraumatic symptoms in adults, essentially dissociative in nature or origin. (p. 196)

To understand, however, the encoding, storage, and retrieval of traumatic childhood events is an enigma that only recently is revealing its secrets. As Knopp and Benson (1996) noted on the jacket of their book

Some of us have childhoods marred by overwhelming, intolerable traumatic experiences nearly impossible to incorporate into existing schemas or make meaning of. Such traumas appear to affect virtually every chemical in the brain, flooding neural pathways with emergency messages that overwhelm the normal processes of encoding and storage of conscious memory. Memories for these experiences may be retained and remembered differently, as isolated fragments of perception, behavior, or emotion, sometimes without awareness of the connection with past trauma.

Bessel van der Kolk (1993) has noted, for instance, that experiences may be deemed traumatic when they are "evaluated by the amygdala as being of great emotional significance, without the chance for proper categorization of the experience by the septohippocampal system" (p. 231). Because intense emotional experiences are not properly categorized, they are not incorporated into existing schemas that make up our narrative memory. They exist as fragmented, "free-floating," bits of memory, unconnected and segregated. These fragmented memories cannot be recalled as part of the continuous stream of life experience; they are seemingly detached from the narrative that makes up our recollections of past life experiences. Van der Kolk (1993) summed it up very succinctly by saying that "the essence of traumatization is the fragmentation of experience." The problems arising from the improper coding and categorizing of information are the very ones associated with trauma, namely, hyperamnesia, amnesia, and dissociation.

The relatively young field of childhood trauma research has been the subject of more than its share of controversy. As Judith Herman (1992) stated so poignantly

To study psychological trauma means bearing witness to horrible events. When the events are natural disasters or "acts of God," those who bear witness sympathize readily with the victim. But when the traumatic events are of human design, those who bear witness are caught in the conflict between victim and perpetrator. It is morally impossible to remain neutral in this conflict. The bystander is forced to take sides. (p. 7)

Trauma-induced amnesia is just one area of the study of psychological trauma where "witnesses" have taken sides over the authenticity and reliability of recovered memories. The controversy over recovered memories of childhood trauma appears to be rooted not in science but in the courtroom, with adult survivors seeking some form of recompense or accountability on the part of their perpetrators. As of 1994, there were close to 500 cases filed based on memories of abuse recalled in therapy (Schneider, 1994). Schneider (1994) noted that "one experienced attorney has estimated that the next decade will bring a plethora of such cases that may consume over $250 million in court costs alone" (p. 6). Most of this litigation is facilitated by the "delayed discovery rule." In most civil lawsuits, the case must be filed within some specified period of time following the event that gave rise to the suit. Although these statutes of limitations vary from state to state, lawsuits alleging sexual abuse in childhood typically must be filed 1 to 3 years after the victim reaches the age of majority (Schneider, 1994). Despite these statutes of limitations, courts generally recognize the need for an exception when the plaintiff had no awareness of the injury during the stipulated limitations period. This exception, the "delayed discovery rule," dates back to 1949 and derives from the United States Supreme Court case of *Urie v. Thompson* [337 U.S. 163 (1949)]. In that case, a railroad employee contracted silicosis after years of inhaling silica dust on the job. The Supreme Court

> held that it would be unfair to bar a plaintiff's suit on the basis of the statute of limitations when the plaintiff could not reasonably have known of his injury during the limitations period. Since *Urie*, the delayed discovery rule has gained widespread application—the classic case in the medical malpractice context." (Schneider, 1994, p. 6)

Since the mid-1980s, plaintiffs have routinely sought, with varying degrees of success, to use the delayed discovery rule in cases involving repressed memories of child abuse. In an early landmark case, the Supreme Court of the State of Washington refused to allow the use of the delayed discovery rule [*Tyson v. Tyson*, 727 P.2d 226 (Wash. 1986)] in a case involving a 25-year-old woman who alleged that her father sexually abused her from the age of 3 to the age of 11. The court's hard-fought, deeply conflicted 5–4 decision in *Tyson* was a clear premonition of the struggles that were to come. At the present time, the general trend is for courts to allow the use of the delayed discovery rule.

It is perhaps ironic that Washington became the first state in 1989 to enact legislation that permits the delayed discovery rule in cases of childhood sexual abuse. Washington's law, prompted by the *Tyson* decision, has become the model for similar laws in about half of the states. In 1994, U.S. Representatives Schroeder and Morella cosponsored a Congressional resolution urging all states to pass a delayed discovery law similar to the one in Washington [H.R. Con. Res. 200, 103rd Cong. 2d Sess. (1994)].

It comes as no surprise that among the legion of plaintiffs there were those with less than honorable motives, or those whose recollections are less than accurate. The "fight against repressed memory" has been spearheaded chiefly by the Philadelphia-based False Memory Syndrome Foundation, with chapters throughout the United States. The war cry of the cynical is that the plaintiffs are "recovering" large judgments, not large memories.

We, of course, can offer no insights about the veridicality of individual reports. They must be examined on a case-by-case basis. We would suggest, however, (again, cynically) that in the absence of recovered memory litigation, there would be no need for a "false memory syndrome," and few would question the clinical or empirical basis for trauma-induced amnesia.

As noted, there is a very substantial empirical literature documenting traumatic amnesia in cases of child sexual abuse (Briere & Conte, 1993; Burgess & Hartman, 1992; Burgess, Hartman, & Baker, 1995; Burgess, Hartman, & Clements, 1995; Cameron, 1994; Elliott & Briere, 1995; Feldman-Summers & Pope, 1994; Freyd, 1996; Herman, 1992, 1995; Herman & Schatzow, 1987; Loftus, Polonsky, & Fullilove, 1994; Polusny & Follette, 1996; Pynoos, 1994; Roe & Schwartz, 1996; Roesler & Wind, 1994; Terr, 1988, 1991, 1994; van der Kolk, 1994; van der Kolk & Fisler, 1993, 1995; van der Kolk & Greenberg, 1987; van der Kolk & Saporta, 1991; Williams, 1994).

In addition, most major professional mental health organizations have acknowledged the existence of recovered memory. In 1993, the American Psychiatric Association issued a Statement on Memories of Sexual Abuse, noting that severely abused children and adolescents cope with their trauma in a variety of ways, including losing conscious awareness of the abuse for varying periods of time. According to APA's Statement, awareness of the abuse may return after years. In 1994, the American Medical Association issued its Report of the Council on Scientific Affairs, entitled "Memories of Childhood Abuse." According to the Council's Report, "recovered memories [of childhood sexual abuse] proved to be correct" in some cases. In 1995, the British Psychological Association issued its Report by the Working Group on Recovered Memories, concluding that between one-third and two-thirds of victims of childhood sexual abuse experience time periods in which they partially or totally forget the abuse. BPA's Report further noted that there is "much less evidence on the creation of false memories," and that the false memory syndrome was an "extreme" response. In 1996, the American Psychological Association issued its Final Report from the Working Groups on Investigation of Memories of Childhood Abuse, concluding that recovered memories in some cases of child sexual abuse-related traumatic amnesia have been legitimate. APA's Final Report stated that "it is possible for memories of abuse that have been forgotten for a long time to be remembered." Brief overviews of these organizational reports were provided by Murphy (1998).

Hypothetical Risk Factors

We can hypothesize, moreover, what conditions place children at increased risk to repress trauma.

Protracted, Inescapable Abuse

When the abuse is ongoing, in some cases for many years, and the child is incapable of avoiding or escaping the abuse, the child must learn to "accommodate" to the abuse. Occasionally, this means psychologically fleeing or dissociating from the abuse or encapsulating the abuse (i.e., stuffing the abuse into a hermetically sealed black box). These are the boxes that, metaphorically, are opened after years of being sealed.

Severity of Abuse

The other powerful mechanism leading to traumatic amnesia is violence. The more invasive and violent the experience, the higher the likelihood that the child will repress the experience. This conclusion is based on a wide range of studies pointing to various forms of repression resulting from traumatic experiences such as combat in wartime.

Close Relationship to the Perpetrator

This last factor is less conclusive. Some have argued that a close relationship to the perpetrator is more likely to result in feelings of betrayal and shattered trust, and that the closer the relationship and the worse the abuse, the greater the sense of betrayal. Freyd (1996), in fact, developed a "betrayal trauma theory" that seeks to explain repression or "motivated forgetting." Freyd argued that one reason we forget traumatic events is to avoid remembering things that "threaten a necessary attachment" (i.e., a major betrayal by someone who must be trusted).

The abuse may become "normalized" and the child becomes increasingly confused about who is responsible and whether or not it really is abuse. The abuse becomes a secret that effectively insulates it from the rest of the family or, in other cases, the family colludes to deny the existence of the abuse. This is, of course, the well-known Child Sexual Abuse Accommodation Syndrome (CSAAS) that was described by Roland Summit (1983) over 15 years ago. In brief, Summit observed that sexually abused children often: (1) act secretive about the abuse, (2) feel helpless to escape the abuse, (3) blame themselves for their own victimization, (4) are conflicted about disclosing the abuse, and (5) tend to recant after disclosing the abuse and experiencing the repercussions of their disclosure. Parenthetically, CSAAS evidence has often been entered in court cases with varying degrees of success (Kalman, 1998).

In conclusion, it is not clear to what extent, and under what circumstances, feelings of betrayal and the "normalization" of the abuse are associated with traumatic amnesia. It would seem, at face value, that if the child was able to "normalize" the abuse, the abuse would not have to be repressed.

Although the task of examining the short-term impact of sexual abuse within the context of the extended family environment, taking into account the numerous factors that potentially influence outcome, is an extraordinarily difficult one, this is the essential "next step" in research on childhood abuse. It is relatively easy to gauge the short-term effects of isolated cases of abuse that are perpetrated by strangers. Impact becomes increasingly difficult to assess when the abuse is protracted, when the perpetrator is known, and when the onset of the abuse has been at a young age. Indeed, the clear need for a developmental perspective on the effects of sexual abuse has been articulated in several important reviews. Cole and Putnam (1992) stated, for instance, that "one major difficulty in this research is the lack of a developmentally-sensitive model for conceptualizing short- and long-term effects and continuity and discontinuity of effects over time" (p. 174). Finkelhor and Dziuba-Leatherman (1994b) concluded that "the field needs a more developmental perspective on child victimization. This would start with an understanding of the mix of victimization threats that face children of different ages" (p. 182). In addition to a more sophisticated approach to investigating the complex interplay of risk factors at different developmental stages, Finkelhor and Dziuba-Leatherman (1994b) also underscored the need for "research that cuts across and integrates the various forms of child victimization" (p. 182). This latter point is especially important, since it is relatively rare that abuse is isolated to only one "form" (e.g., sexual abuse in the absence of any form of psychological or emotional abuse, physical abuse, and neglect).

OVERVIEW OF IMPACT

When sexual abuse is an isolated incident, noninvasive (e.g., caressing or fondling), without physical violence and perpetrated by a stranger, and where there is crisis counseling provided, the child often can recover without major disruption to normal development. Indeed, Briere and Elliott (1994) pointed out that "as many as one-fourth of all sexually abused children either report no initial abuse-related problems or may no longer present with demonstrable symptomatology within two years of their abuse" (p. 63). Quite often, however, the abuse that children suffer is protracted and is perpetrated by a member of the nuclear, extended, step or foster family. Moreover, these children often are subjected to other forms of pathology within the family, such as physical abuse, emotional or psychological abuse, domestic violence, alcohol and drug abuse, promiscuity and inappropriate or blurred sexual boundaries, and neglect of emotional as well as physical needs. In these instances, the sexual abuse invariably is associated with psychiatric sequelae that are manifested in a variety of maladaptive outcomes, including many forms of self-destructive or other-destructive behavior. Although these destructive behaviors often emerge in adolescence, they begin to take a significant toll in adulthood. Indeed, it is quite clear at this point

Table 1. Maladaptive Outcomes of Childhood Sexual Abuse and Their Impact on the System

Maladaptive adult outcomes	System impact
Deficits in educational and vocational skills	Unstable employment
	Underemployment (below potential)
	Public assistance/Welfare
Depression and suicidality	Outpatient treatment
	Possible hospitalization
Severe mental illness (e.g., Borderline PD, Dissociation/MPD, and PTSD)	Unstable employment
	Underemployment
	Dysfunctional and abusive relationships
	Outpatient treatment
	Periodic hospitalization
	Neglect and abuse of children leading to placement
Alcohol and drug abuse	Unstable employment
	Neglect and abuse of offspring (DHS response)
	Outpatient treatment
	Possible hospitalization
	Possible criminal justice system response
Eating disorders	Outpatient treatment
	Possible hospitalization
Prostitution and promiscuous behavior	Medical treatment for STDs
	Criminal justice system response
	Possible imprisonment
	Unplanned/unwanted pregnancies
	Border babies (abandoned)
Revictimization (e.g., wife abuse)	Substance abuse
	Neglect and abuse of offspring
	Unstable employment
	Use of community shelters
	Use of restraining orders
	Emergency medical response
	Death
Victimization of others	Outpatient treatment
	Criminal justice system response
	Possible imprisonment
	Treatment of victim(s)
	Continuation of the cycle of abuse

Note. Adapted from Prentky (1999) by permission.

that childhood sexual abuse has the potential to cast a long shadow into adulthood, effectively undermining normal adult adaptation in a variety of different ways.

Because the adulthood manifestations of childhood abuse are so varied, we rarely think of them as falling under one umbrella with common roots. As we attempted to illustrate in Table 1, this heterogeneous group of maladaptive and destructive behaviors imposes, however, an enormous burden on many facets of the system, from outpatient medical clinics, emergency rooms, and inpatient hospitalization to the Department of Human Services, the police, the court system, the prison system, and Public Assistance/ Welfare. Effective treatment of child victims of sexual abuse *can* reduce the long-term maladaptive consequences of the abuse, and thus the burdens imposed on our already beleaguered medical, social service, and criminal justice systems.

CHAPTER 3

Diagnosis and Classification

In this chapter we attempt to survey the copious clinical and empirical literature on classification of sexual offenders. Because of the enormity of the task, we have divided the chapter into four major sections. In the first section, we look at the various ways in which a valid system for classifying sexual offenders can assist in our clinical and forensic work with this population. In that section, we also address the utility of the DSM-IV for classifying sex offenders, as well as other psychiatric considerations in the classification of sex offenders. In the second section, we discuss a number of the prominent single dimensions that have been used for classifying sex offenders. In some cases, such as sex of victim, these single dimensions have enjoyed widespread use. Although single dimension classification has limited utility, the research spawned by these efforts has contributed significantly to our thinking about the taxonomic problems presented by sex offenders. In the third section, we focus on child molesters, the many clinical systems that have been proposed for these offenders, common types that have more or less consistently appeared in these systems, and finally a brief presentation of an empirically based taxonomy for child molesters. In the fourth section, we focus on rapists, the clinical systems proposed for these offenders, followed by a brief discussion of an empirically based taxonomy for rapists. We have not included in this chapter detailed descriptions of the programmatic research that produced these empirical systems. The interested reader will be referred to the relevant literature for information on the development and validation of these models.

POTENTIAL UTILITY OF CLASSIFICATION FOR SEX OFFENDERS

Science has traditionally proceeded by simplifying complex, diverse domains of information. Simplification is typically achieved through a methodical process of assigning members of a large heterogeneous group to subgroups that possess common characteristics, thereby bringing some degree of order to diversity. The science of classification (*taxonomy*) is fundamental to all science. The task is to uncover the laws and principles that underlie the optimal differentiation, or "carving up," of a domain into subgroups that have theoretically important similarities. The more heterogeneous the area of inquiry, the more critical classification is. The resulting subgroups or subtypes are not simply notational; they connect the content of science to the real world. One might argue, in fact, that classification reflects a normal cognitive process of integration and reduction. Through such a process of classification we make sense of our experiences. The process that helps us to apprehend our world at the sensory level is the same process that scientists use to order and simplify their world at the empirical level. Structurally, a classification system is like a transposable dwelling erected to house an aggregate of experience. The dwelling is intended precisely to reflect its contents, and hence the architecture must change to track the protean nature of experience.

Over the past 40 years, classification systems have been designed, implemented, and tested on virtually every aspect of human behavior. The profusion of these systems during the past several decades resulted from the proliferation of clinical data and the need for an organized approach to complex and diverse behavioral domains. One area that certainly has been the beneficiary of classificatory efforts has been depression. We have witnessed something of a revolution in the treatment of depression and anxiety-related disorders through the identification of increasingly homogeneous subgroups. The clinical literature clearly indicates that valid classification models can lead to greater therapeutic efficacy.

Despite these rather buoyant introductory remarks, Brennan (1987) reminded us that

> The promise of taxonomic work in both theory and practice has not been realized. New typological findings have generally not been well assimilated either in theory or in practice.... Many researchers appear infatuated with classification techniques per se or with creating typologies as ends in themselves. (p. 202).

Classifications possessing the greatest efficacy begin, at the outset, with a clear statement of purpose. In other words, *what* is the intended mission or purpose of the system? Classification systems do not—or at least should not—emerge as the product of a "feels right" exercise. In the criminology domain, the clear purpose of most taxonomic efforts has been to increase the accuracy of predictions of dangerousness or reoffense risk.

In criminology applications, it is evident, moreover, that we *must* embark on a taxonomic course with utmost care and caution. Classification is a rather odd tool. When applied properly, it can help to reveal profound insights into intractable problems. When applied improperly or misused, it can wreak havoc. In an article three decades old on the "care and feeding of typologies," Toch (1970) warned that

> Classifying people in life is a grim business which channelizes destinies and determines fate. A man becomes a category, is processed as a category, plays his assigned role, and lives up to the implications. Labelled irrational, he acts crazy. Catalogued dangerous, he becomes dangerous, or he stays behind bars. (p. 15).

Hans Toch, who has spent much of his professional life attempting to classify violent people, reminds us that "the game of labelling has consequences" and that "individuals can be jailed as representatives of a probable category" (p. 18). Toch's message, which is as true today as it was 30 years ago, is a sobering one. We must not turn back from the task of classification, because it is potentially a very powerful tool. However, we must adhere to rigor in development and utmost care in application. In short, casual or careless assignment of individuals to categories is far worse than no assignment at all. And improper use of a system is far worse than no use at all.

One of the few indisputable conclusions about sexual offenders is that they constitute a markedly heterogeneous group (Knight, Rosenberg & Schneider, 1985). The childhood and developmental histories, adult competencies, and criminal histories of sexual offenders differ considerably. The motives and patterns, moreover, that characterize their criminal offenses differ considerably. As such, it would be misleading, at the very least, to suggest that sex offenders have a single "profile," or that we can pronounce judgments about *all* sex offenders with any degree of accuracy (e.g., "sex offenders cannot be treated," or for that matter, "sex offenders can be treated"). Indeed, it would be equally misleading, not to mention erroneous, to suggest that there is a profile for all rapists or for all child molesters. Classification research reveals that rapists and child molesters are *very* heterogeneous and that each offender group may include a half dozen to a dozen discrete subtypes:

Diversity among rapists

- Teenagers who "pull trains"
- College students who coerce coeds to have sex
- Married men who force their spouses to have sex
- Employers who coerce their employees to have sex
- "Impaired professionals" who coerce their subordinates to have sex
- Career criminals with a lengthy track of crime who rape once
- Serial rapists with no known nonsexual offenses
- Rapists who stalk and terrorize their victims
- Rapists who are highly sadistic to their victims
- Rapists who ask their victims for "dates" after the rape

Diversity among child molesters

- Married men who fondle their own children
- Married men who rape their own children
- Married men who molest unknown children
- "Impaired professionals" who molest children in their care
- Molesters with an exclusive sexual preference for children
- Molesters who are predatory and exploitative in their offenses
- Molesters whose work and social/recreational activities involve children
- Molesters who access, produce, and traffic in child pornography
- Molesters who are overtly sadistic to children

What is equally remarkable, however, is our failure, at least until recently, to take seriously the extraordinary diversity among child molesters and rapists and to develop valid classification models for reducing this diversity. As noted in the above list, there are substantial, fundamental differences between, for instance, married men who molest their own children, pedophiles with an exclusive sexual preference for children, and child molesters who abduct and aggressively assault children. Similarly, there are manifest differences between juveniles who participate in a gang rape (i.e., "pull trains"), college students who coerce a coed into sexual activity, career criminals with a single known rape, and serial rapists. Although sexual offenders have been the subject of intense clinical interest and speculation for at least 50 years, it is only within the past 20 years that progress has been made on the development of empirically validated systems for classifying this population.

We should begin by emphasizing that classification systems do *not* serve all purposes. As noted, classification research typically begins by pinpointing the purpose that the resulting model is intended to serve. For example, a taxonomy may be designed to classify the structural, biochemical, or reproductive characteristics of a particular genus or species of plant or animal. In the case of sexual offenders, the same principle holds. Those who set out to develop a system should have a specific purpose in mind. A classification system that is intended to assist with treatment planning and clinical decision-making may look quite different from a classification system that is intended to inform forensic decision-making (e.g., risk).

Ways in Which Classification May Help

There are a variety of *potential* areas of usefulness for valid taxonomic models of sexual offenders.

Investigative Profiling

In temporal order, the first relevant "event" is the crime itself. Thus, the first possible benefit of a classification system would be in aiding the apprehension of the offender through investigative profiling. Profiling, in its general application, involves the use of crime scene data to draw inferences about the offender in order to aid with apprehension. The use of a classification system introduces two stages into this process. Victim statements (assuming that there is a live victim) and crime scene data are used to bootstrap a classification of the offender. Assuming that it is possible to estimate, with reasonable confidence, the offender's subtype, the profile of that subtype is then used to assist with apprehension. We discuss the general topic of forensic (or criminal) profiling in Chapter 7.

Informing Decisions within the Criminal Justice System

The second relevant "event," after the offender has been apprehended and convicted, involves the discretionary and dispositional decisions made by the criminal justice system. In this capacity, a valid classification system can indeed inform the many "players" within the criminal justice system about issues such as reoffense risk, risk of violence, appropriateness for probation, custody level (i.e., security risk), and so forth. At the point of consideration for parole or discharge from community-based treatment, risk decisions once again become important. This clearly is an area where classification could serve a very useful purpose. Although there has been relatively little research on validating a classification system for this purpose, recent validity studies on several empirically derived taxonomies are promising.

Treatment Planning

The third relevant "event" after the offender has been returned to the community, either on probation or parole, is treatment. Indeed, treatment often becomes available even while the offender is still within an institution. Thus, the third possible benefit of a classification system would be to inform treatment planning and clinical decision-making (e.g., increasing the specificity and accuracy of treatment plans). To the extent that rehabilitation within the criminal justice system remains a goal and to the extent that limited resources require strict allocation, classification systems that attempt to shed light on treatment planning will be very important. Twenty-five years ago, Quay (1975) remarked, "This question of the match between offender characteristics and treatment modalities, i.e., differential classification and treatment, remains perhaps the most important problem for research in applied corrections" (p. 412). In his chapter on classification for treatment, Sechrest (1987) made the following observation. "Lamentably, I conclude that we do not know very much about the classification of criminal offenders for treatment" (p. 318). Thirteen years later, we have made no more progress.

Etiology

The fourth possible benefit of classification, which was alluded to above, is etiology. Classification systems can tell us something about the course of life events that led to the onset of sexual offenses. Indeed, it may be possible to discern the unique roots of each subtype (i.e., the path that led from childhood or adolescence to becoming a particular *type* of sexual offender). For example, the pattern of life events that led to an outcome of becoming a Type 2 rapist might be, hypothetically, quite different from the pattern of life events that led to an outcome of becoming a Type 4 rapist. Most empirical work to date has focused on the development of "path models" that predict taxonomic outcome from familial, childhood, and adolescent variables. Concurrent validity studies of current classification models have begun to shed light on the different life experiences that lead to different taxonomic outcomes (i.e., different subtypes).

Psychiatric Classification

The *Diagnostic and Statistical Manual* (DSM) of the American Psychiatric Association (APA, 1952, 1968, 1980, 1987, 1994) has consistently included a category for pedophilia. In the original DSM, published in 1952, pedophilia was included under Sexual Deviation. Sexual Deviation was one of four Sociopathic Personality Disturbances (along with Antisocial Reaction, Dyssocial Reaction, and Addiction) included within the broader category of Personality Disorders. In the 1952 edition of the DSM, an assignment to the category of Sexual Deviation was guided by the following statement:

> This diagnosis is reserved for deviant sexuality which is not symptomatic of more extensive syndromes, such as schizophrenic and obsessional reactions. The term includes most of the cases formerly classified as "psychopathic personality with pathologic sexuality." The diagnosis will specify the type of the pathologic behavior, such as homosexuality, transvestism, pedophilia, fetishism and sexual sadism (including rape, sexual assault, mutilation). (pp. 38–39)

No specific criteria for classifying pedophilia, or any of the other Sexual Deviations, were provided.

In the DSM-II, published in 1968, pedophilia was again included under Sexual Deviation and again no classification criteria were provided. In the DSM-III, published in 1980, pedophilia was classified under Psychosexual Disorders. The age of onset was identified as "frequently middle age" and the course was stated to be "unknown." Two criteria were provided: (1) the act or fantasy of engaging in sexual activity with prepubertal (age not specified) children is a repeatedly preferred or exclusive method of achieving sexual excitement and (2) if the subject is an adult, the victim is at least 10 years younger; if the subject is a late adolescent, no age difference is required.

In the revision of the third edition of the DSM (III-R), published in 1987, pedophilia was included under Sexual Disorders. The age of onset was revised to "usually begins in adolescence" and the course was now identified as "usually chronic." The DSM-III-R provided more specific, behavioral criteria for pedophilia, including: (1) recurrent intense sexual urges or fantasies involving sexual activity with a prepubescent child (generally age 13 or younger) for at least 6 months, (2) the subject has acted on these urges *or* is markedly distressed by them, (3) the subject is at least 16 years old and at least 5 years older than the victim, and (4) late adolescents who are involved in ongoing relationships with 12- or 13-year-olds are *excluded*. The DSM-III-R also required that the clinician specify: (1) whether the client's victims were all males, all females, or both, (2) whether the offenses were limited to incest, and (3) whether the client is an "exclusive type" (i.e., attracted only to children) or a nonexclusive type.

The DSM-IV, published in 1994, included pedophilia under Sexual and Gender Identity Disorders. The age of onset, course, criteria, and specifications were the same as in the DSM-III-R. The only technical difference is that the first criterion in the DSM-IV added the word *behaviors* to urges and fantasies.

Although the DSM-III-R and DSM-IV provide greater specificity and clarity when it comes to classifying someone as a "pedophile," the clinician who uses the DSM is still left with a single categorical diagnosis for all those who engage in sexual activity with children. From a taxonomic standpoint, the critical question is whether the classification system does an adequate job of capturing as many individuals as possible (i.e., "coverage") and sorting them accurately into theoretically meaningful groups. If the intent is to classify the larger world of child molesters, the DSM fails to provide adequate coverage. One may reasonably argue, of course, that the intent of the DSM was *not* to classify all child molesters but rather to define and capture a subset of individuals with a distinct paraphiliac attraction to children. The DSM-III-R and IV certainly accomplish that narrow goal more effectively than any preceding version of the DSM. In general, however, the DSM is *not* a useful taxonomic system for classifying child molesters.

The DSM has never included a diagnostic category for rapists. Indeed, the use of the DSM to classify sexual offenders has been a matter of not inconsequential controversy. Discussions of including a diagnostic category for rapists have been met with fierce opposition. It has been argued that since the DSM was not designed to classify the broad range of criminals and clearly sexual offenders are criminals, categories for child molesters and rapists have no place in the DSM. There are, after all, no diagnostic categories for bank robbers, burglars, arsonists, and so forth. So why sex offenders? A more specific concern, however, has been raised by victim advocates and others, who argue that a DSM diagnosis may serve to "medicalize" the offending behavior and thus detract from criminal responsibility in a legal proceeding.

Psychiatric Status

The personality disorder most frequently used to identify a subtype in past classification systems for both rapists and child molesters has been APD (Antisocial Personality

Disorder). Many systems have isolated an impulsive, exploitative type whose sexual offenses are simply one part of an extensive criminal history and antisocial lifestyle.

A small but noteworthy group of offenders, ranging from about 8 to 30%, has been found either entirely free of psychopathology (that is, not classifiable into any category within the diagnostic system that was being used) or as sexually deviant in the absence of any other disorder (Apfelberg, Sugar, & Pfeffer, 1944; Brancale, Ellis, & Doorbar, 1952; Brancale, MacNeil, & Vuocolo, 1965; Frosch & Bromberg, 1939). The variation in these rates can be accounted for by sample differences (those referred for psychiatric evaluation would be expected to show a higher incidence of psychopathology) and by variability in the diagnostic systems and criteria employed. Although differences in diagnostic criteria and samples make cross-study comparisons difficult, if not unwise, it is reasonable to conclude that the most frequently diagnosed personality disorder for rapists and extrafamilial child molesters is APD and that traits associated with APD constitute a cohesive subtype for both rapists and child molesters.

Several conclusions may be drawn from the literature regarding the "psychiatric status" of sexual offenders. First, in assessments of personality disorders, sexual offenders have been found to be quite heterogeneous. Indeed, Rosenberg (1981) and Schneider (1981) reported that in their sample of rapists and child molesters every DSM-III personality disorder was represented.

Second, although only a relatively small proportion of sexual offenders have been diagnosed as psychotic (about 10–15%, depending on the sample), such atypical offenders could add considerable noise to any classification system. One way of addressing this problem is to separate out all such offenders, as Gebhard et al. (1965) and Rada (1978b) did. Such a solution considers the offense behavior to be of secondary diagnostic importance to a primary presenting problem of psychosis or mental retardation. We have generally maintained that if the intention is to classify sexually aggressive behavior, it makes little sense to isolate subtypes based exclusively on the presence of psychosis or mental retardation (e.g., Prentky, Cohen, & Seghorn, 1985). Our reasoning is spelled out in subsequent discussion on Disinhibiting Factors.

SINGLE-DIMENSION DIFFERENTIATION

Sex of Victim

The classification of child molesters on the basis of the sex of their victims was one of the earliest discriminators to be examined empirically (Fitch, 1962; Gebhard et al., 1965; Mohr, Turner, & Jerry, 1964). Trichotomization of child molesters into same-sex, opposite-sex, and mixed-sex groups has been shown to have some cross-temporal stability (Fitch, 1962; Langevin, Hucker, et al., 1985) as well as predictive validity (Fitch, 1962; Frisbie, 1969; Frisbie & Dondis, 1965; Quinsey, 1986). In addition, sexual preference among child molesters appears to have some concurrent validity. It has been shown to covary in a systematic way with penile plethysmographic responsiveness to stimuli depicting specific ages and sexes (e.g., Freund, 1965, 1967a,b; Laws & Osborn, 1983; Quinsey & Chaplin, 1988). Indeed, Quinsey (1986; Earls & Quinsey, 1985) has argued that a trichotomization of child molesters on the basis of victim-sex, coupled with a subdivision based on victim-relatedness (incest offenders versus pedophiles) should serve as a "null hypothesis" criterion against which the incremental validity of any new classification system can be evaluated.

Other variables also have been found to relate to the victim-sex preferences of child molesters. For example, offenders against boys, when compared to offenders against girls, have been found to be less aggressive (Gebhard et al., 1965), younger, better educated, more often single, and more often diagnosed as sociopathic (Frisbie & Dondis, 1965) and have higher reoffense rates (Fitch, 1962; Frisbie & Dondis, 1965; Radzinowicz, 1957). Offenders against boys have also been found to choose older victims (Mohr et al., 1964), to abuse unrelated children more often (Dixon, Arnold, & Calestro, 1978; Quinsey, 1977), to report less frequent alcohol consumption during their offenses (Rada, 1976), and to recount different sexual histories (Nedoma, Mellam, & Pondelickova, 1971).

The sex-of-victim distinction has *not*, however, received consistent support. Langevin, Hucker, Handy, Hook, Puring, & Russon (1985), for example, found that same-sex offenders had the fewest criminal charges (8%, compared with 22% for the opposite-sex group). Abel, Becker, Murphy, and Flanagan (1981) found that their opposite-sex child molesters reported over twice as many victims as their same-sex child molesters (62.4 and 30.6%, respectively). Abel, Mittelman, Becker, Rathner, and Rouleau (1988) subsequently reported that mixed-sex preference, as opposed to single-sex preference, accounted for a larger portion of their child molesters who reoffended.

Marques (1995) reported victim sex differences in reoffense rates among 110 treated child molesters. Again, contrary to prediction, the opposite-sex child molesters had a slightly higher rate of recidivism than the same-sex child molesters (13.9 and 12.1%, respectively). The treated mixed-sex group of offenders had the highest recidivism rate (16.7%), supporting the findings of Abel et al. (1988). Among the volunteer controls, however, Marques found that the same-sex offenders had a 5.5% higher recidivism rate than the opposite-sex offenders (13.9 and 8.4%, respectively).

In the most recent panel of data analyzed by Marques, the rates shifted in support of the sex of victim hypothesis (Marques & Day, 1998). Among those offenders who completed the treatment program, opposite-sex child molesters had the lowest rate of recidivism (8.9%), approximately 4% lower than the same-sex child molesters (13.2%) and the mixed-sex child molesters (13.3%). Among the volunteer controls, the spread was even greater, with the opposite-sex child molesters reoffending at a rate of 9.7%, compared with 18.2% for the same-sex offenders and 17.7% for the mixed-sex offenders.

In a 24-year follow-up study of 111 child molesters, we found *no* differences in sexual recidivism rates for the three victim sex groups (Prentky, Knight, & Lee, 1997). The recidivism rates were .33, .35, and .38 for opposite-, mixed-, and same-sex victim groups, respectively. The results of a logistic regression analysis confirmed the lack of predictive power of victim sex in that study. In the analysis with greatest theoretical chance of showing a group difference (opposite-sex versus same-sex victim groups), the beta was 0.23 ($p < .63$). All other logistic regression analyses yielded similar results.

We concluded that one plausible explanation for our failure to find any reoffense differences between our victim sex groups was sampling differences (Prentky, Knight, & Lee, 1997). That is, the group of child molesters who we examined had an average of three known sexual offenses prior to their release. Thus, our sample had a higher base rate probability of reoffense than would be observed in an unscreened sample of child molesters recruited from the general prison population. Among child molesters who are at higher risk to reoffend, sex of victim may have less predictive importance than other variables such as degree of sexual preoccupation with children and impulsivity.

Two additional problems have clouded the sex preference distinction and might have contributed to some of the discrepancies in the literature. The first problem concerns the adequacy with which sexual preference has been operationally defined. The most frequent definition has focused on the sex of victims in reported crimes (Quinsey, 1977). The large number of unreported sexual assaults on children (Abel, 1982; Finkelhor, 1984), possible biases against reporting homosexual encounters, situational factors that might lead to assaults on the less preferred sex, and incarceration after a single assault might all contribute to unreliability in the assignment of offenders to victim-sex categories.

The second problem involves confounding variables that may artifactually contribute to victim-sex subtype differences. Many studies, for instance, have not distinguished between incest and nonincest offenders. Incest cases differ from nonincest cases in several important ways. Most importantly, incest offenders are almost exclusively heterosexual in their choice of victims (Dixon et al., 1978; Langsley, Schwartz, & Fairbairn, 1968). Assuming that "true" (i.e., exclusive) incest offenders constitute a clinically and theoretically meaningful group of child offenders, characterized by unique personality and motivational features (Cormier, Kennedy, & Sangowicz, 1962; Henderson, 1972; Rosenfeld, 1977) and an independent taxonomic structure (Summit & Kryso, 1978), the proportion of such cases in any particular sample might artifactually affect the differences between "boy offenders" and "girl offenders."

Thus, studies that do not take this confounding factor into account may attribute to sexual preference differences that may result in part from the offender's relation to his victims. Incest offenders, for example, reportedly have low recidivism rates (Frisbie & Dondis, 1965; Gibbens, Soothill, & Way, 1978). Follow-up studies that do not differentiate between incest and nonincest offenders might find recidivism differences between boy-only and girl-only offenders exaggerated by the inclusion of incest-only offenders in the girl-only group. The finding that boy-only offenders more often choose unrelated victims might also partially reflect the number of incest offenders that were included in the comparison group of girl-only offenders.

Disinhibiting Factors

A number of factors have been called *disinhibitors* (Finkelhor & Araji, 1983), because they hypothetically circumvent normal controls, thereby increasing the probability of a variety of sexually anomalous behaviors, including child molestation and rape. These factors are alcoholism, psychosis, organicity/senility, and mental retardation. Specifying the role that each of these factors play in sexually deviant and aggressive behavior remains, however, quite problematic. Some writers have concluded that these factors are sufficiently critical to the offense behaviors and life adaptations of the offender that they deserve their own types. Gebhard et al. (1965) included separate types for all four factors (Mentally Defective, Senile Deteriorates, Psychotics, Drunken). Fitch (1962) provided one type, the Pathological offender, that included those who were psychotic, mentally retarded, or organically impaired. Swanson (1971) included a Brain-Damaged type and McCaghy (1967) included a Senile type.

A somewhat broader conceptualization of disinhibition was provided by Schwartz

(Gould, 1997; Schwartz, 1988, Schwartz & Cellini, 1995). In the dynamic model developed by Schwartz, the first two components are motivation and inhibition. The second component comprises those factors that restrain the impulse to commit a sexual assault. These factors include not only the aforementioned ones (substance abuse, mental retardation, psychosis, and organicity/senility) but others that also erode inhibitions against acting out (e.g., stress, peer pressure, lack of empathy, and criminal thought processes). Thus, in Schwartz's model, disinhibitors must be examined on a case-by-case basis. The importance of disinhibition in this model is that it is a moderator for sexually aggressive behavior when motivation for the behavior is relatively low. Disinhibition is thus a centerpiece of the Schwartz model.

We have proposed a slightly different approach to understanding the contribution that these factors make to criminal outcome. We have argued that disinhibiting factors contribute to the relaxation of controls and the expression of a *preexisting* tendency to engage in a particular behavior (Prentky et al., 1985). No matter how intoxicated someone is, it is highly unlikely that that person will molest a child or rape a woman unless the inclination to do so existed prior to getting drunk. Similarly, those who are mentally retarded, psychotic, or organically impaired are not, *simply by virtue of their debility*, at increased risk to commit a sexual offense. Given the pre-existence of an inclination to aggress sexually, however, each of these factors may increase the likelihood of acting out.

Knight (1989) found that these four "disinhibitors" covary with MTC:CM3 classifications in clinically and theoretically meaningful ways. Knight found, for instance, that psychosis was related to increased physical injury and low contact on Axis II of MTC:CM3 (i.e., Types 5 and 6 were more likely to be psychotic). He found, moreover, that neurocognitive deficits were negatively related to social competence. That is, neurocognitive deficits were more likely to be found among the low-social-competence offenders (Types 0 and 2 on Axis I). In addition, we found that 25 offenders (16.7% of the sample) had pregnancy and birth complications. Of those 25, 22 were classified as low in social competence and high in fixation (Type 0). Finally, we found that alcohol abuse differentiated among subtypes as well (Prentky, Knight, Rosenberg, & Lee, 1989). Offenders who were low in fixation (Types 2 and 3 on Axis I) were higher in alcohol abuse than offenders who were high in fixation. Offenders who were low in amount of contact with children (Types 3–6) were higher in alcohol abuse than offenders that were high in contact. Offenders who caused greater physical injury to the child (Types 5 and 6 on Axis II) were higher in alcohol abuse than offenders who caused less physical injury.

MULTIDIMENSIONAL CLASSIFICATION OF CHILD MOLESTERS

Clinically Derived Classification Systems

One of the earliest classification systems for child molesters was proposed by Fitch in 1962. Fitch described five types, two of which were defined on the basis of whether the child molestation was seen as a preferred and longstanding form of sexual behavior (Immature type), or as a reaction to some sexual or emotional frustration at the adult level (Frustrated type). A third type, simply labeled Sociopathic, included offenders whose sexual crimes were part of a generalized social nonconformity. Child molesters whose sexually assaultive behavior was seen as secondary to psychosis, mental defect, or some organic condition constituted Fitch's fourth type, which he called Pathological. Fitch allowed a fifth, Miscellaneous category for offenders who could not be classified into one of the previous groups. Child molesters in this group typically had offenses that were isolated, impulsive, and appeared unrelated to any obvious pattern of emotional difficulty.

Kopp (1962) subdivided child molesters into two groups. His Type I is similar to Fitch's Immature type—an individual seen as timid, passive, and somewhat withdrawn in his relationships with peers. This offender was described as feeling more comfortable around children, and as not viewing his preference for their company as inappropriate. This contrasts with Kopp's Type II who, like Fitch's Frustrated type, is much more assertive and self-important. This offender often marries and may actively participate in the adult community. His sexual offenses were therefore seen as inconsistent with his typical level and quality of psychosexual adaptation.

In a 1964 paper Gebhard and Gagnon reported that four categories accounted for "virtually all of the child-offenders" whose victims were aged 5 or younger. This sub-sample consisted of 60 men out of a larger group of 1356 white males convicted of some sexual offense. It is noteworthy, along with the young age of the victims, that all but 7 of the men in the subsample had been convicted of offenses against female children. The four groups that Gebhard and Gagnon described were: (1) pedophiles (46% of the subsample), (2) mental defectives (25% of the subsample), (3) sociosexually underdeveloped (percentage not indicated), and (4) severe alcoholic involvement (10% of the subsample). The authors concluded that "in general, intelligent and/or aggressive males were conspicuous by their absence among child-offenders, indicating a different etiology for offense behavior involving aggression" (p. 579).

Gebhard, Gagnon, and their colleagues proposed a much more elaborated classification system in their 1965 book. Their system stands in marked contrast to the systems that both preceded and followed it. Unlike these other systems, their typology lacks an underlying theoretical framework to organize the distinctions among types. As a result, the types they proposed appear much more descriptive in nature. That is, each is characterized by a singular, major theme, as opposed to a systematic integration of multiple dimensions. This system also differs from the others reviewed here because of its explicit attention to two separate subgroups of offenders against nonadults (offenders against minors [ages 12–15] and offenders against children [ages 0–11]). Gebhard, Gagnon, and their colleagues subdivided their sample at the outset on the basis of several considerations, including victim sex and presence of aggression in the offense. Additionally, as just mentioned, they employed a three-way breakdown of victim age, considering offenders against "minors" as a group separate from either offenders against children or against adults. Their discussion of types therefore focused on each of six relatively discrete subgroups that resulted from crossing three factors: heterosexual or homosexual, nonaggressive or aggressive, and child or minor. The resulting six groups were: (1) heterosexual, nonaggressive offenders against children; (2) homosexual, nonaggressive offenders against children; (3) heterosexual, nonaggressive offenders against minors; (4) homosexual, nonaggressive offenders against minors; (5) heterosexual, aggressive offenders against children; and 6) heterosexual, aggressive offenders against minors. Aggressors were too infrequent in the homosexual group to justify including the last two groups (i.e., homosexual, aggressive offenders against minors and children).

Among nonaggressive offenders against children, eight types were presented that differed in incidences in the heterosexual and homosexual groups. The most frequent type was the Pedophile, who accounted for 25–33% of the heterosexuals and 50% of the homosexuals. This type appears to be distinguished primarily by the extent of the offender's sexual activity with children and the ease with which he accepts children as sexual partners. In contrast to the other classification systems, an exclusive preference for children and the development of affectionate relationships with them are not necessary for inclusion in the Pedophile group. A second type, accounting for 10% of the heterosexual group, was labeled Sociosexually Underdeveloped. This type was characterized by his comparatively young age (generally under 30) and his failure to establish mature heterosexual relations. The Sociosexually Underdeveloped offender seems to overlap with both Fitch's Frustrated and Immature types, since his offenses may appear either as "continuations of prepubertal sex play" or as a response to unsuccessful attempts to develop relationships with women. Immaturity clearly characterized the offenses of the Mentally Defective type, which was observed in 20% of the heterosexual molesters and 10% of the homosexuals. A fourth type, the Amoral Delinquent, is distinguished by offenses that are impulsive, opportunistic, and part of a pervasive, antisocial makeup and criminal history. The remaining child molester types described by Gebhard, Gagnon, and their colleagues were relatively infrequent. Two additional types, the Senile Deteriorates and the Psychotics, were classified on the basis of a single offender characteristic and accounted for about 10% of the heterosexual offenders (5% each). Two others, the Drunken and Situational offenders, were classified on the basis of offense features only and included a diversity of individuals.

Many of these same individuals were observed in the group of nonaggressive heterosexual offenders against *minors*, 20% of whom could be classified into one of the child molester types described above and 8% of whom had committed offenses against children and minors. Two unique types were, however, proposed for the offenders against minors: (1) the Subcultural offender, who belongs to a social milieu in which young adolescent girls are considered acceptable sexual partners; and (2) the Near-Peer offender, whose proximity in age or maturity to his victim makes the sexual relationship "psychologically and socially appropriate, although illegal." Two types were also posited for the nonaggressive homosexual offenders against minors. The first, accounting for one-third to one-half of the sample, was labeled the Hebephile and defined as an individual who turns from adult homosexual relations to relationships with minors because of the greater availability and lesser demands of younger partners. The second, in contrast, remains sexually active with adult males but has some encounters with boys as a result of either periodic "lapses of normal control and judgement" or a general lack of concern for the age of partners.

Finally, Gebhard, Gagnon, and their colleagues proposed types for the aggressive offenders against children and minors. The majority of aggressive child molesters, though difficult to classify, seemed to be differentiated by a cluster of attributes that included alcoholism or problem drinking, mental impairment or illness, and very low socioeconomic status. The heterosexual aggressors against minors seemed to fall in the gap between rapists of adult women and nonaggressive offenders against minors. Thus, the two most prevalent types of heterosexual aggressors against minors had counterparts in each of the two other classifications. The first of these is the Amoral Delinquent, representing one-third of the observed cases. The second displays features of the Amoral Delinquent, but also resembles the Subcultural offender against minors and the Double Standard rapist, and shares the name of the latter. These individuals, although less antisocial than the Amoral Delinquents and unlikely to assault strangers or use extreme violence, employ force to achieve sexual relations with young girls who are construed to have behaved in an inviting manner.

McCaghy (1967) proposed a six-group classification of child molesters, based in part on an empirical study of the relation between characteristics of the offender and of the offense. This classification system was based on clinical observations, as well as findings from an empirical investigation. He obtained data on 181 molesters from both interviews and official record sources and, unlike many studies, included molesters on probation (one-third of his sample) in addition to incarcerated offenders. McCaghy went beyond simply describing salient features of this sample and tested several theoretically based hypotheses. The hypothesis that appears to be most relevant for classification concerned the child's *meaning* for the offender. He proposed that individual differences in the child's "meaning" for the offender would be manifested in offense behavior. McCaghy operationally defined this meaning in terms of the extent of nonoffense interactions with children and subdivided his total sample into the following three groups: (1) high-interaction molesters, consisting of 18 offenders with numerous contacts with children not from their home or neighborhood; (2) limited interaction molesters, consisting of 103 offenders who interacted with children either in their own home, in their extended family, or in their neighborhood; and (3) minimal-interaction molesters, consisting of 60 offenders with little or no contact with children apart from their offenses.

These groups were compared on four aspects of offense behavior: (1) the familiarity of the victim, (2) the amount of coercion, (3) the context of the encounter immediately preceding the offense, and (4) the nature of the sexual behavior. Consistent differences were found in the anticipated direction (all statistically significant at least at the .05 level), most of which clearly distinguished the *high*-interaction molester from the other two groups. This high-interaction offender rarely molested strangers, did not employ overt physical coercion, was usually engaged in some nonsexual interaction with the child prior to the offense (not simply for the purpose of enticement), and was more likely to fondle or caress the child than to seek genital contact.

Since the minimal- and limited-interaction offenders did not show such clear-cut patterns of behavior, McCaghy concluded that the only type to receive strong empirical support from this study was the high-interaction molester. This type, though relatively infrequent in McCaghy's study, is similar to the various pedophilic types described by other investigators. McCaghy tentatively suggested five other types, two of which, the Career Molester and the Spontaneous-Aggressive Molester, were described in too little detail to allow for comparisons to other systems. He noted, however, that the Spontaneous-Aggressive Molester is characterized by features directly contrasting with those of the High Interaction Molester. Two others, the Senile Molester and the Asocial Molester, have counterparts in other systems. McCaghy created a separate category for the Incestuous Molester. Interestingly, he found that almost half of the offenders characterized as having *limited* interactions with children lived with children to whom they were usually related, but these offenders rarely had contact with children outside the home. He contrasted this pattern with that of the High Interaction offenders who, although well-acquainted with their eventual victims, did not offend against children over whom they had some authority (e.g., as teachers or parents).

Swanson (1971) described four groups of child molesters. His Classic Pedophiliac is similar to Fitch's Immature type, Kopp's Type I, and McCaghy's High Interaction Molester, and was described as an individual with a consistent, often exclusive interest in children. Swanson noted that the Classic Pedophiliac may, at the outset, simply want to play with and care for the children whom they ultimately abuse. In contrast, the Inadequate Sociopathic Violator does not show a specific sexual attraction to children, and may exploit an older female child if she is a convenient or available source of gratification. The Situational Violator was described as one for whom environmental circumstances and situational events are particularly important. He is likely to have sustained a long-term relationship with a peer and may well have been married. His offenses tend to be impulsive and later regretted. He most closely resembles Fitch's Frustrated type and Kopp's Type II. He differs from the Inadequate Sociopathic Violator in that he is typically more stable in other areas of functioning, such as employment history, and is described as being more shy and schizoid. Swanson's Brain-damaged type is similar to Fitch's Pathological type and refers to an individual whose molesting is a function of (or of secondary importance to) some other clinical condition, such as senility or mental retardation.

The Massachusetts Treatment Center (MTC) Classification System for Child Molesters

Classification systems having roots in these earlier typologies derived from collaborative work at the Massachusetts Treatment Center in Bridgewater (Cohen, Garofalo, Boucher, & Seghorn, 1971; Cohen, Seghorn, & Calmas, 1969; Groth & Birnbaum, 1979). Typologies for child molesters and for rapists was proposed by Cohen, Seghorn, and their colleagues. Similar typologies for rapists and for child molesters were developed by Groth and his colleagues.

Cohen and Seghorn's Typology

In the classification system reported by Cohen, Seghorn, and Calmas in 1969, three types of "pedophilia" were described. The "pedophile-fixated type" consists of those offenders whose criminal behavior suggests an apparent arrest in psychosocial development, characterized by an inability to develop and sustain mature relationships with peers at any point in their life. This is the offender with a longstanding, exclusive preference for children as both sexual and general social companions. Few of these offenders have married and there is a negligible history of dating or peer interaction in adolescence or adulthood. Frequently the child is known to the offender in the context of some platonic relationship before any sexual behavior occurs. Offense behavior typically involves minimal if any force or aggression, and the sexual acts pursued are typically nongenital in nature, i.e., fondling, caressing, kissing, or sucking. The victims are usually known to the offender, and the offenses often occur after a period of "courtship." This offender usually has average or near-average intelligence, and his social skills are adequate for day-to-day management, although he is described as shy, timid, and passive. His work history may be steady, although it may be at a level below his apparent capabilities. Cohen and Seghorn noted the difficulty in treating this individual, who typically is not anxious about or disturbed by his behavior or his exclusive preference for children. In addition, these offenders were reported to settle easily into an institutional setting, where they usually create no management problems. Although the least dangerous of the child molester types in terms of physical damage done to any victims, this group was noted to be the most recidivistic.

The "pedophile-regressed type" is similar to the Fixated type in that aggression in the offense, if present, is instrumental and the primary aim is sexual. The most distinctive features of this group are the typically higher levels of social and sexual adaptation achieved. Indeed, adolescent development appears to be normal with respect to peer relationships, dating, and heterosexual experiences. The offender has usually established adult relationships and is likely to have married and to have made a satisfactory work adjustment. Although adult adaptation in major areas of life (e.g., education, military service, employment, marriage) appears to be adequate and appropriate, the adaptation is fragile and tenuous. In the face of severe stress in which the offender's sense of competence and adequacy is questioned, he may regress and turn to an inappropriate object. The offenses tend to be impulsive and are more likely to involve female children who are unknown to the offender. The offense behavior is frequently dystonic for the offender, and he may experience guilt, remorse, or disbelief afterwards. There is typically no sexual fixation on the child so that recidivism depends on the offender's subsequent ability to cope appropriately with whatever sources of stress preceded the offenses.

The third group described by Cohen, Seghorn, and Calmas is the "pedophile-aggressive type." In this group, the primary aim is aggression rather than sex, although the offenses always contain both sexual and aggressive features. Like the sadistic rapists, there is a tendency for the aggression and violence to be focused on sexual areas. Victims are more likely to be male, and the aggression "is expressed in cruel and vicious assaults ... The sexual excitement increases as an apparent function of the aggression" (Cohen et al., 1969, p. 251). There is typically a long history of poor adult adaptation in both sexual and nonsexual areas; as a result these offenders are considered very difficult to treat. Because of the fused aggressive and sexual components, they are also considered quite dangerous. Fortunately, as Groth (1978) noted in discussing his comparable Sadistic child molesters, they are the least common type.

Seghorn added a fourth type in 1970. This Exploitative type, in marked contrast to the Fixated and Regressed types, exploits the inherent weakness of the child and uses the child to gratify his own sexual needs. Genital sexual acts are commonly attempted, and aggression, while typically instrumental, is often used if the offender feels it will ensure the child's compliance. As Seghorn noted, this is a highly narcissistic man who does not care about the emotional or physical well-being of the child, who is typically unknown to him. This offender is descriptively similar to Fitch's (1962) Sociopathic and Swanson's (1971) Inadequate Sociopathic Violator types. He frequently shows many features of the antisocial personality disorder, including a history of antisocial and possibly criminal acts, a chaotic childhood, pervasively poor impulse control, and unstable relationships with peers. Cohen and Seghorn noted that these Exploitative child molesters tend to be less socially facile than many individuals labeled psychopathic; they lack the charm or glibness frequently associated with that disorder. Cohen and Seghorn hypothesized that the markedly defective interpersonal skills of these offenders may in fact contribute substantially to their choice of children for their offenses.

This fourth type was formally incorporated into their classification system in a 1979 article authored by Cohen, Seghorn, and their colleagues Richard Boucher and Jed

Mehegan. In addition to presenting the exploitative offender, the authors identified three descriptive dimensions that were used to derive the four types of child molesters: (1) the motivation of the act (including the quality of the offender's perception of the child as a sexual object), (2) the degree to which the offense reflects a lifelong fixation on the child as a preferred object (versus a regression from a more mature level of psychosexual relationships with adults), and (3) the quality and role of aggression in the offense.

Groth's Typology

Groth also distinguished between the offender who manifests a persistent pattern of child molestation reflecting fixation at a psychosexually immature stage and the offender whose molestation represents a regression from a more mature level of psychosexual adaptation. In a chapter of a book that Groth coauthored with his colleagues Burgess, Holmstrom, and Sgroi in 1978, he distinguished between two *patterns* (fixated or regressed) and between three *motivations* (sex-pressure, sex-force, and incest). In the Sex-Pressure type the offender entices or bribes the child and may desist if the victim actively refuses or resists. This offender is seen as caring for the child on some level, as in Fitch's (1962) Immature type, Kopp's (1962) Type I, McCaghy's (1967) High Interaction molester, and Swanson's (1971) Classic Pedophiliac. Within Groth's second group of Sex-Force child molesters there are two identified subtypes. The first, labeled Exploitative, uses threats or force to overcome victim resistance and shows little regard for the child's feelings. This type corresponds to the Inadequate Sociopathic Violator described by Swanson and the Exploitative offender described by Cohen and Seghorn. The second of the Sex-Force types, the Sadistic child molester, has no specified counterpart in any other system except that developed by Cohen and Seghorn, which they referred to as the Aggressive type. This group is comprised of offenders for whom force and aggression have become eroticized, and thus the offenses are often characterized by cruelty, rage, and degradation.

It was unclear from his chapter whether Groth intended for the two patterns (Fixation and Regression) to be fully crossed with the four motivations (Sex-Pressure, Sex-Force : Exploitative, Sex-Force : Sadistic, Incest), yielding eight types, or whether the types were independent of one another. This question was clarified in Groth's 1981 revision of his typology, in which he classified offenders as *child molesters* (in which case they were typed as Fixated or Regressed) or as *child rapists* (in which case they were typed as Anger, Power, or Sadistic), yielding five separate groups.

A system that has gained particular favor in the criminal investigative field (Lanning, 1986) is the one originally devised by Dietz (1983). As Lanning (1986) pointed out, the distinct advantage of this typology is that its purpose is to assist with the apprehension of child molesters. Dietz subdivided child molesters into two major categories, the Situational offender and the Preferential offender. Although the Situational offender is a variant of Fitch's Frustrated offender, Kopp's Type II offender, Swanson's Situational Violator, Gebhard's Situational offender, and the Regressed offender of Cohen/Seghorn and Groth, this offender category subsumes much more varied motivations than any of the other similar types. The Situational offender category includes four subtypes, the Regressed offender, the Morally Indiscriminate offender (the manipulative, exploitative type), the Sexually Indiscriminate offender (sexual experimentation with children out of boredom), and the Inadequate Offender (includes those suffering from psychosis, eccentric personality disorders, mental retardation, and senility). The Preferential offender is, by name and description, very similar to Fitch's Immature type, Kopp's Type I, McCaghy's High Interaction type, Gebhard's Pedophile, and the Fixated type of Cohen/Seghorn and Groth. Like the Situational group, the Preferential group also is more inclusive than any of the similar types described by other writers. The Preferential category includes three subtypes, the Seduction offender (clear sexual preference for children, offender likely to collect child pornography), the Introverted offender (a socially and interpersonally deficient version of the Seduction offender), and the Sadistic offender.

Another classification scheme developed to assist law enforcement was proposed by Douglas, A. W. Burgess, A. G. Burgess, and Ressler (1992). In their *Crime Classification Manual*, Douglas and his colleagues provided a comprehensive DSM-like list of primary categories with embedded subtypes. In this system, child molesters could be classified in any of the following categories: (1) Nuisance offenses (any one of four subtypes), (2) Domestic sexual assault (child domestic sexual abuse), (3) Entitlement rape (child victim), (4) Subordinate rape (child victim), (5) Power-reassurance rape (child victim), (6) Exploitative rape (child victim), (7) Anger rape (child victim), (8) Sadistic rape (child victim), (9) Child/adolescent pornography (any one of three subtypes), (10) Historical child/adolescent sex rings (any one of three subtypes), (11) Multidimensional sex rings (any one of three subtypes), and (12) Abduction rape (child victim). With the exception of "specialty" categories, such as pornography, sex rings, and abduction, most of these subtypes borrow from preceding systems. As Douglas et al. noted, "The subtypes described here attempt to capture components judged to be critical across taxonomic systems" (p. 193).

Three Common Subtypes

It is noteworthy that most child molester systems have included a type with an exclusive and longstanding sexual and social preference for children ("fixated") and contrasted this type with a second whose offenses were seen as a regression from an adult level of psychosexual adaptation in response to stress ("regressed"). Most systems also described a third type comprised of antisocial individuals with very poor social skills who turned to children largely because they are easy to exploit, not because they were preferred or desired partners.

- Child molester with an exclusive and longstanding sexual and social preference for children
- Child molester whose offenses represent a regression from an adult level of psychosocial adaptation in response to stress
- An exploitative or sociopathic child molester with very poor social skills who turned to children because they were easy prey

Fixated Type

This is an offender with a longstanding, exclusive preference for children as both sexual and social companions. Few of these offenders have married and there is a negligible history of dating or peer interaction in adolescence or adulthood. Frequently the child is known to the offender before any sexual contact occurs. Offense behavior typically involves minimal if any force or aggression, and the sexual acts are typically nongenital, such as fondling, caressing, kissing, or sucking.

Regressed Type

The regressed type is similar to the fixated in that aggression in the offense, if present, is instrumental and the child is seen as a love object. There is a higher likelihood with this group, however, that the offense behavior will include more genital sex. The most distinctive features of this group are the typically high levels of social and sexual adaptation achieved. This offender has usually established adult relationships and is likely to have married and to have made a satisfactory work adjustment. These adaptations may be quite tenuous, however, and in response to severe stress in which the offender's sense of competence and adequacy is questioned, he may regress and turn to an inappropriate object. This behavior is frequently ego-dystonic for the offender, and he may experience remorse, guilt, and shame afterwards.

Exploitative Type

The exploitative child molester is quite different. This offender exploits the weakness of the child and uses him or her specifically to gratify his own sexual needs. Genital sexual acts are common, and aggression, while typically instrumental, will be used if the offender believes that it is needed to ensure compliance. He does not care about the emotional or physical well-being of the child, who is typically unknown to him. This offender is descriptively similar to Fitch's (1962) Sociopathic type, Swanson's (1971) Inadequate Sociopathic Violator and Groth and Burgess's (1977b) Sex-Force : Exploitative type.

The Regression/Fixation Conundrum

The classification of child molesters into categories that are roughly analogous to fixation and its counterpart—regression—is the most common discrimination in the clinical literature on such offenders. As clinicians, we have lived with these descriptive terms for over a quarter of a century. The terms are widely used, sometimes with passing consideration for "criteria" but more often in a casual or informal way. One could reasonably conclude that, at this point, these two terms have become part of the clinical lore surrounding child molesters.

The use of the terms *fixation* and *regression* in connection with child molesters first came into prominence in the writings of Cohen and his students Calmas, Seghorn, and Groth. Although the term fixation had been used previously by Benjamin Karpman in the mid-1950s, it was applied in the psychodynamic sense (i.e., the offender was fixated *on* someone, typically his mother). The first *descriptive* use of the term (i.e., the offender was fixated or "stuck" *at* some earlier stage of psychosexual development) was probably in Calmas's 1965 dissertation. For all practical purposes, however, the terms *fixation* and *regression* did not appear in print in its present usage until Cohen, Seghorn, and Calmas's 1969 article. In that 1969 paper, three offender types were described (Fixated, Regressed, and Aggressive).

In a book that Groth coedited with Burgess, Holmstrom, and Sgroi, Groth distinguished the offender who manifests a persistent pattern of molesting that reflects fixation at a psychosexually immature stage from the offender whose molestation represents a regression from a more mature level of psychosexual adaptation (Groth, 1978). This fixation/regression distinction could be applied to all molesters, and was independent of motivational intent. In Groth's 1981 revision, he classified offenders as child molesters (either fixated or regressed) or child rapists (either anger, power, or sadistic).

Cohen, Seghorn, and Calmas (1969) noted the following about the "Pedophile-fixated type":

- "The offender has never been able to develop or maintain mature object relationships with his male or female peers at any stage of his adolescent, young adult, or adult life. He is socially comfortable only with children and seeks them out as companions or seeks out employment where he can work or be near them."

Cohen, Seghorn, and Calmas (1969) noted the following about the "Pedophile-regressed type":

- "There is a history of an apparently normal adolescence with good peer relationships, some dating behavior, and heterosexual experiences.... There is frequently a history of an inability to deal with the normal stresses of adult life and alcoholic episodes become increasingly more frequent and result in the breakdown of a relatively stable marital, social, and work adjustment."
- "In almost all cases, the victim of the offenders in [this] group is a female child, with homosexual pedophilia extremely rare."

Groth (1981) provided these selected characteristics of fixated and regressed molesters:

- Fixated
  - Little or no seuxal contact initiated with agemates. Offender is usually single or in a marriage of convenience
  - Characterological immaturity, poor sociosexual peer relationships
  - Male (same sex) victims are primary targets
- Regressed
  - Sexual contact with a child coexists with sexual contact with agemates. Offender is usually married or in a common-law relationship
  - More traditional lifestyle, but underdeveloped peer relationships
  - Female (opposite sex) victims are primary targets

Despite this legacy a few intrepid souls have suggested that the venerable concept of fixation/regression may have shortcomings. Conte's (1985) noteworthy concern was that the fixated–regressed dichotomy evolved solely out of clinical experience and had never been subjected to any form of empirical validation. Finkelhor and Araji (1986) raised a more theoretical problem. In their four-factor model, they distinguished between "emotional congruence" (which involves arrested development and low self-esteem) and "blockage" (which involves fear of adult females, poor social skills, and marital disturbance). Finkelhor and Araji's important conceptual and theoretical contribution suggested that social and interpersonal competence may have to be considered independently of fixation. Implicit, or explicit, in the various systems that have described fixated and regressed types is an assessment of achieved level of social competence. Fixated offenders are typically differentiated from regressed offenders by marital status, number and quality of age-appropriate heterosexual relationships, acquired level of education, and achieved skill level. The fixated child molester is likely to have a negligible history of dating or peer interaction in adolescence or adulthood and, if married, the quality of the relationship will be very poor.

Consistent with generally accepted practice, we combined, in an earlier version of our child molester classification system (MTC:CM2; Knight & Prentky, 1990), primary object choice for sexual partners (i.e., children or adults) and achieved social competence in order to differentiate fixation and regression. We found that a serious reliability problem was created by the large number of cases in which object choice and social competence were not coupled (e.g., cases where the primary object choice was children but level of social competence was high). We reasoned that *all* child molesters manifested some degree of fixation simply by virtue of their choice of children as sexual partners. Thus, the dichotomy of fixation or regression (which implies the absence of fixation) was misleading. It made more sense to think of fixation as a continuum (i.e., degree of fixation) rather than as present or absent. We further reasoned, along with Finkelhor and Araji, that social competence and fixation may be confounded and that independent assessments of these two dimensions might enhance reliability as well as validity. Thus, in the current version of our classification system (MTC:CM3), fixation and social competence are independent (and dichotomous) decisions yielding four types (see Knight, Carter, & Prentky, 1989).

In our own research, we defined fixation as unequivocal, direct evidence that children have been a central focus of the offender's sexual and interpersonal thoughts and fantasies for a period of at least 6 months (Knight et al., 1989, p. 13). This definition pinpoints an exclusive preference for children as social and sexual companions and does not include competency in any other sphere of human endeavor. The "classic" fixated offender (i.e., as described by Cohen, Seghorn, and Groth) would be classified as "0," while the "classic" regressed offender (as described by Cohen, Seghorn, and Groth) would be classified as "3." Based upon a sample of 177 incarcerated child molesters, we found that one-third of the offenders were classified into one of the other two categories (Type 1: High Fixation/ High Social Competence or Type 2: Low Fixation/Low Social Competence) (Knight, 1989). In other words, even in a prison sample, where one would expect to find mostly high-fixated and lower-social-competence child molesters, 16.4% of the men were classified as low fixated and 24.3% were classified as high in social competence (see Knight, 1989).

Disentangling social competence and fixation in MTC:CM3 has served the intended purpose of increasing interrater reliability to an acceptable level. In addition, validity studies have supported many a priori speculations about how these groups would differ (Knight, 1989, 1992; Prentky, Knight, Rosenberg, & Lee, 1989).

Noteworthy Type 1's

Of some historical note are two very well known British writers and academics who would be classified as type "1" on Axis I (i.e., high social competence and high fixation) of MTC:CM3.

Charles Lutwidge Dodgson (a.k.a. Lewis Carroll) taught mathematics at his alma mater, Christ Church College, Oxford, for close to three decades. His scientific contributions were prolific, including 10 books and hundreds of papers and articles. His fictional writings included, among other works, six children's books. He was ordained a deacon in the Church of England, and was a prominent member of the Tory Party. Despite lifelong commitments of considerable responsibility, he was never entirely at ease in the company of adults. At social gatherings he was acutely shy, sitting for hours contributing little to conversation. His scientific contributions were said to have suffered because of his reluctance to actively engage in dialogue with his colleagues. Marriage apparently was never a consideration despite numerous acquaintanceships and, in at least one case, friendship (with the well-known actress Ellen Terry). Throughout his entire life the only objects of his love were young girls (12 or younger). He truly loved his young companions, and was very much at ease with them. Reportedly, the only time when he did not stutter was when he was in their company. The interested reader is referred to an article by Gopnik (1995) on "Lewis Carroll and the loves of his life."

Sir James Matthew Barrie was a freelance dramatist and novelist who was lord rector of St. Andrews University from 1919 to 1922, appointed to the Order of Merit in 1922, and elected president of the Society of Authors in 1928. He served as chancellor of Edinburgh University from 1930 until shortly before his death in 1937. He was made a baronet in 1913. Barrie married Mary Ansell, an actress, in 1894. The marriage was dissolved in 1909, childless and apparently unconsummated. In 1887, Barrie met Sylvia Llewellyn Davies. Sylvia died 4 months after he ended his marriage with Mary Ansell. He adopted Sylvia's five sons and had intense love affairs with two of the boys (George and Michael) (Birkin, 1979). For George and Michael, Barrie wove the early tales of *Peter Pan*.

Dodgson was the creator of an imaginary world where one very special girl never grew up (because in Wonderland time stood still). Barrie was the creator of an imaginary world where boys (female visitors were not allowed in Never-Never Land) never grew up. Dodgson and Barrie are classic examples of highly fixated pedophiles who also achieved indisputably very high levels of competence in many spheres of their lives.

We have outgrown our earlier, simpler notions about how the world of child molesters is organized. Our understanding of child molestation is more sophisticated than it was 20 years ago. In keeping with current wisdom we should be examining a variety of factors that may contribute—independently or in combination—to our understanding of child sexual abuse. One such factor that captures an important albeit smaller part of the world than previously thought is fixation. Fixation remains a useful organizing principle as long as it is well-defined (e.g., the degree or strength of an individual's sexual preoccupation with children) and its boundaries well-drawn. Other potentially useful factors, however, include social competence, the amount of contact that the offender has with children, the nature of the sexual acts, and the degree of injury to the victim (Table 1).

Classification of Incest Offenders

It is clear that, as a group, incest offenders are as heterogeneous as nonincest child molesters (e.g., Rist, 1979; Summit & Kryso, 1978). It would thus be misleading, if not specious, to draw inferences and makes decisions about incest offenders under the assumption that they constitute a coherent, cohesive group. Nevertheless, incest offenders are invariably referred to as if they were a homogeneous group, and very few attempts have

Table 1. Comparable Subtypes on Child Molester Classification Systems

Fitch (1962)	Kopp (1962)	Gebhard et al. (1965)	McCaghy (1967)	Swanson (1971)	Groth (1981)	Dietz (1983)/ Lanning (1986)	Knight et al. (1989) (MTC:CM3)
				Common Type 1			
Immature	Type I	Sociosexually Underdeveloped	High Interaction Molester	Classic Pedophiliac	Molestation: Fixated	Preferential: Seduction or Preferential: Introverted	Axis I: Fixated/Low Social Competence Axis II: Interpersonal or Narcissistic
				Common Type 2			
Frustrated	Type II	Situational		Situational Violator	Molestation: Regressed	Situational: Regressed type	Axis I: Lo Fixated/Hi Social Competence Axis II: Interpersonal or Narcissistic or Exploitative
				Common Type 3			
Sociopathic		Amoral Delinquent	Asocial Molester	Inadequate Sociopathic Violator	Rape: Power	Situational: Morally Indiscriminate	Axis I: any type Axis II: Exploitative or Muted Sadistic

Types Characterized by Expressive Aggression

	Spontaneous/ Aggressive	Rape: Anger Type; Rape: Sadistic Type	Preferential: Sadistic Type	Situational: Sexually Indiscriminate; Incestuous; Situational: Inadequate	Axis I: Low Social Competence Types; Axis II: Aggressive or Sadistic
Types characterized by psychosis, mental defect, or organicity					
Pathological	Mentally Defective; Senile Deteriorate; Psychotic	Incestuous Molester; Senile Molester; Brain damage			
Additional unrelated types					
Miscellaneous	Drunken		Career Molester[a]		

Note. Adapted from Prenky (1999) by permission.

[a] Comparability for these types in unclear.

been made to develop any classification system, clinical or empirical. Indeed, to the best of our knowledge, there have been no attempts to implement and test the validity of any classification system for incest offenders.

One of the earliest attempts to classify incest offenders was that of Weinberg (1955). Weinberg described two incest families: (1) the ingrown family whose members fail to develop relationships outside the family and relate primarily to each other, and (2) the promiscuous family where sexual boundaries are inappropriate or nonexistent.

Summit and Kryso (1978) provided a much more elaborated "spectrum" of incest cases:

- Incidental Sexual Contact typically involves isolated expressions of erotic interest or dependency needs. These behaviors often include sexual "games" that are not considered abusive.
- Ideological Sexual Contact is motivated by the parent's belief that expression of sexual instincts and feelings is beneficial to the child.
- Psychotic Intrusion accounts for those instances in which psychotic thinking contributes to the abuse.
- Rustic Environment refers to the folkloric notion that isolated and remote communities promote incest behavior. This category accounts for those cases in which families who have lived in rural settings for generations accept as natural the practice of incest.
- True Endogamous (within marriage) Incest represents the largest class of incest offenders. The dynamics governing endogamous incest were described in the now-classic paper by Cormier, Kennedy, and Sangowicz (1962) and in papers by Herman and Hirschman (1977) and Rosenfeld (1977; Rosenfeld, Nadelson, Krieger, & Backman, 1977). The endogamous incest father, as described by Summit and Kryso, appears to be a relatively well-adjusted individual in many areas of his life (such as work, community activities, avocational pastimes). Disappointments, failures, and stressful life events contribute to role distortion in which the father eroticizes his relationship with his daughter. The mother, for her part, is often disillusioned with the relationship and dissatisfied with her husband. The more that she disengages from the relationship, the more she leaves a vacuum to be filled by her daughter. The daughter gradually assumes many of her mother's familial roles, such as preparing dinner and satisfying her father's ego needs. Boundaries become increasingly blurry and limits increasingly bent until the daughter becomes her father's surrogate "lover." Although there are many ways of understanding the complex interplay of factors that contribute to and foster endogamous incest, it would appear that family dynamics represent the kernel of the pathology.
- Misogynous Incest is a variant of True Endogamous Incest in which hatred of women is the principal driving force behind the abuse. The father's sexual abuse of his daughter may be seen as an act of anger directed at his wife or as a form of punishment of his daughter.
- Imperious Incest represents an admixture of elements found in Ideological, Rustic, and Misogynous incest cases. These offenders reign as "emperors" of their family. In a caricature of male chauvinism, they exercise sovereign power over their wife and children. Their perceived authority embraces all aspects of family functioning.

The daughters become vassals of the feudal lord and their sexual "favors" acts of fidelity.

- Pedophilic Incest comprises those offenders who have an erotic attraction to children. This category includes men who have sexually victimized both their own children and children unknown to them, as well as men who have resisted their fantasies of molesting children outside the home but eventually are overwhelmed by the availability of their own children and give in to their urges.
- Child Rape refers to those, typically surrogate, fathers who are fundamentally inadequate men who nourish power, need to punish, and are attracted to violence. Their generalized tendency to antisocial behavior occasionally includes the sexual assault of their own children.
- Perverse or Pornographic Incest is a category aptly described by Summit and Kryso as "kinky, unfettered lechery." "These cases become more bizarre, more frankly erotic, more flagrantly manipulative and destructive than those in earlier categories" (p. 56). There is a ritualistic, "pornographic" quality to these offenses that clearly reflects the driving force of an intrusive fantasy life.

The prototypic classification system of Summit and Kryso is a helpful clinical contribution to the incest literature, clearly illustrating the marked heterogeneity of men who commit incestuous offenses. This very heterogeneity provides some support for the possibility that some of the dimensions that have successfully discriminated among nonincest child molesters may be relevant for discriminating among incest offenders.

The Usefulness of MTC:CM3 for Classifying Incest

In our own classification research, we have been studying incarcerated samples of child molesters in which exclusive incest cases are infrequent (Knight & Prentky, 1990). As a result we have focused only on offenders who have molested children who were not related to them by blood or marriage, or who have started sexually abusing their own children *after* they had molested other children. The more circumscribed nature of the offenses of incest fathers and the fact that by definition all of them are (or were) married suggest that the usefulness of MTC:CM3 for differentiating among them is limited. All exclusive incest offenders, for instance, would, according to current operational criteria, be high in Social Competence and high in Fixation. At the very least, MTC:CM3 criteria for dimensions of Fixation, Social Competence, and Amount of Contact with Children would have to be amended if the system was to be applied to incest offenders.

Fixation

The fixation distinction of Axis I in MTC:CM3 separates child molesters into those with an enduring focus on children as sexual objects and those without such an enduring pedophiliac interest. Since high fixation in MTC:CM3 is defined, in part, by evidence of a relationship with a child that lasts for 6 months or longer, the strict application of this criterion would mean that virtually all exclusive incest offenders would be classified as "high" in fixation.

It appears, however, that a similar fixation distinction may be useful for incest cases. A small subgroup of incest offenders have deviant sexual arousal to children (Abel, Becker, et al., 1981; Marshall, Barbaree, & Christophe, 1986). It has also been estimated that as many as 25–35% of incest offenders have pedophilic erotic preferences (Langevin, Day, Handy, & Russon, 1985). Finally, there is some evidence that a large number of incest offenders (40–50%) have molested children *outside* of their families (Abel, Mittelman, Becker, Cunningham-Rathner, & Lucas, 1983). Thus, it is reasonable to conclude that a group of incest offenders may be fixated. This group is, in essence, Summit and Kryso's Pedophilic Incest group.

Social Competence

The social competence distinction of Axis I in MTC:CM3 separates child molesters into those who have demonstrated some degree of mastery of social, interpersonal, and vocational skills and those who have not. *Non*incest child molesters have consistently been found deficient as a group in their social skills (Marshall & Christie, 1981; Overholser & Beck, 1986; Quinsey, 1977; Segal & Marshall, 1985). Given that incest offenders were married at the time of their offenses, one might reasonably infer that they are likely to be more competent, as a group, than nonincest offenders in their social and interpersonal skills. In fact, because of their marital status and possibly, but not necessarily, their involvement in parenting, incest fathers would likely be rated as "high" in social competence on MTC:CM3. It would be *incorrect*, however, to conclude that incest fathers, as a group, are highly socially skilled. Indeed, incest fathers report low levels of group involvement (Quinn, 1984). In addition, about one-third of incest offenders report that they have almost no friends (Parker, 1984) and incest fathers report higher levels of introversion than controls on psychological tests (Kirkland & Bauer, 1982; Langevin, Day, Handy, & Russon, 1985; Scott & Stone, 1986).

At this point it is reasonable to conclude that (1) social competence may serve as an important discriminator for incest offenders, and (2) social competence, as operationalized in MTC:CM3, should be revised for use with exclusive incest offenders.

Amount of Contact with Children

The Amount of Contact decision on Axis II of MTC:CM3 yields two types that have high contact with children and four types that have low contact with children. The high-contact types tend to be more passive and dependent while low-contact types tend to be more impulsive and antisocial. Once again, simply by virtue of the fact that the exclusive incest offender lives with his victim, most incest offenders would be classified as "high" in Amount of Contact.

Several studies suggest, however, that a similar distinction may be found among incest offenders. A number of studies reported that incest offenders were more passive, anxious, or reserved than controls (e.g., Kirkland & Bauer, 1982; Langevin, Paitich, Freeman, Mann, & Handy, 1978; Quinn, 1984; Scott & Stone, 1986). In contrast, other studies have described incest fathers as dominant, authoritarian, even tyrannical (Green, 1988). Summit and Kryso's (1978) Misogynous, Imperious, and Child Rape incest offenders would all fall in this category. Incest fathers have been reported to dominate their families with the use of

Table 2. Profiles of MTC:CM3 Axis II Subtypes

Type 1: Interpersonal
  High Contact with children
  Nongenital, nonorgasmic sexual acts (e.g., fondling, caressing, frottage)
  Offender knew victim prior to sexual assault
  Offender often has long-term relationship or multiple contacts with the same victim
  Offenses reflect a high degree of planning
Type 2: Narcissistic
  High Contact with children
  Primary motive is sexual gratification; interests are self-centered
  Phallic sexual acts (i.e., primary aim is achieving orgasm; victim is used as a masturbatory object)
  Victims often are strangers
  Offenses are usually single encounters with each victim
  Offenders tend to be promiscuous (i.e., many victims)
  Offenses are likely to appear more spontaneous with little planning
Type 3: Exploitative
  Low Contact with children
  Relatively little physical injury to victims (i.e., no more aggression or force than necessary to gain the compliance of the victim)
  There is *no* evidence that the aggression in the offense was eroticized or sexualized
  Sexual acts are likely to be phallic, with sexual gratification being the primary aim
  Victims are typically strangers
  Offenses have very little evidence of planning
Type 4: Muted Sadistic
  Low Contact with children
  Relatively little serious physical injury to victims
  Evidence that aggression was eroticized (e.g., sexual acts include bondage, spanking, urination, use of feces, bizarre, peculiar, or ritualized acts, insertion of nondamaging foreign objects, use of "props" that suggest sadistic fantasy, or offender reports the presence of sadistic fantasies)
  Victims are typically strangers
  Offenses reflect a moderate degree of planning
Type 5: Aggressive
  Low Contact with children
  High degree of physical injury to victims (injury may be accidental, resulting from th eoffender's clumsiness or ineptitude, or from aggression rooted in anger at the victim; in the latter case, the amount of aggression or force clearly exceeded what was necessary to gain the victim's compliance))
  Sexual acts are likely to be phallic; there is no evidence of sadism (i.e., that the aggression was eroticized)
  Victims are typically strangers
  Offenses reflect very little evidence of planning
Type 6: Overt Sadistic
  Low Contact with children
  High degree of physical injury to victims
  Offender is highly aroused or derives pleasure from putting the victim in fear or subjecting the victim to pain
  Presence of force, violence, or threats of violence appears to increase sexual arousal
  Presence of bizarre, ritualized, or peculiar sexual acts, insertion of foreign objects, or use of bondage or other forms of restraint
  Victims are typically strangers
  Offenses reflect a high degree of planning

Note. Abstracted from Knight & Prentky (1990).

force (Herman, 1981) and to frequently abuse their wives (Paveza, 1987; Truesdell, McNeil, & Deschner, 1986). Feltman (1985) compared incest fathers with fathers of daughters who had been referred to a juvenile court, finding that approximately the same percentage of both groups (19%) were reported to have beaten their daughters or to have threatened or abused them with a weapon. Such abusive, aggressive behavior is consistent with the elevation on the MMPI Psychopathy scale often found among samples of incest fathers (e.g., Hall, Maiuro, Vitaliano, & Proctor, 1986; Kirkland & Bauer, 1982; Scott & Stone, 1986).

As with the dimensions of Fixation and Social Competence, a revised Amount of Contact dimension may be an important component of a model for classifying incest offenders.

Other Incest/Nonincest Similarities

Developmental Antecedents

The developmental histories of both incest and nonincest child molesters also have sufficient similarities to suggest that the two groups might share common developmental antecedents. A large proportion of both groups have reported histories of sexual abuse in their own childhood (Baker, 1985; Bard et al., 1987; Seghorn, Prentky, & Boucher, 1987). Seghorn et al. (1987) found that 57% of a sample of 54 nonincest child molesters had been sexually victimized during their childhood or adolescence. Groth and Burgess (1977b) found that 32% of a sample of 106 child molesters reported being sexually victimized during their childhood. Langevin, Day, Handy, and Russon (1985) found over five times as many incidents of sexual abuse in the childhoods of their incest offenders as compared to their nonoffender controls. In addition, comparably high proportions of both incest and nonincest offenders have experienced a significant amount of physical abuse and emotional neglect during their upbringing (Bard et al., 1987; Brandon, 1985; Lustig, Dresser, Spellman, & Murray, 1966; Parker & Parker, 1986; Seghorn et al., 1987; Weiner, 1962). For both groups there is ample evidence of disruptive, unstable, rejecting relationships with parents (Baker, 1985; Bard et al., 1987; Cavallin, 1966; Justice & Justice, 1979; Kaufman, Peck, & Tagiori, 1954; Maisch, 1972; Parker & Parker, 1986; Prentky, Knight, Sims-Knight, et al., 1989). Indeed, paternal attitudes and behaviors have been identified as particularly problematic for both groups (Baker, 1985; Parker & Parker, 1986; Prentky, Knight, Sims-Knight, et al., 1989; Seghorn et al., 1987).

Relationship of Offender to Victim

Preceding discussion has focused, implicitly or explicitly, on the father as the perpetrator. Although father–daughter and stepfather–daughter incest is the most common form of within-family sexual abuse, it may account for no more than one-third of all incest cases (Finkelhor, 1984). If a full accounting of all incest is to be achieved, we must not, as Finkelhor cautioned, discount or dismiss incest that is perpetrated by older brothers, uncles, grandfathers, and other significant family caregivers. In 250 consecutive admissions of child victims to Joseph J. Peters Institute (Philadelphia, PA) between 1987 and 1992, there were 53 different types of relationships between the child victim and her/his perpetrator.

Father–daughter *and* stepfather–daughter cases accounted for *less* than one-quarter of the sample. It appears that the relationships between incest offenders and their victims may be as varied as the relationships between nonincest offenders and their victims. In both cases the relationship between offender and victim may have etiologic as well as clinical importance.

Similarities between Incest and Nonincest Subtypes

Similarities between the subtypes proposed by Summit and Kryso (1978) and subtypes of nonincest offenders are noteworthy. For example, Summit and Kryso's Pedophilic Incest offender is very similar to the Interpersonal child molester in MTC:CM3, as well as other nonincest subtypes (e.g., Gebhard's Pedophile, Swanson's Classic Pedophiliac, and Fitch's Immature type). Summit and Kryso's Child Rape incest offender is similar to the Exploitative child molester in MTC:CM3, as well as other nonincest offender types (e.g., Groth's Rape-Power type, and Swanson's Inadequate Sociopathic Violator). Summit and Kryso's Misogynous Incest offender bears some resemblance to the Aggressive child molester in MTC:CM3, as well as other nonincest offender types (e.g., Groth's Rape-Anger type). Finally, Summit and Kryso's Perverse Incest offender shares many common features with those nonincest types that have been labeled sadistic (e.g., the bizarre, ritualistic, "pornographic" quality of the sexual acts, the polymorphous perverse nature of the sexual outlets, the playing out of highly detailed, intrusive fantasies).

Overview of Taxonomic Needs for Incest Offenders

As a starting point for beginning to develop a taxonomic model for classifying incest offenders, the following four dimensions would seem relevant: (1) a revised construct along the lines of what we refer to as Fixation in MTC:CM3; presumably, such a construct would take into consideration the varying degrees of sexual preoccupation with children observed in samples of incest offenders, (2) a revised Social Competence construct that would take into account the obvious differences in social, interpersonal, and vocational skills observed in samples of incest offenders, (3) a dimension that accounts for variability in impulsive, antisocial behavior in the histories of incest offenders, and (4) a dimension that would account for the marked differences in intrusiveness, force, and violence observed in samples of incest offenders.

An Empirically Derived Classification System for Child Molesters

At the invitation of Seghorn and Cohen, Knight began a program of empirical research on classification of sexual offenders at the Massachusetts Treatment Center in 1978. He was subsequently joined by Prentky in 1980. Together with their many colleagues, including Lee, Cerce, Martino, Carter, Rosenberg, and Schneider, they have developed, validated, and revised two typologies, one for rapists and one for child molesters. Both systems are presently in their third iteration and are referred to as MTC:R3 and MTC:CM3 (Massachusetts Treatment Center: Rapist version 3 and Child Molester version 3). The development and revision of earlier versions of these systems will not be discussed in detail here. The best single source for the development of both systems is Knight and Prentky (1990).

The reader also is referred to validity studies on the child molester system (Knight, 1988, 1989, 1992; Prentky, Knight, Rosenberg, et al., 1989) and the rapist system (Knight & Prentky, 1987; Prentky, Burgess, & Carter, 1986; Prentky & Knight, 1986; Prentky, Knight, & Rosenberg, 1988; Rosenberg, Knight, Prentky, & Lee, 1988). The MTC research program on taxonomic models for classification of sexual offenders has been generously supported for the past 20 years by the National Institute of Mental Health and the National Institute of Justice. In the present forum, we will present only the current versions of both systems and clinical profiles of the subtypes. Interested readers should contact Knight or Prentky directly for detailed updates on classification criteria and validity studies.

The MTC Classification System for Child Molesters

Axis I

The present version of our classification system for child molesters (MTC:CM3; Figure 1) has two independent axes (Knight et al., 1989). On Axis I, the old fixation/ regression distinction has been partitioned into two dichotomous decisions: Degree of Sexual Preoccupation with Children (High versus Low) and Social Competence (High versus Low). When crossed, these two decisions yield four possible subtypes:

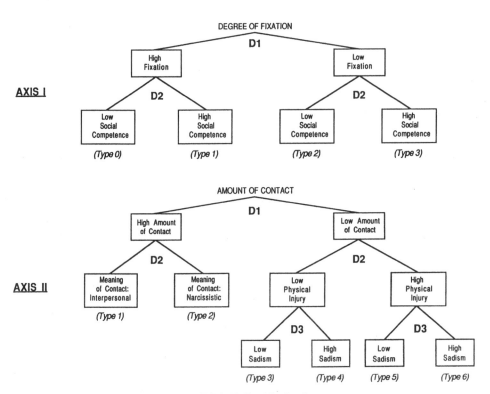

Figure 1. MTC:CM3 Classification System.

- Type 0 (High Sexual Preoccupation with Children/Low Social Competence)
- Type 1 (High Sexual Preoccupation with Children/High Social Competence)
- Type 2 (Low Sexual Preoccupation with Children/Low Social Competence)
- Type 3 (Low Sexual Preoccupation with Children/High Social Competence)

Fixation

The Degree of Sexual Preoccupation decision, which we still refer to as fixation simply because it is an easier shorthand label, attempts to assess the strength of an offender's pedophiliac interest (i.e., the extent to which children dominate an offender's thoughts and fantasies).

Low Fixation. An offender is classified as low fixated (Types 2 or 3) if he is over 20 years of age and *all* of his sexual contact with children (charged and uncharged) occurred within a 6-month period. Children are youngsters who are at least 5 years younger than the offender. If an offender is 20 years old or younger, and all of his known contact with children occurred within 6 months, he may still be classified as *high* fixated if he meets the criteria for high fixation or there is clear evidence of major deficits in his peer relationships.

High Fixation. An offender is classified as high fixated (Types 0 or 1) if he meets any of the following criteria: (1) there is evidence of three or more sexual contacts with children, and the time between the first and last contact is greater than six months; these contacts may involve multiple offenses with a single victim; contacts are *not* limited to charged offenses; (2) there is evidence that the offender has had enduring relationships with children (excluding parental contact); (3) the offender has initiated contact with children in numerous situations over his lifetime.

Social Competence

There are five criteria for assessing level of social competence. To be classified as high in social competence, the offender must meet two or more of the criteria:

1. Offender has had a single job lasting 3 or more years; multiple jobs within 3 years must reflect professional advancement or be characteristic of the profession.
2. Offender has been in a sexual relationship with an adult, involving marriage or cohabitation, for 1 year or longer.
3. Offender has assumed significant responsibility in parenting a child for 3 years or longer.
4. Offender has been an active member in an *adult*-oriented organization; membership must reflect more than just attendance (i.e., active participation for 1 year or longer with frequent adult contact).
5. Offender had a friendship with an adult, not involving marriage or cohabitation, lasting 1 year or longer and involving active contact and shared activities.

A Caveat on Bifurcating the Human Condition

We recognize that the tendency to bifurcate the human condition is, as Wolfgang Pauli said, "an attribute of the devil." The devilish quality of dichotomization is the tendency to incorporate far more into the explanatory domain than the heuristic value of the dichotomy could possibly serve. The drive to simplicity lures us into the false belief that, for instance, someone who is "high" in social competence is "high" in all spheres of human endeavor; or that all individuals classified as "high" in fixation are equally preoccupied with children and have equal propensities to molest children. In reality, of course, degree of sexual preoccupation with children is just that, a matter of degree. In the real world, *sexual preoccupation with children is a dimension with numerous gradations*. Having raised this issue, we must consider the psychometric alternative. If we scaled fixation and social competence, we would increase their sensitivity but decrease substantially their reliability. If fixation and social competence were rated on a 3-point scale, for instance, our matrix would have nine subtypes instead of 4 (3 × 3). Two 4-point scales would yield 16 subtypes, and so forth. From the standpoint of interrater reliability, the system would be cumbersome, impractical, and unreliable. We have thus opted for decisions that are easier to make and thus more reliable, at the expense of more refined subgroups. In the hope that it might provide a clearer picture of each of these four Axis I types, we have included case examples, details of which have intentionally been altered to protect the confidentiality of the individuals.

Axis II

Axis II consists of several hierarchical decisions. The first decision, which is preemptory, assesses the Amount of Contact with Children. In other words, the *initial* decision of high or low Contact leads either to a final subtype decision in the case of *high* Contact (Type 1 or Type 2) or to two subsequent decisions in the case of *low* Contact (Types 3–6). These subsequent decisions assess degree of Physical Injury and Sadism. The *only* exception is when *high* contact occurs *with high* physical injury to the victim. In these cases, the high physical injury takes precedence and the offender is classified as either Type 5 or Type 6. The assumption that the need for this exception would be infrequent was confirmed in a study of 177 child molesters, where it was used only 5% of the time (Knight, 1989).

Amount of Contact with Children

Amount of Contact with Children is a *behavioral* measure of the time that the child molester spends with children or around children in both sexual *and* nonsexual situations. Those who are classified as high in Contact spend a considerable amount of time in close proximity to children. Our preceding caveat about the dangers of dichotomizing complex dimensions of behavior applies here as well. Amount of Contact with Children and Physical Injury obviously are matters of degree. Sadism can be more easily categorized as present or absent.

Several studies, however, have supported the validity of the Amount of Contact dimension. In one early study, the distribution of 177 classified child molesters clearly supported the structural hypotheses that gave rise to MTC:CM3 (Knight, 1989). In another early study, child molesters who were classified as *high* in Amount of Contact evidenced (1) *fewer* school-related acting out problems, (2) *more* academic and interpersonal problems as children, (3) a lower incidence of alcohol abuse, and (4) *less* aggression and impulsivity in adulthood when compared with child molesters classified as low in Amount of Contact (Prentky, Knight, Rosenberg, et al., 1989). Amount of Contact significantly discriminated between those child molesters who did and those who did not recommit violent and/or nonsexual, victim-involved crimes in a 24-year follow-up of 111 offenders (Prentky, Knight, et al., 1997). Amount of Contact had absolutely *no* effect when it came to discriminating between those who recommitted sexual offenses and those who did not. As noted above, the Fixation dimension was much more useful when it came to sexual recidivism.

High Amount of Contact with Children.   For an offender to be classified as high in Contact, there must be clear evidence of regular contact with children in both sexual *and* nonsexual contexts. Evidence of nonsexual contact includes any structured or nonstructured social, recreational, avocational, or occupational activity that involves contact with children, such as schoolteacher, bus driver, carnival worker, newspaper delivery, riding stable attendant, nursery or day-care worker, baby-sitter, Cub Scout leader, Boy Scout leader, Little League, Babe Ruth League, soccer or gym coach, YMCA volunteer, and so forth. Needless to say, this does *not* mean that all men who are engaged in these occupations and activities are child molesters or would-be child molesters. For those *already known* to be child molesters, these occupations and activities help to determine whether someone is high in contact.

Other evidence for high contact may include regular visits from neighborhood children to the offender's home or place of employment, or the offender acting as an adopted father or big brother. Lastly, repeated sexual (nonincest) contact with the same child may imply the development of a "relationship" that goes beyond momentary sexual gratification. For that reason, we classify as high in contact offenders who have molested the same victim on three or more occasions.

High-contact child molesters are further classified as Interpersonal (Type 1) or Narcissistic (Type 2), primarily on the basis of the inferred *meaning* of the contact (i.e., interpersonal or exclusively sexual). Whereas the Interpersonal type is interested in children as social as well as sexual companions, the Narcissistic type is exclusively interested in gratifying sexual needs. Profiles of these two subtypes are provided below.

Low Amount of Contact with Children.   The low contact offender, by definition, has relatively little contact with children in his job or in social and recreational activities. His only designed or premeditated contact with children is in the context of a sexual assault. Offenders who are classified as low in contact, are further classified according to the amount of physical injury sustained by the victim and according to the presence or absence of sadism. There are two subtypes in which there is a *low* amount of physical injury to the child: Type 3 (Exploitative) and Type 4 (Muted Sadistic). There also are two subtypes in which there is a *high* amount of physical injury to the child: Type 5 (Aggressive) and Type 6 (Sadistic).

For the purpose of assessing degree of physical injury, *low* injury is characterized by such acts as pushing, shoving, slapping, or holding the child and the absence of any lasting physical injury, such as cuts, bruises, contusions, or abrasions. *High* injury includes any acts that cause physical injury to the child, including hitting, punching, choking, restraint that is injurious (e.g., results in bruises), and forced ingestion of urine or feces.

MTC:CM3 in Perspective

MTC:CM3 requires one additional revision in which the two primary axes are collapsed. The crossing of Axis I and Axis II yields 24 possible types, far more than realistically exist. Indeed, Knight (1989) found, in a sample of 177 incarcerated child molesters, six cells (possible types) that were empty and another six cells that had fewer than 2% of the offenders assigned to them. Thus, half of the possible types resulting from the cross of Axis I with Axis II either were empty or had very few cases assigned to them. Naturally, some of these empty or low-prevalence cells may reflect the sample. Indeed, one would expect that a sample of nonincarcerated child molesters would have a high proportion of high socially competent offenders (in the study mentioned above, five of the six empty cells were high social competence). Thus, only further generalization studies will allow us to determine which of these cells should be dropped.

In addition, at least four other aspects of MTC:CM3 must be further examined empirically: (1) the relation between sexual preference and the various subtypes, (2) the relation between fixation and social competence, (3) the relation between fixation and the low contact subtypes (Axis II, Types 3–6), and (4) the relation between social competence and the high-contact subtypes (Axis II, Types 1 and 2).

The logic, however, that led to the adoption of independent axes was critical to our understanding of the taxonomic structure of child molestation and has served the purpose of validating key constructs that discriminate among child molesters. Thus, although the individual subtypes may not provide optimal differentiation, the constructs that provide the framework for MTC:CM3 (particularly Fixation and Amount of Contact) appear to be reliable and valid (Knight, 1988, 1989, 1992; Prentky, Knight, Rosenberg, et al., 1989; Prentky, Knight, et al., 1997). Indeed, in a study of 111 child molesters who had been discharged from prison after varying lengths of incarceration, Fixation was found to be a significant risk factor for sexual recidivism and Amount of Contact was found to be a significant risk factor for nonsexual recidivism (Prentky, Knight, et al., 1997).

CLINICALLY DERIVED CLASSIFICATION SYSTEMS FOR RAPISTS

Guttmacher (1951) and Guttmacher and Weihofen (1952) described three types of rapists (Table 3). In the first type, called the "true sex offenders," the rape is an explosive expression of a pent-up sexual impulse. In the second type, the offense is sadistic, and in the third type, the rape is part of a general pattern of criminal behavior.

Kopp (1962) dichotomized rapists on the basis of whether the rape could be characterized as "ego-syntonic" or "ego-dystonic." In the former case, the rapist is an antisocial, psychopathic individual who experiences no guilt or remorse. In the latter case, the rape results from a breakdown in the individual's defensive armor and is likely to produce some sense of guilt and/or remorse.

In their study of 1356 sexual offenders, Gebhard et al. (1965) identified seven types of sexually coercive males. The most frequent type was Assaultive (described as "sadistic"),

Table 3. Comparable Subtypes on Rapist Classification Systems

Guttmacher & Weihofen (1952)	Kopp (1962)	Gebhard et al. (1965)	Cohen et al. (1969)	Rada (1978b)	Groth (1979)	Hazelwood (1987)[a]	Knight & Prentky (1990) (MTC:R3)
Types characterized by a predominantly sexual drive							
True Sex Offenders	Type I (Remorseful; Ego-dystonic)	Double Standard	Compensatory	Masculine Identity Conflict	Power Reassurance or Power Assertive	Power Reassurance or Power Assertive	Sexual Non-Sadistic (Types 6 & 7)
						Opportunistic	Opportunistic (Types 1 and 2)
Types characterized by antisocial and psychopathic behavior							
Aggressive	Type II (Aggressive; Ego-syntonic)	Disorganized Egocentric Hedonist (Amoral Delinquent)	Impulsive	Sociopathic			
Types characterized by sadism							
Sadistic		Sadistic	Sex Aggression Defusion	Sadistic	Anger Excitation	Anger Excitation	Sadistic (Type 4)
Types characterized by nonsadistic aggression							
		Explosive (Episodic Dyscontrol)	Displaced Anger		Anger Retaliation	Anger Retaliation	Pervasive Anger (Type 3) or Vindictive (Types 8 & 9)
Types characterized by psychosis, mental defect, or organicity							
		Mentally Defective Psychotic	Psychotic				
Additional unrelated types							
		Alcoholic	Situational Stress				

[a]Hazelwood uses Groth's four Types plus Opportunistic.

followed in frequency by the Amoral Delinquent (described as "disorganized egocentric hedonists") and the Drunken rapist. The Explosive rapist was characterized by episodic dyscontrol. A fifth group was called the Double Standard type. This individual is a less criminal, less asocial version of the Amoral Delinquent, and usually has a "machismo" interpersonal style and attitudes. These five types accounted for about two-thirds of the 1356 men in their sample. The remaining 30% was composed of "mental defectives" and "psychotics."

Amir (1971) described several types of rapists. One type consisted of those men whose offenses were idiosyncratic to the aberrations of their personality. For these men, the rapes were "devoid of direct social role significance." Another type consisted of men whose offenses represented "role-supportive acts." In other words, the rapes were motivated by, or at least influenced by, the demands of "youth culture."

Rada (1978b) described five types of rapists: (1) the sociopathic offender (characterized by a general record of impulsive, antisocial behavior), (2) the masculine identity conflict offender (characterized by feelings of social and sexual inadequacy and a hypermasculine interpersonal style and attitudes), (3) the situational stress offender (characterized by agitated depression and postassault feelings of shame and guilt), (4) the sadistic offender (characterized by arousal or pleasure in response to the degradation, humiliation, or pain of the victim), and (5) the psychotic offender (characterized by exceptionally bizarre and violent behavior).

The classification system proposed by Douglas et al. (1992) in their *Crime Classification Manual* includes an exhaustive list of categories for rape of adult women. In this system, rapists could be classified in any of the following categories: (1) Criminal enterprise rape, (2) Felony rape (primary or secondary), (3) Nuisance offenses, (4) Domestic sexual assault (adult domestic sexual abuse), (5) Entitlement rape (adult victim), (6) Subordinate rape (adult victim), (7) Power-reassurance rape (adult victim), (8) Exploitative rape (adult victim), (9) Anger rape, (10) Sadistic rape (adult victim), (11) Multidimensional sex rings (Adult survivor sex rings), (12) Abduction rape (adult victim), (13) Formal gang sexual assault, and (14) Informal gang sexual assault. Once again, with the exception of "specialty" categories, such as criminal enterprise rape, abduction rape, and gang rape, most of these subtypes borrow from preceding systems.

MTC Classification Systems for Rapists

Cohen and Seghorn's Typology

In their 1969 paper, Cohen, Seghorn, and Calmas described four types of rapists based on the relative contributions of aggression and sex in the offense.

In the Compensatory type, the motive is more sexual than aggressive. Aggression is used to gain the compliance of the victim. The offender is preoccupied by rape fantasy and highly aroused by the rape. The offender, hypothetically, has pervasive feelings of inadequacy, which the sexual assault "compensates" for.

In the Displaced Aggression type, the sexual assault is an expression of anger (or rage) at the victim, and the intent is to physically harm, degrade, defile, demean, and humiliate the victim. The offender often experiences the assault as an "uncontrollable impulse." In theory, the assault follows some precipitating event involving a significant woman in the offender's life (e.g., mother, wife, girlfriend, close relative, employer). Thus, the offender was said to be "displacing" his anger from the source or sources of aggravation onto an innocent victim.

In the Sex-Aggression-Defusion type, the assault is sadistic or has elements of sadism. In true clinical sadism, feelings of sexual arousal and anger coexist so that the individual cannot experience one without the other. The two feelings are synergistically related. As anger increases, sexual arousal increases. Alternatively, as sexual arousal increases, feelings of anger increase. Because the aggression in the assault is so primitive, lacking any neutralization by sexual feelings, the offense was called sex-aggression-defusion.

In the Impulse type, neither sexual nor aggressive motives appear to be central to the assault. The offense is predatory and represents part of a more generic pattern of impulsive, antisocial behavior.

In their 1971 paper, Cohen, Garofalo, Boucher, and Seghorn examined the two primary motives of sex and aggression and the "undifferentiated" case of sexual sadism. There was a growing concern among the investigators that simply focusing on the two primary motives of sex and aggression was overly simplistic and failed to capture the heterogeneity of the rapists observed at the Massachusetts Treatment Center. The need to examine other sources of motivation and how they are lived out in the offenses was discussed by Seghorn and Cohen (1980).

Groth's Typology

The typology subsequently developed by Groth and his colleagues Burgess and Holmstrom made very similar conceptual distinctions to Cohen and Seghorn's system. Groth described a classification system that underscored power and anger as the two primary motivating factors in rape (Burgess & Holmstrom, 1974a, 1976; Groth, 1979; Groth & Burgess, 1977a; Groth, Burgess, & Holmstrom, 1977). The classification system presented in Groth and Birnbaum's 1979 book included four types, two of which use sexual aggression to satisfy needs for power (Power-Assertive and Power-Reassurance) and two of which use sexual aggression to express anger (Anger-Retaliation and Anger-Excitation):

- The Power-Reassurance rapist alleviates feelings of sexual inadequacy and confirms his sense of masculinity through his sexual assaults. This type is analogous to the Compensatory rapist of Cohen and Seghorn.
- The Power-Assertive rapist expresses potency, mastery, and dominance through his sexual assaults. Doubts about adequacy and effectiveness are more generalized and pervasive than with the Power-Reassurance offender.
- The Anger-Retaliation rapist expresses rage toward women through his sexual assaults. He is seeking some form of revenge, and he does so by degrading and humiliating his victim. This type is analogous to the Displaced Aggression rapist of Cohen and Seghorn.
- The Anger-Excitation rapist is a sadist who obtains sexual gratification from the pain and/or suffering of his victim. This type is analogous to the Sex-Aggression-Defusion rapist of Cohen and Seghorn.

The incorporation of the work of Burgess and Holmstrom on sexual dysfunction among rapists during their offenses and patterns of victim resistance associated with the four types of offenders are distinguishing features of Groth's typology.

EMPIRICALLY DERIVED CLASSIFICATION SYSTEM FOR RAPISTS

The MTC Classification System for Rapists: Version 3

Unlike previous versions of our rapist classification system, the current version (MTC:R3) is prototypic rather than hierarchical (see Knight & Prentky, 1990). That is, rather than a series of hierarchical decisions that lead to a classification, each subtype possesses its own independent set of specific criteria for assigning cases and its own, presumably unique, "profile" of features and characteristics. Each subtype can be thought of as a prototype or model against which new cases can be judged or assessed. In its prototypic design, MTC:R3 is similar to the *Diagnostic and Statistical Manual* of the American Psychiatric Association (APA, 1994).

As can be seen in Figure 2 and Table 4, MTC:R3 includes nine subtypes. They are arranged so that each type is adjacent to the types that are most similar to it in cluster analytic profiles on critical variables (antisocial behavior, sexualized aggression, offense impulsivity, and substance abuse). In all instances except the opportunistically motivated types, high and low social competence variants of a type naturally fell out of the various analyses in close proximity and thus were placed next to each other. The nine types actually "wrap around," so that Type 9 is most similar to Types 8 and 1.

MTC:R3 is a "motivation-driven" system in that it consists of four primary presumptive motivating factors: (1) opportunity, (2) pervasive anger, (3) sexual gratification, (4) vindictiveness. These four differentiating motivational components appear to be related to enduring behavioral patterns that distinguish particular groups of offenders. Assignment of an individual to a subtype is determined by judging the offender on specific criteria that define each subtype. These criteria reflect our attempt to operationalize many of the

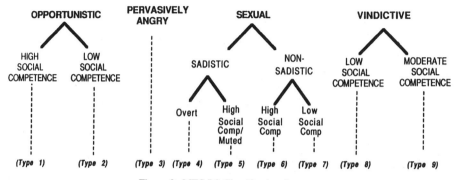

Figure 2. MTC:R3 Classification System.

dimensions that have been identified as important for discriminating among rapists (Prentky & Knight, 1991). The MTC:R3 classification model includes the following major dimensions: Expressive Aggression, Juvenile and Adult Antisocial Behavior, Social Competence, Global or Pervasive Anger, Sadism, Sexualization (e.g., sexual thoughts and fantasies; paraphiliac behaviors), and Offense Planning. The specification of these dimensions was discussed in detail in Knight and Prentky (1990), and the operational criteria are presented in a User's Manual available from the authors.

The individual subtypes are defined, in part, by the hypothesized differential importance of these dimensions for each type. For a given subtype, some dimensions are hypothesized to be of lesser importance while other dimensions are hypothesized to be critically important (i.e., the dimension represents a core characteristic of that type). Expressive Aggression, for instance, may range from verbal coercion and minimal force (i.e., no more than was necessary to gain victim compliance) all the way to brutal assault and murder. Thus, for some subtypes (e.g., Pervasively Angry, Sadistic, and Vindictive types) the *presence* of *high* Expressive Aggression is required for classification. For other subtypes (e.g., Opportunistic), the *absence* of *high* Expressive Aggression is required for classification. Similarly, the role of Sexualization may range in importance from negligible (i.e., no apparent preexisting rape fantasies; the rape appeared to be highly impulsive) to highly salient and critical (e.g., there was evidence of longstanding preoccupation with sexual fantasies that involve rape). In the Opportunistic types sexual fantasy is hypothesized to be relatively *un*important as a motivator for the offenses. For the Overt and Muted Sadistic types and the Nonsadistic, Sexual types, however, sexual fantasy is hypothesized to be a core feature.

Opportunistic Motivation

For the Opportunistic types, the primary motive in the sexual assaults is hypothesized to be impulsive exploitation. That is, the offenses are typically unplanned, predatory acts, driven more by situational and immediately antecedent factors than by any obvious protracted or stylized sexual fantasy. The sexual assault for these individuals appears to be simply one among many instances of poor impulse control, as evidenced by an extensive history of unsocialized behavior in many domains. Such offenders will often have an impulsive lifestyle, as evidenced by instability of employment, numerous short-term or casual relationships, and many changes in residence. In their assaults, they typically show no evidence of gratuitous force or aggression and exhibit relatively little anger except in response to victim resistance. Their behavior suggests that they are seeking immediate sexual gratification and are willing to use whatever force is necessary to achieve their goal. As a group, Opportunistic rapists are most likely to appear "hypermasculine," and to hold characteristic "macho" attitudes about women and sexuality, most notably that sex is their birthright as men and that "refusal" is not an option for women. Although distorted attitudes about women and sexuality are common to all rapists, those attitudes that reflect hypermasculinity seem particularly characteristic of this group of rapists. Because these offenders have little or no empathy for their victims, they are likely to demonstrate a callous indifference to the victim. If the victim resists the assault and fights back, the offender may become angry and use greater physical force, including slapping, punching, or physical restraints. There is no evidence, however, of gratuitous or sexualized violence.

Table 4. Profiles of MTC:R3 Types

Types 1: Opportunistic–High Social Competence

    Aggression is likely to be instrumental; no gratuitous violence and no evidence of pervasive anger

    Moderate impulsive, antisocial behavior in adulthood

    Relatively high level of social and interpersonal competence

    Offenses do *not* typically appear to be sexualized; no history of paraphilias, and no evidence of sadism

    Offenses to *not* appear to be compulsive, offense planning is minimal, and there is little evidence of premeditation

Type 2: Opportunistic–Low Social Competence

    Aggression is likely to be instrumental; no gratuitous violence and no evidence of pervasive anger

    Moderate impulsive, antisocial behavior in adolescence and adulthood

    Relatively low level of social and interpersonal competence

    Offenses do *not* typically appear to be sexualized; no history of paraphilias, and no evidence of sadism

    Offenses do *not* appear to be compulsive, offense planning is minimal, and there is little evidence of premeditation

Type 3: Pervasive Anger

    Characterized primarily by a high level of aggression and gratuitous violence in most aspects of the offender's life

    A history of aggression directed at men *and* women

    Moderate impulsive, antisocial behavior in adolesence and adulthood

    Offenses do *not* typically appear to be sexualized; history of paraphilias is unlikely, and no evidence of sadism

    Offenses do *not* appear to be compulsive, offense planning is minimal, and there is little evidence of premeditation

Type 4: Overt Sadism

    Characterized primarily by a high level of aggression and gratuitous violence, most notably in sexual offenders

    A history of pervasive or generalized anger may be present

    Sexual offenses are marked by sadism (fusion of aggression with sexual arousal); there must be clear evidence of a connection between sexual acts and the pain, suffering, or humiliation of the victim

    Moderate amount of impulsive, antisocial behavior in adolescence and adulthood

    History of other paraphilias often is present

    Offense planning and premeditation are evident

Type 5: Muted Sadism

    Aggression is likely to be instrumental; no gratuitous violence is evident

    Although impulsive, antisocial behavior may be present, it is not a critical feature of this type

    Sexual offenses are marked by sadism with a low level of violence and limited physical injury to victims; sexual acts tend to be symbolic and noninjurious; key difference between Overt and Muted is the relative absence of aggression in the Muted type

    History of other paraphilias may be present

    Offense planning and premeditation are evidence

Type 6: Sexual–High Social Competence

    Aggression is likely to be instrumental; no gratuitous violence and no evidence of pervasive anger

    Minimal impulsive, antisocial behavior in adolesence

    Moderate impulsive, antisocial behavior may be present in adulthood

    Relatively high level of social and interpersonal competence

    Sexual offenses marked by a high degree of sexualization, rape fantasy, and expressed interest in victim as a sexual object

    Although a history of other paraphilias often is present, there is *no* evidence of sadism

    Offense planning and premeditation are evident

Type 7: Sexual–Low Social Competence

    Aggression is likely to be instrumental; no gratuitous violence and no evidence of pervasive anger

    Minimal impulsive, antisocial behavior in adolescence

    Moderate impulsive, antisocial behavior may be present in adulthood

Table 4. (*Continued*)

Relatively low level of social and interpersonal competence

Sexual offenses marked by a high degree of sexualization, rape fantasy, and expressed interest in victim as a sexual object

Although a history of other paraphilias often is present, there is *no* evidence of sadism

Offense planning and premeditation are evident

Type 8: Vindictive–Low Social Competence

  Characterized primarily by a high level of aggression and gratuitous violence that is directed specifically at women, both in sexual offenses and otherwise

  Anger is misogynistic; there is *no* history of pervasive anger

  Minimal impulsive, antisocial behavior in adolescence

  Moderate impulsive, antisocial behavior may be present in adulthood

  Relatively low level of social and interpersonal competence

  Offenses do *not* typically appear to be sexualized; no history of paraphilias, and no evidence of sadism

  Offenses do *not* appear to be compulsive, offense planning is minimal, and there is little evidence of premeditation

Type 9: Vindictive–High Social Competence

  Characterized primarily by a high level of aggression and gratuitous violence that is directed specifically at women, both in sexual offenses and otherwise

  Anger is misogynistic; there is *no* history of pervasive anger

  Minimal impulsive, antisocial behavior in adolescence

  Although some impulsive, antisocial behavior may be present in adulthood, it is *not* extensive

  Relatively high level of social and interpersonal competence

  Offenses do *not* typically appear to be sexualized, no history of paraphilias, and no evidence of sadism

  Offenses do *not* appear to be compulsive, offense planning is minimal, and there is little evidence of premeditation

---

Note. Abstracted from Knight & Prentky (1990).

Pervasively Angry Motivation

The primary motivation for the Pervasively Angry offender is hypothesized to be undifferentiated (or global) anger. These offenders appear to be angry at the world, with little apparent differentiation as to the targets of their anger. Men are as likely to be targets of their anger as women. Pervasively Angry rapists have a history of fighting and nonsexual assaults and may "seek out" opportunities for expressing their anger, such as going to bars to pick fights. Their aggression *is* gratuitous and often occurs in the absence of any victim resistance. They may inflict very serious physical injury on their victims, up to and including death. Although they may sexually assault their female victims, their rage does *not* appear to be sexualized. There is no evidence that their assaults are driven by preexisting rape fantasies and little evidence that their assaults are well-planned or premeditated. The two cardinal features of the Pervasively Angry offender are extreme difficulties with impulsive control and a very deep reservoir of undifferentiated or global anger. From childhood and adolescence through adulthood, their life histories are marked by difficulties controlling their impulses and unbridled expressions of anger that often include fighting and assaultiveness in childhood and adolescence and, with lower frequency, cruelty to animals.

Sexual Motivation

Sexualization essentially refers to a high degree of preoccupation with gratifying one's sexual needs. Sexual preoccupation is typically evidenced by highly intrusive, recurrent sexual and rape fantasies, frequent use of pornography, reports of frequent uncontrollable sexual urges, use of a variety of "alternative" outlets for gratifying sexual needs (e.g., massage parlors, X-rated movies, sex clubs, strip bars), and engaging in other deviant sexual behaviors (paraphilias), such as voyeurism, exhibitionism, or fetishism. The sexual assaults of these offenders are often well-planned, as evidenced by a clear, scripted sequence of events, possession of assault-related paraphernalia, and an apparent plan to procure the victim and elude apprehension after the assault.

Four rapist types are hypothesized to possess a high degree of sexual preoccupation. All four types have in common the presence of protracted sexual and rape fantasies that motivate their sexual assaults and influence the way in which their offenses occur. In MTC:R3, there are two major subgroups based on the presence or absence of sadistic fantasies or behaviors—the Sadistic and Nonsadistic groups. The Sadistic group includes two subtypes (Overt Sadist and Muted Sadist), and the Nonsadistic group includes two subtypes (High Socially Competent and Low Socially Competent). Thus, these four types are differentiated primarily by the content of the fantasies and the ways in which the fantasies are expressed through behavior. In brief, Type 4 is characterized by overtly expressed sadistic acts and a high level of Expressive Aggression. Type 5 is characterized by the presence of sadistic fantasies, the muted expression of those fantasies, and a lower level of aggression. Types 6 and 7 are characterized by an absence of sadistic fantasy and sadistic behavior, and a relatively low level of aggression.

Sadistic Types.   Both of the Sadistic types show evidence of poor differentiation between sexual and aggressive drives, and a frequent co-occurrence of sexual and aggressive thoughts and fantasies. For the Overt Sadistic type the aggression is manifested directly in physically injurious behavior in their sexual assaults. For the Muted Sadistic type the aggression is expressed either symbolically or through covert fantasy that is not acted out behaviorally. Thus far in preliminary analyses conducted by Knight, this overt-muted distinction has correlated highly with social competence, the Overt type being low and the Muted type being high. That is, the presence of a higher level of social competence may "mute" or attenuate the level of expressed aggression.

To be classified as an Overt Sadistic rapist, an offender's behavior must reflect his *intention* to inflict fear or pain on the victim and to manifest a high level of aggression. Moreover, since the defining feature of sadism is the synergistic relationship between sexual arousal and feelings of anger, there must be some evidence that the aggression either contributed to sexual arousal, or at least did not inhibit such arousal. Since the two feelings (sexual arousal and anger) have equal ability to enhance or increase the other, the sexual acts may precede aggression or the aggression may precede the sexual acts. The cardinal feature, in either case, is the intertwining or "fusing" of the two feelings such that increases in one lead to increases in the other. As a group, Overt Sadistic rapists appear to be angry, belligerent people, who, except for their sadism and the greater planning of their sexual assaults, look very similar to the Pervasively Angry rapists.

To be classied as a Muted Sadistic rapist, there must be evidence that the victim's fear or discomfort, or the fantasy of violence, contributed to the offender's sexual arousal (or did not inhibit such arousal), and that the amount of physical force in the sexual assault did *not* exceed what was necessary to gain victim compliance. Symbolic expressions of sadistic fantasy characterize these offenders, who may employ various forms of bondage or restraints, noninjurious insertion of foreign objects, and other sexual "aids," such as Vaseline or shaving cream. What is absent is the high level of Expressive Aggression that is clearly manifest in Overt Sadism. As noted, the higher social competence of Muted Sadistic offenders may explain the difference in aggression, with the greater social "sophistication" of Muted Sadistic rapists attenuating or "muting" the aggression. In general, Muted Sadistic offenders, except for their sadistic fantasies and their slightly higher lifestyle impulsivity, resemble the High Social Competence, Nonsadistic rapists.

Nonsadistic Types. For the *non*sadistic sexualized rapists, the thoughts and fantasies that are associated with their sexual assaults are devoid of the synergistic relation of sex and aggression that characterizes the Sadistic types. Indeed, these two rapist types (Types 6 and 7) are hypothesized to manifest *less* aggression than any of the other rapist types. If confronted with victim resistance, these offenders may flee rather than force the victim to comply. Their fantasies and behaviors are hypothesized to reflect an amalgam of sexual arousal, distorted "male" cognitions about women and sexuality, feelings of social and sexual inadequacy, and masculine self-image concerns. Compared to the other rapist types, these offenders have relatively few problems with impulse control in domains outside of sexual aggression.

Vindictive Motivation

The core feature and primary driving force for the Vindictive types is anger at women. Unlike the Pervasively Angry rapist, women are the central and exclusive focus of the Vindictive rapist's anger. Their sexual assaults are marked by behaviors that are physically injurious and appear to be intended to degrade, demean, and humiliate their victims. The misogynistic anger evident in these assaults runs the gamut from verbal abuse to brutal murder. As noted, these offenders differ from Pervasively Angry rapists in that they show little or no evidence of anger at men (e.g., instigating fights with or assaulting men).

Although there is a sexual component in their assaults, there is no evidence that their aggression is eroticized, as it is for the Sadistic types, and no evidence that they are preoccupied with sadistic fantasies. Indeed, the aggression in the sexual assault is often instrumental in achieving the primary aim of demeaning or humiliating the victim (e.g., forcing the victim to fellate the offender). Vindictive rapists also differ from both the Pervasively Angry and Overt Sadistic offenders in their relatively lower level of lifestyle impulsivity (i.e., they have relatively fewer problems with impulse control in other areas of their lives).

The Role of Social Competence

As may be noted in Figure 2, the Opportunistic rapists, Nonsadistic Sexual rapists, and Vindictive rapists are subdivided into high and low social competence groups. In these three cases, differences in life management skills (i.e., employment, social and interpersonal competence) among offenders suggested that high and low subtypes would further reduce heterogeneity and yield theoretically and clinically meaningful groups. Classifying a rapist as *high* in Social Competence requires that the offender meet both of two criteria (stability of employment and stability of interpersonal attachments). Including high Social Competence variants of the Opportunistic and Nonsadistic Sexual subtypes (Types 1 and 6) may provide a practical and theoretical bridge for applying this system to noninstitutionalized rapists.

Distribution of Sexualization

Fantasy involving sexually coercive and aggressive behavior and paraphiliac behavior (e.g., exhibitionism, voyeurism, fetishism) may well be pathognomonic of outcome, particularly in highly repetitive (or "serial") offenders. It would seem, however, that not only is the presence of rape fantasy important, but that characteristics of the fantasy (e.g., how persistent or recurrent it is, how distracting and preoccupying it is, whether or not it is internally generated) may be critically important for assessing the likelihood that the fantasy will be acted on. Although MTC:R3 includes four subtypes that are hypothesized to be high in Sexualization (Types 4–7), at this point it seems unlikely that Sexualization is in fact a type-defining dimension (i.e., some types have it, while other types do not). Sexualization is most likely present in varying degrees among all types, and the crucial questions may involve such issues as (1) the relative importance of sexualization as a motivator for sexual assault for each of the nine subtypes, (2) the differential importance of components of sexualization for each of the nine subtypes, and (3) the role of sexualization in designing treatment and intervention plans for each of the subtypes.

MTC:R3 in Perspective

The process of developing and refining a classification system for rapists has been immeasurably more complex than the equivalent task of developing a system for child molesters. Sexually coercive and aggressive behavior directed at adult women, in its multitude of manifestations, subsumes a much larger proportion of the general male population than the equivalent behavior that targets children. A survey of the general male population would reveal that a very small, albeit stable, percentage of men have sexual thoughts and fantasies involving children. Assuming veridical responding, an equivalent survey would reveal that a large percentage of the general adult male population have sexual fantasies that include dominance, control, and rape. Thus, it is much easier to place child molestation under the taxonomic microscope and be confident that a reasonably accurate and complete representation of the behavior is present. When it comes to forced sexual contact with adult women, rape supportive attitudes and rape fantasies are so widely held and so casually endorsed in the general male population and sexually coercive behavior occurs with so many shades of gray (i.e., so many levels of subtlety) that it has been difficult to develop a taxonomic model that effectively embraces the totality of the manifestations of this behavior. How well, for instance, does a model developed on incarcerated rapists apply in cases of social acquaintance or date rape, or in cases of marital rape, or in cases of job-related sexual coercion? This question can only be answered by further studies that attempt to apply MTC:R3 to diverse samples of sexually aggressive and sexually coercive individuals. These studies already are under way and have begun to yield remarkable insights about the dimensions that are of putative importance for diverse samples of offenders and (presumptive) nonoffenders.

Although MTC:R3 is a marked improvement over preceding models and validity studies have been very encouraging, there remain important issues that must be addressed, including (1) the utility of MTC:R3 for noninstitutionalized sexually coercive individuals, (2) the role of "sexualization" (e.g., rape fantasy, sexual urges and sexual drive, paraphilias) in each of the subtypes, (3) the relation between themes of control and dominance and the various subtypes, (4) the operationalization of sadism, and (5) the refinement of the Social Competence dimension for application to higher socially competent offenders (e.g., "impaired professionals") and to younger offenders, such as college students, for whom long-term, stable relationships would be unlikely.

CONCLUDING THOUGHTS

In conclusion, classification systems are inherently temporary and artificial, an *a priori* structure serving a time-limited purpose. Few systems endure, and those that do undergo modifications in keeping with current thought. Like any substitute for the "real thing," surrogate systems replace one another as our understanding of the real world changes. If a particular system proves useful, we may report presumptive evidence supporting it. As evidence for new relations appear and the system no longer seems useful, it is modified or discarded. In sum, to seek the "ultimate order" of things is an admirable though somewhat quixotic quest. To *assume* the ultimate order of things negates the purpose of classification, since one is, in effect, hermetically sealing the boundaries of knowledge.

We have made significant strides in our classificatory efforts over the past 20 years or so. Notwithstanding the "tyranny of taxonomy" so eloquently described by Gould (1982), the cautious and prudent application of increasingly sophisticated mathematical techniques to the rational, systematic, and patient ordering of clinical experience has gone a long way to solving some of the vexing problems of classifying sexual offenders. The application of a reliable and valid classification system to forensic and clinical decisions promises to replace bootstrapping and guesswork with a structured, systematically applied procedure for dispositional planning and discretionary decision-making. The task demands cooperation and collaboration between researchers who seek to gather and transform data into tentative answers and clinicians who, as practitioners in the real world, apply and test the tentative answers.

CHAPTER 4

Assessment

THE BUTTERFLY EFFECT

In science, as in all of life, it is well known that a chain of events can reach a crisis point in which very small changes become magnified. In the world of science, this phenomenon is occasionally referred to as the *butterfly effect*, the notion that a tiny, insignificant insect fluttering its wings in the air over London can affect storm systems the next month in New York. In introducing his theory of chaos, Gleick (1988) spoke of the butterfly effect, commenting that "errors and uncertainties multiply, cascading upward through a chain of turbulent features, from dust devils and squalls up to continent-size eddies that only satellites can see" (p. 20). In scientific terms, the butterfly effect reflects "sensitive dependence on initial conditions." Chaos refers, in essence, to the natural and inherent unpredictability of life. It is our task, when seeking to assess and predict human behavior, to improve on this natural order by examining, as accurately as possible, the "initial conditions" that lead to specific outcomes.

The butterfly effect reminds us of the awesome complexity of human nature, and hence the prodigious demands and challenges that confront us when seeking to assess and predict the sequences of events that lead to atypical, often low-frequency behaviors (e.g., sexual offenses). The task is, at once, both daunting because of its complexity and urgent because of its ubiquity. Within the criminal justice system, the assessment of "dangerousness" is indeed ubiquitous. In an excellent review of the public policy issues attendant to dangerousness, Shah (1981) listed no less than 16 different areas in which legal decisions are based on an assessment of dangerousness. Of those 16 areas, at least 6 bear directly on selective incapacitation and another 5 on "insanity" decisions resulting in involuntary, often indeterminate, commitments.

The one category of dangerous criminals most subject to special statutes involving legal proceedings for commitments to segregated units or mental health facilities as well as other ad hoc discretionary and dispositional decisions are sexual offenders. As Cormier and Simons (1969) concluded, the sexual offender poses an especially difficult problem for the forensic clinician and if indeterminate custody is justifiable for any criminal, it may be justifiable for the sexual offender. Indeed, one could reasonably argue that the pervasive impact of decisions on dangerousness throughout the judicial system have their greatest impact on judicial decisions involving sexual offenders. Thus, the routine demand to assess dangerousness within the crimninal justice system is *most* taxing when it comes to sexual offenders.

In the next two chapters we will discuss two common demands of forensic clinicians who work with sex offenders, gathering, assimilating, and interpreting data for the purpose of evaluating a client ("assessment"), and using the data to augur judgments about the likelihood of specific outcomes ("prediction"). There is a symbiosis, of sorts, between assessment and prediction. Assessment provides the "gruel" for prediction (i.e., prediction typically relies on the data culled from an assessment), and the adequacy of our efforts to predict can be no better than the adequacy of the data culled from assessment.

Although we may assess an offender for a multitude of specific reasons, there are, generally speaking, three broad areas: (1) clinical [or needs assessment], (2) risk prediction, and (3) risk reduction. In this chapter we focus on *clinical* assessment. In Chapter 5, we discuss a priori risk assessment (risk prediction), and in Chapter 8 we discuss risk management (risk reduction). Although there clearly are overlapping purposes among these three domains of assessment (e.g., assessing treatment outcome and dispositional planning might occur in both clinical and management categories; assessing risk factors might occur in both management and risk categories), these three assessment domains seem to make practical and theoretical sense. Indeed, in several excellent articles on the subject, Kirk Heilbrun and his colleagues spelled out these distinctions (Heilbrun, 1997; Heilbrun, Nezu, Keeney, Chung, & Wasserman, 1998). In both articles, Heilbrun contrasted prediction and management models for sex offenders, noting the following:

- *Goal* (violence prediction in the former case, risk reduction in the latter case)
- *Nature of risk factors* (static and dynamic in the former case; dynamic only in the latter case)
- *Postassessment control* (variable in the former case; high in the latter case)
- *Number of times administered* (once in the former case; multiple times in the latter case)
- *Sensitivity to change in risk status* (low in the former case; high in the latter case)
- *Implications for intervention* (minimal in the former case; strong in the latter case)

Figure 1. Principal domains of assessment.

- *Research measures* (traditional indices of predictive accuracy, RIOC, ROC in the former case; efficacy and compliance with risk interventions in the latter case)
- *Validation designs* (regression-based in the former case; random or matched assignment to experimental and control groups or between-groups comparisons in latter case)

Data gathered in the course of a forensic assessment will invariably include archival and self-report information, and may also include psychometric and psychophysiological information. There is *no* single, uniformly accepted, standardized protocol for the assessment of sex offenders. Protocols typically are tailored to the needs of a particular case. Thus, although many domains of information—actuarial, clinical, psychometric, physiological—may be useful in accomplishing a comprehensive clinical assessment, the problems posed by a risk assessment require us to telescope in on those variables determined empirically to be most efficacious.

JUNCTURES ALONG THE ASSESSMENT ROUTE

In addition to the many decision points within the system that may require assessments, the *purposes* of the assessments vary. With adult sex offenders, the stages or junctures within the system most frequently requiring assessments are:

A. Apprehension
B. Pretrial investigation
C. Trial
D. Sentencing
E. Prison
F. Release
G. Probation/parole

The *purpose* of the assessment at each stage may be for:

A	Investigative profiling/crime scene analysis
B, C, D	Determination of motive/criminal responsibility
C, D, F, G	Dangerousness and reoffense risk
E	Institutional dangerousness/security risk/escape risk
D, E, F, G	Discretionary decisions
D, E, F, G	Treatment amenability
E, F	Treatment planning
G	Discharge from treatment

With juvenile sex offenders, the decision points within the juvenile justice system may be even more confusing, because there are, potentially, many "parties" involved. Asssessments may occur:

- In the Dispositional Planning Unit of Family Court
- By a probation officer prior to adjudication
- In court during the adjudicatory process

- By Department of Human Services caseworkers responding to reports of sexually acting out boys
- By clinicians considering discharging adolescents from residential placement,
- By clinicians receiving postadjudication referrals for treatment

Although, for the most part, the above-mentioned assessment needs are *not* unique to sexual offenders, the demand for these assessments, as noted, appears to be greatest with sex offenders. In addition, the questions posed for those examining sex offenders may be more esoteric than the relatively straightforward question of whether someone is likely to commit another sexual offense. In the course of doing forensic evaluations, for instance, we have been asked on different occasions to assess: (1) the likelihood that a client will escalate, (2) the likelihood that a client will abduct, (3) the likelihood that a client will progress from a paraphilia to a criminal sexual offense, (4) the likelihood that a client is a "serial" offender, (5) the "signature" of a serial offender, (6) the MOs from two different crime scenes, and so forth.

It is probably sufficient at this point simply to acknowledge that not all assessment tasks are the same and that the specific legal or clinical questions posed (by a therapist, an attorney, a parole agent, a police investigator, or the judge) should drive the assessment (i.e., the assessment protocol should be designed to answer specific questions). We have *not* approached the level of sophistication needed for making informed recommendations about the strategies for rendering optimal decisions across a variety of different conditions. We can, however, set forth reasonable guidelines, recognize the "don'ts," and try to avoid the innumerable sandtraps. We will first review what we do know, partitioned into three sections: (1) interviewing (clinical and psychopathy), (2) psychological testing, and (3) sexual preference assessments. As noted, comprehensive assessments should include data gathered from *multiple* domains, including review of archival documents. The criticality of this point was emphasized by Heilbrun (1992), who noted that forensic examiners often render opinions leading to dispositions that are not subject to revision and that impact, at times dramatically impact, human lives. Heilbrun (1992) stated that

> legal decision making by the factfinder should require the closest possible approxima-
> tion to the truth, rather than hypotheses or speculations to be confirmed or refuted
> through further intervention. Because of this premium on the accuracy of information
> provided to the factfinder, the results of psychological tests should not be used in
> isolation from history, medical findings, and observations of behavior made by others.
> (p. 263)

A related point that cannot be overemphasized is that the procedure as well as the report itself *must* be absolutely defensible. The "ecology" of the assessment (where, when, and how it is conducted) and the components of the assessment (type of interview, psychological tests administered, sexual preference assessments, review of archival documents) must be defensible (i.e., appropriate and adequate). It is too late, once one is in deposition or on the stand, to admit that a particular test has no relevant validity or that critical documents were mistakenly overlooked. Similarly, when a report is to be introduced as evidence, we recommend rereading the completed report with an adversarial eye *prior* to submitting it (i.e., try to discredit your own report). As Mosier and Altieri (1998) put it, "the report should be written so as to be able to withstand ruthless criticism during cross-examination in a courtroom setting" (p. 19). Although there are practical reasons for presenting an unassailable case (e.g., to avoid embarrassment), there are much more important ethical reasons. In the legal arena, the stakes typically are very high, often involving liberty interests (for the defendant) and safety interests (for victims or potential victims). Although error and miscalculation are inevitable, our search for the closest approximation of the "truth" should be uncompromising.

INTERVIEWING

Clinical

A critical component of all assessments is the clinical interview. Clinical interviews typically are open-ended, and relatively little has been written specifically on interviewing procedures for sex offenders. In one of the few articles to address this subject, McGrath (1990) made many useful recommendations about conducting clinical interviews with sex offenders, including interviewing strategies:

- Being familiar with the research on sex offenders (more than a mere recommendation, this should be considered imperative).
- Remain in control of the interview.
- Interview "collaterals" (spouses, family members, victims, witnesses, and so on) separately.
- Use multiple data sources (again, this should be imperative).
- Emphasize *what happened*, and not *why it happened*.
- Always use *behavioral* descriptors and *not* lay, technical, or legal terms.
- Ask direct, straightforward questions in a matter-of-fact manner, avoiding hesitancy and uncertainty as much as possible.
- Try to develop a "yes" response set at the beginning of the interview (i.e., ask questions in which the offender's response will be "yes").
- Try to avoid "tipping your hand" (i.e., offenders may try to determine what the evaluator knows about the details of his/her offense history and then only admit to those details that are known; it is much better for the evaluator to imply that a great deal is known but to remain vague about the specifics).
- At the beginning of the interview, ignore statements believed to be evasive or untruthful; it will be easier, as the interview evolves and the offender relaxes somewhat, to repeat and rephrase questions requiring clarification (i.e., avoid, as much as possible, a confrontative response set at the beginning of the interview).
- Place the burden of denial on the offender, making it as difficult as possible for the offender to deny responsibility (e.g., always ask questions such as "When did you first ..." or "How often did you ..." rather than "Have you ever ...").
- Embedding multiple assumptions in questions further increases the burden on denial; offenders more often deny what they consider to be the more "deviant" aspects of the behavior (e.g., penetration), while taking responsibility for the comparatively less deviant behaviors (e.g., fondling); thus, questions can be crafted that include assumptions about multiple behaviors (e.g., "During the 2 months before your wife discovered you were having intercourse with Jane, how often when you masturbated did you have thoughts about Jane or other children?").

- Use "successive-approximation" strategies (rather than confronting a highly resistant offender immediately with the charged [or convicted] behavior, begin by establishing as "fact" approximate behaviors [e.g., that the offender knew the victim, that the offender had spent time with the victim at a party, that the offender left the party with the victim, that the offender offered to give the victim a ride home, and so forth]).
- Repeat the same question, or a variation of the same question, at various times during the interview, particularly around points for which the offender has been guarded or less than candid; repeating questions can elicit additional information.
- Avoid multiple questions (asking multiple questions at the same time can be confusing, interrupts the flow of the interview, and, most importantly, may allow the offender to avoid answering parts of the question [e.g., asking the offender "Have you ever had fantasies about sex with girls under the age of 12 or had sex with them?" allows him/her to respond that he/she has never had sex with a young girl while avoiding answering whether he/she has ever had sexual fantasies about young girls]).
- Asking questions in a rapid-fire manner permits the evaluator to cover more topics and, more importantly, forces the offender to answer questions more spontaneously; the less "downtime" between questions, the less time that the offender has to "waffle" and to concoct "alternative" answers.
- Alternate support and confrontation (offenders generally are most disclosive when they feel supported and understood and, at the same time, held accountable for "sharing" a truthful personal history).
- Frame disclosure as a positive action (offenders will be well aware of the risks inherent in disclosing deviant behavior but are unlikely to be aware of the benefits of "taking responsibility" [e.g., admission will be viewed favorably by the court and is the first constructive step to getting help]).
- Use the fatigue factor (at the beginning of the interview, an offender can be expected to be on his/her best behavior; an offender's resistance may deteriorate as fatigue increases; a day-long assessment, which intersperses interviews, psychometric testing, and psychophysiological testing, may capitalize on the fatigue factor by permitting the evaluator to observe the offender under conditions of decreased resistance).
- By the end of the interview, the evaluator should have taken the opportunity to "test the limits" by "pushing" the offender to see how far he/she will go in taking responsibility for all aspects of the offenses; this strategy is *not* intended to abuse the offender but to elicit a clear demarcation between the "official" version of the offense (or the victim's report) and the offender's report; testing the limits is the most effective means of examining the offender's reactions when confronted and can be the best way of eliciting cognitive distortions about the offense.

There is, of course, no substitute for preparation. The very best clinical interview requires the very best preparation *prior* to the interview. This means acquainting oneself with *all* archival material, all legal documents, all historical material that has been made available. Not only is such preparation essential for framing questions, it is indispensable for assessing the duplicity (or veridicality) of the offender's answers. The importance of preparation will be all-the-more evident when we examine the unique demands of psychopathy interviews.

Interviewing to Assess Psychopathy

There is an abundant empirical literature demonstrating the efficacy of the construct of psychopathy when examining reoffense risk and criminal dangerousness for offenders. Consequently, assessment of psychopathy has become an increasingly important component of an overall evaluation of reoffense risk for sexual offenders. In addition, however, assessment of psychopathy may also be important when designing treatment and management plans. Although there certainly is debate as to whether psychopaths can (and indeed should) be treated (e.g., Schwartz, 1999), the fact remains that many offenders who are not classifiable as psychopaths using the Psychopathy Checklist-Revised (PCL-R) may still present with a number of Factor I criteria that bear importantly on treatment (e.g., lack of empathy, lack of affect, lack of remorse, manipulativeness, and lying). Moreover, if the characteristic lack of responsiveness to negative feedback or punishment in psychopaths is attributable to deficient response modulation, hindering the processing of peripheral information when engaged in goal-directed behavior (Newman, Schmitt, & Voss, 1997; Patterson & Newman, 1993), rather than fearlessness, as postulated by Lykken over 40 years ago (1957, 1995), it certainly would bear on the treatment process. In sum, being informed about critical features that make up the mosaic of psychopathy, even in individuals who do not "make" the technical cutoff of 30 on the PCL-R, cannot help but be valuable in designing and implementing a treatment plan.

In this section, we will describe, for those unfamiliar, the variables that comprise the construct of psychopathy and offer some caveats and tips when conducting interviews.

The Construct

The dubious "father" of psychopathy is Hervey Cleckley, who first described the pattern of traits associated with this "condition" more than 50 yeras ago [1941]. Although Cleckley's well-known list of 16 behavioral features of the psychopath were strongly influenced by his psychodynamic orientation, most of these characteristics were operationalized by Hare (1980) and have had a profound impact on empirical research on psychopathy. Subsequent editions of Cleckley's classic text, *The Mask of Sanity*, evidenced an evolution in his own thinking about psychopathy, moving from an early conception of psychopathy as a form of "semantic dementia" to a later conceptualization (Cleckley, 1976) that was closer to Kernberg's (1984) notion of borderline personality disorder (see Meloy, 1988, for a more thorough discussion).

The Cleckley criteria

1. Superficial charm and good intelligence
2. Unreliability
3. Untruthful and insincere
4. Lack of remorse or shame
5. Inadequately motivated antisocial behavior

6. Poor judgment and failure to learn from experience
7. Pathologic egocentricity and incapacity for love
8. Poverty of affect
9. Little or no insight
10. Unresponsive in interpersonal relationships
11. Failure to follow any life plan
12. Sex life is impersonal, trivial, and poorly integrated
13. Threats of suicide, rarely carried out
14. "Uninviting" behavior, often with alcohol
15. Absence of delusions and irrational thinking
16. Absence of "nervousness" or neurotic symptoms

The current procedure for assessing psychopathy is the well-known semistructured interview (PCL-R) developed 20 years ago by Robert Hare (Hare, 1980, 1991). Subsequent articles have reported on the factor structure, reliability, and validity of the scale (e.g., Hare, 1998; Hare et al., 1990; Hare, Hart, & Harpur, 1991; Harris, Rice, & Cormier, 1991; Hart, Cox, & Hare, 1995; Hart & Hare, 1997; Hart, Hare, & Forth, 1993; Hart, Hare, & Harpur, 1992; Serin, 1991; Serin & Amos, 1995).

The 20 items comprising the PCL-R include:

Factor I: Selfish, callous, and remorseless use of others

1. Glibness and superficial charm
2. Grandiose sense of self-worth
3. Pathological lying and deception
4. Conning, lack of sincerity, manipulative
5. Lack of remorse or guilt
6. Lack of affect/shallow affect
7. Callous/lack of empathy
8. Failure to accept responsibility for own actions

Factor II: Chronically unstable and antisocial lifestyle

9. Need for stimulation/proneness to boredom
10. Parasitic lifestyle
11. Poor behavioral controls/short-tempered
12. Early behavior problems
13. Lack of realistic, long-term goals
14. Impulsivity
15. Irresponsible behavior as a parent
16. Juvenile delinquency
17. Revocation of conditional release

Additional items not loading on the two primary factors

18. Promiscuous sexual behavior
19. Many short-term marital relationships
20. Criminal versatility (many types of offenses)

Assumptions about the Construct of Psychopathy

Assumption #1: Factor Structure. Two oblique dimensions are necessary and reasonably sufficient to provide a comprehensive description of psychopathic personality. Research has supported this assumption, suggesting that psychopathy has an underlying structure consisting of two correlated factors. The two factors tend to correlate about .50.

The first dimension (Factor I) is positively correlated with clinical ratings of psychopathy and negatively correlated with measures of anxiety and empathy.

The second dimension (Factor II) is the impulsive, antisocial component of psychopathy, positively correlated with DSM-IV Axis II APD diagnoses, and measures of criminal and antisocial behavior.

Assumption #2: Chronicity. The second assumption is that psychopathy is a *chronic* disorder, having discernible roots in early childhood (e.g., Lyman, 1997) and persisting into adulthood. Chronicity is further supported by the clinical and empirical evidence suggesting the relative *in*efficacy of treatment for altering psychopathic behavior. The so-called "burnout" phenomenon is misleading. Although certain types of criminal conduct (e.g., property offenses) diminish after age 45, the core behavioral traits associated with psychopathy remain. Stated otherwise, although impulsivity may diminish with age (reflecting a drop in Factor II), the clinical traits associated with psychopathy (Factor I) should remain relatively stable through the life span.

Assumption #3: Deception. The third assumption is that deception, deceitfulness, lying, and manipulation are cardinal traits of psychopathic personality. The critical point is that a major source of data for making our diagnosis (self-report) is likely to be contaminated when we are interviewing a psychopath (i.e., we should expect dissimulation in the presence of psychopathy, directly assess deception, and control for deception in making judgments about other features of the disorder).

Assumption #4: No Corner on the Market. The fourth assumption is that psychopathy and criminality are related but *distinct* constructs. Although psychopaths certainly have a greater tendency to engage in criminal behavior than nonpsychopaths and prison populations have a higher base rate of psychopathy than community residents, this statement must *not* be interpreted to mean that all psychopaths are criminals or that all criminals are psychopaths. There certainly are many individuals who are high on Factor I and relatively low on Factor II, who spend their lives manipulating and taking advantage of others, always skating on the thin edge of the law, not to mention propriety. In sum, psychopathy may be associated with law-abiding behavior, and it may be associated with the most unspeakably cruel and vicious crimes of interpersonal violence. We find elements of psychopathy in unprincipled businessman, shyster lawyers, unethical physicians, crooked politicians, unscrupulous salespeople, a wide variety of imposters, conmen, and scam artists, the most successful spies, and an assortment of criminals.

From the standpoint of assessment, the critical issue is that we must be prepared to examine both facets of the behavior.

Assumption #5: Dimensionality. The fifth assumption complements Assumption #4. Psychopathy is a complex construct that falls along a dimension of severity (i.e., the symptoms of psychopathy may be manifest in varying degrees). Psychopathy is *not* simply "present" or "absent." Although for practical purposes we use a cutoff score of 30 on the PCL-R to denote psychopathy, in reality psychopathy falls on a continuum of severity. In addition, other factors, such as degree of intelligence, level of social competence, and influential life experiences (such as childhood abuse), may play critical roles in determining the overall behavioral outcome. A high level of intelligence and "social refinement" is part of the profile of a very successful imposter, whereas severe childhood abuse, sadistic fantasy, and elements of schizotypal personality are often part of the profile of a serial sexual killer.

Clinical Features of the Psychopath

Administration of the PCL:SV or PCL-R interview and proper coding of the items using archival and interview-derived data require considerable training and supervised experience. The information provided here is *not* adequate for conducting a proper PCL-R interview. What we hope to do is to provide the reader with a glimpse of the psychopathic personality by examining each of the eight Factor I variables on the PCL-R, describing each and providing some suggestions when interviewing offenders. These "tips" can be useful even when conducting a general interview (i.e., not a PCL-R or PCL:SV interview) with an offender. Since these Factor I variables are the ones correlated with clinical ratings of psychopathy, they are the ones that evaluators should be *most* vigilant to during an interview. Please keep in mind that in each case we are describing the "prototypic" psychopath. Many offenders will evidence some of these features in varying degrees, often making the ultimate task of diagnosing psychopathy a difficult one.

1. Glibness and Superficial Charm. The psychopath is loquacious and verbally fluent, relating highly unlikely although convincing stories that place him in a positive light, typically as a hero or as a victim. He may be an amusing, entertaining conversationalist. He generally succeeds in presenting himself well and is quite likeable. He is *very* adept at controlling an interview, all the while appearing friendly and superficially cooperative. In reality, it is difficult, if not impossible, to elicit any honest or candid responses from him as he rarely answers questions with more than passing references to the truth. Indeed, his responses give the superficial appearance of being related to the question, when in reality they often are tangential and wind up addressing a completely unrelated issue.

The interviewer is often fooled, because the good psychopath is so skilled at controlling and manipulating conversations. Seasoned interviewers must constantly ask themselves, "Did he *really* answer my question, or am I being taken on another detour?" When the interviewer begins to "feel" manipulated, the antennae immediately go up for the remainder of the interview. Preparation (preinterview review of all available archival documents) is critically important, enabling the interviewer to casually inquire about apparent inconsistencies or improbabilities.

2. Grandiose Sense of Self-Worth/Egocentricity. The psychopath tends to be self-assured and confident, even cocky. They do not see themselves as failures or social outcasts. Their present circumstances (if in prison) are the result of bad luck, taking a rap or a fall for someone else, or being the victim of "the system." They often report the intention to pursue a career with high status, often law or law enforcement, oblivious to how unrealistic it may be. They often report having great wealth or access to great wealth, expensive cars, fancy homes, and influential friends or "associates." Their self-esteem appears exaggerated, particularly when compared to their actual accomplishments.

The interviewer must scrutinize their *actual accomplishments* (educational and vocational) and judge the veracity of their statements against those real-life accomplishments.

3. Pathological Lying and Deception. Psychopaths often are extravagant and very adept liars. They may be so adept at "molding" reality that they have completely different, fictitious "life histories." They are very likely to have concocked or "canned" stories about their upbringing, their life accomplishments, and, of course, their criminal offenses. They are likely to perpetrate hoaxes, have aliases, and be charged with such offenses as fraud, forgery, impersonation, and perjury.

The interviewer must be acutely aware of the following paradox: the intent of the interview is to discern if a client is a psychopath; if he is a psychopath, he will most likely provide false data that the interviewer is relying on to make a reliable judgment. The essential task is to cross-check critical self-reported information against the archival documents. Enough instances of disagreement suggest intentional deception. Since for psychopaths lying is a game, a con, they will fabricate about matters of minimal or even trivial importance (whether or not they graduated from high school or specific activities they claim to have participated in while in high school, usually great accomplishments in sports; whether or not they served in a war zone while in the military or how they were discharged from the military; the longest period of employment or specific types of employment; and so forth). Since many, if not most, sex offenders will deny or at least minimize their sexual offenses, inconsistencies about other matters of seemingly little importance are more likely to signal pathological lying.

4. Conning and Manipulative. Psychopaths are often characterized as con men, hustlers, and manipulators, viewing others as "objects" or pawns in an endless variety of scams. The "con" is something like a cat and mouse game and psychopaths tend to be highly skilled players. Since most nonpsychopaths don't play the game, or at least don't play it well, psychopaths easily win. In the world of crime, these cons usually involve criminal enterprise (i.e., making money) or interpersonal violence (i.e., luring victims). In the gray world of noncrime, these cons usually involve skimming the edge of legality to take advantage of an unsuspecting party, usually for monetary gain.

Once again, the interviewer must be constantly on guard against manipulation. The psychopath will have an "impression" or a "persona" that he wants to convey to the interviewer and will craft his responses to form that impression. A psychopath may manipulate the interviewer to feel sorry for him, to appreciate his intrinsic "goodness," to identify with him (e.g., "we have so many things in common or so many shared life experiences..."), to be impressed by his remarkable accomplishments, or to actually do things for him (e.g., mailing letters, calling lawyers or family).

5. Lack of Remorse or Guilt. Psychopaths rarely, if ever, experience remorse or feel guilt, no matter what they verbalize. They are likely to deny or minimize the gravity of their antisocial behavior, often feeling that the sentence they received was much too severe for such a petty act or that they were caught unfairly or that someone else was really responsible. Disowning responsibility is very common, including blaming the victim for being vulnerable or blaming society for enforcing stupid laws.

The interviewer can easily "test" statements that appear to reflect remorse or guilt by pushing the limits on the individual's ability to go beyond superficial pronouncements of remorse or guilt and describe *feelings* associated with the "words" they are using. Beware of tears. Psychopaths can cry on command. What psychopaths have a tougher time doing is telling you exactly how something felt, since they rarely have the actual experience of *feeling* what they are claiming they felt.

6. Lack of Affect or Shallow Affect.   No matter what appears on the surface, very little is going on below the surface. Psychopaths *never* appear to be truly affected by anything. Nothing ruffles their proverbial feathers; no one rattles their cage. Although they may verbalize strong feelings toward others (e.g., hatred, love), they report them with no affect and cannot describe *feelings* associated with the emotion (other than in intellectual terms). A psychopath may say, for instance, that he was very upset when his father died, and in the same breath remark that he never liked his father. Cleckley was so struck by this feature he was prompted to comment that "the psychopath's objective experience is so bleached of deep emotion that he is invincibly ignorant of what life means to others."

Although all affect tends to be shallow, the most noteworthy feature is the seeming absence of anxiety. In situations that would make most people *very* anxious, psychopaths appear calm, composed, unruffled. The absence of even a trace of anxiety is a hallmark. Even under conditions that produce paralyzing anxiety for us, they remain calm.

Perhaps the most famous example is Ian Fleming's character James Bond, who repeatedly stares death in the face and doesn't as much as blink. There are, of course, many *real* James Bonds, such as the British ace spy (Reilly) on whom Bond's exploits were supposed to have been based. Psychopaths do, in fact, make the very best spies. In screening candidates for counterintelligence assignments during World War II, the Office of Strategic Services found that the very best agents were, in effect, psychopaths.

One particularly remarkable case exemplifies the profound absence of anxiety. The case is that of the grisly serial killer Herman Mudget (alias H. H. Holmes). Mudget retired at the normal hour the night before his execution. He fell asleep quickly, slept soundly, and awakened feeling refreshed. He told the cell guard, "I never slept better in my life." He reported having a "hearty appetite," and ate a large breakfast one hour before he was scheduled to be hanged. Until the very moment that the trap door was released, he was calm and amiable, chatting with those around him as if it was just an ordinary day.

These are, of course, extreme cases. Psychopaths will, however, evidence this hallmark trait in some degree. If at all uncertain, the interviewer can ask many "what do you think it would be like" statements in reference to high-anxiety situations, such as jumping out of an airplane or bungee jumping off a 200-foot-high tower. The interviewer might also inquire, "Other than anger, what's the strongest feeling you've ever had?" "Describe the feeling in detail" (i.e., what did the feeling do to your body?). "Rate your worst anger on a scale of 1 to 10." "Now rate the other feeling using the same scale."

7. Lack of Empathy/Callous Indifference.   Psychopaths evidence a callous indifference to the feelings and welfare of others. They may be arrogant, considering others to be stupid or inferior. They are intolerant of other people, and quick to take offense. They are crass and indifferent to the needs, concerns, and problems of others. Their humor may be cruel and mocking, and their interpersonal style may be likened to a schoolyard bully. The more socially "refined" the psychopath is, the more refined and even subtle the cruel remarks will be. They seem to be detached and unconnected to other human beings. Thus, what happens to other human beings is of little concern to them. This fundamental disregard for others may take the form of outright hostility and be expressed in perverse pleasure in the misfortunes of others.

Psychopathic detachment or indifference is usually evident in the course of an interview. It may come across in remarks about their parents or other caregivers, siblings, teachers, supervisors or fellow employees at work, and, most notably, their victims.

8. Failure to Take Responsibility.   Psychopaths avoid taking personal responsibility for their actions. They engage in massive justification and minimization, if not outright denial. Denial usually takes the form of saying that the victim lied, or they were framed, or even lapsed memory because of intoxication. Minimization usually involves denial that the victim suffered any ill effects. They seem to have a particular proclivity for blaming the victim or blaming the circumstances surrounding the crime. It should be emphasized, however, that this item covers failure to take responsibility in all facets of the individual's life. During the course of an interview, it is not unusual to hear, for instance, that the individual was not responsible for innumerable things, including job losses, failed relationships, speeding tickets, and court martials. This item overlaps somewhat with the behaviors assessed in item #5 (lacks remorse or guilt).

Antisocial Behavior and Psychopathy

It is quite apparent that one need not evidence the constellation of signs and symptoms associated with psychopathy to engage in antisocial behavior. Conversely, the presence of psychopathic features provides no assurance that the individual will be a criminal offender. Thus, there is no precise overlap between psychopathy and antisocial behavior. Indeed, there has been so much diagnostic variance in the broad category variously described as antisocial, psychopathic, sociopathic, or asocial that the category has, in the past, been dismissed as a diagnostic wastebasket. Psychopathy, as it is assessed using Hare's PCL-R, incorporates criteria that address inferred traits of personality that have been consistently associated with the psychopath, including a propensity to run afoul of the law. As noted, in Hare's diagnostic formulation of psychopathy, *both* components (the antisocial component captured by Factor II and the clinical component captured by Factor I) are critical. The greater emphasis placed by DSM-IV on criminal conduct in diagnosing APD is undoubtedly responsible for the imperfect match between an APD diagnosis on the DSM-IV and the PCL-R. Although there is almost universal acceptance of the PCL-R as the standard for assessing psychopathy, there continue to be divergent opinions, those who would argue that psychopathy can be satisfactorily assessed by looking only at Factor II behaviors and those who take the more orthodox position that psychopathy should only be conceptualized using Factor I. The incidence of "pure" psychopathy (as measured by the PCL-R) is about 1% in the general population and about 20% in the prison population, substantially lower than the estimated 50 to 75% of the prison population that may be classified with APD.

There are numerous cases of infamous criminals, usually killers, who were psychopaths, and there are an equal number of books that tell their tales. We will briefly mention two cases that are particularly well-known, followed by a somewhat lengthier description of the exploits of one of the greatest imposters of all time who plied his many "trades" with *no* track record of antisocial or criminal behavior (except, of course, for impersonation). We included these brief biosketches to provide a "flavor" of the remarkable feats of "highly accomplished" psychopaths.

The Case of Henri Landau (Alias Bluebeard).   Born in Paris in 1869, Bluebeard truly was a rogue, who was said to have "loved" 283 women and murdered at least 10 of them. He forged, swindled, seduced, and killed. He assumed a variety of occupations, including a toy salesperson, a physician, a lawyer, and an engineer. His habit was to seduce women, charmingly persuade them to hand over their wealth for safekeeping, and, if they caught on and protested too vigorously, he killed them. He was hanged in 1920 at the age of 51.

The Case of Neville Heath.   Heath had an extraordinary career, most of it in the Armed Forces. He was commissioned as an officer and dishonorably discharged on three separate occasions (once in the British Royal Air Force, once in the Royal Armed Service Corps, and once in the South African Air Force).

He flew in a fighter squadron with the RAF until he was court-martialed for car theft at age 19. He then committed a series of thefts and burglaries, and was sentenced to Borstal Prison. He was pardoned in 1939, joined the Royal Armed Service Corps but was discharged for forging documents.

On his way home to England, he jumped ship. He traveled to South Africa, forged necessary documents, and obtained a commission in the South African Air Force. His past eventually caught up with him, and he was court-martialed—for the third time.

This charming, handsome, supremely confident, and extremely bright fighter pilot and officer was shipped back to England, where he proceeded to commit two of the most brutal, sadistic sexual murders in British history.

The Case of Ferdinand Waldo Demara, Jr. (Alias the Great Imposter).   Ferdinand Demara began his "illustrious" career as a Trappist monk. Prompted by the desire to teach, he joined the Army. Soon thereafter he went AWOL, joined the United States Navy, and awaited a commission based on forged documents. When he realized that he was in danger of being exposed after a routine security check, he devised a successful fake suicide. He left his clothing at the end of a pier with a note saying, "This is the only way out."

Demara next obtained the credentials of a Dr. French who held a Ph.D. in psychology from Harvard. "Dr. French," with his newfound credential in hand, got a job as a dean of philosophy at a college in Canada. He successfully taught a variety of psychology courses, and assumed full administrative responsibilities of a dean.

During his stint as a dean, he befriended Joseph Cyr, a physician. He managed to obtain and duplicate all of Dr. Cyr's relevant documents, including his birth, baptism, and confirmation certificates, his school records, his diplomas, and his medical license. He used these documents to obtain a commission in the Royal Canadian Navy as "Dr. Cyr."

During the Korean War, the new "Dr. Cyr" was assigned to a destroyer in the combat zone. The destroyer encountered a small Korean junk carrying seriously wounded men, who were brought on board for emergency medical care. Three of the men required emergency surgery to save their lives. Although Demara had never even observed an operation, he quickly reviewed several medical texts. With no knowledge, no training, and no skill, he operated all through the night. From one man he removed a bullet that was near the heart, and from another man he removed shrapnel lodged in the groin. For the third man, Demara collapsed a lung that had been perforated by a bullet. By dawn he not only had saved the lives of all three men, but he successfully treated 16 other wounded men as well.

The heroic accomplishments of the pseudosurgeon were broadcast over the ship's radio, and distributed, along with his picture, to the press. The *real* Dr. Cyr immediately exposed Demara. The Canadian Navy, in order to avoid further embarrassment, allowed Demara to leave without prosecution.

Undaunted, Demara went to England and obtained his medical license. His fame, not to mention notoriety, followed him, however, and he lost job after job when it was discovered who he was. Ironically, his last medical job was at a state hospital for the criminally insane. He began drinking heavily and decided that it was time to move on. He obtained the credentials of a Ben W. Jones and joined a chapter of Alcoholics Anonymous. He obtained a few fraudulent references through ingenious means and got a job as a guard in a state penitentiary. He did a commendable job and was promoted to assistant warden for maximum-security inmates. He remained in this capacity until one of his own reforms came back to haunt him. He had encouraged the local townspeople to contribute old magazines for the prisoners. An issue of *Life* magazine included his picture and his story. He determined that it was time to leave the prison before he ended up behind the bars. He was in fact jailed for a very brief time and released.

The last tracking of Demara was in the early 1970s. He was functioning successfully as a minister for a church in a small, northwestern town, reportedly with the congregation's knowledge of his past.

PSYCHOMETRIC ASSESSMENT

A vast array of different inventories, questionnaires, and scales are used by different clinicians to assess sex offenders (see Prentky & Edmunds, 1997). By any rigorous psychometric standard, *very few* of those inventories and questionnaires should be used. To begin with, the psychometric properties (e.g., internal consistency, interrater reliability, validity) for most of these scales are unknown (i.e., unpublished or available but not distributed). Additionally, very few of these instruments have been validated on sex offender samples and very few have normative data from sex offender samples. Indeed, of the many standardized personality inventories used with sex offenders, the only one with a track record of published studies using sexual offenders is the Minnesota Multiphasic Personality Inventory (MMPI). Of the dozens and dozens of instruments that purportedly measure some relevant aspect of sexual behavior and thus are of focal interest in assessing sex offenders, *very few* have been validated on samples of sexual offenders. In general, risk assessment studies that have included psychometric instruments, find that psychometric data are not particularly useful in predicting recidivism in sexual offenders (e.g., Proulx et al., 1997). Since most psychometric instruments were never designed to assess reoffense risk, this finding is not surprising.

We should *not* conclude that these instruments should be abandoned. We should conclude that the cardinal principle that applies to the use of psychometric instruments with all other populations applies to sex offenders as well: *tests should only be used for those purposes for which they were intended.* If assessing Axis II character disorder is a critical part of the evaluation, then it makes sense to include the MMPI or Millon's Clinical Multiaxial Inventory (MCMI-III). It would be highly inappropriate, however, to use the MCMI or the MMPI to assess sexual preference. Similarly, if assessing traumatic victimization, depression, or anger is central to an evaluation, one would undoubtedly choose specialized instruments for accomplishing that goal (e.g., Briere's Traumatic Symptom Inventory, Beck's Depression Inventory, or Spielberger's State-Trait Anger Expression Inventory).

Assessing sexual pathology and sexual aggression falls into the same category (i.e., requiring specialized instruments). As noted, although there are many instruments "on the street" that are used for assessing various aspects of sexually deviant and sexually aggressive behavior, very few have been subjected to empirical scrutiny. In general, psychometric instruments should have their greatest utility when they are wisely chosen and when they are used as clinical tools to complement an evaluation.

Heilbrun (1992) has provided useful general guidelines for psychological testing in forensic assessments. Although Heilbrun may have set the bar for minimum standards a bit high for those who do forensic assessments on sex offenders (the field has a surfeit of "home-grown," unvalidated scales and instruments with no norms and no known psychometric characteristics), all of his standards are worthy of our most earnest consideration. His standards (see 1992, pp. 264–267) are the following:

- *Selection* (the test is commercially available and adequately documented in two sources; it is accompanied by a manual describing its development, psychometric properties, and procedure for administration; it is listed and reviewed in a readily available source).
- *Reliability* (the use of tests with a reliability coefficient of less than .80 is not advisable; the use of less reliable tests would require an explicit justification by the psychologist).
- *Relevance* (the test should be relevant to the legal issue, or to a psychological construct underlying the legal issue; whenever possible, this relevance should be supported by the availability of validation research published in refereed journals). Relevance in legal proceedings is often operationalized as "reasonably relied on" by other professionals in the field (Federal Rules of Evidence, Rule 703). The importance of "relevance" cannot be overstated. As Heilbrun pointed out, "The issue of relevancy is the underlying predicate for all expert testimony, however, even when courts impose the additional demands that expert evidence be *reasonably relied on* or *generally accepted in the field*," (1992, p. 260).
- *Administration* (standard administration should be used, with testing conditions as close as possible to the quiet, distraction-free ideal). Obviously, this becomes problematic when screenings or rapid assessments are done in courthouses, jails, and prisons, which are inherently noisy settings. However difficult, we should be mindful, at the very least, of the need for reasonable testing conditions.
- *Interpretation* (applicability to this population and for this purpose should guide both test selection and interpretation; the results of a test should not be applied toward a purpose for which the test was not developed; population and situation-

specificity should guide interpretation; the closer the "fit" between a given individual and the population and situation of those in the validation research, the more confidence can be expressed in the applicability of the results).

- *Test and Actuarial Data* (objective tests and actuarial data combination are preferable when there are appropriate outcome data and a "formula" exists).
- *Response style* (response style [conscious fabrication or gross exaggeration; conscious denial or gross minimization] should be explicit assessed using approaches sensitive to distortion, and the results of psychological testing interpreted within the context of the individual's response style; when response style appears to be malingering, defensive, or irrelevant rather honest/reliable, the results of psychological testing may need to be discounted or even ignored and other data sources emphasized to a greater degree).

Heilbrun concluded by noting that

> When used in the manner just described, it seems clear that the contribution of any test to a forensic assessment should be weighed according to how well it measures psychological constructs that are relevant to the legal issue and assists the evaluator in formulating and testing hypotheses.... Properly used, psychological tests should not be expected to provide direct information about legal issues, and this criticism should only apply to evaluators who misuse them in such a fashion. (p. 269)

We should reemphasize this last point. There is *no direct connection between test results and a particular legal issue.* Test results pertain to psychological constructs, which in turn support, or refute, hypotheses about legal issues. If, for instance, the legal issue under scrutiny is diminished capacity, and we administer Briere's Trauma Symptom Inventory (TSI), there is no direct connection between the score on the Dis scale of the TSI and diminished capacity. The Dis scale tells us something about the psychological construct of Dissociation, which, along with many other sources of data, confirms or disconfirms hypotheses about the role of trauma in supporting diminished capacity.

The final critical point is that information obtained from psychological tests should *never* be used in isolation to draw conclusions about legal questions. Psychometric data should be integrated with psychosocial history, clinical interview data, offense history, actuarial data, neuropsychological data (if gathered), psychophysiological data (if gathered), and as complete and reliable a picture of behavior as can be gleaned. This point has been made on numerous prior occasions by Heilbrun (1992), Melton, Petrila, Poythress, and Slobogin (1987), Rogers (1986), Shapiro (1991), and others.

With the above-mentioned caveats in mind, we will briefly look at two widely used standardized personality questionnaires (MMPI and MCMI), three lengthy questionnaires that have been designed specifically to assess paraphiliac and nonparaphiliac sexual thoughts, fantasies, attitudes, and behaviors, and two other noteworthy research scales that have been used primarily to assess sexual coercion/aggression among nonoffenders (college students). We will not, however, survey the dozens and dozens of instruments that are used, primarily for clinical purposes, by those who work with sexual offenders. There are two resource guides for practitioners that describe many of these instruments, one published by Safer Society Press (Prentky & Edmunds, 1997) and one developed by Hanson, Cox, and Woszcsyna (1991a) under contract for the Corrections Branch, Ministry of the Solicitor General of Canada. The review by Hanson, Cox, and Woszcsyna covers fewer instruments than the Safer Society Press guide but goes into far greater detail in discussing each one. We certainly would concur with Hanson and colleagues concluding statement, again supported by the findings of Proulx et al. (1997), that "most of the measures reviewed appear to have limited utility in the risk management of sexual offenders" (p. 78).

Standardized Personality Tests

Minnesota Multiphasic Personality Inventory (MMPI)

The MMPI is the only standardized personality test that has been widely used with sexual offenders (e.g., Erickson, Luxenberg, Walbek, & Seely, 1987; Hall, Maiuro, et al., 1986; Kalichman & Henderson, 1991; Langevin, Wright, & Handy, 1990; Mann, Stenning, & Borman, 1992; Marshall & Hall, 1995; Shealy, Kalichman, Henderson, Szymanowski, & Mckee, 1991). In their study of 406 child molesters, Hall, Maiuro, et al. (1986) found that although Scales 4 and 8 were both significantly elevated in the mean profile of the sample, only 7% of the sample had a 2-point (4–8) code. Two-thirds of their sample had more than two scale elevations. Overall, in the Hall, Maiuro, et al. (1986) study *no* single 2-point code was predominant. In a mixed sample of 403 sex offenders, including rapists, incest offenders, and extrafamilial child molesters, Erickson et al. (1987) found (1) *no* differences in code frequency between molesters of male and female children, (2) *no* differences in code frequency between incest and nonincest child molesters, (3) more profiles associated with assaultiveness (4–9 code) among rapists than child molesters, and (4) more 4–5 and 4–8 profiles than are usually found in generic samples of prisoners. In a sample of 120 rapists, Kalichman, Szymanowski, McKee, Taylor, and Craig (1989) found essentially five distinct subgroups based on MMPI profiles (Pd; Pd + Ma; D, Pd, Pa, + Sc; F, Pd, Sc, + Ma; D, Pd, Pa, Pt, Sc, + Ma). In a follow-up study on 90 child molesters, Shealy, Kalichman and their colleagues (Shealy et al., 1991) used cluster analysis to identify four profile subgroups: two subgroups had mean profiles within normal limits, one subgroup had a mean profile characterized by anger and aggression (Pd, Pa, and Sc), and one subgroup had a mean profile characterized by severe psychopathology (7 of the 10 clinical scales were significantly elevated).

In a review of the psychometric literature on sex offenders, Knight et al. (1985) noted that the utility of the MMPI for classification purposes is "limited by its failure to sample several domains important for understanding sex offenders (e.g., level and quality of psychosexual adaptation, preferred sexual orientation, and sexual practices and attitudes)" (p. 240). Knight et al. (1985) went on to point out that it was these very limitations of the MMPI that led Thorne and his colleagues to develop their Sex Inventory (Thorne, 1966). We would concur with Hall, Maiuro, et al. (1986) in their conclusion that "the most conservative conclusion would be that the MMPI is of limited clinical utility in asessing and differentiating (offense) patterns among populations of men who have sexually as-saulted children" (p. 496). In the most recent review of MMPI studies with sex offenders, Marshall and Hall (1995) concluded that "this review of the evidence makes it clear that MMPI responses, however they are scored or represented, do not satisfactorily distinguish any type of sexual offender from various other groups of subjects including, more partic-ularly, nonoffenders" (pp. 216–217). Once again, these conclusions underscore the key point. The MMPI does an excellent job at doing what it was designed to do, and a very poor job at doing what it was never designed to do.

Millon Clinical Multiaxial Inventory

There are very few studies on the use of the MCMI with sex offenders. In one of the very few published studies, Chantry and Craig (1994) administered the MCMI to 603 violent offenders. Included in this sample were 201 child molesters and 195 rapists. Although both sex offender groups were more passive-aggressive than the non-sex offender criminals, the child molesters were more dependent, anxious, and depressed than the rapists and the nonsexual offenders. Chantry and Craig concluded that their results were consistent with the MMPI literature on sex offenders, indicating that rapists were more like non-sex offenders (e.g., aggressive and narcissistic) while child molesters distinguished themselves as being emotionally detached and emotionally labile. Bard and Knight (1986) administered the MCMI to 101 sex offenders (67% were rapists and 31% were child molesters). Cluster analysis of the combined sample yielded four distinct subgroups: (1) a detached group with MCMI elevations on Avoidant, Asocial, and Submissive, (2) a "criminal" group characterized by narcissism, aggression, and gregariousness, (3) a group very similar to Group 2 with elevations on Aggressive and Negativistic, and (4) a group with *no* significant elevations on any of the clinical scales. As a group, the rapists were characterized by Gregariousness (24.5% of the sample) and Negativistic (48.1% of the sample). No other MCMI scale accounted for more than 7.5% of the rapist sample. The child molesters, on the other hand, were characterized by Avoidance (26.4% of the sample), Negativistic (26.4% of the sample), and Submissive (16.7% of the sample).

Although the MCMI, like the MMPI, tells us something about the character pathology of sex offenders, the information derived from these assessments tell us relatively little about offense-related treatment issues and, for the most part, nothing about risk. Like the MMPI, the MCMI was not designed as a measure of pathology for sexually aggressive individuals.

Assessing Normal and Paraphiliac Sexual Fantasies and Behaviors

Clarke Sex History Questionnaire

The Clarke Sex History Questionnaire (SHQ) provides an in-depth assessment of sexual experiences. The first six sections inquire about the frequency of sexual experiences with females by age group (age 16 or older, 13–15 years old, age 12 or younger) and males by age group (same breakdown as for females). The last section assesses paraphiliac experiences. The SHQ contains 189 questions and takes about 45 minutes to complete. The original 225-item version of the SHQ was first reported in the literature over 20 years ago (Paitich, Langevin, Freeman, Mann, & Handy, 1977) and has the longest track record of any currently available instrument for assessing sexual deviance.

The revised SHQ, as Knight, Prentky, and Cerce (1994) noted, is based on a model involving the concept of orgasmic preference and a stimulus–response matrix and represented a major psychometric contribution to the assessment of paraphiliac behavior. A number of studies over the past 20 years, primarily by Ron Langevin and his colleagues, have examined the internal consistency, concurrent validity, and discriminant validity of the SHQ (see Langevin, Handy, Paitich, & Russon, 1985). The current version of the SHQ, authored by Ron Langevin and Dan Paitich, is now published by Multi-Health Systems (MHS) in North Tonawanda, New York 14120.

Multiphasic Sex Inventory

The Multiphasic Sex Inventory (MSI) is a questionnaire that is designed to assess a wide range of psychosexual characteristics of identified sexual offenders. The version of the MSI that was originally developed by Nichols and Molinder in 1977 included 200 items. It was expanded to 222 items in 1983, and expanded once again to 300 items in 1984. The first major revision of the MSI was completed in 1990, and the MSI-II was field tested for the next 5 years. Unlike the SHQ, which is intended for adults (age 18 or older), the MSI has a version for juveniles (ages 14–19). The MSI-II, which also takes about 45 minutes to complete, includes norms derived from a nationally standarized sample of 2000 subjects. Although MSI-II documents indicate psychometric characteristics that include generally high test-reliability, high internal consistency of the scales, and good discriminant validity, there are still relatively few studies in the empirical literature. Noteworthy published studies on the MSI include Kalichman, Henderson, Shealy, and Dwyer (1992), Miner, Marques, Day, and Nelson (1990), Schlank (1995), and Simkins, Ward, Bowman, and Rinck (1989). At the present time, the MSI is the most widely used instrument for general assessment of sexual offenders.

Multidimensional Assessment of Sex and Aggression

The Multidimensional Assessment of Sex and Aggression (MASA) is the most recent attempt to develop a reliable and valid self-report measure for sexual offenders. Work on MASA began approximately 10 years ago, with the goal of developing a focal interview to assist with our taxonomic research on classification of rapists. Thus, MASA was developed as a comprehensive inventory that would assess all domains relevant for evaluating rapists. Since the completion of MASA-I in 1990, the interview has been expanded to accommodate other subgroups of sex offenders. A version of MASA was developed for juvenile sex offenders and a version, in its most rudimentary stages at the present time, has been developed and tested on female sex offenders. In addition, items sufficient for the evaluation of child molesters have been added.

Thus, MASA is much longer and much broader in its coverage than the MSI or SHQ. In addition to assessing sexual and aggressive thoughts, fantasies, and behaviors, MASA also includes in-depth assessments of early life experiences (detailed histories of abuse, caregiver instability, history of placements and institutionalization, and so forth), behavior management problems in childhood and delinquency in adolescence, history of substance use, exposure to and use of pornography, antisocial behavior in adulthood, and social, interpersonal, and work history. In addition to providing profiles on all a priori (classification) scales, embedded within MASA are attitudinal scales (e.g., hostility toward women, hypermasculinity, misogynistic anger, and global anger), behavioral scales (e.g., psychopathy, episodic dyscontrol), and sexualization scales (e.g., compulsivity, sexual preoccupation, paraphilias, guilt, inadequacy, sexual coercion).

MASA is administered on computer and takes approximately two hours to complete. Unlike the MSI and the SHQ, both of which were initially developed over 20 years ago, MASA is still under development and has not been released for general use. There is one published paper that reports on the development, reliability, and validity of an earlier version of MASA (Knight et al., 1994). The development of MASA has been generously supported by grants from the National Institute of Mental Health and the National Institute of Justice, and a recent NIMH award to Knight will permit the testing and validation of the final version of the interview (MASA-IV), and the development of algorithms for profiling.

Assessing Sexual Coercion

Sexual Experiences Survey

The Sexual Experiences Survey (SES) was developed by Mary Koss and her colleagues to assess "hidden" or unidentified victims of rape and "undetected" or unidentified perpetrators of rape (Koss & Gidycz, 1985; Koss & Oros, 1982). The original 12-item version of the SES has been reduced to 10 dichotomously scored items. Although there was a 13th women-only item in the original version that asked about rape, all other items were descriptive and avoided use of such terms as *aggression, coercion,* and *rape.* Positive responses to items such as "Have you given in to sexual intercourse when you didn't want to because you were overwhelmed by a man's continual arguments and pressure?" and "Have you had sexual intercourse when you didn't want to because a man used his position of authority to make you?" denote either sexual victimization or sexual coercion (depending on how the item was phrased). The SES has been widely used as a research instrument to assess the incidence and prevalence of rape.

Attraction to Sexual Aggression Scale

The Attraction to Sexual Aggression Scale (ASA) was developed by Neil Malamuth and his colleagues for use with college students to assess the components of male sexual aggression among those who are prone or predisposed to such behavior (Malamuth, 1989a,b; Malamuth & Dean, 1991). The ASA was an outgrowth of earlier work by Malamuth on assessing attraction to sexual aggression using two correlated constructs: the likelihood that a subject would rape a woman if he was guaranteed that he would get away with it (LR) and the likelihood that a subject would force a woman to have sex (LF). Items comprising the LR scale, which 16 to 20% of respondents answered positively to, and items comprising the LF scale, which 36 to 44% of respondents answered positively to, were used in the development of the ASA scale (see Malamuth, 1989a,b).

The ASA includes nine questions, with each question having from 13 to 17 items. The questions ask the subject to estimate how frequently people engage in a variety of sexual behaviors, whether the subject finds these behaviors to be "attractive," what percentage of men and women find those behaviors to be sexually arousing, what percentage of the subject's male friends have engaged in those behaviors, and what is the likelihood that the subject himself would engage in those behaviors. The five components that emerged from factor analysis of the ASA are Attraction to Conventional Sex, Attraction to Bondage, Attraction to Homosexuality, Attraction to Unconventional Sex (e.g., anal intercourse, group sex), and Attraction to Deviant Sex (e.g., pedophilia, transvestism).

Sexual Preference Assessments

Penile Plethysmograph

Penile plethysmography (PPG) is used to assess sexual preference (primarily among child molesters) and sexual arousal to depictions of coercion, aggression, and sadism. A PPG assessment quantifies an erectile response to auditory or visual stimuli depicting normative and deviant sexual themes. There are two approaches to quantifying erections: circumferential and volumetric. Kurt Freund (1963) developed the first volumetric device that was designed to measure changes in penile blood volume. Essentially, a glass cylinder is placed over the penis and a cuff is inflated to make an airtight seal. When blood enters the penis, thereby increasing volume, a pressure transducer records the changes in air displacement. Fisher, Gross, and Zuch (1965) developed a PPG that displaced water rather than air. McConaghy (1967) subsequently developed an air-filled volumetric PPG. The volumetric PPG that is presently being used is essentially the one designed by Freund.

The circumferential procedure quantifies erections by measuring changes in the circumference of the penis. These devices are much simpler than the volumetric PPG. The mercury strain gauge is simply a fine-bore rubber tube (in appearance it looks like a rubber band) that is filled with mercury (or an indium-gallium alloy) and sealed at the ends. As blood enters the penis and circumference increases, the tube stretches, and the mercury column inside the tube increases its diameter. Since the resistance of the mercury varies directly with the diameter of the column, changes in resistance reflect changes in circumference of the penis. The mercury strain gauge has the distinct advantages of being inexpensive, relatively unobtrusive, and easily placed on the penis by the subject. One of the early disadvantages, a short shelf life of about 3 months for the gauges, has long since been addressed. Depending on amount of use and proper care, gauges now last up to 1 year.

A variation of the mercury strain gauge was developed by Johnson and Kitching (1968) and Barlow, Becker, Leitenberg, and Agras (1970). This electromechanical gauge, sometimes referred to as the "Barlow gauge," looks like a metal cuff that fits around the penis. The device is made of two arcs of surgical spring steel that are joined together by two mechanical strain gauges. When the penis increases in circumference, the two steel arcs expand, flexing the strain gauges, producing changes in resistance. The electromechanical gauge was modified several years later by Laws and Pawlowski (1973). The advantage of the electromechanical gauge is that it is much more durable than the traditional mercury strain gauge. A disadvantage, at least of the earlier electromechanical gauges, is that they are more susceptible to artifact if they move or if the ends of the steel arcs touch (Geer, 1980). Another potential disadvantage is that since the electromechanical gauge does not fully enclose the penis (as the mercury strain gauge does), the full circumferance of the penis must be estimated using a calibration device.

At least one study has compared mercury strain with electromechanical gauges using 25 undergraduate college students (Janssen, Vissenberg, Visser, & Everaerd, 1997). Janssen et al. (1997) found that

> The electromechanical gauge as calibrated on the circular device resulted in greater penile circumference changes than the indium/gallium-in-rubber gauge. Mean circumference changes were not different for the two strain gauges when the oval calibration

device was used. The use of an oval calibration device improves ecological validity of calibration of penile strain gauges. Standard inclusion of this method in studies on male sexual response will increase comparability of research findings. (p. 717)

Parenthetically, the rationale for this finding, and the author's recommendation, is that "if penises are more likely to approximate an oval shape in cross-section, the electromechanical gauge will overestimate its circumferance when calibrated on a circular device" (p. 717).

Standardization of procedures for conducting PPG assessments has, for inexplicable reasons, been a matter of controversy among clinicians and has, thus far, *not* been accomplished (see Maletzky, 1995). Indeed, Howes (1995) conducted a survey of labs throughout North America that conduct PPG examinations specifically to look at the variability of methodology. His findings "clearly revealed a field in which there is abundant inconsistency in both plethysmographic assessment procedures and data interpretation" (p. 9). Howes concluded with understatement and charity, noting that "over the course of 30 years plethysmographic assessment does not appear to have evolved as quickly and as fully as practitioners would have wished" (p. 21). With minor exceptions (e.g., Laws, Gulayets, & Frenzel, 1995), there have been no systematic efforts to standarize procedures for PPG assessments. The closest that we have come to providing guidance for practitioners is the Guidelines for the Use of the Penile Plethysmograph, published by the Association for the Treatment of Sexual Abusers in 1993 (ATSA, 1993), and articles such as the one by Lalumiere and Harris (1998) that sought to answer questions most frequently asked by those who do plethysmographic assessments.

Why the PPG should be exempt from the minimal expectations that we demand of all other assessment procedures is perplexing, to say the least. Two examiners could assess the same individual using different procedures and obtain quite different findings. The result, as Howes noted, is ambiguity of comparability of PPG findings across examiners. There is, moreover, no standardized training and certification process for examiners. Thus, there is no procedure for controlling for the competence of examiners who perform PPG assessments. As we will see, these issues bear importantly on the admissibility of PPG data in legal proceedings.

The consensus among practitioners is that PPG assessments should be done in a clinical setting and only for clinical purposes. Indeed, there appears to be a general concensus that PPG assessments should *not* be used for forensic decision-making (see an exhaustive review by Murphy & Barbaree, 1994). McConaghy (1989) has questioned the ethicality of using PPG findings in legal matters, and Pithers and Laws (1988) advised against the use of PPG data in rendering predictive judgments. Travin, Cullin, and Melella (1988) concluded that at this point the "only purpose that erectile measurements have in a forensic setting would be as one evaluative element contributing to an expert opinion offered to the court regarding potential treatment" (p. 248).

At this point, a fair and balanced appraisal of the PPG would conclude the following. The PPG is, as Barker and Howell (1992) noted, "the best objective measure of male sexual arousal because blood flow to the genital area does not seem to be influenced by factors other than sexual eroticism" (p. 22). When used properly, the PPG is an excellent measure of sexual arousal and preference. There are, however, two major problem areas that can generally be referred to as (1) methodological, and (2) forensic. The former case includes, most importantly, lack of standardization of stimuli and procedures, lacks of standards and requirements for training, variable interpretations of the data, and lack of norms for non-offenders and relevant subgroups of sex offenders. The latter case includes, most notably, the overinterpretation of data and data-based predictions of a client's guilt, innocence, or risk of offending. Such predictions, based exclusively or even predominantly on PPG results, are irresponsible. The ample literature on the predictive validity of the PPG, as impressive as it is, does *not* permit conclusions about probability of engaging in the target behavior.

Abel Assessment for Interest in Paraphilias

Gene Abel has developed a method for assessing interest in paraphilias, especially pedophilia, that is noninvasive (involves no measurement of erection), requires no stimuli depicting nudity, and always yields some response (i.e., there are no "nonresponders" or "flat-liners" as one occasionally observes with the PPG) (Abel, Lawry, Karlstrom, Osborn, & Gillespie, 1994). Although the Abel Assessment is *not* a psychophysiological procedure, its purpose (assessing sexual preferences) makes it a close cousin of the PPG, and its mode of operation (reaction time) makes it sufficiently distinct to include it in this section. Parenthetically, it would be very easy to complement the Abel Assessment with psycho-physiological recordings of peripheral nervous system activity (e.g., heart rate) to refine assessment of deception and pupillometry to examine details of stimulus fixation (e.g., precisely what parts of the image are the subjects focusing on). The downside, of course, is that this would make the Abel Assessment much more expensive and less portable.

The Abel Assessment has two components, a questionnaire that asks about sexual thoughts, fantasies, and behavior, and a computerized assessment of self-reported arousal to slides depicting images of boys and girls in the age range of 8–10, male and female teenagers in the age range of 14–17, adult men and women, and scenes suggesting sadism against men and women, exhibitionism, voyeurism, and other paraphilias. Abel et al. (1994) discussed the development, reliability, and validity of the Abel Assessment. In general, the efficiency (overall predictive accuracy) of the Abel Assessment is better with same-sex child molesters than opposite-sex child molesters. The reported efficiency was approx-imately 97% in the former case and 78% in the latter case. When used with opposite-sex child molesters, the procedure has good sensitivity (86–91%) but only moderate specificity (77%). Since sensitivity (the ability of the procedure to correctly identify those who have pedophilic interests) is generally of greater concern than specificity, the lower specificity with opposite-sex offenders may be of only marginal interest. Overall, the Abel Assessment was most accurate with child molesters who prefer pubescent-age boys (90% sensitivity and 98% specificity). The data reported in Abel et al. (1994) are only the "earliest returns" on a promising new technology that certainly should complement and enhance efforts to assess sexual preferences.

Assessment of Dissimulation

Polygraph

The polygraph has been increasingly used over the past 30 years, primarily with sex offenders, to deter reoffending (Abrams & Ogard, 1986; Edson, 1991), to overcome denial

(Abrams, 1992; Priest & Smith, 1992), and to verify compliance with parole conditions (English, 1998; Matte, 1996). The rationale for the use of the polygraph with sex offenders was provided by Pullen (1996), who noted that

> Not only does the polygraph promote the disclosure of information important for both the parole/probation officer and the treatment provider, it also makes possible the identification of additional victims for whom treatment can be provided, often at the perpetrator's expense. In addition, it serves to promote public safety by providing a scientific tool that ensures the disclosure of inappropriate and criminal acts committed while an offender is under community supervision" (p. 15/6).

As Pullen noted, polygraph examinations with sex offenders are generally conducted for two reasons: (1) to verify the sex offense history of an individual (sometimes referred to as the disclosure examination), and (2) to check up on a known offender who is being supervised in the community (referred to as the maintenance examination).

Increased use of the polygraph to examine deception, for both clinical and forensic purposes, has also placed polygraphy under legal scrutiny. Although polygraphy does *not* share a common purpose with phallometry, the former being to detect deception and the latter being to assess sexual preference, both are physiological procedures that are being used with increasing frequency in forensic evaluations. Polygraphy is much more likely than phallometry to be "farmed out" to trained examiners and thus the procedure is less well-known to clinicians. Consequently, we have included a brief discussion on the procedure itself. We discuss problems associated with admissibility of polygraphy in Chapter 7.

The two most common procedures used for physiological detection of deception, both of which have been the subject of considerable empirical research, involve the guilty knowledge test (GKT) and the control question test (CQT). In the GKT, the subject (i.e., suspect or defendant in a criminal matter) is presented with a series of questions, several of which inquire about a crime. If the subject "possesses guilty knowledge," he is expected to respond differently to the critical questions. An innocent individual, one who does *not* possess guilty knowledge, will respond no differently to the critical questions than to the noncritical questions. The "response" that is being monitored, of course, is physiological, essentially an autonomic nervous system response to the anxiety of harboring guilty knowledge. The GKT has practical limitations, however, by assuming that only the guilty party possesses the critical information. In reality, when the details of a crime are widely reported by the media, innocent people may also acquire "guilty knowledge" and evidence physiological responses to questions involving that knowledge. In addition, field studies (real criminal investigations) have reported high-false negative error rates using the GKT procedure (Elaad, 1990; Elaad, Ginton, & Jungman, 1992). In those field studies, the examiner was aware of the relevant items. A more recent study by Elaad (1997) involved a mock situation in which the examiner either knew, or did not know, the relevant items. Elaad (1997) found that "participants yielded weaker responses to relevant items when the examiner was aware of them than when he did not have the knowledge" (p. 107). As Elaad (1997) concluded, these results suggest that uninformed or "blind" examiners may get better results than informed examiners when assessing guilty examinees. This is of practical significance, since, in real life, examiners almost always know which items are critical.

Because of the aforementioned problems associated with the GKT, the CQT has been more widely adopted. In the CQT, subjects are asked three sorts of questions: relevant questions, control questions, and irrelevant questions. *Relevant questions* inquire *directly* about *specific* offense-related issues, e.g., "Did you take Ms. Doe home from the bowling alley on the evening of Saturday January 31, 1998?" *Irrelevant questions* inquire about strictly neutral issues that have nothing to do with the crime, such as "Do you like pistachio ice cream?" Irrelevant questions are intended to provide a response baseline. *Control questions* inquire about general criminal behavior that a large proportion of the population may have done and that has nothing to do with the offense under investigation, such as "When you were a teenager, did you ever steal anything?" Guilty people will, hypothetically, respond much more strongly to the Relevant Questions than to the Control Questions. Simply stated, guilty people will be far more "concerned" about the Relevant Questions than about the Control Questions. By way of contrast, innocent people are expected to be more responsive to the Control Questions than to the Relevant Questions. An innocent person, after all, can state unequivocally that he was not in the bowling alley on the evening of January 31, 1998. When he is asked, however, if he ever stole anything when he was a teenager, his immediate recollection of a trivial incident is likely to produce some physiological response.

The dependent measures for both the GKT and the CQT are typically respiration, electrodermal activity (skin conductance or skin resistance), and cardiovascular activity. The assumption with both the GKT and the CQT is that these indices of peripheral nervous system activity are correlates of an emotional state that is triggered by feelings of guilt or deception-related anxiety. Although not yet introduced into general clinical or forensic practice, criticism of standard procedures of detecting deception has resulted into a new GKT procedure that uses late positivity in the event-related brain potential (ERP) as the dependent measure. ERP deception research, which has been done by Rosenfeld and his colleagues (e.g., Rosenfeld, Angell, Johnson, & Qian, 1991; Rosenfeld, Nasman, Whalen, Cantwell, & Mazzeri, 1987; Rosenfeld et al., 1988), Farwell and Donchin (1986, 1988), and Fort, Hart, Hare, and Harpur (1988), has sought to develop an index that is at least partly, if not wholly, cognitive, rather than relying entirely on an emotional response.

As Abrams (1991) discussed in some detail, in addition to the GKT and CQT tests, the third procedure, used almost exclusively with sex offenders, is the disclosure test. The disclosure test, as the name implies, is intended to assist the clinician in breaking through denial. The disclosure test is used about 3 months after treatment has begun, and, as noted, has the singular purpose of encouraging the offender to acknowledge responsibility. The CQT and GKT tests are referred to as "periodic" by Abrams (1991), since repeated examination is common, particularly when used to verify compliance with conditions of parole. As Abrams pointed out, testing someone every 6 months for years, or in some cases for life, is quite a different matter from the administration of a single test. The validity of "serial" polygraph tests must be examined.

In brief, polygraphy has experienced something of a meteoric rise in popularity as an additional tool for protecting the community from known sex offenders. The popularity of polygraphy is, not surprisingly, linked to the wave of state and federal legislation that has focused on sex offenders during the decade of the 1990s, and the consequent need for improved strategies for reducing reoffense risk among convicted sex offenders living in the community. In her many writings on the subject, Kim English (e.g., English, 1998; English, Pullen, & Jones, 1996) has described her three-cornered containment model: (1) criminal justice supervision and surveillance plans tailored to the offender's unique set of high-risk factors, (2) sex offense-specific therapy, and (3) polygraphic examinations. As English (1998) stated,

> The postconviction polygraph examination is to sexual offenders what the urinalysis drug test is to drug offenders. It is an independent source of information that is not contingent on the offender's self-report.... The value of the postconviction polygraph seems undisputed among those who use it." (p. 228)

For the time being, at least, we can assume that polygraphy will become an increasingly familiar part of the criminal justice system's repertoire for managing sex offenders in the community.

The Interface of Assessment with Treatment

The treatment model most often used with sexual offenders (relapse prevention) is characterized by a clear interdependence of risk assessment and treatment goals. For most of the offenders whom we treat, a unique series (or chain) of events and feelings contributed to their sexual crimes. These precursors or "risk factors" lead, in some sequential fashion, to an offense. These events or risk factors occur with some degree of regularity (i.e., a cycle) and lead to maladaptive responses, such as withdrawal and isolation, substance abuse, domestic violence, improperly managed and expressed anger, altercations at work, motor vehicle offenses, and sexually coercive and aggressive behavior. Although these risk factors do *not always* lead to an offense, they do place the individual at high risk to commit an offense. The co-occurrence of these high-risk factors *and* opportunity is likely to lead to some form of relapse.

Our task as therapists is to identify, as accurately as possible, the unique risk factors that exist for each client, and to help our clients internalize those factors so that they become a part of their conscious awareness. The client must learn to recognize when he is at risk and when the risk is increasing. Metaphors are simple (e.g., only through knowing what poison ivy looks like, can we learn to avoid it). It is critical to remember that these risk factors not only will be different for everyone, they can be, quite literally, anything. Quite often, risk factors involve *legal* activities (e.g., hanging out at a bar, "cruising" near school grounds, being gainfully employed as a carnival worker, a school bus driver, or a camp counselor). Quite often risk factors involve *normative* activities (e.g., having "normal" sex with an age-appropriate consenting partner). That these activities are legal and/or normative does *not* mean that they are not risky. It is *not* our task to make value judgments or legal judgments about a given behavior. It is our task to clearly identify those activities that place our clients at risk and to help our clients avoid them or respond more appropriately to them.

The role of assessment in this process should be as clear as it is vital. The task of the assessment phase of treatment, which typically occurs at intake, is to identify, as accurately as preliminary data permit, the most critical antecedent factors that contributed to the governing offense. Although it is not always the case, most of the time these antecedent factors are the core treatment issues, as well as the high-risk factors. Treatment cannot, or at least should not, proceed without the benefit of an informed, comprehensive sex offender-specific assessment. Unfortunately, there are no standardized or even commonly accepted models for conducting such an assessment. All that we can offer is that most comprehensive assessments will include the following components: (1) a standard psychosocial history, (2) a psychopathy interview (PCL:SV or PCL-R), (3) a sexual preference assessment (if deemed necessary), (4) psychological testing, which may include standardized personality inventories but more commonly includes instruments targeted at specific concerns (such as identification with children, cognitive distortions, anxiety and social avoidance, hyper-masculinity and hostility toward women, anger, empathy, self-esteem, affect, depression, and traumatic symptomatology), and (5) review of archival documents and completion of an actuarial risk assessment instrument. In addition, comprehensive assessments may also include one of the inventories designed to measure normal and paraphiliac sexual fantasies and behaviors (e.g., Clarke, MSI, MASA).

CHAPTER 5

Prediction

Predicting "Dangerousness" for the Courts: Historical Perspective

The two most commonly employed models for predicting generic dangerousness evolved out of federal court orders. The *psychiatric model* emerged from a 1974 court-ordered reevaluation of all residents in Ohio's maximum-security prison for the criminally insane. The *sociopsychological model* emerged from a 1976 court-ordered reevaluation of all inmates in the Alabama correctional system. Pfohl (1979) reviewed the merits of both of these models and concluded that "neither the so-called Ohio nor Alabama models can claim to validly assess the likelihood of future dangerousness" (p. 77). This conclusion has generally been echoed by examiners, clinicians, and investigators alike. In Rappaport's book, *The Clinical Evaluation of the Dangerousness of the Mentally Ill*, Usdin (1967) stated that "we cannot predict even with reasonable certainty that an individual will be dangerous to himself or to others" (p. 43). In a recent World Health Organization study, teams in Brazil, Denmark, Egypt, Swaziland, Switzerland, and Thailand examined the application of the concept of dangerousness (Harding & Adserballe, 1983). These investigators found no evidence to indicate that psychiatrists agree among themselves on the assessment of dangerousness any more than nonpsychiatrists. Psychiatrists *did*, however, tend to rate patients as *more* dangerous than did nonpsychiatrists. Harding and Adserballe concluded by saying that dangerousness is a medicolegal concept that is widely used but rarely with a precise or uniform meaning and criteria and that psychiatric expertise does not increase the reliability of the assessment of dangerousness. An old review article went so far as to call the assessment process "flipping coins in the courtroom" (Ennis & Litwack, 1974).

Predicting Risk for the Courts in the Year 2000

The concept of "dangerousness" remains explicit in our laws. Dangerousness is one of two constitutionally required components of civil commitment (Janus & Meehl, 1997), and the unambiguous justification of the civil commitment of sex offenders is that we are protecting society from the "most dangerous" perpetrators. In years past, the most dangerous sex offenders were called *sexual psychopaths*. At the present time, they are called *sexual predators*. Although the labels change, what constitutes dangerousness has not. Janus and Meehl (1997) cited the four components of dangerousness enumerated by Professor Brooks in a 1974 article: "(a) the magnitude of harm, (b) the probability that the harm will occur, (c) the frequency with which the harm will occur, and (d) the imminence of the harm" (p. 37). Common language in statutes boils down to "repetitive and/or violent" (a + c). Although, as Janus and Meehl (1997) noted, courts have traditionally been "hostile to constitutional attacks on the second of Brooks's dangerousness components" (p. 38) (i.e., the probability that harm will occur), this very component is implicitly embedded in civil commitment statutes for sex offenders. In asserting that only the most dangerous sex offenders are civilly committed, we make the following four assumptions:

> (a) the probability of dangerousness is susceptible of measure, (b) there is a way to discriminate between predictions of higher and lower probability, (c) there are standards that allow commitments based on the former while excluding confinement based on the latter, and (d) these standards are, in fact, enforced. (Janus & Meehl, 1997, p. 38).

Thus, those decisions that are *most* problematic, and arguably more indefensible, for clinicians, asserting the probability of the recurrence of a sexual offense, are the very decisions that are crucial to the integrity of the civil statutes (i.e., the ability to screen for dangerousness and select those who are *more* dangerous by assessing the probability of being dangerous). In a paradoxical way, forensic examiners are increasingly compelled, whether it is their inclination or not, *to dance with mathematics*, an outcome foreseen and criticized by Tribe (1971) (see Trial by Mathematics).

Monahan and Wexler (1978) sought to clarify the court's use of "probability," or more specifically, the probability standards used in civil commitments. Monahan and Wexler proposed a bifurcated standard: a standard of proof and a standard of commitment. The standard of proof is applied in resolving uncertainties in the evidence. The standard of proof is operationalized in the courtroom with such phrases as "clear and convincing evidence" and "beyond a reasonable doubt." The standard of commitment assesses the probability of being dangerous, and is typically associated with such terms as *likely* and *highly likely*. As Monahan and Wexler (1978) submitted, and as Janus and Meehl (1997) discussed, the relationship between these two standards is "intricate and complex," and, at times, intertwined.

For reasons that hopefully will be apparent, clinicians and forensic examiners are increasingly moving away from use of the term *dangerousness* and adopting, in its place, *risk* (see Borum, 1996; Grisso & Tomkins, 1996; Hanson, 1998; Harris, Rice, & Quinsey, 1998; Heilbrun et al., 1998). Risk implies the presence of a potential hazard, and the probability of occurrence of that hazard. Risk reduction implies reduction in the probability of the occurrence of the hazard. *Risk* has greater utility and more flexibility than *dangerousness*. First, risk is clearly thought of as dimensional and continuous, whereas dangerousness is too often (and too easily) thought of in dichotomous terms (i.e., either the offender *is* dangerous or *is not* dangerous). It is much easier to pose the question "What degree of risk does the offender present?" than "What degree of dangerousness does the offender present?" Second, *dangerousness* captures a narrow swath of human behavior, typically acts of interpersonal violence, whereas *risk* captures a much broader range of behaviors (e.g., we may speak about an offender's risk of eloping, of violating parole, of drinking, of using drugs, of depression and/or suicide). Third, the occurrence of risk is more likely to be seen as some calculable probability, whereas dangerousness is more likely to be thought of in absolute terms (as noted above). Fourth, the use of risk brings criminology "in line" with numerous other disciplines, from measuring health care outcomes (where the term *risk adjustment* is used) and environmental protection (environmental health risk management) to meteorology (Monahan & Steadman, 1996).

Using a risk assessment model from meteorology, Monahan and Steadman (1996) delineated the reasons for the remarkable success of weather forecasters that were identified in the National Research Council's 1989 report, *Improving Risk Communication*. The five principal reasons for the success of meteorologists are: (1) frequent practice ("numerous forecasts of the same kind"), (2) base-rate information (availability of vast amounts of data on average probabilities of the events being predicted), (3) actuarial support (availability of computer-generated predictions prior to making forecasts), (4) feedback (reliable, quick feedback about predictive accuracy), and (5) education (meteorologists acknowledge their fallibility and the consequent need for training). As Monahan and Steadman (1996) pointed out, the five conditions identified by the National Research Council for meteorologists have clear applicability for prognostications of risk in the mental health arena. (1) For those mental health practitioners and forensic examiners who routinely assess risk, frequent practice is a given. We would benefit greatly, however, if the experiences of individual clinicians and examiners were aggregated, uniformly treated (i.e., coded), and electronically "fed back" to practitioners. A data set containing thousands of experiences would be much more informative than one examiner's caseload of several hundred experiences. (2) As Monahan and Steadman noted, base rates of interpersonal violence among different subgroups of clients, civil and forensic, are increasingly becoming available. Reliable base-rate data on diverse subgroups of sex offenders are not presently available, however, and the highest premium should be placed on the acquisition of such data. (3) The use of actuarial data to complement risk assessments, and the use of actuarial risk assessment instruments are well accepted and widely practiced. The critical necessity for the field will be patience. We must apply empirical honing stones to our actuarial risk predictors to achieve greater degrees of precision. The task is abundantly clear, and our success will only be delayed or thwarted by premature implementation of unvalidated or poorly validated procedures. (4) Given that the ultimate outcome criterion is reoffense and the commonly accepted dictum that some sex offenders take a long time to reoffend, "feedback" time is often measured in years. The trend, however, has been to shorten and tighten the leash on sex offenders, resulting in much better documentation of failures. Moreover, feedback would be improved by defining the criterion in much broader terms. In other words, by conceptualizing outcome in a variety of ways (e.g., progress in therapy, success on the job, quality of relationships), we can get feedback much sooner and possibly abort an imminent reoffense. (5) Again, as Monahan and Steadman observed, training programs, workshops, and conferences, as well as training materials, are readily available. This certainly is true of the sex offender field as well. The problem is not the proliferation of training opportunities in this field but quality control. There is no uniformity of training curricula, no universally agreed on corpus of knowledge, and no procedure for assuring the competence of trainers.

In sum, there is a clear, if not urgent, mandate for risk-relevant decisions within the criminal justice system, and an equally clear path to follow in developing and testing sophisticated assessment procedures guided by methods successfully employed in other fields. If there is any question about the ubiquity of risk-relevant decisions within the court system, a list was prepared by Heilbrun et al. (1998):

> (a) *civil commitment* (in which a sex offender had a co-occurring diagnosis that would meet the criterion for mental disorder and whose risk for sexual offending was linked to the disorder and provided evidence of danger to others), (b) *sentencing* (following the conviction of a sex offense in some jurisdictions, the issue of aggravating and mitigating circumstances generally, or the questions of specialized treatment needs and sexual offense risk more specifically, are invoked), (c) *postsentence commitment* (as in a *Hendricks* context—whether a convicted inmate at the end of a sentence, without mental illness but nonetheless presenting a significant risk for sexual reoffending, can be civilly committed), (d) *postsentence community notification* (involving informing the local police and community members that a convicted sexual offender is about to be released and plans to reside in their community), (e) *the granting and conditions of probation or parole*, and (f) *child custody*. (p. 153)

ELEMENTARY PROBABILITY THEORY AND PREDICTION

Hopefully, in the past 25 years, we have progressed beyond flipping coins in the courtroom. Advances in risk prediction derive entirely from the application of rigorous scientific methods to the task of assessing risky behavior. In this chapter we will attempt to provide a framework for risk prediction, beginning with (1) a few elementary principles of probability that form the basis for many of our assumptions, (2) the conventional 2 × 2 contingency table now familiar to most forensic examiners, (3) the insuperable problems associated with accurate prediction, and (4) finally what the empirical literature suggests about those factors that are most robust in differentiating between high- and low-risk individuals.

A probability statement tells us what we may expect about the relative frequency of occurrence of some event (or behavior) given that a sufficiently large number of random observations have been made. In theory, if we observe enough instances of the event (or behavior), the relative frequency of occurrence of that event should approach the probability of the event. This basic principle was set forth and proved by James Bernoulli and is usually referred to as *Bernoulli's theorem*. The theorem itself was included in Bernoulli's book *Ars conjectandi* (*The Art of Conjecture*), published in 1713 after his death.

The simplest possible probability distribution includes only two outcomes (e.g., a coin toss in which there are only two possibilities—heads or tails). Such simple probability distributions, with only two possible outcomes, are referred to as *Bernoulli trials* or *Bernoulli processes*. The two outcomes in such cases are often referred to as *success* and *failure*. This is highly relevant for future discussion about risk prediction, which typically involves an estimation of the likelihood (or probability) that an offender will ("fail") or will not ("succeed") commit another criminal act. Thus, the model that is used for examining risk, the 2 × 2 contingency table, crosses *actual* outcome (success [i.e., no evidence of failure] *or* failure) with *predicted* outcome (predicted to succeed or predicted to fail).

The methodology for analyzing this simple 2 × 2 contingency table was developed by the English clergyman Thomas Bayes. In his original paper in 1763, Bayes, in essence, revised classic probability theory to include *prior* information along with present sample (or case) information that might inform and improve our estimates of risk. Classical approaches to statistical inference are, for the most part, limited to sample data (in our context, data gathered in the course of evaluating a client), and do not include consideration of prior data. A wide array of problems involving decision-making in the face of uncertainty, from domains as diverse as economics, business management, natural resource development, medicine, military applications, criminology, and forensic sciences, have benefited from the application of Bayesian methods in which *all* relevant data, including prior information, will be brought to bear on decision-making. This is, of course, what makes Bayesian methods so attractive to social scientists and forensic examiners who render risk decisions based on statistical evidence. In the last 40 years or so, there has been an enormous resurgence of interest in developing Bayesian methods and applying them to a wide range of complex problems where decision-making is critical. Examiners who are called on to make risk decisions about violent behavior clearly have been the beneficiary of this renaissance of interest in Bayesian methods.

One important caveat is that Bayesian methods are often appealing for their apparent simplicity. In reality, it would be a grave mistake to treat these methods as "simple." Although the results of classical and Bayesian methods may appear similar, the interpretation of the results may differ substantially. This is in part the case, because classical and Bayesian approaches to statistical inference begin with different interpretations of probability. The net result is that it often requires considerable mathematical and statistical sophistication to develop a clear, accurate rationale for the results of a Bayesian analysis.

TRIAL BY MATHEMATICS

In practice, psychologists have routinely employed Bayes's theorem as a model for aggregating base-rate data (Koehler, 1996). Meehl and Rosen (1955) recommended the use of base rates for clinical decisions, and over the past 40 years the application of Bayesian methodology to many other decision-making domains has been recommended (Koehler, 1996). Acceptance of the application of more sophisticated mathematical techniques to address some of the elusive riddles that confront forensic examiners should not escape passing reference to the eloquent arguments of Tribe (1971), denouncing "trial by mathematics." Tribe maintained that even if mathematical procedures could be demonstrated to enhance the accuracy of the trial process, there lies an "inherent conflict" between the goals of jurisprudence, particularly with respect to the fact-finding process, and the uncompromising rationality and objectivity of mathematics. The inherent "problem" of induction, that scientific theories are never conclusively verified, is starkly at odds with the deliberative mission of the trier of fact. The merits of Tribe's many arguments notwithstanding, it is quite evident that we live in a less kind and less gentler time when the highest premium is placed on the kind of precision and accuracy in decision-making that relies on mathematics.

Moreover, we live at a time when the rapid pace of technology threatens to overwhelm the "presumption of innocence." Tribe recounted an example in which a palm print found on a murder weapon was similar to that of the defendant, sufficiently similar that an expert could testify that such prints are found in no more than 1 case in a 1000 (see pg. 1355). The question, as Tribe noted, is "how the jury might best be informed of the precise incriminating significance of that finding" (p. 1355). Less than 30 years after Tribe's thesis, we have moved from palm prints and probabilities of 1:1000 to DNA typing and probabilities that range from 1:500,000 to 1:738,000,000,000,000. Even at the "lower end" of this range, how does a juror process that the probability of a chance match between a DNA sample and the defendant is about 1 in a million and still maintain a presumption of innocence? Or, in Tribe's terms, what is the "incriminating significance" of 1 in a million, or for that matter, 1 in a quadrillion?

Trial by mathematics in the sex offender courtroom has even greater relevance (see Janus, 1997b, for a general discussion). The integrity of constitutionally fragile legislation often rests on science. As an obvious case in point, the civil commitment laws rely on a sound scientific basis for assessing risk. Janus (1997b) concluded that

> Science is used both too much and too little in sex offender commitments. Too much deference to science at the adjudication stage permits standardless decisions, divorcing adjudication from the social (commonsense) context that ought to determine the boundary conditions in law. Too little science at the legislative fact stage countenances the adoption of decisions grounded on false generalizations. (p. 386)

The 2 × 2 Contingency Table

Risk classification compares predicted with actual outcomes. Risk classes are defined as the range of the predicted probability of some event (Copas & Tarling, 1986), usually new criminal offenses in criminology applications. One common method is to classify subjects into one of two groups, recidivist or nonrecidivist, based on whether they were recharged, rearrested, or reconvicted of a new offense and examine the ability of selected "risk" variables to discriminate between those who did, and those who did not, re-offend. This method yields four possibilities: the individual did or did not actually reoffend *and* our prediction that the individual would or would not reoffend. A standard 2 × 2 contingency table is used to depict these four possibilities (Figure 1). The contingency table simply crosses two dichotomous outcomes, yielding the following four cells:

		ACTUAL OUTCOME: Yes	ACTUAL OUTCOME: No
PREDICTED OUTCOME	Yes	True Positives (TP)	False Positives (FP)
PREDICTED OUTCOME	No	False Negatives (FN)	True Negatives (TN)

Figure 1. Simple 2 × 2 contingency table.

- *True positives* (TP): We predicted that the subject would reoffend *and* he did reoffend.
- *False positives* (FP): We predicted that the subject would reoffend *but* he did *not* reoffend.
- *True negatives* (TN): We predicted that the subject would *not* reoffend *and* in fact he did not reoffend.
- False negatives (FN): We predicted that the subject would *not* reoffend *but* he did reoffend.

The word *reoffend* can, of course, be substituted for any assortment of other predicted outcomes. As is obvious, there are two different types of errors—FPs (we said someone would reoffend and he didn't) and FNs (we said someone wouldn't reoffend and he did). All indices of predictive accuracy rely, one way or another, on these simple categorizations and all of these indices treat the two errors (FPs and FNs) as equivalent. As Gottfredson (1987) pointed out, these two errors may not be, indeed typically are not, of equal importance when considered in monetary, social, or ethical terms. The consequences assigned to one type of error or the other can dramatically impact the evaluation of predictions (Loeber & Dishion, 1983). It is ironic that assessing the utility of prediction instruments based on the differential weighting of FP and FN errors is common in many contexts but *not* in the criminal justice system in general and not with sex offenders in particular.

The "Downside" to 2 × 2 Contingency Tables

As Hart, Webster, and Menzies (1993) observed, there are reasons for not using the 2 × 2 contingency table, which, for sake of thoroughness, should at least be mentioned. Hart, Webster, and Menzies (1993) noted the following four problems.

First, 2 × 2 tables are, by their very nature, artificial (i.e., they do not reflect the manifest complexity of predictor *or* outcome variables in the area of violence prediction). Such variables cannot be neatly or easily dichotomized. The multidimensional nature of violence dictates, for instance, that all outcomes are not equivalent (e.g., actual rapes, attempted rapes, and threatened rapes, all of which may be classified as the same outcome, may in fact be qualitatively very different outcomes).

Second, reliance on 2 × 2 tables sets a bad example for practitioners. That is, in forensic contexts, the use of 2 × 2 tables by examiners may encourage "absolute" judgments, discourage qualifying judgments with regard to confidence levels and (related) discourage the use of probabilistic statements. The implication of absolute confidence in judgments about violence, whether 2 × 2 tables are used or not, reflects, at the very least, bad practice and, at the worst, unethicality.

Third, Hart, Webster, and Menzies pointed out that 2 × 2 tables are deceptively simple. In reality, understanding what a 2 × 2 table is telling us about predictive accuracy requires at least rudimentary knowledge of probability and Bayesian statistics. Most practitioners are not acquainted with and trained in the statistical methods that are used to assess the predictive accuracy of these tables.

Fourth, 2 × 2 tables may draw the focus of the reader's attention to FP errors, thereby introducing a kind of myopia to the field. In reality, we are not likely to abandon 2 × 2 tables in the near future, and many of the problems that are raised, certainly the second and fourth problems described above, reflect "human error" (or human foibles) and not flaws inherent in the tables themselves. The third problem, while not reflecting human error, is a matter that can be easily rectified with training and, once again, does not suggest an inherent weakness of the 2 × 2 table.

THE ALBATROSS OF OVERPREDICTION

Of perhaps even greater concern than the number of errors (i.e., incorrect predictions) is the direction in which errors most often occur—overprediction or "false positives." For every accurate assessment of dangerousness there are numerous incorrect assessments of dangerousness. Dershowitz (1969) has argued that of all those presently incarcerated on the basis of psychiatric assessments of dangerousness, "there are a few who would, and many more who would not, actually engage in such conduct if released" (p. 47). The problems posed by FPs extend far beyond the obvious ones articulated by civil libertarians (i.e., the antiprotectionist argument that it is morally wrong to detain three or more individuals in order to prevent only one of them from reoffending). First, overprediction places a tremendous burden on our already strained custodial institutions. In the judicial system, the buck eventually stops at the prison gate, and our overcrowded prisons cannot absorb many more bucks. Thus, from a strictly utilitarian standpoint, the tendency to overpredict dangerousness places an impossible demand on the penal system. The concept of selective incapacitation will not be viable until we improve the accuracy with which we select for dangerousness. Second, we cannot dismiss the likelihood that some percentage of those who were *not* dangerous prior to incarceration become dangerous as a result of incarceration. Thus, we may be aggravating the problem by adding to the ranks of the dangerous through the socialization and adaptation process of prison life.

In John Monahan's classic 1981 tome, *Predicting Violent Behavior: An Assessment of Clinical Techniques*, he identified five primary factors that contribute to overprediction: (1) political influences, (2) illusory correlations, (3) cultural differences, (4) conceptual and contextual problems, and (5) low base rates for violence. Before discussing each of these primary factors, it is necessary to digress briefly and describe the prediction table (2 × 2 contingency table) that will be referred to hereafter.

Monahan's Primary Factors Associated with Overprediction

Political influences refer to the *consequences* for the examiner, often adverse, if the offender commits another violent act. If the examiner finds the defendant *not* dangerous and no further acts of violence occur, everything is copacetic. If the examiner finds the defendant *not* dangerous and there is a subsequent violent act, there could be severe repercussions, such as negative media coverage and lawsuits. To avoid the *very real* risks of such negative consequences, the safest response is to err on the side of dangerousness. Taking the safe path, will inevitably result in a different kind of error, proclaiming to be dangerous many of those who are not. Although political consequences take their toll with all miscalculations of dangerousness, it is safe to say that the worst political consequences are reserved for erroneous judgments of sexual dangerousness (i.e., proclaiming to be not dangerous those who subsequently reoffend).

Illusory correlations occur when a relationship between two variables is believed to exist even when it has been empirically demonstrated that no such relationship exists or that the relationship is weak. In other words, examiners may base their decisions about dangerousness on the presence or absence of factors that are unrelated or only weakly related to dangerousness. It is not at all unusual, for instance, in a civil commitment proceeding for examiners to conclude that the defendant is potentially dangerous *because* of his mental illness, an opinion that derives from the incorrect belief that the two are correlated.

To further complicate matters, some variables are much more importantly related to dangerousness for some defendants than for other defendants. For some defendants, for example, alcohol and/or drug use may be highly correlated with their violent behavior, while for other defendants alcohol and drugs may have nothing at all to do with their violence. When predicting dangerousness, alcohol or drugs may account for a large percentage of the variance on some occasions and none of the variance on other occasions. This becomes a very serious problem with sexual offenders, wherein highly idiosyncratic sexual assault cycles may include many different risk factors, some of which may be highly critical for certain offenders and not relevant for other offenders.

Cultural differences refer to the errors in clinical judgment that may arise when the examiner and the defendant are of different racial or ethnic backgrounds. The obvious case would be examiners who are white male psychiatrists or psychologists from middle- or high-income families and defendants who are black or Hispanic males from inner-city, low-income, low-SES families. Resentment over racial and cutural differences may undermine rapport. Even when rapport is developed, the defendant's life experiences may be so foreign to the examiner that the relevance of those experiences for predicting violence may be very poorly understood by the examiner.

Conceptual and contextual problems refer to the training and indoctrination of most mental health professionals, principally psychiatrists and psychologists, who render judgments about dangerousness. All psychiatrists and most psychologists are trained to look for and diagnose "psychopathology." Consequently, dangerousness or propensity to violence is conceptualized as a trait and described in terms of clinical signs and symptoms. This approach may limit the scope of the inquiry into dangerousness, thereby excluding social, situational, and interactional variables that, in some instances, are important predictors.

Diagnoses lend themselves, moreover, to categorical predictions (i.e., that an individual *is* or *is not* dangerous). In reality, of course, no individual is 100% likely, or 0% likely, to be dangerous all of the time. Even those who are demonstrably high risk are *not* high risk all of the time. A more accurate model would conceptualize risk as a "temperature" that fluctuates, often rising or falling in the course of a day. Thus, predictions of risk are inherently probabilistic (i.e., an individual has X probability of dangerousness under a specifiable set of conditions or circumstances).

Low base rates may be the single most important and least understood factor contributing to error in prediction. Since base rates are, arguably, the most conceptually complicated, we have left discussion for the end. Despite the most emphatic statements about the criticality of base rates in rendering forecasts, the use of base rates remains largely ignored. As Steve Gottfredson (1987) noted,

> In 1955 Meehl and Rosen summarized the consequences of failure to consider base rates and concluded that "almost all contemporary research reporting neglects the base rate factor and hence makes evaluation of ... usefulness difficult or impossible" (p. 215).

Although Reiss (1951) clearly and dramatically illustrated this point over thirty years ago in a classic review of Glueck's *Unraveling Juvenile Delinquency* (1950), failure to consider base rates remains an unfortunately common practice. (pp. 25–26)

What was true in 1950 remains true today. As Howard Barbaree (1997) clearly demonstrated in his excellent paper, failure to establish more reliable base rates for recidivism among subgroups of sexual offenders severely undermines any attempt to demonstrate the efficacy of treatment.

In Glaser's (1987) review of the risk classification literature, he defined the "criterion base rate" as the percentage of individuals who are expected to exhibit the criterion. Since the criterion is usually "reoffense," the base rate is simply the proportion of a sample that will reoffend. Using the contingency table, the base rate can also be defined as: (TPs + FNs)/ total sample.

Criticality of Base Rates

Because the criterion base rate for sexual offenders is, almost invariably, reoffense or recidivism, the base rate for recidivism becomes a critical issue. Assuming that recidivism rates are stable across studies, which they are *not*, we must conclude that the *known* sexual recidivism rates that have been reported in most studies of sexual offenders have been rather low (e.g., Hanson & Bussiere, 1998; Hanson, Steffy, & Gauthier, 1993; Marques, Day, Nelson, & West, 1993, 1994). Hanson and Bussiere (1998) concluded from their meta-analysis that,

> The present findings contradict the popular view that sexual offenders inevitably re-offend. Only a minority of the total sample (13.4% of 23,393) were known to have committed a new sexual offense within the average 4- to 5-year follow-up period examined in this study. (p. 357)

Barbaree (1997) observed that most sexual offender recidivism studies have reported base rates ranging from 0.10 to 0.40. Remarkably low base rates have been reported for endogamous incest offenders and juvenile sexual offenders. In our short-term (12 month) follow-up study of 75 juveniles, for example, we were able to detect only three cases of sexual recidivism, amounting to 4.5% of the sample (Prentky, Harris, Frizzell, & Righthand, 1999). When the base rate is that low, the least-error prediction is that no one in the sample will reoffend. In other words, when the base rate is as low as 10%, the best prediction is that no one will reoffend. We will be wrong only 10% of the time. A risk assessment scale would have to be accurate 91% of the time to do better than the simple conclusion that no one will reoffend. In reality, calculation of recidivism rates is a complicated matter, which we discuss in Chapter 9 as a "special topic," and the *long-term* base rates (e.g., 10 years or more) for sexual reoffense are probably much higher.

Importantly, when we hear a base rate cited, the implication is there is a single number (*one* base rate) that holds true for all offenders over time. This is *highly* misleading. A base rate, as the term implies, is a *rate*. A rate is the amount or degree of something in relation to a unit of something else (e.g., *rate* of speed per hour or *rate* of pay per week). The critical unit for offender recidivism is *time* (i.e., rate of recidivism per some time period, often 1 year). It would make no sense, for instance, to say that we are driving 60 miles, unless, of course, we are talking about distance and not speed. If the reference was to speed, we would automatically "fill in" the miles per hour (i.e., "I'm driving 60"). We should, just as automatically, *assume* that a recidivism rate implies some time frame and that the rate conveys no meaning without knowing the time frame.

If we hear that the base rate for sexual recidivism is 10%, it most likely means that 10% of a group of sexual offenders can be expected to reoffend within 1 year of discharge. The base rate naturally will increase as the time period increases. The same group of sex offenders with a 10% base rate at Year 1 may have a 30% base rate at Year 5. Indeed, we observed in a sample of 136 rapists that the base rate for sexual recidivism increased from 9% at Year 1 to 19% at Year 5, 31% at Year 15, and 39% at Year 25 (Prentky, Lee, Knight, & Cerce, 1997). The base rates for sexual recidivism for 115 child molesters increased from 6% at Year 1 to 19% at Year 5, 39% at Year 15, and 52% at Year 25. Thus, all of the following statements would be accurate for that sample of child molesters: (1) the base rate for sexual recidivism at Year 1 was 6%, (2) the base rate for sexual recidivism at Year 25 was 52%, and (3) the *average* base rate over 25 years was approximately 2% per year. As a rule of thumb, the longer the follow-up time, the higher the base rates.

The statement "the recidivism rate for our sample of sex offenders was 25%" also seems to imply that every offender in the sample has an equal probability of reoffending. That too is *highly* misleading. The figure 25% represents an average. In reality, each offender will have a different propensity to reoffend. For some the probability will be much higher than the sample base rate and for others the probability will be lower than the sample base rate. Indeed, there may be dramatic *within-subject* variability in risk to reoffend. A given individual may be at much higher risk to reoffend on one day than another day. On Tuesday, a sex offender goes to work and is informed that he is getting a raise. It makes his day. He feels good about himself, and good about life. On Thursday, he wakes up, gets into an argument with his wife, drives aggressively on his way to work, and gets a ticket. At work, his supervisor reprimands him. By the end of the day he is steaming and heads for the nearest bar for relief. His reoffense risk on Tuesday and Thursday will be dramatically different. Although this principal is perfectly obvious to those who treat sex offenders, we often speak of risk as if it was fixed and stable.

To apply an admittedly crude metaphor, the base rate can be thought of as a target that we trying to hit. If the base rate is 30%, then the "bull's eye" is roughly 30% of the surface area of the target. Using this simplistic example, it would seem to make intuitive sense that the smaller the base rate, the smaller the bull's eye and the larger the base rate, the larger the bull's eye. Thus, if we were to predict, for instance, whether a random sample of adult males would shave in the morning, the "target" would be very large and the task of rendering an accurate prediction would be easy. If, on the other hand, we were to predict whether our random sample of men would ride bicycles to work in the morning, the target would be quite small (i.e., the base rate would be very small) and difficult to hit.

Although appealing to common sense, our simplistic example of a target is misleading. In reality, the difficulty of predicting events increases as the base rate *differs from .50* (Meehl & Rosen, 1955). In other words, the accuracy of our predictions is greatest when the base rate is roughly 50%. As the base rate drops below 50% or rises above 50%, we begin to make more errors, and, importantly, we begin to shift the region of error. With very infrequent events, the percentage of FPs will be very high. That is, in attempting to predict failure (i.e., sexual recidivism) when the base rate for failure is very small (e.g., 5%), we will end up predicting that a large number of individuals will fail when in fact they won't.

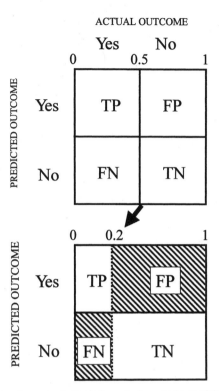

Figure 2. Influence of low base rates on predictive judgments. Increased potential false positive error region and decreased potential false negative error region are associated with a low base rate.

Conversely, with very frequent events, the percentage of FNs is likely to be very high. If the base rate for failure was very high (e.g., 80%), we will end up predicting that a large number of people will *not* fail when in fact they will fail.

Figure 2 illustrates the case of a very low base rate (.20). The shaded area is the increased potential FP error region and the decreased FN error region associated with such a low base rate. As the base rate shrinks, the potential for FP errors increases. Figure 3 illustrates the case of a very high base rate (.80). The shaded area is the increased potential FN error region and the decreased FP error region associated with such a high base rate. As the base rate increases, the potential for FN errors increases.

If we take the above sample of 111 child molesters, it would have been very difficult to predict accurately who would reoffend sexually within the first 12 months, since the target that we would have to hit contained only 7 individuals (6% of 111). With a base rate of only 6%, we would have predicted that a very large number of men were successes (i.e., not recidivists) when in fact they ultimately failed. After 25 years, with a base rate of .52, our ability to predict accurately would have been optimal. In general, as Swets (1992) noted, "Probabilities of rare events are estimated with little reliability" (p.525). Although Swets' examples concerned applications in engineering and infectious disease, his remarks are absolutely as appropriate for application to criminology. He went on to state that "benefits and costs are notoriously difficult to judge when human lives are at stake and are often in

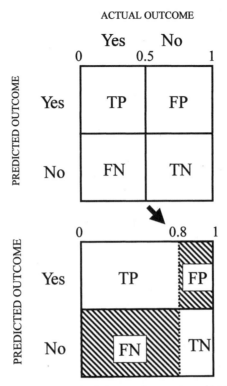

Figure 3. Influence of high base rates on predictive judgments. Increased potential false negative error region and decreased potential false positive error region are associated with a high base rate.

conflict when a balance must be struck between an individual's and society's concerns" (p. 525).

Since the base rate for violence is very low in the *general population,* even when predictor variables possess high predictive validity there may be a large number of FPs. Consider the following simple example:

Take: A general population with 100,000 people.

Assume: That 15% have some potential for committing a violent act (i.e., 15,000). Thus, 85,000 people do not.

Assume: That our examiner has a screening test for dangerousness that accurately classifies 80% of each group. This assumption is, of course, a highly optimistic one.

Conclude: If our examiner screens this population, he or she will identify 12,000 people who *are* potentially violent (15,000 × .80) *and* 17,000 people who are false positives or are not potentially violent (85,000 × .20). Thus, the examiner will be wrong 58.6% of the time (17,000/12,000 + 17,000). That is, 17,000 out of 29,000 people judged to be potentially violent are not violent.

Thus: Assuming a base rate of potential violence of 15% and using a screening device with an 80% correct hit rate, our examiner will now be wrong more than half of the time.

As the base rate shrinks and/or as the predictive accuracy of our screening instruments decrease, the overall correct hit rate for dangerousness decisions will decrease. Although criminal acts are plentiful, extreme violence is, in fact, rare. This holds true for both sexual violence and nonsexual violence. The most obvious and extreme case is homicide. There are roughly 20,000 homicides per year, and about 1,800,000 nonhomicidal acts involving interpersonal violence. Thus, the base rate for homicide is about 1/90 that of nonhomicidal violence [20,000/1,800,000 = 1/90]. This very fact, that the greater the level of violence the harder the task of prediction, is at dramatic odds with the needs of the criminal justice system (i.e., the greater the potential for extreme violence, the greater the need for an accurate prediction of violence).

There is good news, however, from the standpoint of accurate forecasting of violence. The very fact that most violence is rare, an atypical event, means that it doesn't have to occur many times before the likelihood of reoccurrence can be predicted more accurately, which is, of course, why one of the most consistently robust predictors of reoffense is number of priors. A noncriminal atypical event that we might use as an example is skydiving. If we were asked to predict whether someone who had *never* jumped out of a plane would do so, we would be doing little more than hazarding a guess. If you were asked to predict whether someone who jumped out of a plane *once* and had no history of skydiving would do it again, it would be extremely difficult to predict accurately. If that same individual skydived three times, however, the likelihood of a fourth dive would be considerably greater than the likelihood of a second dive in the first instance (i.e., when you knew *only* that the individual had made *one* jump). The same principle holds true with acts of violence, which is, in part, why sex offenders attain the "status" of being classified as "serial" after being convicted of only three (or more) sexual assaults.

The "Downside" to Base Rates

After having devoted ample time to discussing the logic and the importance of base rates for improving the accuracy of our predictions, we must take a step back and examine the potential problems with base-rate data. The best analysis of these problems was provided by Koehler (1996) in his review article on the base rate fallacy. Koehler made (at least) two major points relevant to the present discussion. First, from an empirical standpoint, base rates are more likely to be used by practitioners when they are reliable and relatively diagnostic. At the present time, base rates on sexual offender recidivism are quite unreliable. The informed clinician may eschew base rates, because of their unreliability. The uninformed clinician may apply erroneous base-rate information, based on preconceived notions about the high (or low) likelihood that sex offenders will reoffend.

Second, from a methodological perspective, Koehler (1996) maintained that we fail "to consider how ambiguous, unreliable, and unstable base rates of the real world are and should be used" (p. 1). Koehler concluded that when our assumptions and goals vary and when the criteria are complex, the traditional Bayesian model is not sufficient. It is indisputable that in assessing sexual dangerousness, our assumptions vary and the criteria are complex *and* unstandardized.

Koehler also made a relevant point in arguing that predictive accuracy is not the sole criterion for evaluating the adequacy of our judgments. Within the criminal justice system, for example, the cost of error often leads to inaccurate judgments. As Koehler pointed out, for instance, in a criminal matter, guilt must be established "beyond a reasonable doubt." This standard of proof reduces the likelihood of false convictions relative to lesser standards, such as "preponderance of evidence." Juries may (and do) return *not* guilty verdicts even when they believe that the defendants are guilty, because they were not convinced "beyond a reasonable doubt." Built into the system is a mechanism that is intended to reduce the likelihood that innocent defendants will be convicted and possibly incarcerated (i.e., FPs). Although base-rate information is not relevant to this example, it does illustrate the often profound impact of social and *real* costs associated with bad judgments (e.g., false incarceration) and how those costs persuade clinicians and courts to render inaccurate judgments. In the case of sexual offenders, the bias may actually be in reverse. The perceived costs to society of an FN judgment may persuade clinicians and courts to err in the opposite direction, finding individuals dangerous when the evidence is less than compelling.

Lastly, in an earlier article on this general topic, Cohen (1981) argued that base rates should be ignored unless it can be demonstrated that the case under consideration "shares all of the relevant characteristics" (p. 329) of the sample from which the base rate data were drawn. This is highly relevant to our discussion of sexual offender base rates. It would mean, for instance, that an incest offender should be evaluated with base-rate data from samples comprised entirely of incest offenders, that a highly impulsive, antisocial rapist should be evaluated with base-rate data from samples comprised entirely of impulsive, antisocial rapists, that a pedophile should be evaluated with base-rate data from samples comprised entirely of similar pedophiles, and so forth. We could even go a step further and say that same-sex pedophiles should be evaluated with base-rate data from samples comprised entirely of same-sex pedophiles. Although it is eminently plausible, indeed essential, that base-rate data be "relevant," it is all too clear that in forensic contexts it often is not. Perhaps the simplest summary is that consideration of base-rate data is indeed critical to accurate decision-making, but that (1) the unreliability of such data on sex offenders compromises their usefulness and (2) the overarching goal of community safety may place a higher premium on inaccuracy.

The "Human" Factor

In Freudenburg's (1988) article on the Art of Probabilistic Risk Assessment, he observed that the corpus of evidence from the physical and biological sciences indicated that the Achilles heel of risk assessment is "human error." Freudenburg addressed three problem areas: (1) calibration and overconfidence, (2) statistical vulnerability of low-probability estimates, and (3) monetary and political pressures. Overconfidence results in a failure to take note of factors that introduce error into estimates, including insensitivity to the fragility of our assumptions and to problems of small sample sizes, and failure to take into account interrelations or interactions among individual factors, each of which, when taken alone, may be of relatively minor importance.

Low-probability estimates refer, in Freudenburg's article, to extremely infrequent events (e.g., events that may be expected to occur once in a million operating hours). Because the prevailing assumption is that the event will *never* occur, when it does occur, the response often is one of profound shock. Let's take, as an example, one isolated event that has occurred only once in history, the explosion of a space shuttle. The explosion of the

Challenger, indeed the explosion of any commercial airplane, is something of a "signal" event (Slovic, 1987), resulting in highly publicized, very lengthy, expensive inquiries. In the case of the *Challenger*, the mission of the nation's entire space program was scrutinized. Although the reoccurrence of sexually aggressive behavior is vastly more likely than the explosion of a space shuttle, there are noteworthy similarities. Extremely violent, sadistic, often homicidal, sexual crimes, although extremely rare, are signal events, resulting in exhaustive press coverage, *ad hoc* legislative committees, and new statutes. The sexual murder of a young girl that resulted in the federal and state laws governing community notification is an obvious example.

Freudenburg's commentary about monetary and political pressures speaks, as Monahan did, to the nonscientific forces that contrive to influence, if not bias and distort, the interpretation and meaning of risk assessment. The empirical world, as Freudenburg (1988) notes, "is not always so tidy" and "scientists are sometimes subjected to distinctly unscientific pressures" (p. 46). We attempted to illustrate in Figure 4 how the impact of "conservatism" (the tendency to "lean toward" finding individuals dangerous or the reluctance to find individuals not dangerous) increases the potential FP error region and decreases the potential FN error region. That is, the "conservative" bias toward finding individuals to be dangerous will increase the number of FP judgments. Alternatively, Figure 5 shows how "liberalism" (the tendency to find individuals *not* dangerous or the reluctance to find individuals dangerous) increases the potential FN error region and decreases the potential FP error region. The "liberal" bias toward finding individuals to be not dangerous will increase the number of FN judgments. With the pressure that we all feel not to make a mistake about dangerousness, there is an overwhelming tendency to "err on the conservative," resulting in a higher than necessary FP rate. In speaking about "Quantification of Sacrifice," Tribe (1971) noted that

> there is something intrinsically immoral about condemning a man as a criminal while telling oneself, *I believe that there is a chance of one in twenty that this defendant is innocent, but a ½₀ risk of sacrificing him erroneously is one I am willing to run in the interest of the public's—and my own—safety.* (p. 1372)

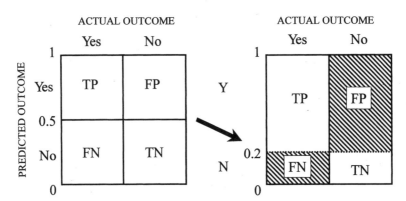

Figure 4. Influence of "conservatism" on predictive judgments. Increased potential false positive error region and decreased potential false negative error region are associated with being conservative (reluctant to find someone *not* dangerous).

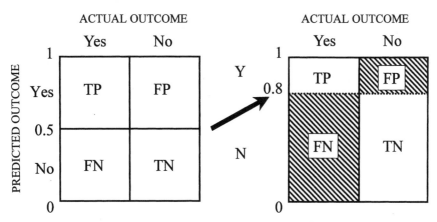

Figure 5. Influence of "liberalism" on predictive judgments. Increased potential false negative error region and decreased potential false positive error region are associated with being liberal (reluctant to find someone dangerous).

We would submit, with all due respect to Professor Tribe, that the pressure to err on the conservative derives *less* from the protectionist motive of community safety than from the practical, self-serving motive of avoiding potential lawsuits resulting from a judgment gone awry.

Overview of Methodological Problems in Prediction

It has been pointed out that the hiatus between assessment and follow-up (or outcome), as well as differences in environments at the time of assessment and outcome, decrease the probability of predictive accuracy (Cohen, Groth, & Siegel, 1978; Monahan, 1978, 1981). It is clear, moreover, that unstandardized or idiosyncratic definitions of, or criteria for, sexual dangerousness and the application of those criteria to highly heterogeneous groups of sexual offenders contribute to low predictive accuracy, high FP rates, and a maximal "drag" on the efficiency of processing sexual offenders. In assessing the probability that anyone will commit an act of violence, clinicians appear to be no more immune to a reliance on illusory correlations and a neglect of statistical rules and base-rate information than are laypersons. In addition, available evidence suggests that clinicians typically employ only a small, albeit important, portion of the data at hand (e.g., severity of previous offenses, Steadman & Cocozza, 1978). Finally, the trait-oriented emphasis that is so pervasive in forensic psychology and psychiatry appears to lead clinicians away from consideration of specific behaviors that occur as a function of the interaction of person and context, toward global attributions of "dangerousness" limited in their long-term, cross-situational validity (Monahan, 1981). Actuarial assessment procedures circumvent most of the serious pitfalls of clinical prediction (e.g., the clinician's inherent biases and limited fund of data to draw on, the use of questionnaires and inventories that were never designed to assess sexual dangerousness among juveniles, random responses and response distortions on those inventories, judgments based on the presence or absence of variables that are unrelated or only weakly related to dangerousness [illusory correlations], and failure to take into account base rates [incidence of target behavior]). Reliance on actuarial methods should, at this point, provide an "upper bounds" (Dawes, Faust, & Meehl, 1989) in our ability to predict sexual dangerousness.

METHODS FOR ASSESSING THE ACCURACY OF PREDICTIVE JUDGMENTS

To illustrate the application of these methods for examining predictive accuracy, we will use one of our studies that focused on risk assessment with child molesters (Prentky, Knight, et al., 1997). In this study, which we will simply refer to as CMRA, we collected follow-up data on the 111 offenders who were discharged from the Massachusetts Treatment Center between 1960 and 1984 and examined the accuracy of 10 rationally derived, archivally coded variables for predicting: (1) any new charge for a serious sexual offense (i.e., involving physical contact with the victim), (2) any new charge for a nonsexual, victim-involved offense, and (3) any new charge for a violent offense. In each case, we used discriminant analysis to determine how effectively our 10 variables discriminated between those who did and those who did not reoffend (i.e., charged with a new offense during the 25-year follow-up). The first two analyses, using (1) sexual and (2) nonsexual, victim-involved reoffense, are reported in Tables 1 and 2.

In the first analysis, we considered only victim-involved sexual offenses and excluded what are commonly called nuisance (or victimless) sexual offenses. As may be noted in Table 1, Group 1 (those who were never charged with a new sexual offense) consisted of 73 offenders and Group 2 (those who were charged with one or more new sexual offenses) consisted of 40 offenders. The three variables that significantly discriminated between the groups were Fixation (high), Paraphilias, and Number of Prior Sexual Offenses. Offenders who recidivated were high in fixation, evidenced more paraphilias, and had a greater number of prior sexual offenses.

Table 1. Discriminant Function Analysis Using Sexual Reoffense as the Criterion

Scale variables	Group 1[a]	Group 2[a]	r[b]	F[c]
Amount of Contact	0.411/0.49	0.475/0.51	.13	0.42
Fixation	0.767/0.43	0.925/0.27	.41	4.52*
Impulsivity	−0.76/0.67	0.100/0.72	.25	1.68
Paraphilias	−0.129/0.33	0.440/1.69	.53	7.70**
Juvenile Antisocial Behavior	0.020/0.91	0.097/0.99	.08	0.17
Adult Antisocial Behavior	0.027/0.50	0.005/0.65	−.04	0.34
Alcohol Abuse	−0.106/1.02	−0.211/0.92	−.10	0.29
Number of Prior Sexual Offenses	3.475/3.56	5.425/3.51	.65	11.19***
Victim Gender	0.757/0.70	0.825/0.81	.07	0.14
Social Competence	−0.101/0.87	0.100/0.76	.24	1.51

Note. From Prentky, Knight, & Lee (1997). Copyright © 1997 by the American Psychological Association. Adapted with permission.
[a]Group 1 ($N = 73$): No evidence of sexual recidivism (M/σ). Group 2 ($N = 40$): Charged with one or more new sexual offenses) M/σ).
[b]Correlation between component and criterion.
[c]Univariate F value, df 1, 111.
*$p < .05$; **$p < .01$; ***$p < .001$.

Table 2. Discriminant Function Analysis Using Nonsexual Victim-Involved Reoffense as the Criterion

Scale variables	Group 1[a]	Group 2[a]	r^b	F^c
Amount of Contact	0.500/0.50	0.105/0.32	−.51	10.81***
Fixation	0.819/0.39	0.842/0.37	.04	0.56
Impulsivity	−0.53/0.87	0.232/0.77	.32	2.92*
Paraphilias	−0.056/0.48	0.709/2.33	.55	8.61**
Juvenile Antisocial Behavior	−0.088/0.88	0.709/1.15	.55	12.11***
Adult Antisocial Behavior	0.050/0.53	0.401/0.81	.58	9.84**
Alcohol Abuse	0.146/0.96	−0.125/1.11	.02	0.71
Number of Prior Sexual Offenses	3.061/3.56	3.145/3.51	−.05	0.68
Victim Gender	0.766/0.77	0.895/0.94	.12	0.41
Social Competence	−0.019/0.87	−0.084/0.68	−.06	0.84

Note. From Prentky, Knight, & Lee (1997). Copyright © 1997 by the American Psychological Association. Adapted with permission.
[a]Group 1 ($N = 94$): No evidence of nonsexual victim-involved recidivism (M/σ). Group 2 ($N = 10$): Charged with one or more nonsexual, victim-imvolved offenses (M/σ).
[b]Correlation between component and criterion.
[c]Univariate F value, df 1, 111.
*$p < .09$; **$p < .005$; ***$p < .001$.

In the second analysis we considered only charges for *nonsexual*, victim-involved offenses. There were 94 nonrecidivists and 19 recidivists in this analysis. The four scale variables that significantly discriminated between the groups were Amount of Contact with children (low), Paraphilias, Juvenile Antisocial Behavior, and Adult Antisocial Behavior (see Table 2). Impulsivity was marginally significant ($p < .09$). The significance of low Amount of Contact with children is consistent with previous findings that those who are low tend to be more impulsive. Those who recidivated with a nonsexual, victim-involved offense were, in essence, higher in impulsive, antisocial behavior.

TRADITIONAL INDICES OF PREDICTIVE ACCURACY

The "first-generation" approach to measuring predictive accuracy employed a variety of indices that are based on the 2 × 2 contingency table illustrated in Figure 1.

The "fit" of the 2 × 2 contingency table (Predicted Failure—Yes or No versus Actual Failure—Yes or No) can be examined by looking at Kendall's rank correlation tau (Kendall, 1970) and Goodman and Kruskal's gamma (Goodman & Kruskal, 1963). These are measures of degree of association, however, and provide, at best, an indirect assessment of how a prediction instrument will work in practice.

In addition to reporting the simple percentage of TP, FP, TN, and FN, the overall chance-corrected predictive accuracy is the accuracy of *both* positive and negative predictors taking prior probabilities into account (prior probability determined using base rate and selection rate). Kappa and phi statistics are the two most widely used indices in calculating change-corrected predictive accuracy (e.g., Fleiss, 1981). Hart, Webster, et al. (1993) recommended calculating the positive predictive power (PPP), the negative predictive power (NPP), and an overall measure, such as kappa or phi. PPP refers to the accuracy of

ACTUAL OUTCOME

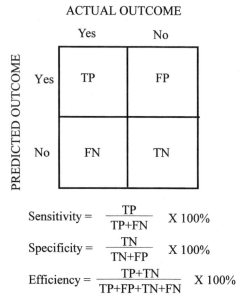

$$\text{Sensitivity} = \frac{TP}{TP+FN} \times 100\%$$

$$\text{Specificity} = \frac{TN}{TN+FP} \times 100\%$$

$$\text{Efficiency} = \frac{TP+TN}{TP+FP+TN+FN} \times 100\%$$

Figure 6. Indices of predictive accuracy.

predictions that individuals *are* dangerous [TP/(TP × FP)], while NPP refers to the accuracy of predictions that individuals are *not* dangerous [TN/(TN + FN)].

The number of TP, TN, FP, and FN classifications from the CMRA study are reported in Table 3, as well as the chance-corrected predictive accuracy (kappa score) for each of the analyses. The kappa was quite good (about .40) for sexual and nonsexual, victim-involved offenses but dropped to .23 for violent offenses (a distinctly rare event for child molesters). In the analysis of sexual recidivism (see Table 1), 73% of the cases were correctly classified, with the highest percentage of errors being FNs (= 15/40 or 37.5% for sexual charges). The equivalent FP rate was 15/73 or 20.5%. In the analysis of nonsexual, victim-involved recidivism, 79.65% of the cases were correctly classified, once again with the highest percentage of errors being FNs (= 6/19 or 31.6%). The FP rate was 17/94 or 18.1%.

Table 3. Classification of Criterion Variables

Criterion	TP	FN	FP	TN	κ	σ	z	p
Victim-Involved								
Sexual	25	15	15	58	.42	.09	4.46	.001
Nonsexual	13	06	17	77	.41	.09	4.53	.001
Violent	10	07	25	71	23	.09	2.69	.01

Note. From Prentky, Knight, & Lee (1997). Copyright © 1997 by the American Psychological Association. Adapted with permission. TP = true positive; FP = false positive; FN = false negative; TN = true negative; $z = \kappa/\sigma$.

Base Rate and Selection Ratio

Loeber and Dishion (1982, 1983) have discussed the importance of the base rate (BR) and the selection ratio (SR). The BR, as noted, is the proportion of the sample that actually reoffended (in the case of recidivism studies). The SR is the proportion of the sample that was predicted to reoffend. The BR can be calculated as: $(TP + FN)/T$, where T is the total sample. SR, on the other hand, can be calculated as: $(TP + FP)/T$. The BR and the SR are the two marginal distributions of an expectancy table. Taken together, the BR and SR determine the chance expectancies for the table. When the SR is larger than the BR, the number of FPs will be greater than the number of FNs. When the BR is larger than the SR, the number of FNs will be greater than the number of FPs.

Loeber and Dishion noted that the BR and SR determine the greatest number of correct predictions that are possible for a given assessment instrument, as well as a certain number of correct predictions that would be expected by chance alone. Loeber and Dishion proposed the use of the RIOC index (relative improvement over chance), which provides a measure of how the instrument performs relative to what would be expected and relative to its best possible performance given the BR and the SR. After calculating the BR and the SR, the RIOC index can be calculated as: $[AC - RC]/[MC - RC]$, where AC = the actual number of correct predictions, RC = the randomly expected number of correct predictions, and MC = the maximum possible number of correct predictions. If we substitute the familiar terms into the equation, $RIOC = [TP \cdot TN - FP \cdot FN]/[TP + min(FN,FP)][TN + min(FN,FP)]$

Sensitivity and Specificity

It is customary to further summarize the accuracy of binary assessments using sensitivity and specificity (Somoza & Mossman, 1990). Sensitivity refers to the probability that the assessment will be positive (TP) when applied to a truly dangerous individual. Sensitivity equals the *true* positive rate $[TP/(TP + FN)]$. Specificity refers to the probability that the assessment will be negative (TN) when applied to a truly nondangerous individual. Specificity equals the *true* negative rate $[TN/(TN + FP)]$. Efficiency simply refers to the *overall* percentage of cases that are correctly classified $[(TP + TN)/(TP + TN + FP + FN)]$.

Selected indices of predictive accuracy in the CMRA study are presented in Table 4. Because of the relatively high number of FNs compared to TPs, the sensitivity is fairly low. Although the actual number of FNs is only 6 and 7 for nonsexual victim-involved and violent charges, respectively, the number of TPs in those categories is very low (13 and 10, respectively). Again, because of the relatively low FP rate, specificity is reasonably good. Higher specificity is, of course, a function of the large number of TNs, particularly in the nonsexual victim-involved and violent domains.

Positive predictive power (PPP) and negative predictive power (NPP) are different ways of conceptualizing predictive accuracy, referring to the accuracy of predictions that child molesters *will* reoffend (PPP) and the accuracy of predictions that child molesters will not reoffend (NPP). Because PPP reflects the proportion of individuals predicted to be violent who were violent at follow-up, it takes into consideration the percentage of those incorrectly predicted to be violent (i.e., FPs). Again, given the higher proportion of FPs,

Table 4. Indices of Predictive Accuracy for Classification of Criterion Variables

Index	Sexual	Nonsexual Victim-Involved	Violent[a]
Sensitivity 100% × TP/(TP + FN)	62.5	68.4	58.8
Specificity 100% × TN(TN + FP)	79.5	81.9	74.0
Positive Predictive Power 100% × TP/(TP + FP)	62.5	43.3	28.6
Negative Predictive Power 100% × TN/(TN + FN)	79.5	92.8	91.0
Efficiency 100% × (TP + TN)/(TP + FP + FN + TN)	73.5	79.6	71.7

Note. From Prentky, Knight, & Lee (1997). Copyright © 1997 by the American Psychological Association. Adapted with permission. TP = true positive; FP = false positive; FN = false negative; TN = true negative.
[a]Incluees sexual and nonsexual violent offenses.

PPP was inferior to NPP, particularly in criminal offense domains involving nonsexual victim-involved and violent charges. In reality, the actual number of FN and FP errors in predicting sexual reoffense was identical (15; see Table 3). The critical difference was that there were more than twice as many TN cases (58) as TP cases (25). The Efficiency Index simply reflects the overall classification accuracy. The efficiency of this scale is around 75%, varying slightly depending on the domain of criminal offenses that is used.

We further sought to demonstrate with our sample of child molesters in the CMRA

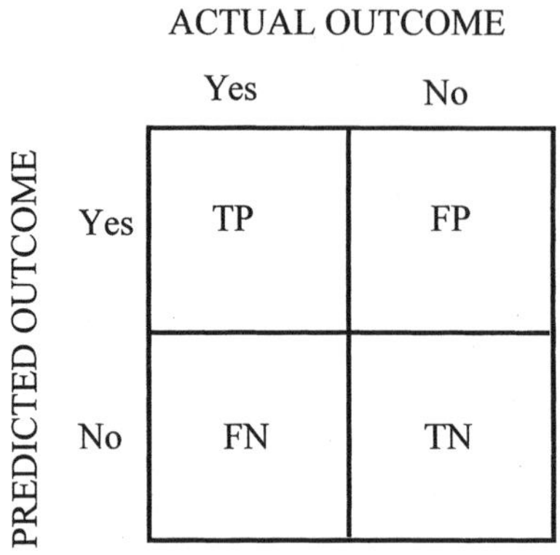

ACTUAL OUTCOME

$$\text{Positive Predictive Power} = \frac{TP}{TP+FP} \times 100\%$$

[the accuracy of predictions that individuals will be violent]

$$\text{Negative Predictive Power} = \frac{TN}{TN+FN} \times 100\%$$

[the accuracy of predictions that individuals will not be violent]

Figure 7. Predictive power.

Table 5. Sensitivity and Specificity Values for Different Prior Probabilities

	Sexual offense		Nonsexual Victim-Involved Offense		Violent Offense	
C-statistic	.778		.787		.732	
Prior probability	Sensitivity[a]	Specificity[a]	Sensitivity	Specificity	Sensitivity	Specificity
.05	1.00	.03	.90	.33	1.00	.15
.10	1.00	.11	.84	.52	.82	.47
.15	.98	.19	.68	.70	.59	.69
.20	.90	.36	.68	.80	.47	.81
.25	.83	.52	.58	.86	.41	.90
.30	.78	.67	.53	.88	.35	.95
.40	.60	.82	.42	.95	.12	.97
.45	.50	.86	.26	.95	.12	.98
.50	.45	.93	.21	.99	.06	.99
.60	.30	.95	.11	1.00	.06	1.00
.70	.25	.96	.05	1.00	.06	1.00
.80	.13	.97	.05	1.00	.06	1.00
.90	.08	.99	.05	1.00	.06	1.00

Note. From Prentky, Knight, & Lee (1997). Copyright 1997 by the American Psychological Association. Adapted with permission.
[a]Sensitivity = TP/(TP + FP); specificity = TN/(TN + FN).

study that the sensitivity and specificity values change considerably as the prior probability changes. Table 5 reports the sensitivity and specificity values for a range of prior probabilities, from .05 to .90, for each of the three criminal offense domains in our sample of child molesters. Based on that sample, the optimal prior probability for predicting a sexual offense for child molesters was about .30. The optimal prior probability for predicting a nonsexual victim-involved offense, a more rare event with child molesters, was about .20, whereas the optimal prior probability for predicting a violent offense, an even more rare event, dropped to between .15 and .20. For the prediction of sexual offenses, the composite of risk variables for child molesters that we tested obtained optimal sensitivity at a prior probability of about .25 or lower and an optimal specificity at a prior probability of about .40 or greater. For the prediction of nonsexual victim-involved offenses or very violent offenses, the risk assessment composite obtained optimal sensitivity at a prior probability of about .10 and optimal specificity at a prior probability of about .20 or greater.

Receiver Operating Characteristic Analysis

Mossman (1994b) has argued that any of the traditional contingency table-derived indices of predictive accuracy can be misleading, because "2 × 2 tables conflate intrinsic ability to detect future violence with the level of risk that might prompt one to take action" (p. 588). Mossman (1994b) noted that receiver operating characteristic (ROC) analysis enables the individual to see the relationship between level of risk and decision choice. In other words, ROC analysis permits one to assess the trade-offs between sensitivity and specificity. Moreover, the area under the ROC curve is a preferable index of predictive accuracy, because it is invariant of BRs (Hanson, 1998).

In order to derive ROC curves (Metz, 1978; Mossman, 1994a) for each of the criminal domains in the CMRA study, we used the SAS (1994) procedure PROC LOGISTIC since it provides the C-statistic. Although there is no uniformly accepted index of accuracy for predictive models employing dichotomous dependent variables (Ash & Schwartz, 1994), the C-statistic is generally regarded as an index that should be reported (Harrell, Lee, Califf, Pryor, & Rosati, 1984). The C-statistic is equivalent to the area under the ROC curve (Ash & Schwartz, 1994). The area under the curve corresponds to the probability of accurately predicting that a randomly selected, truly dangerous individual is more likely to be dangerous than a randomly selected, truly nondangerous individual. Near-perfect accuracy in discriminating between dangerous and nondangerous individuals would yield a C-statistic that approached 1.00. Chance prediction would yield a C-statistic of .50. The ROC curve is derived by plotting sensitivity by 1-specificity. In general, models possessing good discrimination have high sensitivity (i.e., high TP rates and relatively low FP rates).

As may be observed by examining the C-statistics in Table 5, the risk assessment scale derived for child molesters in the CMRA study provided comparable discrimination for all three domains of criminal behavior. The C-statistics in all three cases suggested, moreover, discrimination that was substantially better than chance. The C-statistics ranged from .73 for violent offenses, to .78 and .79 for sexual and nonsexual, victim-involved offenses, respectively. As a basis for comparison, Mossman (1994b) examined 58 studies of violence prediction, finding that the median area under the ROC curve for all 58 studies was .73 and the weighted average was .78.

EMPIRICAL RESEARCH ON PREDICTION OF SEXUAL DANGEROUSNESS

Given the indisputably high profile of sexual offenders in the media as well as in the criminal justice system, and the prevailing opinion that these offenders are at considerable risk to reoffend and progress from less to more serious offenses, one would expect that this domain of criminal behavior would have been the focus of rigorous programmatic efforts to enhance the accuracy of predictive decisions. Unfortunately, this has not, until quite recently, been the case. Although there is ample evidence demonstrating the predictive superiority of actuarial methods over clinical judgment (e.g., Dawes et al., 1989), only within the past half-dozen years or so have there been any concerted, empirical efforts to develop and test actuarial prediction devices for sexual offenders.

First-Generation Research on Risk Assessment

Sex of Victim

The early research on risk was essentially univariate, focusing on single variables thought to be importantly related to reoffense. One of the earliest of these risk markers, specific to child molesters, was a typological distinction based on the sex of the victim. As we discussed in Chapter 3, these early reports suggested that the reoffense rates among same-sex child molesters were higher than the rates for opposite-sex child molesters (e.g., Fitch, 1962; Frisbie & Dondis, 1965; Radzinowicz, 1957). These findings were reviewed by Ortmann (1980) and Quinsey (1977), prompting Quinsey to conclude in his 1986 review that "a simple grouping of child molesters into heterosexual and homosexual and related and unrelated victim classes represents a large increase in our ability to predict recidivism" (p. 153). Hanson et al. (1993) also found support for the predictive power of victim sex. In their follow-up study, offenders against boys were at higher risk to recidivate than offenders against girls, and the mixed group was intermediate, not differing significantly from either of the other two groups. Hanson (1997a) subsequently included "male victims" as one of four items on his Brief Actuarial Risk Scale for Sexual Offense Recidivism. Proulx and his colleagues also found that the child molesters in their follow-up study (64½ months) who recidivated were more likely to have male victims (Proulx et al., 1997).

As we also noted in Chapter 3, however, the sex-of-victim distinction has not received consistent support. Langevin, Harper, et al., (1985) found that the same sex offenders evidenced the fewest number of criminal charges (8%, compared to 22% for the opposite-sex group). Abel, Becker, et al., (1981) found that their opposite-sex child molesters reported over twice as many victims as their same-sex child molesters (62.4 and 30.6%, respectively). Abel et al., (1988) reported that mixed sex preference, as opposed to single sex preference, accounted for a larger portion of their recidivating subjects. Marques (1995) reported sex-of-victim differences in reoffense rates among 110 treated child molesters. The opposite-sex child molesters had a slightly higher rate of recidivism than the same-sex child molesters (13.9 and 12.1%, respectively). The treated mixed sex group of offenders had the highest reoffense rate (16.7%), a finding that would support Abel et al. (1988).

In our CMRA study referred to earlier, we found no evidence for the utility of sex of victim as a predictor of reoffense (Prentky, Knight, et al., 1997). The sexual recidivism rates for opposite-sex, mixed, and same-sex offenders were .33, .35, and .38, respectively. In a series of discriminant function analyses, using different domains of criminal behavior as the criterion, the univariate F values for victim sex in all three analyses were <0.50, and the correlations between victim sex and the criterion were .07 (opposite), .12 (mixed), and −.03 (same).

Strength of Sexual Preoccupation with Children

A second variable specific to child molesters has received reasonably consistent support as a predictor of recidivism, namely, the strength or intensity of an offender's preoccupation with children as sexual objects (i.e., "fixation"). Strength of sexual preoccupation with children is repeatedly identified as a critical marker (e.g., Abel, Becker, et al., 1981). An offender's degree of preoccupation with children as sexual objects has been measured in two ways. The first uses phallometry to assess behaviorally the offender's sexual arousal to depictions of children of various ages. Although such a direct measure is appealing and sexual arousal patterns have been shown to predict sexual recidivism (Quinsey, Lalumiere, Rice, & Harris, 1995), it has its drawbacks, including the logistical problems of obtaining phallometric data, the cost of the assessment procedure, and the increased likelihood in forensic contexts that dissimulation may compromise the validity of the assessment.

We have developed another measure of fixation for use in our taxonomy for classification of child molesters (MTC:CM3, Knight et al., 1989) that may serve as a reliable proxy for phallometric assessment. The construct of fixation in MTC:CM3 assesses the strength of an offender's pedophilic interest (i.e., the extent to which children are a major focus of the offender's thoughts and attention) from archivally reported preoccupation with children as sexual objects or from the report of specific patterns of child-related behaviors from which such preoccupation can be inferred. In the CMRA study, the archivally measured construct of fixation was significantly related to sexual recidivism.

Barbaree, Seto, and Serin's (1994) recent study of MTC:CM3 compared high- to low-fixated child molesters. They found that the high-fixated child molesters had a larger number of victims and evidenced greater sexual arousal on the plethysmograph to stimuli depicting prepubescent and pubescent children. Their study provides the first empirical evidence that the behaviorally anchored, but archivally based MTC:CM3 assessment of fixation may serve as a suitable substitute for phallometric assessment.

Although risk assessment procedures that rely exclusively on archival data may never achieve the efficiency of procedures that such as the Abel Screen (Abel et al., 1994) or the penile plethysmograph, the advantages of an archivally assessed behavioral measure include its ease of use (i.e., it does not require the compliance or even the presence of the offender), cost-efficiency, and relatively high reliability. Despite these presumptive advantages, it must be demonstrated that such an archivally based procedure possesses reasonable discrimination across samples.

Prior Sexual Offenses

The general criminal literature certainly demonstrates the predictive efficacy of prior acts of violence (e.g., Wolfgang, Figlio, & Sellin, 1972) and the same findings apply to sexual offenders (e.g., Quinsey, Lalumiere, et al., 1995). For sexual offenders, a higher number of prior offenses increases the risk for reoffense. This finding has been consistently supported for both child molesters and rapists (e.g., Abel et al., 1988; Fitch, 1962; Frisbie, 1969; Hall & Proctor, 1987; Hanson, Scott, & Steffy, 1995; Hanson et al., 1993; Prentky, Knight, et al., 1997; Proulx et al., 1997; Quinsey, Lalumiere, et al., 1995; Radzinowicz, 1957; Rice, Quinsey, & Harris, 1991; Romero & Williams, 1985).

Substance Abuse and Social Competence

Sexual offenders who have a substance abuse history and/or have never been married are hypothesized to be at higher risk to reoffend. The literature suggests that there is weak support for the predictive efficacy of alcohol abuse (Frisbie, 1969) and variously defined measures of social competence (Abel et al., 1988; Frisbie, 1969; Hanson et al., 1993; Rice et al., 1991). Seto and his colleagues reported that substance abuse was weakly, albeit significantly, associated with criminal outcome, and social competence was not predictive of outcome. It is reasonable to conclude that these two factors do *not* explain sufficient predictive variance to be considered in isolation. That is, the presence (or absence) of a history of substance abuse and the presence (or absence) of high social competence, taken alone, are insufficient to make predictive judgments. Both variables may become important, however, in the presence of other variables, such as deviant sexual arousal or a history of antisocial behavior. We have hypothesized, for instance, that social competence may be a moderator for aggression in muted sadistic rapists (MTC:R3, Type 5). That is, among rapists with sadistic sexual fantasies, a higher level of social competence for some of these offenders may attenuate the manifest level of aggression.

Antisocial Behavior & Psychopathy

Abel, Becker, et al. (1981) found that child molesters with a high Pedophilic Aggression Index (psychophysiologically assessed degree of arousal to scenes depicting aggressive sexual acts compared to scenes depicting nonaggressive sexual acts) were in fact the most dangerous (in terms of their actual behavior). In our CMRA study, we found that level of aggression or violence was better predicted by a history of impulsive, antisocial behavior than solely by an assessment of the strength of sexual attachment to children. Although our measure of pedophilic attachment was behavioral rather than physiological, as was the case in the Abel et al. study, it makes clinical sense that those offenders who are high in impulsive, antisocial behavior will be distinguished by a greater degree of callousness and indifference to the welfare of their victims.

Psychopathy, assessed using Hare's (1991) Psychopathy Checklist-Revised, is clearly related to violence (e.g., Grann, Langstrom, Tengstrom, & Kullgren, 1999; Serin, 1991, 1996) and thus has been identified as a critical factor in the assessment of dangerousness (e.g., Brandt, Kennedy, Patrick, & Curtin, 1997; Hart, 1998a,b; Hart & Hare, 1996; 1997; Salekin, Rogers, & Sewell, 1996; Serin & Amos, 1995). Although a high level of psychopathy is most certainly a marker for interpersonal violence, the relation between psychopathy and sexual deviance is less certain. Serin, Malcolm, Khanna, and Barbaree (1994) examined 65 sexual offenders, half rapists and half child molesters. The correlation between deviant sexual arousal, assessed using the PPG, and psychopathy was significant although *low* ($r =$ .28). The relation between deviant arousal and psychopathy was *most* apparent for extra-familial child molesters. As Serin et al. (1994) pointed out, however, the mean scores on the PCL-R for all groups were quite low, well below the cutoff for psychopathy. It may well be the case that a clearer relationship between psychopathy and deviant sexual arousal becomes apparent at a higher level of psychopathy.

Brown and Forth (1997) divided 60 rapists into those with PCL-R scores of 30 or greater (21, 35% of the sample) and those with PCL-R scores of 29 or less (39, 65% of the sample). Brown and Forth found that psychopathy was *not* related to sexual offense history, age of onset of sexual offending, or victim injury. Psychopathy was positively (and strongly) related to prior nonsexual offenses, and negatively related to age of onset of general criminal activity, number of sexual victims, and the intensity of negative emotions experienced prior to sexual offenses. Nonpsychopaths were significantly more likely to report feeling alienated and stressed, whereas psychopaths were more likely to report feeling positive emotions. From a taxonomic perspective, psychopaths were twice as likely to have been classified as Opportunistic (Types 1/2) and Pervasively Angry (Type 3) on MTC:R3. Sexual, Nonsadistic (Types 6/7) rapists were much more likely to be classified as nonpsychopathic. Almost all of the rapists classified as sadists (6 of the 7) were *non*-psychopaths. Although Brown and Forth concluded by recommending that psychopathy be considered when developing intervention strategies for rapists, the precise role that psychopathy plays in sexually aggressive behavior is evidently quite complex.

As Hart and Hare (1996) candidly observed, although the weight of evidence clearly indicates that psychopathy is a critical risk factor, it is not apparent precisely *why* it is so important. Hart and Hare offered three possible explanations: (1) psychopaths may have "cognitive schemata that predispose them to perceive hostile intent in the actions of others," (2) psychopaths "are prone to violence that occurs as part of a more general pattern of impulsivity," or (3) psychopaths "may have a generalized emotional deficit that prevents them from experiencing empathy, guilt, fear," emotions that would otherwise inhibit the expression of violent impulses (p. 382). None of these explanations are, of course, *specific* to sexual offending, and any one of them or combination of them may apply when assessing sex offenders. We can conclude at this point that (1) psychopathy is *not* relevant for a large number of sex offenders (e.g., most incest offenders), (2) when psychopathy *is* present, the criminal track record is typically much worse and the outcome often is bleak (i.e., a high probability of reoffense), and (3) psychopathy is invariably present in the most dangerous, serial offenders, many of whom kill their victims. Thus, although psychopathy is *not* universally observed among sex offenders, it is a factor that must be reckoned with when it is present.

Second-Generation Research on Risk Assessment

The "second generation" of empirical research on risk assessment was launched primarily by a large, prolific group of researchers in Canada, including Howard Barbaree, Karl Hanson, Grant Harris, Steve Hart, Vern Quinsey, Marnie Rice, Ralph Serin, Michael Seto, and Chris Webster. Rather than focusing on single item or single construct differentiation, the more recent research has, for the most part, sought to develop multivariate prediction scales and test the properties and utility of the scales using more sophisticated procedures, such as ROC analysis.

Actuarial Risk Assessment Scales

There is an ever-increasing number of actuarial risk assessment scales, spawned in good measure by the wave of state legislation that mandates these assessments. Not surprisingly, most of these scales share common variables. Although the variables themselves are not precisely the same, they are tapping similar variance (e.g., variables that, in one way or another, measure sexual deviance and variables that measure antisociality). Most of these scales are too new to have demonstrated track records of empirical validation. In this section, we provide descriptive overviews of a number of these scales, some well-known and others not. Most of these scales are presented in greater detail in the Appendix. The information provided here is not adequate for the proper use of these scales. If the reader wishes to use of any of these instruments, it is necessary to obtain detailed coding and psychometric information from the scale's authors.

VRAG.   Perhaps the most frequently reported instrument in the empirical literature is the Violence Risk Appraisal Guide (VRAG: Harris et al., 1993; Quinsey, Harris, Rice, & Cormier, 1998; Rice & Harris, 1995, 1997; Webster, Harris, Rice, Cormier, & Quinsey, 1994). The VRAG was developed to assess violent recidivism using mentally disordered offenders who had been committed to the Mental Health Centre in Penetanguishene, Ontario. The VRAG consists of 12 variables (see the Appendix for the full scale):

  1.   Lived with both biological parents to age 16
  2.   Elementary school maladjustment
  3.   Alcohol abuse history

4. Marital status
5. Criminal history (nonviolent offenses)
6. Failure on prior conditional release
7. Age at index offense
8. Victim injury in index offense
9. Female victim in index offense
10. DSM-III diagnosis of any personality disorder
11. DSM-III diagnosis of schizophrenia
12. Hare's Psychopathy Checklist score

In the initial heterogeneous construction sample of 618 men who had been committed to a maximum-security psychiatric hospital as mentally disordered offenders, the correlation between the 12 predictor variables and violent recidivism was .459 (Harris et al., 1993). The two predictors with the highest univariate correlations were the Psychopathy Checklist (.34) and elementary school maladjustment (.31). The weakest predictors were female victim in index offense (.11), alcohol abuse history (.13), victim injury in index offense (.16), and a DSM-III diagnosis of schizophrenia (.17). It should be noted, however, that this sample included relatively few sex offenders. Harris et al. (1993) reported that 14% of those who recidivated and 7% of those who did not recidivate had index offenses with a sexual motive. Thus, apparently only about 57 of the 618 offenders had a sexually motivated index offense.

A cross-validation study, using 159 sex offenders who were not included in the original construction sample, yielded similar results (Rice & Harris, 1997). That is, the correlation of the VRAG with violent recidivism (sexual and nonsexual) was quite comparable (.47) to the correlation of .46 observed in the original study. The VRAG appears to do much better at predicting generic violence (nonsexual as well as sexual) than at predicting the *full gamut* of sexual recidivism, which inevitably includes many crimes that are on the low end of a violence continuum. In the cross-validation study, for instance, the VRAG's correlation with sexual recidivism (i.e., *only* sexual crimes) was .20 (Rice & Harris, 1997). In an earlier examination of the predictive efficacy of the VRAG, Rice and Harris (1995) concluded that "the ROCs suggest that the VRAG performed equally well in prediction of violent acts that varied in seriousness from common assault to homicide," and that "its predictive ability seemed to be robust over a broad range of high-risk offenders, over a broad range of violent offenders, and over a broad range of follow-up times" (p. 745). Rice and Harris (1997) subsequently concluded, after their cross-validation study, that

> The present data support the use of the VRAG for both sex offenders and other violent offenders, and the prediction of violent, rather than specifically sexual, recidivism. Although the factors related to future sex offending may be of theoretical interest, the practical issue has more to do with the prediction of future violence (both sexual and nonsexual offenses). (p. 239)

As Rice and Harris (1997) clearly state, the mission for VRAG is interpersonal violence. Thus, it is not surprising that the VRAG falls short when it comes to differentiating among samples exclusively comprised of sexual offenders, many of whom have minimal (or no) track records of violence. The VRAG variable with the greatest weighting is the PCL-R score (Rice & Harris, 1995), and none of the 12 items capture the sexual pathology (e.g., sexually deviant thoughts/fantasies, intensity of sexual preoccupation with children, amount of contact with children) that would seem to be critical for most child molesters and some types of rapists. In their meta-analysis of sexual offender recidivism studies, Hanson and Bussiere (1998) found that "sexual offense recidivism was best predicted by measures of sexual deviancy (e.g., deviant sexual preference, prior sexual offenses) and, to a lesser extent, by general criminological factors" (p. 348). Thus, it would certainly seem that any attempt to predict sexual recidivism must take into account sexually deviant thoughts and behaviors.

Quinsey, Rice, and Harris (1995) examined the predictive efficacy of a large number of variables (demographic, psychiatric history, criminal history, scores derived from Hare's (1991) Psychopathy Checklist, and plethysmographic assessment) on a sample of child molesters and rapists (predominantly child molesters). On their combined sample, they found support for the predictive validity of ratings on the Psychopathy Checklist, plethysmographic assessment, and prior criminal history.

SORAG.   Quinsey et al. (1998) revised the VRAG for sexual offenders. Ten of the fourteen items on the resulting "SORAG" (see Appendix) are taken from the VRAG. The four new SORAG items are: (1) criminal history score for violent offenses, (2) number of previous convictions for sexual offenses, (3) history of sexual offenses only against girls under 14, and (4) phallometric test results. Quinsey et al. (1998) reported that

> The ability of the SORAG in predicting violent recidivism among sex offenders has so far exceeded that of the VRAG only marginally.... We attribute this lower predictive accuracy for specifically sexual recidivism to three factors. The first is the higher measurement error associated with sexual offending already discussed. The second has to do with the relatively narrow range of risk in our studies of sex offenders *(i.e., relatively few low risk offenders in their sex offender samples)....* The third limitation on the ability of our actuarial instrument to predict sexual recidivism might have to do with our exclusive use of additive linear relationships in the construction of the SORAG. (pp. 156 and 158)

RRASOR.   Hanson (1997a) has reported on the development of an actuarial scale for assessing risk to recidivate among sex offenders. Hanson used aggregate data from seven follow-up studies that included 2592 subjects. Hanson examined seven variables that had emerged as important from their meta-analysis (Hanson & Bussiere, 1998):

1. "Officially recorded" prior sex offenses
2. Stranger victims
3. Any prior nonsexual offenses
4. Age (at time of release for those who were in prison and at time of evaluation for those in the community)
5. Marital status
6. Any nonrelated victims (victims not having a biological, step, or foster relationship with the offender)
7. Any male victims (child or adult)

The resulting scale contained four variables:

1. Prior sexual offenses
2. Age at risk less than 25
3. Extrafamilial victims
4. Male victims

Hanson's four-item Rapid Risk Assessment for Sex Offense Recidivism scale (see Appendix) correlated .27 with sexual recidivism using the scale development samples. The C-statistic from the ROC analysis was .71. The scale correlated .25 with sexual recidivism using the validation sample, and the C-statistic was .67.

SACJ-Min.   A scale similar to the RRASOR was developed by David Thornton (see Grubin, 1998). Like the RRASOR, the Structured Anchored Clinical Judgment was developed as a brief screening scale for predicting sexual recidivism. Unlike the RRASOR, the SACJ is rated using a multistage process. In the first stage, documented convictions are coded in the following five areas:

1. Any current sexual offense
2. Any prior sexual offense
3. Any current nonsexual violent offense
4. Any prior nonsexual violent offense
5. four or more prior (distinct) sentencing occasions

If four or five of the above factors are present, the offender is automatically classified as high risk. If two or three factors are present, the offender is classified as medium risk. If one or none of the factors are present, risk is considered low.

The second stage incorporates one of two sets of variables that are regarded as potentially aggravating factors. Set A includes the following four variables:

1. Any stranger victims
2. Any male victims
3. Never married
4. Convictions for noncontact sex offenses

Set A is relatively easy to code quickly and reliably. Hence, the five Stage 1 variables plus the four Set A variables represent the SACJ-Min—the minimum required for a valid assessment. The four Set B variables, which are more time-consuming and difficult to code, are

1. Substance abuse
2. Deviant sexual arousal
3. Psychopathy
4. Placement in residential care as a child

The SACJ was developed through exploratory analyses on several data sets in England. The SACJ-Min was validated on a different sample of approximately 500 sex offenders released from prisons in 1979. Follow-up data were collected on the complete sample after 16 years. In this validation study, the SACJ-Min correlated .34 with sexual recidivism and .30 with any sexual or violent reoffense (see Hanson & Thornton, 1999).

Static-99.   The Static-99 represents the combined efforts of Hanson and Thornton to integrate the RRASOR and the SACJ-Min (see Hanson & Thornton, 1999). As the name implies, the scale includes only static variables. The year "99" suggests that the scale is a work in progress. The Static-99 includes 10 variables: 8 of the 9 original SACJ-Min variables (current sex offense was dropped) and all 4 of the RRASOR variables. Since 2 of the 4 RRASOR variables were also on the SACJ-Min, only 2 new variables were added to the 8 SACJ-Min variables. The full set of 10 variables on the Static-99 are described in the Appendix.

HCR-20.   Another important contribution to the literature on assessing risk of general violence comes from the work of Webster, Hart, and their colleagues (Webster, Douglas, Eaves, & Hart, 1997; Webster, Eaves, Douglas, & Wintrup, 1995). Webster et al. developed the HCR-20 in 1995 for assessing risk of violence and in 1997 published a slightly revised version 2.

The 10 Historical items ("H" of HCR) are

1. Severity and frequency of previous violence
2. Young age of first violent incident
3. Instability of relationships
4. Employment problems (not stability)
5. Substance use problems
6. History of serious, acute major mental illness
7. Psychopathy as measured by the PCL-R ($0 = \leq 20$, $1 = 21\text{--}29$, $2 = \geq 30$)
8. Early maladjustment (behavioral problems at home and in school)
9. Personality disorder (*any* diagnosis of a personality disorder)
10. Prior supervision failure (serious failure of any community or institutional supervision)

The 5 Clinical items ("C" of HCR) are

1. Lack of insight
2. Negative attitudes
3. Active symptoms of major mental illness
4. Impulsivity
5. Unresponsive to treatment

The 5 Risk management items ("R" of HCR) are

1. Plans lack feasibility
2. Exposure to destabilizers (typically the result of inadequate supervision)
3. Lack of personal support (from friends and relatives)
4. Noncompliance with remediation attempts (likelihood of failure to comply with remediation attempts)
5. Stress (poor adaptation to stressors and likelihood of exposure to serious psychosocial stressors)

SVR-20.   A variant of the HCR-20 was developed specifically for assessing risk of sexual violence (Boer, Hart, Kropp, & Webster, 1997). The SVR-20 (Sexual Violence Risk-20 scale) consists of the following items (see Appendix):

Psychosocial adjustment items

1. Sexual deviance
2. Victim of child abuse
3. Psychopathy (Hare's PCL-R)

4. Major mental illness
5. Substance use problems
6. Suicidal/homicidal ideation
7. Relationship problems
8. Employment problems
9. Past nonsexual violent offenses
10. Past nonviolent offenses
11. Past supervision failures

Sexual offense items

12. High density sex offenses
13. Multiple sex offense types
14. Physical harm to victim in sex offenses
15. Uses weapon or threats of death in sex offenses
16. Escalation in frequency or severity of sex offenses
17. Extreme minimization or denial in sex offenses
18. Attitudes that support or condone sex offenses

Future plans items

19. Lacks realistic plans
20. Negative attitude toward intervention

Two-Tier Model.   A comprehensive risk assessment model was described by Serin, Barbaree, Seto, Malcolm, and Peacock (1997). This model has two tiers. Tier 1 includes two categories of "central risk factors": Criminality (8 variables) and Sexual Deviance (12 variables). Tier 2 includes three categories of "moderating risk factors": Social Competence (7 variables), Substance Abuse (10 variables), and Treatment Readiness (4 variables). This model was tested on 466 sex offenders at Warkworth Prison (Seto, Barbaree, Serin, & Malcolm, 1997). Seto et al. reported that Criminality had the largest and most consistent relationship with various indices of outcome, particularly parole failure and posttreatment risk evaluations. Sexual Deviance and Substance Abuse also were significantly related to indices of outcome. Social Competence had, at best, very weak relationships with outcome. All zero-order correlations that reportedly were significant at the .05 level, were *very* modest, ranging in magnitude from .10 to .36.

CARAT.   The California Actuarial Risk Assessment Tables (CARAT) provides two sets of predictors, one for rapists and one for child molesters (Schiller & Marques, 1998). The nine variables that predicted recidivism for *rapists* were:

1. Under age 25 at time of release from prison (this was the strongest risk factor; rapists released from prison before the age of 25 had 20 times the risk of reoffending as rapists possessing no risk factors; according to the actuarial table, rapists released before the age of 25 had an 11.3% probability of reoffending)
2. Sexually abused as a child (this was the second strongest risk factor; the reoffense rate for those who were sexually abused was estimated to be 28.6%, compared with a 15% rate for those who were not sexually abused)

3. Acquaintance victim
4. Stranger victim
5. Average IQ (having an average IQ was associated with a higher reoffense rate for all types of sexual offenses, as well as parole violations)
6. Age 25–35 (age 25–35 at time of release from prison)
7. One prior sex offense (one prior sex-related arrest and no other risk factors places the individual at 2.2 times the risk of reoffense compared with rapists having none of the other risk factors)
8. Two or more prior sex offenses (two or more prior sex-related arrests and no other risk factors places the individual at 2.6 times the risk of reoffense compared with rapists having none of the other risk factors)
9. Has prior (nonsexual) felonies (one prior nonsexual felony and no other risk factors places the individual at 1.8 times the risk of reoffense compared with rapists having none of the other risk factors)

CARAT variables not predicting recidivism for rapists. Those variables that were *not* significant predictors of recidivism for the rapists were: (1) injury to victim in index offense, (2) whether subject used a weapon, (3) whether subject verbally abused victim, and (4) whether subject expressed concern for the welfare of the victim. Moreover, none of the above variables predicted whether a sexual reoffense would be violent.

The six variables that predicted recidivism for *child molesters* were:

1. Under age 25 at time of release from prison (as with the rapists, this was the strongest risk factor; child molesters released from prison before the age of 25 had 4.46 times the risk of reoffending as child molesters possessing no risk factors)
2. Two or more prior sex offenses (the second strongest risk predictor for child molesters was having two or more prior sex-related arrests and no other risk factors places the individual at 2.6 times the risk of reoffense compared with child molesters having none of the other risk factors)
3. Molest boys only (the next strongest risk factor for child molesters is having all boy victims)
4. Age 25–35 (the fourth strongest risk factor for child molesters was being between the ages of 25 and 35 at time of release from prison)
5. Stranger victim (having any victim who was a stranger)
6. Victim under 6 years of age

CARAT variables not predicting recidivism for child molesters. Those variables that were *not* significant predictors of recidivism for the child molesters were: (1) injury to victim, (2) use of a weapon, (3) verbal abuse of victim, and (4) expressing concern for the victim's welfare. Parenthetically, whether the offender had been physically or sexually abused as a child was *not* significantly associated with reoffending for the child molesters.

RRAS. New Jersey's Registrant Risk Assessment Scale (RRAS) was specifically developed to assist in assigning convicted sex offenders to one of three risk tier classifications (low, moderate, and high risk), which is, in turn, linked to corresponding levels of community notification (Ferguson, Eidelson, & Witt, 1998). The 13 variables comprising the RRAS are divided into four categories:

1. Seriousness of Offense (degree of force, degree of contact, age of victim)
2. Offense History (victim selection, number of offenses/victims, duration of offensive behavior, length of time since last offense, history of antisocial acts)
3. Characteristics of Offender (response to treatment, substance abuse)
4. Community Support (therapeutic support, residential support, employment/educational stability)

Each of the 13 variables are scored according to low (score 0), moderate (score 1), or high risk (score 3). The three Seriousness of Offense variables are multiplied by 5, and the five Offense History variables are multiplied by 3. Thus, both of these categories are equally "weighted," with a possible 45 points each. The two Characteristics of Offender variables are multiplied by 2 (possible 12 points), and the three Community Support variables are multiplied by 1 (possible 9 points).

MnSOST-R. The Minnesota Sex Offender Screening Tool-Revised (MnSOST-R) is a 16-item scale that was developed for the Minnesota Department of Corrections (Epperson, Kaul, & Hesselton, 1998). The 16 items (see Appendix) are the following:

1. Number of legal sex/sex-related convictions
2. Length of sex offending history
3. Was the offender under any form of supervision when he committed a sex offense?
4. Was any sex offense committed in a public place?
5. Was force or the threat of force ever used to achieve compliance in any sex offense?
6. Has any sex offense involved multiple acts on a single victim within any single contact event?
7. Number of different age groups victimized across all sex/sex-related offenses
8. Offended against a 13- to 15-year-old victim and the offender was more than 5 years older than the victim at the time of the offense?
9. Was the victim of any sex/sex-related offense a stranger?
10. Is there evidence of adolescent antisocial behavior?
11. Is there any pattern of substantial drug or alcohol abuse?
12. Stability of employment history?
13. Discipline history while incarcerated?
14. Chemical dependency treatment while incarcerated?
15. Sex offender treatment while incarcerated?
16. Age at release from institution?

J-SOAP. The Juvenile Sex Offender Assessment Protocol was initially developed by Robert Prentky, Bert Harris, and Kate Frizzell at the Joseph J. Peters Institute in Philadelphia and revised with the collaborative assistance of Sue Righthand in Maine (Prentky et al., 2000). J-SOAP consists of four rationally derived factors: two historical factors (Sexual Drive/Preoccupation and Impulsive, Antisocial Behavior) and two dynamic factors (Intervention and Community Stability/Adjustment) (see Appendix). The initial intention in developing J-SOAP was to provide an instrument for assessing risk prior to treatment and at time of discharge. Thus, J-SOAP has a moderately strong representation of dynamic variables (10 out of 26). All J-SOAP variables are scored equally using a three-point scale (0, 1, 2). There is *no* differential weighting. Eight of the eleven variables comprising the Impulsive, Antisocial Personality Factor represent the Adolescent Psychopathy Taxon developed by Harris et al. (1994).

J-SOAP continues to be tested on juveniles in Philadelphia, Massachusetts, and Maine, and revised accordingly. One concurrent and predictive validity was completed based on a sample of 96 juveniles who were treated and released from Peters Institute (see Prentky et al., 2000). These preliminary findings provided tentative support for the reliability and validity of the scale.

Sexual Drive/Preoccupation Factor

1. Prior legally charged sex offenses
2. Duration of sex offense history
3. Evidence of sexual preoccupation/obsessions
4. Degree of planning in sexual offense
5. Gratuitous sexual exploitation of victim

Impulsive, Antisocial Behavior Factor

6. Caregiver consistency
7. History of expressed anger
8. School behavior problems
9. School suspensions or expulsions
10. History of conduct disorder (before age 10)
11. Juvenile antisocial behavior (age 10–17)
12. Ever arrested before the age of 16
13. Multiple types of offenses
14. Lifestyle impulsivity
15. History of substance abuse
16. History of parental alcohol abuse

Intervention Factor

17. Accepts responsibility for sexual offense
18. Internal motivation for change
19. Understands sexual assault cycle and relapse prevention
20. Evidence of empathy, remorse, guilt
21. Absence of cognitive distortions

Community Stability/Adjustment Factor

22. Evidence of poorly managed anger in the community
23. Stability of current living situation
24. Stability of school
25. Evidence of support systems in the community
26. Quality of peer relationships

A-SOAP.   Like J-SOAP, the Adult Sex Offender Assessment Protocol (A-SOAP) was initially developed by Robert Prentky at the Joseph J. Peters Institute and revised with the collaborative assistance of Sue Righthand in Maine. The initial intention in developing A-SOAP, like J-SOAP, was to assess risk among adult sex offenders for our outpatient treatment program. Thus, A-SOAP also has a strong representation of dynamic variables (10 out of 21). All A-SOAP variables are scored equally using a three-point scale (0, 1, 2), and, once again, there is *no* differential weighting.

A-SOAP is presently being used with adults, incarcerated and outpatient, in Philadelphia, Massachusetts, and Maine. Although data continue to be gathered on A-SOAP, the predictive validity of the scale still has not been examined. As with J-SOAP, A-SOAP consists of four rationale factors: two historical factors (Sexual Drive/Preoccupation and Impulsive, Antisocial Behavior) and two dynamic factors (Intervention and Community Stability/Adjustment) (see Appendix).

Sexual Drive/Preoccupation Factor

1. Prior legally charged sex offenses
2. Duration of sex offense history
3. Evidence of sexual preoccupation/obsessions
4. Degree of planning in sexual offense
5. Gratuitous sexual exploitation of victim

Impulsive/Antisocial Behavior Factor

6. History of expressed anger
7. Multiple types of offenses
8. Lifestyle impulsivity
9. History of substance abuse
10. Juvenile antisocial behavior (age 10–17)
11. Adult antisocial behavior (age 18 or older)

Intervention Factor

12. Accepts responsibility for sexual offense
13. Internal motivation for change
14. Understands sexual assault cycle and relapse prevention
15. Evidence of empathy, remorse, guilt
16. Absence of cognitive distortions

Community Stability/Adjustment Factor

17. Evidence of poorly managed anger in the community
18. Stability of current living situation
19. Stability of employment
20. Evidence of support systems in the community
21. Quality of peer relationships

Will One Risk Assessment Scale Predict Sexual Recidivism?

Rice and Harris (1997) stated, rather matter-of-factly, that "predictive accuracy for sexual recidivism cannot match that possible for violent recidivism" (p. 239). This is, of course, an empirical question. There is no reason, in principle, why sexual recidivism cannot be predicted with comparable accuracy to violent recidivism, assuming that the same basic principles are adhered to. As a rule of thumb, the more frequently the target behavior (e.g., violence) has been expressed, the greater the likelihood that it will be expressed again. As Hanson and Bussiere (1998) noted, "One of the simplest and most defensible approaches to recidivism prediction is to identify a stable pattern of offending" (p. 348). What makes the prediction of violent recidivism reliable is reliance on *prior* acts of violence. Risk assessment for violence targets a relatively narrow domain of expressed behavior.

The most obvious source of *un*reliability and *in*accuracy when assessing risk of sexual crimes is the manifest heterogeneity of the behavioral domain that has been targeted. It is likely that no *single* risk assessment procedure for sex offenders will ever achieve optimal reliability. It is obvious, for instance, that degree of sexual preoccupation with children is a very important risk factor for extrafamilial child molesters and of no importance in assessing risk among rapists. Similarly, impulsive, antisocial behavior and psychopathy are very important risk factors for rapists and much less important for child molesters. In sum, prediction of sexual recidivism among child molesters is sufficiently different from prediction of sexual recidivism among rapists to require an entirely unique set of predictor variables. Indeed, this supposition is supported by Hanson and Bussiere's (1998) finding that one of the highest weighted average correlations between sexual recidivism and a risk predictor was sexual interest in children as measured by phallometry ($r = .32$). The correlation for "any deviant sexual preference" dropped to .22. Criminological variables did rather poorly in predicting sexual recidivism ($r = .12$ for "criminal lifestyle"). Hanson and Bussiere's meta-analysis included recidivism data on 9603 child molesters and 1839 rapists. The strongest risk predictors reflect the disproportionate number of child molesters. If Hanson and Bussiere had looked at the sample of 1839 rapists separately, criminal lifestyle undoubtedly would have been a much stronger risk predictor. Although rapists and extrafamilial child molesters should, at the very least, be treated separately, we would argue that, ideally, there should also be separate risk assessment procedures for exclusive incest offenders and for juvenile sex offenders.

Recent Studies on Correlates of Recidivism

Proulx et al. (1997) examined correlates of recidivism in samples of 113 rapists and 269 child molesters. There were relatively few differences between those rapists who reoffended sexually and those who did not. Rapists who recidivated were more likely to be younger and have prior convictions. Comparatively, there were far more differences among the child molesters. Child molesters who recidivated sexually had: (1) a higher pedophilic index, (2) more previous sexual charges, (3) were younger, (4) more likely to have male victims, (5) more likely to have extrafamilial victims, and (6) more likely to be living alone.

Knight (1999) reviewed existing validity data on MTC:R3 (rapist classification system described in Chapter 3). The strongest support for *predictive* validity (i.e., recidivism) came from four dimensions: Juvenile Antisocial Behavior, Adult Antisocial Behavior, Pervasive Anger, and Offense Planning. We can reasonably infer that these four dimensions are critical risk predictors for rapists. As we described in Chapter 3, Pervasive Anger captures a longstanding pattern of undifferentiated, *non*sexualized, gratuitous anger that often results in serious physical injury to the victims. All three dimensions—Juvenile and Adult

Antisocial Behavior and Pervasive Anger—reflect chronic problems controlling aggression, and general problems controlling impulsivity in most domains of the offender's lives. Thus, these results are entirely consistent with many other studies supporting the robust predictive importance of impulsive antisocial lifestyle. The inclusion of Offense Planning in Knight's (1999) results presumably broadens the scope of prediction from generic violence to include sexual crimes.

Hanson and Bussiere (1998) examined 69 possible predictors of sexual recidivism, 38 predictors of nonsexual, violent recidivism, and 58 predictors of any form of recidivism, using a combined sample of 28,972 sex offenders. Hanson (1998) noted that "although many of the effects were moderate to small, the consistency of the findings across numerous studies suggests that these are reliable factors to consider in sexual offender risk assessments" (p. 57). The 10 most reliable predictors, with an average correlation greater than .10, were:

1. Sexual preference for children, based on phallometric assessment ($r = .32$)
2. *Any* deviant sexual preference ($r = .22$)
3. Prior sexual offenses ($r = .19$)
4. Failure to complete treatment ($r = .17$)
5. Antisocial personality disorder or psychopathy ($r = .14$)
6. Any prior offenses ($r = .13$)
7. Age (young) ($r = .13$)
8. Never married ($r = .11$)
9. Any unrelated victims ($r = .11$)
10. Any male child victims ($r = .11$)

Perhaps equally noteworthy were those potential predictors that, in Hanson and Bussiere's (1998) meta-analysis, were completely *un*related to recidivism. These predictors included measures of general psychological maladjustment, such as low self-esteem, and a history of childhood sexual abuse ($r = -.01$). Moreover, those sex offenders who denied their sex offense were at no higher risk of reoffending than other sex offenders ($r = .02$).

Consistently reported *clinical* risk factors for child molesters and rapists are the following:

Clinical risk factors for child molestors

- Degree of sexual preoccupation with children, enduring "relationships" with children, child pornography
- Proximity and access to children
- Amount of contact with children
- Sex (gender) of victims
- Impulsive, antisocial behavior
- Substance abuse
- Poor social and interpersonal skills, social discomfort with peers, feelings of inadequacy
- Attitudes (anger toward victims; distortion about children and sexuality; self [low self-esteem]; defensive justification)
- Denial of problems
- Failure to comply with parole conditions

Clinical risk factors for rapists

- Impulsive, antisocial behavior
- Psychopathy
- Rape fantasy and urges to act on fantasies
- Attitudes (anger toward victims; misogynistic anger; global anger; hypermasculine/ macho, con; self [low self-esteem]; indifference)
- Substance abuse
- Poor social and interpersonal skills
- Dominance/control needs
- Poor community adjustment
- Denial of problems
- Failure to comply with parole conditions

We use the word *clinical* to imply that many of these risk factors make "intuitive sense" but have not received empirical support. Of those that have received empirical support, the strength of the suppport varies considerably. Although it is entirely reasonable to consider *all* of these factors, as well as others not mentioned here, when doing a comprehensive risk assessment, caution must be taken when attributing significance to any single risk factor, particularly when the risk assessment may be used for forensic purposes. A number of these risk factors, although critically important for treatment planning, do not stand alone as robust predictors of reoffense. Poor social skills and distorted attitudes obviously fall in this category. Neither of these variables is a robust predictor of reoffense, which is to say that neither differentiate reliably between those who recidivate and those who do not. This is not surprising when considering that the vast majority of sex offenders have distorted attitudes and a large proportion of them have suboptimal social skills. Poor social skills and distorted attitudes, however, may well increase the potential dangerousness of an individual who also presents with a track record of impulsive, antisocial behavior and/or a high sexual drive that includes rape fantasies. A perhaps even better example is substance abuse. Substance abuse, when examined alone, is rarely identified as a reliable predictor of sexual recidivism. Again, this undoubtedly is attributable to the fact that a very large proportion of sex offenders abuse alcohol, drugs, or both. What is common to a large proportion of the sample will not differentiate among the sample. One surely would be remiss, however, in ignoring the presence of active substance abuse in an offender who was being evaluated, particularly an offender with a history of acting out when high or intoxicated.

To further complicate matters, it is obvious that risk factors rarely operate in isolation, independent of one another. The presence of certain combinations of risk factors may be far more critical than other combinations. Our example of substance abuse is an obvious case in point. Although substance abuse when taken alone is a very weak predictor of sexual recidivism, substance abuse in combination with deviant sexual arousal may result in higher estimated risk than if deviant sexual arousal were observed alone. Although the calculus of risk factor interactions is far beyond the current state of the art, it behooves us to at least keep in mind this fragile interplay when assigning importance to risk factors on a case-by-case basis.

The logic of considering such "clinical" factors was clearly articulated by Hanson (1998), who noted that

> The risk factors that are most easily justified are those with empirical support, but they
> are not the only factors that need to be considered. Some factors are so obviously related
> to sexual offender recidivism that to ignore them would strain common sense. Although
> I am aware of no study that has examined the relationship between behavioral intentions
> and sexual offense recidivism, it would be foolish for an evaluator to dismiss an
> offender's stated intention to reoffend. Evaluators need to be cautious, however, in
> admitting factors based only on plausibility. What is common sense to one evaluator
> may be patent nonsense to another. (pp. 60–61)

The empirical risk factors for predicting reoffense for chld molestors and rapists are as
follows:

Child molesters

- Degree of sexual preoccupation with children
- Sexual drive strength
- Paraphilias
- Number of prior sexual offenses
- Sex (gender) of victims
- Amount of contact/impulsivity

Rapists

- Impulsive, antisocial behavior
- Psychopathy
- Sexual drive strength
- Sexual coercion and rape fantasies
- Number of prior sexual offenses
- Offense planning
- Attitudes (global/pervasive anger, hypermasculine/macho, con/criminal)

The empirical literature supports the predictive efficacy of essentially four factors: psychopathy, a history of impulsive, antisocial behavior, prior sexual offenses, and a factor that may be generally referred to as sexual deviance or "sexual drive," depending on the sample of sex ofenders. These four factors are sufficiently robust that when observed individually or in combination they must be taken very seriously.

When looking over the multitude of variables incorporated into the risk assessment scales described here, it may appear as though there are far more than four factors that are predictive. As noted earlier, most of the risk variables are variations on common themes (i.e., different ways of assessing essentially the same construct). The SORAG includes Criminal History for Violent Offenses, Number of Previous Convictions for Sex Offenses, and the PCL-R to cover APD and the PPG (phallometric assessment) to cover sexual deviance. The HCR-20 includes Past Nonsexual Violent Offenses and the PCL-R to cover APD and Sexual Deviance, High Density Sex Offenses, and Multiple Sex Offense Types to cover sexual deviance. The Two-Tier model of Serin et al. includes 8 Criminality variables and 12 Sexual Deviance variables. The RRAS includes 8 Offense History and Seriousness of Offense variables. The MnSOST-R includes 8 variables about Sex Offense History and

History of Adolescent Antisocial Behavior. The SOAP includes 5 variables for Sexual Deviance and 6 variables for APD.

We should reiterate, however, that (1) there are marked typological (or subtype) differences, the most obvious being those factors that predict for child molesters and those factors that predict for rapists (e.g., as illustrated in Tables 4 and 5), and (2) there are criminal domain differences (i.e., factors that predict risk of sexual recidivism are often quite different from factors that predict risk for nonsexual recidivism and violent recidivism).

A Caveat on Defensibility

As Mosier and Altieri (1998) admonished, reports "should be written so as to be able to withstand ruthless criticism during cross-examination in a courtroom setting" (p. 19). Since risk assessments often are used in forensic contexts, they *must* be defensible. Defensible means that the assessments utilized instruments and procedures that are supported by the empirical literature and that the conclusions reached are related directly to the data culled from those instruments and procedures. Defensible means that conclusions drawn and the opinions rendered do not stray beyond what the data support. Defensible means that whenever and wherever possible, conclusions are based on multiple data sources, and that the conclusions are no stronger than the weakest link in the chain of data. As Harre (1976) pointed out,

> The certainty of a conclusion is the certainty of the weakest link in the chain of deduction, that is, of the least certain premise.... Whichever way we look at it, predictions based upon data and arrived at by the use of a theory are no more certain than the certainty of the most dubious of the elements entering into a prediction. (pp. 10–11)

The Ethicality of Auguring Reoffense Risk

Prevailing wisdom has, over the years, asserted that our ability to predict violence falls well below a threshold of accuracy that justifies the use of such predictions in legal proceedings (e.g., Cocozza & Steadman, 1976; Ennis & Litwack, 1974; Ewing, 1983, 1985, 1991; Megargee, 1981; Monahan, 1981). Indeed, Ewing's unambiguous conclusions are well known and often cited. Ewing noted in 1983 that "the psychiatrist or psychologist who makes a prediction of dangerousness violates his or her ethical obligation to register judgments that rest on a scientific basis" (pp. 417–418). Again, in 1991, Ewing asserted that there "is good reason to conclude that psychologists and psychiatrists act unethically when they render predictions of dangerousness that provide a legal basis for restricting another person's interest in life and liberty" (p. 162). The issues are considerably more complex than the "arbitrary" judgment of the level of accuracy of predictive judgments, arbitrary because of the unfathomably complicated interactions of the competence of the examiner, the variable difficulty of rendering decisions in different cases, the variable quality and quantity of data for rendering decisions in different cases, and the different social forces that contrive to influence decisions in different cases. Thus, even if we hold constant the predictive instrument and assume a decent level of accuracy for that instrument, all of the aforementioned factors would still come into play. In addition, as Grisso and Appelbaum (1992) pointed out, "A careful analysis of predictions of future violence demonstrates that there are several types of predictive testimony, varying along at least three ethically relevant dimensions: the nature, foundation, and consequences of the prediction" (p. 632). Grisso and Appelbaum argued that, although there may well be "circumstances in which predictive statements cannot be considered ethical," "this conclusion cannot blithely be generalized to all other contexts. Therefore, we would not advise psychology, psychiatry, or the courts to conclude that all predictions of dangerousness are unethical" (p. 632).

The ethicality of assessing risk may, however, be academic. As Witt, DelRusso, Oppenheim, and Ferguson (1996) pointed out, "Risk assessment is ubiquitous. Despite decades of hand wringing by mental health experts, risk assessment occurs at every stage and in every venue of the criminal justice system" (p. 367). Since we may fairly assume that the problem of sexual violence is unlikely to abate in the near future, the demand for assessments and predictions of sexual dangerousness also will not abate. Based on overwhelming evidence suggesting little or no relationship between *clinical* predictions of dangerousness and criminally dangerous behavior, we are advised, with good reason, to question the ethicality of rendering unreliable judgments. Thus, if we abandon prediction based solely on clinical judgments we must have some satisfactory alternative method of assessment. The "second generation" of empirical research discussed here has added immeasurably to our understanding about how to approach assessments of risk with improved reliability. We have shifted the focus from the abolition of all assessments of risk to a more cautious optimism that basic research has begun to render such assessments more reliable. There are, of course, no magical solutions to the problem of assessing highly idiosyncratic facets of human behavior. Our only recourse is to persist in our best efforts to find empirically based answers to assist in predicting dangerousness in different situations, for different types of offenders, and, most importantly, with a consistent and uniform approach. Those best efforts have resulted in marked progress over the past 10 years, yielding a number of empirically validated assessment scales. The cloud of "ethicality" overshadowing risk assessment will, moreover, begin to recede as the scientific integrity of the assessments improves.

CHAPTER 6

Legal Responses
to Sexual Violence

THE EVOLUTION OF SEXUAL PSYCHOPATH STATUTES AND SOCIAL POLICY

It may fairly be concluded at this point that virtually all discretionary decisions about sexual offenders are firmly, perhaps hopelessly, embedded in a quagmire of social and political logomachy. Indeed, the heat of political and social debate far exceeds the light that is cast on the problem of sexual violence. The age-old struggle, dating back to the Old Testament, between the visceral need to inflict punishment and the occasional recognition of the potential shortcomings of punishment is manifestly evident in the legislative ambivalence that has enacted, repealed, and reenacted sexual psychopath laws throughout the United States for the last half century. There is no evidence that anything has changed over the past 60 years. Indeed, all available evidence indicates that the pattern is alive and well. As we move into the next millennium, we find ourselves in the throes of profound social and legislative ambivalence regarding the efficacy of the predator laws that have swept the country for the past decade.

A History of Laws Governing Sex Offenders

There are two clear "generations" of sexual offender laws separated by a period of dormancy (see Lieb, Quinsey, & Berliner, 1998). The "first generation" could be dubbed the Era of Sexual Psychopath laws and lasted from the late 1930s to about 1975, roughly a 35-year period. The intermediate period could be dubbed the Era of Dormancy and Repeal, lasting from 1975 to 1990, a period of about 15 years. The "second generation" of statutes designed to manage sexual offenders could be dubbed the Era of Sexual Predator laws. As with the previous generation of sexual psychopath laws, the current wave of sexual predator legislation makes a substantial demand on a veritable army of forensic clinicians and practitioners to assist the courts in implementing these laws.

The Era of Sexual Psychopath Laws

The era of sexual psychopath legislation in the United States began in 1937 when Michigan passed the first such law. Michigan's law was quickly challenged and declared unconstitutional by the courts. In 1938, Illinois adopted the Criminal Sexual Psychopath Law, which passed constitutional muster (Meeks, 1963), and in 1939 both California and Minnesota followed suit. The Illinois statute had noteworthy limitations, however, and over a period of 17 years only 83 offenders were committed under it (Meeks, 1963). The most important limitations noted by Meeks were lack of a conditional release program, absence of the privilege of jury waiver, and the requirement of a criminal indictment. Minnesota succeeded in drafting and passing a model statute that became a template for numerous laws in other states (Minn. Sess. Laws 1939, ch. 369, sec. 1). In what may well be the first and most significant opinion rendered by the U.S. Supreme Court on sexual psychopath legislation until the recent *Hendricks* decision [*Kansas v. Hendricks*, 117 S.Ct. 2072 (1997)], the Supreme Court upheld the constitutionality of Minnesota's statute, finding that the indefinite civil commitment of individuals with "psychopathic personality disorder" did not violate due process [*Minnesota ex rel. Pearson v. Probate Court* (309 U.S. 270, 1940)].

Between 1937 and 1976, variants of the Minnesota legislation were passed in 30 other states. Thus, by 1976 well over half of the states in the United States had sexual psychopath statutes. In a period of just six years, between 1975 and 1981, half of those statutes were repealed. As of 1985, these laws existed in only 13 states, and were regularly enforced in just 6 states (Brakel, Parry, & Weiner, 1985).

Sexual Psychopathy as a Diagnostic Entity

It is clear that the statutory use of the term *psychopathy* is strictly legal and bears little or no relation to the clinical use of the term. As noted, this was pointed out quite clearly over 20 years ago by the Group for the Advancement of Psychiatry: "Sexual psychopathy is not a psychiatric diagnosis. It is a term used with a variety of confusing meanings and applications but with no precise clinical meaning" (GAP, 1977, p. 840).

Although some statutes actually refer to "psychopathic personality" (e.g., Minnesota and Massachusetts), no statutes define this entity in accordance with the criteria set forth originally by Hervey Cleckley in 1941 or more recently by Robert Hare and his colleagues (e.g., Hare, 1991; Hare et al., 1990, 1991.) The psychopathic personality, according to the Massachusetts statute, refers to "persons who by an habitual course of misconduct in sexual matters have evidenced an utter lack of power to control their sexual impulses" (MGL, ch. 123A, sec. 1). Washington's statute was even less specific. A sexual psychopath was defined as "any person who is affected in a form of psychoneurosis or in a form of psychopathic personality, which form predisposes such person to the commission of sexual offenses in a degree constituting him a menace to the health or safety of others." The GAP (1977) study reviewed sexual offender statutes in 28 jurisdictions, and identified seven features that many of those laws shared: (1) commission of a sexual offense, (2) the notion that the offending behavior is "dangerous," (3) repetition, (4) high probability of re-offense, (5) need for community protection, (6) the presence of some mental illness, mental disorder, or mental deficiency (typically unspecified) in the offender, (7) need for treatment (without concern for amenability for treatment).

Importantly, none of these features suggest the clinical component of psychopathy (Factor 1 of Hare's Psychopathy Checklist-Revised [PCL-R]). At best, these statutes may be selecting for the antisocial component (Factor 2 of the PCL-R) along with a predisposition to sexually aggressive behavior. As Lieb et al. (1998) pointed out, "Diagnosing psychopathy meant perceiving what was lacking in a human being, a difficult target for precision" (p. 57). In other words, unlike civil commitments in which an examiner is evaluating the *presence* of specific symptoms or behaviors (e.g., hallucinations or delusions), in the case of "psychopathy" examiners are asked to judge the *absence* of something, typically the absence of the ability to control sexual impulses (e.g., "an utter lack of power to control his impulses" in California's definition of the "mentally abnormal sexual offender"). The clinical criteria for psychopathy, as spelled out by Cleckley or Hare, certainly never appeared in these laws.

In those instances where diagnostic criteria may be inferred, the predominant behavioral criterion for the sexual psychopath statutes involved some form of volitional impairment (i.e., an inability to control impulses to engage in acts of sexual aggression). This conclusion is consistent with the GAP finding that most statutes have in common notions of repetition and high risk of reoffense. Impaired impulse control is associated with repetitive offenses. Thus, the "modal" individual committed under these statutes is a repetitive or habitual sex offender. Given the apparent intent of these statutes, descriptive and diagnostic accuracy would be achieved by referring to these laws as *habitual sex offender* statutes and avoiding the use of the term *psychopath*. Even here, however, the category of habitual sex offender is nosologically heterogeneous, characterized by a wide variety of DSM-IV Axis II (personality) disorders (APA, 1994), as well as multiple DSM-IV Axis I disorders (e.g., mood disorders, anxiety disorders, substance abuse, impulse disorders) (APA, 1994). Thus, DSM-IV comorbidity in men classified under these statutes is an important empirical question.

As Grubin and Prentky (1993) commented, in this regard,

> Most of the statutes are framed so that individuals who are mentally handicapped or "legally insane" are excluded. Thus, as in England, the laws in effect create a type of mental disorder by legislative edict, one that would seem to absolve the individual from responsibility for his actions. The sexual psychopath, after all, is by definition not able to control his sexual behavior and is therefore not a free agent who can reasonably be held accountable for what he does: indeed, the Minnesota statute actually states that the individual is rendered "irresponsible for habitual courses of conduct with respect to sexual matters." Nevertheless, the legislation usually makes clear that a finding of sexual psychopathy is not a defense to a criminal charge. (p. 383)

The essential point, of course, is the legislative *intent* of the sexual psychopath laws. If the primary intent of the law is preventive detention, as Pacht (1976) argued 25 years ago, and treatment is merely thrown in so that the law will pass constitutional muster, then it is very *un*likely that the law will promote a marked diminution in recidivism among released offenders. The task of effecting behavior change in seriously characterologically disordered individuals is, in itself, considerable. When these individuals have not chosen treatment but are placed in treatment by the court (as is often the case), and when the treatment occurs in the context of a dangerous prison environment where the goal is survival and not therapy (as is often the case), then the task becomes immeasurably more difficult. When the treatment provided is suboptimal, the conditions (i.e., prison) are highly problematic, and the therapists are inadequately trained and supervised, the task may well be impossible. Under these onerous conditions it would be an egregious error to draw any conclusions about the efficacy (or inefficacy) of treatment with sex offenders.

Era of Dormancy and Repeal

The rapidity of the diffusion and repeal of these statutes has been the subject of much scholarly discourse. In his classic article on the diffusion of sexual psychopath legislation, Edwin Sutherland (1950a) described the pattern of events that lead to the enactment of such laws. The first event that Sutherland identified was "a state of fear" that has "been aroused in a community by a few serious sex crimes committed in quick succession" (p. 144). Typically, this "state of fear" follows a single, particularly heinous sex crime, often the sexual murder of a child. The attention given to the crimes by the media exacerbates the fear, which then "readily bursts into hysteria" (p. 145). Sutherland argued that "hysteria" alone was insufficient to explain enactment. According to Sutherland, citizens driven by fear and outrage, appeal to their legislators directly and indirectly through letters to the media or their representatives, or band together in committees.

Legislators, reacting to public outrage, set up ad hoc committees to "study the problem." These ad hoc committees (Sutherland's third factor) consist of "experts," such as lawyers and mental health professionals. The committees' mission of gathering "facts" (Sutherland's quotation marks) conveys, in Sutherland's view, an appearance of scientific credibility to the recommendations issued by the committee. The committee's recommendations eventuate in statutes that ostensibly are designed to address "the problem." The role of "public response" as a catalyst for these laws was clearly understood in the 1940s and 1950s. Apfelberg, Sugar, and Pfeffer (1944) remarked that, "the community demands swift, severe punishment for all sex offenders, even when there is little or no injury to society," and Deutsch (1950) noted that "action against sex crimes usually evolves in an atmosphere of hysteria; such action is often useless and frequently harmful" (cited in Karpman, 1951). A 1948 Massachusetts Report stated, quite simply, that "after a particularly revolting sex crime, the public clamors for harsher penalties" (cited in Sadoff, 1964, p. 249). Sadoff (1964) provided an interesting analysis of the seemingly temporally stable public over-reaction to sexual offenders, noting that

> We react to our own sexual drives in many ways. Those that are acceptable, we express at the appropriate time and under the proper circumstances. The immature and socially unacceptable ones we must handle by the classical defenses of denial and repression. This would suffice if all people were successful in their defenses. But there are those who would dare to express these unacceptable and even dangerous urges, thereby reminding us of our own drives which need to be suppressed even further.... The stronger the repressed drives are, the harsher need be the controls. (p. 251)

Perhaps consistent with Sadoff's explanation, once public outcry has dissipated and the crimes that gave rise to it are largely forgotten, the laws become the target of persistent criticism. Couched in Sadoff's terms, once we have effectively suppressed our own deviant fantasies and urges stimulated by the crime, we examine the resulting law with greater dispassion and recognize shortcomings.

Factors Contributing to the Repeal of these Statutes

The Feminist Movement.   The rapid repeal or modification of these statutes has been attributed to a number of factors, including the growing influence of the feminist movement, which held that rape was solely an act of aggression and that the perpetrators should be treated no differently from those who commit nonsexual battery crimes. Feminist writings helped to dispel the myth that rape was strictly a crime of sex perpetrated by a "lustful" man against a "bad" woman. Although it was consistent with the myth that men who committed rapes were in need of treatment to learn how to control their desires, the reinterpretation of rape held that it was an act of aggression and that the perpetrators should be treated the same way that nonsexual battery cases are treated. Perhaps the singular most influential book that drew attention to the differential processing and treatment of offenders who assaulted women was Brownmiller's (1975) *Against Our Will.* Brownmiller vigorously challenged the substance of rape statutes, the enforcement of those statutes, and the treatment of the rape victim by the criminal justice system. The influence of the feminist movement, beginning in 1966 with the founding of the National Organization for Women, may be responsible, in part, for the following noteworthy changes: the passage of rape shield laws that protect the identity of the victim, the legislative modification of the common law exception of spousal rape, the creation in many metropolitan and state police departments of special sex crime units, and the training of hospital workers and police officers in the treatment of the rape victim and safeguarding evidence of the rape. Perhaps the most important and compelling change has been in limiting the cross-examination of rape victims. Questions concerning the complainant's sexual background, sexual practices, contraceptive use, and other matters are now inadmissible (i.e., not germane).

Many of these changes have come about as a result of a changed public perception of the offender's motive in committing a rape. The mythology of rape regards the offender as either an oversexed or sexually unfulfilled but otherwise normal man or as a disturbed man carried away by a sudden uncontrollable impulse. The myth included an image of the rapist's victim as a comely, not-so-innocent young woman who may have by acting provocatively or seductively and brought the rape on herself. The myth simply was that rape was a crime of sex perpetrated by a "lustful" man against a "bad" woman. There certainly was no understatement in the finding of Schwartz and Clear (1978) that

> Ever since Dean John Henry Wigmore entombed in his monumental opus on evidence his own *almost obsessive concern with female sexual derangements*, the American legal profession has taken as an article of faith the proposition that rape-fantasizing or scheming shrews falsifying police reports make up a significant amount of the reported crime. Under the American precept that convicting an innocent man is far worse than letting a guilty one go unpunished, it is logical for a state that believes in the natural inclination of women to lie to build a system that requires a rape victim to undergo a virtual ordeal by fire to prove her veracity. (p. 314).

The myth has been challenged by feminist writers (e.g. Brownmiller, 1975; French, 1992; Griffin, 1971; Greer, 1971), as well as many professionals in the field (e.g., Burgess & Holmstrom, 1974a; Chappell, Geis, & Geis, 1977; Cohen et al., 1971; Groth, 1979; Herman, 1990; Rada, 1978b; Russell, 1975; Schwartz & Clear, 1978; Schwendinger & Schwendinger, 1974; Seghorn & Cohen, 1980).

Dissatisfaction among Professionals.   Another factor that contributed to the repeal of these statutes was the growing dissatisfaction of examiners (primarily psychiatrists) who were charged with the responsibility of evaluating the offenders under the provisions of the statute (see Carter & Prentky, 1993, p. 117). Psychiatrists, and in some cases psychologists, are charged with the responsibility of assessing offenders under the provisions of the statute, and, at a later point, determining "dangerousness" for release decisions. This *decision-making* process, however onerous, is not substantially different than that employed by psychiatrists in most civil commitments where "danger to self or others" is a key element. The apparent resistance was not to the assessment process itself but to the specific decisions required under the statutes (e.g., determining "sexual dangerousness"). Indeed, a report from the New Jersey Diagnostic Center concluded, from a review of 300 sex offenders, that "legal designation and classification of sex offenders were found to be quite confused, illogical and overlapping and to have little relationship to scientific classification of the offenders" (cited in Sadoff, 1964, p. 242).

In 1950, the Committee on Forensic Psychiatry of the Group for the Advancement of Psychiatry (GAP) published *Psychiatrically Deviated Sex Offenders.* This influential committee expressed serious reservations about such laws. Ultimately, however, the Committee "set forth a tentative proposal intended for eventual formulation of a model for legislation applicable to sex offenders" (p. 2). The proposal "anticipated the participation of psychiatry in the disposition of the sex offender" (p. 2).

The 1950 GAP report reflected the view of then-prominent writers in the field. For example, Guttmacher, in a series of lectures published in 1950, praised Maryland's defective delinquent statute and other similar laws as "representing great social progress" "since they recognize deficiencies of will and the anomalous and borderline status of the psychopath and the neurotic character." Yet Guttmacher, in the same lectures, criticized some of the other statutes on the same grounds expressed as reservations by GAP.

Similarly, Karpman (1954) argued for the institution of special sexual psychopath laws that permitted the "encompassing of many potential offenders" (p. 224) and "longer, indefinite sentences [that] would enable more study and more therapy" (p. 225). Although Karpman echoed the criticisms enunciated by Guttmacher and Sutherland, he nevertheless followed the guidelines of GAP in supporting the designs of a model statute. In sum, it appears that although psychiatrists in the 1950s were not enthusiastic about the new sexual psychopath laws, they did cooperate in the development and implementation of the laws.

By 1977, dissatisfaction with these laws had grown to such a degree that the second GAP report on sexual offenders concluded that such statutes were "social experiments that have failed and that lack redeeming social value" (p. 840). The 1977 GAP report stated unequivocally that (1) the term *sexual psychopath* is not a psychiatric diagnosis and hence has "no precise clinical meaning" (p. 840), (2) "reliable conclusions about the efficacy of treatment are most difficult to reach" (p. 869), (3) "predictions about sexual dangerousness are unreliable" (p. 939), and (4) "constitutional questions are involved on many levels" (p. 937). The conclusion of the report was blunt in its recommendation: "sex psychopath statutes should be repealed. This is a beginning step toward justice" and "when an experiment has failed, it is time to say so rather than continue an exercise in futility" (p. 942).

Due Process Concerns.   A third factor that has been held responsible for the repeal or modification of these statutes is the "due process revolution." The suits filed on behalf of mental patients raised both procedural and substantive due process issues, and rights, heretofore denied, were granted to those institutionalized under sexual psychopath statutes. It thus became necessary to justify indeterminate detainment of sex offenders with such due process considerations as treatment and annual reviews of dangerousness. Since the statutes, for the most part, served the singular purpose of preventive detention (Pacht, 1976), they were found to be unconstitutional and repealed or modified. The view of Norval Morris (1982) was terse and succinct. He lamented that the sexual psychopath laws spread "like a rash of injustice across the United States" (p. 135). Morris concluded that "little in principle can be said in defense" of the laws (p. 136). These laws, Morris noted, were an "immediate legislative reactions to sensational sexual crimes and illustrate a legislative capacity to conceal excessive punishments behind a veil of psychiatric treatment" (p. 136). Morris took some solace in observing that the laws were "rarely and sporadically applied, except in California, Indiana, and Wisconsin, where mistaken enthusiasm has outrun both good sense and a sense of justice" (p. 136). In a similar vein, Sadoff (1964) quoted a 1952 University of Pittsburgh Law Review article on the Pennsylvania Sex Crimes Act as commenting that "the fact that certain types of sexual psychopaths are an epithet of repugnance and evil does not form the basis for relaxing constitutional safeguards" (Sadoff, 1964, p. 251).

Displeasure with Treatment of Sex Offenders. The fourth factor that should be mentioned is a wave of social disapprobation with treatment of sex offenders. Treatment increasingly grew out of favor with an angry public that did not want to pay to rehabilitate sex offenders and, moreover, felt that these men deserved punishment. Thus, among those jurisdictions that did provide treatment for offenders, the grass-roots sentiment opposing treatment prompted legislators to withdraw support for such programs. When treatment programs were reduced or eliminated, the principal support for the constitutionality of the statutes was withdrawn, rendering the laws vulnerable in court.

The Pendulum Swings On

Over the ensuing decades, the reform of rape laws, the introduction of new treatment techniques, and changing attitudes about the efficacy of treatment and the reliability of prediction, as well as the enduring societal plea to ensure safety through protracted incarceration, have ensured the perpetual motion of the pendulum described by Sutherland. Indeed, it is quite apparent that the Sutherland phenomenon of enactment (and repeal) of statutes governing the disposition of sexual offenders is the same today as it was half a century ago. As Lieb et al. (1998) also observed, "The circumstances surrounding passage of sexual predator laws often bear an uncanny resemblance to Sutherland's description from the 1950s" (p. 66). Indeed, the situation-specific, reflexive nature of these laws was most evident when, in 1989, two jurisdictions in the United States, Washington and Massachusetts, rendered opposite recommendations at almost exactly the same time. The committee reports containing these recommendations were issued within two months of each other. The Governor's Task Force on Community Protection for the State of Washington (November 1989) recommended the institution of a civil commitment for "sexually violent predators" that will be "constitutionally sound and provide necessary procedural rights" (pp. II-23). The Governor's Special Advisory Panel on Forensic Mental Health for the Commonwealth of Massachusetts (September 1989) recommended the repeal of Chapter 123A (the 1959 statute under which sex offenders could be civilly committed for "one day to life" (Governor's Special Advisory Panel, 1989, p. 10).

As Carter and Prentky (1993) commented,

> The enactment–repeal phenomenon may be understood as a legislative—or political—response to the social debate over incarceration [i.e., determinate sentencing] or rehabilitation [i.e., civil commitment]. Importantly, the struggle over whether or not to provide treatment for those who have committed egregious acts should *not* be confused with the potential efficacy of treatment for reducing risk of reoffense for those offenders. The struggle seems to be an expression of our need to inflict punishment on those whose behavior we find repugnant, and our occasional recognition that the effectiveness of punishment for the redress of wrongdoing has its limitations. (p. 118)

The question of treatment efficacy is, as Carter and Prentky (1993) noted, an empirical one, not a social or political one. Unfortunately, we must conclude that the social debate over management of sex offenders is fueled by impassioned feelings about sex offenders, and typically is insensitive to rational input and uninformed by empirical data. Hacker and Frym (1955) used more colorful language in referring to the motives of those who promote these laws as "an unholy coalition of vengeance tendencies with sexual excitement" (p. 780).

In sum, what the "Sutherland phenomenon" reflects, as noted at the outset, is clear ambivalence and confusion about how best to respond to the problem of sexual violence. Indeed, what we have observed historically with sex offenders is a magnification of the phenomenon so eloquently described by Wolfgang (1988). One would hope that at some point we can fill "the empty cup of our ignorance" (Wolfgang) with gains from the scientific community rather than relying on the "good intentions" (Wolfgang, p. 120) of the lay community. The "nothing works doctrine" (Thornton, 1987, p. 182) is not only nihilistic, it is an inaccurate representation of current wisdom. The questions that the advisory panels and committees entertain can, and should, be informed by the knowledge acquired through patient, systematic empirical inquiry. The question, for instance, of whether or not to treat sex offenders should be answered impartially and empirically, not emotionally. Once equipped with sound, reliable information on the efficacy of treatment for reducing recidivism and the cost of treatment relative to long-term incarceration, the decision to provide treatment falls squarely in the hands of policymakers. As Prentky and Burgess (1990) concluded,

> If the overriding goal is the reduction of victimization rates, as well as the costs incurred by victimization, and if rehabilitation of offenders can be shown to reduce the likelihood of repeated offenses, then it is imperative that we overcome our resistance to treating (sex offenders)—not for the sake of the offenders, but for the sake of the victims. (p. 116)

Era of Sexual Predator Laws

The Era of Sexual Predator laws (also referred to as Sexually Violent Predator [SVP] laws) was heralded in 1990 with the passage of the first of the new statutes in the State of Washington. Four years passed before Kansas, Wisconsin, and Minnesota passed variants of Washington's sexual predator law. Enactment of similar laws became more rapid in 1996, and by early 1999, 10 more states had passed sexual predator laws (Illinois, New Jersey, North Dakota, Arizona, Florida, Iowa, South Carolina, Missouri, Oklahoma, and California) (Fitch, 1998b). An additional 13 states had active bills that were expected to pass in 1999 (Arkansas, Indiana, Maine, Louisiana, Massachusetts, Michigan, Montana, North Carolina, Ohio, Oregon, Texas, Virginia, and West Virginia) (Fitch, 1998b). It is noteworthy that the pace of newly enacted statutes slowed considerably. Only 3 of the 13 states with active bills succeeded in passing sexual predator legislation in 1999 (Virginia, Texas, and Massachusetts). The Virginia law will not be implemented for 1 year. The Texas law appears to be truly unique among the predator statutes. Although it is a civil commitment, it calls for placement in a community-based treatment program coupled with other features of intensive aftercare. Thus, as of the end of 1999, a total of 17 states had passed sexual predator legislation. It would appear that the extraordinary cost of these sexual predator laws has already begun to have an impact.

In 8 of the first 14 states with sexual predator laws, the Department of Mental Health operates the facility (Arizona, California, Florida, Minnesota, North Dakota, Oklahoma, South Carolina, and Wisconsin). In the other 6 states, the Department of Corrections operates the facility and the Department of Mental Health is responsible for providing clinical services (Illinois, Iowa, Kansas, Missouri, New Jersey, and Washington) (Fitch, 1998b). Thus far, it appears that only 3 states have made any extensive use of their predator laws: California with 122 men committed, Minnesota with 125 men committed, and Wisconsin with 116 men committed (Fitch, 1998b).

The sexual predator laws all use civil commitment procedures to detain sex offenders after they have completed serving criminal sentences for their crimes (Janus, 1997b). All of these civil commitment laws have essentially the same four elements. Janus (1997b) noted that the laws

> require proof, by the state, of (1) a history of sexually violent acts, (2) a current mental disorder or abnormality, (3) the likelihood of future sexually harmful acts, and (4) a nexus between the first two elements and the third. Procedurally, these laws impose a burden of proof on the state that is at least at the *clear and convincing level* and in some cases at the *beyond a reasonable doubt* level. Some laws provide for trial by jury, others do not. All provide for confinement that is essentially indefinite and all allow for the release of an individual committed when it is shown that he or she is no longer dangerous by reason of a mental disorder. (pp. 348–349)

Hendricks: The Precedent-Setting Case for SVP Laws

Without doubt the single most influential court decision regarding sexual offenders in the decade of the 1990s has been *Kansas v. Hendricks*, -U.S.-, 117 S.Ct. 2072 (1997). In 1994, Kansas enacted the Sexually Violent Predator Act, which established procedures for civil commitment of persons who, because of a "mental abnormality" or a "personality disorder" are likely to engage in "predatory acts of sexual violence" [Kan. Stat. Ann. sec. 59-29a01 *et seq.*(1994)]. The State invoked the Act for the first time to commit Leroy Hendricks, a 60-year-old man with a long history of taking "indecent liberties" with children, and who was scheduled for release from prison shortly after the Act became law. Hendricks challenged his commitment on, *inter alia*, "substantive" due process, double jeopardy, and ex post facto grounds.

Double jeopardy refers to the Fifth Amendment guarantee (enforced through the Fourteenth Amendment) protecting citizens against second prosecution for the same offense after disposition (acquittal or conviction) *and* against multiple punishments for the same offense. Ex post facto, literally, means after the fact and refers to laws passed after the occurrence of a crime that retrospectively change the legal consequences of that crime. In effect, these are (1) laws that provide for the infliction of punishment for an act which, when the act was committed, carried no punishment, or (2) laws that change the punishment or inflict greater punishment than the law governing the crime when the crime was committed, or (3) laws that change the rules of evidence. The concept of "due process of law," as it is embodied in the Fifth Amendment, requires that laws are not unreasonable, arbitrary, or capricious. Due process rights refer to all of those rights that are of such fundamental importance as to require compliance with standards of fairness and justice. Citizens have both procedural and substantive rights protecting against government actions that threaten the denial of life, liberty, or property. Substantive due process essentially refers to the doctrine that laws must be fair and reasonable in content as well as in application. The essence of substantive due process is protection from arbitrary and unreasonable laws. As applied to the sexual offender laws, substantive due process generally refers to certain "entitlements," such as treatment for one's "mental disorder" and periodic review of dangerousness (i.e., amelioration of one's mental disorder).

The Kansas Supreme Court invalidated the Act, holding that its precommitment condition of a "mental abnormality" did not satisfy the "substantive" due process require-ment that involuntary civil commitment must be based on a finding of "mental illness" [*In re Hendricks*, 259 Kan. 246, 261, 912 P.2d 129, 138 (1996)]. The State of Kansas petitioned for certiorari. Hendricks subsequently filed a cross-petition in which he reasserted his federal double jeopardy and ex post facto claims. Certiorari was granted on both petitions.

The Hendricks case was argued before the U.S. Supreme Court on December 10, 1996, and decided on June 23, 1997. Hendricks's ex post facto and double jeopardy claims were decided using the same threshold question: Did civil commitment imposed *after* Hendricks served a criminal sentence constitute punishment (Walsh & Flaherty, 1999a)? Justice Thomas, writing for the majority, held that: (1) The Act's definition of "mental abnor-mality" satisfied substantive due process requirements for civil commitment, and (2) The Act did not establish "criminal" proceedings, and involuntary confinement pursuant to the Act was not punitive, thus precluding a finding of any double jeopardy or ex post facto violation. [*Kansas v. Hendricks*, -U.S.-,117 S.Ct. 2072, 2073 (1997)].

Justice Thomas asserted that

> A finding of dangerousness, standing alone, is ordinarily not a sufficient ground upon which to justify indefinite involuntary commitment. We have sustained civil commit-ment statutes when they have coupled proof of dangerousness with the proof of some additional factor, such as a "mental illness" or "mental abnormality." These added statutory requirements serve to limit involuntary civil confinement to those who suffer from a volitional impairment rendering them dangerous beyond their control. The Kansas Act is plainly of a kind with these other civil commitment statutes: It requires a finding of future dangerousness, and then links that finding to the existence of a "mental abnormality" or "personality disorder" that makes it difficult, if not impossible, for the person to control his dangerous behavior. The precommitment requirement of a "mental abnormality" or "personality disorder" is consistent with the requirements of these other statutes that we have upheld in that it narrows the class of persons eligible for confinement to those who are unable to control their dangerousness." [*Kansas v. Hendricks*, -U.S.-,117 S.Ct. 2072, 2080 (1997)]

Hendricks has rapidly generated a substantial scholarly literature. Of the many issues raised, two appear to be key: (1) Departure from reliance on the *parens patriae* interest of the State to civilly commit (Cornwell, 1998; Janus, 1998a; Schopp, 1998) and (2) departure from volitional dysfunction (e.g., Janus, 1998a,b; Winick, 1998).

Departure from Reliance on Parens Patriae

The authority of the state to involuntarily commit individuals for care and protection derives from two sources: (1) the state's *parens patriae* power to provide care for those individuals who are unable to care for themselves because of emotional problems and (2) the state's police power to protect the community from mentally ill individuals who may be dangerous (Cornwell, 1998). Both powers, *parens patriae* and police, are critically important in justifying civil commitment. Janus (1998a) commented, in this regard, that

> Perhaps the most far-reaching and significant aspect of *Hendricks* is the Court's failure to rely at all on the state's *parens patriae* power, either as a limitation on civil commitment or as a justification. The majority opinion in *Hendricks* does not mention the *parens patriae* power, and its argument does not, in its structure, rely on the *parens patriae* power. (p. 302)

The Role of Treatment.   The Court's apparent rejection (or simply ignoring) of *parens patriae* could signal an equal rejection (or ignoring) of the criticality of treatment in justifying civil commitment (Janus, 1998a). This does *not* appear to be entirely the case. The Court apparently envisioned a (limited) role for treatment even in *Hendricks*, which is arguably a police power commitment. The Court seemed to adopt a middle-ground position, indicating that the state may be obliged to provide treatment that is "available" for disorders that are "treatable" (see Janus, 1998a). By the same token, the Court clearly rejected the proposition that *effective* treatment is required to justify civil commitment. Although "treatment takes a central constitutional role if civil commitment is limited to *parens patriae* intervention" (Janus, 1998a, p. 307), treatment is not central to a police power commitment. The rationale under *parens patriae* is that remediation of mental illness through treatment is beneficial to the individual, hence justifying civil commitment and perhaps bolstering the argument for the nonpunitive nature of the state's intent. As Janus (1998a) pointed out, however, treatment is of benefit to the individual *only* if the individual elects treatment, or if the individual is incompetent to make an informed choice. In *Hendricks*, the criticality of treatment in civil commitment is quite ambiguous. If we conclude that *Hendricks* is a police power commitment, in police power commitments treatment may be a right of those committed but it is *not* a justification for commitment. The principal objective is to protect society, not to rehabilitate.

Departure from Volitional Dysfunction

Volitional impairment or dysfunction refers to the linking of presumptive dangerousness with a "mental abnormality" or "personality disorder" that has embedded within it the notion of dyscontrol (i.e., the mental abnormality is defined, in part, by inability, or impaired ability, to control one's dangerous impulses). Janus (1998a) suggested

> that the Court might have had in mind a model of control impairment that goes
> something like this: Sexually violent behavior is "caused" by "mental disorder." Since
> the behavior is "caused," the individual's actions are beyond his or her volitional
> control. (p. 318)

Janus (1998a) went on to note, however, that "many scholars refute this reasoning with a
reductio ad absurdum, since *all* behavior is 'caused...' " (p. 318).

As we have mentioned, the roots of volitional impairment derive from the "utter lack
of power to control" language of the 1939 Minnesota Supreme Court. The view that the
urges of at least some sex offenders were irresistible was shared by the psychiatric
community during the 1940s and 1950s. In his classic tome, *The Sexual Offender and His
Offenses*, Benjamin Karpman (1954) observed that

> There is little doubt that the reactions that are attributed to sexual psychopaths are
> beyond the sphere of conscious or voluntary control and appear as irresistible impulses,
> which explains why in practice these cases do not profit by punishment; uncontrollable
> instinct is beyond any punishment. (p. 483)

Over the past 50 years, however, our notions of behavioral dyscontrol, behavioral disinhibition, or behavioral impulsivity have been informed by considerable empirical research. The
result is a richer appreciation of the complex and multidimensional nature of impulsivity,
which is generally conceptualized as a form of behavioral disinhibition that manifests itself
as a lack of behavioral control.

Although research has consistently and strongly linked impulsivity with psychopathy
and antisociality, there is no clear link to the urges and sexual impulses implied by the language of the 1939 Minnesota Supreme Court. The notion of lack of power (or ability) to control one's sexual impulses, in the clinical literature, usually implies the report of frequent
uncontrollable sexual urges, evidence of compulsive sexual behavior, a high sexual drive,
constant preoccupation with gratification of sexual needs and obsessional thinking about
sex, and highly intrusive sexual and rape fantasy. It certainly would not be surprising to see
evidence of detailed offense planning (e.g., a clear modus operandi, "scripted" offenses,
rape kits or other paraphernalia brought to the crime scene). Importantly, in these cases the
sexual crimes themselves are not impulsive. Indeed, there is often considerable evidence of
planning. Contemporary understanding of sexual impulsivity (see Kafka, 1995a) suggests
an important biological component that contributes to high sexual drive and that may be
remediated psychopharmacologically. We may certainly infer at this point that sexual
impulsivity will be *variably* present in sex offenders, ranging from absent in some cases to
profoundly important in other cases. Unfortunately, what we do know about sexual
impulsivity sheds little or no light on the statutory use of terms implying sexual impulsivity.

Interestingly, the subordinative role of "utter lack of power to control" (volitional
impairment) in *Hendricks* derives *not* from the inherent ambiguity of volitional impairment
but from the ambiguity of mental illness. Since volitional impairment is a symptom of an
unspecified mental illness, if the significance of mental illness is undermined, then the
significance of volitional impairment may also be downgraded. As Walsh and Flaherty
(1999a) noted

> The majority [of the U.S. Supreme Court] dismissed *Foucha's* seeming "requirement"
> that there be a finding of a mental illness by stating that "the term *mental illness* is

devoid of any talismanic significance," as not even psychiatrists agree on what mental
conditions constitute a mental illness justifying civil confinement. (p. 34-3)

Since civil commitment generally requires evidence of some psychological or emotional
aberration, mental illness has been replaced with the even more ambiguous, broader
categories of "mental abnormality" or "mental disorder."

From a strictly legal standpoint, the departure from the "volitional dysfunction"
requirement is particularly noteworthy. As Janus (1997a) quipped, "In *Linehan*, the state
got caught with its hand in the 'preventive detention' till, helping itself to 'civil commitment' without paying the 'utter lack of power to control' price for it" (p. 81). As noted,
evidence that someone's "will" has been overwhelmed by an irresistible or uncontrollable
urge or impulse has been fundamental to a finding of "mental disorder." As Janus (1997a)
pointed out, "It is the inference from behavior (which the individual did not control) to
capacity (which the individual could not control) that furnishes the 'mental disorder'
justification for sex offender commitments" (p. 81). Absent volitional dysfunction or a
substantive replacement, a finding of mental disorder is made all the more problematic.
Although volitional dysfunction provides at least a minimal behavioral benchmark for
forensic examiners, Janus (1997a) noted that such a presumptive dysfunction "has consistently baffled judges, forensic professionals, and philosophers" (p. 81). Although "utter
lack of power to control" may be, as Janus (1997a) stated, an "abstract psychological
construct" (p. 84), it is at least a psychological construct. Mental disorder stands alone as a
legal contrivance with no clear and specific psychological meaning. Janus (1997c) noted, in
this regard, that, "Mental disorder supports civil commitment only when it impairs fundamental psychological capacities like cognition and volition" (p. 49). Thus, only through
some putative aberration of cognition or volition can we infer the presence of a "mental
disorder." When volition is omitted, we are left with an even more flimsy psychological
reed to lean on.

Hendricks, according to the Supreme Court, had a "serious mental disorder" (pedophilia) that rendered him dangerous because of a "specific, serious, and highly unusual
inability to control his actions" (from Justice Breyer's dissenting opinion) (Cornwell, 1998,
p. 397). The clear implication is that *all* pedophiles are incapable of controlling their impulses to molest children. It is not clear if Hendricks was deemed dangerous solely because
he is a pedophile (a disorder that, according to the Court, renders individuals helpless to
control their impulses), or because he was unable to control his impulses and his impulses
happened to be pedophilic.

As Winick (1998) pointed out

> People addicted to TV, chocolate, tobacco, coffee, or even jogging, and people who
> abuse alcohol and illicit drugs, often experience themselves as being out of control and
> unable to resist the object of their strong desires.... People who have strong desires,
> particularly those rooted in unconscious psychological needs or "drives," may find their
> desires difficult to resist.... There is, however, a considerable difference between a
> desire not resisted and an irresistible desire. (pp. 520–521)

Winick (1998) further noted that

> people who act impulsively are acting to fulfill certain desires, for example, to obtain the
> object of their gratification or to avoid feelings of dysphoria. Acting to achieve such

desires, even when strongly felt, is undeniably goal-directed, intentional, and purposive action. These are impulses not resisted, not irresistible impulses. (p. 522)

Winick (1998) concluded that "there simply is no theoretical or empirical support for the proposition that people with pedophilia are unable to prevent themselves from acting on their strong sexual urges" (p. 521). Although Winick is fundamentally correct, a more precise conclusion would be that child molesters are quite heterogeneous with respect to the strength of their sexual urges and their ability to control those urges.

It is not unreasonable to argue, as Cornwell (1998) did, that anyone with an antisocial personality disorder could be involuntarily committed using the mental abnormality standard as it was applied to Hendricks. If the standard is a personality disorder that leaves individuals unable to control their dangerous impulses, then antisocial personality disorder would seem to qualify. As Cornwell (1998) noted

> states may well argue that antisocial personality disorder is, generally speaking, a sufficient ground for psychiatric commitment because it is characterized, inter alia, by chronic impulsivity, irresponsibility, aggressiveness, and unlawful behavior. (p. 397)

Following this logic, anywhere between 50 and 75% of the prison population might qualify for civil commitment based on an APD diagnosis.

Presumably, one could make a similar argument about other disorders as well. Cornwell (1998), in fact, noted that "*Hendricks* approved the broadening of states' prerogative to label classes of individuals fit candidates for involuntary psychiatric detention" (p. 412). For lack of any coherent explanation as to the Court's reasoning, we are left with considerable ambiguity around the critical question of the state's authority to define a condition as a mental disorder, thereby justifying it as a basis for civil commitment (Winick, 1998).

Parenthetically, there may be a typological bias here. Impulsive, antisocial behavior is more commonly observed among rapists than child molesters and is more likely to be a risk factor for rapists. Lack of power to control *sexual* urges is arguably a more important risk factor for child molesters. This putative statutory bias toward child molesters is not surprising, since most of the laws were enacted after some heinous crime committed by a child molester.

Janus (1998a) observed that

> If the Court's constitutional evocation of control impairment is clarion clear, the actual mechanism by which this form of mental disorder advances the constitutional calculus is as opaque as the meaning of control-impairment itself.... The discourse of "control" and "volition" is, of course, murkily perilous. (pp. 312–313).

Schopp (1998) also remarked that

> The Supreme Court's opinion in *Hendricks* adds nothing substantive to the vague discussion of volitional impairment.... the Court provided no guidance for the lower courts in interpreting and applying their decision and no explanation that would justify committing Hendricks or others under the statute. The appropriate conception of legal mental illness for the statute remains mysterious. (p. 342)

Janus (1998b) elsewhere pointed out that "the 1939 Minnesota Supreme Court almost certainly viewed the "utter lack of power to control" requirement as constitutionally significant, rooted deeply, though ambivalently, in notions of criminal nonresponsibility and incompetence" (pp. 1283–1284). If this is the case, it may explain the ambiguity around the application of the "utter lack of power to control" standard to criminals who, for the most part, *are* criminally responsible and *are* competent.

On a less than sanguine note, Cornwell ended his appraisal of *Hendricks* with the following:

> As we head into the 21st century, civil commitment harkens back increasingly to its 18th- and 19th-century roots. In-as-much as early images of the "furiously mad," enchained and removed from public scrutiny, were replaced by those of the modern hospital and its mission of providing care and treatment to dangerous mentally ill persons, modern sexual predator statutes reflect a reinvigoration of nontherapeutic civil incapacitation founded exclusively on historical notions of societal self-defense. (p. 412)

In Light of Foucha

The analysis and reasoning of the U.S. Supreme Court in *Foucha v. Louisiana* [112 S.Ct. 1780 (1992)] provided a critical precedent for the *Hendricks* case.

Terry Foucha broke into a home with the intention to steal. The couple living in the home fled unharmed. As Foucha was leaving the home, he fired a shot at a police officer who had come to investigate. Foucha was apprehended and charged with burglary and illegal discharge of a firearm. Two psychiatrists evaluated Foucha and testified that, because of a drug-induced psychosis, he could not distinguish between right and wrong at the time of the crime. Foucha successfully pled not guilty by reason of insanity and was committed indefinitely to Louisiana's East Feliciana Forensic Facility. Sometime after his commitment, Foucha sought release and was again evaluated by two psychiatrists. The psychiatrists concurred that Foucha was not, at that time, mentally ill. The psychiatrists diagnosed Foucha with APD, a condition that was deemed untreatable. Because of Foucha's recent history—he had assaulted several people while at Feliciana—the psychiatrists could *not* certify that he was not dangerous. Based on the psychiatrist's testimony, the judge continued Foucha's commitment based *solely* on his presumptive dangerousness. Foucha twice appealed to Louisiana courts and lost. Foucha next appealed to the U.S. Supreme Court. The Court, by a 5 to 4 decision, reversed the lower court's finding, ruling that its own precedents precluded the commitment of an individual free of mental illness based solely on dangerousness [*Foucha v. Louisiana*, 112 S.Ct. 1780 (1992)].

In his analysis of *Foucha*, R. Alexander (1993) noted that

> The Court identified three problems with the state's argument. First, involuntary commitment requires both a determination that an individual is mentally ill and dangerous. Second, Foucha was entitled to a fair procedure that would establish the grounds for his confinement after the initial basis for his commitment dissipated. Third, every individual has a fundamental freedom of liberty, which cannot be extinguished by arbitrary or wrongful state behavior, even if the state has employed a seemingly fair judicial procedure. Furthermore, Justice White reasoned that if the state could incarcerate someone just for being dangerous, then the state could incarcerate a prisoner nearing release from prison because many of them, like *Foucha*, have been diagnosed as having antisocial personalities and being dangerous. (p. 376)

In discussing the implications of *Foucha* for sex offender civil commitment statutes, Alexander (1993) stated that

> *Foucha* challenges sexual psychopath and psychopathic personality statutes, such as those in Washington and Minnesota, because the Court has now held that a person cannot be committed based solely on dangerousness. Civil commitment requires both a finding of mental illness and dangerousness, and the absence of either one deprives the state of the power to commit an individual. An individual's having an antisocial personality and being dangerous is not enough for civil commitment because antisocial personality or psychopathic personality *is not mental illness*. (pp. 377–378)

The Supreme Court rejected the "jurisprudence-of-prevention argument" set forth by Louisiana (Janus, 1996, p. 176). The Court reaffirmed that mental disorder is an essential, constitutionally required, criterion for civil commitment. Janus (1998a) remarked that "learning *Foucha*'s lesson well, each of the states enacting contemporary sex offender commitment statutes framed them as 'dangerousness plus' laws, in which dangerousness is supplemented by mental disorder as a constitutional predicate" (p. 301).

The *Hendricks* decision is entirely consistent with *Foucha* in underscoring the theoretical importance of "mental disorder." Janus (1998a) commented that "although there is substantial ambiguity about how the mental disorder element functions in *Hendricks*, there is no question that the Court considered the element to be the prime limiting and justifying factor in the Kansas scheme" (p. 301). The obvious, and apparently crucial, difference was that Foucha was diagnosed with APD (*not* a mental disorder, according to the Court), whereas Hendricks was diagnosed with pedophilia (a mental disorder, according to the Court). Since APD and pedophilia are both in the DSM-IV, it is not clear why one, but not the other, qualifies as a mental disorder. The law provides little guidance in its analysis of what constitutes a mental disorder. We may reasonably infer that volitional impairment is a key ingredient (i.e., that inability to control one's impulses implies or suggests the presence of a mental disorder). Hence, the Court would argue that volitional impairment is present in the case of pedophilia and not present in the case of APD. If volitional impairment is the singular, or even principal, criterion for mental disorder, clarity might well be advanced by dropping altogether the use of "mental disorder" and referring only to "uncontrollable" urges to engage in dangerous behavior.

Do nonsexual offenders suffer from volitional impairment? Although the courts might well be reluctant to consider as plausible an individual who argues that he has uncontrollable impulses to break into and rob homes, it certainly would seem reasonable to argue that drug-addicted criminals evidence "uncontrollable urges" to steal when they are supporting their habit. We may be forced to conclude, quite simply, that the state has a less compelling need to civilly commit drug addicts, or, for that matter, other nonsexual criminals who evidence uncontrollable impulses.

Overview of the Sexual Predator Laws

The following points overview the initial 14 sexual predator commitment laws: (1) the laws are invoked after a criminal sentence has been served, (2) they do *not* require a diagnosis of mental illness, although they do require a finding of a mental disorder or mental abnormality, (3) they do *not* require impaired volition (i.e., "utter lack of power to control one's impulses"), (4) the standard of proof most often is "beyond a reasonable doubt" (8 of the statutes) and "clear and convincing evidence" in the remainder, (5) the agency responsible for providing clinical services, in *all* instances, is the Department of Mental Health (DMH) (or its state equivalent), (6) the setting in 9 cases is a DMH facility; in the other 6 cases, offenders are committed to a segregated mental health unit within a Department of Correction facility (with DMH responsible for treatment), (7) in all cases, except California, duration of confinement is indeterminate (in California, individuals are committed for 2 years with extensions by the court), and (8) in all cases, except Minnesota and New Jersey, the court is responsible for releasing committed offenders (in Minnesota, it is the Commissioner, and in New Jersey, it is the Parole Board).

Cost as a Delimiting Factor. As is evident, the enactment period has been swift, in good measure because of the role that the federal government has taken. It may reasonably be surmised, however, that the life of these new statutes will be short, given the extraordinary expense that is required to comply with the mandate of these laws (Lieb & Matson, 1998). Based on the initial estimates for housing and treatment from eight states (California, Florida, Kansas, Minnesota, New Jersey, North Dakota, Washington, and Wisconsin), it costs approximately $91,000 a year per offender. Cost estimates have run as high as $120,000 per year in Minnesota and $107,000 in California (Fitch, 1998b). These cost estimates do *not* include legal expenses, which, from ample past experience with the "generation one" sexual psychopath laws, tend to be *very* high. In his detailed accounting of costs associated with sexual predator laws, La Fond (1998) pointed out, for instance, that a predator commitment trial can cost as much as $100,000 (per the Minnesota experience). La Fond (1998) further noted that "lawyers in Washington state describe a predator commitment trial as very similar to a death penalty trial because of the time spent and costs incurred by both the government and the defense" (p. 485). The arithmatic is simple. At $90,000 per offender, it will cost $9 million per year for 100 men. Those same 100 men will cost about $10 million in legal expenses to commit and incalculable additional legal expenses during the course of their detention. If there is no appropriate facility to house those 100 men, the state may have to spend an additional $20 million or so (e.g., New Jersey appropriated $20 million to build a new 150-bed facility).

Conclusion

Sex offender-specific legislation over the past 60 years can be described metaphorically as waxing in tidal waves of revulsion and protest over well-publicized crimes and waning in response to egregious violations of constitutional safeguards. The marriage of sex offenders and civil commitment law clearly is imperfect, characterized by an unremitting tension, and, thus far, refractory to conventional legal "remedies." As Janus (1997a) observed, civil commitments for sex offenders

> do not arise out of a benign, *parens patriae* motive. The subjects of sex offender commitments are *not*, for the most part, incompetent to make decisions about their own mental health treatment. And they have not been found incompetent to stand trial or not guilty by reason of insanity. Sex offender commitments possess many of the qualities that elicit condemnation of preventive detention. Most centrally, unlike standard civil commitments, sex offender commitments are aimed directly at those guilty of criminal

acts, and are explicitly intended to circumvent the traditional strict constitutional limitations on the state's power to incarcerate. In addition, though courts may categorize them as *civil commitment as usual*, sex offender commitments are well outside the traditional boundaries for standard civil commitment. For these reasons, sex offender commitment schemes need special justification or legitimization. (pp. 72–73)

The justification is, of course, community safety. Civil commitment of sex offenders uses preventive detention to accomplish the same purpose that has previously been reserved exclusively for criminal matters (Janus, 1997a). Whereas a criminal sentence will, almost inevitably, return the offender to the community, a civil commitment provides some sense of comfort that the offender may never return to the community. Thus, community safety is pit against protection of constitutional rights. The result is an inexorable tension that has been most visibly manifest in the pendulum of enactment and repeal. Janus (1996) concluded with the following plea

Sex offender commitment laws confuse too many important values. Obscuring the critical role that mental disorder plays in defining the state's police powers, these laws embrace a dangerous jurisprudence of prevention. We must find other, more truthful and more principled ways to prevent sexual violence. (p. 213).

Although they may not be *politically* appealing, there *are* constructive options that substantially increase community safety while not abridging basic constitutional rights. There is little evidence, thus far, that litigation in response to the current wave of sexual predator laws will shed light on the ambiguity of the critical elements that comprise these laws, *or*, for that matter, provide the legal architecture for a comprehensive risk reduction model that could effectively promote community safety. These options are discussed in Chapter 8 under Risk Management.

CASE STUDIES: HISTORIES OF RAPE LEGISLATION IN SIX STATES

Minnesota

Minnesota passed its first sex offender regulatory statute in 1939. This statute sought to develop a "psychopathic personality" commitment standard, defining psychopathic personality as

the existence in any person of such conditions of emotional instability, or impulsiveness of behavior, or lack of customary standards of good judgment, or failure to appreciate the consequences of personal acts, or a combination of any such conditions, as to render such person irresponsible for personal conduct with respect to sexual matters and thereby dangerous to other persons. (1939 Minn. Laws ch. 369, sec. 1)

That same year, the law, deemed to be too vague, was challenged, and the Minnesota Supreme Court narrowed the definition of psychopathic personality, holding that the law applied to individuals who, by a

habitual course of misconduct in sexual matters, have evidenced an utter lack of power to control their sexual impulses and who, as a result, are likely to attack or otherwise inflict injury, loss, pain or other evil on the object of their uncontrolled and uncontrollable desire. [*State ex rel Pearson v. Probate Court*, 205 Minn. 545, 555, 287 N.W. 297, 302 (1939), *aff'd*, 309 U.S. 270 (1940)]

This "psychopathic personality" statute was used routinely during the following two decades, but after 1960 the law was used quite infrequently (Civil Commitment Study Group, 1999). Although most states repealed their equivalent statutes during this period when indeterminate sentences fell out of favor, the Minnesota law remained on the books in a state of relative dormancy. The decade of the 1990s brought renewed challenges to the constitutionality of the psychopathic personality law. In response to these challenges, the State Legislature created a Task Force in 1994 to study the many problems pertinent to the indeterminate confinement of sexual offenders. On August 31, 1994, the State Legislature enacted statutory amendments consistent with those recommended by the Task Force. The Legislature recodified the psychopathic personality law, renaming it the "sexual psychopathic personality" law (SPP). More notably, the legislation added an additional commitment category to Minnesota's Civil Commitment Act (Minn. Stat. ch. 253B). The new category, called "Sexually Dangerous Person" (SDP), applied to an individual who has "engaged in a course of harmful sexual conduct as defined in subdivision 7a, has manifested a sexual, personality, or other mental disorder or dysfunction, and, as a result, is likely to engage in acts of harmful sexual conduct as defined in subdivision 7a." SDP, as defined by this statute, did *not* require that the individual was unable to control his sexual impulses. The SDP category has essentially the same three elements observed elsewhere: (1) a history of sexual crimes (i.e., "harmful sexual misconduct"), (2) a psychological disorder, and (3) the resulting probability of future sexual crimes. Notably, "the legislature retained the old Psychopathic Personality Law (SPP) on the books as a safeguard in case the courts determined that the new law was unconstitutional" (Janus, 1997a, p. 80).

Since September 1, 1994, sex offenders in Minnesota have been committed under both the SPP and SDP statutes. Most civilly committed sex offenders are the result of a screening process initiated by the Department of Corrections. In accordance with Minn. Stat. 244.05, subd. 7, the DOC screens sex offenders and makes commitment referrals 1 year prior to the offender's release date. The number of offenders referred for possible commitment are roughly 10% of the total number released in a given year.

In the 1998 Omnibus Crime Bill passed by the Minnesota Legislature, Section 15 directed the Commissioner of DOC and the Commissioner of Human Services to reexamine the management of sex offenders under SPP and SDP and make recommendations. On April 29, 1998, the Commissioner of DOC appointed a Civil Commitment Study Group (CCSG), and in January 1999, the CCSG issued its findings and recommendations in the "1998 Report to the Legislature" (Civil Commitment Study Group, 1999). The CCSG Report recommended no changes in the DOC referral process, the petition and trial process, and the treatment program. Sex offenders who meet the criteria for civil commitment are sent to the Sexual Psychopathic Treatment Center in Moose Lake or the Minnesota Security Hospital in St. Peter. The Minnesota Supreme Court upheld the constitutionality of the SPP statute in 1994 [*In re Blodgett* 115 S.Ct. 146 (1994)]. The Minnesota Supreme Court also upheld the constitutionality of the SDP statute in December 1996 [*In re Linehan*, 557 N.W.2d 171, 189 (Minn. 1996)].

California

California also enacted its first sexual psychopath law in 1939. Although the law survived, it was the subject of considerable criticism (e.g., Hacker & Frym, 1955). In 1963, the California legislature replaced "sexual psychopath" with "mentally disordered sex offender" (MDSO) (Cal. Welf. & Inst. Code S6300). Mentally Disordered Sex Offenders were committed to state hospitals, primarily Atascadero State Hospital. The law remained the target of persistent criticism, however, with concerns focusing on equal protection and due process issues as well as the quality of treatment services being offerred (Tanenbaum, 1973). In 1976, the California Supreme Court ruled that MDSO "patients" could not be held in state hospitals for any longer than they would have been held in prison for the governing offense. In 1981, California Senate Bill 278 repealed all legislation authorizing the direct commitment of sex offenders to state hospitals, and added Sections 1364 and 1365 to the state Penal Code. S1364 provided for the voluntary transfer of certain sex offenders to the DMH for treatment during the last 2 years of their prison sentence. S1364 further stipulated that this treatment program would be limited to 50 men. S1365 required that "the program described in S1364 shall be established according to a valid experimental design in order that the most effective, newest, and promising methods of treatment of sex offenders may be rigorously tested." The 1981 legislation contained no references to psychopathy, psychopathic personality, MDSO, or any other purportedly clinical nosologic entity, stating that those eligible for treatment are "persons convicted of sex offenses against a person under the age of 14 years or of a sex offense accomplished against the victim's will by means of force, violence, duress, menace, or fear of immediate and unlawful bodily injury to the victim" (California General Laws, C5.5, S1364).

The treatment program provided for in S1364 was implemented in 1985. The Sex Offender Treatment and Evaluation Project (SOTEP), established and directed by Dr. Janice Marques, represented, to this day, the only experimental treatment and evaluation program for sex offenders in the United States. A controlled, longitudinal study, SOTEP included three groups: (1) treated offenders, (2) a group of volunteer controls, and (3) a group of matched, nonvolunteer controls. The volunteers were matched and randomly assigned to the treatment or control groups. The treated offenders spent 2 years at Atascadero, and the controls remained in prison without treatment. The treated offenders received intensive, highly structured therapy designed specifically to reduce the likelihood of relapse among sex offenders. The treated offenders were followed for 1 year after discharge and received treatment as a condition of parole. The controls were seen by their parole officers as a condition of parole. SOTEP included a follow-up phase in which consenting subjects were assessed for 5 years after discharge. The follow-up phase included a quarterly review of the criminal records of all discharged subjects for a period of 5–14 years after release. A detailed explication of the cognitive–behavioral treatment model used by SOTEP and ongoing findings are provided in many reports by Marques and her colleagues (e.g., Marques, 1988; Marques, Day, Nelson, & Miner, 1989; Marques et al., 1993, 1994).

Although SOTEP as a study is no longer in operation, the lessons learned from SOTEP have contributed significantly to California's current Sex Offender Commitment Program (SOCP). SOCP is the outcome of California's SVP civil commitment law. The SVP civil commitment process was established through Chapters 762 and 763, Statutes of 1995 (Assembly Bill 888) and Senate Bill 1143, effective January 1, 1996. These statutes created a new civil commitment for SVPs, defined as individuals previously convicted of specified sex offenses against two or more victims and determined to have a mental disorder that makes it likely that they will engage in further acts of sexual violence after their return to the community. This new law was implemented by the Department of Mental Health as SOCP.

Massachusetts

The Massachusetts legislature enacted its first sexual psychopath statute in the late 1940s. Almost the entire law was taken verbatim from the 1939 Minnesota Sexual Psychopath Law (McGarry & Cotton, 1969). Because of the "awkward and cumbersome provisions of the statute" (McGarry & Cotton, 1969), only one person was committed under the law through 1954. The legislature completely revised Chapter 123A in 1954 in an effort to address numerous problems with the existing law. The term *sexual psychopath* was replaced with *sex offender*, and a treatment center was established within the DMH.

These changes were not to become operative until the Commissioner of DMH established that the treatment center provided for in section 2 of Chapter 123A was adequately staffed. In the fall of 1954 DMH began to provide treatment for a small group of offenders housed in a segregated at Concord Reformatory (now a medium-security state prison).

DMH continued to proceed cautiously until the crisis of 1957. A sex offender was released from prison after serving part of his 10-year-sentence for the near-fatal stabbing of a 12-year-old boy who had resisted his sexual advances. Only a few weeks after his release, he brutally murdered two brothers, aged 10 and 12, and left their burned bodies in a public park. Less than 2 months after his release, he was arrested for the sadistic murders of the boys. He was never tried for these crimes. He was sent directly to Bridgewater State Hospital, where he was found to be mentally ill and incompetent to stand trial. It is ironic perhaps that the man who was principally responsible for the current sex offender statute in Massachusetts was never committed under it.

The murders prompted emergency legislation in September 1957 that further modified the law, providing for the establishment of a treatment center within a correctional facility, indeterminate commitments, and mandatory transfers of inmates who were determined to be "sex offenders" to the treatment center. The law was once again revised in 1958 (Mass. Acts and Resolves, Acts of 1958, ch. 646). The statute as revised in 1958 remained fundamentally unchanged for about 25 years. This version of the law replaced "sex offender" with "sexually dangerous person" and defined that term as

> any person whose misconduct in sexual matters indicates a general lack of power to control his sexual impulses, as evidenced by repetitive or compulsive behavior and either violence, or aggression by an adult against a victim under the age of sixteen years, and who as a result is likely to attack or otherwise inflict injury on the objects of his uncontrolled or uncontrollable desires. (Mass. Gen. Laws, ch. 123A, S1)

In 1959, acting in response to *Commonwealth v. Page* (339 Mass. 313, 159 N.E. 2d 82), the Supreme Judicial Court ordered that branch treatment centers be eliminated and one independent center (i.e., not housed within an existing prison) be established in Bridgewater. The Treatment Center was located in an antiquated building at the Bridgewater prison complex until moving to a new facility in April 1986. Under the then current statute, those men who were deemed to be "sexually dangerous persons" could be civilly committed for an indeterminate period of 1 day to life. Ross and Hochberg (1978) reviewed the innumerable constitutional challenges to the commitment and release provisions of Massachusetts' Sexually Dangerous Persons Act, concluding that

> Chapter 123A has been law for two decades. The science of psychiatry has progressed and the rights of due process and equal protection have expanded. But Chapter 123A remains on the books unscathed. The statute has not survived this progress in law and

medicine because it is intrinsically sound. Nor has it survived because judges, legislators, or patients are satisfied with it. The reason it has survived is neglect. Up to now, the
statute has caused only limited reaction from the legal community of Massachusetts. It
is our conviction that prompt, thorough and meaningful action must be taken to bring the
Sexually Dangerous Person Act up to the minimum standards of fairness and justice
required by the Constitution. (p. 307).

A task force was organized in 1984 to examine the operation of the sex offender
statute. Meeting over a 2-year period, the Task Force's recommendations were incorporated
into Chapter 752 of the Acts of 1985. This new law, which went into effect in April 1986,
eliminated probation as a release option, eliminated a provision that prevented the public
from attending hearings, retained the criminal sentence to be served concurrently with the
civil commitment, and added psychologists, in addition to psychiatrists, as "qualified
examiners" for the purpose of evaluating defendants and testifying at hearings.

Chapter 1 of the legislative Acts of 1988 provided for the establishment of a special
advisory panel. The impetus for this panel was highly publicized problems, including the
death of five inmates, at Bridgewater State Hospital. The Governor's Special Advisory
Panel on Forensic Mental Health focused on three specialized treatment facilities, the State
Hospital, the Treatment Center for Sex Offenders, and the Addiction Center. Recommendations, submitted to the Governor in September 1989, included (1) "Stop the practice of
committing new 'sexually dangerous persons' to the Treatment Center, and to phase out the
statute over the next five years," (2) "develop a pilot voluntary treatment program for sex
offenders in the Department of Correction," (3) "Establish a transitional treatment program for civilly committed sex offenders," (4) "Expand treatment services in county and
state correctional facilities," and (5) "Implement new stricter sentencing guidelines for
repeat sex offenders to assure public safety" (see Governor's Special Advisory Panel,
Executive Summary, September 1989). Effective September 1, 1990, a legislative act
repealed all sections of Chapter 123A *except* for 1, 2, 8, and 9. The most important impact of
this change in Chapter 123A was to halt all further commitments to the Treatment Center.
The last inmate (#600) was committed in August 1990. The remaining sections concern
definitions (e.g., "sexually dangerous person") (S1), the authority of DMH to run the
facility (S2), the functioning of the institutional review board that makes determinations
about sexual dangerousness (S8), and the procedure for periodic review of sexual dangerousness and discharge from the facility (S9).

In response to this legislative enactment, Judge Mazzone of the U.S. District Court
appointed a Special Master on September 2, 1992, "to review and report to the Court on
existing and pending legislation, pending cases filed by residents and the operation of the
Treatment Center" (October 31, 1996, Memorandum and Order of Mazzone, D. J., *King v.
Greenblatt*, C.A. No. 72-788-ADM and *Williams v. Lesiak*, C.A. No. 72-571-ADM, p. 9).
The Special Master filed six reports on September 16, 1993. In 1994, the Massachusetts
State Legislature enacted Statute 1993, Chapter 489, which amended Chapter 123A and
placed control of the Treatment Center solely with the DOC. Immediately thereafter, the
Commonwealth of Massachusetts sought to modify the existing consent decrees. Although
the plaintiffs vigorously opposed modification, Judge Mazzone eventually, on June 29,
1995, allowed the motions to modify. Judge Mazzone's decision was based, in good
measure, on a lengthy, 136-page Management Plan submitted by the DOC. The last section
of the Management Plan proposed the integration of the civilly committed sex offenders at

the Treatment Center with the Prison Program for Sex Offenders. In the above-referenced Memorandum, dated October 31, 1996, Judge Mazzone granted the Commonwealth's motion to introduce a modular unit for 300 state inmates with sexual offenses at the Treatment Center (October 31, 1996, Memorandum and Order of Mazzone, D. J., *King v. Greenblatt*, C.A. No. 72-788-ADM and *Williams v. Lesiak*, C.A. No. 72-571-ADM). In a Memorandum and Order, dated June 21, 1999, Judge Mazzone terminated the consent decrees. The Order terminated consent decrees that were instituted over 25 years ago to govern operations at the Treatment Center.

In 1992, Justice Resource Institute, a private vendor, was contracted by the DMH to provide treatment services. With the departure of all DMH clinicians in 1994, Justice Resource Institute assumed full responsibility for all rehabilitation programs (clinical, educational, vocational) at the Treatment Center. When control of the Treatment Center shifted to the DOC in 1994, the Justice Resource Institute contract was transferred from DMH to DOC. At the present time, under the leadership of Dr. Barbara Schwartz, treatment services are provided to approximately 180 civilly committed sex offenders and 550 state inmates (sex offenders with determinate sentences). Although the Massachusetts Legislature has considered bills that would reintroduce indeterminate commitments for sex offenders, to date no such laws have been passed. Thus, at the present time Chapter 123A remains in effect only for the 180 civilly committed sex offenders that remain at the Treatment Center. As noted, no one has been committed under Chapter 123A since 1990, and the remaining population decreases over time by death and occasional releases via section 9 (finding by the judge that someone is no longer "sexually dangerous").

Effective September 10, 1999, Massachusetts passed legislation that once again revised Chapter 123A, reintroducing civil commitment along the lines of other sexual predator statutes. The Massachusetts statute is actually an omnibus bill with three distinct sections, covering civil commitment, the sex offender registry, and community-based lifetime parole.

New Jersey

New Jersey adopted its first law stipulating the management of convicted sex offenders in April 1949 [N.J.P.L. (1949) c.20, sec. 1]. The law included all those convicted of

> rapes, sodomy, incest, lewdness, indecent exposure, uttering or exposing obscene literature or pictures, indecent communication to females of any nature whatsoever, carnal abuse, or any attempt to commit any of the aforementioned offenses. [N.J.P.L. (1949), c.20, sec. 1]

The law attempted to distinguish between

> those offenders in whom the deviant act was the means utilized in a neurotic attempt at resolution of an intrapsychic conflict from those where the act was situational or just another expression of an anti-social personality pattern rather than compulsive in nature. (Vuocolo, 1969, pp. 36–37)

The "model" sexual psychopath law proposed but not adopted at that time, would have imposed a civil, indeterminate period of confinement. This model law was deemed potentially unconstitutional. Rather than enacting such a law, the state legislature approved a resolution appointing a commission to

make a thorough examination of the existing laws of this state and the practices
thereunder to determine whether they are adequate to cope with the problem of apprehending the habitual sex offender and thereafter providing either preventative treatment
or appropriate institutional confinement of a corrective therapeutic character. (N.J.S.J.R.
No.7, March 10, 1949)

Under the law that was adopted, convicted sex offenders were required to be examined
by two or more psychiatrists appointed by the judge. If the consensus of psychiatric opinion
was that the offender suffered from "any form of abnormal mental illness" [N.J.P.L.
(1949), c.20, sec. 5], the judge committed the offender to an institution for a term not to
exceed the maximum sentence that could be imposed for the crime.

The commission that was established in 1949 submitted its report in February 1950,
and, based principally on its recommendations, a new sex offender statute was adopted on
June 8, 1950. Major changes in the 1950 statute included (1) replacing the obviously vague
"suffering from any form of abnormal mental illness" with a finding that the offender's
conduct was characterized by a pattern of repetitive–compulsive behavior *and* either
violence, or an age disparity in which the victim is under the age of 15 and the offender is an
adult, (2) an alternative to incarceration in which the judge could place the offender on
probation with outpatient treatment, (3) the appointment of the Special Classification
Review Board, which would examine those offenders who were being considered for
parole, and (4) the provision of voluntary admission to the Diagnostic Center for those
individuals who deemed themselves to be potentially sexually dangerous. Since the 1950
statute eliminated what the Commission considered to be petty or nuisance sexual offenses,
keeping only rape, sodomy, carnal abuse, and impairing the morals of a minor, a series of
amendments to the statute reintroduced crimes not originally included. The first amendment in April 1951 added open lewdness and indecent exposure, and a subsequent amendment in July 1954 added assault with intent to commit rape, carnal abuse, or sodomy. An
amendment in January 1959 dropped the word *adult*, since the statute appeared to be
applicable only to those offenders who were 21 years old or older.

Over the years there have been many challenges to the statute, including the transfer of
offenders from hospital settings to prison facilities, resulting in a clarification of the
distinction between a "sentence" and a "commitment to an institution for treatment under
the sex offender act" (see Vuocolo, 1969, for a detailed discussion of the evolution of the
statute through the mid-1960s). Vuocolo (1969) concluded that the most noteworthy features of New Jersey's sex offender law are the establishment of a separate diagnostic
facility for the examination of sex offenders and the establishment of the Special Classification Review Board.

New Jersey's current Sexually Violent Predator Act was enacted August 12, 1998, and
became effective August 12, 1999 [P.L. 1998, c.71 (*N.J.S.A.* 30:4-27.24 *et. seq.*)]. A
Sexually Violent Predator is, according to this statute

a person who has been convicted, adjudicated delinquent or found not guilty by reason
of insanity for commission of a sexually violent offense, or has been charged with a
sexually violent offense but found to be incompetent to stand trial, and suffers from a
mental abnormality or personality disorder that makes the person likely to engage in acts
of sexual violence if not confined in a secure facility for control, care and treatment.
(P.L. 1998, c.71, sec. 3b)

According to this statute, mental abnormality "means a mental condition that affects a person's emotional, cognitive or volitional capacity in a manner that predisposes that person to commit acts of sexual violence" (P.L. 1998, c.71, sec. 3). Under this Act, those classified as sexually violent predators may be committed to a secure facility, operated by the DOC, for custody, care, and treatment. The Division of Mental Health Services (Department of Human Services) provides or arranges for the provision of treatment. Such individuals, age 18 or older, classified as sexually violent predators are civilly committed, for an indeterminate period, to the Adult Diagnostic and Treatment Center.

Wisconsin

The first sexual psychopath law in Wisconsin was enacted in 1947 [Wisc. Stat. sec. 51.37 (1947)]. "Sexual psychopath" was defined in sec. 51.37(1) as

> any person suffering from such conditions of emotional instability or impulsiveness of behavior, or lack of customary standards of good judgment, or failure to appreciate the consequences of his acts, or a combination of any such conditions, as to render the person irresponsible for his conduct with respect to sexual matters and thereby dangerous to himself and to other persons.

The law was deemed to be so clearly unconstitutional that a Public Welfare Board Citizens' Committee was appointed to develop a more reasonable statute and to recommend a plan for a treatment program that would be utilized under the revised law. Recommendations in the Committee's 1951 Report were incorporated into the new Wisconsin Sex Crimes Law [Wisc. Laws ch. 542 (1951)], passed on July 27, 1951. The new Sex Crimes Law apparently was modeled on the New Jersey statute, which had been enacted the year before. The Wisconsin Supreme Court upheld indeterminate commitment in *State ex rel. Volden v. Haas* [264 Wisc. 2d 127, 58 N.W.2d 577 (1951)].

Halleck and Pacht (1960) noted that

> This law specifically recognized the psychological nature of many sex offenses. It established the legal and administrative machinery to both identify and provide specialized treatment for the deviated sex offender. Provisions were also included to protect society from such offenders until such time as they could be safely released. (p. 17)

The new law provided trial judges with the option of sentencing sex offenders to prison or committing them to a forensic hospital for 60-day observation. Sex offenders who were evaluated returned to court with a finding that they were, or were not, "sexually deviated" (a condition that the law did not define). Sex deviates were "essentially inadequate individuals who are impulse-ridden, with poor controls, who verbalize a lack of responsibility for their behavior and express a desire for someone to provide direction for them" (Pacht & Cowden, 1974, p. 13). In practice, a finding of deviated meant that the offender needed treatment *and* could benefit from treatment. Those who remained dangerous, however, could remain in "maximum custody for life" (Pacht, Halleck, & Ehrmann, 1962). Although this law was subsequently revised, setting the maximum time of commitment at the maximum sentence possible for the crime that the offender had been convicted of (Miller, 1988), the burden even under the original Act was not nearly as onerous as the current predator laws. The process by which offenders could be confined beyond their maximum sentence was a request for a 5-year extension from the committing court. During a period of 11 years, from July 1951 to June 1962, 2125 sex offenders were examined under the Act and 52% were found to be in need of specialized treatment and committed (Wisconsin State Department of Public Welfare, 1965). Of the 1105 offenders who were committed, 69 offenders had their commitments extended once and 2 offenders had their commitments extended twice (Wisconsin State Department of Public Welfare, 1965).

The Sex Crimes Act remained in effect for 29 years until it was repealed by the legislature on July 1, 1980. The repeal bill provided for the phasing out of the Sex Crimes Act, so that the only offenders who continued to be confined under the Act were those sentenced prior to the effective date of the repeal bill (Ransley, 1980). Ransley (1980) noted that

> The Wisconsin law was originally hailed as a piece of progressive legislation. It sought both to protect the public and to provide treatment instead of punishment for disturbed individuals who committed sex crimes. In contrast to some other states, Wisconsin gave increasing attention to the protection of the constitutional rights of persons adjudged to be sex deviates. The Act was one of the most widely used sex deviate statutes in the nation; the question that must be asked when considering its repeal is what went wrong. (pp. 941–942).

Certainly in what must be regarded as a prescient observation, Ransley (1980) concluded that

> By the time of its repeal, the Wisconsin Sex Crimes Act was obviously encountering serious legal and administrative problems. Many difficulties stemmed from the attempt to apply the treatment considerations of mental health law to a post-conviction program for sex criminals. The recent trend in mental health law has been to give patients as many rights as is feasible, to ensure that they are examined regularly, and to release them when there is no treatment-based need to keep them institutionalized. The focus in criminal law, meanwhile, seems to have shifted away from considerations of rehabilitation and predictive prevention toward determinate sentencing for purposes of punishing offenders and deterring crimes by others. As the gap between the two fields widened, it became increasingly awkward for the Sex Crimes Act to straddle that gap. The problem of protecting inmate rights under a law that provided for confinement up to and in excess of the maximum term was a subject of frequent litigation. Repeal of the Sex Crimes Act was an obvious way to escape these difficulties. (p. 973).

Wisconsin enacted its predator law in 1994 (Wisc. Laws ch. 980). A "sexually violent person," as defined by this law, is an individual who is "dangerous because of a mental disorder that makes it substantially probable that the person will engage in acts of sexual violence." The law defines "mental disorder" as "a congenital or acquired condition affecting the emotional or volitional capacity that predisposes the person to engage in acts of sexual violence." The constitutionality of this law was upheld by the Wisconsin Supreme Court in December 1995 [*State v. Oldakowski*, No. 94-2357 (S.Ct. Dec. 8, 1995)].

Washington

Washington's sexual psychopath statute was enacted by the State Legislature in 1951 (R.C.W. 71.06.010-140). The statute provided for a 90-day evaluation at a state hospital and possible confinement and treatment until the individual was deemed "safe to be at large." The law was rarely used, however, until 1966, when the State's Department of Institutions established a specialized treatment program for sex offenders at Western State Hospital in Fort Steilacoom. By 1971, this acclaimed program had received the Significant Achievement Award from the American Psychiatric Association (Guided Self-Help, 1973–1974). Thus, for approximately 30 years Washington's law authorized the indefinite commitment of "sexual psychopaths" to state hospitals, the two principal facilities being Western and Eastern State Hospitals.

In 1983 the Sentencing Guidelines Commission was directed by the legislature to reexamine sentencing procedures for sex offenders and to make recommendations. In July 1984 the legislature passed the Sentencing Reform Act, which mandated the following changes: (1) the repeal of the sexual psychopathy law, (2) repetitive sexual offenders and sexual offenders who use weapons and are violent will *not* be eligible for treatment and must be incarcerated, and (3) other sexual offenders may be sentenced under special provisions in the Sentencing Reform Act that provide for treatment in the community or at state hospitals. To be eligible for treatment, the court must determine that both society and the offender could benefit from the offender receiving treatment. During 1985 and 1986 a number of sex offenders escaped from state hospital grounds and committed new offenses. These incidents prompted a study by the Legislative Budget Committee. According to this 1986 study, those who successfully completed treatment programs were as likely to reoffend as those who served prison sentences and were released without treatment. As a result of this study, the legislature eliminated hospital-based treatment for sex offenders who committed their crimes after 1987. The legislature provided, however, for voluntary, prison-based treatment programs for sex offenders with sentences between 1 and 6 years.

In May 1989 a young Tacoma boy was the victim of a brutal sexual assault. One month later, on June 15, the legislature created the Governor's Task Force on Community Protection, with a mandate that it report its findings by December 1, 1989. Tragically, during the months that the Task Force was conducting its work, a Vancouver man sexually assaulted and murdered three boys, further reinforcing the gravity of the problem.

The recommendations of the Task Force were incorporated into the Community Protection Act, adopted by the legislature in 1990 (WA Laws of 1990, ch.3). The Community Protection Act is a comprehensive law that touches on a wide variety of matters, including community notification, special provisions for juvenile offenders, registration of sex offenders, crime victims' compensation, criminal sentencing reforms, civil commitment of offenders, background checks for employees, and special provisions for incest offenders. For present purposes, the most important component of this law involves the adoption of a civil commitment for "sexually violent predators." A sexually violent predator was defined as "a person who has been convicted of or charged with a crime of sexual violence and who suffers from a mental abnormality or personality disorder which makes the person likely to engage in predatory acts of sexual violence" (Governor's Task Force on Community Protection, Final Report, p. II-21). Predatory was defined as "acts directed towards strangers or towards individuals with whom a relationship has been established or promoted for the primary purpose of victimization" (Final Report, p. II-21). During the period of civil commitment the offender will receive treatment, and will be afforded the opportunity to petition the court for release.

In brief, the law provides for: (1) prison-based treatment services for adult offenders with sentences longer than 6 years, and an expansion of the program to include 200 additional beds, (2) community-based treatment services for adult offenders *after* a consideration of the victim's interests, (3) treatment for juvenile sex offenders in residential and outpatient settings, (4) the registration of juveniles convicted of any sex offense, and the establishment of a central registry of sex offenders, (5) polygraph and plethysmograph assessments of sex offenders who are under supervision in the community, (6) testing and certification of all treatment providers who work with sex offenders.

The history of rape legislation in the State of Washington has been the subject of considerable scholarly discourse (e.g., Boerner, 1992; Fujimoto, 1992; Lieb et al., 1998; and the comprehensive report, *Sex Offenses in Washington State: 1998 Update* [Washington State Institute for Public Policy, 1998]).

RECENT FEDERAL LAWS CONCERNING SEXUAL OFFENDERS

The Wetterling Act and Megan's Law

In 1994, the U.S. Congress passed the Jacob Wetterling Crimes Against Children and Sexually Violent Offender Registration Act (42 U.S.C. 14071). Eleven-year-old Jacob Wetterling was abducted in October 1989 near his home in St. Joseph, Minnesota. He is still missing. The Wetterling Act required states to establish registries for sexual offenders and to develop rigorous registration requirements for those sexual offenders deemed to be very dangerous (i.e., "sexually violent predators"). The Act further required all sex offenders to report their addresses every year for 10 years, and for sexually violent predators to report their addresses every 3 months for life. Importantly, states that failed to comply with the provisions of the Act by September 1997 were subject to a mandatory 10% reduction in federal block grant funds for criminal justice purposes under the Byrne Memorial State and Local Law Enforcement Assistance Funding Program.

The Wetterling Act permitted states discretion in deciding whether to release registration information to the public and what information to release. The Wetterling Act was amended by Congress in May 1996 (P.L. No. 104-145, 110 St. 1345). The resulting law, known as Megan's Law, clearly mandated that the designated agency for each state "shall release relevant information that is necessary to protect the public concerning a specific person required to register." Compliance requirements for Megan's Law are the same as for the Wetterling Act. By 1996, all 50 states registered sexual offenders, and approximately 185,000 sex offenders were registered under the respective laws (Matson & Lieb, 1996). As Lieb et al. (1998) pointed out, the principle of community notification has strong public support. Indeed, Lieb et al. (1998) even observed that "Megan's Law" has been included in the New Words section of the 1996 *Random House Webster's College Dictionary*, defined as "any of various laws aimed at people convicted of sex-related crimes, requiring community notification of the release of offenders, establishment of a registry of offenders, etc."

Not surprisingly, the public notification and registration laws have already generated substantial litigation (see Walsh & Flaherty, 1999b,c). The basic premise of these challenges is that public notification constitutes punishment and thus violates the constitutional principles of ex post facto, double jeopardy, cruel and unusual punishment, and bill of attainder (Walsh & Flaherty, 1999b). Although most challenges to these public notification laws have been brought on punishment-related grounds, non-punishment-related challenges have included equal protection, search and seizure, procedural due process, substantive due process, and the Fifth and Sixth Amendments (Walsh & Flaherty, 1999b). Despite the numerous challenges to the community notification (and registration) laws, the legal picture is far from clear, and it would be premature to make any pronouncements regarding the viability of these statutes. As noted, many of these challenges hinge on the issue of punishment, and the jurisprudence of punishment is far from resolved. Among non-punishment-related challenges, some of the most difficult cases have involved due process, particularly when offenders are subject to risk levels or tier levels. Since "enhanced" registration and notification provisions clearly impact the offender, determinations of risk or tier level are highly critical, both to the offender and to the community. Walsh and Flaherty (1999c) stated that "it is expected that this area of law, risk level determination, will continue to generate turmoil in the state and federal courts" (p. 36-6).

The most recent information on sex offender registration may be found in the proceedings of a Bureau of Justice Statistics/SEARCH conference (National Conference on Sex Offender Registries, May 1998) and the sourcebook published by the Civic Research Institute (Walsh & Cohen, 1998).

The Lychner Act

In 1996, Congress also passed the Pam Lychner Sexual Offender Tracking and Identification Act (42 U.S.C. 14072). Pam Lychner was a Houston real estate agent who arrived at a vacant home to show it to a prospective buyer. Lychner was brutally assaulted. Her life was saved when her husband arrived at the house. After the assault, Lychner formed Justice for All, a Texas-based victims' rights advocacy group. The bill was named to honor Lychner and recognize her activism on behalf of victims after she was killed in the crash of TWA flight 800 in July 1996. The Lychner Act directs the FBI to establish a national database of sexual offenders to assist investigators in tracking sex offenders who cross state lines, and to assist states or communities within states that are unable to maintain "minimally sufficient" registration and notification programs. The compliance deadline for the Lychner Act was October 1999.

Center for Sex Offender Management

Although it did not come about as the direct result of federal legislation, the establishment of the Center for Sex Offender Management (CSOM) is undoubtedly the most significant achievement of the federal government in addressing the problem of sexual violence. In November 1996, the Office of Justice Programs (Department of Justice) convened the National Summit: Promoting Public Safety Through the Effective Management of Sex Offenders in the Community. A highly diverse, multidisciplinary group of 180 individuals representing all facets of the spectrum (judges, defense attorneys, prosecutors, probation and parole officers, researchers, clinicians, and victim rights advocates) gathered to make recommendations that would lead to more effective management strategies for sex offenders. One of the recommendations was the creation of a center at the highest level of government that would be not only an informed national resource but also a support system for pilot and experimental programs at the state level. CSOM was formally established in June 1997 as a joint effort by the Office of Justice Programs, the National Institute of

Corrections, and the State Justice Institute. CSOM, which is administered by the Center for Effective Public Policy in Silver Spring, Maryland, has as its primary goal "enhancing public safety by preventing further victimization through improving the management of sex offenders who are in the community."

Community Notification

One of the more recent well-publicized, notorious sex crimes occurred in the Hamilton Township of New Jersey in 1994 when a 7-year-old girl, Megan Kanka, was lured into the home of a released sexual offender, sexually assaulted, and murdered (see Glaberson, 1996). Megan's death, and the revulsion and fear that accompanied it, prompted lawmakers to draft what has come to be called "Megan bills" or "Megan laws." As noted, in 1996 federal legislation required states to adopt community notification laws or risk losing 10% of their federal law enforcement funding under the Byrne Memorial State and Local Law Enforcement Assistance Funding Program. Within approximately 1 year, 47 states had complied. Although these laws differ, in some cases substantially, the core feature of all of these laws is community notification (see Finn, 1997; Lieb et al., 1998; Policy Report from the National Criminal Justice Association, 1997; and Walsh & Cohen, 1998, for comprehensive discussions).

Community notification laws direct the local police or district attorney's office to alert (or "notify") neighbors living in close proximity to a recently released sex offender that a potentially dangerous person is living nearby. Methods used for notification vary considerably, including 800 and 900 telephone lines, placing notices in local newspapers or posting notices in public areas such as schools, playgrounds, and churches, making CD-ROMs available to the public, posting notices on the Internet, and so forth. Needless to say, there are obvious advantages and disadvantages to each of these methods. The 800/900 telephone lines are easily accessible but do not provide photos or "wildcard" search options. The World Wide Web and the Internet provide the widest dissemination, but, by the same token, the dissemination far exceeds the affected community. CD-ROMs provide the greatest control over who accesses the information, but access is relatively inconvenient (individuals must go to a local law enforcement agency).

Community notification is quite separate and distinct from *registration*, the requirement that sex offenders register with the local police department or the district attorney's office. California was the first state to require sex offenders to register; the California registry was established in 1947. As of 1996, all states passed laws requiring sex offenders to register with law enforcement agencies after their release.

Notification of individuals who are *not* connected, in some capacity, with the criminal justice system (e.g., neighbors) raises a variety of problems (e.g., Longo, 1996a,b; Prentky, 1996) that must be addressed. Three primary problems are the following:

First, the presumptive purpose of notifying neighbors is for protection (i.e., so parents can keep their children away from potentially dangerous people). Although the immediate neighbors will be able to warn their children to stay away from an offender, there is nothing to prevent the offender from going to the adjacent community, or getting into his car and driving to an even more distant community.

In other words, we may accomplish nothing more than changing the neighborhood in which the offender looks for victims. There should be nothing surprising about this conclusion. For those with a rudimentary appreciation of the forces that motivate repetitive sex offenders, it is all too obvious that notifying the neighbors will serve no purpose if the man is intent on finding a victim. If we were as concerned about victims in adjacent communities as we are about victims who live in the same neighborhood, we would recognize the profound flaw in the logic of community notification. As Tennyson was wont to observe, this is more than a "little rift within the lute."

Although community notification may be seen as part of community policing laws (Berliner, 1996), the highest-risk offenders will, by and large, not reside in our community. That is, the highly predatory, exploitative, low-social-competence child molester who is most likely to abduct a child and take his victim to a different community or, indeed, a different state, is *not* likely to have a stable, reliable "address" in the community. The offenders who are likely to be *most* impacted by community notification laws are, by and large, the least dangerous (e.g., exclusive incest offenders). These are individuals who are most likely to have a stable job and the financial resources needed to have a home or rent an apartment in the community. These are the individuals who are more likely to be making a good-faith effort to reenter society as law-abiding citizens.

I (R.A.P.) was most struck by this paradox (that notification laws may have their least impact on the most dangerous offenders) when I was asked to evaluate a man in his mid-50s with a long history of molesting young girls. Shortly after his arraignment on the most recent charges, he absconded. The Pennsylvania State Police did an excellent job of tracking him to North Carolina. The North Carolina State Police eventually found an old, abandoned school bus in the woods where he had been staying. When they broke into the school bus, they discovered large quantities of child pornography but no offender. They tracked him down in Tennessee, but by the time authorities in Tennessee discovered his whereabouts, he was gone again. He was eventually picked up in a random tag check in Florida. The outstanding warrant was noted, and he was returned to Philadelphia. Without question, this man posed the greatest possible threat. He could have abducted at will and left a trail of victims that extended 1000 miles from Pennsylvania to Florida. To think of community notification with this man is, to say the least, silly. We would have needed to "notify" the entire Eastern corridor of the United States. The bottom line, of course, is that the *most* dangerous sex offenders rarely are gainfully employed and have stable residences.

Second, we cannot dismiss the possibility that some percentage of offenders will reoffend because of the stress and pressure imposed by a hostile, rejectionist community that has branded the offender as a pariah. Thus, we may be unwittingly increasing the likelihood that some sex offenders reoffend. There is ample clinical evidence to suggest that maintenance in the community is the most difficult part of reducing reoffense risk. Most sex offenders, even those who are released from treatment programs, are returned to the community with few, if any, support systems and expected "to swim." Satisfactory reintegration and adjustment often poses the greatest challenge, even for the most well-intentioned ex-offender.

Lastly, we assume that when the neighbors are informed about the identity of a recently discharged sex offender, they *will act responsibly*. We assume that their actions will remain within the framework of the law, and that they will provide such supervision as is necessary to protect their children from potentially dangerous people. There is no evidence to support that assumption, and, unfortunately, considerable evidence to support the opposite assumption, that people will take "matters" into their own hands and the result will be further violence.

Headlines from many newspapers around the country speak to the reality of what happens when people are frightened and uninformed. The combination of fear and ignorance provides the worst recipe for responsible decision-making. Thus, some degree of vigilantism, resulting in more crime and more injury, is a logical outcome of telling people that an evil menace lurks next door.

Does it make sense that the neighbors would want to know that a potentially dangerous sex offender was living next door? Absolutely! When asked in a radio debate whether I (R.A.P.), as a father of two little boys, would want to know if a child molester was living next door to me, I answered, quite candidly, "Yes, but unfortunately that knowledge would not prevent the man from reoffending, even in my own neighborhood, if he was intent on doing so."

Rather than responding emotionally and reflexively, we should address, head on, what we *can* do that *will* reduce risk and increase the safety of our communities. Since we are not inclined to be the servant only of bad tidings, we would like to offer a number of viable recommendations that will better serve to protect our community from potentially dangerous sex offenders:

First, we can do a reasonably good job of assessing risk. Formal actuarial risk assessment can (and should) be instituted for all sex offenders who, at time of release, are deemed to be potentially dangerous by virtue of violence and/or repetitiveness. Those who are deemed to be at high risk should be mandated for treatment and intensive supervision.

Second, for repeat sex offenders and those who have committed particularly violent acts, lifetime parole should be considered. Lifetime parole is vastly cheaper than imprisonment, much more acceptable than indeterminate sentences on constitutional grounds, and a reasonably good compromise for protecting society. For those offenders who are mandated to be in treatment or who need to be on medication (such as Depo-Provera), lifetime parole increases substantially compliance.

Third, there should be well-coordinated treatment services provided by trained therapists who are experienced in working with sexual offenders. Services should be provided in prison as well as after return to the community. Treatment in the community is particularly critical for adjustment and maintenance. Treatment should be considered one aspect of an overall maintenance program that is coordinated by a parole agent or probation officer.

Fourth, *intensive* parole/probation should be instituted by hiring additional parole agents/probation officers who will carry small caseloads and who are highly trained in assessment, evaluation, and community maintenance of sexual offenders. Caseloads should not exceed about 15 offenders to ensure effective surveillance and supervision. A program of mandatory treatment plus intensive community supervision will be vastly *less* expensive than keeping sex offenders in prison and vastly more effective than mandatory notification alone.

Fifth, the confidential notification of local police departments and the district attorney's office is essential. Registration with the criminal justice system provides one leg of the triad of community maintenance for sex offenders (the other two legs being the parole/ probation officer and clinical service providers).

Registration *alone*, however, is unlikely to deter most sex offenders who have reached a point where they are at high risk to reoffend. Once they have entered their offense cycle, they have started down a slippery slope toward reoffense and the mere awareness that they are registered is unlikely to interrupt the cycle. Given the current state of "wisdom," these recommendations offer the best chance to reduce the risk of sex offenders reoffending.

Between us, we (R.A.P. and A.W.B.) have spent over 50 years working with sex offenders and victims of sex offenders. We know as well as anyone the suffering caused by sex offenders. We have seen children, some as young as 2 years old, who have been subjected to unspeakable abuse. We have seen adults, both men and women, whose lives have been scarred by the trauma of sexual abuse. We say this only to make it absolutely clear that our common mission is the reduction in the number of human beings who are subjected to sexual abuse. There is nothing to be gained by competing for a moral highground in this debate. The singular consideration should be whether community notification will *in fact* reduce victimization rates or whether it will merely provide a dangerous false sense of security. Since there is no compelling evidence to date suggesting that community notification is an effective response to the problem, the only conclusion we are left with is that the latter must be true (i.e., that being notified simply makes us feel better). That is, if danger is pointed out to us, we can try to avoid it and thus increase our sense of control over it. Although we would *not* dismiss the virtue of (possibly) increasing the comfort level of those who live near a sex offender, it is unlikely to decrease the overall victimization rate, and it is a tragically shortsighted response to the problem.

Children and the Internet

With millions of children having access to home computers and online services, the use of the Internet as a vehicle for procuring victims, distributing illegal material, including pornographic images, and promoting criminal sexual abuse of minors, has become a major concern and will, inevitably, be an increasing concern as we enter the twenty-first century. Newspapers are only beginning to run articles with headlines such as "Child Lured by Predator Online" and "Computer Repair Shop Reports Kiddie Porn to Local Authorities." This darker side of the Internet permits criminals to meet, network, transfer illicit material, and commit crimes across state and international borders. Chat rooms are very attractive places for vulnerable children to meet "friendly" adults, making it easy for the online predator to anonymously lure children from the confines of their home. Criminal uses of computer technology range from the online solicitation of children for sexual purposes, the production and transmission of child pornography, and the distribution of pornographic materials. Although the criminal justice system is, by now, well acquainted with the problem, it is still relatively new for researchers and there are few published studies that describe its magnitude (Whitcomb, 1998).

Cyberspace, Children, and the ECU

The online predator uses the chat room to groom his potential victim. An online friendship is initiated with the child, which includes shared hobbies and interests, and possibly leads to the sending of pictures or gifts. The online predator grooms the child, builds trust, and eventually arranges a meeting. This process is, of course, not new. What is new is the vast, limitless playground of the World Wide Web.

The Exploited Child Unit (ECU) was established as a cooperative agreement between the U.S. Department of the Treasury and the National Center for Missing and Exploited Children (NCMEC). The mission of the ECU is to tackle the problem of the online exploitation of children. In principle, the investigative process used by the ECU has not changed. The task, and the challenge, is to adapt investigative, interviewing, and interrogative skills to solve Internet crimes.

Another function of the ECU is to operate the CyberTipline, established in March 1998, to handle online leads from individuals reporting the sexual exploitation of children. Reports include information on child pornography, child prostitution, child sexual tourism, extrafamilial child sexual exploitation, and online enticement of children.

Additional federal responses and resources for protecting children online include the FBI, U.S. Customs Service, and the U.S. Postal Inspection Service. Each of these federal law enforcement agencies works in concert with NCMEC's CyberTipline (Jezycki, 1998). Computer-related sexual exploitation of children most often comes to the attention of law enforcement as a result of a complaint, referrals from commercial service providers, or inadvertently discovered during other investigations. Cases are also proactively identified by undercover agents.

Cyber "Pedophiles"

In an article on "Cyber Pedophiles," FBI Agent Ken Lanning (1998) noted that parents routinely warn their children of the dangers associated with meeting strangers but, thus far, have failed to extend their admonitions to strangers who they "meet" online. The "danger" is perceived to be much less, indeed quite intangible. One is sitting in the relative safety and security of one's home staring at a computer screen. There are no scary people threatening to whisk you away.

Parenthetically, Lanning encourages law enforcement to use the term *preferential* child molesters rather than pedophiles because: (1) it is descriptive, not diagnostic; (2) it is probative, not prejudicial; (3) it can include both offenders who sexually molest children and those who "just" collect child pornography; (4) it can include offenders whose child pornography is only a small portion of their large pornography collection; and (5) it can include those with preferences for adolescent victims and for adolescent pornography.

Evaluate Computer Use

The following information from online computer activity can provide valuable investigative information (Lanning, 1998). This information can often be ascertained from the online service provider and through undercover communication, pretext contacts, informants, record checks, and other investigative techniques (e.g., mail cover, pen register, trash run, surveillance):

- Screen Name
- Screen Profile
- Accuracy of the Profile
- Length of Time Active
- Amount of Time Spent Online
- Number of Transmissions

- Number of Files
- Number of Files Originated
- Number of Files Forwarded
- Number of Files Received
- Number of Recipients
- Site of Communication
- Theme of Messages and Chat
- Theme of Pornography

Use of Computers

Computers provide child molesters with a highly efficient vehicle for meeting their needs: (1) organize their collections, correspondence, and fantasy material, (2) communicate with a much wider, larger, and more diverse audience (victims as well as other offenders), (3) store, transfer, manipulate, and create child pornography, (4) maintain financial records, and (5) elude apprehension more easily than using conventional surface mail and telephone. This is particularly the case with public access computers, making it more difficult to trace the source to the offender. The sex offender using a computer, according to Lanning, is not a new type of criminal. It is simply a matter of pedophiles applying new technology to easily and more efficiently identify and communicate with victims and, ultimately, gratify their sexual needs.

Federal Legislation for Protecting Children Online

In October 1998, Congress passed The Child Online Protection Act, a bill designed to restrict minors' access to adult sexual material on the Internet. The Act would make it illegal for commercial Web site operators to post "material that is harmful to minors" without blocking access to the site through a credit card requirement or other adult verification. The Act defines harmful material as anything of a sexual nature that is obscene or that "the average person, applying contemporary community standards," finds, "with respect to minors," appeals to the "purient interest," and taken as a whole, lacks a serious literary, artistic, political, or scientific value "for minors."

On February 1, 1999, Federal Judge Lowell A. Reed, Jr. blocked the new law on grounds that it was constitutionally flawed. In written remarks, Judge Reed said he reached his decision "despite the court's personal regret that this preliminary injunction will delay once again the careful protection of our children." He acknowledged that many parents would be disappointed by the ruling, but he said "we do the minors of this country harm if First Amendment protections, which they will with age inherit fully, are chipped away in the name of their protection."

RECENT RAPE LAW REFORM

One of the challenges of the criminal justice system has been to close the gap between what legally constitutes sexual assault (under the law) and what constitutes sexual assault in the process of issuing warrants. Rape is, at once, both a classic battery (Loggans, 1985) and an entirely unique offense, unlike any other victim-involved assault. There is reasonable support in the lay community (as well as the criminal justice system) for a simple dichotomy between "real rape" and other sex crimes. Indeed, it has been noted that prosecutors often distinguish between "real crimes" (which occur among strangers) and "junk cases" (which occur between people who know each other) (Silberman, 1978). For no other victim-involved crime is there such strict adherence to a preconceived set of criteria for what constitutes the "real" offense. By tradition, not only must a real rape offense involve penetration, but there must be clear evidence of physical force or threat of violence and no prior sexual contact between the victim and her assailant.

There have been two substantive changes in rape law that address this problem, thereby facilitating prosecution and conviction. In 1977 the legislature of the Commonwealth of Massachusetts passed a Rape Shield Law. This law provides, in part, that "evidence of the reputation of the victim in a rape case shall be excluded from evidence." Such shield laws prevent defense attorneys from shifting the focus from the alleged rape to the sexual history of the victim. As a result, collateral, extraneous "evidence" becomes inadmissible. The second major change in rape law was the institution of "staircasing" legislation. The Massachusetts legislature passed such a statute in 1980. The purpose of staircasing legislation is to circumvent the dictum that "if you didn't meet the criteria for rape, it wasn't rape." Staircasing recognizes the heterogeneity of sexual assaults by graduating offenses from the less serious to the more serious, thus providing increased incentive for juries to convict. Prior to staircasing, the crime of aggravated rape carried (up to) a life sentence. Juries were reluctant to impose a sentence that was punishable by life in prison for what they considered a lesser offense. Staircasing of rape now yields four offense alternatives: indecent sexual assault, assault with intent to commit rape, rape (punishable up to 20 years in prison), and aggravated rape (punishable up to life in prison). The Massachusetts staircasing legislation is a step in the correct direction; however, given the complexity and heterogeneity of sexual assault, the staircase needs additional steps and clarification of representative offense-related behaviors that characterize each step.

Another critical area of rape law reform concerns interspousal immunity from assault liability. In the past, spouses were fundamentally immune from prosecution for physical and sexual assault unless the crime was heinous. There has been a trend to adopt legislation that makes spouses liable—and prosecutable—for all crimes of assault, whether or not the spouses were living together at the time of the alleged assault. Given the estimated frequency of spousal abuse, legislation facilitating the prosecution of all assault-related crimes is imperative.

An area of rape law that has witnessed recent attention is first- and third-party liability in sexual assault (Loggans, 1985). Rape has been successfully prosecuted as an intentional tort, with victims recovering damages against employers and property owners (e.g., landlords, hotel, motel, and theater owners). These cases can be successfully prosecuted when it can be demonstrated that the defendant's action—or inaction—in the face of foreseeable risks may have contributed to an assault. These cases are based, for the most part, on negligence rather than on an intentional tort (i.e., evidence of willful and wanton misconduct). The line between negligence and an intentional tort may be, as Loggans (1985) clearly points out, quite thin. The importance of third-party claims, however, is to bring to public attention, by force of law, the magnitude and gravity of the problem of sexual assault and the responsibility of all citizens to be "noncontributory." It would thus seem useful, for the purpose of clarifying third-party liability, to provide guidelines for "utter indifference" and "conscious disregard" where sexual assault is concerned. For example, a movie theater owner who fails to provide adequate lighting for a dimly lit parking lot *after* a sexual assault would undoubtedly be liable in the event of a subsequent rape. Whether or not he would have been found liable the *first* time is much more uncertain.

Any "model law of rape" *must* include a "well-reasoned principle of non-consent" (Loh, 1981, p. 28). Although nonconsent has been a component of various other crimes (e.g., theft, assault, battery, and trespass) (Estrich, 1987), the crime of rape is unique in its definition of nonconsent, requiring victims "to demonstrate their 'wishes' through physical resistance" (Estrich, 1987, p. 29). Estrich quipped that "the woman who dates a man, or talks to him, is effectively held, absent affirmative evidence (resistance) to the contrary, to assume the risk of unwanted sex in the same way that baseball fans assume the risk of fly balls" (p. 41).

Despite the aforementioned obstacles yet confronting reformers of rape law, Caringella-MacDonald (1988) concluded that "sweeping law reform in sexual assault, marital rape, and domestic violence overlap to reinforce heightened sensitivity and serve an educative, symbolic function" (p. 184). Caringella-MacDonald (1988) noted, however, that "systematic problems" arising from the very reform that was intended to rectify the problems remain. For example, although shield laws restrict evidence on past sexual history in almost all rape reform legislation, marital rape law has become *less* restrictive with respect to the same evidence. The "voluntary social companion" (Finkelhor & Yllo, 1985, p. 149) addendum to the marital rape law is a case in point. With this supplement to the law, "acquaintance rape can ... be seen to be legalized" (Caringella-MacDonald, 1988, p. 185).

A similar discontinuity between California's marital rape law and Michigan's sexual assault law exists. For instance, the California law states that if a wife was raped while unconscious or drugged or if she was mentally handicapped at the time of the offense, it is not rape (Finkelhor & Yllo, 1985, p. 143). Under Michigan law these same factors not only are inclusionary but they define the more serious levels of sexual assault.

Overall, a number of features of rape reform legislation, such as lowering the evidentiary standards, changes in standards for resistance and nonconsent, the adoption of shield laws, changing the legal definition of rape, and (when it has been included) partitioning sexual assault into a series of progressively more serious offenses, have improved victim treatment and cooperation with the criminal justice system and increased the likelihood that cases will be prosecuted (Largen, 1988). Furthermore, there is some evidence that the Michigan model is more effective than most in closing the legal standards gap between sexual assault and other victim-involved crimes (Largen, 1988). Largen (1988) concluded, however, that

> Despite the new statutory appelations applied to rape by many states today, rape remains the only crime in the United States for which the determination of criminality in most states rests on the proven lack of consent of the victim. Regardless of any "reasonableness" standards now applied, rape remains the only crime that victims are expected by law to resist. (pp. 289–290)

Wavering Progress of Rape Law: Two Steps Forward, One Step Back

There has been very little improvement in the past 15 years. Although progress has been made, it can best be described as hesitant. Rape law clearly remains ambivalent about the crime of rape. In no other crime must the victim clearly demonstrate through resistance that she did not want to be victimized. In no other crime is the burden of responsibility for the crime partially shifted to the victim. It would strike all parties as absurd, for instance, if the victim of an armed robbery was interrogated about (1) why she (or he) was walking down a particular street in a particular part of town when accosted, (2) why she (or he) happened to be on the street at the hour that the robbery took place, (3) precisely what she (or he) was wearing at the time that might have given the robber the "wrong idea," (4) precisely what she said that might have encouraged the robber and so on.

If stranger rape could be ambiguous with regard to the mere existence of a crime, it is readily apparent how ambiguous nonstranger sexual coercion is under the law. In an excellent revisionist analysis of rape law, Professor Schulhofer (1998) developed a standard for "sexual autonomy," noting that we are fundamentally unequipped to deal adequately with the full range of the problem of sexual coercion. In speaking of the traditionally "grey area" of sexual coercion, Schulhofer (1998) noted that

> The number of women affected can only be estimated, but it is undoubtedly large—perhaps as many as a million working women per year subjected to the unwelcome advances of their job supervisors, over 200,000 women per year pressured for sex by their teachers in college, thousands or—more likely—tens of thousands of women per year having unwanted sex with their therapists and doctors. (The number of women abused by their lawyers can't be estimated, but it is almost certainly not insignificant.) (p. 278)

Schulhofer is speaking to the failure of rape law to protect what is arguably the most precious of our rights, the right to seek *and refuse* intimacy. Schulhofer's authoritative reflections are worthy of lengthier report:

> Of all our rights and liberties, few are as important as our right to choose freely whether and when we will become sexually intimate with another person. Yet, as far as the law is concerned, this right—the right to sexual autonomy—doesn't exist. Citizens simply do not have a legally recognized claim to protection for their freedom of sexual choice.
>
> The law of rape suffers from well-known practical limitations. But even under the best of circumstances, its coverage is narrow. It prohibits sex with children and with unconscious adults, but in nearly all other situations it protects our sexual freedom *only* against interference by compelling physical force. No other concern that is central to the life of a free person receives such stinting protection.
>
> A well-developed system of criminal law enforcement protects our property, our labor, our right to vote, our privacy, and our confidential information. The criminal law protects these rights against physical violence, of course. But it also does more. It makes these rights meaningful by protecting them *comprehensively*. It punishes interference by nonphysical threats, by coercive "offers," by misuse of authority, by abuse of trust, and by deception. It ensures that we retain these rights until we choose to give them to someone else; we can't simply lose them by default. And the law doesn't say, in the words of those who oppose rape reform, that people facing interference with these rights should just "take responsibility"—that they should scream, fight back physically, or "stop whining" and learn to live with the unpleasant consequences.
>
> We know that we have to accept minor injuries and that life isn't always fair. We know that even for serious threats, self-help is sometimes the most practical remedy. But we also understand that in a civilized community, important interests can't be left to the vagaries of self-help and the rules of the jungle. We understand that vital interests must be nurtured and supported by law.
>
> When interests in sexual autonomy are at stake, our society doesn't see matters this

way. With rare exceptions, protection against physical violence is all the protection we get, as far as the criminal law is concerned. Civil remedies don't extend much farther. For all the fuss about the supposedly stringent character of sexual harrassment laws, their scope remains limited....

In effect, the law permits men to assume that a woman is always willing to have sex, even with a stranger, even with substantial physical force, unless the evidence shows unambiguously that she was *un*willing.

These diverse examples of stinting, inadequate legal protection reflect a common theme—the law's refusal to recognize that sexual autonomy is *important*, an interest deserving protection in its own right. (1998, pp. 274–276)

In reality, the "law's refusal" is *our* refusal, since we are the makers and the custodians of the law. And *our* refusal really translates to male refusal, since it is men who are predominantly responsible for drafting and passing laws. Since sexual autonomy is not a "problem" for most men (i.e., they "have it"), it is not perceived as a problem for women. Schulhofer (1998) remarked that "in countless conversations, acquaintances (mostly but not all men) have told me that unwanted sex, unless compelled by threats of violence, is really not a big deal. 'It just happens, it's over,' they say" (p. 276). It is fair to conclude that rape law will "catch up" with the full gamut of sexual coercion when men acknowledge that women have the right to sexual autonomy.

CHAPTER 7

Forensic Evidence

In this chapter, we focus specifically on the types of evidence, or data, collected by *clinical* forensic examiners (as opposed to medical examiners and police investigators) and problems associated with the admissibility of such data in legal proceedings. Many examiners routinely employ a variety of different paper-and-pencil tests, scales, and questionnaires, and these "psychological tests" are typically *not* challenged in court with regard to admissibility. Many of these tests *should* pose problems, but in reality they do not. As we noted in Chapter 4, many of these tests have never been published; their psychometric properties are unknown; the predictive validity of the tests has never been examined; no sex offender norms are available. Application of the four *Daubert* criteria (testability of the procedure, supportive empirical evidence from peer-reviewed studies, a known error rate, and general acceptance by the scientific community) would most certainly exclude many of these tests. Many other standardized tests (e.g., MMPI and MCMI), although widely used by clinicians, have no validity or very limited validity when used for forensic purposes with sex offenders. A rare study that actually examined whether the Millon Clinical Multiaxial Inventory (MCMI), one of the two most commonly employed standardized instruments for assessing personality disorder, met the *Daubert* standard, found the MCMI to be "markedly deficient with respect to both criterion-related and construct validity" (Rogers, Salekin, & Sewell, 1999, p. 439). Rogers et al. (1999) found that with the exception of Avoidant, Schizotypal, and Borderline personality disorders, "the remaining Axis II disorders have insufficient construct validity for rendering any firm conclusions" (p. 439). If tests with as robust a history of development, validation, and revision as the MCMI and MMPI fall short of the *Daubert* Standard, one can only imagine how the many "home-grown" inventories would fare. Thus, examiners must exercise utmost prudence and caution when using many of these instruments in forensic evaluations, expecting that a *Daubert* test might well render many of the tests inadmissible.

All of the attention with regard to admissibility, however, has focused on much "glitzier" sources of evidence, principally the penile plethysmograph, and increasingly the polygraph and DNA. The reason is fairly obvious. As medical procedures, or medical evidence in the case of DNA, the resulting data can be far more influential and persuasive in the courtroom than a T-score on a psychological test. Thus, there is a far greater need to discredit such evidence or to exclude it entirely.

Forensic Use of PPG and Polygraph Data

Despite concerns about the misuse of the PPG in forensic contexts, the PPG is often incorporated into forensic assessments. It is our recommendation that as long as forensic assessments are being done, there is no prima facie evidence that would preclude the *responsible and appropriate* use of the PPG as an adjunct to such an assessment. The concerns that would ban the PPG from the courtroom are understandable responses to the misuse of the PPG and the misinterpretation or overinterpretation of PPG findings. As with *all* interpretations of data, whether the data are archivally, psychometrically, or physiologically derived, conclusions drawn and recommendations made should never stray beyond the scope of the procedure or the limitations of the data. We are on highly *infirm* ground arguing that the PPG, with decades of empirical research supporting its validity, should be excluded while innumerable psychometric instruments, with no research supporting their validity with sexual offenders, are routinely included. The use of PPG data in the courtroom has, nonetheless, been controversial, not only among clinicians but also among attorneys and judges.

Standards for Admissibility of PPG Data

Because PPG data are so often gathered in sexual offender evaluations, the admissibility of such data is a critical issue. The landmark case that established the criteria for determining whether a scientific procedure or test had acquired sufficient acceptance and credibility within the scientific community to be admissible in court as evidence was *Frye v. United States* [*Frye v. United States*, 293 F. 1013, 1014 (D.C. Cir. 1923)]. As Foster and Huber (1999) noted

> *Frye* was a criminal case. The defendant was accused of murdering a doctor. He had confessed, then recanted. At trial he offered a weak alibi and sought to introduce evidence that he had passed a "systolic blood pressure deception test"—a primitive precursor of the "lie detector" polygraph. The trial court rejected this evidence. In affirming that ruling, the District of Columbia Circuit Court of Appeals articulated the "general acceptance" rule to govern the admission of expert testimony in federal courts. James Alphonso Frye served 18 years in prison. The "*Frye* rule" was applied by federal courts for more than 50 years and is still enforced by many state courts. (p. 225).

The Court of Appeals decision in *Frye v. U.S.* stated that

> Just when a scientific principle crosses the line between the demonstrable stages is difficult to define. Somewhere in this twilight zone the evidential force of the principle must be recognized, and while courts will go a long way in admitting expert testimony deduced from a well-recognized scientific principle or discovery, the thing from which the deduction is made must be sufficiently established to have gained acceptance in the particular field in which it belongs.

For many years, phallometric assessment was subjected to, and often failed, the *Frye* test. We can posit two possible explanations, one legitimate and one not, for the failure of PPG data to meet the *Frye* standard. The legitimate reason, which in reality is probably *not* the real one, concerns the intended use of the PPG data in testimony. The empirical literature is unequivocal in support of the discriminant and the concurrent validity of the PPG. Although some may disagree (e.g., Quinsey, Lalumiere, Rice, & Harris, 1995), we believe that it is reasonable to conclude that the predictive validity of phallometry is less certain. The results of a phallometric assessment should *never* be used to draw conclusions that an offender will, or will not, commit an offense. Phallometric assessment should *never* be used, moreover, to draw conclusions that an offender did, or did not, commit an offense. The PPG informs us about the presence—or possible absence—of deviant sexual arousal. We may properly conclude from the PPG that someone does, or does not, experience sexual arousal to depictions of sexual activity that is deviant and/or aggressive. Phallometry will *not* tell us whether the deviant arousal will result in deviant behavior. Other factors, in conjunction with phallometry, are needed to make more reliable predictions of reoffense risk. Quinsey, Rice, et al. (1995), for instance, found that phallometry in addition to psychopathy and previous criminal history were the best predictors of sexual recidivism. Thus, PPG may have failed to meet the *Frye* standard if the data were being used, out of the context of a comprehensive evaluation, to render forecasts about future dangerousness. In addition to the issue of predictive validity, courts have also been concerned about the lack of standardization of procedures and the lack of standardized norms.

The *less legitimate* and probably more accurate explanation, however, involves the perceived persuasiveness of the evidence. Attorneys have often opposed the admissibility of phallometric data, because data from such a "medical device" may be more persuasive to jurors than other sorts of psychological evidence. If an expert witness holds up a strip chart and points to a trace depicting arousal to a deviant stimulus, the evidence may appear more definitive to a jury than if the witness described the results of several psychological tests.

The General Acceptance Standard changed in 1993 with the case of *Daubert et al. v. Merrill-Dow Pharmaceutical* (U.S. Supreme Court Case #92-102; date of decision: June 28, 1993). The *Daubert* case involved the question of whether an antiemetic drug (Benedictin) caused birth defects and thus had nothing to do with expert witness testimony by social scientists. The *Daubert* case did, however, set forth guidelines for expert testimony. These revised guidelines require that the expert testify that the procedure being employed or the theory underlying the procedure is testable and that there is evidence reported in the literature from peer-reviewed studies supporting the expert's testimony. In addition to testability and peer review, U.S. Supreme Court Justice Blackmun also posited two other considerations: the known or potential error rate, and whether the procedure or theory was generally accepted by the scientific community. Although these four factors were considered to be "nonexclusive" (i.e., none of four would alone be determinative), the first factor (whether the procedure or theory had been properly tested) was considered "a key question." Although the *Daubert* guidelines are not mandated for the state courts, 38 states have adopted the Federal Rules of Evidence on which the *Daubert* decision is based (Goodman-Delahunty, 1997). The *Daubert* decision has clearly changed the judicial standard for qualifying experts and for admitting testimony based on scientific data or principles. The resulting standard is less narrow than the previous *Frye* standard. We can reasonably expect that the *Daubert* case will have an increasing impact on the admissibility of complex scientific evidence, and that the prospects for the admissibility of phallometric data are enhanced by this new standard.

A lengthy discussion and analysis of *Daubert* concluded with the following

> After Daubert, courts bear the responsibility to consider the scientific validity and scientific reliability of factual evidence as a threshold issue. An examination of opinions in which courts have made the effort to evaluate the reliability and relevance of scientific evidence suggests that this responsibility is fully commensurate with judicial capabilities. Daubert did not, however, hand judges a step-by-step guide to applying scientific principles. Similarly, *Daubert* left unanswered the question whether a study's statistical significance level goes to admissibility or to the burden of proof.... Although courts should predicate admissibility on the parties' presentation of the scientific evidence with an associated level of significance, courts should address both the magnitude of the results and the level of statistical significance as burden of proof issues. Only under this interpretation of *Daubert* can courts effectively assimilate the scientific method into, rather than impose the scientific method upon, the legal process. (Confronting the New Challenges of Scientific Evidence, 1995, pp. 1556–1557)

Foster and Huber (1999) commented that

> The comparison of *Frye* and *Daubert* thus ends where it began: With the original, commonlaw standard of *Frye* and with the Federal Rules of Evidence that replaced it in 1975. *Frye* referred to "general acceptance" in the scientific community; the Federal Rules refer, more cryptically, to "scientific knowledge." For practical legal purposes, the two may not be so very different. The law is constructed out of language, and the key words in the Federal Rules are "scientific knowledge...." For judges applying Rule 702, "scientific knowledge" is reliable only if it is the knowledge of a community rather than an individual. This does not seem very different from what an appellate court wrote in *Frye* seven decades before *Daubert*. (pp. 251–252)

STANDARDS FOR ADMISSIBILITY OF POLYGRAPHIC DATA

In at least four respects, polygraphy seems to bear some resemblance to penile plethysmography. Like the PPG, the polygraph is widely used. Honts and Perry (1992) noted, for instance, that

> Every law enforcement agency in the federal government has a staff of polygraph examiners, and approximately 100 new federal examiners are trained each year at the federal government's Department of Defense Polygraph Institute. (p. 357)

Second, despite the widespread practice of polygraphy, standardization of procedures and training of examiners have been seriously wanting. Honts and Perry (1992) commented that

> Polygraph examiners in the United States, as a whole, are poorly trained. Their techniques lack standardization, and polygraph tests are subject to manipulation by unethical examiners. Given this state of affairs, the probative value of the work-product of most of the polygraph professionals should rightly be questioned. (p. 375)

Third, like the PPG, there is a large, credible research literature on detection of deception, which, by and large, has *not* informed and advanced the practice of polygraphy. Fourth, like the PPG, evidence from polygraph testing has generally been excluded from the courts. Honts and Perry (1992) remarked that

> The continued widespread exclusion of polygraph tests appears to lie in a continued distrust of the polygraph based on concerns about logical relevance.... Judicial objections that polygraph evidence will overwhelm juries have found no support in the scientific literature; all the available evidence from jury studies clearly suggests that juries can evaluate and give appropriate weight to polygraph evidence. (p. 375)

In sum, the same standards for admissibility of PPG data apply to the admissibility of polygraph data, and in both cases, for very similar reasons, courts have tended to exclude evidence derived from the PPG or the polygraph.

We may expect, however, that this condition will change, first because of a relaxation in the admissibility standard, and second because of the increasing volume of empirical research that hopefully will impact and advance the state of the art for both techniques. Penile plethysmography and polygraphy clearly have utility in both forensic and clinical domains, and should be treated as potentially important components of an examiner's armamentarium. What appears to be lacking in both cases is an infusion of empiricism into practice (i.e., into the application of PPG and polygraphy in clinical and forensic settings). Variability of procedural application seems to be particularly problematic for the PPG (i.e., the absence of a clear process for training, supervising, and credentialing PPG examiners results in inevitable variability in competence of administration of the PPG and interpretation of PPG findings). It is thus particularly incumbent on the court to scrutinize the relevant background of a witness presenting PPG findings.

Despite these shortcomings, recent rulings have upheld the admissibility of PPG and polygraph evidence. The Sixth Circuit recently upheld a decision of the district court to use periodic polygraph and PPG assessments with sex offenders [*U.S. v. Marvin R. Wilson*, 1998 US App. LEXIS 32005 (6th Cir. 1998)]. In deliberating whether to admit the PPG and polygraph evidence, the Sixth Circuit considered that there was "sufficient indicia of reliability to support its probable accuracy" and noted that "probable accuracy" was equivalent to the "preponderance of evidence" standard set forth in *U.S. v. Silverman* [976 F.2d 1502 (6th Cir. 1992)]. With respect to the above-noted case of *U.S. v. M. R. Wilson*, it was noted that

> In rejecting the defendant's contention that the tests were so inaccurate as to constitute "unreasonable special conditions of release," the court affirmed the lower court's admission of the test results because that court had found the tests to be sufficiently, although not perfectly, reliable and only a "part in the analysis." Since the assessment was based on a wide variety of tests and interviews, these particular tests were allowed to be admitted given that the weight of their results would be balanced by other factors. The court also deemed that their use would be beneficial both for the defendant and for the safety of the public. (Offender Programs Report, 1999, p. 90)

The message from the Sixth Circuit analysis in this case is that the polygraph and the PPG are sufficiently accurate to be admitted as evidence when part of a comprehensive assessment that includes multiple sources of data.

Qualifying as an Expert Polygrapher or PPG Examiner

Federal Rules of Evidence (FRE 702) allows a witness to offer expert testimony in the form of an opinion. The testimony is intended to assist the judge and the jury in understanding the facts of a case. Although the process of qualifying someone as an expert, at least in federal courts, is relatively simple, with considerable discretion granted to the trial judge, the routine documentation of the witness's experience and training often differs according to the nature of the testimony. If an expert will be testifying about "the treatment of sex offenders," little may be expected beyond an assertion that the expert has treated sexual offenders for X number of years. If the expert will be testifying about a PPG exam or a polygraph exam, presumably the expert must demonstrate sufficient expertise to be considered an "expert." Unlike the PPG, where commonly accepted standards of practice, training, and credentialing are virtually nonexistent, polygraphers can document appropriate training and requisite apprenticeships or internships leading to licensure or accreditation (Honts & Perry, 1992).

Although qualifying someone as an expert to present evidence based on a PPG assessment often is much less stringent than qualifying someone to present polygraphic evidence, in both instances a judgment must be made about the relevance and the reliability of the data being presented. It is reasonable to assume that judges will exclude evidence that is deemed not relevant or evidence that has been misapplied to the issues being litigated. Similarly, judges are likely to exlude evidence based on unvalidated procedures or instruments. In the aftermath of the *Daubert* decision, judges are likely to take increasing authority as "gatekeepers" of expert evidence. At the same time, the U.S. Supreme Court recently held that a judge's decision to admit or exclude expert scientific testimony under Daubert is subject to appellate review under the "abuse of discretion" standard [*General Electric Co. v. Joiner*, U.S. Supreme Court No. 96-188 (Dec. 15, 1997)]. It is clear that the parameters of the *Daubert* decision will continue to be tested for years to come.

For experts, however, there should be one immutable standard for scientific evidence presented in a trial court, namely, data-based testimony must rely on evidence that was gleaned from demonstrably valid procedures and instruments, and that is indisputably relevant to the issues being litigated. As experts, we can expect, indeed we should expect, that substandard testimony will be impeached and possibly excluded.

FORENSIC USE OF DNA TYPING

In 1980 Wyman and White first reported the discovery of a hypervariable DNA polymorphism in the human genome, and 5 years later Jeffreys, Wilson, and Thein showed that such hypervariability was widespread in humans (Chakraborty & Kidd, 1991). Forensic scientists realized immediately the import of these discoveries for identifying criminals from biological samples left at crime scenes. DNA evidence was first introduced in court in the United States in a 1988 rape case in Florida (Roberts, 1991). Courts in the United States and England now routinely admit DNA evidence in criminal as well as civil cases. By 1990, over 2000 court cases in 49 states and the District of Columbia admitted evidence from DNA tests (Chakraborty & Kidd, 1991). When DNA typing was first introduced, "it was heralded as a tool of stunning precision, the greatest forensic advance since the advent of fingerprinting itself," (Roberts, 1991, p. 1721).

In a crude sense, DNA types can be thought of as roughly analogous to blood types. One critical difference, of course, is that instead of having four major blood types, there are more than 2000 DNA polymorphisms that have been identified and catalogued (Chakraborty & Kidd, 1991), thereby illustrating the difference in chance findings between blood and DNA typing. Proponents of DNA typing have maintained that the probability of two DNA samples matching by chance alone is virtually nonexistent, citing figures that range from 1:500,000 to 1:738,000,000,000,000 (quadrillion) (Roberts, 1991). In a disarmingly quaint article on DNA typing, Dawkins (1998) noted that

> As a tool for identifying people, DNA is unmatched. A gene is a body's version of a bar code: the DNA in each of my cells [with minor exceptions] is identical to the DNA in all my other cells. It differs from the DNA in every one of your cells—and not in some vague, impressionistic way, either, the way our faces or signatures differ. It differs at a precise number of positions dotted along the billions of DNA base pairs that we both possess. (pp. 20–21).

DNA typing is a powerful tool not only because of its extraordinarily high level of discrimination among individuals but also because of its flexibility (i.e., DNA typing can be done on samples collected from sources that would be entirely unusable for traditional blood typing). Thus, from a criminal investigative standpoint, DNA typing opens up a much wider window of potential evidence that can be secured at a crime scene.

Chakraborty and Kidd (1991) pointed out, however, that approximately 60 to 65% of all criminal cases in which DNA evidence has been examined resulted in one of two negative outcomes: (1) the DNA typing was inconclusive because of insufficient DNA from the sample or because of technical problems with the test, or (2) the DNA profiles of the relevant samples do not match, in which case the evidence may be deemed exculpatory. In 35 to 40% of criminal cases, a match is found. Although the significance of a match, strictly speaking, is a legal and not a scientific question, significance often is defined in terms of chance probability (i.e., what is the probability that the match occurred by chance and that the defendant is not linked to the sample?). Dawkins (1998) observed that "if the entire set of genes in both samples were written down, the probability of a false conviction would be one in billions and billions" (p. 21). This matter ultimately was addressed by the National Academy of Sciences committee, created in 1989 to examine the full gamut of technical and social issues raised by DNA typing. Roberts (1992) reported, in this regard, that "the most extravagant probability estimates will be replaced with numbers in the range of 1 in several hundred thousand or a million" (p. 301). That we should struggle over how "conservative" our estimates should be—1 in a quarter of a million or 1 in a billion—is amusing when we consider that our conventional standard is 5 in 100.

Disagreement over such relatively mundane issues as a standard range for estimating probability of matches is the proverbial tip of the iceberg. The heat of debate is, arguably, in direct proportion to the potential power of the technique as it is applied in the courtroom. Since DNA evidence can have a profound influence on the outcome of a criminal trial, it must, in the adversarial climate of the courtroom, be hotly contested. In opposing the admissibility of DNA evidence, or in seeking to discredit matches, attorneys have generally favored "problems" that are easily lendable to scientific inquiry (e.g., scientists do not agree among themselves on how to calculate whether a match between two samples has occurred; scientists do not agree on reasonable probability estimates for matched DNA profiles, with current estimates based on insufficient population sampling; since laboratory procedures are not rigorously controlled, there is some likelihood that errors may occur; when there is insufficient intact DNA, the preferred, more sensitive, RFLP [restriction fragment length polymorphism] method is substituted with polymerase chain reaction [PCR] which amplifies gene segments, as well as any contaminants, resulting in possible contamination). Thus, although there clearly are technical (i.e., scientific) questions that must be addressed, the more profoundly difficult questions are sociolegal and ethical.

A review of DNA evidence in criminal cases concluded that

> Although some challenges to the admissibility of inculpatory DNA test results have been successful, the inexorable trend of both state court rulings and state legislation favors a general policy of admitting DNA evidence, yet allowing defense attorneys to challenge and undermine confidence in the particular results. (Confronting the New Challenges of Scientific Evidence, 1995, pp. 1557–1558)

The same review goes on to observe that

> Inculpatory DNA evidence presents formidable difficulties for defense attorneys. Claims of "genetic fingerprinting" may exert tremendous persuasive power, even when the reality of the testing procedures falls short of what is advertised. Such appearances may be difficult to overcome merely through cross-examination and verbal rehearsal of the possible hazards and disputable interpretations encountered in the process. (p. 1559)

The review concludes that

> Exonerative DNA testing promises to provide fairly conclusive proof, not mere suggestion of innocence. Thus, although other relevant evidence may be elusive or stale when such scientific evidence is unearthed, this problem is of less concern given the remarkably high degree of certainty provided by exculpatory DNA tests. (pp. 1577–1578)

Moreover, from a practical standpoint, DNA evidence is highly complex and inherently probabilistic, which may place it out of the realm of comprehension for some jurors. Now that DNA evidence is finding its way into the courtroom with increasing frequency, the question of how jurors interpret, process, and weigh such information is being scrutinized (e.g., Schklar & Diamond, 1999). Twenty-five years ago concern was expressed that jurors may accept some scientific evidence with a sense of "mystic infallibility" [*United States v. Addison*, 498 F.2d 741 (1974)]. Thus, the issue of how scientifically unsophisticated jurors utilize and weigh complex, technical evidence may *not* be new at all, only the nature and perhaps the degree of complexity of the information.

CODIS

The FBI's Combined DNA Index System (CODIS) was initiated in 1986, at least a decade before DNA profiling began to receive widespread attention in the media. CODIS has two principle objectives: (1) assist law enforcement in the identification of suspects of violent crimes and (2) increase the effectiveness and efficiency of forensic laboratories by providing advanced software to calculate genotype frequency. CODIS has created a national repository of DNA information, enabling investigators throughout the country to share findings and to cross-reference information with other investigators. Cross-referencing makes it possible to uncover DNA matches among previously unrelated cases. Although CODIS software is designed to work with RFLP and the PCR, advances in DNA analysis will undoubtedly result in updates of the software.

CODIS is a database that operates on DOS-compatible computers. At the present time CODIS organizes DNA profiles into three indices or categories according to the origin of the sample: (1) Convicted Offender Index (used to generate investigative leads in criminal investigations and missing person investigations), (2) Forensic Index (contains DNA records from cases for which there are no suspects), and (3) Population File (contains DNA types and allele frequency data from anonymous individuals representing major population groups in the United States, used to estimate frequencies of DNA profiles) (Loftus, 1999). In the future, CODIS will incorporate the following additional indices or categories: (1) Victim Index (will contain DNA records from victims, living and dead, from whom DNA may have been carried from the crime scene by the perpetrator), (2) Unidentified Persons Index (will contain DNA from individuals whose identities are not known, including unidentified human remains and human body parts, and known persons who cannot, or will not, disclose their identity to the police), (3) Unidentified Persons Reference Index (will contain DNA records from missing persons and their close biological relatives, will be searched against the Unidentified Persons Index to identify persons and body parts) (Loftus, 1999).

The FBI assesses the efficacy of CODIS by tracking the number of crimes solved, in part, with CODIS data. The FBI refers to matches as hits, either "cold" hits or "warm" hits. Cold hits are unexpected matches (i.e., investigators had no suspects and CODIS information resulted in successful leads). Warm hits are expected matches based on prior knowledge (i.e., confirmatory evidence about a particular suspect). By the summer of 1998, the 94 laboratories using CODIS were responsible for 218 hits in which two or more forensic profiles were matched (Loftus, 1999). These laboratories made an additional 175 offender hits in which CODIS matched one or more forensic profiles to an offender sample. As a result of these CODIS hits, the number of Investigation Aided cases (cases or investigations that CODIS assisted through a hit) was 578 (Loftus, 1999).

Niezgoda, Loftus, and Burgess (1998) reported the following examples of CODIS hits:

> A 1991 rape/murder in Minnesota was the first United States case solved by searching convicted offender DNA records. The Minnesota Bureau of Criminal Apprehension ran the DNA profile from the crime scene specimen against approximately 1200 convicted offender DNA records. A suspect was identified, arrested, and convicted. (p. 45)

> On the morning of November 25, 1991, a masked man broke into the home of a newly-wed couple in Ritchie, Illinois. He shot and killed the husband and then raped and shot the wife. The attacker presumed the woman to be dead, and drove away in the couple's car. The woman survived, but was unable to identify the attacker, and police were unsuccessful in determining his identity. Two weeks later, the same man raped a 17-year-old girl. This victim was able to identify him, and he was convicted of the offense. On April 6, 1993, forensic scientists at the Springfield Crime Lab were running a routine check of convicted offender DNA profiles against crime evidence in CODIS. The search produced a match between the DNA profile of the Ritchie, Ill. murder/rape and the man convicted of the rape of the 17-year-old girl. The offender, Arthur Dale Hickey, had been a neighbor of the couple in Ritchie, Ill. Hickey was sentenced to death by a jury in Joliet, Illinois. (p. 33)

> In February of 1995, the Florida Department of Law Enforcement linked semen found on a Jane Doe rape-homicide victim to a convicted offender's DNA profile. The suspect's DNA was collected, analyzed, and stored in a CODIS database while he was incarcerated for another rape. The match was timely; it prevented the suspect/offender's release on parole scheduled eight days later. (p. 45)

DNA Identification Act

The DNA Identification Act of 1994 was included in the Violent Crime Control and Law Enforcement Act of 1994. In brief, the DNA Identification Act authorizes the FBI's director to gather DNA information in the following instances: (1) on persons convicted of crimes, (2) on samples recovered from crime scenes, and (3) on samples recovered from unidentified human remains. DNA information is to be made available to (1) criminal justice agencies for law enforcement purposes, (2) for judicial proceedings (if deemed admissible), and (3) for criminal defense purposes. The DNA database may be used for other purposes (e.g., population statistics, research, quality control), if identifying information is removed.

Postconviction Use of DNA

The DNA "door" swings in two directions. Just as DNA evidence has been a powerful tool in achieving convictions, the same evidence has become an equally powerful tool in achieving postconviction exculpation. It has been noted that

> dramatic post-conviction uses of DNA evidence have proliferated. Scores of convicted felons are petitioning courts to allow tests to be performed on preserved samples, and more than seventeen of those exonerated by post-conviction DNA testing have been released. (Confronting the New Challenges of Scientific Evidence, 1995, p. 1571)

The same review goes on to conclude, however, that remedies following exonerative postconviction DNA testing are far from certain, noting that all too often

> Convicted defendants encounter substantial barriers to relief even when evidence has been preserved and access to it has been granted. Those who have been exonerated by such test results still face the difficulty of obtaining their freedom postconviction. (p. 1577)

FORENSIC PROFILING

The definition of "profile" that comes closest to its forensic application is "a vivid and concisely written sketch of the life and characteristics of a person" (*Random House Dictionary of the English Language*, 1967). The sketch is a "best guess" of the personality and behavioral characteristics of the offender based on the crime that was committed. The sketch is compiled from crime scene evidence and (if available) victim data. This process is generally referred to in law enforcement application as investigative profiling, criminal personality profiling, criminal investigative analysis, psychological profiling, behavior profiling, or simply, forensic profiling.

In the *Crime Classification Manual* (Douglas et al., 1992), Munn stated that

> The FBI defines *criminal investigative analysis* as an investigative process that identifies the major personality and behavioral characteristics of the offender based on the crimes he or she has committed. This process involves a behavioral approach to the offense from a *law enforcement perspective*, as opposed to a mental health viewpoint. This law enforcement perspective focuses on the identification and apprehension of the offender,

while the mental health viewpoint centers on diagnosis and treatment. The process generally involves seven steps:

(1) evaluation of the criminal act itself;
(2) comprehensive evaluation of the specifics of the crime scene/s;
(3) comprehensive analysis of the victim;
(4) evaluation of preliminary police reports;
(5) evaluation of the medical examiner's autopsy protocol;
(6) development of the profile, with critical offender characteristics;
(7) investigative suggestions predicated on the construction of the profile. (p. 310).

A different application of the term *profiling*, occasionally employed by forensic clinicians, involves the use of psychometrically or taxonomically derived sketches (or profiles). In these applications, each subtype from a classification system would have its own unique "profile" of characteristics (taxonomic), or a profile of scale scores (raw scores, T scores, percentiles, and so on) would derive from a single test or test protocol psychometric).

Taxonomic and Psychometric Profiling of Sex Offenders

We have little to say regarding the use of psychometric instruments or taxonomic systems for profiling criminal suspects. To the best of our knowledge, there are *no* sex offender classification systems that have been developed for this purpose and none that have been validated for this purpose. Similarly, there are no psychometric instruments that have been validated for this purpose. Although the goal is a worthy one, and quite conceivably attainable, we are a long way off from reaching it.

There are two requirements for using a classification system to apprehend an unknown subject. The first requirement involves "bootstrapping" a classification (i.e., extrapolating from available data what the probable subtype of the suspect is). Thus, the first requirement is highly contingent on whether there are adequate data from the crime scene to permit a reliable classification. In a homicide case, the absence of a live victim makes the task extraordinarily difficult. In the case of rape, the presence of a live victim makes the task somewhat easier. The second requirement is using whatever knowledge is available about the subtype to assist in apprehending the suspect. To date, no classification system, including the MTC system, has been validated for this purpose.

The taxonomic "profiling" of sex offenders essentially started with a deductive methodology using the systems first developed by Murray Cohen and Nick Groth in the 1960s and 1970s. The system developed by Cohen and Seghorn, which was conceptually very similar to Groth's system, was put to empirical test by researchers at the Massachusetts Treatment Center in the 1980s (discussed in Chapter 3). The current classification model for rapists (MTC:R3) is the second major revision of the original Cohen–Seghorn system. MTC:R3 is the only classification system to date that has been examined empirically with regard to efficacy in crime scene analysis.

The *only* study that applied a classification system (MTC:R3) to crime scene data used an FBI dataset on 116 rapists and a second data set on 254 repetitive rapists incarcerated at the Massachusetts Treatment Center to predict MTC:R3 subtypes (Knight, Warren, Reboussin, & Soley, 1998). If we are to profile repetitive offenders with any degree of accuracy, we must demonstrate that the evidence and behaviors are more or less consistently observed across crimes. Knight et al. (1998) looked at across-crime consistency, finding that a few variables, such as gun or rifle present, victim's clothing cut or slashed, excessive response to victim resistance, victim bound, how restraints were obtained, what the restraints were, how the victim was bound, and planning of the rape, had *high* consistency, while most of the other variables (31 of the 54 examined) had *low* to *no* consistency. In general, however, the composite scales had greater consistency than the individual items that comprised them.

Knight et al. (1998) attempted to predict rapist classifications (MTC:R3) using crime scene variables that were determined to be very similar to those dimensions that had shown the greatest consistency in the FBI sample. The dimension of Expressive Aggression yielded the best overall predictive accuracy, followed by the dimensions of Adult Anti-social Behavior and Sadism, which were moderately accurate. The remaining dimensions of Sexualization, Compensatory/Pseudoselfish Behavior, Pervasive Anger, and Vindictiveness, were marginal or did not predict at all. In sum, the study by Knight et al. (1998) suggested that crime scene variables were good predictors of Expressive Aggression and Adult Antisocial Behavior (two dimensions in MTC:R3). Other dimensions (Sadism, Offense Planning, and Relationship with Victim) had high internal consistency within individual offenses and good across-crime consistency, but did not work well at predicting classification. The task presumably would be to identify better crime-scene indicators for those dimensions.

In sum, the use of classification to assist this process introduces two major potential sources of error: (1) correctly classifying the offender based on limited information (in some cases, *very* limited information), and (2) drawing reliable conclusions about the offender's appearance, adaptational characteristics (e.g., job history and living situation), offense patterns, and predicted future behavior based on nothing more than what one knows about a particular subtype.

Investigative Profiling in Historical Perspective

Teten and Turvey (1998) provided a historical overview of investigative or criminal profiling. They noted that the first recorded profiling of a criminal was accomplished by Dr. Thomas Bond in the late 1880s and involved the grisly Whitechapel murders (Jack the Ripper). Dr. Bond worked with Dr. George Phillips, the pathologist who examined one of the victims (Mary Jane Kelly). Dr. Bond's notes, written after the postmortem examination of Kelly, provided, in Teten and Turvey's words, "a wealth of forensic information about the Whitechapel murders, as well as the foundation for the most competent behavioral insights about the true abilities of the person responsible for the crimes" (p. 1).

A psychiatrist, William Langer (Langer, 1972), was hired by the Office of Strategic Services to profile the personality of Adolf Hitler. Teten and Turvey noted that one of the most celebrated early profilers was Dr. James Brussels, a psychiatrist in New York City. For a period of about 10 years, from the late 1950s to the early 1960s, Dr. Brussels consulted on many famous cases, including the Mad Bomber (New York) and the Boston Strangler (Massachusetts). Beyond the recognition of a few notable clinicians working on their own, the actual origins of criminal profiling are unclear (Ault & Reese, 1980; Pinizzotto & Finkel, 1990).

The modern history of crime scene profiling, however, is entirely embraced by one agency, namely the FBI. Profiling was initiated in the late 1960s by Howard Teten, who was influenced by many very prominent instructors teaching at the School of Criminology at the University of California, Berkeley. Teten taught the first course in profiling in 1970 to the Suffolk County, New York Police Department and "profiled" his first actual case in 1970 in Amarillo, Texas. Teten taught the first profiling course (called Applied Criminology) to the FBI National Academy in 1970.

The Behavioral Science Unit (BSU) was founded in 1972, coincident with the opening of the new FBI Academy in Quantico, Virginia, and Jack Kirsch was named as the Unit's first director. During the early 1970s, Special Agents of the FBI's BSU began profiling criminals on an informal basis by using crime scene information to deduce certain offender characteristics. Because these characteristics proved useful in identifying offenders, local authorities requested such assistance in increasing numbers. As a result, the FBI's criminal profilng service became available to all law enforcement agencies.

John Phaff succeeded Kirsch as director of the BSU, and Phaff was succeeded by Roger DePue in 1978. In the 6 years that Roger DePue headed the Unit, there was enormous growth, including many of the most well-known Special Agents (e.g., Dick Ault, Alan Burgess, John Douglas, Bill Hagmaier, Roy Hazelwood, Ken Lanning, Gregg McCrary, Judson Ray, Jim Reese, Bob Ressler, Peter Smerick, Clint VanZandt, and Jim Wright). In 1984, DePue retired and John Douglas took over as head of the Unit. Douglas headed the Unit for 10 years until his retirement in 1994. Before leaving the unit, Douglas changed the title of the Profiling Unit to Criminal Investigative Analysis.

President Ronald Reagan announced the establishment of the National Center for the Analysis of Violent Crime (NCAVC) on June 21, 1984, in a speech at the National Sheriff's Association Annual Conference. NCAVC, which became an official part of the FBI (incorporated into the FBI's budget) in October 1985, was to be administered by the BSU. NCAVC originally consisted of four programs (Research and Development, Training, Profiling and Consultation, and VICAP [Violent Criminal Apprehension Program]). In January 1986, the original BSU was split into two separate units, each responsible for two of the four NCAVC programs. The Behavioral Science Instruction and Research Unit (BSIR) was responsible for Research and Development and Training. The Behavioral Science Investigative Support Unit (BSIS) was responsible for Profiling and Consultation and VICAP. Within the BSIS, Robert Ressler was the first program director of VICAP and John Douglas was the first program director of the Profiling Unit. Within the BSIR, Dr. Richard Ault was appointed the first program manager for the Research and Development Program.

Investigative Profiling at the BSU

In practice, investigative profiling does *not* typically use any formal taxonomic system for classifying offenders. Profiling, as it is routinely practiced by federal agents and police detectives, assimilates a wide range of forensic and physical evidence from the crime scene and detailed victim accounts (in the case of a live victim) to draw inferences about the personality, behavior, and lifestyle of the offender. Crime scene profiling in cases of serial offenders has proven to be quite helpful, wherein the profiler has a large number of "repeats" from which to draw inferences (see Burgess, Hazelwood, Rokous, Hartman, & Burgess, 1988; Douglas, Ressler, Burgess, & Hartman, 1986; Hazelwood, Reboussin, & Warren, 1989; McCann, 1992; Ressler, Burgess, & Douglas, 1988).

Douglas et al. (1986) delineated a six-step criminal-profile-generating process. Stage 1, Profiling Inputs Stage, gathers all relevant information (complete background data on the victim, autopsy reports with toxicology and serology results, crime scene/victim photographs, medical examiner reports, and so on). Stage 2, Decision Process Models Stage, organizes and arranges all of the information into meaningful patterns with regard to homicide type and style, primary intent (e.g., sexual or criminal enterprise), victim risk (e.g., victim's age, occupation, lifestyle, physical stature, resistance ability), offender risk (i.e., the risk that the offender was taking to commit the crime), escalation, time factors, and location factors. Stage 3, Crime Assessment Stage, involves a reconstruction of the sequence of events and behaviors that led to the crime; this is essentially a complete reconstruction of everything that happened leading up to and including the crime. Stage 4, Criminal Profile Stage, generates a descriptive profile of the type of individual who committed the crime. The profile includes demographic information, physical characteristics, habits, beliefs and values, preoffense behavior leading to the crime, and postoffense behavior. Stage 5, Investigation Stage, yields a report that details the results of Stage 4 and offers recommendations for investigating the crime and apprehending the offender. Stage 6, Apprehension Stage, examines the agreement between the outcome (i.e., the apprehended offender) and the stages in the profile-generating process.

Because this method of identifying offenders was based largely on a combination of experience and intuition, without the benefit of empirical corroboration, it had its failures as well as its successes. Nevertheless, a 1981 FBI evaluation questionnaire sent to field offices regarding the profile service revealed that the criminal personality assessment had helped focus the investigation in 77% of those cases in which suspects were subsequently identified.

Crime Scene and Profile Characteristics

Crime scene characteristics are defined as those elements of physical evidence found at the crime scene that may reveal behavioral traits of the murderer. The crime scene can include the point of abduction, locations where the victim was held, the murder scene, and the final body location. Examples of crime scene characteristics may include the use of restraints, manner of death, depersonalization of the victim, possible staging of the crime, and the amount of physical evidence at the crime scene.

Profile characteristics are those variables that identify the offender as an individual and together form a composite picture of the suspect. Profile characteristics are usually determined as a result of the analysis of the crime scene characteristics and can include age, sex, occupation, intelligence, acquaintance with the victim, residence, and mode of transportation.

The agents involved in criminal profiling were able to classify murders by number, type, and style and murderers as either organized or disorganized in their commission of the crimes. Two publications contributed to the study of homicide. In a study of criminal profiling from crime scene analysis (Douglas et al., 1986), Douglas and colleagues outlined the classifying of homicides by number of victims, type, and style. In a study of 36 sexual killers and their victims (Ressler, Burgess, Douglas, Hartman, & D'Agostino, 1986), crime scene characteristics and profile characteristics were analyzed into two categories or organized and disorganized.

Classifying by Number, Type, and Style of Homicide

Crimes may be classified by type, style, and number of victims. A single homicide is one victim, one homicidal event. A double homicide is two victims, one event, and in one location. A triple homicide has three victims in one location during one event. Anything beyond three victims is classified as a mass murder, that is, a homicide involving four or more victims in one location within one event.

Two additional types of multiple murder are spree murder and serial murder. A spree murder involves killing at two or more locations with no emotional cooling off period between murders (i.e., killing at one location and then moving to a second location and killing again with no emotional "downtime"). The killings constitute a single event, which can be of short or long duration. Serial murders involve three or more separate events, with an emotional cooling off period between homicides (e.g., seven separate homicides over a period of 2 years).

Classifying by Organization and Disorganization of the Crime Scene

Generally, an *organized* murderer is one who plans his murders in a conscious manner and who displays control of the victim at the crime scene. The *disorganized* murderer is less consciously aware of a plan, and his crime scenes display haphazard behavior. Sometimes an offender has elements from both categories and is referred to as mixed. Occasionally, a murderer will begin as highly organized and, after years of killing and eluding apprehension, will become increasingly disorganized (e.g., Ted Bundy).

Organized Murderer.   The crime scene of an organized offender suggests that a semblance of order existed prior to, during, and after the offense. Methodical organization suggests a carefully planned crime that is aimed at eluding apprehension. Hypothetical crime scene characteristics of organized murderers include the following:

- Offense planned
- Victim a targeted stranger
- Personalizes victim
- Controlled conversation
- Crime scene reflects overall control
- Demands submissive victim
- Restraints used
- Aggressive acts prior to death
- Body hidden
- Weapon/evidence absent
- Transports body of victim

Hypothetical personality and lifestyle characteristics of the organized murderer include the following:

- Above-average intelligence
- Socially competent
- Skilled work preferred
- Sexually competent

- High birth order status
- Father's work stable
- Inconsistent childhood discipline
- Controlled mood during crime
- Use of alcohol with crime
- Precipitating situational stress
- Living with partner
- Mobility, with car in good condition
- Follows crime in news media
- May change jobs or leave town

Disorganized Murderer. The crime scene of a disorganized offender suggests that the crime has been committed suddenly and with no set plan of action for avoiding detection. The crime scene shows considerable disarray. It has a spontaneous, symbolic, unplanned quality. The victims may be known to the offender, but the age and sex of the victims do not necessarily matter. Hypothetical crime scene characteristics of disorganized murderers include the following:

- Spontaneous offense
- Victim or location known
- Depersonalizes victim
- Minimal conversation
- Crime scene random and sloppy
- Sudden violence to victim
- Minimal use of restraints
- Sexual acts after death
- Body left in view
- Evidence/weapon often present
- Body left at death scene

Hypothetical personality and lifestyle characteristics of the disorganized murderer include the following:

- Average intelligence
- Socially inmature
- Poor work history
- Sexually incompetent
- Minimal birth order status
- Father's work unstable
- Harsh discipline in childhood
- Anxious mood during crime
- Minimal use of alcohol
- Minimal situational stress
- Living alone
- Lives/works near crime scene
- Minimal interest in news media
- Minimal change in lifestyle

The organized/disorganized distinction, which is applicable to other types of crime, is especially attractive for several reasons. It relies on readily identifiable sources of evidence from the crime scene, and offers a clear and immediate mental picture of the perpetrator, including many hypotheses about the personality and lifestyle of the perpetrator. In addition, it avoids the technical psychological jargon that is often confusing to police investigators.

Classifying Using Inductive or Deductive Methodology

A more recent contribution to the theory of profiling involves the basic scientific principles of induction and deduction. Deductive reasoning reaches conclusions from a set of premises containing no more information than the premises taken collectively. In other words, a "deduced" profile uses only information obtained at the crime scene. Teten and Turvey (1998) gave the following example of Deductive Criminal Profiling:

> The body of a victim was found at a remote forest location with multiple stab wounds to the face and chest area, very little blood was found at the crime scene; tire impressions were found in the mud approximately 50 yards from where the body was found; therefore our offender likely has a vehicle, is mobile, and the location where the body was found is a secondary crime scene (disposal site only, not the site of the attack as indicated by the lack of blood. (p. 6)

Inductive reasoning, by contrast, reaches conclusions by employing *more* information than the observations (or evidence) on which the conclusions are based. Inductive profiles make use of a much larger pool of evidence gathered and assimilated from many prior crime scenes. Teten and Turvey (1998) gave the following example of Inductive Criminal Profiling

> 80% of all serial killers who attack college students in parking lots drive Volkswagen Bugs—Our offender has attacked at least two college students on separate occasions; our offender has attacked both college students in parking lots; therefore, our offender drives a VW Bug. (p. 6)

Inductive Criminal Profiling proceeds, in good Baconian tradition, from specifics (i.e., crime scene data) to general hypotheses about the suspect. The general hypotheses are based on the synthesis of data gathered from many prior crime scenes. Thus, the rigorous application of empiricism teaches us, at least in theory, many things about the features, the behaviors, the idiosyncrasies, of serial killers (as an example). As noted, using evidence collected and analyzed from previous crime scenes, we draw conclusions about specific bits of evidence gleaned from a current crime scene.

Teten and Turvey (1998), perhaps unwittingly, identified a problem, noting that

> More frightening is the increased reliance upon inductive reasoning and statistical analysis from criminal profiling interpretations. The result of this is the continued incrimination by very learned and experienced profilers of innocent people who just happen to "fit a profile," such as the Colin Stagg case in Britain and the Richard Jewell "Olympic Park Bombing" case, both in 1996. (p. 3)

A Caveat.   The problem noted by Teten and Turvey is not unique to criminal profiling. It is fundamental to any consideration of the philosophy of scientific inquiry. Karl

Popper (1975) began his august tome on *The Logic of Scientific Discovery* by discussing the "problem of induction." The basic premise derives from Hume's dictum that no theory can be proven inductively. There is always a "heuristic gap," as Polanyi (1964) expressed it, between observation and theory. Popper's example is very simple. He noted that "no matter how many instances of white swans we may have observed, this does not justify the conclusion that *all* swans are white" (1975, p. 27). The answer, of course, is not to abandon induction but to exercise caution and apply the principles of probability when reporting findings. In other words, no profile may be assumed, a priori, to be entirely accurate. A profile is simply a composite of hypotheses. Every statement about a characteristic of the suspect is, in effect, a hypothesis. Each hypothesis will be based on a unique set of evidence. Hence, some hypotheses will, inevitably, be much stronger than other hypotheses (i.e., based on stronger evidence). Thus, the probability of accuracy for each hypothesis may be different. Since certainty can only be attained if all possible instances have been observed, we must work under the assumption that certainty is not attainable and that our hypotheses are simply that—hypotheses.

Computer-Assisted Profiling

Pinizzotto and Finkel (1990) discussed the *process* by which expert profilers "organize and recall knowledge related to crime scene investigations" (p. 217). Pinizzotto and Finkel (1990) go on to observe that "experienced profilers may be able to give meaning to what might appear to the nonprofiler as random, inconsequential, or illogical" (p. 217). The basic premise is that the most successful profilers assimilate information and draw conclusions from that information that elude other, presumably less talented, profilers. As Pinizzotto and Finkel (1990) pointed out, this basic premise is no different from what is often observed among mathematicians and scientists, namely, that some individuals are more adept at problem solving than others.

There is, of course, an existing technology of artificial intelligence that seeks to identify the complex paths of decision-making and render guidelines to assist the less initiated. The use of AI technology by the FBI dates back to 1983 when a computer-assisted profile successfully identified the arsonist in a series of fires at houses of worship (Icove, 1986). Dr. Icove, then a Senior Systems Analyst with BSIS, described the Violent Crime Systems Analysis Model and NCAVC's AI Knowledge-Based Expert System (Icove, 1986). In describing NCAVC's Expert System, Icove stated that

> the knowledge engineer transforms prior experiences of the crime profiler and the results of violent crime research into a knowledge base. Using artificial intelligence computer software, the knowledge base is transformed into decision rules defining an inference engine. The NCAVC investigators input new cases and receive consultation via a user interface. (p. 29)

Although still in its relative infancy, expert-based, computer-assisted profiling could usher in an entirely new era of "automated" profiling. Such systems can organize and manipulate a vastly larger database of prior cases and prior experiences than any single profiler could possibly handle. As Icove (1986) remarked, such systems can "create and preserve in an active environment a system that is not subject to human failings, will respond to constant streams of data, and can generalize large bodies of knowledge" (p. 30).

A Final Caveat: The Dwarfing of Soft Variables

We noted at the beginning of this chapter that evidence derived from the PPG, a medical device, may be deceptively compelling for the uninformed observer. Indeed, much of the evidence discussed here, such as PPG, polygraphy, and DNA, confer a higher level of confidence than most "softer" clinical evidence, such as interviews, diagnoses, and psychological testing. In discussing this potential problem, Tribe (1971) referred to the "dwarfing of soft variables," commenting that

> The syndrome is a familiar one: If you can't count it, it doesn't exist. Equipped with a mathematically powerful intellectual machine, even the most sophisticated user is subject to an overwhelming temptation to feed his pet the food it can most comfortably digest. Readily quantifiable factors are easier to process—and hence more likely to be recognized and then reflected in the outcome—than are factors that resist ready quantification. The result, despite what turns out to be a spurious appearance of accuracy and completeness, is likely to be sigificantly warped and hence highly suspect. (pp. 1361–1362).

Although it is not at all clear that evidence such as DNA, or even phallometry, is more accessible to lay persons (more readily digestible in Tribe's words), it certainly is the case that such evidence may be disproportionately convincing (i.e., significantly outweigh in importance other, less "scientific," evidence). Unless such evidence is indisputably more compelling than softer evidence, it should be presented conservatively, its limitations underscored, and its overall contribution tempered. Perhaps most importantly, it is invariably the case that multiple diverse sources of data, in the aggregate, are more powerful than any one single source of data.

CHAPTER 8

Remediation

PRIMARY PREVENTION

Primary Prevention Programs for Children and Child Victims

Reppucci and Haugaard (1989) reviewed the progress to prevent sexual abuse of children. Programmatic efforts have focused on (1) schoolchildren, (2) the parents and other care-givers, and (3) day-care centers. School programs have two principal goals, primary prevention and detection (disclosure of past and ongoing sexual abuse). Plummer (1984) observed that about 500,000 children had received some form of preventive education. Reppucci and Haugaard note that since 1984 "such programs have increased by quantum leaps" (p. 1268). These programs are, by and large, driven by well-intended, sincere educators. They provide large coverage per contact hour and hence are relatively cost-efficient. However, the teachers typically receive little preparation (Trudell & Whatley, 1988), and the concepts are often presented in the abstract without examples (Conte, Rosen, & Saperstein, 1984). What appears to be the most serious criticism of these programs is that they avoid the emotionally charged subject of sexuality (Finkelhor, 1986). That is, the format is to emphasize prevention in the abstract without tying it to human sexuality. Trudell and Whatley (1988) argued that by avoiding sexuality, children may learn that "sexuality is essentially secretive, negative, and even dangerous" (p. 108).

Finkelhor (1986) emphasized the potential importance of instructional programs for parents. This component of prevention has been much less popular than school-based programs aimed at children. Several explanations have been offered. The parents who are most likely to attend such programs are the most informed and least in need (i.e., most likely to discuss abuse prevention issues with their children). Porch and Petretic-Jackson (1986) found, for instance, that 57% of the parents who completed a workshop had already discussed sexual abuse with their children before the workshop took place. In addition, Finkelhor (1984) found in his survey that most parents tend to think of their own children as capable of avoiding dangerous situations and don't want to frighten them.

Programs aimed at nonparental caregivers (e.g., teachers, school counselors, nurses, pediatricians, clergy, police, day-care workers) have been constructive in raising awareness of the general problem of sexual abuse and detecting signs in children of possible abuse.

Only three program evaluations have been done, without convincing evidence that the programs translated into an increase in founded reports of abuse. It may be argued that increasing public awareness alone justified the existence of these programs.

The greatest attention has been devoted to day-care programs and comparable school-based programs. Reppucci and Haugaard (1989) pointed out that one interesting outcome of at least four program evaluations, raising cost-benefit questions, was that

> many children had a high degree of knowledge about the concepts being taught even before the prevention programs were started and that any post-program increases, although statistically significant, were quite small in absolute terms. (p. 1271)

Overall, the area of knowledge that evidences the greatest gain seems to be family abuse (i.e., that close, trusted people like members of your own family can abuse you). Curiously, this is also the area that evidences the greatest loss of knowledge on follow-up. In addition, the instruments that are used to measure change apparently have, as Reppucci and Haugaard (1989) noted, a ceiling effect. Thus, either the instruments need to be revised or the program content needs to be upgraded. Lastly, the younger children benefit less from the program than the older children. In fact, retention for preschool children is so short that frequent review sessions are required, raising the question of the value of such programs for children under the age of 6.

Reppucci and Haugaard (1989) identified a number of "untested assumptions" that are noteworthy since they will have to be addressed in subsequent program design and evaluation. One assumption is that we are communicating to children those skills that will make them less vulnerable to abuse. However, since child sexual abuse "comes in many different forms" the skills appropriate for strangers may not be useful for family members. A second assumption is that children will be able to transfer the knowledge acquired from an instructional program to a potentially dangerous situation when confronted by it. A third assumption is that there are no negative consequences to such programs, or, at the very least, the negative consequences pale by comparison to the positive effects. Reppucci and Haugaard (1989) concluded their view with the following caveat: "Unless the usefulness of sexual abuse prevention programs can be demonstrated, the reality is that the prevention of child sexual abuse may indeed be only a myth" (p. 1274).

In a report on Preventing Child Sexual Abuse from the U.S. General Accounting Office (GAO, 1996b), 16 reviews that summarized research on education programs designed to prevent child sexual abuse were examined and synthesized. Although "thirteen of the 16 reviews concluded that education programs were generally effective in teaching children new concepts about sexual abuse," "fifteen of the 16 research reviews concluded that there was no evidence from the empirical studies they reviewed that demonstrated the effectiveness of education programs in actually preventing the occurrence of child abuse" (GAO, 1996b, p. 6). Although it is easy to demonstrate acquisition of personal safety skills and general knowledge about child sexual abuse, it is far more difficult to demonstrate a reduced incidence of such abuse that is linked to the education programs.

An article in the April 1999 issue of the American Psychological Association's *Monitor* on child abuse prevention efforts found that such efforts were far too few, noting that less than 10% of funds spent on abuse and neglect is devoted to prevention (Rabasca, 1999). Dr. Zigler was quoted in the article as commenting on the criticality of a fundamental switch in prevention efforts to focus on support services and education for high-risk families. Rather than placing the burden of responsibility on children for avoiding would-be abusers, the burden should be placed on high-risk adults and high-risk families. Not only is this strategy eminently logical, it is vastly easier to track outcomes and demonstrate efficacy.

Adults and Adult Victims

Unlike the primary prevention programs that have been developed and implemented for children, the focus of intervention for women has been secondary (e.g., rape crisis centers and hot lines, special sexual assault investigative teams, safe houses, and guidelines for medical examinations and evidence collection). The principal modes of *primary* prevention, other than the proliferation of books and pamphlets offering advice on risk reduction, have been strategies intended to "strengthen individual capacities and reduce individual vulnerabilities" and "environmental modification through planned social change" (Koss, 1990, p. 378). As Koss noted, most of these primary prevention programs are designed around offender control or victim control strategies. Victim control prevention models are inappropriate, certainly as an exclusive means of prevention, since they restrict the freedom and mobility of women. Offender control strategies, other than incarceration, have not proved helpful. The informational guides alluded to above come from diverse sources, such as feminists (e.g., Connell & Wilson, 1974; Medea & Thompson, 1974), crisis centers (e.g., The London Rape Crisis Centre, 1984), the Department of Justice (Office of Justice Assistance, Research & Statistics, 1979), journalists (Benedict, 1985), and commissions (e.g., Grossman, 1982). Although clearly helpful, much of the otherwise constructive advice provided in these booklets again places the burden of prevention on the potential victim. A typically unmentioned influence that quite conceivably has had a profound impact on primary prevention by raising to widespread public awareness the magnitude of the problem of rape, is the feminist movement. It should be quite apparent, however, that the general area of primary prevention for women is very weak. We have failed to shift the responsibility for prevention from the potential victim to society-at-large. This might be accomplished by requiring through legislation safety measures that are targeted at high-risk environments (e.g., college and university campuses, hotels and motels, movie theaters, parking lots, apartment buildings, public parks).

Certainly the most volatile, impassioned debate over an intervention strategy concerns the question of how victims should respond in sexually dangerous situations. The question has been ideologically polarized between those who recommended that the victim acquiesce to reduce degree of physical injury (usually law enforcement personnel) and those who recommended that the victim fight her attacker (usually feminists). The studies that have examined this question yielded equivocal results. In fact, two studies with seemingly opposite findings were conducted at approximately the same time on rapists incarcerated at the same institution (Chappell & James, 1976; Queen's Bench Foundation, 1976). Given the marked motivational heterogeneity of rapists, this ambiguous picture is hardly surprising. It makes little sense, given current wisdom, to assume that the same victim response will be responded to in the same way by all rapists.

This assumption was tested in a study that examined the interaction of differentiated subgroups of rapists with combative and noncombative victim responses (Prentky, Burgess, & Carter, 1986). The 389 victims of 108 rapists were partitioned into four subgroups:

173 victims of compensatory rapists, 133 victims of exploitative rapists, 46 victims of displaced anger rapists, and 37 victims of sadistic rapists. Victims using combative resistance any time during the offense (e.g., scratching, kicking, biting, punching) were compared with victims who did not or could not resist the rapist physically. The two groups (combative versus noncombative) were compared with respect to degree and nature of physical injuries sustained. The rapists were further divided into four categories using MTC:R2 (the now-outdated, prior version of our rapist classification system). Among the victims of "sadistic rapists," 100% of those employing combative resistance, compared with 20% of those who did not, suffered medical problems requiring a physician and had cuts, bruises, or abrasions. By contrast, there were *no* significant group differences on these variables for the victims of "exploitative" rapists. Among the victims of "compensatory" rapists, 21.7% of those who were combative, compared with 3.5% of those who were not, required the attention of a physician; 93.8% of those who were combative, compared with 30% of those who were not, received cuts, bruises, or abrasions; 9.7% of those who were combative, compared with 0% of those who were not, were rendered unconscious. For the victims of both "displaced anger" and "sadistic" rapists, about one-third of the victims who were combative, compared with 0% of those who were not, were rendered unconscious.

A subsequent study by Ullman and Knight (1995) used the revised rapist classification system (MTC:R3) and found little evidence that the type of rapist had any bearing on the efficacy of the victim's response. Ullman and Knight (1995) concluded that "level of violence should constitute a major determinant of resistance strategy selection" (p. 279). Level of violence ("expressive agression") is one of the primary dimensions in MTC:R3. Ullman and Knight argued that manifest degree of expressive aggression alone should be enough to inform the victim as to the nature of her response, with other MTC:R3 dimensions (e.g., juvenile and adult antisocial behavior, pervasive anger, or sadism) being of negligible importance. Clearly, these are highly complex questions that require judicious, dispassionate scrutiny.

Overview of Primary Prevention Programs

The general area of primary and secondary intervention is still in a most nascent stage. Educational programs intended to serve as primary prevention for children require standardization of procedures and built-in, standardized, evaluative components. The many yet unanswered questions raised by past educational programs include the age that children can most benefit, how to tailor specialized instructional modules to children of different ages, what instructional approaches and techniques maximize awareness and comprehension while minimizing potential harm resulting from fear and other unwanted side effects, how long-lived the beneficial effects are, and whether periodic booster sessions are helpful (e.g., should children participate in a program each year throughout primary and secondary school?). Importantly, we must begin targeting the most needy and the most vulnerable children. If we have reason to believe that the children from the poorer, inner-city neighborhoods are at higher risk, then we should concentrate our efforts there.

We must anticipate that these intervention efforts may increase, perhaps dramatically, the number of reports of victimization (though that too remains an empirical question). In the event that such an increase does accompany expanded educational programs, the services that respond to such reports will have to be prepared to reply. One of the most crippling problems that undermines our efforts to respond efficiently and effectively is the adversarial relationship that often exists between victim services and offender services. Both sets of service providers are responding to a single problem and their efforts must be wedded so that they are not working at cross-purposes.

One specific recommendation would be longitudinal prospective primary prevention programs beginning in early childhood and extending through middle childhood (i.e., 5–10 years of age). Although the years of middle childhood may well be the most critical time for primary prevention programs, we would also recommend instituting similar didactic programs in high school. A broad range of issues might include health (e.g., STDs, drug/alcohol abuse), attitudes about masculinity and self-esteem, attitudes about women and sex, the appropriate expression and management of anger, developing empathic responses to others, and so forth. A potentially powerful adjunct to these didactic sessions would be group discussions centered around these issues. Similar experimental programs have already been developed for high school students with noteworthy success. To carry this theme one step further, we would recommend that similar educational programs be developed and implemented at the college level.

For purposes of evaluation, these longitudinal educational intervention programs must be fully standardized and uniformly implemented. It will not otherwise be possible to assess whether these programs effect changes in attitudes that translate into a reduction in the incidence of abusive and assaultive behavior.

Insofar as primary prevention programs for adult women are concerned, we are essentially at the drawing boards. We must employ whatever reasonable means necessary to shift the burden of prevention to society. As briefly noted later in this chapter, there are ample places to begin designing and implementing pilot prevention projects. A threefold effort should target high-risk public places (such as parks), high risk private places (such as parking lots), and the major institutional forums for the inculcation of beliefs and attitudes (e.g., educational system, advertising industry, entertainment industry, news media).

Secondary Intervention

Offender Therapy

The mechanics and, to a lesser extent, efficacy of sex offender treatment have been quite thoroughly discussed (e.g. Longo & Knopp, 1992; Laws, 1989; Maletzky, 1991a; Marques et al., 1993; Marshall, 1993; Marshall & Barbaree, 1990; Marshall, Jones, Ward, Johnston, & Barbaree, 1991; Murphy, 1990; Pithers, 1990, 1993; Schwartz & Cellini, 1995, 1997) and we will not attempt to restate what has been extensively discussed elsewhere. Instead, we will focus on the rationale for sex offender treatment. The rationale for the modification of any unwanted behavior stems from the informed consideration of those factors that are most importantly associated with the emergence and the sustenance of the behavior. Although cognitive behavior therapy has become the designer treatment of the 1990s, its principles have been around for a very long time. Indeed, one might argue that the first behavior therapist was Cicero, the Roman statesman and philosopher. Cicero observed, over 2000 years ago, that "in the beginning, the world was so made that certain signs come before certain events."

From the ample research on addictive disorders, particularly alcoholism, smoking, and obesity, there has emerged a substantial literature on preventing relapse (Brownell, Marlatt, Lichtenstein, & Wilson, 1986). Relapse prevention, as a model, has been revised and adapted for use with sex offenders (see Laws, 1989). Although sexual aggression derives from a substantially more complex amalgam of factors than most addictive disorders and typically reflects a chronic pattern of maladaptive behaviors, the underlying principles remain the same. That is, before designing strategies for modifying sexually aggressive behavior, we first must identify those factors that are most importantly related to the behavior (i.e., determinants of relapse). Although the factors discussed here are, by no means, inclusive, they do represent the core components of most contemporary treatment programs.

Core Elements of Most Treatment Programs for Sex Offenders

Impaired Adult Relationships

Impaired relationships with adults reflect a broad dimension of social competence that is temporally stable and multiply determined. Becker, Abel, Blanchard, Murphy & Coleman (1978), for instance, identified three components of social skills: heterosexual behavior, assertive behavior, and empathetic behavior. Although social skills training is one of the most frequently included components of treatment for sex offenders (McFall, 1990), its role in relation to sexual aggression remains unclear. Because there are many facets to social competence, specifying what aspect one is assessing is critical. For instance, there is reasonable support for the conclusion that rapists have assertiveness problems (e.g., Stermac & Quinsey, 1986), but differences in other areas of social competence are less evident. Some child molesters, such as "pedophiles" (i.e., those with a longstanding sexual preoccupation with children), often are acutely deficient in their social and interpersonal skills (e.g., initiating and sustaining conversations with adults), feel socially awkward around adults, and generally are more comfortable with younger companions (e.g., Araji & Finkelhor, 1985). Segal and Marshall (1985) found that child molesters were more heterosocially inadequate than rapists, and Williams and Finkelhor (1990) concluded that social isolation and poor social skills were noteworthy features of incestuous fathers.

Although the question of the etiologic importance of social competence remains inconclusive, the inclusion of techniques to address social skills deficits may still be clinically appropriate (Segal & Marshall, 1985; Whitman & Quinsey, 1981). In addition to social skills training, the modalities that are most often used to improve relationships with adults include assertiveness training, relaxation training, systematic desensitization, sex education, and self-esteem enhancement. Despite a long tradition of social skills training, however, the available evidence that supports its efficacy remains questionable (McFall, 1990).

Lack of Empathy

In all domains of interpersonal violence, a general lack of empathetic relatedness for one's victim can be regarded as a powerful disinhibitor. Alternatively, the presence of empathetic concern will serve to inhibit aggression. As Hildebran and Pithers (1989) stated,

"Victim empathy gives [the sex offender] the pivotal reason for not reoffending, for, with empathy, he can no longer not perceive his victim's pain" (p. 238). Although these two statements are hypotheses, ample data have been generated over the years to support them (e.g., Bandura, 1973; Bandura, Underwood, & Fromson, 1975; Feshbach, 1987; Feshbach & Feshbach, 1982; Mehrabian & Epstein, 1972; Parke & Slaby, 1983). Thus, although the empirical evidence of specific deficits in empathy among subgroups of sex offenders is inconclusive, there is a clear clinical rationale for assuming the presence of such deficits and targeting interventions to enhance empathy (Longo & Pithers, 1992; Marshall, 1993; Pithers, 1993).

Although capacity for emotional relatedness and empathetic concern have long been a focus of treatment for sex offenders, these issues have, until recently, been included in the larger topic of social skills deficits. As noted, for example, the third component of Becker and colleagues (1978) assessment of social skills was empathetic behavior. More recently, however, it has been argued that deficits in empathy not only characterize many sex offenders, but such deficits may be of critical etiologic importance (Marshall, 1993; Marshall & Barbaree, 1990; Williams & Finkelhor, 1990). Hildebran and Pithers (1989) described the importance of developing empathy for all victims of sexual abuse as an essential first stage of treatment, followed by the development of empathy for one's own victims. At this point most sex offender treatment programs include a separate component for increasing victim empathy. Indeed, Knopp, Freeman-Longo, and Stevenson (1992) found in their survey of treatment programs in North America that 94% included victim empathy training. In addition to the standard exercises and tapes (video and audio) used in victim empathy training (see Longo & Pithers, 1992), expressive therapy may be used to increase the offender's emotional or affective response to the distress of the victim. Some programs introduce victim advocates, victim counselors, and occasionally victims to increase further the emotional ante. Moreover, increasing the offender's affective apprecia-tion of his own childhood experiences of victimization can instill a greater awareness of his victim's experience of abuse. The generalized importance of empathy was captured by Pithers's (1993) conclusion that "if empathy can be established, significant effects may be observed in sexual arousal, cognitive distortions, intimacy within interpersonal relation-ships, realistic self-esteem, and motivation to change and maintain change" (p. 190).

Degree and Nature of Anger

The degree and nature of anger evidenced in the assault have long been assumed to differentiate between offenders who were willing to use extreme force to gain victim compliance and those who were not. Anger, or its behavioral manifestation—aggression—that is used only to force victim compliance, sometimes referred to as "instrumental" aggression, may vary according to victim resistance, the use of alcohol or drugs, the presence of other offenders or victims, and situational or offender-specific factors (e.g., Prentky et al., 1985). Thus, sex offenders who intend only to force victim compliance are likely to vary widely in the amount of aggression evident in their offenses. When the aggression clearly exceeds what was necessary to force victim compliance, sometimes referred to as "expressive" aggression, the motivation and manifestation may also vary considerably (see Prentky et al., 1985). In the case of expressive aggression, the anger may be undifferentiated with respect to victims (i.e., the offender may be globally angry and express his anger at any available target), or the offender may be focally angry at the subgroups represented by his victims. Sex offenders may be generally angry at women (i.e., misogynistic anger) or they may displace their anger on specific groups of women (e.g., elderly women). Similarly, child molesters who intentionally inflict considerable physical injury on their victims may be generally angry at children.

Regardless of how "expressive" the aggression is and how it is manifest, we must assume that in a battery offense, such as sexual assault, aggression must have been present. It is thus impossible to dismiss a component of sexual assault that is obviously so prominent and critical a feature of the behavior. The recognition of the importance of anger as a driving force in sexual offenses has resulted in the inclusion of treatment techniques to reduce and contain anger. The most commonly employed of these techniques is an anger management group which uses cognitive–behavioral strategies to increase self-control as well as the timely and appropriate expression of angry feelings. In addition, Relapse Prevention, which also focuses on increasing self-management skills, and Stress Management can assist the offender to gain control over chronic and situationally induced anger. Lastly, early life experiences of victimization can fuel lifelong anger that is periodically triggered by real or imagined provocations. A group that focuses on childhood victimization can help the offender to master these traumatic events.

Cognitive Distortions

Cognitive distortions are "irrational" ideas, thoughts, and attitudes that serve to: (1) perpetuate denial around sexually aggressive behavior, (2) foster the minimization and trivialization of the impact of sexually aggressive behavior on victims, and (3) justify and sustain further sexually aggressive behavior. Cognitive distortions are presumed to be learned attitudes that are instilled at an early age by caregivers, reinforced by peers during childhood and adolescence, and further strengthened in adulthood by the prevailing social climate.

The social and cultural forces that have been hypothesized to contribute to sexual violence include the permissive responses of a wide variety of social systems and institutions that function to perpetuate rape myths and misogynistic attitudes, the objectification and exploitation of children and women in pornography, and the often similar but more subtle messages conveyed in advertising that support, or at least condone, sexual harassment (see Stermac, Segal, & Gillis, 1990). Indeed, many facets of sexual aggression represent institutionalized, normative behavior that are deeply ingrained in the social fabric.

The causal relation among demeaning and misogynistic attitudes, attributions, moral evaluations, and sexual violence is, arguably, one of the more important areas of inquiry in research on sexual aggression (see Marshall, 1993; Murphy, 1990; Segal & Stermac, 1990). This area of research, emerging both from the laboratories of experimental social scientists and from the writings of feminist theorists, dovetails nicely with the clinical and experimental psychopathology research on cognitive distortions. Whereas social and feminist research has tended to focus on rape-supportive attitudes and rape myths held by the cross section of society (i.e., *non*offenders), the clinical research has focused on the irrational and offense-justifying attitudes expressed by sex offenders.

The importance of cognitions in moderating sexual arousal has been repeatedly demonstrated. Moreover, clinical observations have suggested that many sexual offenders harbor offense-justifying attitudes and that these attitudes are importantly related to the maintenance of the "sexual assault cycle." Thus, the modification of irrational attitudes has been a major focus of treatment intervention. Although there are a variety of treatment modalities that may impact these distortions, the most commonly employed technique is cognitive restructuring. For cognitive restructuring to be most effective, it is critical that cognitive *and* affective components be addressed. That is, it is insufficient merely to confront the "distorted" nature of the attitudes, to discuss the role that such distortions play for the individual, or to provide accurate information about sexual abuse (all cognitive components). It is equally important to create discomfort by focusing on the victim's response (e.g., fright, pain, humiliation)—the affective component. This latter exercise is also integral to victim empathy training.

In addition to cognitive restructuring, a group that focuses on childhood victimization can also be very helpful. Since the origin of these distorted attitudes is often a primary caregiver who was an influential role model, as well as exposure to peer role models—often in institutional settings, a group that focuses on these early life experiences can help to trace the cognitions to their source, thereby challenging their generality and diminishing their sense of "truth" or "reality."

Sexual Fantasy and Deviant Sexual Arousal

Sexual fantasy refers to cognitive activity that focuses on thoughts and images having sexual content, and deviant sexual arousal refers to an arousal response that is prompted by thoughts, stimuli (visual or auditory), or behaviors that are defined as unconventional or antisocial by society. Studies investigating the relation of sexual fantasy to sexual aggression have typically employed plethysmography to assess sexual arousal to auditory and visual stimuli that purportedly tap specific sexual preferences. The guiding premise of these studies has been that deviant sexual fantasy is highly correlated with deviant sexual arousal and that both deviant fantasy and deviant arousal patterns are important precursors of deviant sexual behavior (Abel & Blanchard, 1974).

Substantial evidence has emerged supporting the relation between phallometrically assessed sexual preferences and sexually deviant behavior (see Quinsey & Earls, 1990). For instance, differential arousal patterns to specific sexual/aggressive stimuli have discriminated rapists from nonrapists and differentiated among rapists (Quinsey, Chaplin, & Upfold, 1984). Moreover, more recent studies have provided evidence that deviant sexual arousal patterns are an important identifier of sexually coercive males in noncriminal samples (e.g., Malamuth, 1986, 1989a,b). Finally, phallometrically measured sexual interest in nonsexual violence has been found to be a predictor of both sexual and violent offense recidivism (Rice, Harris, & Quinsey, 1990).

The frequent targeting of such fantasies for therapeutic intervention (e.g., Quinsey & Earls, 1990) reflects the widely held belief that the modification of deviant sexual fantasies and deviant sexual arousal patterns is critical for the successful treatment of sex offenders. Indeed, the presence of deviant sexual fantasies does appear to increase the likelihood of subsequent deviant sexual behavior (Abel & Blanchard, 1974). Moreover, the moderate success at increasing nondeviant arousal and behavior by applying techniques aimed solely at modifying arousal to deviant sexual fantasies (Marshall, Abel, & Quinsey, 1983) supports the hypothesis that deviant fantasies not only lead to and maintain deviant sexual behavior but also impede normal sexual adaptation.

Behavioral techniques for modifying sexual arousal patterns are grouped into two categories, those that decrease deviant arousal (e.g., covert sensitization, aversion, masturbatory satiation, biofeedback, shame therapy) and those that increase appropriate arousal (e.g., systematic desensitization, fantasy modification and orgasmic reconditioning, "fading" techniques, exposure to explicit appropriate sexual material). Although over 20 different behavioral techniques have been reported in the literature, the most widely used method has involved some variant of aversive therapy. Kelly (1982) found, for instance, that 78% of the 32 studies he reviewed employed aversive techniques. Furthermore, most research on methods for reducing deviant sexual arousal has focused on covert sensitization and/or aversion therapy (Grossman, 1985).

Both of these procedures follow a standard classical conditioning paradigm in which a noxious stimulus is paired with auditory or visual stimuli of deviant sexual content. In aversion therapy, the deviant stimuli are typically paired with noxious odors. In covert sensitization, the deviant stimuli are typically paired with negative mental images (e.g., a physically unpleasant experience such as vomiting or having a cavity filled or a psychologically unpleasant experience such as being apprehended by the police and going to prison). Aversive stimuli may be combined with mental images (e.g., presenting a noxious odor with an image of vomiting). The relative efficacy of the different aversive techniques with different types of offenders remains an empirical question. Moreover, the extent to which response inhibition is situation-bound after repeated exposure to aversive experiences remains to be demonstrated.

In addition to the repertoire of behavioral interventions, organic treatment has become increasingly popular as a complement to psychological treatment. These organic or drug treatments consist primarily of antiandrogens (Bradford, 1990) and antidepressants (Kafka, 1991; Kafka & Prentky, 1992). The antiandrogens (e.g., medroxyprogesterone acetate and cyproterone acetate) reduce sexual drive by reducing the level of testosterone. The antidepressants that are used are primarily the selective serotonin reuptake inhibitors such as fluoxetine. Although the neuroregulation of sexual drive remains unclear, there is some evidence that enhanced central serotonin neurotransmission inhibits sexual arousal (Segreaves, 1989). In addition, there is clinical evidence that uncontrollable sexual urges and compulsive sexual behaviors are associated with dysthymia and major depression (e.g., Kafka & Prentky, 1992).

Antisocial Personality/Lifestyle Impulsivity

Impulsivity has long been a cynosure for the general criminal literature and, more recently, the sexual assault literature. In research on sexual offenders, lifestyle impulsivity has proven to be a significant discriminator (e.g., Hall, 1988; Prentky & Knight, 1986; Prentky, Knight, Lee, & Cerce, 1995; Rice et al., 1990). In his postdictive study of the offense histories of 342 nonpsychotic sex offenders who were examined at a state hospital, Hall (1988) found that the frequency of sexual offending against adults was related to a wide range of other criminal offenses, suggesting the presence of antisocial personality. Rice et al. (1990) found that the degree of psychopathy predicted both sexual and violent (sexual and nonsexual) recidivism. In a 25-year follow-up of 106 rapists released from a maximum-security treatment facility, Prentky et al. (1995) found that the hazard rate for the high-impulsivity offenders was at least twice as great as the hazard rate for the low-impulsivity offenders across all domains of criminal behavior. For nonsexual, victimless offenses, the hazard rate was almost four times as great.

There is increasing evidence even within noncriminal samples (e.g., college students) that the likelihood of engaging in sexually aggressive behavior is greater among those who are more impulsive (e.g., Lisak & Roth, 1988; Rapaport & Burkhart, 1984). Lisak and Roth (1988) found, for instance, that college men who reported having been sexually aggressive rated themselves as more impulsive than did nonaggressive college men. The sexually aggressive men also reported having less respect for society's rules.

Clinicians have long recognized the importance of impulsivity for relapse and have introduced self-control and impulsivity management modules into treatment. In addition to groups that focus specifically on impulse control, most treatment programs include components of Relapse Prevention. Relapse Prevention begins by identifying the chain of events and emotions that lead to sexually aggressive behavior. Once this "assault cycle" is described, two interventions are employed: strategies that help the offender avoid high-risk situations, and strategies that minimize the likelihood that high-risk situations, once encountered, will lead to relapse. This is an "internal self-management" system (see Pithers, 1990) that is designed to interrupt the seemingly inexorable chain of events that lead to an offense. Relapse Prevention is potentially helpful for interrupting patterns of behavior that eventuate in specific outcomes, such as sexual assault, as well as patterns of behavior that are more global, such as impulsive, antisocial behavior.

Lastly, there is reasonable evidence in the literature that supports the efficacy of selective serotonin reuptake inhibitors for impulse disorders (e.g., Benarroche, 1990; McElroy, Pope, Hudson, Keck, & White, 1991). The general efficacy of drugs for treating sex offenders is discussed in greater detail in a subsequent section.

What Can We Conclude about Treatment Efficacy?

Variations in recidivism rates associated with different treatment programs are extremely difficult to interpret. Differences among recidivism rates across studies are confounded with legal jurisdiction, duration of follow-up, offender characteristics, differential client attrition rates, differences in program integrity and amount of treatment, amount and quality of posttreatment supervision, and a host of other variables. In addition, recidivism measures tend to be noisy and result in comparisons of low statistical power. Even without attempting to attribute variations in recidivism to treatment program characteristics, the variation in recidivism rates in the published literature is truly remarkable.

Although there have been no comparisons of different treatment approaches within the same study using random assignment of offenders to treatment conditions, there have been some treatment–no treatment comparisons using matched designs or convenience samples. We will describe two such studies.

Using a sample of 35 untreated extrafamilial child molesters, Barbaree and Marshall (1988) found that inappropriate age preference ratios correlated .38 with recidivism and .43 with the number of reoffenses. However, Marshall and Barbaree (1988) found that neither pre- nor posttreatment deviance quotients nor pre–post changes in deviance quotients predicted recidivism in a community sample of 126 treated and untreated child molesters.

Marshall and Barbaree obtained large differences in recidivism rates, as estimated by official police records and unofficial records of police and child protective agencies, between clients given cognitive–behavioral treatment in a community clinic and similar but not randomly assigned clients given no treatment. For extrafamilial child molesters, recidivism rates over approximately 4 years were 43 and 18% for untreated and treated extrafamilial heterosexual child molesters, respectively 43 and 13% for extrafamilial homosexual child molesters, and 22 and 8% for untreated and treated heterosexual incestuous child molesters.

Rice et al. (1991) determined the recidivism rates of 136 extrafamilial child molesters who had received phallometric assessment in a maximum-security psychiatric institution from 1972 to 1983 over an average 6.3-year follow-up period. Fifty of these offenders had participated in a behavioral program designed to alter inappropriate sexual age preferences (Quinsey, Chaplin, Maguire, & Upfold, 1987). Thirty-one percent of the subjects were convicted of a new sexual offense, 43% of the total were known to have committed a violent or sexual offense, and 58% were arrested for any offense or returned to the maximum-security institution. Subjects convicted of a new sex offense had previously committed more sex offenses, had been admitted to correctional institutions more frequently, were more likely to have been diagnosed as personality disordered, were less likely to have ever been married, and had shown more inappropriate sexual preferences in initial phallometric assessment than those who had not. Behavioral laboratory treatment did not affect recidivism.

The difference between the outcomes of the quasiexperimental treatment evaluations reported by Marshall and Barbaree (1988) and Rice et al. (1991) illustrates the difficulties in arriving at definitive conclusions concerning treatment efficacy. Among the more important of the myriad of differences between these studies are the locus of the program (maximum-security psychiatric facility versus the community), severity of the offense history of the clients/patients treated in the program, and differences in the amount of treatment received. Any or all of these or other confounded variables could be responsible for the markedly different results.

In a widely reported meta-analysis on 12 studies of treated sex offenders ($N = 1313$), Hall (1995) found a small but significant overall effect size for treatment versus comparison conditions ($r = .12$). The overall recidivism rate for treated sex offenders was .19, compared with the overall recidivism rate of .27 for untreated sex offenders. The effect sizes were larger in those samples with higher base rates of recidivism, those samples with follow-up periods that were greater than 5 years, those samples that included outpatients, and those studies that used cognitive–behavior therapy or antiandrogen medication. Cognitive–behavior therapy and antiandrogen medication were significantly more effective than behavioral techniques, such as covert sensitization or aversion. Cognitive–behavior therapy and antiandrogen medication appeared to be of equal efficacy (i.e., there was no difference in effectiveness between the two). The treatment effect sizes across the 12 studies were heterogeneous. Hall (1995) posited that the likely causes of the heterogeneity were: (1) highly variable base rates of recidivism, (2) variable length of follow-up after treatment, (3) the degree of "pathology" of the offenders in the different studies, and (4) the types of treatment provided in the different studies.

In an excellent paper on the critical role of base rates for recidivism in treatment outcome studies, Barbaree (1997) concluded that "recidivism studies were found to be quite insensitive to the effects of treatment" (p. 111). The problem is a relatively simple one.

As Barbaree noted, the base rates for sexual recidivism in most studies range from .10 to .40. Sample sizes in most studies are generally small, rarely more than 200 offenders. With a low base rate and a small sample, the treatment effect would have to be very large (greater than .50) to observe significant differences between treated and untreated offenders. It is unrealistic to expect treatment effects of that magnitude. Consequently, as Barbaree demonstrated, it is unlikely that conventional treatment outcome studies will demonstrate significant treatment effects. Although solutions to these problems are evident, each has its own limitations. We could increase substantially the size of our samples. Barbaree (1997) determined "that an N of 495 would be required in the 'average' study in the literature (power = 0.50) to achieve statistical significance" (p. 121). If we increase the power, we increase the sample size. As Barbaree noted, with power set at 0.80, we would need a sample of 916 offenders to obtain significance. Another option is to increase the base rate by increasing the length of the follow-up, or by using a wider array of sources of recidivism data (including "informal" data such as confidential self-report), or by examining presumptively higher risk offenders. As noted, all of these solutions have their problems, primarily time and money. Barbaree (1997) concluded that

> The recognition of the weakness of recidivism studies, namely, their insensitivity to treatment effects, gives greater validity and importance to nonrecidivism studies of treatment efficacy, including studies of within treatment behavior change. (p. 126)

Barbaree's recommendation has been echoed by others. Hanson, Cox, and Woszcsyna (1991b) recommended that treatment be evaluated by assessing change in those factors that are related empirically to risk. Such factors might include minimization and denial, sexual preferences, deviant sexual fantasies, irrational thoughts and attitudes, and cognitive and behavioral deficits. Noting that the low base rate for detected recidivism makes reoffense "an impractical outcome criterion," Hanson (1997b) described three different approaches: (1) large, well-controlled single-site studies, (2) pooling smaller studies by using meta-analysis, and (3) examining within-treatment change on dynamic risk factors.

The first approach, the large, well-controlled study, is extraordinarily expensive and very time-consuming. The gold standard for such studies was California's Sex Offender Treatment and Evaluation Project (SOTEP). Hanson (1997b) noted that SOTEP "has been running for over 10 years and the results are still preliminary" (p. 132). The cost of SOTEP was approximately $2.25 million per year (Hanson, 1997b). Hanson concluded that

> The SOTEP study was exceptionally well designed, but its methodology has one important failing: it is almost impossible to replicate. Long-term projects of this sort require a rare confluence of research talent and political will that is unlikely to be repeated in the foreseeable future. (p. 133)

The second approach described by Hanson is the aggregation of many smaller studies through meta-analysis. At this point, the only meta-analysis on sex offender treatment studies appears to be the one by Hall (1995) discussed above. Although meta-analysis is indisputably a powerful technique for aggregating results from multiple studies, the results can be no more reliable than the reliability of the input data. Aggregating apples and oranges will, inevitably, result in the heterogeneous effect sizes that Hall found. Although the task is to gather studies that are as comparable as possible on relevant dimensions, it would have been impossible for Hall to draw comparability in several critical areas, such as the nature, quality, intensity, and duration of treatment services, and the methods and procedures for collecting and analyzing reoffense data. Hanson (1997b) also pointed out innumerable potential problems, including the lack of well-controlled studies, the classification and comparability of treatment modalities, the comparability of procedures for gathering and analyzing recidivism data, and the relative heterogeneity of sex offenders in the different studies. Hall's meta-analysis was, nonetheless, an invaluable first effort. Indeed, the fact that Hall found a detectable "signal" (i.e., treatment effect) despite the considerable background noise is noteworthy.

Perhaps the most promising short-term solution to assessing efficacy of treatment involves the examination of within-treatment changes on dynamic risk factors. Logically, there must be a demonstrable link between the dynamic factors and recidivism. It isn't enough merely to demonstrate change, the change must take place in areas that are critically related to reoffense. To date, however, "almost all the empirically validated risk factors for sexual offenders are static, historical variables, such as age and offense history" (Hanson, 1997b, p. 141). Hanson (1997b) went on to note that

> Even the most potentially changeable risk factors are extremely stable: never being married, deviant sexual preferences, and antisocial personality disorder. The most dynamic of the empirically validated risk factors are motivation and cooperation with treatment. (p. 141)

Thus, with the exception of assessments of internal motivation for change and degree of cooperativeness with the treatment program, we have scant empirical evidence for the predictive validity of the kind of dynamic variables that can be readily assessed during and after treatment (e.g., cognitive distortions, hypermasculine attitudes, problems with attachment and intimacy, social skills deficits, victim empathy deficits, compulsive sexual urges).

A General Accounting Office study identified and summarized 22 reviews of research on sex offender treatment (GAO, 1996c). The reviews, which were published between 1977 and 1996, covered 550 studies. The gist of the GAO (1996c) report was that the results are promising but inconclusive. The report concluded as follows:

> The most optimistic reviews concluded that some treatment programs showed promise for reducing deviant sexual behavior. However, nearly all reported that definitive conclusions could not be drawn because methodological weaknesses in the research made inferences about what works uncertain. There was consensus that to demonstrate the effectiveness of sex offender treatment more and better research would be required. (p. 11)

Concluding Thoughts about Treatment

Given the failure of more traditional correctional remedies, such as deterrence and incapacitation, for reducing the level of sexual violence in society, other interventions must be actively sought. One potentially effective intervention for known offenders is treatment. Dispassionate conclusions, *un*informed by data, would be that treatment is *un*likely to be effective for *all* offenders *and* that treatment *is* likely to be effective for some offenders. Essentially, such conclusions are accurate and, for most of us, obvious. Given the extraordinary heterogeneity of sex offenders, it would be only logical that some, but not all, offenders would benefit from treatment. Stated otherwise, treatment undoubtedly will restore some offenders to a nonoffending lifestyle and will fail to touch other offenders. The question of "how many" fall into each category is what the heated debate is all about. The question is extremely difficult to answer, beset by a host of methodological problems. The more helpful questions would be "who" and "how." Who are the sex offenders most likely to benefit from treatment, and how best should they be treated? In sum, the verdict as to the efficacy of treatment for sexual offenders will inevitably be a complex one that addresses: (1) optimal treatment modalities for specific subtypes of offenders, (2) optimal conditions under which treatment and follow-up should occur, and (3) selection (or exclusion) criteria for treatment candidates. At the present time, the most informed and dispassionate conclusion must be that we simply do not know what percentage of the aggregated (highly heterogeneous) population of sex offenders can return to a nonoffending lifestyle through treatment. We can also conclude, with equal confidence, that some sex offenders are highly amenable to treatment and pose a negligible risk to reoffend sexually, whereas other sex offenders are highly resistant to treatment and pose a very high risk to reoffend sexually.

The approximate 10% treatment effect that has been reported in the literature thus far is a crude estimate, crude because it collapses across a markedly heterogeneous population of men. As noted above, for some offenders, the treatment effect will be much higher than 10%, whereas for other offenders there will likely be no detectable treatment effect at all. The simple use of dimensions known to differentiate between recidivists and nonrecidivists would bring considerable clarity to estimates of treatment effects. As a simple example, we looked at the utility of lifestyle impulsivity as a discriminator for recidivism among rapists (Prentky et al., 1995). Lifestyle impulsivity was measured using five variables: unstable employment history, disruptiveness at school or work, a history of fighting, repeated instances of aggressive behavior in response to frustration, and reckless behavior with no regard for consequences (e.g., many motor vehicle violations or other risk-taking behaviors). We examined 25-year follow-up data on 109 rapists. In all instances, the hazard rate for the high-impulsivity group was at least as great as the hazard rate for the low-impulsivity group. Perhaps the most remarkable finding, however, concerned the focal analysis of sexual offenses. Because the entire sample of rapists was composed of repetitive and/or violent offenders, it was particularly noteworthy that the hazard rate for the high-impulsivity group was still almost three times higher (for sexual recidivism) than the hazard rate for the low-impulsivity group, with a 22% lower survival rate after 5 years. We can reasonably conclude, based on these results, that a large proportion of treatment failures among rapists are those who are highly impulsive.

Aside from the obvious scientific issues, there are profound social and political issues that obfuscate matters. As Prentky and Burgess (1992) commented, as a society, we appear to resist treating sexual offenders because it is perceived to be a "humane" response to egregious behavior. However, if the overriding goal is reducing the number of victims, as well as the costs incurred by such victimization, and if rehabilitation can be demonstrated to reduce the likelihood of reoffense, then it is imperative that we overcome our resistance to treatment and work toward the optimization of treatment interventions and treatment conditions that reduce risk of reoffense. Clearly, the most compelling motive for offender treatment is the presumptive reduction in victimization rates. To that end, the treatment of sex offenders may be viewed, quite legitimately, as *pro bono publico*, and not *pro bono privato*.

Somatic Therapy

The use of drugs to reduce levels of testosterone in sexual offenders is a natural outgrowth of prior experiences with surgical castration. Since castration involves the removal of the testes and since the testes are responsible for producing 95% of the testosterone in the body, it was logical to conclude that other means of reducing testosterone might produce the same or similar effects on behavior. Thus, if castration was effective in reducing reoffense rates among sexual offenders, the chemical equivalent of castration should also be effective in reducing recidivism. The validity of the first half of this proposition appears to be supported by studies involving thousands of sexual offenders who were castrated.

Orchiectomy

According to Le Maire (1956), the first therapeutic castration was done by Forel in Switzerland in 1892, followed by Maier (1911), Frank (1925) and Kartel and Quervain (1929) (all cited in Le Maire, 1956). In these early years, castration for therapeutic purposes was being done in Switzerland, Holland, Germany, Finland, Iceland, and Denmark. The first law legalizing castration was passed in Denmark in 1929 (Ortmann, 1980). Ortmann (1980) reported that between 1929 and 1959, 738 sexual offenders were castrated under this law. During this period only 10 of the castrated men were known to have reoffended, for an approximate recidivism rate of 1.4%. According to Ortmann, the expected recidivism rate for this group prior to castration was about 50%. In Germany alone at least 2800 offenders were castrated between 1934 and 1944 and another 800 between 1955 and 1977. Langluddeke (1963) (cited in Heim & Hursch, 1979) followed up 1036 castrated offenders and found that 24 (2.3%) recidivated. The recidivism rate for this group prior to castration was about 84%. Bremer (1959) followed 102 castrated offenders for 5 to 10 years, noting a recidivism rate of 2.9%. The precastration reoffense rate for this group was 58%. The single most ambitious study was Sturup's (1968) 30-year follow-up of 900 offenders who were castrated between 1929 and 1959. Sturup reported a recidivism rate of 1.1%. Cornu (1973) (cited in Heim & Hursch, 1979) studied 127 castrated offenders who had been released for a minimum of 5 years, finding a presurgical reoffense rate of 76.8% and a postsurgical reoffense rate of 7.4%. It would appear, based on this cursory look at the recidivism literature on castrated sexual offenders, that the surgical procedure was indeed a powerful mode of intervention. It would thus seem logical to infer that a similar intervention that chemically reduces testosterone levels would have a similar impact on recidivism. If this inference is in fact valid, then "chemical castration" would be much more attractive than surgery. Not only is it less expensive and easier to implement, it is reversible. In addition, it does not carry the stigma of having been castrated. Thus, experience with the presumptive effectiveness of castration provided a rationale for the use of antiandrogen (or testosterone-reducing) medication.

The Use of Drugs to Reduce Sexual Drive

Drugs have been used in the United States to treat sexually aggressive behavior for about 50 years. Female sex hormones (i.e., estrogen) were the most commonly used substances in the late 1940s and early 1950s (e.g., Golla & Hodge, 1949; Whittaker, 1959). Although estrogens were considered to be generally effective in reducing sexual drive, the side effects (such as nausea, vomiting, and feminization) compromised their widespread use. Despite these side effects, as well as more serious ones such as increasing risk of breast cancer (Symmers, 1968), the experimental use of estrogen continued, with estradiol implants eventually being used (Field & Williams, 1970).

The preferred mode of chemical intervention in the 1960s was neuroleptics. Thioridazine (Bartholomew, 1964; Litkey & Feniczy, 1967), fluphenazine enanthate (Bartholomew, 1964), and the butyrophenone benperidol (Sterkmans & Geerts, 1966; Tennent, Bancroft, & Cass, 1974) were all found to suppress sexual drive. The routine use of neuroleptics to reduce sexual drive is hindered, however, by the wide range of side effects, most notably tardive dyskinesia and the extrapyramidal symptoms, that accompany these medications. The advantage of tranquilizers such as benperidol, which is currently used in England (Anquil, Janssen Pharmaceutical Ltd.), is that they are nonsteroidal, thereby avoiding the side effects of steroids (e.g., immunosupression, muscle weakness, and emotional lability).

The Antiandrogens

Until recently, the principal alternative to the neuroleptics has been the antiandrogens. Although there are nonsteroidal antiandrogens (e.g., cimetidine and flutamide), they are relatively weak in their antiandrogenic effect, and they are not antigonadotropic. Thus, the steroids are more commonly used. The most potent of the antiandrogens are, like estrogen, also progestogens. Bradford (1983) noted that Heller, Laidlaw, Harvey, and Nelson (1958) were the first to observe that progestogens reduced sexual drive. The most potent of the progestogens are medroxyprogesterone, chlormadinone, megestrol, and cyproterone. Although the acetates of these 17-hydroxy progesterone derivatives all show strong progestogenic activity, the antiandrogenic effect is most pronounced with cyproterone acetate (CPA) (Mugglestone, 1983). These progestogens are antilibidinal, because they are antiandrogenic (i.e., they blockade androgen receptors) (Laschet & Laschet, 1975). In addition to being antiandrogenic, they are also antiestrogenic and antigonadotropic. None of the hormones mentioned are entirely specific; they each have multiple effects, and the precise mechanisms underlying their antilibidinal properties are far from certain (Whalen, 1984).

During the 1960s a number of potent antiandrogenic agents came into experimental use (Lerner, 1964), including A-norprogesterone (Lerner, Bianchi, & Barman, 1960), CPA (Neumann, von Berswordt-Wallrabe, Elger, & Steinbeck, 1968), and chlormadinone acetate (Rocky & Neri, 1968). While cyproterone actetate is commonly used in Canada, Great Britain, and elsewhere in Europe, it is unavailable in the United States. The agent of choice in the United States has been medroxyprogesterone acetate (MPA; Provera, Upjohn). The Food and Drug Administration (FDA) withdrew its approval for Provera in 1978. Since then Provera has been used in the United States only on an experimental basis with sexual offenders. The decision of the FDA to withdraw approval for Provera is based on the drug's putative carcinogenicity. It is noteworthy, in this regard, that the World Health Organization and approximately 70 foreign governments have concluded that Provera is safe (Sun, 1984). The FDA's reluctance to approve Provera may be understood, in good measure, by the perceived lack of sound empirical data on the health risks associated with its long-term use

(Sun, 1984). In addition to the more common side effects of Provera, such as weight gain, lethargy, cold sweats, hot flashes, nightmares, shortness of breadth, hyperglycemia, reduced testicle size, and hypertension (Berlin, 1983), the drug has also been associated with thrombotic disorders, such as phlebitis, cerebrovascular disorders, pulmonary embolism, and renal thrombosis, and fluid retention. Thus, it can place those with epilepsy, migraine, asthma, and cardiac or renal dysfunction at some potential risk (Bradford, 1983). Despite the ongoing controversy over the possible health risks associated with long-term use of Provera, the drug, along with Androcur (CPA), continues to command considerable attention, from clinicians as well as politicians.

The first programmatic use of MPA for the treatment of sexual offenders was initiated in 1966 with the creation of the Biosexual Psychohormonal Clinic at Johns Hopkins University. In early reports from the Hopkins's Clinic on the use of MPA with sex offenders, Money (1968, 1970) found that MPA reduced a variety of sexually related criminal behaviors. Money and his colleagues subsequently reported that the use of MPA, in combination with a program of counseling, was beneficial in helping sexual offenders control their behavior (Money & Bennett, 1981; Money et al., 1975). In 5 out of 10 cases there was a remission of paraphiliac symptoms (Money et al., 1975). Most of the offenders were pedophiles and exhibitionists rather than rapists. Money and his colleagues concluded that, while MPA had a potent effect on sexual behavior (i.e., suppression of testosterone, suppression of erection and ejaculation, and a decrease in erotic imagery), it did not necessarily alter aggressiveness. This latter finding was based primarily on the results of the administration of MPA to a comparison group of 13 XYY males who were nonsexual offenders.

Murray, Bancroft, Anderson, Tennent, and Carr (1975) examined endocrine changes after treatment in 12 sexual offenders. Three of the 12 subjects had elevated levels of testosterone and sex hormone-binding globulin (SHBG). In one study, tranquilizers (benperidol and chlorpromazine) were compared to a placebo. In the second study, ethynyl estradiol and CPA were compared. The tranquilizers produced no change in plasma testosterone (PT) or luteinizing hormone (LH). Cyproterone acetate reduced levels of PT, LH, and follicle-stimulating hormone (FSH). While ethynyl estradiol did not affect FSH, it produced a 46% increase in PT, a 49% increase in LH, and a 120% increase in SHBG. The unexpected increase in PT and LH was attributed to the increase in SHBG, which produced a rise in bound, inactive testosterone. CPA did not affect SHBG. Despite the differing endocrine changes from the three active treatment conditions, all substances produced similar behavioral changes, including reduced frequency of masturbation and self-ratings of frequency of sexual thoughts, while leaving unaffected both sexual attitudes (measured by the semantic differential) and plethysmographic erectile responses to erotic visual stimuli.

Spodak, Falck, and Rappeport (1978) reported that three of their six patients responded favorably to MPA. The three patients for whom there was apparently no recurrence of paraphiliac behavior were two pedophiles and a sadist. The three patients whose paraphiliac behavior was unaffected by treatment were two pedophiles and an exhibitionist. The efficacy of MPA with respect to paraphiliac sexual drive was certainly equivocal in this study. Curiously, one of the three cases in which the drug *did* prove efficacious involved the sadistic activities of a middle-aged man who beat his wife, shaved her head, and tied her in chains. The drug failed, however, to prove helpful with three much less violent offenders:

a 27-year-old homosexual pedophile who engaged in frottage, a 52-year-old homosexual pedophile, and a 38-year-old exhibitionist.

Gagne (1981) reported on 48 male paraphiliacs who received MPA and milieu therapy for up to 12 months. Of the 48 offenders, 27 were child molesters, 5 were exhibitionists, 4 were compulsive masturbators, 3 were rapists, and the remaining 9 engaged in other offenses (e.g., incest, voyeurism, transvestism, indecent assault, attempted rape). Despite the apparent heterogeneity of the sample, Gagne identified a number of common features: a history of hypersexuality manifested by frequent masturbation, multiple sex partners, inability to refrain from acting on deviant sexual thoughts, and a high frequency of sexual fantasies and erotic dreams. In addition, all of the child molesters had been introduced to sexual activity by an adult before they reached puberty. Gagne found that 40 of the 48 offenders responded positively to treatment, all within 3 weeks. He observed a decrease in the urge to engage in deviant sexual behavior and improved psychosocial functioning. Although he stated that none of the 40 offenders returned to their pretreatment sexual behavior after their testosterone levels restabilized, there was no indication of the length of follow-up.

Berlin and Meinecke (1981) reported on 20 sexual offenders who were treated with MPA. With the exception of two cases of sadomasochism, all other subjects were child molesters or exhibitionists, with one case of voyeurism and one case of transvestism. At the time of the report, 13 offenders had completed or discontinued treatment. Of those 13, 10 relapsed within 1 year after treatment. The three successes (no relapse within the first 12 months) were all same-sex child molesters. It should be pointed out that all relapses were treatment dropouts, whereas two of the three successes satisfactorily completed the treatment program. As Berlin and Coyle (1981) noted, compliance with the treatment regimen is obviously critical and may depend as much on the nature and intensity of sexual drive as on characterological features of the individual, such as a capacity to form and sustain healthy relationships with peers and a tendency to abuse alcohol. It is apparent that in at least one regard the satisfactory treatment of a paraphilia is no different than the satisfactory treatment of other problems with psychological roots. It demands that the patient be firmly committed to changing his or her behavior.

The principal research on the efficacy of CPA on paraphiliac behaviors has been done by Bradford at the Sexual Behaviors Clinic of the Royal Ottawa Hospital (Bradford, 1983, 1985, 1988, 1990, 1996, 1998). Bradford (1988) reported on an ongoing double-blind placebo crossover study of CPA. Among the participants were 12 sexual offenders with a mean of 2.5 prior convictions. For this subgroup, CPA significantly reduced PT, LH, and FSH during the active treatment phase compared to baseline and placebo. In addition, sexual arousal, as measured by the penile plethysomograph in response to slides of erotic stimuli as well as 2 minutes of covert sexual fantasy, was significantly reduced compared to the placebo condition. Bradford also found that CPA significantly reduced "sexual tension, sexual fantasies, libido, sexual potency, nocturnal emission, spontaneous erections in the morning, and masturbation" (p. 198). In a second phase of this study the effect of CPA on sexual arousal to audiotaped narratives of erotic scenes was examined. The narratives were the standard ones used for the assessment of child molesters. Nineteen offenders were divided into two groups based on basal level of testosterone. Bradford gleaned, from a complicated three-way interaction, evidence to suggest the effect of CPA on sexual arousal responses is influenced by the type of stimulus presented as well as the baseline level of testosterone prior to treatment. Perhaps most noteworthy is Bradford's (1988) report on seven unrelated studies conducted between 1973 and 1977. Each of these studies examined recidivism rates after CPA treatment. The follow-up periods ranged from 1 year to 4.5 years. Six of the seven studies found posttreatment reoffense rates to be zero. Bradford noted that these rates were corrected for poor patient compliance, inadequate dosage, and inadequate information on relapse.

Kiersch (1990) examined eight sexual offenders who were court committed to a state hospital. The eight volunteers, serving as their own controls, received 16 weeks of MPA injections and 16 weeks of saline injections. The eight subjects were six pedophiles and two rapists. Most of the subjects evidenced decreased sexual arousal *both* to MPA and to saline. Although subjects reported a decrease in deviant fantasies, this finding was not supported by the laboratory results (using the plethysmograph). Moreover, although MPA reduced sexual drive, it did not alter sexual preference (i.e., pedophiles were still attracted to children). One of Kiersch's conclusions was that "treatment of hard core [sexual offenders] with MPA in this incarcerated setting is inconclusive and an unreliable means of predicting appropriate dosages and probable favorable outcome" (p. 186).

Gottesman and Schubert (1993) administered low-dose MPA to seven subjects who met the DSM-III-R criteria for paraphilias. Three of the seven patients had "contact" paraphilias (i.e., pedophilia and sexual sadism). Six of the seven patients responded to a dosage level of 60 mg/day with testosterone reduction ranging from 50 to 75%. All seven patients reported fewer paraphiliac fantasies and no recurrence of paraphiliac behavior during the study period (average of 15.3 months).

It should be kept in mind that we have accepted at face value the reliability and generalizability of recidivism rates reported in these highly dissimilar studies involving surgical and chemical castration. In reality, methodological variability in determining recidivism rates makes generalizability across studies virtually impossible. Nevertheless, MPA and CPA are enjoying increasingly widespread use with sex offenders and those with noncriminal paraphiliac and nonparaphiliac-related disorders.

More Recent Alternatives and Complements to MPA and CPA

SSRI Antidepressants. A recent major addition to the pharmacological agents for treating sexual offenders is the group of antidepressants classified as selective serotonin reuptake inhibitors (SSRIs). The SSRIs, fluoxetine and clomipramine, enhance central synaptic transmission of serotonin. The side effects of the SSRIs have generally been known to include a high frequency of sexual dysfunction (e.g., loss of sexual desire and erectile dysfunction). The use of this class of drugs to treat sex offenders, however, was only identified about 10 years ago. One of the earliest reports was by Bianchi (1990), who treated an exhibitionist with fluoxetine. During a 2-month follow-up period, the exhibitionist reported a decrease in paraphiliac fantasies. Over the past 10 years an increasing number of studies have reported on the use of fluoxetine to treat sexual offenders, particularly those who are highly preoccupied with sexual thoughts and fantasies and those who report a high sexual drive or high total sexual outlet (e.g., Bradford, 1990, 1998; Emmanuel, Lydiard, & Ballenger, 1991; Kafka, 1991, 1994, 1997a; Kafka & Prentky, 1992; Perilstein, Lipper, & Friedman, 1991; Rubey, Brady, & Norris, 1993; Stein et al., 1992). By the mid-1990s, sample sizes were becoming respectable. Greenberg, Bradford, Curry, and O'Rouche

(1996a) reported their findings on a retrospective study of 58 paraphiliacs treated with fluoxetine, fluvoxamine, or sertraline for a period of 12 months. Greenberg et al. found that the severity of paraphiliac fantasies was markedly reduced. Greenberg, Bradford, Curry, and O'Rouche (1996b) reported their findings from a controlled, retrospective study involving 95 paraphiliacs. The paraphiliacs, who were treated with SSRIs and psychosocial and behavioral interventions, were matched to a control sample of 104 subjects who received only the psychosocial and behavioral interventions. At the end of 12 weeks, the frequency and severity of paraphiliac fantasies and urges were significantly reduced in the SSRI group.

Several reviews have discussed the role of SSRIs in the treatment of paraphiliac and nonparaphiliac sexual disorders (e.g., Federoff, 1993; Greenberg & Bradford, 1997; Kafka, 1995a,b, 1997a; Maletzky, 1991b; Stein et al., 1992). The literature on the use of SSRIs to mitigate hypersexual desire among sex offenders is, by now, substantial and quite promising. Greenberg and Bradford (1997) noted, for instance, that between 1992 and 1997 there had been 14 case reports or open trials supporting the efficacy of SSRIs for treatment of paraphilias. In a recent theoretical paper, Kafka (1997b) proposed a monoamine hypothesis for the pathophysiology of paraphilias:

> paraphilias are disorders characterized by pathological dimensions including altered sexual preference, relative temporal stability, volitional impairment and possibly, increased sexual drive-related behaviors. Multiple paraphilic disorders appear to more commonly occur in affected persons implying that there is a paraphilic disthesis that predisposes to a variety of socially anomalous sexual outlets. In addition, paraphilic disorders can be accompanied by low self-esteem, social anxiety, social skills impairment, low grade anxious and depressive symptoms, and additional expressions of socially deviant impaired impulse control. These symptoms and syndromes may be, in part, mediated by perturbations in central monoamine neurotransmitters and can be ameliorated by pharmacological agents that affect serotonin, norepinephrine and dopamine. (1997b, p. 351)

A Nosologic Footnote. Reduced central serotonin neurotransmission has been associated with a wide variety of psychiatric problems, including most impulse control disorders (e.g., intermittent explosive disorder, kleptomania, pyromania, pathological gambling, and trichotillomania), suicide, major affective disorders, anxiety disorders, panic disorder, consummatory disorders (including alcoholism), obsessive-compulsive disorder (OCD), and aggressive behavior. Although the biological substrates of anxiety, depression, and impulse control disorders are much more clearly described and documented than the equivalent substrates of paraphiliac disorders, there are noteworthy similarities. Kafka (1997b) refers to some paraphiliac disorders as "socially deviant disorders of impulse control" (p. 349). From a nosological standpoint, it would make most sense, given current wisdom, to classify *some* sex offenders with a sexual impulse control disorder. This is the same class of sex offenders, those who report frequent, intense sexual urges, frequent preoccupation with sexual thoughts and fantasies, those who report a high total sexual outlet, that has been referred to by Carnes (1992) as sexual addicts and by Coleman (1987) as sexually compulsive. From a *legal* standpoint, Kafka (1997a) offered a useful clarification of the relationship between hypersexual desire and "utter lack of power to control one's impulses." Kafka observed that

Hypersexual desire, rather than emphasizing the nature of volitional impairment that accompanies PAs and PRDs [paraphilias and paraphilia-related disorders], is a categorical term to describe men with a persistent high frequency of sexual outlet. In a *subset* of these men hypersexual desire apparently either accompanies or predisposes to a spectrum of clinically significant disorders that include time consuming, highly arousing sexual fantasies, urges, and activities with volitional impairment, distress, or significant role dysfunction. (1997a, p. 519)

Although some have found "considerable overlap" between paraphilias and OCD (Bradford, 1996; Greenberg & Bradford, 1997), the two disorders appear to be pathophysiologically distinct. Although it is not yet clear whether paraphilias share a common pathophysiology with mood disorders, as Kafka (1995b) argued, there is increasing evidence that paraphilias are *not* related to OCD. Perhaps the notable evidence to date is the consistent finding that the comorbidity of OCD among paraphilics is only 10–12% (e.g., Kafka & Prentky, 1994, 1998). Given that symptoms of OCD typically express themselves in a variety of different ways in the same individual, one would certainly predict a much higher incidence of OCD symptoms among paraphiliacs were "paraphilia" part of the OCD spectrum. By contrast, the lifetime prevalence of mood disorders was 73.5% among men with paraphilia disorders and 80.8% among paraphilia-related disorders (Kafka & Prentky, 1994). In a subsequent study, the lifetime prevalence of mood disorders was 76.7% among sex offenders, 66.7% among paraphiliac nonoffenders, and 66.7% among those with paraphilia-related disorders (Kafka & Prentky, 1998).

LHRH Agonists and GnRH Inhibiting Factors. Berlin (1983) has described yet another approach to testosterone reduction, the use of gonadotropin-releasing hormone (GnRH). Long-term administration of GnRH paradoxically inhibits the release of FSH and LH from the anterior pituitary gland, which in turn results in decreased testosterone production from the testes. Speculation about a hypothalamic–pituitary–gonadal dysfunction in some cases of paraphilia (Gaffney & Berlin, 1984) has also given rise to the experimental use of luteinizing hormone-releasing hormone (LHRH) agonists with paraphiliacs who are refractory to other chemical interventions (Dickey, 1992; Richer & Crismon, 1993; Rousseau, Couture, Dupont, Labrie, & Couture, 1990). LHRH initially stimulates gonadotropin secretion, which is followed by a loss of LHRH receptors at the gonadotropin-synthesizing cells of the pituitary, resulting in reduced LH secretion and a marked reduction in androgen biosynthesis (Neumann & Kalmus, 1991). This phenonmenon of "receptor downregulation" occurs 2–3 weeks after onset of medication (Neumann & Kalmus, 1991).

In one of the very few empirical studies to date, Rosler and Witztum (1998) administered triptorelin (Decapeptyl-CR), a long-acting agonist analogue of GnRH, to 30 men with "severe longstanding paraphilia" (25 of whom were pedophiles). In this uncontrolled, observational study, Rosler and Witztum found that all of the men experienced a marked decrease in deviant sexual fantasies, from an average of 48 per week before therapy to 0 per week during therapy, as well as a decrease in the number of deviant sexual behaviors, from an average of 5 per month to 0 during therapy. Rosler and Witztum reported that "these effects were evident after 3 to 10 months of therapy and persisted in all 24 men who continued therapy for at least 1 year" (p. 416). Mean serum testosterone levels dropped from an average of 545 ng/dl prior to therapy to an average of 23 ng/dl after 42 months of treatment. Principal side effects included erectile failure, hot flashes, decrease in bone mineral density, and transient pain at the injection site.

Although triptorelin is not presently available in the United States, similar long-acting analogues of naturally occurring GnRH or LHRH are available. The two that are approved by the FDA, leuprolide (Lupron) and goserelin (Zoladex), are indicated for use with prostatic cancer, central precocious puberty, and endometriosis. These synthetic analogues possess greater potency than the natural hormone. The drug that has been most often used in the United States with sex offenders is Lupron. The advantages of drugs like Lupron over the more commonly used antiandrogen (MPA) are that they have relatively fewer side effects than MPA and are more potent than MPA when it comes to suppressing testicular steroidogenesis. The disadvantage is that such drugs, at least at the present time, are more expensive. The GnRH or LHRH analogues represent the latest in the chemical agents used to treat sex offenders. We expect that these drugs will become an increasingly familiar part of the regimen used to treat sex offenders, and that with increased use will come controlled double-blind studies examining not only the efficacy of Lupron but also the comparative efficacy of Lupron, MPA, and fluoxetine. Unltimately, the combination of fluoxetine with an androgen-suppressing agent may be most effective for some sex offenders with exceptionally high sexual drive coupled with volitional dysfunction.

Legal and Ethical Issues Related to Medication

Legal and ethical considerations in the use of antiandrogen medication with sexual offenders have been addressed by Berlin (1989b), Demsky (1984), Kafka (1995b), Maletzky (1991a), Melella, Travin, and Cullen (1989), Miller (1998), and Pallone (1990). In brief, these issues include the administration of a medication for off-label purposes (i.e., not FDA-approved for use with sexual offenders), requiring a detailed statement of informed consent, and legislative efforts to mandate the use of antiandrogen medication.

Informed consent requires that the individual *fully* understand what he is being asked to consent to (i.e., precisely what is involved in taking the medication and what the potential benefits and risks are). Obtaining informed consent varies in difficulty depending on the intervention. Informed consent is relatively easy to obtain if the client is an adult of average intelligence and is being asked to participate in group therapy. Perhaps the most complicated consent process comes about when we ask the client to take antiandrogen medication. In addition, the assumption that consent is voluntary may be questionable. As Halleck (1981) remarked "can anyone facing incarceration or the threat of incarceration provide competent, informed, and voluntary consent to a potentially disabling treatment?" (pp. 642–643). Maletzky (1991a) similarly questioned whether offenders have "free choice" when they are subject to the scrutiny of the legal system. Berlin (1989b) has maintained, however, that when the client is fully informed and voluntary consent can be obtained, the use of antiandrogen medication should pose few legal and ethical concerns.

Perhaps the single most important legal issue as it pertains to surgical or chemical castration is the Eighth Amendment protection against cruel and unusual punishment. As Pallone (1990) has pointed out, the courts are unlikely to impose surgical castration, deemed to be a form of mutilation, since it will be in violation of the Eighth Amendment. Indeed, the U.S. Supreme Court termed castration "barbaric" almost a century ago [*Weems v. United States*, 217 U.S. 349 (1910)]. Pallone reviewed a case in which the South Carolina

Supreme Court vacated the sentence of a trial judge, ruling that "voluntary" castration was not a viable sentencing option (1990, p. 88). The critical issue, as Pallone noted, was *not* whether the defendants possessed free will and could freely choose to be castrated (i.e., whether the decision was truly "voluntary"), but whether the judge had the constitutional right even to offer the option of castration. The answer, at least in this case, was No.

California was the first state to pass a law making compulsory antiandrogen treatment a condition of probation for certain convicted sex offenders (California Assembly Bill 3339). The California statute went into effect January 1, 1997. Within a year, Florida, Georgia, and Montana followed suit (Miller, 1998). Thus far, however, the compulsory antiandrogen medication laws have not fared nearly as well as the sexual predator laws. Similar bills in 23 other states were defeated, died, were withdrawn, or continue to be debated (Miller, 1998). Amazingly, of the 27 bills calling for compulsory antiandrogen treatment, only 5 required any type of medical evaluation prior to the imposition of the condition.

The legal issues raised by statute (or court)-mandated antiandrogen medication include (1) violation of the Eighth Amendment protection against cruel and unusual punishment, (2) violation of the Equal Protection Clause, (3) inability to obtain truly voluntary informed consent, (4) violation of the First Amendment right to privacy, and (5) violation of a constitutional right to be punished based on a "right to personhood" (see Miller, 1998). These various issues, particularly the question of whether compulsory antiandrogen treatment constitutes an infringement of the Eighth Amendment, have been the subject of considerable debate (see Miller, 1998), much of which could be characterized as partisan. There clearly is *legal* (as opposed to clinical) ambiguity around the many issues raised by compulsory treatment of sex offenders with medication. Berlin (1989b) has made a good counterargument, for instance, in noting that *intentionally withholding* antiandrogen medication from fully informed, willing sexual offenders could be considered a violation of the Eighth Amendment.

There are, of course, compliance considerations as well. The compliance issue, seemingly more problematic with medication, is, in fact, a concern with surgical castration too. In both cases, the effects of reduced testosterone can be reversed simply by obtaining supplementary testosterone "on the street." Thus, in either case, a client can feign compliance.

Although there may be legal ambiguity with regard to compulsory antiandrogen treatment, there is *no* clinical ambiguity. Mandating antiandrogen treatment for *all* sexual offenders is clinically indefensible. Miller (1998) observed that

> A blanket requirement that all sex offenders in a given legal (not clinical) class be forced to take them [sex drive-reducing drugs] to be released from prison, regardless of their clinical conditions, is neither sound social policy nor acceptable medical practice. (pp. 194–195)

Miller's point is patently obvious. From a strictly medical/clinical standpoint, there is absolutely no justification for the blanket application of medication, or any other single treatment intervention, for the extraordinarily heterogeneous population of sexual offenders. There are, after all, many sex offenders who do *not* commit their crimes because of a runaway libido. For them, the motives that drove their offenses are likely to be unaffected by antiandrogen medication. As we have noted before, there are *no* silver bullets for a problem as heterogeneous in its manifestation and as widespread as sexually coercive behavior. Miller (1998) concluded with a terse reminder that by using psychiatrists and their medications the criminal justice system is attempting to legitimize and sanitize what are at heart punitive programs. Psychiatrists should not lend credibility to such efforts, but should actively oppose them in the courts and legislatures. (p. 199)

Concluding Comments

Since the explicit purpose of surgical or chemical castration is to reduce sexual arousal and sexual fantasy, it would stand to reason that castration (or the chemical equivalent) would be most effective with those offenders whose behavior is highly repetitive, driven by uncontrollable sexual urges, or where there are highly intrusive, repetitive sexual fantasies. Both surgical castration and antiandrogen drugs clearly suppress or reduce sexual urges. Not surprisingly, however, the net effect of accomplishing this aim in humans is complex. There is evidence, for instance, that the reduction of testosterone functions primarily to alter the *affect* associated with sexual drive and only secondarily to suppress hypothalamic releasing factors and pituitary gonadotropins (Cooper, 1981). Thus, the principal effect of reducing testosterone may be to blunt the phenomenological experience of sexual arousal and hence to diminish the strength of one's sexual drive.

These conclusions are based on the supposition that there is a correlation between strength of sexual desire and testosterone level. This remains an empirical question. At the present time, most of the empirical literature addresses the relation between testosterone level and aggressive behavior, not sexual behavior (see Prentky, 1985, for a review). Indeed, Rada, Laws, and Kellner (1976) found that rapists who were rated as being most violent had, on average, significantly higher testosterone levels than normals, child molesters, *and* less violent rapists. Thus, within a sample of sexual offenders, testosterone correlated with degree of manifest violence. Rada (1981) once again found that the most violent sexual offenders, in this case a subgroup of child molesters, had the highest average testosterone levels. In yet a third study, Rada, Laws, Kellner, Stivastava, and Peake (1983) found a nonsignificant trend in the same direction. Sexual offenders who evidenced more violence had higher levels of testosterone. Thus, based on the work of Rada and his colleagues, it appears that testosterone level is more directly related to the feeling of anger than to the feeling of sexual arousal.

In conclusion, antiandrogen drugs should *never* be used as exclusive treatments for paraphiliac and aggressive sexual behaviors. The clinic at Johns Hopkins University has coupled medication with counseling since the inception of the program in 1966. From a therapeutic standpoint, antiandrogen medication has a very important place in the armamentarium of clinicians who work with sexual offenders. It makes no more sense, however, to give antiandrogen medication to every sexual offender than it does to give antidepressant medication to every sexual offender. Antiandrogen medication is *not* appropriate for all sexual offenders and should never be administered indiscriminately to all sexual offenders. As antiandrogen medication continues to prove efficacious with specifiable subtypes of paraphiliacs and sex offenders, its maximum effectiveness will be realized when it is fully integrated into treatment regimens that are tailored to the needs of the individual.

This is one instance in which William of Ockham would agree. There are no simple solutions or easy answers to the problem of sexual violence. Much as we might otherwise like to believe, the mandated use of antiandrogen drugs provides not even a tarnished bullet. Effective interventions will, inevitably, be as complex as the manifest behavior.

QUANDARIES IN THE MEASUREMENT OF REOFFENSE RATES

There is perhaps no single piece of information that is more sought after than the *rate* at which sex offenders recommit their crimes. The *rate* of sexual recidivism has become something of the Holy Grail of our field. It is much coveted, in part, because it can be used as a powerful weapon to bring to bear on social policy and rape law. Depending on one's philosophical bent, treatment services can be fervently supported, or condemned with equal passion. The absence of solid empirical data (representing multiple sites and diverse populations) that address the question of recidivism rates among different groups of sexual offenders fosters heated debate (i.e., there are so many published rates that one can pick and choose whatever rates one wishes in order to support one's "case").

Studies examining reoffense rates among sex offenders have varied in a number of critical dimensions (Tracy, Donnelly, Morgenbesser, & McDonald, 1983), such are: (1) the study sample, (2) the criterion for recidivism, which includes the source of criterion information, the types of outcome criminal activity assessed, and the operationalization of recidivism, and (3) the length and consistency of the follow-up period.

The sources of outcome data and the criteria for recidivism, in terms of both the criminal behavior domains considered (only sexual offenses, all violent offenses, any offense, and so on) and the legal definition of what constitutes recidivism (a new arrest, a new conviction, any parole violation, and so on) have varied considerably among studies. Whereas some studies have accessed only a single fallible outcome source like FBI records (Hall & Proctor, 1987) or probation records (Romero & Williams, 1985), others (e.g., Rice et al., 1990, 1991) have assessed outcome using multiple record sources. Some studies have analyzed only global sex versus nonsex offense outcome categories (e.g., Romero & Williams, 1985), whereas other investigators have examined more differentiated subcategories of offenses (e.g., Hall & Proctor, 1987). Finally, studies have differed in how recidivism was operationalized. Some have defined recidivism as an arrest for a crime (Hall & Proctor, 1987; Romero & Williams, 1985); others have used conviction (Hanson et al., 1993; Rice et al., 1990, 1991); and still others have targeted sentencing (Christiansen, Elers-Nielsen, Le Maire, & Sturup, 1965). Such definitional variation could yield significant fluctuation in recidivism estimates. Variations in the length of the follow-up period could also affect recidivism estimates and may even be differentially important for different types of offenders.

Studies to date vary widely in the at-risk follow-up period, with the 15- to 30-year follow-up of Hanson et al. (1993) being one of the longest. Miller (1984), by contrast, found that 55 out of 68 (81%) reports of recidivism rates in the United States and Canada were based on a period of 12 months or less. Maltz (1984) confirmed that 1 year is the most common observation period. Moreover, within studies offenders may vary in their time at risk (e.g., 12 to 24 years in Christiansen et al., 1965, and 15 to 30 years in Hanson et al., 1993). Commenting on the Christiansen et al. (1965) study, Soothill and Gibbens (1978) noted a probable shortcoming of the study that may well mean that it tends to underestimate the recidivism of sexual offenders over a long period. Soothill and Gibbens argued that the at-risk or exposure times were improperly calculated in the Christiansen et al. study. The sample in the Christiansen et al. study was gathered from a 10-year period (1929–1939), but all cases were followed-up in the early 1950s, yielding a variable period at risk. Soothill and

·Gibbens (1978) acknowledged that their own study (Soothill, Jack, & Gibbens, 1976) was vulnerable to the same criticism, and they proposed that the problem be addressed using life-table methodology. The life table developed by Soothill and Gibbens revealed an overall reconviction rate of 48% by the end of the their maximum observation period (22nd year), compared with an equivalent estimate of 38.5% using the conventional procedure of calculating the percent failures each year. Using their life table, Soothill and Gibbens recalculated the sexual recidivism rate at the end of the follow-up period, noting an increase from 18.4% to 23%. Perhaps the most important consequence of their readjusted figures was the observation that only half of the reconvictions for a violent offense (sexual or nonsexual) occurred within the first 5 years.

Since recidivism will, inevitably, be the centerpiece for the evaluation of treatment effectiveness, we will at least provide some commentary on the areas that are most contributory to noncomparability across recidivism studies with sex offenders. The data that we will present come from a 25-year follow-up of 251 sex offenders (136 rapists and 115 child molesters) who were discharged from the Massachusetts Treatment Center between 1959 and 1984 (Prentky, Lee, et al., 1997). Although the study period was fixed at 25 years, from 1959 through January 1985, the actual exposure time varied considerably among the subjects, depending on their discharge date.

The most common method of estimating recidivism is to calculate the simple percentage or proportion of individuals who reoffended during the study period. This method will *underestimate* the rate of recidivism, because some of those individuals who were in the community for a briefer period of time may still reoffend. This problem is addressed by using survival analysis, a collection of methods for analyzing time-to-reoffense outcomes that takes into account not only whether members of each group commit subsequent crimes, but also the length of time between release and criminal activity. Recidivism may be operationalized in a variety of different ways. As noted, the most common method is to report the simple proportion of individuals known to have reoffended during the study period. We calculated this simple proportion to illustrate the magnitude of underestimation. We report the proportion here (in the text and tables) as percentages. We also operationalized recidivism as a failure rate (FR), calculated as the proportion of individuals who reoffended using survival analysis. Failure rate is an estimate that takes into account the amount of time each offender has been on the street and thus able to reoffend. Again, as noted, procedures that take into account time at risk (or exposure time) yield much more accurate estimates of recidivism. In both instances, of course, recidivism is limited only to those criminal offenders who were detected.

Analysis of Criminal Offense Categories

In the first analysis, we examined changes in detected recidivism as a function of criminal offense category. Criminal offense charges were classified into one of three groups (sexual, victim-involved; nonsexual, victim-involved; and nonsexual, victimless). The number of noncensored observations (NC; the number of individuals who reoffended), the number of censored observations (C; the number of individuals not known to have reoffended), the corresponding Weibull parameters for each offense domain and the composite, the mean (average exposure time before reoffense) and its standard deviation (σ) are

**Table 1. First Occurrence of Each Disposition
for Each Category of Criminal Activity (Rapists, N = 136)**

Classification by disposition	Classification of criminal activity			
	Composite	Sexual (victim)	Nonsexual (victim)	Nonsexual (victimless)
Charge				
NC	76	35	45	48
C	58	101	91	86
α/γ	.224/.554	.091/.528	.113/.552	.124/.574
M/σ	2.70/1.81	4.55/1.90	3.95/1.81	3.64/1.74
Conviction				
NC	60	21	27	30
C	74	115	109	104
α/γ	.139/.597	.042/.608	.065/.542	.061/.636
M/σ	3.31/1.68	5.20/1.64	5.05/1.85	4.39/1.57
Prison				
NC	42	18	20	10
C	94	118	116	126
α/γ	.097/.545	.042/.540	.047/.533	.028/.465
M/σ	4.28/1.83	5.87/1.85	5.72/1.88	7.70/2.15

Note. Adapted from Prentky, Lee, Knight, & Cerce (1997). Conviction includes those who went to prison. Prison is a subset, and includes those who were convicted *and* imprisoned. C: number of censored observations; NC: number of noncensored observations. α: Weibull scale parameter; γ: Weibull shape parameter. M: mean number of years; σ: standard deviation.

presented in Tables 1 (rapists) and 2 (child molesters) and the two estimates of recidivism based on the simple proportion (%) and survival analysis (FR) are presented in Table 3.

For rapists, the percentage of new sexual offenses at the end of the study period (25 years) was 26%, with an average of 4.55 years before sexual reoffense. By comparison, the FR at the end of the study period was *39%*. The percentage of new nonsexual offenses were somewhat higher, 33% for victim-involved and 36% for noncontact crimes. The average exposure time prior to committing these offenses was 3.95 and 3.64 years, respectively. The FR for these two offense domains were 49% and 54%, respectively. The percentage for any new offense (using any criminal charge from the three domains) was 57%, with an average exposure time of 2.70 years before an offense. The FR for any charge by the end of the study period was 74%.

For child molesters, the percentage of new sexual offenses at the end of the study period was 32%, with an average of 3.64 years before reoffense. The FR for sexual offenses by the end of the study period was 52%. The percentage of new nonsexual, victim-involved offenses was considerably lower (14%), with an average exposure time of 5.58 years before reoffense. The FR for this category was 23%. The percentage of new nonsexual, noncontact offenses was comparable to the equivalent estimate for sexual offenses (30%), with a similar average exposure time (3.90 years). The FR for nonsexual, noncontact crimes was 48%. The percentage for any new offense (any criminal charge) was 54%, with an average

**Table 2. First Occurrence of Each Disposition
for Each Category of Criminal Activity
(Child Molesters, $N = 115$)**

Classification by disposition	Classification of criminal activity			
	Composite	Sexual (victim)	Nonsexual (victim)	Nonsexual (victimless)
Charge				
NC	62	37	16	34
C	52	78	99	80
α/γ	.150/.688	.063/.758	.042/.569	.089/.620
M/σ	2.75/1.45	3.64/1.32	5.58/1.76	3.90/1.61
Conviction				
NC	44	29	07	14
C	70	86	108	100
α/γ	.081/.729	.043/.791	.017/.576	.029/.671
M/σ	3.45/1.37	3.98/1.27	7.05/1.74	5.28/1.49
Prison				
NC	35	26	05	07
C	80	89	110	108
α/γ	.063/.707	.039/.776	.015/.496	.016/.613
M/σ	3.92/1.42	4.17/1.29	8.50/2.02	6.78/1.63

Note. Adapted from Prentky, Lee, Knight, & Cerce (1997). Conviction includes those who went to prison. Prison is a subset, and includes those who were convicted *and* imprisoned. C: number of censored observations; NC: number of noncensored observations. α: Weibull scale parameter; γ: Weibull shape parameter. M: mean number of years; σ: standard deviation.

exposure time of 2.75 years before an offense. The FR for any charge by the end of the study period was 75%.

Analysis of Legal Disposition

In the second analysis, we examined changes in detected recidivism as a function of disposition (charge, conviction, or prison).

Of the 136 rapists (Table 1), 101 received no new charges for a sexual offense during the study period. Of the remaining 35 offenders, 14 were charged but never convicted, 3 were convicted but not imprisoned, and 18 were convicted and imprisoned. The percentage for charge was 26%, followed by 15% for conviction and 13% for prison. The equivalent FRs for these three dispositional categories were 39, 24, and 19%. Thus, the difference in FR between charge and conviction for a sexual offense was 15% and the difference in FR between charge and imprisonment was 20%. The underestimation when using percentage was greatest for convictions (38%). The underestimation was 33% for charges and 32% for imprisonment. Changes in percentage for the three dispositional categories were similar for nonsexual offenses. Percentages, with FRs in parentheses, for nonsexual, victim-involved offenses were 33% (49%), 20% (31%), and 15% (23%) and for nonsexual, victimless offenses were 36% (54%), 22% (38%), and 7% (12%). For the composite, the percentage

**Table 3. Comparison of Recidivism Rates
for Charge, Conviction, and Prison at Year 25**

Classification by disposition	Composite	Classification of criminal activity		
		Sexual (victim)	Nonsexual (victim)	Nonsexual (victimless)
Rapists, $N = 136$				
Charge				
%	57%	26%	33%	36%
FR	74%	39%	49%	54%
Conviction				
%	45%	15%	20%	22%
FR	60%	24%	31%	38%
Prison				
%	31%	13%	15%	07%
FR	42%	19%	23%	12%
Child molesters, $N = 115$				
Charge				
%	54%	32%	14%	30%
FR	75%	52%	23%	48%
Conviction				
%	39%	25%	06%	12%
FR	56%	41%	10%	22%
Prison				
%	30%	23%	04%	06%
FR	44%	37%	07%	21%

Note. Adapted from Prentky, Lee, Knight, & Cerce (1997). $: simple proportion of detected reoffenses in each category. FR: failure rate, derived from survival analysis.

and the FR for the three dispositional categories were 57% (74%), 45% (60%), and 31% (42%).

Of the 115 child molesters (Table 2), 78 received no new charges for a sexual offense during the study period. Of the remaining 37 offenders, 8 were charged but never convicted, 3 were convicted but not imprisoned, and 26 were convicted and imprisoned. The percentage of new sexual offenses, with FRs in parentheses, was 32% (52%) for charges, 25% (41%) for conviction, and 23% (37%) for prison. Thus, the difference in FR between charge and conviction for a sexual offense was 11% and the difference in FR between charge and imprisonment was 15%. Underestimation among child molesters when using the percentage was similar for all three dispositional categories (38% for charges, 39% for convictions, and 38% for imprisonment). Child molesters were more likely than the rapists to have been charged with a victimless than a victim-involved offense (30% versus 14%). Although somewhat more likely to be convicted for a victimless offense (12% versus 6%), child molesters were rarely imprisoned for either offense category (6% versus 4%). The percentages and the FRs for nonsexual, victim-involved offenses were 14% (23%) for charges, 6% (10%) for convictions, and 4% (7%) for imprisonment. Percentages and FRs for nonsexual, victimless offenses were 30% (48%), 12% (22%), and 6% (21%) for charges, convictions, and prison, respectively. For the composite, the percentages and FRs for the three dispositional categories were 54% (75%), 39% (56%), and 30% (44%) for charges, convictions, and prison, respectively.

Analysis of Exposure Time

In the third analysis, we examined the cumulative failure rates for new charges for sexual offenses only (Table 4) and for new charges for any offense (Table 5) using nine time gates, broken down by charge, conviction, and prison. Among the rapists, there was a stable 2–3% recidivism rate for new *sexual* charges per year through the 5th year. The rate drops to about 1% per year every year thereafter through the 25th year (end of the study period). If we restricted our follow-up to the conventional exposure period of 12 or 24 months, we would err by approximately 30 or 25%, respectively. If we extended our follow-up to 60 months, we would still miss approximately 20% of the new charges. The rate of recidivism using conviction or incarceration was one-half that of the rate using charge during the first 5 years and slightly less than one-half thereafter. By the end of the study period, the conviction and incarceration rates were 24 and 19%, respectively, compared to the charge rate of 38%.

Among the child molesters, the cumulative failure rate for new *sexual* charges is 4% per year through the 3rd year, dropping to 3% in the 4th year and 2% in the 5th year. After Year 5, the charge rate continues to increase at noteworthy increments, 11% between Year 5 and Year 10, 9% between Year 10 and Year 15, 7% between Year 15 and Year 20, and 6% between Year 20 and Year 25.

If we restricted our follow-up to the conventional exposure period of 12 or 24 months, we would err by approximately 45 or 40%, respectively. If we extended our follow-up to 60 months, we would still miss approximately 30% of the new charges. The rate of recidivism using conviction or incarceration was two-thirds that of the rate using charge throughout the study period. By the end of the study period, the conviction and incarceration rates were 41 and 37%, respectively, compared to the charge rate of 51%.

Table 4. Cumulative Failure Rates
for Sexual Offenses over Nine Time Gates

| | Time gates (years) | | | | | | | | |
Disposition	1	2	3	4	5	10	15	20	25
			Rapists						
Charge	.09	.12	.15	.17	.19	.26	.31	.36	.39
Conviction	.04	.06	.08	.09	.11	.16	.20	.23	.24
Prison	.04	.06	.07	.08	.10	.14	.17	.19	.19
			Child molesters						
Charge	.06	.10	.14	.17	.19	.30	.39	.46	.52
Conviction	.04	.07	.10	.12	.14	.23	.31	.37	.41
Prison	.04	.07	.09	.11	.13	.21	.28	.33	.37

Note. Adapted from Prentky, Lee, Knight, & Cerce (1997).

**Table 5. Cumulative Failure Rates
for All New Offenses over Nine Time Gates**

Disposition	Time gates (years)								
	1	2	3	4	5	10	15	20	25
				Rapists					
Charge	.20	.28	.34	.38	.42	.55	.63	.69	.74
Conviction	.13	.19	.23	.27	.30	.42	.50	.56	.60
Prison	.08	.13	.16	.19	.21	.29	.35	.39	.42
				Child molesters					
Charge	.14	.22	.27	.32	.37	.52	.62	.69	.75
Conviction	.08	.13	.16	.20	.23	.35	.44	.51	.56
Prison	.06	.10	.13	.15	.18	.27	.35	.41	.44

Note. Adapted from Prentky, Lee, Knight, & Cerce (1997).

The cumulative failure rates for *any* new offense are provided in Table 5. Among the rapists, there was a steady increase throughout the follow-up period. Although the new charge rate was 42% by the end of the 5th year, the rate continued to climb after Year 5, reaching 74% by the end of the study period. The gap between the charge rate and the conviction rate was consistently between 11 and 13% throughout the study. The rate for incarceration declined throughout the study, with the gap between conviction and incarceration starting out at 5% in Year 1 and steadily increasing to 9% after Year 5 and 18% by the end of the study.

Among the child molesters, there was a steady increase in charges for new offenses throughout the follow-up period, with the rate starting out at 14%, increasing to 37% at Year 5 and 75% by the end of the study. The gap between the charge rate and the conviction rate increased steadily, from 6% in Year 1 to 14% by Year 5, 17% by Year 10, and 18% throughout the remainder of the study. The gap between conviction and incarceration rates steadily increased, from 2% in Year 1, to 5% at Year 5 and 12% by the end of the study.

Slow and Constant "Decay"

It is quite apparent for both of these samples that the "decay process" is relatively slow and constant. Contrary to conventional wisdom, most reoffenses did not occur within the first several years. As Gibbens et al. (1978) found more than 20 years ago and Hanson et al. (1993) reported more recently, child molesters are at risk to reoffend sexually throughout their lives. The FR for sexual charges between Year 20 and Year 25 was 6% among the child molesters in our sample. Indeed, the cumulative FR among the child molesters *after Year 10* until the end of the study period was 22%. It is equally important to note, however, that we observed the constant decay among the rapists as well. Among the rapists, the cumulative FR for sexual charges *after Year 10* was 13%.

Hanson et al. (1993) noted that the greatest risk period for their child molesters seemed to be the first 5–10 years. Given the temporal stability of failure in our sample, it would be difficult to impose a single high-risk window. The sexual FR for child molesters was 4%/

year through Year 3. Thereafter, however, the FR was stable at 2–3%/year through Year 15, and slightly over 1%/year for the next 10 years. The pattern was the same for the rapists, only at a slightly lower rate. The sexual FR for rapists was 3%/year through Year 3, 2%/year through Year 5, and 1–1.5%/year thereafter until Year 20. If we adopted the common risk period of 5 years, we would miss slightly under two-thirds (63%) of new sexual charges for child molesters and half (51%) of new sexual charges for rapists.

Sampling Differences

As Tracy et al. (1983) observed, it certainly appears that sampling differences, in addition to the other factors examined in this study, contributed considerable variability to recidivism rates. It has been well established, for example, that antisociality, psychopathy, lifestyle impulsivity, and number of prior sexual offenses are factors known to be correlated with reoffense risk for sexual offenders (Hanson & Bussiere, 1998; Hanson et al., 1993; Prentky & Knight, 1991; Prentky, Knight, et al., 1995; Prentky, Knight, et al., 1997; Quinsey et al., 1995a,b; Rice et al., 1990). Thus, in any given sample, the higher the proportion of offenders with a history of impulsive, antisocial behavior and known prior sexual offenses, the higher the predicted reoffense rate is. It truly is ironic that the arguably more difficult task of empirically confirming constructs that differentiate sexual offenders with respect to reoffense risk has been successfully addressed, while the patently easier task of controlling for methodological variability has not been achieved.

What Will the Holy Grail Reveal?

We suggested at the beginning that politicians, reporters, and clinicians are all in search of *the true* recidivism rate, the Holy Grail of our field. If found, what would the Holy Grail reveal? It would inform us, quite discreetly no doubt, that we have been chasing wild geese. Simply put, there can be *no* single rate at which sex offenders reoffend. First, the word *rate* implies a certain quantity or amount of something in relation to a unit of something else (e.g., a rate of 60 miles *per* hour or $6.00 *per* pound, or $20 *per* hour). A recidivism *rate* must specify the precise unit, typically measured in years (e.g., 8% in 1 year, 30% in 5 years). Thus, the rate will change depending on the intended unit (length of exposure time). Second, as we have attempted to illustrate, the rate will change depending on a variety of other factors, such as how we measured recidivism, how we defined recidivism, and the quality of the data that we used to determine recidivism. Third, as a group, sex offenders are extremely heterogeneous with respect to rates of reoffense. Not only do child molesters, as a group, differ from rapists, as a group, but within those two groups there are marked differences in recidivism rates. Although we will most likely never achieve this level of specificity, we should, ideally, posit *ranges* for clearly specified *legal dispositions* (e.g., new arrests for sexual recidivism among incest offenders) and *exposure time or length of follow-up* (within 5 years). For example, the 5-year sexual recidivism rate, based on new arrests, for exclusive endogamous incest offenders might be 5 to 10%; the 3-year sexual recidivism rate, based on new arrests, for highly fixated extrafamilial child molesters might be 12 to 18%; or the 10-year sexual recidivism rate, based on new arrests, for rapists with an extensive history of impulsive, antisocial behavior might be 25 to 30%. (The ranges provided here are strictly for purposes of illustration.)

Forensic Implications

Sex offenders constitute a subsample of dangerous criminals who both elicit a disproportionate number of special statutes involving legal proceedings for commitments to segregated units of prisons or mental health facilities, and require an inordinate number of ad hoc discretionary and dispositional decisions. Forensic risk assessments of sex offenders are ubiquitous. Clinicians are routinely asked to examine sex offenders in child protection cases, juvenile preventative detention and juvenile waiver hearings, domestic violence cases, bail hearings, during pretrial and sentencing, at time of parole, and in connection with civil commitments (Witt et al., 1996). In addition, states that have "sexual predator" laws typically have examining boards that require clinicians to apply these laws to offenders. The problem of sexual aggression is not likely to abate in the foreseeable future, and the consequent demand for statutes governing these offenders and the accompanying requisite forensic decisions about their status is not apt to decline.

Despite this demand for accurate decisions about sex offenders, the judges, attorneys, examiners, and clinicians, who are required to implement the "special" sex offenders laws, have had to rely on extant assumptions of dangerousness and reoffense risk that often are ill-informed or erroneous. Inaccurate decisions lead to suboptimal dispositions and increase the likelihood of further victims and additional expense. Indeed, all facets of the social and political response to sexual violence from the enactment of more effective legislation to enhancing the efficacy of discretionary decisions rely on an informed, empirically sound understanding of the reoffense risks posed by different groups of sex offenders.

Methodological variability in follow-up time and outcome operationalization constitute major sources of the marked inconsistencies in recidivism rates across studies. There are, moreover, striking differences in outcome among different types of sex offenders (Knight, 1999; Prentky et al., 1995; Prentky et al., 1997a) that go well beyond the apparent differences between rapists and child molesters that may be observed in the study that we just described. There is a paucity of information on base rates for recidivism among subgroups of sex offenders. Clearly, there is an urgent need to address these methodological problems so that more accurate and standardized base rates can be determined, thereby improving the accuracy of risk-based, high-stakes decision-making about sex offenders.

Clinical Implications

These base rate problems also affect the evaluation of treatment outcome. As Barbaree (1997) clearly demonstrated, failure to establish more reliable base rates for recidivism among subgroups of sexual offenders severely undermines any attempt to demonstrate the efficacy of treatment for sexual offenders. The temporal stability of recidivism that we found in our study suggests that intensive community supervision and aftercare should be the centerpiece of any secondary intervention strategy. This, of course, is not a novel recommendation. It was recommended almost 30 years ago in an article by Meeks (1963) on criminal sexual psychopaths. At the present time, the most effective known technique for reducing risk of relapse is intensive supervision by trained probation officers or parole agents and an aftercare plan that includes treatment (e.g., Marques et al., 1993). It appears that such supervision, at least for higher-risk offenders, should be long-term. The cost of long-term supervision is relatively trivial when compared to the costs associated with revictimization (Prentky & Burgess, 1990).

Policy Implications

The recommendation for intensive community supervision and informed aftercare plans impacts on policy decisions about sex offenders. The decision, now in vogue, to require sex offenders to serve all, or most, of their sentences is a matter of public policy. The role of empirical data in such decisions is oftentimes moderated by other considerations, including social and moral issues and practical concerns, such as resource allocation (Rice, 1997). The data in the study reported here suggest, however, that, unless one is willing to impose indeterminate sentences with all of their concomitant problems, public safety would best be served by instituting prolonged supervision after release. When offenders are returned to the community, reintegration under supervision will provide a far more effective safety net than returning offenders to the community with no supervision. As Rice (1997) pointed out, even among the more dangerous, less treatment responsive psychopathic offenders, supervision increases the likelihood of detection. Given the proclivity of a core subgroup of sexual offenders to reoffend, close monitoring and supervision may be the most effective secondary intervention that we have at the present time. Such a conclusion is, of course, inconsistent with the recent trend to require sex offenders to serve their entire sentence, thereby eliminating parole. Although this policy will keep offenders off the street for longer periods of time and will satisfy the need to appear punitive, it will return offenders to the community unsupervised. If community safety is more important than retribution, supervision must be prioritized over "maxing out."

A PATH NOT YET TAKEN

The path into the twenty-first century must move us beyond the "high drama" of sexual assault that is fueled by the media and responded to by politicians who draft myopic, reactive laws. The model that we propose treats sexual assault as a public health problem, indeed a very serious public health problem. The branches of this pervasive, dendritic problem insinuate into and directly affect *all* aspects of society. Despite the hypervigilant attention to sexual crimes by the media and the draconian responses to those crimes by many politicians, our legal and social remedies are woefully inadequate and fail to address the preponderance of individuals who violate the sexual autonomy of others. By and large, those who sexually intimidate and sexually coerce others do so with impunity. Even clear instances of aggravated sexual assault may be treated by the entertainment industry as normative behavior. In sum the number of individuals who are apprehended, charged, and convicted for their sexual crimes is greatly eclipsed by the total number of men (and women) who engage in the full gamut of sexually coercive and abusive behavior.

The *totality* of the problem of sexual coercion in our society is incalculable. In its *larger* context, sexual coercion permeates all of society, affects hundreds of thousands of people each year, places an incalculable financial burden on society, and makes vast demands on systemic resources. Society now spends hundreds of millions of dollars each year to cope with the direct and indirect effects of the problem. A complex system of laws, state and federal, attempt to contain the problem. Clearly, by *any* definition, sexual coercion must be regarded as a public health problem.

In this last section, we would like to propose an adaptation of a public health model for managing and deescalating the problem of sexual assault and sexual coercion. If we are to make any progress, it is clear that we must "break set" by (1) accepting the full measure and gravity of the problem, and (2) contriving new, different, more constructive and efficacious methods for addressing the problem.

Adaptation of a Risk-Assessment and Risk-Management Model

Proper risk management is deceptively complex. Fortunately, however, the task of managing the risk posed by sexual offenders is not fundamentally different from the task of managing the risks posed by other social and environmental "hazards" that scientists must contend with. One area of inquiry that we may be able to benefit from involves environmental hazards. The Presidential/Congressional Commission on Risk Assessment and Risk Management (1997a,b) completed a *Framework for Environmental Health Risk Management*. The Commission developed a six-step process for risk assessment and risk management. This model, taken from a vastly different field with different concerns and different problems, can easily be adapted for use with sexual offenders. Step 1 is Problem/Context, and requires us to place the problem in a public health context. Step 2 is Risks, and refers to all elements of risk assessment, including the technical feasibility of risk reduction, the distribution of benefits and costs of risk reduction to the community, political, social, and cultural perspectives on risk reduction. Step 3 is Options, which refers to currently available risk management options and the need to increase the number of options through the identification of more cost-effective methods of reducing risk. Step 4 is Decisions, and refers to the costs and unintended consequences of risk reduction for different agencies or factions within society. Step 5 is Actions, which refers to actions that are taken from decisions that emerge from risk assessments, and Step 6 is Evaluation, which refers to the evaluation of the efficacy of risk management decisions. These six steps are diagrammed as spokes of a wheel with "Stakeholders" being at the center. The stakeholder in the case of sexual offenders is, of course, society or the community.

Step 1

- Identify the parameters of the problem of sexual crime.
- Place sexual crime in a public health context.
- Determine the risk management goals; first and foremost is to reduce to a minimum the risk associated with a reoffense by a known sex offender; risk management goals *must* also include, however, primary prevention strategies for reducing incidence; risk management goals must also include the economics of risk reduction.
- Identify the "risk managers" who possess the authority and responsibility for exercising necessary action to minimize risk; in addition to the criminal justice system, this would include all those who provide services (e.g., therapist) or support (e.g., pastor, support groups, work supervisor) for the offender.
- Implement a process for engaging the community (presumably, a more constructive, restorative process than simply notifying the community of the offender's address), such as a series of ongoing community/town meetings facilitated by trained risk managers that would be generally informative and noninflammatory; the virtue of constructively engaging the community is that it reduces fear, increases the knowledge base for informed decision-making by those living in the

community, ensures that the voices of victims or those in fear of victimization are heard, increases the accountability of the offender to the community.

Step 2

- The assessment of risk considers the nature and likelihood of the risk to the health of the community, which individuals are at greatest risk, how severe are the anticipated adverse effects of failure, what are the uncertainties in the calculation of risk, how confident is the risk analyst about the prediction of risk, what is the range of informed views about the nature and probability of the risk.
- Risk assessment provides the scientific foundation for risk management decision-making; risk assessment will continue to evolve and improve as risk analysts and other members of the scientific and risk management community work to develop and validate increasingly sophisticated procedures.

Step 3

- Identifying potential risk management options and evaluating their efficacy, their feasibility, their potential benefits, their potential costs, any unintended consequences, and any social impacts, adverse or otherwise, from the options. Several excellent examples of risk management options that could be subjected to such analysis would be the community notification laws and the compulsory anti-androgen treatment laws. The most obvious risk management option for known sex offenders that must be the focus of rigorous analysis is treatment, both psycho-therapeutic and somatic. The most critical risk management options for known offenders also include monitoring, surveillance, polygraphy, and supervision, all of which must be subjected to an efficacy, feasibility, and cost-benefit analysis.
- If we are to succeed, we must prioritize success over punitiveness; the essential issue, in this regard, is the indispensability of aftercare, a supervisory program for discharged offenders that includes close surveillance and monitoring, a network of approved supports, therapy, urine screens if warranted, and possibly polygraphy. Such "containment approaches" have been described in detail by Kim English and her colleagues (English, 1998; English et al., 1996). For all of its demonstrated worth, this strategy is ignored when sex offenders are required to serve their maximum sentence and are returned to the community with *no* supervision, *no* monitoring, *no* surveillance, and *no* enforceable stipulation of treatment.

Step 4

- Review of the information gathered during Steps 2 and 3 by decision-makers in order to select the best solutions; decision-makers will usually have a variety of options from which to choose, the most optimal of which will depend on the particular offender and situation.
- Sound risk management decisions are characterized by the following six criteria: (1) based on the best available clinical, actuarial, psychological, and economic information, (2) account for multisource and multirisk contexts, (3) are feasible, with anticipated benefits reasonably related to costs, (4) give priority to preventing risk, not just controlling risk, (5) are sensitive to social and political, as well as victim, considerations, and (6) include incentives for evaluation and research.

Step 5

- Implementation, actions typically initiated and orchestrated by the criminal justice system; in practice, however, action-takers may also include public health agencies, mental health agencies, child protection agencies, community groups, the church, employers, and others.

Step 6

- Evaluation of the efficacy of the actions taken in Step 5; the evaluation typically documents whether the actions were "successful" (i.e., accomplished what was intended), whether modifications would improve success, whether the paucity of information in critical areas hinders success, whether new information now indicates that decisions need to be revisited, and whether the lessons learned from the evaluation process can guide and improve future risk management decisions.

The Health Care System and Accountability

In the late 1980s, concerns about the causes and consequences of various health care practices brought about the "Era of Assessment and Accoutability," which has been dubbed the third revolution in U.S. health care after World War II (Lezzoni, 1994). Unlike the second revolution of Cost Containment during the 1970s to the early 1980s, the Era of Assessment and Accountability emphasizes not only costs but clinical outcomes (i.e., the effectiveness of care). Outcomes are essentially report cards on the variable degree of success (or failure) of our interventions. We are inevitably accountable to those who underwrite our intervention efforts, since all interventions come with a price tag. Thus, for better or for worse, society (the "underwriters") makes the (presumptively rational) decision as to whether the effectiveness of the intervention warrants the cost of the intervention. Because the "system" often requires sex offenders to be in treatment, it does *not* exempt clinicians who work with sex offenders from the burden of clearly demonstrating the efficacy of their interventions.

When it comes to sexual violence, however, these maxims are familiar, and uncomfortable. After all, if *no* intervention is provided, or if the intervention is inappropriate or suboptimal, we may well have multiple casualties, not just one. Thus, clinicians are likely to argue, perhaps with some merit, that any constructive intervention is better than none at all. However virtuous, that argument will *not* pass muster in the current health care climate of accountability and cost containment.

Roughly 15 years ago, Medicare adopted a payment system for hospitals based on diagnosis-related groups (DRGs). There was an implicit, if not explicit, linkage between severity of diagnosis and magnitude of resources required for appropriate intervention. Thus, the most severe cases (e.g., organ failure) required the most costly treatment (organ transplant). Parenthetically, severity is also, more or less, equatable with risk (i.e., the higher the severity, the greater the likelihood of a poor outcome). Notwithstanding the many purported limitations of DRGs (e.g., the occasional insensitivity of DRGs to severity of illness), and indeed the trend to move away from the use of DRGs, the analogy to sexual offenders is not far-fetched. The rationale for proposing such an analogy is quite simple. Sex offenders are the only category of criminals who are selectively removed from the mainstream of the criminal justice system and given "special treatment" in the form of involuntary civil commitment. Thus, out of a perceived need to manage sex offenders through indeterminate confinement, we have placed sex offenders in a public health arena that presumes some form of "mental abnormality" that requires treatment. The inevitable consequences include such matters as (1) adequacy of treatment intervention, (2) cost of treatment interventions, and (3) accountability in the form of demonstrable efficacy of treatment interventions. These "consequences" are no different from any other area of health care.

The roots and motivating factors behind sexual violence vary enormously, ranging in severity from cases of exclusive endogamous incest to serial sexual homicide. Just as the severity of these cases varies considerably, the costs associated with intervention (including the intervention of preventive detention) vary, ranging from outpatient therapy to lifetime incarceration. When the field of "sex offender management" comes of age, we may witness the rough equivalent of DRG's, precisely defined categories of behavior that correspond to severity (or risk) and intensiveness of treatment.

Risk-Relevant Interventions and Risk Management

Volume 2 of the Final Report of the Presidential/ Congressional Commission, entitled *Risk Assessment and Risk Management in Regulatory Decision-Making*, is an excellent guide for those who assess risk of sex offenders. Although the Commission's purview, environmental health and safety, is substantially different from the management of hazards posed by sex offenders, the problems addressed, the conclusions reached, and the recommendations made are certainly on target with respect to sexual offenders.

The closest that we have now come to applying the principles of risk management articulated in more sophisticated areas of inquiry, such as environmental health and safety, may be found in the writings of Kirk Heilbrun (e.g., Heilbrun, 1997). In Heilbrun's excellent paper, he delineated two models of risk assessment, an *a priori* model that emphasizes *risk prediction*, and a *management* model that emphasizes *risk reduction* (Chapter 4, figure 1). Very few risk assessment procedures to date come close to addressing Heilbrun's distinction.

In the *a priori* model, the goal clearly is maximally accurate risk prediction. This is *a priori* risk assessment in that it relies, primarily, on historical (static) variables. To date, most risk assessment procedures fall into this category (i.e., they are designed to *predict* risk based on historical data). These instruments will be relatively insensitive to risk *reduction*.

In the management model, the goal is risk reduction. The variables chosen for risk assessment are dynamic and risk-relevant and are intended to relect change. Rather than focusing on prediction of risk based on past behavior (*a priori* model), the focus is on reduction of risk through compliance and progress with risk interventions. Unlike instruments designed for risk prediction, risk reduction instruments should be sensitive to changes in risk status.

The overemphasis on risk prediction derives, of course, from the ubiquitous laws that rely on such assessments. Ironically, the very laws that mandate involuntary civil commitment, and rely for their constitutionality on a "mental disorder" that requires treatment, do *not* typically embrace notions of risk assessment that might reflect reduction of risk.

As the field of research on sexual offenders continues to evolve and mature, we will, in our estimation, increasingly focus on (1) empirically corroborated dimensions of risk, (2) risk-relevant interventions, and (3) risk management.

We have made substantial progress in identifying and validating dimensions of risk, the fruits of which are being reaped in the risk scales that are proliferating. Subsequent generations of these risk scales will be specialized, addressing, for instance, the unique risks posed by rapists as opposed to child molesters. Subsequent generations of these risk scales will, moreover, interlace static and dynamic risk factors. Although we have made admirable progress, our risk scales are in a puerile stage of development. As difficult as it may be, we must resist the pressure to produce unvalidated or inadequately validated risk assessment scales to comply with the urgent needs of the legal system. Ironically, risk decisions deriving from the premature use of inadequately validated scales may well be "at risk" for inadmissibility in a *Daubert* challenge.

The most relevant risk-based interventions fall, broadly, into two large categories: (1) internal modification of behavior through therapy and medication and (2) external modification of behavior through intensive community supervision and surveillance. Although increasingly risk-sensitive and risk-relevant interventions continue to be explored, the field seems to be evolving along twin, parallel tracks, with those most invested in treatment in one group and those who promote and advance the cause of community-based supervision, including surveillance and polygraphy, in another group. There appears to be a perception among some clinicians that some supervision strategies are more retributive than restorative. In our estimation, the importance of aftercare is indisputable. As is often the case in this field of "rediscovered wheels," the importance of supervision for sex offenders has been known for a long time. Almost 40 years ago, Meeks (1963), a sociologist with the Illinois Department of Public Safety, concluded his discussion of criminal sexual psychopaths by stressing the importance of supervision for reducing the risk of released "sexually dangerous persons." What is "new" in 1999 is that we have replaced supervision with "aftercare," a term that reflects a more comprehensive management model, including intensive supervision, psychotherapy, somatic therapy (if needed), polygraphy, urine screens (if needed), and appropriate, full-time employment.

Meeks (1963) further commented that the conditional release program at the Joliet Diagnostic Depot was, at that time, "at a virtual standstill." Ironically, in 1999, most programs either have no conditional release program, or, if they do, the programs are at a "virtual standstill." This is a clear example of prioritizing retribution, or retributive satisfaction, over community safety. When sex offenders are required to "max out" (serve their entire sentence), they end up being released back to the community unleashed—no parole supervision and no mandated therapy. The only leash for these men is the one provided by the registry board, and it is an extremely minimal leash indeed.

The critical tasks that face us are the same for both treatment and community-based aftercare. We must continue to develop and test sound intervention strategies and determine which of those strategies are most effective with which types of offenders. The same dictum applies, whether we are talking about relapse prevention, medication, phallometry, polygraphy, electronic monitoring, random urine checks, or surveillance. The interventions must be demonstrably effective, and they must be selected for the unique needs posed by the individual. There are some communities that already are moving in the direction of team-based, interdisciplinary approaches to community-based aftercare, with a restorative mission and a focus on case plans that are tailored to the specific needs of individual offenders. Aftercare can be made sufficiently "tight" to reduce risk to a minimum for many offenders and will be vastly less expensive than indeterminate confinement.

Lastly, in our estimation, the importance of somatic treatments for many sex offenders is indisputable and *must* be considered a critical part of treatment planning. We are *not* suggesting that all sex offenders can benefit from medication. We are suggesting, however, that medication should be as natural a consideration as anger management, social skills training, or any other commonly employed mode of therapy.

Risk management is, in effect, the "big picture," the large umbrella that includes all risk-relevant interventions, as well as all other strategies for risk reduction. The management model provides a much more holistic and realistic framework for addressing the full range of sexually deviant, coercive, and aggressive behavior. A management model, for instance, must incorporate risk reduction strategies for domestic/partner rape, sexual coercion and intimidation in the workplace, sexual coercion among adolescents, sexual coercion on college campuses, sexual exploitation and abuse of children in myriad contexts, and so forth.

Once again, what we are proposing is neither novel nor original. Twelve years ago, for instance, Mercy and O'Carroll (1988) placed interpersonal violence in a public health context, highlighting four priority areas for immediate attention: (1) developing surveillance systems for morbidity associated with interpersonal violence, (2) precisely identifying risk groups for nonfatal violent events, (3) applying case-control methods to the exploration of potentially modifiable risk factors for violent behaviors, and (4) rigorously evaluating extant programs that are intended to prevent interpersonal violence or modify suspected risk factors. These priority areas, identified by Mercy and O'Carroll for interpersonal violence, conform to a management model that clearly applies to sexual coercion as well. Indeed, within the past several years there has been an increasing trend to place sexual violence in a public health context (Mercy, 1999; McMahon, 2000, McMahon & Puett, 1999).

Attenuation of unwanted sexual behavior, however it manifests itself, requires a reconceptualization of the problem, a focus on reducing risk associated with all facets of unwanted sexual behavior, and a commitment to, as Professor Schulhofer (1998) termed it, the right to sexual autonomy. This *right* is taken for granted by most adult heterosexual men. Why should this *right* be denied women and children? Although the answer to this question is deceptively complex, the necessary steps to address the problem are not. What is required is a three-pronged effort: (1) a wholly revised jurisprudence of rape, consistent with the recommendations of Schulhofer (1998), (2) implementation of a comprehensive management model for rape, and (3) support for programmatic research that informs and guides the management model. In commenting on the unalienable rights set forth in our Constitution, the Honorable Charles Gill (1992) observed that

> The truths, the rights, justice and the blessings of liberty were not extended to all people by our fundamental documents. Slaves, children, and, to a large degree, women were excluded. They were property, mere chattel, in varying degrees. Slaves had no rights, since they were property, and the child-citizens, similarly, had no rights except to someday succeed to the rights of their fathers. (p. 4).

The bequeathing of unalienable rights to other than adult white males has come at an agonizingly unhurried pace. One of the tragic consequences of this legacy is the relative absence of rights to sexual autonomy for women and children.

CHAPTER 9

Special Topics

This chapter includes a number of general areas that occasionally come up in forensic evaluations, such as pornography (or more specifically trafficking over the Internet) or the complex role of sexual fantasy in assessing risk. Although the mission of this book clearly is not etiologic, we chose to begin this chapter with a brief discussion of the social and cultural factors that are so intrinsically important in sustaining sexual violence.

SOCIAL AND CULTURAL ROOTS OF SEXUAL VIOLENCE

The social and cultural factors that have been implicated in sexual violence include the permissive response of a wide variety of social systems and institutions that functions to perpetuate rape myths and misogynistic attitudes, objectify and exploit children and women in pornography, as well as the more subtle messages conveyed in advertising, and support, or at least condone, sexual harassment (Stermac et al., 1990). Sexual aggression, in its many facets, represents institutionalized, normative behavior. The response is deeply ingrained and indelibly embedded in the social fabric.

The Feminist Model

The social and cultural forces that coalesce to foster a rape conducive climate have been extensively discussed by many feminist writers (e.g., Brownmiller, 1975; Darke, 1990; Gager & Schurr, 1976; Griffin, 1979; Herman, 1990; Morgan, 1980; Russell, 1975; Wood, 1975) as well as a growing cohort of social scientists (e.g., Alder, 1985; Malamuth, 1984; Malamuth & Billings, 1985; Riger & Gordon, 1981; Sanday, 1981). Although there is reasonable agreement as to what those forces are, there is little resolution as to how they interrelate with other variables (situational and characterological) to increase risk of violence. Indeed, there is an implicit working assumption that these forces impact differentially those individuals who, in varying degrees, are more vulnerable to their pernicious effects (e.g., those men who are more "prone" to rape, as Malamuth expressed it).

The feminists have long maintained that sexual intimidation through threat of assault or outright assault serves the function of subjugating women, keeping women "in their place" and exercising power over women (e.g., Brownmiller, 1975). A diverse body of data has accumulated that supports this general thesis, from the prevalence of sexual aggression in the media to the tolerance of sexual harassment in the workplace, the widespread, unthinking acceptance of myths about rape, the very high self-reported (unofficial) victimization rates, and the failure of the criminal justice system to effectively prosecute, convict, and punish perpetrators. The institutions of society (e.g., news media, entertainment industry, advertising industry, criminal justice system) are perceived to be permissive with respect to the sexualization and exploitation of women and children. Victims, whether they are adults or children, tend to be blamed for their victimization and the consequences of the assault are minimized or trivialized. In her excellent "social analysis" of the feminist model, Herman (1990) concluded, after reviewing evidence from cross-cultural studies, epidemiological studies, studies on irrational attitudes and rapes myths, and psychiatric studies, that "the weight of evidence supporting a feminist analysis of sexual assault is overwhelming" (p. 178). The feminist model has been a rich trove for generating and, in many instances, corroborating, hypotheses. In addition, the model has contributed significantly to theory development.

Perhaps the most tangible symptom of a climate of sexual violence is that potential victims live in chronic fear of sexual assault (e.g., Riger & Gordon, 1981; Warr, 1985). Simple questions such as when to go the laundromat, when to leave work in the evening, what mode of transportation to use, where to park the car, where it is safe to walk or jog, and whether to use your first name on your mailbox or in the phone book become major concerns for women, especially in larger cities. Similarly, questions for parents such as choosing day care or baby-sitters, permitting unsupervised outside play, and providing adult escorts at school bus stops are taken for granted and accepted as part of the "norm" of our society. Thus, fear alone acts as an agent of social control. As Griffin (1979) noted, "The fear of rape keeps women off the streets at night. Keeps women at home. Keeps women passive and modest for fear they be thought provocative" (p. 21).

Based on their 1977 telephone survey of 1620 people living in Philadelphia, San Francisco, and Chicago, Riger and Gordon (1981) found that 41% of the women interviewed reported the use of "isolation tactics" (limiting movement) all or most of the time and 74% of the women reported frequent use of "street savvy tactics" (i.e., risk management). Parenthetically, 90% of the men said that they "rarely" used street savvy tactics.

In sum, sexual exploitation and aggression perpetrated against women and children is, according to the feminist model, socially and culturally institutionalized. Indeed, it is so deeply embedded in the fabric of our society that it has become normative behavior. One such example was cited by Finkelhor (1984). In January 1982 a judge in Lancaster, Wisconsin, sentenced a man to 90 days in a work-release program on the charge of sexually assaulting the 5-year-old daughter of the woman he lived with. Finkelhor noted, "In explaining this lenient sentence, the judge said: 'I am satisfied we have an unusually sexually promiscuous young lady. And he [the defendant] did not know enough to refuse. No way do I believe he initiated sexual contact' " (p. 108). Astonishing as it may seem to most of us, a judge found that a 5-year-old girl was "an unusually sexually promiscuous young lady" and implicitly, if not explicitly, responsible for sexual contact with an adult man.

Rape Prone Societies

Sanday's (1981) now-classic study of tribal societies suggested characteristics of "rape-prone" and "rape-free" societies. The former were distinguished by clearly defined markings of male dominance, a prevailing ideology of male toughness, the relegation of women, in one form or another, to the role of property or chattel, and the segregation of women and men into distinct, insulated groups. Rape-free societies, however, were characterized by equality between women and men with respect to the contributions that each make to society, a clear sense of the criticality and integrality of the contributions made by women, and a very low level of general interpersonal violence. As interpersonal violence becomes an increasingly viable option for solving problems and increasingly accepted as a way of life, the incidence of rape inevitably rises.

Sanday (1981) tested on her tribal samples four "Western" hypotheses derived from the work of Amir (1971), Abrahamsen (1960), Brownmiller (1975), LeVine (1959), and Wolfgang and Ferracuti (1967). She found strong support for two hypotheses: (1) intergroup and interpersonal violence is enacted in male sexual violence and (2) rape is an expression of a social ideology of male dominance. She found very weak support for the influence of parent–child relations and child-rearing characteristics and no support for the role of sexual repression. A tentative extension of Sanday's findings on tribal societies to Western society is readily available from the work of Wolfgang and Ferracuti (1967) on subcultures of violence. Such subcultures are distinguished by a core group of disenfranchised males who are afflicted by chronic, inescapable poverty and experience themselves as emasculated and powerless. One response to this condition is to place a high premium on physical aggression as a sign of prowess and potency. In the sexual arena, when one's sense of manhood depends on toughness, the use of force and coercion will be an inevitable by-product of the fulfillment of the need to be tough. Jaffee and Straus (1987) found rape rates to be associated with a cluster of variables often considered part of the subculture of violence (e.g., degree of urbanization and poverty) as well as pornographic magazine readership.

Social Attitudes and Likelihood of Rape

The causal relation between demeaning and misogynistic attitudes, attributions, moral evaluations, and sexual violence is, arguably, one of the more important areas of inquiry in the domain of social science research. Parenthetically, this area of research, emerging both from the laboratories of experimental social psychologists and from the writings of feminist theorists, dovetails nicely with the clinical and experimental psychopathology research discussed earlier on irrational cognitions. The former social and feminist research has tended to focus on rape myths and rape-supportive attitudes held by the cross section of society (i.e., *non*offenders), while the latter clinical research has focused on the irrational and offense-justifying attitudes expressed by offenders (i.e., child molesters and rapists). Despite a consensus on the theoretical importance of this general area, there are a paucity of studies that have focused on the development and testing of multifactorial models that seek to explain the translation of irrational attitudes (or violent fantasies) into behavior. A major contribution to this general issue is the research that sought to assess "likelihood of rape" (LR) or proclivity to rape (Malamuth, 1981) using the Attraction to Sexual Aggression scale (see Malamuth, 1989a,b). In general, men (primarily college students) with high LR scores have more callous attitudes about rape and endorse rape myths more than individuals with low LR scores. In summarizing findings from several studies, Malamuth (1981) reported that approximately 35% of the subjects indicated "some likelihood" of raping and about 20% indicated higher likelihoods of raping. These self-reports from nonoffenders typically are elicited with two conditions: (1) the word *rape* is replaced by *coerced* or *forced* and (2) the subject is instructed to respond within the context of immunity (i.e., there will be no legal repercussions).

In Burt's (1980) widely cited random survey of 598 adult men and women in Minnesota using the Rape Myth Acceptance Scale, the startling finding was that over half of the sample believed that rape reports usually resulted from women either concealing a pregnancy or seeking reprisal against a man. The subjects also believed that in the majority of rape cases the victim was promiscuous or had a bad reputation. Costin (1985) administered a rape scale (stereotyped beliefs about rape) and a women's social roles scale to 762 subjects comprising four groups (female and male college students, employed women, employed men). Factors were derived and three hypotheses were tested: women's responsibility for rape, the role of consent in rape, and the rapist's role and motivation in the assault. Costin found that the correlations for all three factors across all four groups were significant at the .01 probability level (magnitudes of the *r* values ranging from .42 to .66). In all instances, negative stereotypes and rape myths were positively related to beliefs that women's social roles and rights should be more restricted than those of men.

Rape tolerance research (rape-prone attitudes and beliefs) is the subject of a growing body of literature (e.g., Hall, Howard, & Boezio, 1986; Mosher & Anderson, 1986; Schultz & DeSavage, 1975; Stille, Malamuth, & Schallow, 1987). The gist of what these reports suggest is that there is a continuum of rape proneness within the general male population. As an individual approaches the middle to higher end of the continuum, he may be identified as at "high risk." This cognitive or attitudinal factor is assumed to interact with other factors. Several empirical questions emerge from this research: (1) whether this cognitive factor alone is sufficient to motivate rape and (2) what the critical interactive factors are that tend to be associated with different rapist types.

The Role of the Media

Media Effects on Individual Behavior

There is ample evidence from studies of newspaper and television reporting of salient violent crimes to support the hypothesis that the mass media can have an effect on individual violent behavior. For instance, Phillips (1974, 1979) documented that after well-publicized suicides the number of suicides went up significantly, and there was a positive relation between the amount of newspaper space devoted to reporting the incidents and the number of suicides in the areas exposed to the stories. Moreover, after a well-publicized suicide there were sharp increases in the number of automobile fatalities, especially single-car accidents, that may mask suicides. Indeed, Phillips (1974) estimated that in the two months after Marilyn Monroe's suicide there were 303 more suicides in the United States than would have normally occurred in this period. Highly publicized murders such as the multiple murders committed by Richard Speck and Charles Whitman or the assassination of President Kennedy were also followed by increases in violent crime (Berkowitz &

Macaulay, 1971). Although it is not clear whether such accounts of violence incite more people to model violent behavior, whether they increase the rate of violence in already violent individuals, or whether they simply increase the severity of violent acts that would have occurred anyway, the association between media reporting and individual violence has nonetheless been consistently documented.

The Biasing Effects of Individual Cases

A growing body of empirical literature has documented the thinking and reasoning fallacies to which humans are prone. The fallacies that have consistently been demonstrated provide an explanation for the vulnerability to hysterical conclusions that we cited above, and suggest that the news media selection of cases for public consumption is particularly likely to feed these fallacies. These studies indicate that both experts and novices form opinions quickly and on the basis of remarkably little and weak evidence. For example, mental health professionals form their initial diagnostic impressions within the first 5 minutes of contact with the patient (Gauron & Dickinson, 1969; Sandifer, Hordern, & Green, 1970). People rely on snippets of knowledge that "stick in their minds" rather than considering alternative hypotheses and the widest range of data that might differentially support these alternative hypotheses. To make matters worse, these snippets may be inadequate or misleading. Thus, it is critical to investigate the nature of the news media's selection criteria to determine the representativeness of their choices. Not only do people make quick first impressions, but a considerable body of empirical research has consistently found that when people know (or know about) one or two people who purportedly epitomize a particular belief, they will consider that belief supported without even asking whether those cases are typical or atypical (see review by Taylor & Thompson, 1982). Anderson's (1983) study clearly exemplifies this phenomenon. One group of undergraduates read two case studies supporting the hypothesis that good firefighters are high risk takers. In one case the firefighter was good at his job and was also a high risk taker. In the other case the firefighter was poor at his job and was a low risk taker. Another group of undergraduates were given comparable case studies exemplifying the opposite relation (good firefighters are low risk takers). Most subjects had no difficulty forming a causal hypothesis on the basis of the two case studies. The subjects were then informed that the case studies were fictitious and subsequently asked about their true beliefs about the relation. The subjects acted as if the causal relation in the cases they had been exposed to was true—they used it to make predictions about five additional case studies, for example—and they still held that belief a week later.

To summarize the research described so far, people tend to form initial impressions very rapidly and typically on the basis of whatever constructs happen to be available to them at the time, whether or not they are appropriate (Higgins & King, 1981). This in and of itself may not be such a bad thing, if only they would then search for additional evidence and keep their minds open to changing their opinion. Unfortunately, the opposite appears to be true. After forming an initial impression, people tend then to seek evidence to support that belief rather than seeking evidence in an unbiased fashion. Wason (1960) demonstrated this phenomenon very clearly, and it has been replicated and extended frequently since (see Wason & Johnson-Laird, 1972, pp. 202–214). Subjects were told that the three numbers 2, 4, 6 conformed to a simple relational rule. Their job was to discover this rule by generating triads of numbers. After each triad they were told whether the triad conformed to the rule. They were allowed to keep records on paper and were to show the rule to the experimenter only when they were highly confident that they had discovered it. Very few people were able to get the rule correct on the first try. Of 45 scientists and ministers in Mahoney and DeMonbreun's (1977) study, only 2 discovered the rule on their first guess. Fewer than half ever found the right rule. Why is this task so difficult? It is because people are likely to form an initial hypothesis very quickly—that the rule is "increasing by twos" or "even numbers." They then spend their time creating tests that would confirm their hypothesis, e.g., 100, 102, 104. Other rules are, of course, possible, including the correct rule: "numbers increasing in order of magnitude." To test whether this alternative rule might be correct, subjects would have to use a disconfirmation strategy, e.g., seeing if the sequence 10, 11, 12 conformed to the rule. People rarely do this. Even when they are told "even numbers" is incorrect, the majority persevere in their error by reconfirming a previously falsified hypothesis. The confirmatory bias is so strong that (1) initial impressions last even if people are told that the data they had just studied were false (e.g., Anderson, 1983; Anderson, Lepper, & Ross, 1980) and (2) people find data that support their hypotheses even when the data provided contains no systematic support for that hypothesis (Chapman & Chapman, 1967, 1969). To make matters worse, much of the research described so far has involved designs that contrasted impressionistic data (representativeness, available memories, knowledge, and stereotypes, case studies) with statistical data. These studies have shown that when people have access to both impressionistic data and statistical data, most ignore the statistical data and form their predictions or conclusions on the basis of the impressionistic data (e.g., Nisbett & Borgida, 1975). Consequently, this cognitive literature suggests that the small number of cases that the news media reports to the public are likely to be the basis of the conclusions that the public forms, and that these conclusions are likely to be impervious to subsequent correction through more representative and scientific information.

PORNOGRAPHY

For feminists, the most egregious manifestation, as well as the most obtrusive symbol, of male dominance and subjugation of women is pornography. Consequently, a very considerable lay and scientific literature has addressed the issue of pornography. Because of the social, theoretical, and empirical importance of pornography, as reflected by extant literature, conferences, and commissions that have focused on it, discussion of pornography will be in some detail.

The issue of pornography is clearly one of the most socially and politically charged of all topics that potentially bear on sexual violence. Although the magnitude of the problem, as measured by the commercial availability of pornography, is a matter of speculation, several estimates place it in the range of $4 billion (McCarthy, 1980) or $5 billion (McCally, 1981, as cited by O'Brien, 1983) a year. If these figures are even remotely accurate, they exceed the combined revenues of the movie and record industries (McCarthy, 1980; Steinem, 1980). In reality, since hard-core pornography is a clandestine business, produced, marketed, and sold underground, it is virtually impossible to estimate with any accuracy the size of the "business." We may infer the size of the market, however, from the

1986 U.S. Commission on Pornography's seemingly exhaustive review of "adults only" magazines and book titles in six cities (Washington, D.C., Baltimore, Miami, New York, Philadelphia, and Boston). Members of the Commission managed to identify 3050 separate and distinct titles at those locations. Presumably, the market is large enough to support such extraordinary diversity, not to mention the absolute number of competing items.

The Feminist Response

The subject of pornography has been discussed at considerable length by feminist writers (e.g., Brownmiller, 1975; Dworkin, 1981; Gager & Schurr, 1976; Griffin, 1981; Morgan, 1980; Russell, 1980; Steinem, 1980), who generally conceive of it as sexist propaganda that serves the purpose of sanctioning and promoting the subjugation of women. The social and ideological underpinnings of the feminist model were discussed by Malamuth and Billings (1986). In brief, the model contends that the pernicious effects of pornography extend well beyond the momentary fantasies stimulated by the depictions. Women—or children—are degraded, dehumanized, and objectified as sources of sexual pleasure. The net effect is to reinforce attitudes about women—or children—that are consonant with the depictions (e.g., depictions of rape will foster attitudes that condone rape), thereby increasing the likelihood of the translation of fantasy into behavior. Although the link between irrational attitudes and sexually aggressive behavior is correlative and not causal, Malamuth and Billings (1986) did conclude that "considerable data clearly reveal that exposure to sexually violent media affect perceptions, attitudes, beliefs in a manner that may contribute to a cultural climate that is more accepting of violence against women" (p. 99). Lottes (1988) also concluded in her review of a different subset of studies that support for the "sociocultural etiology of rape" reveals that "men with a history of sexual aggression and men who indicate a tendency to commit sexually aggressive acts report greater acceptance of callous rape attitudes" (p. 213). There is no question that media depictions of sexual violence *will* affect the attitudes of those *predisposed* to sexual violence (i.e., rape prone). Such depictions, however, may also affect those who are not predisposed by desensitizing them to violence.

Changes in Pornography Content

One of the concerns that has spirited debate is whether the content of pornography is becoming increasingly violent and/or demeaning. A number of content analyses of pornographic books and magazine covers, pictorials, and cartoons revealed a marked increase in depictions of rape, bondage, and dominance (e.g., Dietz & Evans, 1982; Malamuth & Spinner, 1980; Smith, 1976). In 1986, the Attorney General's Commission on Pornography concluded that pornography has indeed become more violent over the past two decades. However, this conclusion, and others rendered by the Commission, have been considered suspect since they were not supported by a thorough examination of the empirical literature (see the critique by the American Civil Liberties Union, 1986, as well as comments by Malamuth, 1989c, and Scott & Schwalm, 1988). A more recent 30-year longitudinal study of *Playboy* magazine found that "the number of sexually violent depictions has always been extremely small, and the number of such depictions has decreased in recent years" (Scott & Cuvelier, 1987, p. 538). It is unclear, of course, whether the finding reported by

Scott and Cuvelier (1987) can be generalized to more explicit "hard-core" pornography. Since the base rate for violence or sham violence depicted in hard-core pornography is much higher than the equivalent base rate in soft-core pornography, it would be necessary to look at trends in violence separately in soft- and hard-core publications. Lebegue (1991) reviewed the 3050 "adults only" titles identified by the U.S. Commission on Pornography, noting that "sadomasochism was by far the most common paraphilia (49.9%)" (p. 43) depicted in the magazines and books. Lebegue (1991) also pointed out that Dietz, Harry, and Hazelwood (1986) described an entire domain of "literature," characterized as pornography for the sexual sadist, that the Commission did not look at—detective magazines. In sum, we must be very careful inferring trends in sexual violence depicted in magazines.

The Association between Pornography and Aggression

The focal concern among social scientists has been the extent to which pornography precipitates or encourages sexual aggression against women and children. The hypothesis that pornography serves as a model for imitation, hence instigating the behavior that it depicts, has a considerable following, among feminist theorists (e.g., Bart & Jozsa, 1980; Brownmiller, 1975; Diamond, 1980; Russell, 1980; Russell & Vandeven, 1976) as well as social scientists. This hypothesis argues that pornography operates at two levels. At the conscious level, it endorses and thus condones the depicted behavior. At the unconscious level, it may awaken a sexually dangerous appetite that is sated through aggressive behavior.

In 1970, the President's Commission on Obscenity and Pornography reported, after 2 years of reviewing research, that there was no evidence to support an association between pornography and antisocial behavior. The ensuing decade of empirical research sought to identify and tease apart the more subtle nuances of the hypothetical relation between pornography and aggression. Many studies examined the modeling effect of pornography using college students (e.g., Baron, 1974; Baron & Bell, 1977; Donnerstein & Barrett, 1978; Donnerstein, Donnerstein, & Evans, 1975; Frodi, 1977; Jaffe, Malamuth, Feingold, & Feshbach, 1974; Smeaton & Byrne, 1987; Zillman, 1971). Some studies reported that exposure to pornography inhibited aggression (e.g., Baron, 1974; Frodi, 1977), while other studies found that although mildly erotic stimuli inhibited aggression, highly erotic stimuli increased reported aggression in a laboratory setting (e.g., Baron & Bell, 1977; Donnerstein et al., 1975). Overall, it may be concluded from these laboratory studies that when males are exposed to pornography with *violent* content (e.g., rape) there is an increase in self-reported likelihood of raping, as well as an increase in the endorsement of misogynistic attitudes and myths about rape (see Donnerstein, 1983; Malamuth & Donnerstein, 1982, for reviews). The key ingredient appears to be *violent* content. The President's Commission (1970) based its conclusions on nonviolent depictions of nudity and sexual acts. One caveat regarding this research, noted by Gray (1982), Mould (1988), and others, is that laboratory-induced anger in college students may not be an accurate—or even appropriate—facsimile of the pathological aggression evidenced in sexual offenders. Boeringer (1994) simply looked at the association between pornography use and rape proclivity in a sample of 515 college males, finding clear evidence that there were strong correlations between self-reported sexual coercion or the will to be sexually coercive and exposure to hard-core violent and rape pornography. As Boeringer (1994) concluded

> Exposure to soft-core pornography was not correlated with likelihood of rape and actual physical coercion. Higher exposure to pornography depicting violent and rape behavior appeared to be significantly related to both engaging in sexual aggression and believing oneself capable or likely of engaging in sexual aggression. (pp. 298–299)

The impact of pornography on sexual offenders and nonoffenders who harbor sexually aggressive fantasies is, arguably, of immediate concern. Although feminists are undoubtedly correct in arguing that pornography may contribute to the general subjugation of women (e.g., Brownmiller, 1975; Gager & Schurr, 1976; Morgan, 1980; Russell, 1980), the most critical empirical question is whether pornography increases the likelihood of violent *behavior* among those predisposed to engage in such behavior. A number of penile tumescence studies have demonstrated that the sexual arousal patterns of rapists differ from the arousal patterns of nonrapists (e.g., Abel, Barlow, Blanchard, & Guild, 1977; Barbaree, Marshall, & Lanthier, 1979; Quinsey et al., 1984). Moreover, it has been found that these deviant arousal patterns among rapists include responses to *non*sexual violence involving female victims (Abel et al., 1977; Quinsey et al., 1984). This latter finding suggests that the cues eliciting the response in both sexual and nonsexual violence are similar (i.e., the presence of a female who is being aggressively victimized). Although rapists appear to differ from nonrapists in their response to sexual violence, they do *not* seem to differ from nonrapists when the stimuli portray consenting sexual acts. That is, rapists seem to be more or less equally aroused by stimuli depicting rape and stimuli depicting consenting sex (e.g., Abel et al., 1977; Abel, Becker, & Skinner, 1980; Abel, Becker, Blanchard, & Djenderedjian, 1978; Barbaree et al., 1979; Hinton, O'Neill & Webster, 1980; Quinsey, Chaplin, & Varney, 1981).

Baron (1990) reported that the sales of the eight major "men's magazines" were five times higher per capita in Alaska and Nevada than other states, and lowest of all in North Dakota. Rape rates in Alaska and Nevada were six times higher per capita than in North Dakota. Importantly, however, Baron (1990) *also* found positive correlations between rape rates and gender inequality, social disorganization, urbanization, economic inequality, and unemployment. Baron concluded that "a macho culture pattern independently influences men to purchase more pornography and commit more rapes" (p. 364). In summary, on the question of whether pornography *causes* rape, Kimmel (1993) concluded that

> The results of research are inconclusive. In aggregate studies and in the laboratory, researchers have not been able to isolate pornography as the cause of violence against women. The pervasiveness of rape and violence, even in the absence of a single causal mechanism, means that we have a larger and more diffuse constellation of masculine attitudes to confront. (p. 8)

Kimmel is absolutely correct. There is no single *causal* mechanism for rape. Among those who are predisposed to rape, pornography certainly will act as a disinhibitor or a catalyst for rape fantasy and perhaps even behavior. It cannot be concluded, however, that pornography *caused* the predisposed individual to rape, since there were preexisting conditions that placed the individual at greater than average risk. Thus, even among predisposed individuals, pornography will not reliably elicit rape. Opportunity and many other factors come into play. Among those with no predisposition to rape, pornography will most certainly not prompt rape behavior.

Sex Magazine Circulation Index

Several studies have examined the relation between pornography and rape by developing a "sex magazine circulation index" and correlating it with rape rates. Baron and Straus (1984) devised such an index using the number of sale copies of eight sexually explicit magazines during 1979. The number of copies sold was converted to a rate per 100,000 population for each state. The index was highly correlated with the UCR rape rate ($r = .63$) but not with UCR rates for murder ($r = .24$), robbery ($r = .24$), or aggravated assault ($r = .16$). A similar study by Scott and Schwalm (1988) employed an index based on 10 soft-core magazines (the two studies had six magazines in common) with sales in the year 1982. The Scott and Schwalm index also was correlated with the UCR rape rate ($r = .54$; $\rho = .36$) but not with UCR rates for murder ($r = .15$), robbery ($r = .15$), or aggravated assault ($r = .12$). Although the conclusion that pornography seems to be related to the likelihood of rape is a compelling one based on these results, both studies appropriately caution that the results may be related to mediating factors. In particular, jurisdictional differences with respect to reporting, investigating, and prosecuting rape cases must be examined, as well as within-state estimates of rape rates (as opposed to UCR estimates) and, if possible, a distinction between soft-core (which both studies used) and hard-core pornography.

Overview

There is, at present, no theoretical model that effectively embraces and explains these findings. Several reviews, however, discussed the presumptive mediating factors that connect media-depicted, socially sanctioned sexual aggression with overt behavior (Ceniti & Malamuth, 1984; Malamuth, 1984, 1989c; Rule & Ferguson, 1986). These hypothetical factors include attributions and moral evaluations, degree of satiation or emotional habituation after repeated exposure, aggression augmented by increases in autonomic arousal, individual differences with respect to information processing and retrieval (e.g., "priming effects") as well as patterns of conditioning, and the role of specific stimulus parameters (e.g., stimulus intensity and interstimulus interval). Berkowitz (1986) has argued persuasively that the relevant empirical question is no longer *whether* some people respond to observed violence with aggression but *under what circumstances* the response occurs. Murrin and Laws (1990) concluded their review with the following conundrum: "In a cultural environment where people are not considered to be sexual objects, pornography use probably would have little effect on sexual crime. Ironically, in such a culture, pornography itself would most likely not exist" (p. 89).

The Role of Fantasy in Sex Violence

The role of fantasy in deviant, aggressive sexuality was proposed 25 years ago by Abel and Blanchard (1974), and over the ensuing several decades there has accumulated "abundant evidence" to support it (Marshall et al., 1983). The commonly accepted explanatory model pairs fantasy with sexual arousal. The rehearsed fantasy is reinforced through masturbation. The deviant fantasy eventually becomes sufficiently reinforced, and inhibitions sufficiently eroded, to place the individual at high risk to act on the fantasy. Although such a simple classical conditioning model may have some utility in explaining how markedly deviant fantasies become translated into behavior, the model stops short of suggesting what mechanisms may originate and drive the fantasy. Moreover, from an etiologic perspective, such a model fails to account for the virtual absence of paraphiliac sexuality in females relative to the observed incidence in males (Gosselin & Wilson, 1984). In this section of the chapter, we explore the complex world of fantasy, its putative biological roots, and its presumptive role as a critical antecedent of sexually deviant behavior.

Advances in Model Development

Burgess, Hartman, Ressler, Douglas, and McCormack (1986) reported on a fantasy-based motivational model for sexual homicide. The model, which has five interactive components (impaired development of attachments in early life; formative traumatic events; patterned responses that serve to generate fantasies; a private, internal world that is consumed with violent thoughts and that leaves the person isolated and self-preoccupied; a feedback filter that sustains repetitive thinking patterns), was tested on a sample of 36 sexual murderers. In this initial study Burgess et al. (1986) found evidence for daydreaming and compulsive masturbation in over 80% of the sample in both childhood and adulthood. Using the same sample, Ressler and Burgess (1985) examined the role of the organized/disorganized dichotomy, which has proven to be a relatively powerful discriminator in two important areas (crime scene investigation and life history variables). Classification as organized or disorganized is made with the use of data present at the scene of a murder, and is based on the notion that highly repetitive, planned, well-thought-out offenses will be distinguishable from spontaneous, random, sloppy offenses. According to prediction, the former, organized, case should be much more characterized by a fantasy life that drives the offenses than the latter, disorganized, case. Ressler, Burgess, Douglas, Hartman, and D'Agostino (1986) found support for numerous differences between organized and disorganized offenders with respect to acts committed during the offense.

Repetitive Sexual Homicide

Another study examined the role of fantasy as a drive mechanism for repetitive (i.e., serial) sexual homicide (Prentky, Burgess, et al., 1989). The role of fantasy was examined by looking at putative differences between serial and solo sexual murderers. The working hypothesis was that serial sexual murderers were more likely to have an underlying internal mechanism that drives the assaultive behavior than solo sexual murderers. This internal drive mechanism was hypothesized to take the form of an intrusive fantasy life manifested in (1) a higher incidence of paraphilias, (2) a higher incidence of "organized" crime scenes, and (3) a higher incidence of fantasy.

The serial sexual murderer sample consisted of 25 of the 36 murderers drawn from an earlier study by the FBI (Burgess, Hartman, Ressler, Douglas, & McCormack, 1986; Ressler et al., 1986, 1988). Only those men with three or more sexual homicides were included in this study. The men were interviewed by special agents of the FBI in various U.S. prisons between 1979 and 1983. Data collection included information retrieved from official records (e.g., psychiatric and criminal records, pretrial records, court transcripts, interviews with correctional staff, and prison records). Information derived from these structured interviews and archival sources were coded using a questionnaire.

The solo sexual murderer sample consisted of seven offenders in the FBI sample who had murdered once and ten men residing at the Massachusetts Treatment Center who murdered once. The data source for the Treatment Center subjects was archival. The clinical files were coded using a questionnaire similar to the one employed in the FBI study.

Since the age of the offender at the onset of violent criminal activity could be a critical factor, we compared the two samples on the mean age at the time of the first sexual homicide. The samples were remarkably similar ($X^2 = 1.02, p < .80$). The only noteworthy comparison concerned intelligence. As a group, the serial murderers had a higher IQ than the solo murderers, though the difference was not statistically significant ($X^2 = 3.14, p < .21$). Over half of the serial group (58%) was above average in IQ, compared with less than one-third of the solo group (29%). This apparent trend is entirely consistent with theoretical expectation and essentially parallels the difference between the groups with respect to organization of crime scene. That is, organized murderers are predicted to be higher in IQ than disorganized murderers (Ressler & Burgess, 1985). While intelligence seems to have very little bearing on the quality or content of the fantasy, it may influence how well the fantasy is translated into behavior (i.e., "organized"), and how successfully the offender eludes apprehension.

Operational Considerations for Dependent Measures: Fantasy

Fantasy is a rather inclusive term that covers a wide range of cognitive processes. Our use of the term is based on an information processing model that interprets thoughts as derivations of incoming stimuli that have been processed and organized (Gardner, 1985). Daydreaming has been defined as any cognitive activity representing a shift of attention away from a task (Singer, 1966). A fantasy, as it was defined in the study, is an elaborated set of cognitions (or thoughts), characterized by preoccupation (or rehearsal), anchored in emotion, and having origins in daydreams. A fantasy is generally experienced as a collection of thoughts, although the individual may be aware of images, feelings, and internal dialogue. For the purposes of the study, a crime fantasy (either rape, murder, or both) was positively coded if interview or archival data indicated daydreaming content that included intentional infliction of harm in a sadistic or otherwise sexually violent way.

Organized/Disorganized Crime Scenes

The homicide was classified as organized if the crime scene suggested that a semblance of order existed prior to, during, and after the offense and that this order was aimed at eluding detection (Ressler & Burgess, 1985). The homicide was classified as disorganized if the crime scene was characterized by great disarray, suggesting that the assault had been committed suddenly and with no apparent plan for avoiding detection. The crime scene classifications were made by two special agents from the FBI, using crime scene data only. Such data consist of physical evidence found at the crime scene that are hypothesized to reveal behavioral and personality traits of the murderer. The crime scene may include the point of abduction, locations where the victim was held, the murder scene, and the final body location. Examples of crime scene data include use of restraints, manner of death, presence of weapon, depersonalization of the victim (i.e., rendering the victim unidentifiable through disfigurement), evidence that the crime was staged, and physical evidence (e.g., personal artifacts of the victim or offender).

The degree of "organization" of the sexual assaults is hypothesized to be related to the elaborateness of the fantasy and the length of rehearsal prior to the assault. In other words, well-organized assaults reflect well-rehearsed fantasies. The critical mediating factors that are hypothesized to differentiate the organized from the more disorganized offender are social competence and impulsivity. That is, the organized offenders are predicted to be higher in intelligence, more socially skilled and interpersonally adept, more vocationally competent, and more stable in most aspects of lifestyle. In addition to being less accomplished in all of these domains, the disorganized offender is predicted to have a much more impressive track record of vehicular and criminal offenses beginning at an early age.

Paraphilias

The paraphilias may be understood as the behavioral expression of an underlying fantasy. Money (1980) noted, in this regard, that "the paraphiliac's ideal is to be able to stage his/her erotic fantasy so as to perceive it as an actual experience" (p. 76). The paraphilias were coded as present if there was clear, unambiguous evidence in the archives or via self-report that the behavior was practiced and that it was not happenstance. The paraphilias were defined in concrete, behavioral terms with examples provided—for the subject in the case of self-report and for the coders in the case of archival retrieval.

Results

Eight variables were identified in the FBI database and the Treatment Center database that were conceptually identical and theoretically meaningful for testing a series of hypotheses regarding these two samples. The two sets of variables were merged to create a new set of dichotomous variables. The dichotomous variables were analyzed using the chi-square statistic.

The a priori hypothesis regarding fantasy was strongly supported ($X^2 = 14.02$, $p <$ .001). Well over three-quarters of the serial group (86%), compared with less than one-quarter of the solo group (23%), evidenced sufficiently obtrusive fantasy to be noted in the records or through self-report.

To the extent that the paraphilias do indeed provide behavioral evidence of fantasy life, the difference between the two groups was again supported. There was a higher incidence of all five paraphilias in the serial group than in the solo group, with the last two—fetishism and cross-dressing—being statistically significant at the .05 level ($X^2 =$ 4.54 and 4.38, respectively).

Our a priori hypothesis regarding the organization or disorganization of the crime scene also was supported ($X^2 = 8.00$, $p < .005$). Over two-thirds of the serial murderer's first sexual homicide were organized, while three-quarters of the solo sexual homicides were disorganized.

Assumptions of a Fantasy-Based Drive Model

Preliminary findings from these studies, based on relatively small samples of offenders, provide tentative support for the hypothesis that fantasy life may be importantly related to repeated acts of sexual violence. Although the precise function of fantasy is speculation, we concur with MacCulloch, Snowden, Wood, and Mills (1983) that once the restraints inhibiting the acting out of the fantasy are no longer present, the individual is likely to engage in a series of progressively more accurate "trial runs" in an attempt to "stage" the fantasy as it is imagined. Since the trial runs can never precisely match the fantasy, the need to restage the fantasy with a new victim is established.

We attempted to provide an operationalized drive mechanism for repetitive behavior that is characterized by deviant sexual fantasy in which aggression is a distinctive feature (Prentky & Burgess, 1991). Our work was been guided by a number of implicit assumptions:

The first assumption is that the individual has created an inner world (a fantasy life) that is intended to satisfy, often in disguised or symbolic fashion, needs that cannot be satisfied in the real world (see Kardener, 1975). As such, this inner world can host a seemingly unlimited range of possible wishes and needs. Our present concern involves those inner worlds that are dominated by a maelstrom of sexual and aggressive feelings.

The second assumption is that the mechanisms that drive the fantasies and the factors that permit the enactment and reenactment of the fantasies are at least as important, if not more important, than understanding the specific content of the fantasies. This is a critical point, since it is commonly accepted that "normal" people often have sexually deviant fantasies (Crepault & Couture, 1980). Thus, merely having sadistic or homicidal fantasies does *not* mean that those fantasies will ever be acted out (Schlesinger & Revitch, 1983).

The third assumption is that the script or content of the sexual fantasy derives from explicit, protracted sexually deviant and pathological experiences first sustained at a young age. In this regard it was noted by Gosselin and Wilson (1984) that if "human males have certain broad 'innate releasing mechanisms' for sexual arousal, it would appear that these can be distorted or over-detailed by traumatic events in childhood" (p. 106). Kardener (1975) was even more explicit in his comments about children who are forced to "fill in the blanks with distortions, feelings of badness and primitive mythologies" (p. 53). He remarked that "there is a horrible fascination for the grotesque distortions of what sex means contained in a vacuum of alternate expression that compels the murderer to master his distortions through acting out his forbidden fantasies" (p. 53).

The fourth assumption is that the parameters governing fantasy life in "normals" are different from the equivalent parameters in repetitive sexual offenders. The fantasies that are associated with sexually deviant or coercive behavior in "normals" are not typically rehearsed and are not typically preoccupying. The fantasies are usually associated with an exteroceptive stimulus and diminish in intensity, or extinguish entirely, after the withdrawal of the stimulus. Assuming that the fantasies are not acted upon and assuming that the fantasies are not so disturbing that they interfere with daily living, they are of little concern other than to those who would speculate about why sexually aggressive fantasies appear to be so common among males.

We are concerned about those sexually aggressive fantasies that are *intrusive* (distracting and preoccupying), *reiterative* (persistent and recurrent), and *interoceptive* (internally generated). From an empirical standpoint, we are exploring those factors that serve to disinhibit and facilitate the enactment of such fantasies and what factors promote the reoccurrence of such fantasies.

Putative Biological Mechanisms

Fantasy or imagery, at least as it exists in humans, is not strictly a property of the visual system but is a cognitive process (Gazzaniga, 1985; Hebb, 1968; Lang, 1979, 1985). Fantasy has been conceptualized as an activated perceptual–motor memory (Kosslyn, 1988; Lang, 1985), and our own conceptualization of fantasy embraces these notions, as well as incorporating the elements of rehearsal and emotion. The imagery literature affords greater specificity.

Vividness of Fantasy

The vividness of a fantasy is a function of the amount of endogenous visual cortical activity (Farah, Steinhauer, Lewicki, Zubin, & Peronnet, 1988). In the case of sexual fantasies, the more vivid or "real" the fantasy is, the greater the sexual arousal. Smith and Over (1987) reported that the extent to which men can induce erection through fantasy is a function not only of the sexual content of the fantasy but of the vividness of the fantasy as well. Consistent with this finding, it has also been reported that during a sexual fantasy the genital response and sexual arousal increase when subjects complement sexual scenes with imagined physical responses during sex acts (Dekker & Everaerd, 1988). In a related finding, visceral activity during emotional imagery varied positively with imagery ability (Miller et al., 1987). It thus appears that fantasies that incorporate more detailed visceral responses are more arousing. While this is not a particularly startling conclusion, it does underscore the wide range of individual differences with respect to the "richness" or vividness of fantasies, ranging from drab, dull, poorly organized images to exciting, dynamic, three-dimensional images.

Location of Fantasy

Speculations about the "location" of fantasy are relevant. It has been argued that the left hemisphere, not the right, appears to be responsible for generating fantasy (Gazzaniga, 1985). Although the orgasmic response seems to be localized in the nondominant hemisphere, the "script" for the orgasm (that is, the content of the fantasy accompanying sexual arousal) seems to be localized in the dominant hemisphere (Flor-Henry, 1980; Gosselin & Wilson, 1984). Flor-Henry (1980) noted that

> Pathologic neural organization of the dominant hemisphere provides the substrate for the abnormal ideational representations of the sexual deviations and lead to (or are associated with) perturbed interhemispheric interactions so that only these abnormal ideas are capable of eliciting, or have a high probability of inducing, the orgasmic response. (p. 260)

It has thus been concluded that *left* hemispheric dysfunction is more likely to impact the *content* of the fantasy, resulting in bizarre or deviant images, than right hemispheric dysfunction (Gosselin & Wilson, 1984). Although it is clear that the act of generating a fantasy is considerably more complicated than what is suggested here, there is reliable evidence to support at least two separate processes with hemispheric specialization for each process (Kosslyn, 1988).

Some confirmatory evidence, as well as neuroanatomical specificity, was provided by a study that employed PET scans on a small sample ($N = 8$) of males viewing three types of films (sexually explicit, humorous, and emotionally neutral) (Stoleru et al., 1999). Visually evoked sexual arousal was described by three stages of activation: first, bilateral activation of the inferior temporal cortex; second, two paralimbic areas (right insula and right inferior frontal cortex); third, left anterior cingulate cortex (a paralimbic area that controls autonomic and neuroendocrine function). Activation was positively correlated with plasma testosterone levels. Stoleru et al. (1999) proposed a model for visually evoked sexual arousal that has three components: (1) a first stage perceptual–cognitive component, with the function of assessing the stimuli; activation is observed in the right and left inferior temporal cortices; (2) a second stage emotional/motivational component, linking what is perceived with emotional content; activation is observed in the right inferior frontal cortex and the left cingulate cortex; (3) a third stage endocrine and autonomic component, with the function of generating a physiological response to the stimuli; activation is noted in the left anterior cingulate cortex.

Temporal Lobe. Another area of research suggests further specificity. Flor-Henry (1980), in fact, referred to "the astonishing specificity of abnormal limbic mechanisms in the genesis of some of the sexual deviations" (p. 258). Two paraphilias in particular, fetishism and transvestism, have been associated with temporal lobe damage (see Langevin, 1983, for a discussion). It has thus been concluded that *dominant* temporal lobe dysfunction may be associated with fetishism, transvestism, and psychopathic sexual impulses (Flor-Henry, 1980). Although we certainly cannot conclude that temporal lobe dysfunction *causes* paraphiliac behavior, Langevin (1983) has argued that very early onset paraphilias "may be organic in origin since most sexually anomalous behavior is only prominent about the time of puberty" (p. 251). It is interesting to note in this regard that of the five paraphilias that we examined, the two with the largest group differences were fetishism and transvestism.

Limbic System. To go one step further, we have proposed that the coexistence of a dominant hemisphere dysfunction in the limbic system (particularly the hippocampus) increases the likelihood that abusive experiences in childhood may become encoded in memory and retrieved in the form of sexually pathological fantasy. Such a dysfunction is hypothesized to have occurred prenatally, at birth, or early in development.

There exists a sizable literature demonstrating that animals with hippocampal lesions act as if they lacked internal inhibition (e.g., Douglas, 1967; Kimble, 1968) and habituate more slowly than controls as a result of a deficit in response inhibition (e.g., Jarrard & Korn, 1969; Kimble, 1968; Leaton, 1965). It is noteworthy in this regard that one study found that humans who reported more vivid images responded with *slower* electrodermal habituation to imagined electric shock (Drummond, White, & Ashton, 1978). The logic of this finding, as presented by the authors, is simple and straightforward. Imagined stimuli produce similar physiological changes to real stimuli. Imagining a scene that provokes fear or anxiety produces autonomic responses that are more or less in proportion to the vividness of the image. Drummond et al. (1978) argued that "if more vivid images do produce larger physiological responses, then individual differences in imagery vividness should affect rate of habituation to images, since it is well known that larger responses take longer to habituate" (p. 193). The Drummond et al. study may provide an important theoretical link between presumptive autonomic correlates of fantasy and autonomic correlates of hippocampal impairment. That is, hippocampal impairment may be associated with slow habituation caused by a deficit in response inhibition. Slow habituation may also be associated with increased vividness of imagery.

In addition, Sano, Sekino, and Mayanagi (1972) related ergotropic (posteromedial hypothalamus near the lateral wall of the third ventricle) dominance to "violent, aggressive, restless behaviours or rage" (p. 72). Isaacson (1972) noted that "the hippocampal influence upon the hypothalamus could be the inhibition of the ergotropic systems in the posterior hypothalamus" (p. 514). Thus, hippocampal impairment may also be associated with disinhibition of the ergotropic system.

There is also evidence that electrical stimulation of the hippocampus suppresses the release of adrenocortical steroids (Rubin, Mandell, & Crandall, 1966). As Venables (1974) pointed out, the relatively rapid recovery of the skin conductance response after hippocampal lesioning may result from chronic increases in ACTH, and hence elevated levels of adrenocortical hormones leading to faster sodium reabsorption. Although this pattern would suggest the presence of high levels of 17 hydroxycorticosteroids (17-OHCS), one might predict that the more important hormone is not a glucocorticoid (e.g., 17-OHCS) but the polypeptide ACTH, which directly affects PT level (Prentky, 1985). Interestingly, a chronic high level of ACTH may chronically *suppress* PT level, explaining why research on PT has failed to provide convincing evidence of markedly elevated levels among sex offenders. While there is predictably a high "arousal" state among serial offenders, the arousal may not be driven by testosterone. In the event of a limbic-related condition of chronic primary adrenocortical excess, it would not be surprising to see some Cushing's-like side effects, such as elevated blood glucose, suppression of the inflammatory response with a resulting susceptibility to infections and, tangentially, a high cholesterol level (Prentky, 1985). The latter prediction (susceptibility to infections) is also consistent with the hypothesis of Geschwind and Galaburda (1987) regarding an increased incidence of autoimmune disorders.

In a very interesting study in which sexual arousal to erotic movies was monitored using penile plethysmography, the reported fantasies were grouped according to those that were neutral, those that were avoided, and those that were common (Kling, Borowitz, & Cartwright, 1972). Common fantasies correlated positively with sexual arousal and negatively with plasma levels of 17-OHCS. Violent fantasies (the avoided ones) were negatively associated with sexual arousal and positively associated with 17-OHCS (i.e., levels increased). We would speculate that among serial sexual offenders violent fantasies would be positively associated with sexual arousal and 17-OHCS. In the case of 17-OHCS, the association would not be a stimulus-specific response to aversive images but a steady-state condition.

Brain pathology, such as we have discussed, is, of course, "quite subtle" (Langevin, 1990), and there is no empirical basis for drawing any firm conclusions. The studies discussed here are drawn from disparate areas of inquiry and represent preliminary excursions into a relatively uncharted terrain, beset by a variety of extraordinarily challenging problems, such as interpreting the influence of a target lesion on a specific behavior—or constellation of behaviors—and generalizing from that case to a larger subset of cases with common behavioral aberrations.

Neurochemical Considerations

Serotonin.   Extreme cases of intrusive, recurrent fantasies may be associated with a state of chronic, undifferentiated arousal, defined as elevations in adrenocortical hormones and catecholamines, particularly norepinephrine (3–methoxy–4–hydroxyphenylglycol, or MHPG). If this arousal state is mediated by catecholamines, it is reasonable to conjecture that acetylcholine (ACh)—and perhaps serotonin—should suppress arousal by antagonizing the catecholamines (Mabry & Campbell, 1978). Thus, along with higher levels of MHPG we might also expect to find lower levels of serotonin (5-hydroxytryptamine, or 5-HT) and its metabolite 5-HIAA (5-hydroxyindoleacetic acid) and ACh. The most impressive effects of 5-HT depletion on male sexual behavior have been observed in the rat, where increased sexual excitement, increased mounting behavior, and increased chasing/rolling have been noted (Prentky, 1985). For the most part, however, the results of studies employing monkeys and humans have generally been negative (Prentky, 1985). That is, the administration of 5-HT biosynthesis inhibitors (e.g., parachlorophenylalanine) did not affect sexual behavior. It is noteworthy, however, that until recently no human studies have used as subjects men with manifestly high levels of sexually deviant and/or aggressive behavior. Kafka (1991) examined the effects of fluoxetine, a 5-HT reuptake blocker, in 10 men with diagnosed paraphilias (exhibitionists, fetishists, and transvestites), finding amelioration of deviant sexual behaviors and a reduction of sexual drive toward normative levels in 9 of the 10 subjects. This is, of course, a single study on a small group of volunteers, although it does offer some support for future inquiry into the relation of serotonin to sexually compulsive and anomalous behavior in humans. Clearly, the relation, if indeed one exists, will be vastly more complex than what has thus far been observed in rats and rabbits.

Sex Hormones.   The last important consideration concerns the relation between testosterone and sexual aggression. Although there is ample clinical evidence to suggest that gonadal hormones are involved in human aggression (Valzelli, 1981), the relatively few empirical studies have yielded conflictual and inconclusive results (Prentky, 1985). One finding that is of theoretical importance, as well as being reasonably reliable (Rose, 1978), suggests a relationship between markedly elevated levels of PT and extreme violence and/ or a long history of aggressive behavior beginning at a young age (Rose, 1978). Kreuz and Rose (1972) reported that prisoners with histories of more violent crimes in adolescence had significantly higher PT levels than prisoners without histories of adolescent violence. Bain, Langevin, Dickey, and Ben-Aron (1987) and Langevin, Ben-Aron, Wright, Marchese, and Handy (1988) have reported elevated PT levels in violent offenders.

Despite many clinical reports and some reliable empirical evidence, we are still unable to draw any firm conclusions regarding the role of circulating androgens and aggression in adult humans. This may be explained, in good measure, by the complex interaction of other variables, such as social learning, environmental factors, and disinhibiting agents.

There are two periods during development when testosterone may be influential with respect to aggressive behavior. The first period occurs *in utero*. The fact that male children are more aggressive than female children has been attributed to the presence of testosterone in males and its absence in females during a restricted period of *in utero* development

(Simon, 1981). The second period when testosterone may be influential occurs during puberty, when there is a 10-fold increase in testosterone production (Brown, 1981).

Within the last decade a related area of inquiry has provided a potentially important glimpse at the relationship between testosterone and aggression. This window is *in utero*, the first developmental epoch when testosterone may be influential with respect to aggressive behavior. In fact, one study found that the plasma free-testosterone level of male fetuses during midpregnancy may be more than twice as high as in adulthood (Stahl, Gotz, Poppe, Amendt, & Dorner, 1978). As Kopera (1983) noted, "sex hormones exert regulatory influences on the central nervous system, particularly during limited 'critical' periods in the rapidly developing embryonic, foetal, postnatal brain" (p. 52). These influences "organize the sexually undifferentiated brain, with regard to neuroendocrine function and patterns of not only sexual but also non-sexual behavior" (Kopera, 1983, pp. 58–59).

The process of masculinization of the developing male brain is not, however, a simple, dualistic phenomenon. The amount of testosterone *in utero*, as well as the sensitivity of target tissues to testosterone and the metabolic inactivation of testosterone, may vary considerably. Thus, masculinization or feminization is, in reality, a matter of degree (Money, 1986), subject to a wide variety of factors such as the aforementioned "individual" differences, as well as endocrine abnormalities of the fetus, hormone-producing tumors in the mother, stress that alters the pregnant mother's own hormone levels, and substances— including steroid hormones—that enter the placenta after having been ingested or absorbed by the pregnant mother (Ehrhardt, 1978; Meyer-Bahlburg, 1978; Ward, 1984). Of the various congenital or drug-induced abnormalities, e.g., Turner's syndrome (see Ehrhardt, Greenberg, & Money, 1970), androgen insensitivity (Money, Ehrhardt, & Masica, 1968), and adrenogenital syndrome (Ehrhardt, 1977), the latter case of congenital adrenal hyperplasia (adrenogenital syndrome, CAH) is of particular interest. CAH can be induced by androgenic progestins, such as Provera, given to the pregnant mother to counteract toxemia. Studies of CAH and non-CAH female siblings found masculinized gender role behavior in the CAH sibs (Ehrhardt & Baker, 1974). The "feminizing" effects of estrogens in boys have also been noted. Yalom, Green, and Fisk (1973) reported that the sons of diabetic mothers who had been prenatally exposed to elevated estrogen demonstrated feminized gender role behavior (i.e., fewer "masculine" interests and reduced assertiveness and aggressiveness). Reinisch and Sanders (1982) pointed out that medications containing barbiturates (e.g., sleeping pills), which may have a feminizing effect on the fetus, were taken by millions of pregnant women.

In order to draw any inferences about the prenatal influence of sex hormones on subsequent aggressive and/or sexually deviant behavior, it is necessary to follow "exposed" subjects into late adolescence when such behavior is expressed (Money, 1986). In one widely cited study, 17 females and 8 males who were exposed during gestation to synthetic progestins were compared to their sex-matched unexposed siblings on a paper-and-pencil inventory designed to assess potential for aggressive behavior (Reinisch, 1981). The mean physical aggression scores for the progestin-exposed females and their unexposed sisters were 4.0 and 2.6, respectively. The mean physical aggression scores for the progestin-exposed males and their unexposed brothers were 9.75 and 4.88, respectively. In both cases group differences were significant at the .01 confidence level. An excellent review by Meyer-Bahlburg and Ehrhardt (1982) concluded that research to date provides tentative support for the hypothesis that prenatal exposure to exogenous sex hormones may influence the development of human aggressive behavior. Another review of this research also concluded that "sexual deviations in the human may be based, at least in part, on discrepancies between the genetic sex and a sex-specific sex hormone level during brain differentiation" (Dorner, 1980, p. 192). Dorner (1980) further observed, based on the examination of 84 human fetuses, that the critical period for sex-specific brain differentiation is between the fourth and seventh months of gestation. Lack of statistical power resulting from small samples and methodological problems (e.g., the unaccounted effect of the pregnancy abnormality for which the hormones were administered, and the period during gestation when exposure to the hormones occurred) again obviates any firm conclusions.

The influence of excess testosterone, or increased sensitivity to testosterone, *in utero* is the subject of Geschwind and Galaburda's (1987) remarkable and controversial cross-disciplinary, theoretical integration. They suggested that excess testosterone slows the development of the left hemisphere, resulting in an increased incidence of autoimmunity in left-handers by suppressing development of the thymus gland in the fetus (Geschwind & Galaburda, 1987). Geschwind and Galaburda (1987) noted that the male fetal gonads, which owe their development to the H-Y antigen—a protein on the Y chromosome—produce testosterone at levels that may be comparable to that of adult males. It is interesting, in this regard, that Goodman (1983), in a brief comment on the paraphilias, cited Federman (1981) as stating that "variations in the H-Y antigen complex … may well affect an individual's sexual profile" (p. 219). This speculation is supported by at least one study of transexuals (Eicher et al., 1979). Eicher et al. (1979) examined the white blood cells of their subjects, looking for the presence or absence of H-Y antigen. Typically, H-Y antigen is present on the cell surface of males and absent in females. In some of their subjects Eicher et al. (1979) found that the experienced or "felt" gender corresponded with the absence or presence of H-Y antigen rather than with the individual's body phenotype (external appearance).

In reality, the extent to which pre- or perinatal androgen excess potentiates aggressive and/or sexual behavior in humans is a vastly complex question, complicated by the inevitable influences of environment and rearing. It may well be, however, that such exposure does introduce a biological vulnerability, thereby increasing the risk for those individuals whose childhood and adolescent development is severely compromised by pathological experiences.

Following masculinization of the male brain *in utero* there is a surge of testosterone at about 2 weeks of age that ends at about 3 months of age (Money, 1986). Thereafter, there is a sex-hormone dormancy until the *onset of puberty* (Migeon & Forest, 1983), at which time there is, as noted, a 10-fold increase in production of testosterone (Brown, 1981). When the sex hormone tap is turned on again at puberty, testosterone and its metabolites activate a brain that has already been differentiated with respect to, as Money (1986) put it, "eroto-sexual programs." That is, the sex hormones activate the intricate developmental "software" that has been written over the preceding 13 years.

This abrupt increase in release of testosterone provides an opportunity for "naturalistic" studies on developmentally related changes in testosterone level and a concomitant onset of aggressive behavior. Konner (1982) reported that, in one study of male prison inmates, the higher the testosterone level the earlier the age of first arrest. Kreuz and Rose (1972) also found a significant correlation between the age of first occurrence of more violent or aggressive crimes and PT levels ($r = -.65$). If the age-related changes in criminal behavior can be tied to developmentally related changes in PT, it would provide important correlative support for the contribution of sex hormones.

Overview

As noted earlier, we have elsewhere proposed and begun to test a fantasy-based information processing model of repetitive sexually aggressive behavior (Burgess et al., 1986; Prentky & Burgess, 1991). In Prentky and Burgess (1991), we explored hypothetical biological correlates of the model. We began with a working assumption that fantasy is a cognitive process, essentially a retrieved memory. Moreover, we hypothesized that there are marked individual differences with regard to the strength or vividness of sexual fantasies and the intrusiveness and reiterativeness of sexual fantasies, and that the presence of these two factors will be pronounced in cases of repetitive sexual assault.

A fully integrated theoretical model must address three questions: (1) What coexisting "conditions" motivate the offense behavior? (2) What antecedent factors are associated with these conditions? (3) What constitutional and situational factors serve to increase or decrease the likelihood of the occurrence of the behavior? We proposed a highly speculative answer to question #1. We argued that the presumptive "condition" motivating the offense behavior is an intrusive, sexually deviant fantasy life and that the parameters governing the salience of these fantasies (e.g., their vividness and intrusiveness) have a biological underpinning. The origin of the deviant fantasies (question #2) was hypothesized to be protracted experiences of abuse in childhood. Mediating or disinhibting factors that increase or decrease the likelihood of acting on the fantasies (question #3) were not discussed.

Concluding Caveat

Overall, it is not known what link, if any, in the causal chain of human sexual aggression is occupied by biology. Were it possible to identify the neural circuitry that underlies different aggressive behaviors, complex exogenous factors (i.e., social learning and the environment), which may alter the endogenous response, would still defy simple explanations. Focusing on one aspect of sexual aggression, that which involves *repeated* assault, narrows somewhat the frame of reference by excluding all those who have committed no acts of sexual aggression or only a single known acts of sexual aggression. Even here, however, it is obvious that biological factors cannot be examined in a vacuum. The most compelling evidence to date underscores the powerful effect of social learning on the manner in which individuals learn to cope with and react to emotional experiences. Research on biological correlates of human sexual aggression must not only integrate theoretically meaningful social and developmental variables, but do so in models that permit the examination of complex interactions and temporal changes.

Risk Assessment Instruments

In this Appendix, we provide some of the more commonly used or well-known risk assessment instruments for sexual offenders. We have not been inclusive, and apologize for the inadvertent omission of equally useful instruments. Indeed, risk assessment scales are proliferating so fast, and existing scales are being revised in accordance with the results of validity studies, that it would be impossible to "capture" a rapidly evolving field.

In each case, we have reported the items from the most recent version of the instrument along with coding options and weights (if applicable). Importantly, the information provided here is not sufficient for the reliable use of these instruments. The reliable use of any of these instruments requires, in effect, a User's Manual that provides detailed coding and scoring instructions, cutoff scores or ranges (if available), psychometric characteristics of the instrument (if available), predictive validity data (if available), and sufficient "rehearsals" to achieve adequate interrater reliability. Thus, for each instrument, we have attempted to provide the reader with referral sources to obtain the aforementioned information. Anyone interested in using any of these scales should contact the authors directly.

Rapid Risk Assessment for Sexual Offense Recidivism (RRASOR)

Author: R. Karl Hanson, Ph.D.

Principal Author Affiliation:

Karl Hanson, Ph.D.
Senior Research Officer
Corrections Directorate
Department of the Solicitor General of Canada
Ottawa, Ontario
Canada K1A 0P8

Source: Public Works and Government Services Canada.
   User Report entitled: *The development of a brief actuarial risk scale for sexual offense recidivism.*
   Cat. No. JS4-1/1997-4E (User Report 97-04)

Items:

1. Prior sex offenses (not including index offenses; include arrests and/or convictions)
   none (no known priors)   = 0
   1 conviction *or* 1 or 2 charges   = 1
   2 or 3 convictions *or* 3, 4, or 5 charges = 2
   4 or more convictions *or* 6 or more charges = 3

2. Age at release (current age at time of assessment)
   age 25 or older = 0
   age 18–24.99* = 1
   *(RRASOR is not intended for those younger than 18 at time of exposure to risk)

3. Victim gender
   Only female victims = 0
      (all known sexual offenses are against females)
   Any male victim   = 1
      (if offender has ever committed a sexual offense against a male victim)

4. Relationship to victim
   Only related victims = 0
   (related victims include spouses, biological and stepchildren, parents, grand-
      children, in-laws, nieces, nephews, cousins, and so forth; offenders in a parental
      role to a victim living in the same household are related)
   Any unrelated victims = 1

The RRASOR score is the sum of the four items, ranging from 0 to 6.

Structured Anchored Clinical Judgment (SACJ-Min)

Author: David Thornton, Ph.D.

Principal Author Affiliation:

David Thornton, Ph.D.
Offender Behaviour Programmes Unit
Room 701
HM Prison Service
Abell House
John Islip Street
London SW1P 4LH
England

Source: Grubin, D. (1998). *Sex offending against children: Understanding the risk.*
          Police Research Series Paper 99. London: Home Office.

Items:

   1. Male victims
   2. Never married
   3. Noncontact sex offenses
   4. Stranger victims

5. Any current sex offense
6. Any prior sex offense
7. Any current nonsexual violent offense
8. Any prior nonsexual violent offense
9. Four or more prior sentencing occasions

Static-99

Authors: R. Karl Hanson, Ph.D., and David Thornton, Ph.D.

Principal Author Affiliations:

Karl Hanson, Ph.D.
Senior Research Officer
Corrections Directorate
Department of the Solicitor General of Canada
340 Laurier Avenue West
Ottawa, Ontario
Canada K1A 0P8

David Thornton, Ph.D.
Offender Behaviour Programmes Unit
Room 701
HM Prison Service
Abell House
John Islip Street
London SW1P 4LH
England

Source: Hanson, K. R., & Thornton, D. (1999). *Static 99: Improving actuarial risk assessments for sex offenders.* Public Works and Government Services Canada User Report. Cat. No. J2-165/1999 (User Report 99-02)

Items:

1. Prior sex offenses
   (all officially recorded offenses, including parole and probation violations, violations of conditional release, and institutional violations)

2. Prior sentencing dates
   (the number of distinct occasions on which the offender has been sentenced for criminal offenses of any kind; the number of charges and/or convictions does *not* matter, only the number of sentencing dates; exclude court appearances that result in acquittals)

3. Noncontact offenses
   (number of convictions for noncontact sexual offenses, such as exhibitionism, obscene telephone calls, and voyeurism; exclude self-reported offenses)

4. Index nonsexual violence
   (convictions for nonsexual assault that are dealt with on the same sentencing occasion as the index sex offense; may involve the same victim as in the index sex offense or a

different victim; examples include assault, assault and battery, robbery, weapons offenses, murder, arson, and threatening)

5. Prior nonsexual violence
   (any conviction for nonsexual violence prior to the index sentencing occasion)

6. Unrelated victim
   ("related" implies a relationship where marriage would ordinarily be prohibited, such as parent, grandparent, uncle, stepbrother)

7. Stranger victim
   (a victim is considered a stranger if the victim did not know the offender 24 hours before the offense)

8. Male victim
   (all sexual offenses involving male victims; exclude possession of child pornography that includes boys)

9. Young
   (offender's age at the time of the risk assessment; if the assessment concerns *current* risk level, use current age; if the assessment concerns projected risk [e.g., on release], use age at time of release)

10. Single
    (offender is considered single if he has never lived with a lover [male or female] for a period of at least 2 years; exclude legal marriages involving less than 2 years of cohabitation)

Items 1–5 are coded using archival ("official") documents.
Items 6–10 are coded using *all* available information, including self-report, victim statements, and collateral reports.

Sexual Violence Risk-20 (SVR-20)

Authors: Douglas Boer, Ph.D., Stephen Hart, Ph.D., Randall Kropp, Ph.D., and Christopher Webster, Ph.D.

Principal Author Affiliation:
Mental Health, Law, and Policy Institute
Simon Fraser University
Burnaby, British Columbia
Canada V5A 1S6

Source: Published by Psychological Assessment Resources, Odessa, Florida 33556, and Mental Health, Law, and Policy Institute. Copyright © 1997 by Dr. Stephen D. Hart of the Mental Health, Law, and Policy Institute, Simon University, Burnaby, Columbia, VSA 1S6. Fraser British Canada. All rights reserved. Reproduced by permission.

Items:

1. Sexual deviation
   (deviant sexual preference, as inferred from a pattern of behavior or from a plethysmographic assessment)

2. Victim of child abuse
   (presence of "serious" physical or sexual abuse or neglect, resulting in substantial physical or psychological harm, occurring on multiple occasions, to a dependent minor age 17 or younger)

3. Psychopathy
   (as assessed by the PCL-R or the PCL:SV; on the PCL-R, scores of 30 or higher are coded Y [yes or present], scores 21 to 29 are coded ?, and scores of 20 or lower are coded N [no or absent]; the corresponding cutoffs for the PCL:SV are Y [18 and higher], ? [13 to 17], and N [12 and lower])

4. Major mental illness
   (includes serious cognitive or intellectual impairment [e.g., dementia or mental retardation] and psychosis [delusional disorders, schizophrenia, major depression, bipolar disorder], based on DSM-IV criteria)

5. Substance use problems
   (includes illicit as well as licit drugs [alcohol and prescribed medication]; "serious problems" require use that results in substantial impairment of the individual's health and/or social functioning)

6. Suicidal/homicidal ideation
   (includes thoughts, impulses, and fantasies about causing, as well as intent to cause and attempts to cause, serious harm or death to self or others; "serious" means that the ideation is experienced as persistent and intrusive, or involves high lethal methods, or that the level of intent is moderate to high)

7. Relationship problems
   (refers to intimate [sexual] relationships that are marital or common-law between adults [same or opposite sex]; "problems" refer to multiple relationship breakdowns, serious marital conflict, and spousal violence; if the individual is a minor, this item is coded based on the stability of the relationship with his or her family of origin)

8. Employment problems
   (legal employment, including self-employment and job-related education and training in the community; "problems" refer to a history of frequent job changes or long periods of unemployment; if the individual is a minor, this item is coded based on the stability of his or her educational history)

9. Past nonsexual violent offenses
   ("violence" refers to actual, attempted, or threatened physical harm of another person; "serious" means that violence caused [or could have caused] substantial physical or psychological harm to the victim, or that it occurred on multiple occasions; "nonsexual" means that the violence did not involve actual, attempted, or threatened contact or communication of a sexual nature and that it was not intended to further a sexual offense)

10. Past nonviolent offenses
    ("criminal conduct" refers to antisocial behavior and delinquency that constitutes a violation of the law; "serious" means that the criminal conduct resulted in a charge or arrest or that it occurred on multiple occasions; "nonviolent" means that the conduct did not involve actual, attempted, or threatened physical harm of another person; "nonsexual" means that the conduct did not involve actual, attempted, or threatened

contact or communication of a sexual nature and was not intended to further a sexual offense)

11. Past supervision failures
    ("supervision in the community" means that the individual was residing in the community subject to civil or criminal court orders [bail, peace bond, restraining order, outpatient commitment] or was granted conditional release from a correctional or mental health facility [e.g., parole, day pass]; "serious violations" include all acts that resulted [or could have resulted] in termination of release and/or criminal charges)

12. High density sex offenses
    ("high density" means multiple acts of sexual violence occurring in a relatively short time period when the individual was "at risk" [i.e., had an opportunity to commit sexual crimes])

13. Multiple sex offense types
    (implies that the individual's history includes acts that vary in terms of nature and victim selection, including a number of paraphilias, varying degrees of coercion, victims of differing ages and relationships to the offender, and so forth)

14. Physical harm to victim(s) in sex offenses
    ("physical harm" means that a victim suffered bodily injury as a direct result of the actions of the individual and that the actions were deliberate and intended to cause harm or were reckless; "serious" means that the physical harm required medical attention or treatment, or resulted in death; "while committing" means that the injury occurred during a sexual offense or to further a sexual offense)

15. Uses weapons or threats of death in sex offenses
    ("weapons" include firearms, knives, clubs, ligatures, and any other object or device used to threaten or harm a victim; "threats of death" refer to any statement expressing a willingness or desire to kill a victim; "while committing" means that the use of weapons and/or threats to kill occurred during a sexual offense or to further a sexual offense)

16. Escalation in frequency or severity of sex offenses
    ("history of sexual violence" includes all acts of sexual violence committed by the individual; "escalation in frequency" means that the individual committed more sexual offenses recently than he or she did in the past, taking time "at risk" into account; "escalation in severity" means that, relative to earlier sexual offenses, the individual's more recent sexual offenses were more likely to involve victim contact, included more serious physical harm to the victim, included weapons or more lethal weapons, and included increasingly credible threats to kill)

17. Extreme minimization/denial of sex offenses
    ("extreme minimization or denial" means that the individual denies many or all past acts of sexual violence, denies personal responsibility for many or all past acts, or denies the serious consequences of many or all past acts)

18. Attitudes that support or condone sex offenses
    (attitudes that support or condone sexual violence include sociopolitical, religious, cultural or subcultural, and personal beliefs and values that encourage or excuse sex offenses)

19. Lacks realistic plans

("plans for the future" are the individual's intentions concerning adjustment in the community, including relationships, employment, place of residence, health care, and compliance with conditions of supervision and registration; "realistic" means the individual's intended plans are explicit, stable, and reasonable, reasonable being judged in light of the individual's history)

20. Negative attitude toward intervention

("negative attitude toward intervention" includes personal beliefs and values that encourage or excuse lack of participation in treatment, management, or support services; lack of participation in treatment programs includes refusal to attend, premature termination ["dropping out"], and superficial participation ["shamming"])

Other considerations:

The SVR-20 allows for the inclusion of "rare but important risk factors not included as separate items in the SVR-20," such as (a) acute mental disorder that does not meet the criteria for Major Mental Illness (item #4), (b) recent loss of social support network not attributable to Marital Breakdown (item #7) or Loss of Employment (item #8), and (c) frequent contact with potential victims not resulting from Lack of Realistic Plans (item #19) or Poor Attitude toward Intervention (item #20).

The 20 SVR items constitute three rationally derived groups: Psychosocial Adjustment (items 1–11), Sexual Offenses (items 12–18), and Future Plans (items 19 and 20). All items are coded as: Yes (present), ? (questionable), or No (absent).

Violence Risk Appraisal Guide (VRAG) and Sex Offense Risk Appraisal Guide (SORAG)

Authors: Vernon Quinsey, Ph.D., Grant Harris, Ph.D., Marnie Rice, Ph.D., and Catherine Cormier, M.A.

Principal Author Affiliations:

Vernon L. Quinsey, Ph.D.
Psychology Department
Queen's University
Kingston, Ontario
Canada K7L 3N6

Grant Harris, Ph.D., Marnie Rice, Ph.D., and Catherine Cormier
Research Department
Mental Health Centre
Penetanguishene, Ontario
Canada L9M 1G3

Source: Quinsey, V. L., Harris, G. T., Rice, M. E., & Cormier, C. (1998). *Violent offenders: Appraising and managing risk*. Washington, DC: American Psychological Association. Copyright © 1998 by the American Psychological Association. Adapted with permission.

Violence Risk Appraisal Guide

Items:

1. Lived with both biological parents to age 16 (except for death of parent due to natural causes)
   Yes = −2
   No = +3

2. Elementary school maladjustment
   No Problems   = −1
   Slight or Moderate Problems = +2
   (minor discipline or attendance problems)
   Severe Problems   = +5
   (frequent disruptive behavior and/or attendance or behavior resulting in expulsion or serious suspensions)

3. History of alcohol problems (one point is allotted for each of the following: parental alcoholism, teenage alcohol problem, adult alcohol problem, alcohol involved in a prior offense, alcohol involved in the index offense)
   0   = −1
   1 or 2 =   0
   3   = +1
   4 or 5 = +2

4. Marital status
   Ever Married   = −2
   (or lived common-law in the same home for at least 6 months)
   Never Married = +1

5. Criminal history score for nonviolent offenses (using the Cormier–Lang system, see Source Appendix A)
   Score 0   = −2
   Score 1 or 2   =   0
   Score 3 or above = +3

6. Failure on prior conditional release (includes parole or probation violation or revocation, failure to comply, bail violation, any new arrest while on conditional release)
   No =   0
   Yes = +3

7. Age at index (governing) offense (at most recent birthday)
   39 or over   = −5
   34 through 38 = −2
   28 through 33 = −1
   27   =   0
   26 or under   = +2

8. Victim injury (for index offense; the most serious is scored)
   Death   = −2
   Hospitalized   =   0
   Treated and Released = +1

None or Slight   = +2
(no victim also scored as +2)

9. Any female victim (for index offense)
Yes = −1
No = +1
(no victim also scored as +1)

10. Meets DSM-III criteria for any personality disorder
No = −2
Yes = +3

11. Meets DSM-III criteria for schizophrenia
Yes = −3
No = +1

12. Psychopathy checklist (PCL-R) score
  4 and under = −5
  5 through 9 = −3
10 through 14 = −1
15 through 24 =   0
25 through 34 = +4
35 and over   = +12

Sex Offence Risk Appraisal Guide

1. Lived with both biological parents to age 16 (except for death of parent due to natural causes)
Yes = −2
No = +3

2. Elementary school maladjustment
No Problems   = −1
Slight or Moderate Problems = +2
(minor discipline or attendance problems)
Severe Problems   = +5
(frequent disruptive behavior and/or attendance or behavior resulting in expulsion or serious suspensions)

3. History of alcohol problems (one point is allotted for each of the following: parental alcoholism, teenage alcohol problem, adult alcohol problem, alcohol involved in a prior offense, alcohol involved in the index offense)
0   = −1
1 or 2 =   0
3   = +1
4 or 5 = +2

4. Marital status
Ever Married = −2
(or lived common-law in the same home for at least 6 months)
Never Married = +1

5. Criminal history score for nonviolent offenses (using the Cormier–Lang system, see Source Appendix A)
   Score 0   = −2
   Score 1 or 2   =   0
   Score 3 or over = +3

6. Criminal history score for violent offenses (using the Cormier–Lang system, see Source Appendix B)
   Score 0   = −2
   Score 1 or 2   =   0
   Score 3 or over = +6

7. Number of previous convictions for sexual offenses (pertains to all known convictions, based on all available documents, for hands-on sexual offenses *prior* to the index [or governing] offense)
   0   = −1
   1 or 2 = +1
   ⩾ 3   = +5

8. History of sex offenses only against girls under 14 (including index offenses; if offender was less than 5 years older than victim, always score +4)
   Yes =   0
   No = +4

9. Failure on prior conditional release (includes parole/probation violation or revocation, failure to comply, bail violation, any new arrest while on conditional release)
   No =   0
   Yes = +3

10. Age at index (governing) offense (at most recent birthday)
    39 or over   = −5
    34 through 38 = −2
    28 through 33 = −1
    27   =   0
    26 or under   = +2

11. Meets DSM-III criteria for any personality disorder
    No = −2
    Yes = +3

12. Meets DSM-III criteria for schizophrenia
    Yes = −3
    No = +1

13. Phallometric test results
    All test results indicate nondeviant sexual preferences = −1
    Any test result indicates deviant sexual preferences = +1

14. Psychopathy checklist (PCL-R) score
    4 and under = −5
    5 through 9 = −3
    10 through 14 = −1

15 through 24 =   0
25 through 34 = +4
35 and over = +12

Minnesota Sex Offender Screening Tool-Revised (MnSOST-R)

Authors: Douglas Epperson, Ph.D., James Kaul, and Denise Hesselton

Principal Author Affiliation:

Douglas Epperson, Ph.D.
Department of Psychology
Iowa State University
W112 Lagomarcino Hall
Ames, IA 50011-3180

Source: *Final report on the development of the Minnesota Sex Offender Screening Tool—Revised.* Presented at the 17th Annual Research and Treatment Conference of the Association for the Treatment of Sexual Abusers, Vancouver, Canada. Available from:

Minnesota Department of Corrections
SO/CD Services Unit
1450 Energy Park Drive, Suite 200
St. Paul, MN 55108-5219

Items:

1. Number of legal sex/sex-related convictions (including the current conviction)
   One = 0, Two or more = +2

2. Length of sex offending history
   Less than 1 Year   = −1
   1 to 6 Years   = +3
   More than 6 Years =   0

3. Was the offender under any form of supervision when he committed any sex offense for which he was eventually charged or convicted?
   No = 0, Yes = +2

4. Was any sex offense (charged or convicted) committed in a public place?
   No = 0, Yes = +2

5. Was force or the threat of force ever used to achieve compliance in any sex offense (charged or convicted)?
   No force in any offense   = −3
   Force present in at least one offense =   0

6. Has any sex offense (charged or convicted) involved multiple acts on a single victim within any single contact event?
   No = −1, Yes = 1

7. Number of different age groups victimized across all sex/sex-related offenses (charged or convicted)

Check all age groups of victims that apply:
  Age 6 or younger
  Age 7 to 12 years
  Age 13 to 15 (offender more than 5 years older than victim)
  Age 16 or older
No age groups or only one age group checked =   0
Two or more age groups checked   = +3

8. Offended against a 13- to 15-year-old victim AND the offender was more than 5 years older than the victim at the time of the offense (charged or convicted)
   No = 0, Yes = +2

9. Was the victim of any sex/sex-related offense (charged or convicted) a stranger?
   No victims were strangers   = −1
   At least one victim was a stranger   = +3
   Neither of the above can be confirmed, due to missing data =   0

10. Is there evidence of adolescent antisocial behavior in the file?
    No indication   = −1
    Some relatively isolated antisocial acts =   0
    Persistent, repetitive pattern   = +2

11. Pattern of substantial drug or alcohol abuse (12 months prior to the instant offense or revocation)
    No = −1, Yes = +1

12. Employment history (12 months prior to the instant offense)
    Stable employment for 1 year or longer prior to arrest   = −2
    Homemaker, retired, full-time student, or disabled/unable to work = −2
    Part-time, seasonal, unstable employment   =   0
    Unemployed or significant history of unemployment   = +1
    File contains no information about employment   =   0

13. Discipline history while incarcerated (does not include discipline for failure to follow directives to successfully complete treatment)
    No major discipline reports or infractions =   0
    One or more major discipline reports   = +1

14. Chemical dependency treatment while incarcerated
    Treatment recommended and successfully completed or in program at time   = −2
      of release
    No treatment recommended/Not enough time/No opportunity   =   0
    Treatment recommended but offender refused, quit, or did not pursue   = +1
    Treatment recommended but terminated   = +4

15. Sex offender treatment while incarcerated
    Treatment recommended and successfully completed or in program at time   = −1
      of release
    No treatment recommended/Not enough time/No opportunity   =   0
    Treatment recommended but offender refused, quit, or did not pursue   =   0
    Treatment recommended but terminated   =   3

16. Age at release from institution
    Age 30 or younger = +1
    Age 31 or older   = −1
    Actual age: _____

JJPI-Maine Juvenile Sex Offender Assessment Protocol (JSOAP)

Authors: Robert Prentky, Ph.D., Bert Harris, M.A., Kate Frizzell, M.A., and Sue Right-
           hand, Ph.D.

Principal Author Affiliations:

R. A. Prentky, Ph.D.
Justice Resource Institute
Massachusetts Treatment Center
30 Administration Road, Box 554
Bridgewater, MA 02324

Bert Harris, M.A.
Joseph J. Peters Institute
260 S. Broad Street, #220
Philadelphia, PA 19102

Sue Righthand, Ph.D.
Senior Consultant
State Forensic Service
151 State House Station
Augusta, Maine 04330

Source: Prentky, R. A., Harris, B., Frizzell, K., & Righthand, S. (2000). An actuarial
          procedure for assessing risk with juvenile sex offenders. *Sexual Abuse: A Journal
          of Research and Treatment*, 12, 71–93.

Juvenile Sex Offender Assessment Protocol

I.   Sexual Drive/Preoccupation Factor

  1. Prior legally charged sex offenses (conviction not necessary)
     None = 0   1 Offense = 1   > 1 Offense = 2

  2. Duration of sex offense history (*not* limited to legally charged offenses; include
     credible reports and self-report)
     Only one known sexual offense and no other history of sexual aggression   = 0
     (governing or index offense is the only known sexual offense)
     Multiple sex offenses within a brief time period (6 months or less), whether one   = 1
     victim or multiple victims
     Multiple sex offenses that extend over a period greater than 6 months, whether   = 2
     one victim or multiple victims

  3. Evidence of sexual preoccupation/obsessions (preoccupation with sexual fanta-
     sies and gratification of sexual needs, frequent uncontrollable sexual urges,

multiple paraphilias [such as exposing, peeping, cross-dressing, fetishes], compulsive masturbation, excessive use of pornography, cruising, stalking)
No = 0   Somewhat = 1   Yes = 2
("Somewhat" signifies present but minimal or occasional; "Yes" signifies clearly present and observed on multiple occasions)

4. Degree of planning in sexual offense(s)
    Impulsive Offense(s) (opportunistic, sudden, without any apparent planning)   = 0
    Moderate Planning (clear evidence that the subject thought about or fantasized   = 1
        about the sexual offense *beforehand*, but minimal evidence of actual planning [i.e., no clear modus operandi]; grooming or "setting up" the victim typically reflects moderate planning)
    Detailed Planning (a clear modus operandi; offenses may appear "scripted,"   = 2
        particular victim and crime location targeted; rape "kit" or paraphernalia brought to crime, including weapon and/or restraints)

5. Gratuitous sexual exploitation of victim (exploiting the victim as a sexual object by making the victim view or participate in pornography, prostituting the victim, subjecting the victim to repeated sexual assaults during protracted confinement)
    No = 0   Somewhat = 1   Yes = 2
    ("Somewhat" signifies present but minimal or occasional; "Yes" signifies clearly present and observed on multiple occasions)

II.   Impulsive, Antisocial Behavior Factor

6. Caregiver consistency (key issue is frequency of *change* in caregivers)
    Stable (lived with biological parents until current age or age 16 if subject is   = 0
        older than 16)
    Unstable (lived with only one biological parent *or* lived with one stepfamily or   = 1
        one foster family until current age or the age of 16)
    Highly unstable (multiple changes in caregivers)   = 2

7. History of expressed anger (as evidenced by verbal aggression, angry outbursts; threatening and intimidating behavior; nonsexual assaults, destruction of property; suspensions or expulsions from school due to anger; loss of jobs due to anger; physical violence directed at peers, caregivers, teachers, or other "authority figures," and cruelty to animals)
    None/Minimal   = 0
    Moderate (1 or 2 different criteria present) = 1
    Strong (3 or more different criteria present) = 2

8. School behavior problems (code for kindergarten through eighth grade only; "problems" include school failure, repeated truancy, fighting with peers and/or teachers, or other evidence of serious behavioral problems at school)
    No = 0   Mild = 1   Severe = 2

9. School suspensions or expulsions (code for kindergarten through eighth grade only)
    No = 0   Once = 1   More than once = 2

10. History of conduct disorder (before age 10) (a persistent pattern of behavioral disturbance, with early onset, characterized by repeated failure to obey rules, violating the basic rights of others, and engaging in destructive and aggressive conduct at school, home, and in the community)

None/Minimal = 0

Moderate   = 1 (1 or 2 different criteria present)

Strong   = 2 (3 or more different criteria present)

11. Juvenile antisocial behavior (age 10–17) (as evidenced by delinquent behavior, such as a history of vandalism and destruction of property, other nonsexual, victimless crimes, nonassaultive offenses, fighting and physical violence, owning or carrying a weapon, or other serious rule violations)

None/Minimal   = 0

Moderate (1 or 2 different criteria present) = 1

Strong (3 or more different criteria present) = 2

12. Ever arrested before the age of 16 (includes current *and* other sexual and nonsexual offenses)

No = 0   Once = 1   More than once = 2

13. Multiple types of offenses (not limited to legally charged offenses. Include self-report or other credible reports. Check as many different types of offense categories as apply and score according to the total number checked)

___ a. *Sexual offenses* (such as rape, indecent assault and battery, gross sexual assault, unlawful sexual contact, open and gross lewdness)

___ b. *Person offenses—nonsexual* (such as assault, assault and battery, assault causing bodily harm, robbery, armed robbery, kidnapping, attempted murder, manslaughter, murder, terrorizing)

___ c. *Property offenses* (such as theft, burglary, possessing burglary tools, larceny, breaking and entering, criminal trespass, malicious destruction of property, arson, receiving/possessing stolen property, embezzlement, extortion of property)

___ d. *Fraudulent offenses* (such as fraud, forgery, passing bad checks, using stolen credit cards, impersonation, identity fraud, counterfeiting)

___ e. *Drug offenses* (such as possession of drugs, drug trafficking)

___ f. *Serious motor vehicle offenses* (such as operating to endanger, operating under the influence, reckless driving, chronic speeding, leaving the scene of an accident, vehicular homicide)

___ g. *Conduct offenses* (such as disorderly conduct, running away, vagrancy, malicious mischief, resisting arrest, habitual truant, habitual offender)

___ h. *Other rule-breaking offenses* (there is no clear victim but the law has been broken, such as escape from legal custody, failure to appear, conspiracy, accessory before or after the fact, possession of a firearm without a permit, obstruction of justice, violation of conditions of probation or other release, violation of a protection/restraining order, prostitution)

1 Type = 0   2 Types = 1   > 2 Types = 2

14. Impulsivity (evidence of a highly impulsive lifestyle, as evidenced by truancy
    and absenteeism, running away, a history of escapes, fighting and assaultive
    behavior, unstable work history, numerous brief relationships, reckless driving,
    and driving to endanger)
    None/Minimal   = 0
    Moderate (1 or 2 different criteria present) = 1
    Strong (3 or more different criteria present) = 2

15. History of substance abuse (recent or continuing problems associated with substance
    abuse, such as driving violations, physical illness, school, work, family, or legal
    problems; if in prison or secure juvenile placement, consider period prior to being in
    custody)
    No or Occasional (no problems associated with abuse)   = 0
    Moderate Abuse (some problems associated with abuse)   = 1
    Chronic or Severe Abuse (multiple problems associated with abuse) = 2

16. History of parental alcohol abuse
    No or Occasional (no problems associated with abuse)   = 0
    Moderate Abuse (some problems associated with abuse)   = 1
    Chronic or Severe Abuse (multiple problems associated with abuse) = 2

III. Intervention Factor

17. Accepts responsibility for sexual offense(s)
    Accepts *full* responsibility; No evidence of minimization   = 0
    Accepts some responsibility; Occasional minimization; No evidence of denial   = 1
    Accepts *no* responsibility, or partial denial and/or minimization   = 2

18. Internal motivation for change
    Appears to be distressed by sexual offenses *and* to have a genuine desire to   = 0
      change behavior
    Some degree of internal conflict and distress, mixed with a clear desire to avoid = 1
      the "consequences" of reoffending
    No internal motivation. Does not perceive a need to change, feels hopeless and   = 2
      resigned about life in general, or motivation for treatment is *solely* external
      (e.g., to avoid arrest, incarceration, or residential placement)

19. Understands sexual assault cycle and relapse prevention
    Good understanding and demonstration of knowledge of cycle, knows triggers;   = 0
      knows cognitive distortions (thinking errors), knows high-risk situations,
      knows and uses relapse prevention concepts
    Incomplete or partial understanding of cycle and relapse prevention; demon-   = 1
      stration of knowledge may be present, but inconsistent
    Poor or inadequate understanding of cycle, triggers, distortions, high-risk situa- = 2
      tions, and relapse prevention. Cannot identify triggers, distortions, high-risk
      situations, or prevention strategies

20. Evidence of empathy, remorse, guilt   = 0
    Appears to have genuine remorse and can generalize to other victims; Remorse
      appears to be internalized at an affective level

Some degree of remorse or guilt; Possible egocentric motives (e.g., shame or   = 1
embarrassment); May be internalized at a cognitive (thinking) level
Little or no evidence of remorse or empathy for victims   = 2

21. Absence of cognitive distortions (thinking errors)
No expression of thoughts, attitudes, or statements that are demeaning to   = 0
others, or that minimize, distort, or justify criminal conduct
Occasional comments, attitudes, or statements that minimize, distort, or justify = 1
criminal conduct
Frequent comments, attitudes, or statements that minimize, distort, or justify   = 2
criminal conduct

IV. Community Stability/Adjustment Factor
(Code the Remaining Items for the Past 6 Months)
Communities include residential treatment programs

22. Evidence of poorly managed anger in the community (physical or verbal
assaults on family members, peers, and authority figures, such as teachers,
supervisors, employers, probation officers, therapists)
Not a problem (no known incidents)   = 0
Moderate problem (1 or 2 incidents)   = 1
Serious problem (3 or more incidents) = 2

23. Stability of current living situation (instability evidenced by household members [caregivers, partners, or siblings] engaging in: substance abuse, having a
known criminal history, frequent changes in sexual partners, frequent moves,
poor boundaries, use of pornography, family violence and/or child neglect;
instability may also be indicated by frequent changes in subject's living situation, or subject is in a high-risk living situation or high-risk location [i.e., near a
bar or a playground]. If subject is in residential placement with an impending
discharge, consider discharge situation. If plan is unknown, score 2)
Stable (presence of no more than 1)   = 0
Unstable (presence of 2 or 3)   = 1
Highly Unstable (presence of 4 or more) = 2

24. Stability of school (unstable school history as evidenced by truancy, fighting
with peers or teachers; suspensions or expulsions; history of running away from
school; carrying weapons at school; use of alcohol/drugs at school)
Stable (no evidence of any of the above)   = 0
Unstable (presence of 1 or 2 of the above)   = 1
Highly unstable (presence of 3 or more of the above) = 2

25. Evidence of support systems in the community (evidence of cooperation and
compliance with juvenile caseworkers/probation officers and/or treatment program; apparently supportive family, extended family, foster family, friends, or
others; participation in organized, after-school sports; involvement in church
and church-related functions; clear evidence of continued involvement with a
delinquent peer group requires a score of 2; if subject is in a residential
treatment program with an impending discharge, consider likely discharge
situation)

Considerable Support Systems (2 or more of the above apply) = 0
Some Support Systems (1 of the above applies)   = 1
No Known Support Systems/Negative Support Systems   = 2

26. Quality of peer relationships

Socially active, peer-oriented, and rarely alone; often with friends in structured   = 0
and unstructured social and/or sports activities; friends are *non*delinquent

A few friends, some involvement in structured or unstructured activities;   = 1
occasional social life

For the most part, withdrawn from peer contact and socially isolated; no   = 2
"good" friends, just "acquaintances" or all peers are part of a delinquent
group

Scoring Procedure

STATIC/HISTORICAL FACTORS

Sexual Drive/Preoccupation Factor Score: (Add items 1–5)   _____

Impulsive-Antisocial Personality Factor Score: (Add items 6–16)   _____

Note: I-A P Factor includes Harris, Rice, and Quinsey (1994) Adolescent Psychopathy
Taxon (items 6, 8–10, 12, 14–16)

DYNAMIC FACTORS

Intervention Factor Score: (Add items 17–21)   _____

Community Stability Factor Score: (Add items 22–26)   _____

TOTAL SCORE	MAXIMUM POSSIBLE	% Present Score/Max
Sexual Drive/Preoccupation Factor Score	10	_____
Impulsive-Antisocial Personality Factor Score	22	_____
Intervention Factor Score	10	_____
Community Stability Factor Score	10	_____
TOTAL Score	52	

JJPI/Maine Adult Sex Offender Assessment Protocol (A-SOAP)

Authors: Robert Prentky, Ph.D., and Sue Righthand, Ph.D.

Principal Author Affiliations:

R. A. Prentky, Ph.D.
Justice Resource Institute
Massachusetts Treatment Center
30 Administration Road, Box 554
Bridgewater, MA 02324

Sue Righthand, Ph.D.
Senior Consultant

State Forensic Service
151 State House Station
Augusta, ME 04330

Source: Authors (unpublished, available from authors)

I.   Sexual Drive/Preoccupation Factor

1. Prior legally charged sex offenses (charge or arrest; conviction *not* necessary)
   None = 0   1 Offense = 1   > 1 Offense = 2

2. Duration of sex offense history (*not* limited to legally charged offenses; include
   credible reports and self-report)
   Only one known sexual offense and no other history of sexual aggression   = 0
      (governing or index offense is the only known sexual offense)
   Multiple sex offenses within a brief time period (6 months or less), whether one   = 1
      victim or multiple victims
   Multiple sex offenses that extend over a period greater than 6 months, whether   = 2
      one victim or multiple victims

3. Evidence of sexual preoccupation/obsessions (preoccupation with sexual fantasies and gratification of sexual needs, frequent uncontrollable sexual urges,
   multiple paraphilias [such as exposing, peeping, cross-dressing, fetishes], compulsive masturbation, excessive use of pornography, cruising, stalking)
   No = 0   Somewhat = 1   Yes = 2
   ("Somewhat" signifies present but minimal or occasional; "Yes" signifies
   clearly present and observed on multiple occasions)

4. Degree of planning in sexual offense(s)
   Impulsive Offense(s) (opportunistic, sudden, without any apparent planning)   = 0
   Moderate Planning (clear evidence that the subject thought about or fantasized   = 1
      about the sexual offense *beforehand*, but minimal evidence of actual plan-
      ning [i.e., no clear modus operandi]; grooming or "setting up" the victim
      typically reflects moderate planning)
   Detailed Planning (a clear modus operandi; offenses may appear "scripted,"   = 2
      particular victim and crime location targeted; rape "kit" or paraphernalia
      brought to crime, including weapon and/or restraints)

5. Gratuitous sexual exploitation of victim (exploiting the victim as a sexual
   object by making the victim view or participate in pornography, prostituting the
   victim, subjecting the victim to repeated sexual assaults during protracted
   confinement)
   No = 0   Somewhat = 1   Yes = 2
   ("Somewhat" signifies present but minimal or occasional; "Yes" signifies
   clearly present and observed on multiple occasions)

II.   Impulsive/Antisocial Behavior Factor

6. History of expressed anger (as evidenced by verbal aggression, angry outbursts;
   threatening and intimidating behavior; nonsexual assaults, destruction of property; loss of jobs due to anger; physical violence directed at children or partners;
   and cruelty to animals)

None/Minimal   = 0
Moderate (1 or 2 different criteria present) = 1
Strong (3 or more different criteria present) = 2

7. Multiple types of offenses (include current offense) (not limited to legally charged offenses. Include self-report or other credible reports. Check as many different types of offense categories as apply and score according to the total number checked)
    __ a. *Sexual offenses* (such as rape, indecent assault and battery, gross sexual assault, unlawful sexual contact, open and gross lewdness)
    __ b. *Person offenses—nonsexual* (such as assault, assault and battery, assault causing bodily harm, robbery, armed robbery, kidnapping, attempted murder, manslaughter, murder, terrorizing)
    __ c. *Property offenses* (such as theft, burglary, possessing burglary tools, larceny, breaking and entering, criminal trespass, malicious destruction of property, arson, receiving/possessing stolen property, embezzlement, extortion of property)
    __ d. *Fraudulent offenses* (such as fraud, forgery, passing bad checks, using stolen credit cards, impersonation, identity fraud, counterfeiting)
    __ e. *Drug offenses* (such as possession of drugs, drug trafficking)
    __ f. *Serious motor vehicle offenses* (such as operating to endanger, operating under the influence, reckless driving, chronic speeding, leaving the scene of an accident, vehicular homicide)
    __ g. *Conduct offenses* (such as disorderly conduct, running away, vagrancy, malicious mischief, resisting arrest, habitual truant, habitual offender)
    __ h. *Other rule-breaking offenses* (there is no clear victim but the law has been broken, such as escape from legal custody, failure to appear, conspiracy, accessory before or after the fact, possession of a firearm without a permit, obstruction of justice, violation of conditions of probation or other release, violation of a protection/restraining order, prostitution)
    1 Type = 0   2 Types = 1   > 2 Types = 2

8. Impulsivity (evidence of a highly impulsive lifestyle, as evidenced by truancy and absenteeism, running away, a history of escapes, fighting and assaultive behavior, unstable work history, numerous, brief relationships, nomadic [living in many different places for a brief time], reckless driving and driving to endanger)
    None/Minimal   = 0
    Moderate (1 or 2 different criteria present) = 1
    Strong (3 or more different criteria present) = 2

9. History of substance abuse (recent or continuing problems associated with substance abuse, such as driving violations, physical illness, work, family, or legal problems. If in prison, consider period prior to being in custody)
    No or Occasional (no problems associated with abuse)   = 0
    Moderate Abuse (some problems associated with abuse)   = 1
    Chronic or Severe Abuse (multiple problems associated with abuse) = 2

10. Juvenile antisocial behavior (age 10–17) (as evidenced by delinquent behavior, such as a history of vandalism and destruction of property, other nonsexual,

victimless crimes, nonassaultive offenses, fighting and physical violence, owning or carrying a weapon, or other serious rule violations)

None/Minimal   = 0
Moderate (1 or 2 different criteria present)   = 1
Strong (3 or more different criteria present) = 2

11. Adult antisocial behavior (age 18 or older) (as evidenced by a history of
vandalism and other nonsexual, victimless crimes; assaultive offenses, physical
violence directed at children or partners, owning or carrying a weapon; coincident substance abuse and acting out)

None/Minimal   = 0
Moderate (1 or 2 different criteria present)   = 1
Strong (3 or more different criteria present) = 2

III. Intervention Factor

12. Accepts responsibility for sexual offense(s)
Accepts *full* responsibility; No evidence of minimization   = 0
Accepts some responsibility; Occasional minimization; No evidence of denial   = 1
Accepts no responsibility, or partial denial and/or minimization   = 2

13. Internal motivation for change
Appears to be distressed by sexual offenses *and* to have a genuine desire to   = 0
  change behavior
Some degree of internal conflict and distress, mixed with a clear desire to avoid   = 1
  the "consequences" of reoffending
No internal motivation. Does not perceive a need to change, feels hopeless and   = 2
  resigned about life in general, or motivation for treatment is *solely* external
  (e.g., to avoid arrest, incarceration, or residential placement)

14. Understands sexual assault cycle and relapse prevention
Good understanding and demonstration of knowledge of cycle, knows triggers;   = 0
  knows cognitive distortions (thinking errors), knows high-risk situations,
  knows and uses relapse prevention concepts
Incomplete or partial understanding of cycle and relapse prevention; demon-   = 1
  stration of knowledge may be present, but inconsistent
Poor or inadequate understanding of cycle, triggers, distortions, high-risk situa-   = 2
  tions, and relapse prevention. Cannot identify triggers, distortions, high-risk
  situations, or prevention strategies

15. Evidence of empathy, remorse, guilt
Appears to have genuine remorse and can generalize to other victims; Remorse   = 0
  appears to be internalized at an affective level
Some degree of remorse or guilt; Possible egocentric motives (e.g., shame or   = 1
  embarrassment); May be internalized at a cognitive (thinking) level
Little or no evidence of remorse or empathy for victims   = 2

16. Absence of cognitive distortions (thinking errors)
No expression of thoughts, attitudes, or statements that are demeaning to   = 0
  others, or that minimize, distort, or justify criminal conduct
Occasional comments, attitudes, or statements that minimize, distort, or justify   = 1
  criminal conduct

Frequent comments, attitudes, or statements that minimize, distort, or justify   = 2
criminal conduct

IV.   Community Stability/Adjustment Factor
      (Code for the Remaining Items for the Past 6 Months)

17. Evidence of poorly managed anger in the community (physical or verbal
     assaults on family members, peers, and authority figures, such as supervisors,
     employers, probation officers, parole agents, and therapists)
     Not a problem (no known incidents)   = 0
     Moderate problem (1 or 2 incidents)   = 1
     Serious problem (3 or more incidents) = 2

18. Stability of current living situation (instability evidenced by household mem-
     bers [caregivers, partners, or siblings] engaging in: substance abuse, having a
     known criminal history, frequent changes in sexual partners, frequent moves,
     poor boundaries, use of pornography, family violence and/or child neglect;
     instability may also be indicated by frequent changes in subject's living situa-
     tion, or subject is in a high-risk living situation or high-risk location [i.e., near a
     bar or a playground]. If subject is in prison with an impending discharge,
     consider likely discharge situation. If living situation is unknown, score 2)
     Stable (presence of no more than 1)   = 0
     Unstable (presence of 2 or 3)   = 1
     Highly Unstable (presence of 4 or more) = 2

19. Stability of employment (stability and consistency of employment history). If
     self-employed, unemployed, or disabled, code stability of activities that occupy
     the day. If subject is incarcerated, code for employment stability at the time of
     the governing offense. If subject is incarcerated with an impending discharge,
     consider likely postdischarge employment options. If postdischarge employ-
     ment situation is unknown, score 2)
     Stable (consistently employed, holding jobs for a minimum of 6 months;   = 0
        termination not the result of being fired or quitting impulsively)
     Unstable (1 or 2 instances of short-term jobs [less than 6 months], or unem-   = 1
        ployed with some structured use of time)
     Highly unstable (3 or more instances of short-term jobs; the only exception   = 2
        would be if termination was related to a progression in responsibility or skill
        level [i.e., getting "better" jobs]; no structured use of time)

20. Evidence of support systems in the community (evidence of cooperation and
     compliance with probation officers, parole agents, and treatment programs;
     apparently supportive spouse/partner, family, friends, or extended family, par-
     ticipation in appropriate social and recreational activities [such as church and
     church-related functions, men's support groups; organized adult-oriented hob-
     bies and sports activities]. Clear evidence of continued involvement with an
     antisocial peer group requires a score of 2, unless incarcerated. If subject is
     incarcerated with an impending discharge, consider likely support systems)
     Considerable Support Systems (2 or more of the above apply) = 0
     Some Support Systems (1 of the above applies)   = 1
     No Known Support Systems/Negative Support Systems   = 2

21. Quality of peer relationships

    Socially active, peer-oriented, and rarely alone; often with friends in structured   = 0
and unstructured social and/or sports activities; friends are *not* part of an
antisocial peer group

    Socially active with a few friends and/or a spouse or partner; some involvement   = 1
in structured or unstructured activities; occasional social life

    For the most part, withdrawn from peer contact and socially isolated; no   = 2
"good" friends, just "acquaintances" who may be part of an antisocial peer
group

Scoring Procedure

STATIC/HISTORICAL FACTORS

Sexual Drive/Preoccupation Factor Score: (Add items 1–5)   _____

Impulsive-Antisocial Personality Factor Score: (Add items 6–11)   _____

DYNAMIC FACTORS

Intervention Factor Score: (Add items 12–16)   _____

Community Stability Factor Score: (Add items 17–21)   _____

TOTAL SCORE	MAXIMUM POSSIBLE	% Present Score/Max
Sexual Drive/Preoccupation Factor Score	10	_____
Impulsive-Antisocial Personality Factor Score	12	_____
Intervention Factor Score	10	_____
Community Stability Factor Score	10	_____
TOTAL Score	42	

Sexual Predator Risk Assessment Screening Instrument

Authors: Kim English and Paul Retzlaff, Ph.D.

Principal Author Affiliation:

Kim English
Research Director
Office of Research and Statistics
Division of Criminal Justice
Colorado Department of Public Safety
700 Kipling Street, Suite 1000
Denver, CO 80215

Paul Retzlaff, Ph.D.
Department of Psychology
University of Northern Colorado
Greeley, CO 80639

Source: English, K. (1999, June). *Adult Sex Offender Risk Assessment Screening Instru-*
           ment: Progress Report 1.a, Colorado Division of Criminal Justice, Denver,
           Colorado.

Part 1:   Defining Sexual Assault Crimes

The offender has been convicted of one or more of the following crimes:

> Sexual Assault in the First Degree
> Sexual Assault in the Second Degree
> Sexual Assault in the Third Degree
> Sexual Assault on a Child
> Sexual Assault on a Child by one in a position of Trust

Part 2:   Relationship

(The offender must meet one of the following three relationship definitions: 1) Stranger,
2) Established A Relationship, or 3) Promoted A Relationship)

   1) *Stranger.* The victim is a stranger to the offender when the victim has never known
or met the offender, or has met the offender in such a casual manner as to have little or no
familiar or personal knowledge of said offender, prior to the current offense.

   2) *Established A Relationship.* The offender established a relationship primarily for
the purpose of sexual victimization when any *two* of the following criteria are present:

- the offender has a history of multiple victims and similar behavior;
- the offender has actively manipulated the environment to gain access to the victim;
- the offender introduced sexual content into the relationship, such as, but not limited
  to, pornography or inappropriate discussion of sexual relations with a child;
- the offender persisted in the introduction of sexual content or inappropriate behavior of a sexual nature despite lack of consent or the absence of the ability to
  consent.

   3) *Promoted A Relationship.* The offender promoted an existing relationship primarily for the purpose of sexual victimization when the first item below is present and any other
item is present:

- the offender took steps to change the focus of the relationship to facilitate the
  commission of a sexual assault, such as, but not limited to, planning, increased
  frequency of contact, introduction of inappropriate sexual contact, stalking, seduction, or drugging of the victim;

and

- the offender engaged in contact with the victim that was progressively more
  sexually intrusive, or
- the offender used or engaged in threat, intimidation, force, or coercion in the
  relationship, or
- the offender engaged in repetitive non-consensual sexual contact, or

- the offender established control of the victim through means such as, but not limited to, emotional abuse, physical abuse, financial control, or isolation of the victim in order to facilitate the sexual assault.

Part 3: DCJ Sex Offender Risk Scale

Items:

(Items 1–10 are dichotomous: Y/N)

1. The offender has one or more juvenile felony adjudications.
2. The offender has one or more prior adult felony convictions.
3. The offender was employed less than full time at arrest.
4. The offender failed first or second grade.
5. The offender possessed a weapon during the current crime.
6. The victim had ingested or was administered alcohol or drugs during or immediately prior to the current crime.
7. The offender was NOT sexually aroused during the sexual assault.
8. The offender scored 20 or above on the CO-SOMB Denial scale.
9. The offender scored 20 or above on the CO-SOMB Deviancy scale.
10. The offender scored 20 or *below* on the CO-SOMB Motivation scale.

(Total Sex Offender Risk Scale Score is derived by adding the number of "yes" responses to items 1–10)

Part 4 Mental Abnormality

The offender meets the Mental Abnormality criterion when he scores:

18 or more on the Psychopathy Checklist: Screening Version;
or 30 on the Psychopathy Checklist-Revised;
or 85 or more on *each* of the following MCMI-3 scales: Narcissistic, Antisocial, and Paranoid

The offender meets the SVP standard when he meets the criteria for: (Part 1) + (Part 2) + (Part 3 or Part 4)

References

Abel, G. (1982, July). Viewpoint: Who is going to protect our children? *Sexual Medicine Today*, 32.

Abel, G. G., Barlow, D. H., Blanchard, E. B., & Guild, D. (1977). The components of rapists' sexual arousal. *Archives of General Psychology, 34*, 895–908.

Abel, G. G., Becker, J. V., Blanchard, E. B., & Djenderedjian, A. (1978). Differentiating sexual aggressives with penile measures. *Criminal Justice and Behavior, 5*, 315–332.

Abel, G. G., Becker, J. V., Mittelman, M. S., Cunningham-Rathner, J., Rouleau, J. L., & Murphy, W. D. (1987). Self-reported sex crimes of nonincarcerated paraphilics. *Journal of Interpersonal Violence, 2*, 3–25.

Abel, G. G., Becker, J. V., Murphy, W. D., & Flanagan, B. (1981). Identifying dangerous child molesters. In R. B. Stewart (Ed.), *Violent behavior: Social learning approaches to prediction management and treatment* (pp. 116–137). New York: Brunner/Mazel.

Abel, G., Becker, J., & Skinner, L. (1980). Aggressive behavior & sex. *Psychiatric Clinics of North America, 3*(1), 133–151.

Abel, G. G., & Blanchard, E. B. (1974). The role of fantasy in the treatment of sexual deviation. *Archives of General Psychiatry, 30*, 467–475.

Abel, G. G., Lawry, S. S., Karlstrom, E., Osborn, C. A., & Gillespie, C. F. (1994). Screening tests for pedophilia. *Criminal Justice and Behavior, 21*, 115–131.

Abel, G. G., Mittelman, M. S., Becker, J. V., Cunningham-Rathner, J., & Lucas, L. (1983 December). *The characteristics of men who molest young children.* Paper presented at the World Congress of Behavior Therapy, Washington, DC.

Abel, G. G., Mittelman, M., Becker, J. V., Rathner, J., & Rouleau, J. L. (1988). Predicting child molesters response to treatment. In R. A. Prentky & V. L. Quinsey (Eds.), *Human sexual aggression: Current perspectives* (pp. 223–234). New York: New York Academy of Sciences.

Abel, G. G., & Rouleau, J. L. (1990). The nature and extent of sexual assault. In W. L. Marshall, D. R. Laws, & H. E. Barbaree (Eds.), *Handbook of sexual assault: Issues, theories and treatment of the offender* (pp. 9–21). New York: Plenum Press.

Abrahamsen, D. (1960). *The psychology of crime.* New York: Columbia University Press.

Abrams, S. (1991). The use of polygraphy with sex offenders. *Annals of Sex Research, 4*, 239–263.

Abrams, S. (1992). A response to Wygant's critique of the Discovery Test. *Polygraph, 21*, 248–253.

Abrams, S., & Ogard, E. (1986). Polygraph surveillance of probationers. *Polygraph, 15*, 174–182.

Alder, C. (1985). An exploration of self-reported sexually aggressive behavior. *Crime and Delinquency, 31*, 306–331.

Alexander, P. C. (1993). The differential effect of abuse characteristics and attachment in the prediction of long-term effects of sexual abuse. *Journal of Interpersonal Violence, 3*, 346–362.

Alexander, R. (1993). The civil commitment of sex offenders in light of *Foucha v. Louisiana. Criminal Justice and Behavior, 20*, 371–387.

Amir, M. (1971). *Patterns in forcible rape.* Chicago: University of Chicago Press.

American Civil Liberties Union. (1986). *Polluting the censorship debate: A summary and critique of the Final Report of the Attorney General's Commission on Pornography*. Washington, DC: Author.

American Psychiatric Association. (1952). *Diagnostic and statistical manual of mental disorders*. Washington, DC: Author.

Aerican Psychiatric Association. (1968). *Diagnostic and statistical manual of mental disorders* (2nd ed.). Washington, DC: Author.

American Psychiatric Association. (1980). *Diagnostic and statistical manual of mental disorders* (3rd ed.). Washington, DC: Author.

American Psychiatric Association. (1987). *Diagnostic and statistical manual of mental disorders* (3rd ed. rev.). Washington, DC: Author.

American Psychiatric Association. (1994). *Diagnostic and statistical manual of mental disorders* (4th ed.). Washington, DC: Author.

Anderson, C. A. (1983). Abstract and concrete data in the perseverance of social theories: When weak data lead to unshakable beliefs. *Journal of Experimental Social Psychology, 19*, 93–108.

Anderson, C. A., Lepper, M. R., & Ross, L. (1980). Perseverance of social theories: The role of explanation in the persistence of discredited information. *Journal of Personality and Social Psychology, 39*, 1037–1049.

Anderson, G., Yasenik, L., & Ross, C. A. (1993). Dissociative experiences and disorders among women who identify themselves as sexual abuse survivors. *Child Abuse and Neglect, 17*, 677–686.

Apfelberg, B., Sugar, C., & Pfeffer, A. Z. (1944). A psychiatric study of 250 sex offenders. *American Journal of Psychiatry, 100*, 762–769.

Araji, S., & Finkelhor, D. (1985). Explanations of pedophilia: Review of empirical research. *Bulletin of the American Academy of Psychiatry and the Law, 13*, 17–37.

Ash, A. S., & Schwartz, M. (1994). Evaluating the performance of risk-adjustment methods: Dichotomous measures. In L. I. Lezzoni (Ed.), *Risk adjustment for measuring health care outcomes* (pp. 313–346). Ann Arbor, MI: Health Administration Press.

Association for the Treatment of Sexual Abusers (ATSA). (1993). *The ATSA Practitioner's Handbook*. Lake Oswego, Oregon.

Attorney General's Commission on Pornography. (1986). *Report of the Attorney General's Commission on Pornography: Final report*. Washington, DC: U.S. Government Printing Office.

Ault, R., & Reese, J. T. (1980). A psychological assessment of crime profiling. *FBI Law Enforcement Bulletin, 49*, 22–25.

Badgley, R. (1984). *Sexual Offenses against Children: Report of the Committee on Sexual Offenses against Children and Youth*. 2 vols. Ottawa: Ministry of Supply and Services, Canada.

Bagley, C. (1991). The long-term psychological effects of child sexual abuse: A review of some British and Canadian studies of victims and their families. *Annals of Sex Research, 4*, 23–48.

Bain, J., Langevin, R., Dickey, R., & Ben-Aron, M. (1987). Sex hormones in murderers. *Behavioral Sciences and the Law, 5*, 95–101.

Baker, D. (1985). Father–daughter incest: A study of the father. *Dissertation Abstracts International, 42*, 951B. (University Microfilms No. 85-10,932)

Baker, T., Burgess, A. W., Davis, T., & Brickman, E. (1990). Rape victims' concern about possible exposure to AIDS. *Journal of Interpersonal Violence, 5*, 49–60.

Bandura, A. (1973). *Aggression: A social learning analysis*. Englewood Cliffs, NJ: Prentice–Hall.

Bandura, A., Underwood, B., & Fromson, M. E. (1975). Disinhibition of aggression through diffusion of responsibility and dehumanization of victims. *Journal of Research in Personality, 9*, 253–269.

Barbaree, H. E. (1997). Evaluating treatment efficacy with sexual offenders: The insensitivity of recidivism studies to treatment effects. *Sexual Abuse: A Journal of Research and Treatment, 9*, 111–128.

Barbaree, H. E., & Marshall, W. L. (1988). Deviant sexual arousal, offense history, and demographic variables as predictors of reoffense among child molesters. *Behavioral Sciences and the Law, 6*, 267–280.

Barbaree, H. E., Marshall, W. L., & Lanthier, R. D. (1979). Deviant sexual arousal in rapists. *Behavior Research and Therapy, 17*, 215–222.

Barbaree, H. E., Seto, M. C., & Serin, R. C. (1994). *Comparisons between low- and high-fixated child molesters: Psychopathy, criminal history, and sexual arousal to children*. Unpublished manuscript.

Bard, L. A., Carter, D. L., Cerce, D. D., Knight, R. A., Rosenberg, R., & Schneider, B. (1987). A descriptive study of rapists and child molesters: Developmental, clinical and criminal characteristics. *Behavioral Sciences and the Law, 5*, 203–220.

Bard, L. A., & Knight, R. A. (1986, March 8). *Sex offender subtyping and the MCMI*. Paper presented at the Conference on the Millon Clinical Inventories, Miami, FL.

Barker, J. G., & Howell, R. J. (1992). The plethysmograph: A review of recent literature. *Bulletin of the American Academy of Psychiatry and Law, 20,* 13–25.

Barlow, D. H., Becker, R., Leitenberg, H., & Agras, W. S. (1970). A mechanical strain gauge for recording penile circumference change. *Journal of Applied Behavior Analysis, 3,* 73–76.

Baron, L. (1990). Pornography and gender equality: An empirical analysis. *Journal of Sex Research, 27,* 363–380.

Baron, L., & Straus, M. A. (1984). Sexual stratification, pornography and rape. In N. M. Malamuth & E. Donnerstein (Eds.), *Pornography and sexual aggression* (pp. 185–209). New York: Academic Press.

Baron, R. A. (1974). The aggression-inhibiting influence of heightened sexual arousal. *Journal of Personality and Social Psychology, 30,* 318–322.

Baron, R. A., & Bell, P. A. (1977). Sexual arousal and aggression by males: Effects of type of erotic stimuli and prior provocation. *Journal of Personality and Social Psychology, 35,* 79–87.

Bart, P., & Jozsa, M. (1980). Dirty books, dirty films, and dirty data. In L. Lederer & A. Rich (Eds.), *Take back the night: Women on pornography.* New York: Morrow.

Bartholomew, A. A. (1964). Some side effects of thioridazine. *Medical Journal of Australia, 1,* 57–59.

Becker, J. V., Abel, G. G., Blanchard, E. B., Murphy, W. D., & Coleman, E. (1978). Evaluating social skills of sexual aggressives. *Criminal Justice and Behavior, 5,* 357–367.

Becker, J. V., Kaplan, M. S., Cunningham-Rathner, J., & Kavoussi, R. (1986). Characteristics of adolescent incest sexual perpetrators: Preliminary findings. *Journal of Family Violence, 1,* 85–97.

Beebe, D. K. (1991). Emergency management of the adult female rape victim. *American Family Physician, 43,* 2041–2046.

Benarroche, C. L. (1990). *Trichotillomania symptoms and fluoxetine response.* In New Research Program and Abstracts of the 143rd Annual Meeting of the American Psychiatric Association, New York. Abstract NR 327.

Bender, L., & Blau, A. (1937). The reaction of children to sexual relations who had atypical sexual experience. *American Journal of Orthopsychiatry, 7,* 500–518.

Bender, L., & Grugett, A. (1952). A follow-up report on children who had atypical sexual experiences. *American Journal of Orthopsychiatry, 22,* 825–837.

Benedict, H. (1985). *Recovery.* New York: Doubleday.

Berkowitz, L. (1986). Situational influences on reactions to observed violence. *Journal of Social Issues, 3,* 93–106.

Berkowitz, L., & Macaulay, J. (1971). The contagion of criminal violence. *Sociometry, 34,* 238–260.

Berlin, F. S. (1983). Sex offenders: A biomedical perspective and a status report on biomedical treatment. In J. G. Greer & I. R. Stuart (Eds.), *The sexual aggressor: Current perspectives on treatment.* New York: Van Nostrand–Reinhold.

Berlin, F. S. (1988). Issues in the exploration of biological factors contributing to the etiology of the "sex offender," plus some ethical considerations. In R. A. Prentky & V. L. Quinsey (Eds.), *Human sexual aggression: Current perspectives* (pp. 183–192). New York: New York Academy of Sciences.

Berlin, F. S. (1989a, January). *Differential diagnosis and pharmacological treatment of sex offenders.* Paper presented at the meeting of the American Association for the Advancement of Science, San Francisco.

Berlin, F. S. (1989b). The paraphilias and Depo-Provera: Some medical, ethical and legal considerations. *Bulletin of the American Academy of Psychiatry and Law, 17,* 233–239.

Berlin, F. S., & Coyle, G. S. (1981). Sexual deviation syndromes. *The Johns Hopkins Medical Journal, 149,* 119–125.

Berlin, F. S., & Meinecke, C. F. (1981). Treatment of sex offenders with antiandrogenic medication: Conceptualization, review of treatment modalities, and preliminary findings. *American Journal of Psychiatry, 138,* 601–646.

Berliner, L. (1996). Community notification of sex offenders: A new tool or a false promise. *Journal of Interpersonal Violence, 11,* 294–295.

Bianchi, M. D. (1990). Fluoxetine treatment of exhibitionism [Letter to the editor]. *American Journal of Psychiatry, 147,* 1089–1090.

Biden, J. R. (1993). Violence against women. The Congressional response. *American Psychologist, 48,* 1059–1061.

Birkin, A. J. M. (1979). *Barrie and the Lost Boys: The love story that gave birth to Peter Pan.* New York: Clarkson N. Potter.

Boer, D. P., Hart, S. D., Kropp, P. R., & Webster, C. D. (1997). *Manual for the Sexual Violence Risk—20.* Vancouver, BC: The Mental Health, Law, and Policy Institute and Simon Fraser University.

Boeringer, S. B. (1994). Pornography and sexual aggression: Associations of violent and nonviolent depictions with rape and rape proclivity. *Deviant Behavior: An Interdisciplinary Journal, 15,* 289–304.

Boerner, D. (1992). Confronting violence: In the act and in the word. *University of Puget Sound Law Review, 15,* 525–577.

Boney-McCoy, S., & Finkelhor, D. (1995). Psychosocial sequelae of violent victimization in a national youth sample. *Journal of Consulting and Clinical Psychology, 63*(5), 726–736.

Borum, R. (1996). Improving the clinical practice of violence risk assessment. *American Psychologist, 51,* 945–956.

Bradford, J. M. W. (1983). Hormonal treatment of sexual offenders. *Bulletin of the American Academy of Psychiatry and the Law, 11,* 159–169.

Bradford, J. M. W. (1985). Organic treatments for the male sexual offender. *Behavioral Sciences and the Law, 3,* 355–375.

Bradford, J. M. W. (1988). Organic treatment for the male sexual offender. In R. A. Prentky & V. L. Quinsey (Eds.), *Human sexual aggression: Current perspectives* (pp. 193–202). New York: New York Academy of Sciences.

Bradford, J. M. W. (1990). The antiandrogen and hormonal treatment of sex offenders. In W. L. Marshall, D. R. Laws, & H. E. Barbaree (Eds.), *Handbook of sexual assault: Issues, theories, and treatment of the offender* (pp. 297–310). New York: Plenum Press.

Bradford, J. M. W. (1996). The role of serotonin in the future of forensic psychiatry. *Bulletin of the American Academy of Psychiatry and the Law, 24*(1), 57–72.

Bradford, J. M. W. (1998). Treatment of men with paraphilia. *New England Journal of Medicine, 338,* 464–465.

Brakel, J., Parry, J., & Weiner, B. A. (1985). *The mentally disabled and the law.* Chicago: American Bar Foundation.

Brancale, R., Ellis, A., & Doorbar, R. R. (1952). Psychiatric and psychological investigations of convicted sex offenders: A summary report. *American Journal of Psychiatry, 109,* 17–21.

Brancale, R., MacNeil, D., & Vuocolo, A. (1965). Profile of the New Jersey sex offender: A statistical study of 1,206 male sex offenders. *The Welfare Research Report, 16,* 3–9.

Brandon, C. (1985). Sex role identification in incest: An empirical analysis of the feminist theories. *Dissertation Abstracts International, 46,* 3099B. (University Microfilms No. 86-22,829)

Brandt, J. R., Kennedy, W. A., Patrick, C. J., & Curtin, J. J. (1997). Assessment of psychopathy in a population of incarcerated adolescent offenders. *Psychological Assessment, 9,* 429–435.

Braun, B. G., & Sachs, R. G. (1985). The development of multiple personality disorder: Predisposing, precipitating, and perpetuating factors. In R. P. Kluft (Ed.), *Childhood antecedents of multiple personality* (pp. 37–64). Washington, DC: Psychiatric Press.

Bremer, J. (1959). *Asexualization: A follow-up study of 244 cases.* New York: Macmillan.

Brennan, T. (1987). Classification: An overview of selected methodological issues. In D. M. Gottfredson & M. Tonry (Eds.), *Prediction and classification: Criminal justice decision making* (pp. 201–248). Chicago: University of Chicago Press.

Briere, J. N. (1992). *Child abuse trauma.* Newbury Park, CA: Sage.

Briere, J. N., & Conte, J. (1993). Self-reported amnesia for abuse in adults molested in childhood. *Journal of Traumatic Stress, 6,* 21–31.

Briere, J. N., & Elliott, D. M. (1994). Immediate and long-term impacts of child sexual abuse. *Sexual Abuse of Children, 4,* 54–69.

Briere, J., & Runtz, M. (1988). Symptomatology associated with childhood sexual victimization in a nonclinical adult sample. *Child Abuse and Neglect, 12,* 51–59.

Briere, J. N., & Runtz, M. (1989). University males' sexual interest in children: Predicting potential indices of "pedophilia" in a nonforensic sample. *Child Abuse and Neglect, 13,* 65–75.

Briere, J., & Runtz, M. (1990a). Differential adult symptomatology associated with three types of child abuse histories. *Child Abuse and Neglect, 14,* 357–364.

Briere, J., & Runtz, M. (1990b). Augmenting Hopkins SCL scales to measure dissociative systems: Data from two nonclinical samples. *Journal of Personality Assessment, 55,* 376–379.

Briere, J., & Runtz, M. (1993). Childhood sexual abuse long-term sequelae and implications for psychological assessment. *Journal of Interpersonal Violence, 8,* 312–330.

Briere, J. N., & Zaidi, L. Y. (1989). Sexual abuse histories and sequelae in female psychiatric emergency room patients. *American Journal of Psychiatry, 146,* 1602–1606.

Brown, G. R., & Anderson, B. (1991). Psychiatric morbidity in adult inpatients with childhood histories of sexual and physical abuse. *American Journal of Psychiatry, 148,* 55–61.

Brown, S. L., & Forth, A. E. (1997). Psychopathy and sexual assault: Static risk factors, emotional precursors, and rapist subtypes. *Journal of Consulting and Clinical Psychology, 65,* 848–857.

Brown, W. A. (1981). Testosterone and human behavior. *International Journal of Mental Health, 9,* 45–66.

Browne, A. (1992). Violence against women: Relevance for medical practitioners. *Journal of the American Medical Association, 267,* 3184–3189.

Browne, A., & Finkelhor, D. (1986). Impact of child sexual abuse: A review of the research. *Psychological Bulletin, 99,* 66–77.

Brownell, K. D., Marlatt, G. A., Lichtenstein, E., & Wilson, G. T. (1986). Understanding and preventing relapse. *American Psychologist, 41,* 765–782.

Brownmiller, S. (1975). *Against our will: Men, women and rape.* New York: Simon & Schuster.

Bryer, J. B., Nelson, B. A., Miller, J. B., & Krol, P. A. (1987). Childhood sexual and physical abuse as factors in adult psychiatric illness. *American Journal of Psychiatry, 144,* 1426–1430.

Bulik, C. M., Sullivan, P. E., & Rorty, M. (1989). Childhood sexual abuse in women with bulimia. *Journal of Clinical Psychiatry, 50,* 46–64.

Bureau of Justice Statistics. (1984). *National Crime Survey.* Washington, DC: U.S. Department of Justice.

Bureau of Justice Statistics. (1985). *National Crime Survey.* Washington, DC: U.S. Department of Justice.

Burge, S. K. (1989). Violence against women as a health care issue. *Family Medicine, 21,* 368–373.

Burgess, A. W., & Hartman, C. R. (1992). Memory, cognition, and childhood trauma. In A. W. Burgess (Ed.), *Child trauma I: Issues and research* (pp. 61–86). New York: Garland Publishing.

Burgess, A. W., Hartman, C. R., & Baker, T. (1995). Memory presentations of childhood sexual abuse. *Journal of Psychosocial Nursing, 33,* 9–15.

Burgess, A. W., Hartman, C. R., & Clements, P. T. (1995). Biology of memory and childhood trauma. *Journal of Psychosocial Nursing, 33,* 9–16.

Burgess, A. W., Hartman, C. R., & McCormack, A. (1987). Abused to abuser: Antecedents of socially deviant behaviors. *American Journal of Psychiatry, 144,* 1431–1436.

Burgess, A. W., Hartman, C. R., Ressler, R. K., Douglas, J. E., & McCormack, A. (1986). Sexual homicide: A motivational model. *Journal of Interpersonal Violence, 1,* 251–272.

Burgess, A. W., Hazelwood, R. R., Rokous, F. E., Hartman, C. R., & Burgess, A. G. (1988). Serial rapists and their victims: Reenactment and repetition. In R. A. Prentky & V. L. Quinsey (Eds.), *Human sexual aggression. Current perspectives* (pp. 277–295). New York: New York Academy of Sciences.

Burgess, A. W., & Holmstrom, L. L. (1974a). *Rape: Victims of crisis.* Englewood Cliffs, NJ: Prentice–Hall.

Burgess, A. W., & Holmstrom, L. L. (1974b). Rape trauma syndrome. *American Journal of Psychiatry, 131,* 981–986.

Burgess, A. W., & Holmstrom, L. L. (1976). Coping behavior of the rape victim. *American Journal of Psychiatry, 133,* 413–418.

Burgess, A. W., & Holmstrom, L. L. (1979a). Rape: Sexual disruption and recovery. *American Journal of Orthopsychiatry, 49,* 648–657.

Burgess, A. W., & Holmstrom, L. L. (1979b). *Rape: Crisis and recovery.* Bowie, MD: Robert J. Brady Co.

Burnam, M. A., Stein, J. A., Golding, J. M., Siegel, J. M., Sorenson, S. B., Forsythe, A. B., & Telles, C. A. (1988). Sexual assault and mental disorders in a community population. *Journal of Consulting and Clinical Psychology, 56,* 843–850.

Burt, M. R. (1980). Cultural myths and support for rape. *Journal of Personality and Social Psychology, 38,* 217–230.

Cameron, C. (1994). Women survivors confronting their abusers: Issues, decisions and outcomes. *Journal of Child Sexual Abuse, 3,* 7–35.

Caringella-MacDonald, S. (1988). Parallels and pitfalls: The aftermath of legal reform for sexual assault, marital rape, and domestic violence victims. *Journal of Interpersonal Violence, 3,* 174–189.

Carnes, P. (1992). *Out of the shadows. Understanding sexual addiction.* Minneapolis, MN: CompCare Publishers.

Carter, D. L., & Prentky, R. A. (1993). Forensic treatment in the United States: A survey of selected forensic hospitals. Massachusetts Treatment Center. *International Journal of Law and Psychiatry, 16,* 117–132.

Cavaiola, A., & Schiff, M. (1988). Behavioral sequelae of physical and/or sexual abuse in adolescents. *Child Abuse and Neglect, 12,* 181–188.

Cavallin, H. (1966). Incestuous fathers: A clinical report. *American Journal of Psychiatry, 122,* 1132–1138.

Ceniti, J., & Malamuth, N. M. (1984). Effects of repeated exposure to sexually violent or nonviolent stimuli on sexual arousal to rape and nonrape depiction. *Behavioral Research Therapy, 22*, 535–548.

Chakraborty, R., & Kidd, K. K. (1991). The utility of DNA typing in forensic work. *Science, 254*, 1735–1739.

Chantry, K., & Craig, R. J. (1994). Psychological screening of sexually violent offenders with the MCMI. *Journal of Clinical Psychology, 50*, 430–435.

Chapman, L. J., & Chapman, J. P. (1967). Genesis of popular but erroneous psychodiagnostic observations. *Journal of Abnormal Psychology, 72*, 193–204.

Chapman, L., & Chapman, J. (1969). Illusory correlations as an obstacle to the use of valid psychodiagnostic signs. *Journal of Abnormal Psychology, 74*, 271–280.

Chappell, D. (1989). Sexual criminal violence. In N. A. Weiner & M. E. Wolfgang (Eds.), *Pathways to criminal violence* (pp. 68–108). Newbury Park, CA: Sage.

Chappell, D., Geis, R., & Geis, G. (Eds.). (1977). *Forcible rape*. New York: Columbia University Press.

Chappell, D., & James, J. (1976, September). *Victim selection and apprehension from the rapist perspective: A preliminary investigation*. Unpublished paper presented at the Second International Symposium on Victimology, Boston.

Christiansen, K.O., Elers-Nielsen, M., Le Maire, L., & Sturup, G. K. (1965). Recidivism among sexual offenders. In K. O. Christiansen (Ed.), *Scandinavian studies in criminology* (pp. 55–85). London: Tavistock.

Chu, J. A., Dill, D. L., & McCormack, A. (1990). Dissociative symptoms in relation to childhood physical and sexual abuse. *American Journal of Psychiatry, 147*, 887–892.

Civil Commitment Study Group. (1999, January). *1998 report to the legislature*. St. Paul: Minnesota Department of Corrections.

Cleckley, H. (1941). *The mask of sanity*. St. Louis: Mosby.

Cleckley, H. (1976). *The mask of sanity*. St. Louis: Mosby.

Cocozza, J., & Steadman, H. (1976). Prediction in psychiatry: An example of misplaced confidence in experts. *Rutgers Law Review, 29*, 1084–1101.

Cohen, L. J. (1981). Can human irrationality be experimentally demonstrated? *Behavioral and Brain Sciences, 4*, 317–331.

Cohen, M. L., Boucher, R. J., Seghorn, T. K., & Mehegan, J. (1979, March). *The sexual offender against children*. Paper presented at the meeting of the Association for Professional Treatment of Offenders, Boston.

Cohen, M. L., Garofalo, R. F., Boucher, R., & Seghorn, T. (1971). The psychology of rapists. *Seminars in Psychiatry, 3*, 307–327.

Cohen, M. L., Groth, A. N., & Siegel, R. (1978). The clinical prediction of dangerousness. *Crime and Delinquency, 24*, 28–39.

Cohen, M. L., Seghorn, T. K., Boucher, R., & Mehegan, J. (1979). *The sexual offender against children*. Paper presented at the meeting of the Association for Professional Treatment of Offenders, Boston.

Cohen, M. L., Seghorn, T. K., & Calmas, W. (1969). Sociometric study of sex offenders. *Journal of Abnormal Psychology, 74*, 249–255.

Cole, P. M., & Putnam, F. W. (1992). Effect of incest on self and social functioning: A developmental psychopathology perspective. *Journal of Consulting and Clinical Psychology, 60*, 174–184.

Coleman, E. (1987). Sexual compulsivity: Definition, etiology, and treatment considerations. In E. Coleman (Ed.), *Chemical dependency and intimacy dysfunction*. New York: The Haworth Press, Inc.

Coller, S. A., & Resick, P. A. (1987). Women's attributions of responsibility for date rape: The influence of empathy and sex-role stereotyping. *Violence and Victims, 2*, 115–125.

Condy, S. R., Templer, D. I., Brown, R., & Veaco, L. (1987). Parameters of sexual contact of boys with women. *Archives of Sexual Behavior, 16*, 379–394.

Confronting the New Challenges of Scientific Evidence. (1995, May). *Harvard Law Review, 108*, 1481–1605.

Connell, N., & Wilson, C. (Eds.). (1974). *Rape: The first sourcebook for women*. New York: New American Library.

Conte, J. R. (1985). Clinical dimensions of adult sexual abuse of children. *Behavioral Sciences and the Law, 3*, 341–354.

Conte, J. R. (1988). The effects of sexual abuse on children: Results of a research project. In R. A. Prentky & V. L. Quinsey (Eds.), *Human sexual aggression: Current perspectives* (pp. 310–326). New York: New York Academy of Sciences.

Conte, J. R., Rosen, C., & Saperstein, L. (1984, September). *An analysis of programs to prevent the sexual victimization of children*. Paper presented at the Fifth International Congress on Child Abuse and Neglect, Montreal, Canada.

Coons, P. M. (1986). Psychiatric problems associated with child abuse: A review. In J. J. Jacobson (Ed.), *Psychiatric sequelae of child abuse* (pp. 169–200). Springfield, IL: Charles C. Thomas.

Coons, P. M., Bowman, E. S., Pellow, T. A., & Schneider, P. (1989). Posttraumatic aspects of the treatment of victims of sexual abuse and incest. *Psychiatric Clinics of North America, 12*, 325–335.

Cooper, A. J. (1981). A placebo-controlled trial of the antiandrogen cyproterone acetate in deviant hypersexuality. *Comprehensive Psychiatry, 22*, 458–465.

Copas, J. B., & Tarling, R. (1986). Some methodological issues in making predictions. In A. Blumstein, J. Cohen, J. A. Roth, & C. Visher (Eds.), *Criminal careers and "career criminals"* (Vol. II, pp. 291–313). Washington, DC: National Academy Press.

Cormier, B., Kennedy, M., & Sangowicz, J. (1962). Psychodynamics of father–daughter incest. *Canadian Psychiatric Association Journal, 7*, 203–217.

Cormier, B. M., & Simons, S. P. (1969). The problem of the dangerous sexual offender. *Canadian Psychiatric Association Journal, 14*, 329–335.

Cornwell, J. K. (1998). Understanding the role of the police and *parens patriae* powers in involuntary civil commitment before and after *Hendricks. Psychology, Public Policy, and Law, 4*, 377–413.

Costin, F. (1985). Beliefs about rape and women's social roles—A four nation study. *Archives of Sexual Behavior, 14*, 319–325.

Crepault, C., & Couture, M. (1980). Men's erotic fantasies. *Archives of Sexual Behaviour, 9*, 565–581.

Crowell, N. A., & Burgess, A. W. (1996). *Understanding violence against women.* Washington, DC: National Academy Press.

Darke, J. L. (1990). Sexual aggression: Achieving power through humiliation. In W. L. Marshall, D. R. Laws, & H. E. Barbaree (Eds.), *Handbook of sexual assault: Issues, theories, and treatment of the offender* (pp. 55–71). New York: Plenum Press.

Davidson, J. R., & Foa, E. B. (1991). Diagnostic issues in posttraumatic stress disorder: Considerations for the DSM-IV. *Journal of Abnormal Psychology, 100*, 346–355.

Davidson, J. R., & Foa, E. B. (1993). *Posttraumatic stress disorder: DSM-IV and beyond.* Washington, DC: American Psychiatric Press.

Davis, R., Taylor, B., & Bench, S. (1995). Impact of sexual and nonsexual assault on secondary victims. *Violence and Victims, 10*(1), 73–84.

Dawes, R. M., Faust, D., & Meehl, P. E. (1989). Clinical versus actuarial judgment. *Science, 243*, 1668–1674.

Dawkins, R. (1998). Arresting evidence. *The Sciences, 38*, 20–25.

Deblinger, E., McLeer, S. V., Atkins, M. S., Ralphe, D. L., & Foa, E. (1989). Posttraumatic stress in sexually abused, physically abused, and nonabused children. *Child Abuse and Neglect, 13*, 403–408.

Dekker, J., & Everaerd, W. (1988). Attentional effects on sexual arousal. *Psychophysiology, 25*, 45–54.

Demsky, L. S. (1984). The use of Depo-Provera in the treatment of sex offenders: The legal issues. *Journal of Legal Medicine, 5*, 295–322.

Dershowitz, A. (1969, February). Psychiatrists' power in civil commitment. *Psychology Today, 2*, 47.

Deutsch, A. (1950, November 25). Sober facts about sex crimes. *Collier's, 170*.

Diamond, I. (1980). Pornography and repression: A reconsideration of "who" and "what." In L. Lederer & A. Rich (Eds.), *Take back the night: Women on pornography* (pp. 187–203). New York: Morrow.

Dickey, R. (1992). The management of a case of treatment-resistant paraphilia with a long-acting LHRH agonist. *Canadian Journal of Psychiatry, 37*, 567–569.

Dietz, P. E. (1983). Sex offenses: Behavioral aspects. In S. H. Kadish (Ed.), *Encyclopedia of crime and justice* (pp. 1485–1493). New York: Free Press.

Dietz, P. E., & Evans, B. (1982). Pornographic imagery and prevalence of paraphilia. *American Journal of Psychiatry, 139*, 1493–1495.

Dietz, P. E., Harry, B., & Hazelwood, R. R. (1986). Detective magazines: Pornography for the sexual sadist? *Journal of Forensic Science, 31*, 197–211.

Dixon, K. N., Arnold, E., & Calestro, K. (1978). Father–son incest: Underreported psychiatric problem? *American Journal of Psychiatry, 135*, 835–838.

Donnerstein, E. (1983). Erotica and human aggression. In R. Geen & E. Donnerstein (Eds.), *Aggression: Theoretical and empirical reviews* (Vol. 2, pp. 127–154). New York: Academic Press.

Donnerstein, E., & Barrett, G. (1978). The effects of erotic stimuli on male aggression toward females. *Journal of Personality and Social Psychology, 36*, 180–188.

Donnerstein, E., Donnerstein, M., & Evans, R. (1975). Erotic stimuli and aggression: Facilitation or inhibition. *Journal of Personality and Social Psychology, 32,* 237–244.

Dorner, G. (1980). Neuroendocrine aspects in the etiology of sexual deviations. In R. Forleo & W. Pasini (Eds.), *Medical sexology. The Third International Congress.* Littleton, MA: PSG Publishing.

Douglas, J. E., & Burgess, A. E. (1986). Criminal profiling: A viable investigative tool against violent crime. *FBI Law Enforcement Bulletin, 55,* 9–13.

Douglas, J. E., Burgess, A. W., Burgess, A. G., & Ressler, R. K. (1992). *Crime classification manual.* New York: Lexington Books.

Douglas, J. E., Ressler, R. K., Burgess, A. W., & Hartman, C. R. (1986). Criminal profiling from crime scene analysis. *Behavioral Sciences and the Law, 4,* 401–421.

Douglas, R. J. (1967). The hippocampus and behavior. *Psychological Bulletin, 67,* 416–442.

Drummond, P., White, K., & Ashton, R. (1978). Imagery vividness affects habituation rate. *Psychophysiology, 15,* 193–195.

Dubowitz, H., Black, M., Harrington, D., & Verschoore, A. (1993). A follow-up study of behavior problems associated with child sexual abuse. *Child Abuse and Neglect, 17,* 743–754.

Dunn, S. F., & Gilchrist, V. J. (1993). Sexual assault. *Primary Care, 20,* 359–373.

Dutton, D. G. (1992). *Empowering and healing the battered woman: A model for assessment and intervention.* Berlin: Springer.

Dworkin, A. (1981). *Pornography: Men possessing women.* New York: Putnam.

Earls, C. M., & Quinsey, V. L. (1985). What is to be done? Future research on the assessment and behavioral treatment of sex offenders. *Behavioral Sciences and the Law, 3,* 377–390.

Edson, C. F. (1991). *Sex offender treatment.* Medford, OR: Department of Corrections.

Ehrhardt, A. A. (1977). Prenatal androgenization and human psychosexual behavior. In J. Money & H. Musaph (Eds.), *Handbook of sexology* (pp. 245–257). Amsterdam: Excerpta Medica.

Ehrhardt, A. A. (1978). Behavioral effects of estrogen in the human female. *Pediatrics, 62,* 1166–1170.

Ehrhardt, A. A., & Baker, S. W. (1974). Fetal androgens, human CNS differentiation, and behavior sex differences. In R. C. Friedman, R. M. Richart, & R. L. Vande Wiele (Eds.), *Sex differences in behavior* (pp. 53–76). New York: Wiley.

Ehrhardt, A. A., Greenberg, J., & Money, J. (1970). Female gender identity and absence of fetal gonadal hormones: Turner's syndrome. *Johns Hopkins Medical Journal, 126,* 237–248.

Eicher, W., Spoljar, M., Cleve, H., Murken, J.-D., Richter, K., & Stangel-Rutkowski, S. (1979). H-Y antigen in transsexuality. *Lancet, 2,* 1137–1138.

Elaad, E. (1990). Detection of guilty knowledge in real-life criminal investigations. *Journal of Applied Psychology, 75,* 521–529.

Elaad, E. (1997). Polygraph examiner awareness of crime-relevant information and the Guilty Knowledge Test. *Law and Human Behavior, 21,* 107–120.

Elaad, E., Ginton, A., & Jungman, N. (1992). Detection measures in real-life criminal guilty knowledge tests. *Journal of Applied Psychology, 75,* 521–529.

Elliott, D. M., & Briere, J. (1992). The sexually abused boy: Problems in manhood. *Medical Aspects of Human Sexuality, 26,* 68–71.

Elliott, D. M., & Briere, J. (1995). Posttraumatic stress associated with delayed recall of sexual abuse: A general population study. *Journal of Traumatic Stress, 8,* 629–647.

Emmanuel, N. P., Lydiard, R. B., & Ballenger, J. C. (1991). Fluoxetine treatment of voyeurism [Letter]. *American Journal of Psychiatry, 148,* 950.

English, K. (1998). The containment approach: An aggressive strategy for the community management of adult sex offenders. *Psychology, Public Policy, and Law, 4,* 218–235.

English, K., Pullen, S., & Jones, L. (Eds.) (1996). *Managing adult sex offenders: A containment approach.* Lexington, KY: American Probation and Parole Association.

Ennis, B. J., & Litwack, T. R. (1974). Psychiatry and the presumption of expertise: Flipping coins in the courtroom. *California Law Review, 62,* 693–752.

Epperson, D. L., Kaul, J. D., & Hesselton, D. (1998). *Final report on the development of the Minnesota Sex Offender Screening Tool-Revised* (MnSOST-R). St. Paul: Minnesota Department of Corrections.

Erickson, W. D., Luxenberg, M. G., Walbek, N. H., & Seely, R. K. (1987). Frequency of MMPI two-point code types among sex offenders. *Journal of Consulting and Clinical Psychology, 55,* 566–570.

Estrich, S. (1987). *Real rape.* Cambridge, MA: Harvard University Press.

Ewing, C. (1983). "Dr. Death" and the case for an ethical ban on psychiatric and psychological predictions of dangerousness in capital sentencing proceedings. *American Journal of Law and Medicine, 8*, 407–428.

Ewing, C. (1985). *Schall v. Martin*: Preventive detention and dangerousness through the looking glass. *Buffalo Law Review, 34*, 173–226.

Ewing, C. (1991). Preventive detention and execution: The constitutionality of punishing future crimes. *Law and Human Behavior, 15*, 139–163.

Farah, M. J., Steinhauer, S. R., Lewicki, M. S., Zubin, J., & Peronnet, F. (1988). Individual differences in vividness of mental imagery: An event-related potential. *Psychophysiology, 25*, 444–445.

Farwell, L. A., & Donchin, E. (1986). The "brain detector": P300 in the detection of deception [Abstract]. *Psychophysiology, 24*, 434.

Farwell, L. A., & Donchin, E. (1988). Event-related potentials in interrogative polygraphy: Analysis using bootstrapping [Abstract]. *Psychophysiology, 25*, 445.

Federal Bureau of Investigation. (1993). *Uniform Crime Reports*. Washington, DC: U.S. Department of Justice.

Federman, D. D. (1981). The requirements for sexual reproduction. *Human Genetics, 58*, 3–5.

Federoff, J. P. (1993). Serotonergic drug treatment of deviant sexual interests. *Annals of Sex Research, 6*, 105–121.

Fehrenbach, P. A., Smith, W., Monastersky, C., & Deisher, R. W. (1986). Adolescent sexual offenders: Offender and offense characteristics. *American Journal of Orthopsychiatry, 56*, 225–233.

Feldman-Summers, S., & Pope, K. S. (1994). The experience of "forgetting" childhood abuse: A national survey of psychologists. *Journal of Consulting and Clinical Psychology, 62*, 636–639.

Feltman, R. I. (1985). A controlled, correlational study of the psychological functioning of paternal incest victims. *Dissertation Abstracts International, 46*, 3592B. (University Microfilms No. 85-26,512)

Ferguson, G. E., Eidelson, R. J., & Witt, P. H. (1998). New Jersey's Sex Offender Risk Assessment Scale: Preliminary validity data. *Journal of Psychiatry and Law, 26*, 327–351.

Feshbach, N. D. (1987). Parental empathy and child adjustment/maladjustment. In N. Eisenberg & J. Strayer (Eds.), *Empathy and its development* (pp. 271–291). New York: Cambridge University Press.

Feshbach, N. D., & Feshbach, S. (1982). Empathy training and the regulation of aggression: Potentialities and limitations. *Academic Psychology Bulletin, 4*, 399–413.

Field, L. H., & Williams, M. (1970). The hormonal treatment of sexual offenders. *Medicine, Science and the Law, 10*, 27.

Figley, C. R. (Ed.) (1985). *Trauma and its wake: The study and treatment of posttraumatic stress disorder*. New York: Brunner/Mazel.

Finkelhor, D. (1984). *Child sexual abuse: New theory and research*. New York: Free Press.

Finkelhor, D. (1986). Prevention: A review of programs and research. In D. Finkelhor & Associates (Eds.), *A sourcebook on child sexual abuse* (pp. 224–254). Newbury Park, CA: Sage.

Finkelhor, D. (1994). The international epidemiology of child sexual abuse. *Child Abuse and Neglect, 18*, 409–417.

Finkelhor, D., & Araji, S. (1983, July). *Explanations of pedophilia: A four factor model*. Paper presented at the American Academy of Psychiatry and Law, Portland, OR.

Finkelhor, D., & Araji, S. (1986). Explanations of pedophilia: A four factor model. *Journal of Sex Research, 22*, 145–161.

Finkelhor, D., Araji, S., Baron, L., Browne, A., Peters, S. D., & Wyatt, G. E. (1986). *A sourcebook on child sexual abuse*. Newbury Park, CA: Sage.

Finkelhor, D., & Asdigian, N. L. (1996). Risk factors for youth victimization: Beyond a Lifestyles/Routine Activities Theory approach. *Violence and Victims, 11*, 3–19.

Finkelhor, D., & Dziuba-Leatherman, J. (1994a). Children as victims of violence: A national survey. *Pediatrics, 94*, 413–420.

Finkelhor, D., & Dziuba-Leatherman, J. (1994b). Victimization of children. *American Psychologist, 49*, 173–183.

Finkelhor, D., & Lewis, I. S. (1988). An epidemiologic approach to the study of child molestation. In R. A. Prentky & V. L. Quinsey (Eds.), *Human sexual aggression: Current perspectives* (pp. 64–78). New York: New York Academy of Sciences.

Finkelhor, D., & Yllo, K. (1985). *License to rape: Sexual abuse of wives*. New York: Holt, Rinehart & Winston.

Finn, P. (1997, February). Sex offender community notification. *National Institute of Justice Research in Action*. Washington, DC: Office of Justice Programs, DOJ.

Fisher, C., Gross, J., & Zuch, J. (1965). Cycle of penile erection synchronous with dreaming (REM) sleep. *Archives of General Psychiatry, 12*, 29–45.

Fitch, J. H. (1962). Men convicted of sexual offenses against children: A descriptive follow-up study. *British Journal of Criminology, 3*, 18–37.

Fitch, W. L. (1998a). Sex offender commitment in the United States. *The Journal of Forensic Psychiatry, 9*, 237–240.

Fitch, W. L. (1998b, October). *NASMHPD update: Civil commitment of sex offenders in the U.S.* Paper presented to the meeting of the National Association of State Mental Health Program Directors, St. Petersburg, FL.

Fleiss, J. L. (1981). *Statistical methods for rates and proportions* (2nd ed.). New York: Wiley.

Flor-Henry, P. (1980). Cerebral aspects of the orgasmic response: Normal and deviational. In R. Forbes & W. Pasini (Eds.), *Medical sexology. The Third International Congress* (pp. 256–262). Littleton, MA: PSG Publishing.

Fort, A. E., Hart, S. D., Hare, R. D., & Harpur, T. J. (1988). Event-related potentials and detection of deception [Abstract]. *Psychophysiology, 25*, 446.

Foster, K. R., Bernstein, D. E., & Huber, P. W. (Eds.). (1999). *Phantom risk: Scientific inference and the law.* Cambridge, MA: MIT Press.

Foster, K. R., & Huber, P. W. (1999). *Judging science: Scientific knowledge and the federal courts.* Cambridge, MA: MIT Press.

French, M. (1992). *The war against women.* New York: Summit Books.

Freudenburg, W. R. (1988). Perceived risk, real risk: Social science and the art of probabilistic risk assessment. *Science, 242*, 44–49.

Freund, K. (1963). A laboratory method for diagnosing predominance of homo- and hetero-erotic interest in the male. *Behavior Research and Therapy, 1*, 85–93.

Freund, K. (1965). Diagnosing heterosexual pedophelia by means of a test for sexual interest. *Behavior Research and Therapy, 3*, 229–234.

Freund, K. (1967a). Diagnosing homo- and heterosexuality and erotic age preference by means of a psychophysiological test. *Behavior Research and Therapy, 5*, 209–228.

Freund, K. (1967b). Erotic preference in pedophilia. *Behavior Research and Therapy, 5*, 339–348.

Freyd, J. J. (1996). *Betrayal trauma.* Cambridge, MA: Harvard University Press.

Friedrich, W. N. (1988). Behavior problems in sexually abused children: An adaptational perspective. In G. E. Wyatt & G. J. Powell (Eds.), *Lasting effects of child sexual abuse.* Newbury Park, CA: Sage.

Friedrich, W. N. (1993). Sexual victimization and sexual behavior in children: A review of recent literature. *Child Abuse and Neglect, 17*, 59–66.

Friedrich, W. N., Beilke, R. L., & Urquiza, A. J. (1987). Children from sexually abusive families: A behavioral comparison. *Journal of Interpersonal Violence, 2*, 391–402.

Friedrich, W. N., & Luecke, W. (1988). Young school age sexually aggressive children. *Professional Psychology: Research and Practice, 19*, 155–164.

Friedrich, W. N., & Reams, R. A. (1987). Course of psychological symptoms in sexually abused young children. *Psychotherapy, 24*, 160–170.

Friedrich, W. N., Urquiza, A. J., & Beilke, R. L. (1986). Behavioral problems in sexually abused young children. *Journal of Pediatric Psychology, 11*, 47–57.

Frieze, I. H., Hymer, S., & Greenberg, M. S. (1987). Describing the crime victim: Psychological reactions to victimization. *Professional Psychology, 18*, 299–315.

Frisbie, L. V. (1969). Another look at sex offenders in California. *California Mental Health Research Monograph*, No. 12, State of California Department of Mental Hygiene.

Frisbie, L. V., & Dondis, E. H. (1965). Recidivism among treated sex offenders. *California Mental Health Research Monograph*, No. 5, State of California Department of Mental Hygiene.

Frodi, A. (1977). Sexual arousal, situational restrictiveness, and aggressive behavior. *Journal of Research in Personality, 11*, 48–58.

Fromuth, M. E., Burkhart, B. R., & Jones, C. W. (1991). Hidden child molestation. An investigation of adolescent perpetrators in a nonclinical sample. *Journal of Interpersonal Violence, 6*, 376–384.

Frosch, J., & Bromberg, W. (1939). The sex offender: A psychiatric study. *American Journal of Orthopsychiatry, 9*, 761–776.

Fujimoto, B. K. (1992). Sexual violence, sanity, and safety: Constitutional parameters for involuntary civil commitment of sex offenders. *University of Puget Sound Law Review, 15*(3).

Furby, L., Weinrott, M.R., & Blackshaw, L. (1989). Sex offender recidivism: A review. *Psychological Bulletin, 105*, 3–30.

Gaensbauer, T. J. (1973). Castration in treatment of sex offenders: An appraisal. *Rocky Mountain Medical Journal*, *70*, 23–28.

Gaffney, G. R., & Berlin, F. S. (1984). Is there hypothalamic-pituitary-gonadal dysfunction in paedophilia? A pilot study. *British Journal of Psychiatry, 145*, 657–660.

Gager, N., & Schurr, C. (1976). *Sexual assault: Confronting rape in America*. New York: Grosset & Dunlap.

Gagne, P. (1981). Treatment of sex offenders with medroxyprogesterone acetate. *American Journal of Psychiatry, 160*, 127–137.

Gardner, H. (1985). *The mind's new science*. New York: Basic Books.

Garland, R. J., & Dougher, M. J. (1990). The abused-abuser hypothesis of child sexual abuse: A critical review of theory and research. In J. R. Feierman (Ed.), *Pedophilia: Biosocial dimensions* (pp. 488–509). Berlin: Springer-Verlag.

Gauron, E. F., & Dickinson, J. K. (1969). The influence of seeing the patient first on diagnostic decision-making in psychiatry. *American Journal of Psychiatry, 126*, 199–205.

Gavey, N. (1991). Sexual victimization prevalence among New Zealand university students. *Journal of Consulting and Clinical Psychology, 59*, 464–466.

Gazzaniga, M. S. (1985). *The social brain. Discovering the networks of the mind*. New York: Basic Books.

Gebhard, P. H., & Gagnon, J. H. (1964). Male sex offenders against very young children. *American Journal of Psychiatry, 121*, 576–579.

Gebhard, P. H., Gagnon, J. H., Pomeroy, W. B., & Christenson, C. V. (1965). *Sex offenders: An analysis of types*. New York: Harper & Row.

Geer, J. H. (1980). Measurement of genital arousal in human males and females. In L. Martin & P. H. Venables (Eds.), *Techniques in psychophysiology* (pp. 431–458). New York: Wiley.

General Accounting Office. (1996a, September). *Cycle of sexual abuse*. Report to the Chairman, Subcommittee on Crime, Committee on the Judiciary, U.S. House of Representatives. Washington, DC: Author.

General Accounting Office. (1996b, July). *Preventing child sexual abuse*. Report to the Chairman, Subcommittee on Crime, Committee on the Judiciary, U.S. House of Representatives. Washington, DC: Author.

General Accounting Office. (1996c, June). *Sex offender treatment*. Report to the Chairman, Subcommittee on Crime, Committee on the Judiciary, U.S. House of Representatives. Washington, DC: General Accounting Office.

Geschwind, N., & Galaburda, A. M. (1987). *Cerebral lateralization. Biological mechanisms, associations, and pathology*. Cambridge, MA: MIT Press.

Gibbens, T. C. N., Soothill, K. L., & Way, C. K. (1978). Sibling and parent–child incest offenders. *British Journal of Criminology, 18*, 40–52.

Gill, C. D. (1992). Essay on the status of the American child, 2000 A.D.: Chattel or constitutionally protected child-citizen? In A. W. Burgess (Ed.), *Child trauma I: Issues & research* (pp. 3–48). New York: Garland Publishing.

Glaberson, W. (1996, May 6). At the center of "Megan's Law" Case, a man the system couldn't reach. *New York Times*, p. C10.

Glaser, D. (1987). Classification for risk. In D. M. Gottfredson & M. Tonry (Eds.), *Prediction and classification. Criminal justice decision making* (pp. 249–291). Chicago: University of Chicago Press.

Gleick, J. (1988). *Chaos. Making a new science*. New York: Penguin Press.

Gold, E. R. (1986). Long-term effects of sexual victimization in childhood: An attributional approach. *Journal of Consulting and Clinical Psychology, 54*, 471–475.

Goldfarb, L. A. (1987). Sexual abuse antecedent to anorexia nervosa, bulimia, and compulsive eating: Three case reports. *International Journal of Eating Disorders, 6*, 665–680.

Golding, J. M. (1994). Sexual assault history and physical health in randomly selected Los Angeles women. *Health Promotion, 13*, 130–138.

Golding, J. M., Siegel, J. M., Sorenson, S. B., Burnam, M. A., & Stein, J. A. (1989). Social support sources following sexual assault. *Journal of Community Psychology, 17*, 92–107.

Golla, F. L., & Hodge, R. S. (1949). Hormone treatment of sex offenders. *Lancet, 1*, 1006–1007.

Gondolf, E. W. (1990). *Psychiatric responses to family violence: Identifying and confronting neglected danger*. Lexington, MA: Lexington Books.

Goodman, L. A., Koss, M. P., Fitzgerald, L. F., Russo, N. F., & Keita, G. P. (1993). Male violence against women. Current research and future directions. *American Psychologist, 48*, 1054–1058.

Goodman, L. A., & Kruskal, W. H. (1963). Measures of association for cross classifications III. *Journal of the American Statistical Association, 58*, 310–364.

Goodman, R. E. (1983). Biology of sexuality: Inborn determinants of human sexual response. *British Journal of Psychiatry, 143*, 216–255.

Goodman-Delahunty, J. (1997). Forensic psychological expertise in the wake of Daubert. *Law and Human Behavior, 21*, 121–140.

Goodwin, J. M. (1985). Post-traumatic symptoms in incest victims. In S. Eth & R. S. Pynoos (Eds.), *Post-traumatic stress disorder in children* (pp. 155–168). Washington, DC: American Psychiatric Press.

Gopnik, A. (1995, October 9). Wonderland. Lewis Carroll and the loves of his life. *The New Yorker*, 82–90.

Gordon, M. T., & Riger, S. (1989). *The female fear.* New York: Free Press.

Gosselin, C., & Wilson, G. (1984). Fetishism, sadomasochism and related behaviours. In K. Howells (Ed.), *The psychology of sexual diversity* (pp. 89–110). Oxford: Blackwell.

Gottesman, H. G., & Schubert, D. S. P. (1993). Low-dose oral medroxyprogesterone acetate in the management of the paraphilias. *Journal of Clinical Psychiatry, 54*, 182–188.

Gottfredson, S. D. (1987). Prediction: An overview of selected methodological issues. In D. M. Gottfredson & M. Tonry (Eds.), *Prediction and classification. Criminal Justice Decision Making* (Vol. 9, pp. 21–51). Chicago: University of Chicago Press.

Gould, M. A. (1997). An empirical investigation of floodgates factors in child sexual abusers. In B. Schwartz (Ed.), *The sex offender* (Vol. II, pp. 4-1–4-19). Kingston, NJ: Civic Research Institute.

Gould, P. (1982, May/June). The tyranny of taxonomy. *The Sciences*, 7–9.

Governor's Special Advisory Panel on Forensic Mental Health. (1989, September). *Executive summary* (The Commonwealth of Massachusetts).

Governor's Task Force on Community Protection. (1989, November 19). *Task Force on Community Protection: Final report.* Olympia: Washington State Department of Social and Health Services.

Grann, M., Langstrom, N., Tengstrom, A., & Kullgren, G. (1999). Psychopathy (PCL-R) predicts violent recidivism among criminal offenders with personality disorders in Sweden. *Law and Human Behavior, 23*, 205–217.

Gray, S. H. (1982). Exposure to pornography and aggression toward women: The case of the angry male. *Social Problems, 29*, 387–398.

Green, A. H. (1988). Overview of the literature on child sexual abuse. In D. H. Schetky & A. H. Green (Eds.), *Child sexual abuse. A handbook for health care and legal professionals* (pp. 30–54). New York: Brunner/Mazel.

Greenberg, D. M., & Bradford, J. M. W. (1997). Treatment of the paraphilic disorders: A review of the role of the selective serotonin reuptake inhibitors. *Sexual Abuse: A Journal of Research and Treatment, 9*, 349–360.

Greenberg, D. M., Bradford, J. M., Curry, S., & O'Rourke, A. (1996a). A comparison of treatment of paraphilias with three serotonin reuptake inhibitors: A retrospective study. *Bulletin of the American Academy of Psychiatry and the Law, 24*, 525–532.

Greenberg, D. M., Bradford, J. M., Curry, S., & O'Rourke, A. (1996b). *A controlled study of the treatment of paraphilia disorders with selective serotonin reuptake inhibitors.* Annual Meeting of the Canadian Academy of Psychiatry and the Law, Tremblay, Quebec.

Greenfeld, L. A. (1996). *Child victimizers: Violent offenders and their victims* (NCJ-158625). Washington, DC: U.S. Department of Justice, Bureau of Justice Statistics.

Greenfeld, L. A. (1997). *Sex offenses and offenders. An analysis of data on rape and sexual assault* (NCJ-163392). Washington, DC: U.S. Department of Justice, Bureau of Justice Statistics.

Greenfeld, L. A. (1998). *Violence by intimates* (NCJ-167237). Washington, DC: U.S. Department of Justice, Bureau of Justice Statistics.

Greer, G. (1971). *The female eunuch.* New York: McGraw–Hill.

Griffin, S. (1971, September). Rape, the all-American crime. *Ramparts, 10*, 26–36.

Griffin, S. (1979). *Rape: The power of consciousness.* San Francisco: Harper & Row.

Griffin, S. (1981). *Pornography and silence: Culture's revenge against nature.* New York: Harper & Row.

Grisso, T., & Appelbaum, P. S. (1992). Is it unethical to offer predictions of future violence? *Law and Human Behavior, 16*, 621–633.

Grisso, T., & Tomkins, A. J. (1996). Communicating violence risk assessments. *American Psychologist, 51*, 928–930.

Gross, R. J., Doerr, H., Caldirola, D., Guzinski, G. M., & Ripley, H. S. (1980-1981). Borderline syndrome and incest in chronic pelvic pain patients. *International Journal of Psychiatry in Medicine, 10*, 79–96.

Grossman, C. J. (1985). Interactions between the gonadal steroids and the immune system. *Science, 227*, 257–260.

Grossman, R. (Ed.). (1982). *Surviving sexual assault*. New York: Congdon & Weed.

Groth, A. N. (1978). Patterns of sexual assault against children and adolescents. In A. W. Burgess, A. N. Groth, L. L. Holmstrom, & S. M. Sgroi (Eds.), *Sexual assault of children and adolescents* (pp. 3–24). Boston: Heath.

Groth, A. N. (1979). Sexual traumas in the life histories of rapists and child molesters. *Victimology: An International Journal*, *4*, 10–16.

Groth, A. N. (1981). *Sexual offenders against children*. Distributed by Forensic Mental Health Associates, Webster, MA 01570.

Groth, A. N., & Birnbaum, J. (1979). *Men who rape: The psychology of the offender*. New York: Plenum Press.

Groth, A. N., & Burgess, A. W. (1977a). Rape: A sexual deviation. *American Journal of Orthopsychiatry*, *47*, 400–406.

Groth, A. N., & Burgess, A. W. (1977b). Motivational intent in the sexual assault of children. *Criminal Justice and Behavior*, *4*, 253–264.

Groth, A. N., Burgess, A. W., & Holmstrom, L. L. (1977). Rape: Power, anger, and sexuality. *American Journal of Psychiatry*, *134*, 1239–1243.

Group for the Advancement of Psychiatry. (1950, February). *Psychiatrically deviated sex offenders*. Report #9. New York: The Mental Health Materials Center.

Group for the Advancement of Psychiatry. (1977, April). *Psychiatry and sex psychopath legislation: The 30s to the 80s* (Vol. 9). New York: The Mental Health Materials Center.

Grubin, D. (1998). *Sex offending against children: Understanding the risk*. Police Research Series Paper 99. London: Home Office.

Grubin, D., & Prentky, R. A. (1993). Sexual psychopathy laws. *Criminal Behaviour and Mental Health*, *3*, 381–392.

Guided Self-Help. A new approach to treatment of sexual offenders. (July 1973–June 1974). Annual Report on Treatment Center for Sexual Offenders at Western State Hospital. Olympia: Department of Social & Health Services, State of Washington.

Guttmacher, M. S. (1951). *Sex offenses: The problem, causes, and prevention*. New York: Norton.

Guttmacher, M. S., & Weihofen, H. (1952). *Psychiatry and the law*. New York: Norton.

Hacker, F. J., & Frym, M. (1955). The Sexual Psychopath Act in practice: A critical discussion. *California Law Review*, *43*, 766–780.

Hall, E. R., Howard, J. A., & Boezio, S. L. (1986). Tolerance of rape: A sexist or antisocial attitude? *Psychology of Women Quarterly*, *10*, 101–108.

Hall, G. C. N. (1988). Criminal behavior as a function of clinical and actuarial variables in a sexual offender population. *Journal of Consulting and Clinical Psychology*, *56*, 773–775.

Hall, G. C. N. (1995). Sex offender recidivism revisited: A meta-analysis of recent treatment studies. *Journal of Consulting and Clinical Psychology*, *63*, 802–809.

Hall, G. C. N., Maiuro, R. D., Vitaliano, P. P., & Proctor, W. C. (1986). The utility of the MMPI with men who have sexually assaulted children. *Journal of Consulting and Clinical Psychology*, *54*, 493–496.

Hall, G. C. N., & Proctor, W. C. (1987). Criminological predictors of recidivism in a sexual offender population. *Journal of Consulting and Clinical Psychology*, *55*, 111–112.

Hall, R. C., Tice, L., Beresford, T. P., Wolley, B., & Hall, A. K. (1989) Sexual abuse in patients with anorexia nervosa and bulimia. *Psychosomatics*, *30*, 73–79.

Halleck, S. L. (1981). The ethics of antiandrogen therapy. *American Journal of Psychiatry*, *138*, 642–643.

Halleck, S. L., & Pacht, A. R. (1960, December). The current status of the Wisconsin State Sex Crimes Law. *Wisconsin Bar Bulletin*, 17–26.

Hanson, R. K. (1990). The psychological impact of sexual assault on women and children: A review. *Annals of Sex Research*, *3*, 187–232.

Hanson, R. K. (1997a). *The development of a brief actuarial risk scale for sexual offense recidivism* (User Report No. JS4-1/1997-4E). Ottawa: Department of the Solicitor General of Canada.

Hanson, R. K. (1997b). How to know what works with sexual offenders. *Sexual Abuse: A Journal of Research and Treatment*, *9*, 129–145.

Hanson, R. K. (1998). What do we know about sex offender risk assessment? *Psychology, Public Policy, and Law*, *4*, 50–72.

Hanson, R. K., & Bussiere, M. T. (1998). Predicting relapse: A meta-analysis of sexual offender recidivism studies. *Journal of Consulting and Clinical Psychology*, *66*, 348–362.

Hanson, R. K., Cox, B., & Woszczyna, C. (1991a). *Sexuality, personality and attitude questionnaires for sexual offenders: A review* (Cat. No. JS4-1/1991-13). Ottawa: Ministry of the Solicitor General of Canada.

Hanson, R. K., Cox, B., & Woszczyna, C. (1991b). Assessing treatment outcome for sexual abusers. *Annals of Sex Research, 4*, 177–208.

Hanson, R. K., Scott, H., & Steffy, R. A. (1995). A comparison of child molesters and non-sexual criminals: Risk predictors and long-term recidivism. *Journal of Research in Crime and Delinquency, 32*, 325–337.

Hanson, R. K., Steffy, R. A., & Gauthier, R. (1993). Long-term recidivism of child molesters. *Journal of Consulting and Clinical Psychology, 61*, 646– 652.

Hanson, R. K., & Thornton, D. (1999). *Static 99: Improving actuarial risk assessments for sex offenders* (User Report No. J2-165/1999). Ottawa: Public Works and Government Services Canada.

Harding, T. W., & Adserballe, H. (1983). Assessments of dangerousness: Observations in six countries. *International Journal of Law and Psychiatry, 6*, 391–398.

Hare, R. D. (1980). A research scale for the assessment of psychopathy in criminal populations. *Personality and Individual Differences, 1*, 111–119.

Hare, R. D. (1991). *Manual for the Hare Psychopathy Checklist—Revised.* Toronto: Multi-Health Systems.

Hare, R. D. (1998). Psychopaths and their nature: Implications for the mental health and criminal justice systems. In T. Millon, E. Simonsen, M. Birket-Smith, & R. D. Davis (Eds.), *Psychopathy. Antisocial, criminal, and violent behavior* (pp. 188–212). New York: Guilford Press.

Hare, R. D., Harpur, T. J., Hakstian, A. R., Forth, A. E., Hart, S. D., & Newman, J. P. (1990). The Revised Psychopathy Checklist: Descriptive statistics, reliability and factor structure. *Psychological Assessment: A Journal of Consulting and Clinical Psychology, 2*, 338–341.

Hare, R. D., Hart, S. D., & Harpur, T. J. (1991). Psychopathy and the proposed DSM-IV criteria for antisocial personality disorder. *Journal of Abnormal Psychology, 100*, 391–398.

Harpur, A., Hakstian, R., & Hare, R. D. (1988). Factor structure of the Psychopathy Checklist. *Journal of Consulting and Clinical Psychology, 56*, 227–232.

Harre, R. (1976). *The philosophies of science.* London: Oxford University Press.

Harrell, F. E., Lee, K. L., Califf, R. M., Pryor, D. B., & Rosati, R. A. (1984). Regression modeling strategies for improved prognostic prediction. *Statistics in Medicine, 3*, 143–152.

Harris, G. T., Rice, M. E., & Cormier, C. A. (1991). Psychopathy and violent recidivism. *Law and Human Behavior, 15*, 625–637.

Harris, G. T., Rice, M. E., & Quinsey, V. L. (1993). Violent recidivism of mentally disordered offenders. The development of a statistical prediction instrument. *Criminal Justice and Behavior, 20*, 315–335.

Harris, G. T., Rice, M. E., & Quinsey, V. L. (1994). Psychopathy as a taxon: Evidence that psychopaths are a discrete class. *Journal of Consulting and Clinical Psychology, 62*, 387–397.

Harris, G. T., Rice, M. E., & Quinsey, V. L. (1998). Appraisal and management of risk in sexual aggressors: Implications for criminal justice policy. *Psychology, Public Policy, and Law, 4*, 73–115.

Hart, S. D. (1996). Psychopathy and risk assessment. In D. J. Cooke, A. E. Forth, J. P. Newman, & R. D. Hare (Eds.), *Issues in criminological and legal psychology: No. 24. International perspectives on psychopathy* (pp. 63–67). Leicester, England: British Psychological Society.

Hart, S. D. (1998a). The role of psychopathy in assessing risk for violence: Conceptual and methodological issues. *Legal and Criminological Psychology, 3*, 121–137.

Hart, S. D. (1998b). Psychopathy and risk for violence. In D. J. Cooke, A. E. Forth, & R. D. Hare (Eds.), *Psychopathy: Theory, research, and implications for society* (pp. 355–373). Dordrecht: Kluwer.

Hart, S. D., Cox, D. N., & Hare, R. D. (1995). *The Hare Psychopathy Checklist: Screening Version.* Toronto: Multi-Health Systems.

Hart, S. D., & Hare, R. D. (1996). Psychopathy and risk assessment. *Current Opinion in Psychiatry, 9*, 380–383.

Hart, S. D., & Hare, R. D. (1997). Psychopathy: Assessment and association with criminal conduct. In D. M. Stoff, J. Brieling, & J. Maser (Eds.), *Handbook of antisocial behavior* (pp. 22–35). New York: Wiley.

Hart, S. D., Hare, R. D., & Forth, A. E. (1993). Psychopathy as a risk marker for violence: Development and validation of a screening version of the revised Psychopathy Checklist. In J. Monahan & H. J. Steadman (Eds.), *Violence and mental disorder: Developments in risk assessment* (pp. 81–98). Chicago: University of Chicago Press.

Hart, S. D., Hare, R. D., & Harpur, T. J. (1992). The Psychopathy Checklist: Overview for researchers and clinicians. In J. Rosen & P. McReynolds (Eds.), *Advances in psychological assessment* (Vol. 8, pp. 103–130). New York: Plenum Press.

Hart, S. D., Webster, C. D., & Menzies, R. J. (1993). A note on portraying the accuracy of violence predictions. *Law and Human Behavior, 17*, 695–700.

Hazelwood, R. R., Reboussin, R., & Warren, J. I. (1989). Serial rape. Correlates of increased aggression and the relationship of offender pleasure to victim resistance. *Journal of Interpersonal Violence, 4*, 65–78.

Hebb, D. O. (1968). Concerning imagery. *Psychological Review, 75*, 466–477.

Heilbrun, K. (1992). The role of psychological testing in forensic assessment. *Law and Human Behavior, 16*, 257–272.

Heilbrun, K. (1997). Prediction versus management models relevant to risk assessment: The importance of legal decision-making context. *Law and Human Behavior, 21*, 347–359.

Heilbrun, K., Nezu, C. M., Keeney, M., Chung, S., & Wasserman, A. L. (1998). Sexual offending: Linking assessment, intervention, and decision-making. *Psychology, Public Policy, and Law, 4*, 138–174.

Heim, N., & Hursch, C. J. (1979). Castration for sex offenders: Treatment or punishment? A review and critique of recent European literature. *Archives of Sexual Behavior, 8*, 281–304.

Heller, C. G., Laidlaw, W. M., Harvey, H. T., & Nelson, D. L. (1958). Effects of progestational compounds on the reproductive processes of the human male. *Annals of the New York Academy of Sciences, 71*, 649–665.

Henderson, H. (1981). Exploring the human sexual response. *Sexual Medicine Today, April*, 6–16.

Henderson, J. (1972). Incest: A synthesis of data. *Canadian Psychiatric Association Journal, 17*, 299–313.

Hendricks-Matthews, M. K. (1993). Survivors of abuse: Health care issues. *Primary Care, 20*, 391–406.

Herman, J. L. (1981). *Father–daughter incest*. Cambridge, MA: Harvard University Press.

Herman, J. L. (1986). Histories of violence in an outpatient population: An exploratory study. *American Journal of Orthopsychiatry, 56*, 137–141.

Herman, J. L. (1990). Sex offenders. A feminist perspective. In W. L. Marshall, D. R. Laws, & H. E. Barbaree (Eds.), *Handbook of sexual assault: Issues, theories, and treatment of the offender* (pp. 177–193). New York: Plenum Press.

Herman, J. L. (1992). *Trauma and recovery*. New York: Basic Books.

Herman, J. L. (1995). Crime and memory. *Bulletin of the American Academy of Psychiatry and Law, 23*, 1–17.

Herman, J. L., & Hirschman, L. (1977). Father–daughter incest. *Signs: Journal of Women in Culture and Society, 2*, 735–756.

Herman, J. L., Perry, J. C., & van der Kolk, B. A. (1989). Childhood trauma in borderline personality disorder. *American Journal of Psychiatry, 146*, 490–495.

Herman, J. L., & Schatzow, E. (1987). Recovery and verification of memories of childhood sexual trauma. *Psychoanalytic Psychology, 4*, 1–14.

Higgins, E. T., & King, G. (1981). Accessibility of social constructs: Information-processing consequences of individual and contextual variability. In N. Cantor & J. F. Kihlstrom (Eds.), *Personality, cognition, and social interaction* (pp. 69–121). Hillsdale, NJ: Erlbaum.

Hilberman, E. (1980). Overview: The wife-beater's wife reconsidered. *American Journal of Psychiatry, 137*, 1336–1347.

Hilberman. E., & Munson, K. (1978). Sixty battered women. *Victimology, 2*, 460–470.

Hildebran, D., & Pithers, W. D. (1989). Enhancing offender empathy for sexual abuse victims. In D. R. Laws (Ed.), *Relapse prevention with sex offenders* (pp. 236–243). New York: Guilford Press.

Hinton, J. W., O'Neill, M. T., & Webster, S. (1980). Psychophysiological assessment of sex offenders in a security hospital. *Archives of Sexual Behavior, 9*(3), 205–216.

Holmes, W. C., & Slap, G. B. (1998). Sexual abuse of boys. Definition, prevalence, correlates, sequelae, and management. *Journal of the American Medical Association, 280*, 1855–1862.

Honts, C. R., & Perry, M. V. (1992). Polygraph admissibility. *Law and Human Behavior, 16*, 357–379.

Howes, R. J. (1995). A survey of plethysmographic assessment in North America. *Sexual Abuse: A Journal of Research and Treatment, 7*, 9–24.

Icove, D. J. (1986). Automated crime profiling. *FBI Law Enforcement Bulletin, 55*, 27–30.

Isaacson, R. L. (1972). Neural systems of the limbic brain and behavioral inhibition. In R. A. Boakes & M. S. Halliday (Eds.), *Inhibition and learning* (pp. 497–528). New York: Academic Press.

Jackson, J. L., Calhoun, K. S., Amick, A. E., Madderer, H. M., & Habif, V. L. (1990). Young adult women who report childhood intrafamilial sexual abuse: Subsequent adjustment. *Archives of Sexual Behavior, 19*, 211–221.

Jaffe, Y., Malamuth, N., Feingold, J., & Feshbach, S. (1974). Sexual arousal and behavioral aggression. *Journal of Personality and Social Psychology, 30*, 759–764.

Jaffee, D., & Straus, M. A. (1987). Sexual climate and reported rape: A state-level analysis. *Archives of Sexual Behavior, 16*, 107–123.

James, J., & Meyerding, J. (1977). Early sexual experience and prostitution. *American Journal of Psychiatry, 134*, 1381–1385.

Janssen, E., Vissenberg, M., Visser, S., & Everaerd, W. (1997). An in vivo comparison of two circumferential penile strain gauges: The introduction of a new calibration method. *Psychophysiology, 34*, 717–720.

Janus, E. S. (1996). Preventing sexual violence: Setting principled constitutional boundaries on sex offender commitments. *Indiana Law Journal, 72*(1), 157–213.

Janus, E. S. (1997a). Sex offender commitments: Debunking the official narrative and revealing the Rules-in-Use. *Stanford Law and Policy Review, 8*, 71–102.

Janus, E. S. (1997b). The use of social science and medicine in sex offender commitment. *New England Journal on Criminal and Civil Confinement, 23*, 347–386.

Janus, E. S. (1997c). Toward a conceptual framework for assessing police power commitment legislation: A critique of Schopp's and Winick's explications of legal mental illness. *Nebraska Law Review, 76*(1), 1–50.

Janus, E. S. (1998a). *Hendricks* and the moral terrain of police power civil commitment. *Psychology, Public Policy, and Law, 4*, 297–322.

Janus, E. S. (1998b). Foreshadowing the future of *Kansas v. Hendricks*: Lessons from Minnesota's sex offender commitment litigation. *Northwestern University Law Review, 92*, 1279–1305.

Janus, E. S., & Meehl, P. E. (1997). Assessing the legal standard for predictions of dangerousness in sex offender commitment proceedings. *Psychology, Public Policy, and Law, 3*, 33–63.

Jarrard, L. E., & Korn, J. H. (1969). Effects of hippocampal lesions on heart rate during habituation and passive avoidance. *Communications in Behavioral Biology, 3*, 141–150.

Jenny, C., Hooton, T. M., Bowers, A., Copass, M. K., Krieger, J.N ., Hiller, S. L., Kiviat, N., & Corey, L. (1990). Sexually transmitted diseases in victims of rape. *The New England Journal of Medicine, 322*, 713–716.

Jezycki, M. (1998). How safe is cyberspace? *The APSAC Advisor, 11*(4), 10–11.

Johnson, A. G. (1980). On the prevalence of rape in the United States. *Signs: Journal of Women in Culture and Society, 6*, 1.

Johnson, J., & Kitching, R. (1968). A mechanical transducer for phallography. *Biomedical Engineering*, 416–418.

Justice, B., & Justice, R. (1979). *The broken taboo.* New York: Human Sciences Press.

Kafka, M. P. (1991). Successful antidepressant treatment of nonparaphilic sexual addictions and paraphilias in men. *Journal of Clinical Psychiatry, 52*, 60–65.

Kafka, M. P. (1994). Sertraline pharmacotherapy for paraphilias and paraphilia-related disorders: An open trial. *Annals of Clinical Psychiatry, 6*, 189–195.

Kafka, M. P. (1995a). Sexual impulsivity. In E. Hollander & D. J. Stein (Eds.), *Impulsivity and aggression* (pp. 201–228). New York: Wiley.

Kafka, M. P. (1995b). Current concepts in the drug treatment of paraphilias and paraphilia-related disorders. *CNS Drugs, 3*, 9–21.

Kafka, M. P. (1997a). Hypersexual desire in males: An operational definition and clinical implications for males with paraphilias and paraphilia-related disorders. *Archives of Sexual Behavior, 26*(5), 505–526.

Kafka, M. P. (1997b). A monoamine hypothesis for the pathophysiology of paraphilic disorders. *Archives of Sexual Behavior, 26*(4), 343–358.

Kafka, M. P., & Prentky, R. A. (1992). Fluoxetine treatment of nonparaphilic sexual addictions and paraphilias in men. *Journal of Clinical Psychiatry, 53*, 351–358.

Kafka, M. P., & Prentky, R. A. (1994). Preliminary observations of DSM-III-R Axis I comorbidity in men with paraphilias and paraphilia-related disorders. *Journal of Clinical Psychiatry, 55*(11), 481–487.

Kafka, M. P., & Prentky, R. A. (1998). Attention-Deficit/Hyperactivity Disorder in males with paraphilias and paraphilia-related disorders: A comorbidity study. *Journal of Clinical Psychiatry, 59*(7), 388–396.

Kalichman, S. C., & Henderson, M. C. (1991). MMPI profile subtypes of nonincarcerated child molesters. *Criminal Justice and Behavior, 18*, 379–396.

Kalichman, S. C., Henderson, M. C., Shealy, L. S., & Dwyer, M. (1992). Psychometric properties of the Multiphasic Sex Inventory in assessing sex offenders. *Criminal Justice and Behavior, 19*, 384–396.

Kalichman, S. C., Szymanowski, D., McKee, J., Taylor, J., & Craig, M. (1989). Cluster analytically derived subgroups of incarcerated adult rapists. *Journal of Clinical Psychology, 45*, 149–155.

Kalman, J. Z. (1998). A modest proposal for a new way to use Child Sexual Abuse Accommodation Syndrome evidence. *Sexual Assault Report, 1*, 33–48.

Kanekar, S., & Vaz, L. (1983). Determinants of perceived likelihood of rape and victim's fault. *Journal of Social Psychology, 120,* 147–148.

Kanin, E. J. (1984). Date rape: Unofficial criminals and victims. *Victimology: An International Journal, 9,* 95–108.

Kanin, E. J. (1985). Date rapists: Differential sexual socialization and relative deprivation. *Archives of Sexual Behavior, 14,* 219–231.

Kardener, S. H. (1975). Rape fantasies. *Journal of Religion and Health, 14,* 50–57.

Karpman, B. (1951). The sexual psychopath. *Journal of Criminal Law, Criminology, and Police Science, 42,* 184.

Karpman, B. (1954). *The sexual offender and his offenses, etiology, pathology, psychodynamics and treatment.* New York: Julian Press.

Katz, B. (1991). The psychological impact of stranger versus nonstranger rape on victims' recovery. In A. Parrot & L. Bechhofer (Eds.), *Acquaintance rape: The hidden crime* (pp. 251–269). New York: Wiley.

Kaufman, I., Peck, A., & Tagiori, L. (1954). The family constellation and overt incestuous relations between father and daughter. *American Journal of Orthopsychiatry, 24,* 266–279.

Kaufman, J., & Zigler, E. (1987). Do abused children become abusive parents? *American Journal of Orthopsychiatry, 57,* 186–192.

Kelly, R. J. (1982). Behavioral reorientation of pedophiliacs: Can it be done? *Clinical Psychology Review, 2,* 387–408.

Kemp, A., Rawlings, E. I., & Green, B. L. (1991). Posttraumatic stress disorder (PTSD) in battered women: A shelter example. *Journal of Traumatic Stress, 4,* 137–148.

Kempe, R. S., & Kempe, C. H. (1984). *The common secret: Sexual abuse of children and perpetrators.* New York: Freeman.

Kendall, M. G. (1970). *Rank correlation methods.* London: Griffin.

Kendall-Tackett, K., & Simon, A. (1988). Molestation and the onset of puberty: Data from 365 adults molested as children. *Child Abuse and Neglect, 12,* 73–81.

Kendall-Tackett, K., Williams, L. M., & Finkelhor, D. (1993). Impact of sexual abuse on children: A review and synthesis of recent empirical studies. *Psychological Bulletin, 113,* 164–180.

Krenberg, O. (1984). *Severe personality disorders: Psychotherapeutic strategies.* New Haven, CT: Yale University Press.

Kiersch, T. A. (1990). Treatment of sex offenders with Depo-Provera. *Bulletin of the American Academy of Psychiatry and the Law, 18,* 179–187.

Kilpatrick, D. G., Edmunds, C. N., & Seymour, A. K. (1992). *Rape in American: A report to the nation.* Arlington, VA: National Victim Center.

Kilpatrick, D. G., Saunders, B. E., Best, C. L., Veronen, L. J., Amick, A. E., Villeponteaux, L. A., & Ruff, G. A. (1985). Mental health correlates of criminal victimization: A random community sample. *Journal of Consulting and Clinical Psychology, 53,* 866–873.

Kilpatrick, D. G., Saunders, B. E., Veronen, L. J., Best, C. L., & Von, J. M. (1987). Criminal victimization: Lifetime prevalence, reporting to police, and psychological impact. *Crime and Delinquency, 33,* 479–489.

Kilpatrick, D. G., & Saunders, B. E. (1997, April). The prevalence and consequences of child victimization. *Research Preview.* Washington, DC: U.S. Department of Justice, National Institute of Justice.

Kimble, D. P. (1968). The hippocampus and internal inhibition. *Psychological Bulletin, 70,* 285–295.

Kimerling, R., & Calhoun, K. S. (1994). Somatic symptoms, social support, and treatment seeking among sexual assault victims. *Journal of Consulting and Clinical Psychology, 62(2),* 333–340.

Kimmel, M. S. (1993, June). Does pornography cause rape? *Violence Update, 3,* 1–8.

Kirkland, K. D., & Bauer, C. A. (1982). MMPI traits of incestuous fathers. *Journal of Clinical Psychology, 38,* 645–649.

Kiser, L. J., Ackerman, B. J., Brown, E., Edwards, N. B., McColgan, E., Pugh, R., & Pruiff, D. B. (1988). Posttraumatic stress disorder in young children: A reaction to purported sexual abuse. *Journal of the American Academy of Child and Adolescent Psychiatry, 27,* 645–649.

Kling, A., Borowitz, G., & Cartwright, R. D. (1972). Plasma levels of 17-hydroxycorticosteroids during sexual arousal in man. *Journal of Psychosomatic Research, 16,* 215–221.

Kluft, R. (1985). *Childhood antecedents of multiple personality.* Washington, DC: American Psychiatric Press.

Knight, R. A. (1988). A taxonomic analysis of child molesters. In R. A. Prentky & V. Quinsey (Eds.), *Human sexual aggression: Current perspectives* (pp. 2–20). New York: New York Academy of Sciences.

Knight, R. A. (1989). An assessment of concurrent validity of a child molester typology. *Journal of Interpersonal Violence, 4,* 131–150.

Knight, R. A. (1992). The generation and corroboration of a taxonomic model for child molesters. In W. O'Donohue & J. H. Geer (Eds.), *The sexual abuse of children: Theory, research, and therapy* (pp. 24–70). Hillsdale, NJ: Erlbaum.

Knight, R. A. (1999). Validation of a typology for rapists. *Journal of Interpersonal Violence, 14*, 297–323.

Knight, R. A., Carter, D. L., & Prentky, R. A. (1989). A system for the classification of child molesters: Reliability and application. *Journal of Interpersonal Violence, 4*, 3–23.

Knight, R. A., & Prentky, R. A. (1987). The developmental antecedents and adult adaptations of rapist subtypes. *Criminal Justice and Behavior, 14*, 403–426.

Knight, R. A., & Prentky, R. A. (1990). Classifying sexual offenders: The development and corroboration of taxonomic models. In W. L. Marshall, D. R. Laws, & H. E. Barbaree (Eds.), *The handbook of sexual assault: Issues, theories, and treatment of the offender* (pp. 23–52). New York: Plenum Press.

Knight, R. A., Prentky, R. A., & Cerce, D. (1994). The development, reliability, and validity of an inventory for the multidimensional assessment of sex and aggression. *Criminal Justice and Behavior, 21*, 72–94.

Knight, R., Rosenberg, R., & Schneider, B. (1985). Classification of sexual offenders: Perspectives, methods and validation. In A. Burgess (Ed.), *Rape and sexual assault: A research handbook* (pp. 222–293). New York: Garland Publishing.

Knight, R. A., Warren, J. I., Reboussin, R., & Soley, B. J. (1998). Predicting rapist type from crime-scene variables. *Criminal Justice and Behavior, 25*, 46–80.

Knopp, F. H., & Benson, A. R. (1996). *A primer on the complexities of traumatic memory of childhood sexual abuse.* Brandon, VT: Safer Society Press.

Knopp, F. H., Freeman-Longo, R. E., & Stevenson, W. (1992). *Nationwide survey of juvenile and adult sex-offender treatment programs.* Orwell, VT: Safer Society Press.

Koehler, J. J. (1996). The base rate fallacy reconsidered: Descriptive, normative, and methodological challenges. *Behavioral and Brain Sciences, 19*, 1–17.

Konner, M. (1982). She and he. *Science 82, September*, 54–61.

Kopera, H. (1983). Sex hormones and the brain. In D. Wheatley (Ed.), *Psychopharmacology and sexual disorders* (pp. 50–67). (British Association for Psychopharmacology Monograph No. 4). Oxford: Oxford University Press.

Kopp, S. B. (1962). The character structure of sex offenders. *American Journal of Psychotherapy, 16*, 64–70.

Koss, M. P. (1988). Hidden rape: Sexual aggression and victimization in a national sample of students in higher education. In A. W. Burgess (Ed.), *Rape and sexual assault* (pp. 3–25). New York: Garland Publishing.

Koss, M. P. (1990). The women's mental health research agenda: Violence against women. *American Psychologist, 45*, 374–380.

Koss, M. P. (1993a). Rape. Scope, impact, interventions, and public policy responses. *American Psychologist, 48*, 1062–1069.

Koss, M. P. (1993b). Detecting the scope of rape. A review of prevalence research methods. *Journal of Interpersonal Violence, 8*, 198–222.

Koss, M. P., & Dinero, T. E. (1988). Predictors of sexual aggression among a national sample of male college students. In R. A. Prentky & V. L. Quinsey (Eds.), *Human sexual aggression: Current perspectives* (pp. 133–147). New York: New York Academy of Sciences.

Koss, M. P., Dinero, T. E., Seibel, C. A., & Wisniewski, N. (1988). Stranger and acquaintance rape. *Psychology of Women Quarterly, 12*, 1–24.

Koss, M. P., & Gidycz, C. A. (1985). Sexual Experiences Survey: Reliability and validity. *Journal of Consulting and Clinical Psychology, 53*, 422–423.

Koss, M. P., Gidycz, C. A., & Wisniewski, N. (1987). The scope of rape: Incidence and prevalence of sexual aggression and victimization in a national sample of higher education students. *Journal of Consulting and Clinical Psychology, 55*, 162–170.

Koss, M. P., Goodman, L., Browne, A., Fitzgerald, L., Keita, G. P. & Russon, N. P. (1994). *No safe haven.* Washington, DC: American Psychological Association.

Koss, M. P., & Harvey, M. R. (1991). *The rape victim: Clinical and community interventions.* Newbury Park, CA: Sage.

Koss, M. P., & Heslet, L. (1992). Somatic consequences of violence against women. *Archives of Family Medicine, 1*, 53–59.

Koss, M. P., Leonard, K. E., Beezley, D. A., & Oros, C. J. (1985). Nonstranger sexual aggression: A discriminant analysis of the psychological characteristics of undetected offenders. *Sex Roles, 12*, 981–992.

Koss, M. P., & Oros, C. J. (1982). Sexual Experiences Survey: A research instrument investigating sexual aggression and victimization. *Journal of Consulting and Clinical Psychology, 50,* 455–457.

Koss, M. P., Woodruff, W. J., & Koss, P. (1991). Criminal victimization among primary care medical patients: Prevalence, incidence, and physician usage. *Behavioral Science and the Law, 9,* 85–96.

Kosslyn, S. M. (1988). Aspects of a cognitive neuroscience of mental imagery. *Science, 240,* 1621–1626.

Kreuz, L. E., & Rose, R. M. (1972). Assessment of aggressive behavior and plasma testosterone in a young criminal population. *Psychosomatic Medicine, 34,* 321–332.

Lacey, H. B. (1990). Sexually transmitted diseases and rape: The experience of a sexual assault center. *International Journal of STD and AIDS, 1,* 4405–4409.

La Fond, J. Q. (1998). The costs of enacting a Sexual Predator Law. *Psychology, Public Policy, and Law, 4,* 468–504.

Lalumiere, M. L., & Harris, G. T. (1998). Common questions regarding the use of phallometric testing with sexual offenders. *Sexual Abuse: A Journal of Research and Treatment, 10,* 227–237.

Lang, P. J. (1979). A bio-informational theory of emotional imagery. *Psychophysiology, 16,* 495–512.

Lang, P. J. (1985). The cognitive psychophysiology of emotion: Fear and anxiety. In A. H. Tuma & J. D. Maser (Eds.), *Anxiety and the anxiety disorders* (pp. 131–170). Hillsdale, NJ: Erlbaum.

Langan, P. A., & Harlow, C. W. (1994). *Child rape victims.* Crime Data Brief (NCJ-147001). Washington, DC: U.S. Department of Justice, Office of Justice Programs, Bureau of Justice Statistics.

Langer, W. C. (1972). *The mind of Adolf Hitler.* New York: Basic Books.

Langevin, R. (1983). *Sexual strands: Understanding and treating sexual anomalies in men.* Hillsdale, NJ: Erlbaum.

Langevin, R. (1990). Sexual anomalies and the brain. In W. L. Marshall, D. R. Laws, & H. E. Barbaree (Eds.), *Handbook of sexual assault: Issues, theories, and treatment of the offender* (pp. 103–113). New York: Plenum Press.

Langevin, R., Ben-Aron, M. H., Wright, P., Marchese, V., & Handy, L. (1988). The sex killer. *Annals of Sex Research, 1,* 263–301.

Langevin, R., Day, D., Handy, L., & Russon, A. E. (1985). Are incestuous fathers pedophilic, aggressive, and alcoholic? In R. Langevin (Ed.), *Erotic preference, gender identity, and aggression in men: New research studies* (pp. 161–179). Hillsdale, NJ: Erlbaum.

Langevin, R., Handy, L., Paitich, D., & Russon, A. E. (1985). Appendix A: A new version of the Clarke Sex History Questionnaire for males. In R. Langevin (Ed.), *Erotic preference, gender identity, and aggression in men* (pp. 287–305). Hillsdale, NJ: Erlbaum.

Langevin, R., Hucker, S. J., Handy, L., Hook, H. J., & Purins, J. E., & Russon, A. E. (1985). Erotic preference and aggression in pedophilia: A comparison of heterosexual, homosexual, and bisexual types. In R. Langevin (Ed.), *Erotic preference, gender identity, and aggression in men: New research studies* (pp. 137–160). Hillsdale, NJ: Erlbaum.

Langevin, R., Paitich, D., Freeman, R., Mann, K., & Handy, L. (1978). Personality characteristics and sexual anomalies in males. *Canadian Journal of Behavioral Sciences, 10,* 222–238.

Langevin, R., Wright, P., & Handy, L. (1990). Use of the MMPI and its derived scales with sex offenders: I. Reliability and validity studies. *Annals of Sex Research, 3,* 245–291.

Langsley, D. G., Schwartz, M. N., & Fairbairn, R. H. (1968). Father–son incest. *Comprehensive Psychiatry, 9,* 218–226.

Lanning, K. V. (1986). *Child molesters: A behavioral analysis for law-enforcement officers investigating cases of child exploitation.* Washington, DC: National Center for Missing and Exploited Children.

Lanning, K. V. (1998). Cyber "pedophiles." *The APSAC Advisor, 11*(4), 12.

Lanyon, R. I. (1986). Theory and treatment in child molestation. *Journal of Consulting and Clinical Psychology, 54,* 176–182.

Largen, M. A. (1988). Rape-law reform: An analysis. In A. W. Burgess (Ed.), *Rape and sexual assault, II* (pp. 271–292). New York: Garland Publishing.

Laschet, U., & Laschet, L. (1975). Antiandrogens in the treatment of sexual deviations of men. *Journal of Steroid Biochemistry, 6,* 821–826.

Laws, D. R. (Ed.). (1989). *Relapse prevention with sex offenders.* New York: Guilford Press.

Laws, D. R., Gulayets, M. J., & Frenzel, R. R. (1995). Assessment of sex offenders using standardized slide stimuli and procedures: A multisite study. *Sexual Abuse: A Journal of Research and Treatment, 7,* 45–66.

Laws, D. R., & Osborn, C. A. (1983). How to build and operate a behavioral laboratory to evaluate and treat sexual deviance. In J. G. Greer & I. R. Stuart (Eds.), *The sexual aggressor* (pp. 293–335). New York: Van Nostrand–Reinhold.

Laws, D. R., & Pawlowski, A. V. (1973). A multi-purpose biofeedback device for penile plethysmography. *Journal of Behavior Therapy and Experimental Psychiatry, 4,* 339–341.

Leaton, R. N. (1965). Exploratory behavior in rats with hippocampal lesions. *Journal of Comparative and Physiological Psychology, 59,* 325–330.

Lebegue, B. (1991). Paraphilias in U.S. pornography titles: "Pornography made me do it" (Ted Bundy). *Bulletin of the American Academy of Psychiatry and the Law, 19,* 43–48.

Le Maire, L. (1956). Danish experiences regarding the castration of sexual offenders. *Journal of Criminal Law, Criminology and Police Science, 47,* 295–310.

Lerner, L. J. (1964). Hormone antagonists: Inhibitors of specific activities of estrogen and androgen. *Recent progress in hormone research* (pp. 435–490). New York: Academic Press.

Lerner, L. J., Bianchi, A., & Barman, A. (1960). A-Norprogesterone: An androgen antagonist. *Proceedings of the Society for Experimental Biology and Medicine, 103,* 172–175.

LeVine, R. A. (1959). Gusii sex offenses: A study in social control. *American Anthropologist, 61,* 965–990.

Lezzoni, L. I. (1994). Risk and outcomes. In L. I. Lezzoni (Ed.), *Risk adjustment for measuring health care outcomes* (pp. 1–28). Ann Arbor, MI: Health Administration Press.

Lieb, R., & Matson, S. (1998, September). *Sexual predator commitment laws in the United States: 1998 update.* Olympia: Washington State Institute for Public Policy.

Lieb, R., Quinsey, V., & Beliner, L. (1998). Sexual predators and social policy. *Crime and Justice—Review of Research, 23,* 43–114.

Lindberg, F. H., & Distad, L. J. (1985). Post-traumatic stress disorders in women who experienced childhood incest. *Child Abuse and Neglect, 9,* 329–334.

Liner, D. (1989). *Dissociation in sexually abused children.* Doctoral dissertation. Atlanta: Georgia State University.

Lisak, D., & Roth, S. (1988). Motivational factors in nonincarcerated sexually aggressive men. *Journal of Personality and Social Psychology, 55,* 795–802.

Litkey, L. J., & Feniczy, P. (1967). An approach to the control of homosexual practices. *International Journal of Neuropsychiatry, 3,* 20–23.

Litwack, T. R. (1993). On the ethics of dangerousness assessments. *Law and Human Behavior, 17,* 479–482.

Livingston, R. (1987). Sexually and physically abused children. *Journal of the American Academy of Child and Adolescent Psychiatry, 26,* 413–415.

Loeber, R., & Dishion, T. (1982). *Strategies for identifying at-risk youths.* Unpublished report. Eugene: Oregon Social Learning Center.

Loeber, R., & Dishion, T. (1983). Early predictors of male delinquency: A review. *Psychological Bulletin, 94*(1), 68–99.

Loftus, E. F., Polonsky, S., & Fullilove, M. T. (1994). Memories of childhood sexual abuse: Remembering and repressing. *Psychology of Women Quarterly, 18,* 67–84.

Loftus, P. (1999, January/February). CODIS: The Combined Deoxyribonucleic Acid Index System for DNA typing. *Crime Victims Report, 2*(6), 81–90.

Loggans, S. E. (1985). Rape as an intentional tort. *Trial, October,* 45–55.

Loh, W. D. (1981). Q: What has reform of rape legislation wrought? A: Truth in criminal labelling. *Journal of Social Issues, 37,* 28–52.

London Rape Crisis Centre. (1984). *Sexual violence.* London: The Women's Press.

Longo, R. E. F. (1982). Sexual learning and experience among adolescent sexual offenders. *International Journal of Offender Therapy and Comparative Criminology, 26,* 235–241.

Longo, R. E. F. (1996a). Feel good legislation: Prevention or calamity. *Child Abuse and Neglect, 20,* 95–101.

Longo, R. E. F. (1996b). Prevention or problem. *Sexual Abuse: A Journal of Research and Treatment, 8,* 91–100.

Longo, R. E. F., & Blanchard, G. T. (1998). *Sexual abuse in America: Epidemic of the 21st century.* Brandon, VT: Safer Society Press.

Longo, R. E. F., & Knopp, F. H. (1992). State-of-the-art sex offender treatment: Outcome and issues. *Annals of Sex Research, 5,* 141–160.

Longo, R. E. F., & Pithers, W. D. (1992). *A structured approach to preventing relapse: A guide for offenders.* Orwell, VT: Safer Society Press.

Lottes, I. L. (1988). Sexual socialization and attitudes toward rape. In A. W. Burgess (Ed.), *Rape and sexual assault* (pp. 193–213). New York: Garland Publishing.

Lurigio, A. J., & Resick, P. A. (1990). Healing the psychological wounds of criminal victimization: Predicting postcrime distress and recovery. In A. J. Lurigio, W. G. Skogan, & R. C. Davis (Eds.), *Victims of crime: Problems, policies, and programs* (pp. 51–67). Newbury Park, CA: Sage.

Lustig, N., Dresser, J., Spellman, S., & Murray, T. (1966). Incest. *Archives of General Psychology, 14*, 31–40.

Lykken, D. T. (1957). A study of anxiety in the sociopathic personality. *Journal of Abnormal and Social Psychology, 55*, 6–10.

Lykken, D. T. (1995). *The antisocial personalities.* Hillsdale, NJ: Erlbaum.

Lyman, D. R. (1997). Pursuing the psychopath: Capturing the fledgling psychopath in a nomological net. *Journal of Abnormal Psychology, 106*, 425–438.

Mabry, P. D., & Campbell, B. A. (1978). Cholinergic–monoaminergic interactions during ontogenesis. In L. L. Butcher (Ed.), *Cholinergic–monoaminergic interactions in the brain* (pp. 257–270). New York: Academic Press.

MacCulloch, M. J., Snowden, P. R., Wood, P. J. W., & Mills, H. E. (1983). Sadistic fantasy, sadistic behaviour and offending. *British Journal of Psychiatry, 143*, 20–29.

Mahoney, M. J., & DeMonbreun, B. G. (1977). Psychology of the scientist: An analysis of problem-solving bias. *Cognitive Therapy and Research, 1*, 229–238.

Maisch, H. (1972). *Incest.* New York: Stein & Day.

Malamuth, N. M. (1981). Rape proclivity among males. *Journal of Social Issues, 37*, 138–157.

Malamuth, N. M. (1984). Aggression against women: Cultural and individual causes. In N. M. Malamuth & E. Donnerstein (Eds.), *Pornography and sexual aggression* (pp. 19–52). New York: Academic Press.

Malamuth, N. M. (1986). Predictors of naturalistic sexual aggression. *Journal of Personality and Social Psychology, 5*, 953–962.

Malamuth, N. M. (1989a). The attraction to sexual aggression scale: Part One. *Journal of Sex Research, 26*, 26–49.

Malamuth, N. M. (1989b). The attraction to sexual aggression scale: Part Two. *Journal of Sex Research, 26*, 324–354.

Malamuth, N. M. (1989c). Sexually violent media, thought patterns, and antisocial behavior. *Public Communication and Behavior, 2*, 159–204.

Malamuth, N. M., & Billings, V. (1986). The functions and effects of pornography: Sexual communications versus the feminist models in light of research findings. In J. Bryant & D. Zillman (Eds.), *Perspectives on media effects* (pp. 83–108). Hillsdale, NJ: Erlbaum.

Malamuth, N. M., & Dean, K. E. (1991). Attraction to sexual aggression. In A. Parrot & L. Bechhofer (Eds.), *Acquaintance rape: The hidden crime* (pp. 229–247). New York: Wiley.

Malamuth, N. M., & Donnerstein, E. (1982). The effects of aggressive–pornographic mass media stimuli. In L. Berkowitz (Ed.), *Advances in experimental social psychology* (Vol. 15, pp. 103–136). New York: Academic Press.

Malamuth, N. M., & Spinner, B. (1980). A longitudinal content analysis of sexual violence in the best selling erotica magazines. *Journal of Sex Research, 16*, 226–237.

Maletzky, B. M. (1991a). *Treating the sexual offender.* Newbury Park, CA: Sage.

Maletzky, B. M. (1991b). The use of medroxyprogesterone acetate to assist in the treatment of sexual offenders. *Annals of Sex Research, 4*, 117–129.

Maletzky, B. M. (1995). Editorial: Standardization and the penile plethysmograph. *Sexual Abuse: A Journal of Research and Treatment, 7*, 5–7.

Maltz, M.D. (1984). *Recidivism.* New York: Academic Press.

Mann, J., Stenning, W., & Borman, C. (1992). The utility of the MMPI-2 with pedophiles. In E. Coleman, S. M. Dwyer, & N. J. Pallone (Eds.), *Sex offender treatment. Psychological and medical approaches* (pp. 59–74). New York: Haworth Press.

Marques, J. K. (1988). The sex offender treatment and evaluation project: California's new outcome study. In R. A. Prentky & V. L. Quinsey (Eds.), *Human sexual aggression: Current perspectives* (pp. 235–243). New York: New York Academy of Sciences.

Marques, J. K. (1995, September). *How to answer the question: Does sex offender treatment work?* Paper presented at the International Expert Conference on Sex Offenders: Issues, Research and Treatment, Utrecht, The Netherlands.

Marques, J. K., & Day, D. M. (1998, May). *Sex offender treatment and evaluation project. Progress report.* Sacramento: California Department of Mental Health.

Marques, J. K., Day, D. M., Nelson, C., & Miner, M. H. (1989). The Sex Offender Treatment and Evaluation

Project: California's relapse prevention program. In D. R. Laws (Ed.), *Relapse prevention with sex offenders* (pp. 247–267). New York: Guilford Press.

Marques, J. K., Day, D. M., Nelson, C., & West, M. A. (1993). Findings and recommendations from California's experimental treatment program. In G. C. Nagayama Hall, R. Hirschman, J. R. Graham, & M. S. Zaragoza (Eds.), *Sexual aggression: Issues in etiology, assessment, and treatment* (pp. 197–214). London: Taylor & Francis.

Marques, J. K., Day, D. M., Nelson, C., & West, M. A. (1994). Effects of cognitive behavioral treatment on sex offender recidivism: Preliminary results of a longitudinal study. *Criminal Justice and Behavior, 21,* 28–54.

Marshall, W. L. (1993). A revised approach to the treatment of men who sexually assault adult females. In G. C. Nagayama Hall, R. Hirschman, J. R. Graham, & M. S. Zaragoza (Eds.), *Sexual aggression: Issues in etiology, assessment, and treatment* (pp. 143–166). London: Taylor & Francis.

Marshall, W. L., Abel, G. G., & Quinsey, V. L. (1983). The assessment and treatment of sexual offenders. In S. Simon Jones (Ed.), *Sexual aggression and the law* (pp. 43–52). Criminology Research Centre, Simon Fraser University.

Marshall, W. L., & Barbaree, H. E. (1988). The long-term evaluation of a behavioral treatment program for child molesters. *Behaviour Research and Therapy, 26,* 499–511.

Marshall, W. L., & Barbaree, H. E. (1990). Outcome of comprehensive cognitive-behavioral treatment programs. In W. L. Marshall, D. R. Laws, & H. E. Barbaree (Eds.), *Handbook of sexual assault: Issues, theories, and treatment of the offender* (pp. 363–385). New York: Plenum Press.

Marshall, W. L., Barbaree, H. E., & Christophe, D. (1986). Sexual offenders against female children: Sexual preferences for age of victims and type of behaviour. *Canadian Journal of Behavioural Sciences, 18,* 424–439.

Marshall, W. L., & Christie, M. M. (1981). Pedophilia and aggression. *Criminal Justice and Behavior, 8,* 145–158.

Marshall, W. L., & Hall, G. C. N. (1995). The value of the MMPI in deciding forensic issues in accused sexual offenders. *Sexual Abuse: A Journal of Research and Treatment, 7,* 205–219.

Marshall, W. L., Jones, R., Ward, T., Johnston, P., & Barbaree, H. E. (1991). Treatment outcome with sex offenders. *Clinical Psychology Review, 11,* 465–485.

Matson, S., & Lieb, R. (1996). *Sex offender registration: A review of state laws.* Olympia: Washington State Institute for Public Policy.

Matson, S., & Lieb, R. (1997, October). *Megan's law: A review of state and federal legislation* (Document No. 97-10-1101). Olympia: Washington State Institute for Public Policy.

Matte, J. A. (1996). Psychophysiological veracity examinations using the polygraph in sex offenders. *Forensic psychophysiology using the polygraph: Scientific truth verification-lie detection* (pp. 596–627). Williamsville, NY: J.A.M. Publications.

Mazelan, P. M. (1980). Stereotypes and perceptions of the victims of rape. *Victimology: An International Journal, 5,* 121–132.

McCaghy, C. H. (1967). *Child molesters: A study of their careers as deviants.* New York: Holt, Rinehart & Winston.

McCann, I. L., Sakheim, D. K., & Abrahamson, D. J. (1988). Trauma and victimization: A model of psychological adaptation. *The Counseling Psychologist, 6,* 531–594.

McCann, J. T. (1992). Criminal personality profiling in the investigation of violent crime: Recent advances and future directions. *Behavioral Sciences and the Law, 10,* 475–481.

McCarthy, S. J. (1980). Pornography, rape, and the cult of macho. *Humanist, October,* 11–20.

McConaghy, N. (1967). Penile volume changes to moving pictures of male and female nudes in heterosexual and homosexual males. *Behavior Research and Therapy, 5,* 43–48.

McConaghy, N. (1989). Validity and ethics of penile circumference measures of sexual arousal: A critical review. *Archives of Sexual Behavior, 18,* 357–359.

McElroy, S. L., Pope, H. G., Hudson, J. I., Keck, P. E., & White, K. L. (1991). Kleptomania: A report of 20 cases. *American Journal of Psychiatry, 148,* 652–657.

McFall, R. M. (1990). The enhancement of social skills: An information-processing analysis. In W. L. Marshall, D. R. Laws & H. E. Barbaree (Eds.), *Handbook of sexual assault: Issues, theories, and treatment of the offender* (pp. 311–330). New York: Plenum Press.

McGarry, A. L., & Cotton, R. D. (1969). A study in civil commitment: The Massachusetts Sexually Dangerous Persons Act. *Harvard Journal on Legislation, 6,* 263–306.

McGrath, R. J. (1990). Assessment of sexual aggressors. Practical clinical interviewing strategies. *Journal of Interpersonal Violence, 5,* 507–519.

McLeer, S. V., Deblinger, E., Atkins, M. S., Foa, E. B., & Ralphe, D. L. (1988). Post-traumatic stress disorder in sexually abused children. *Journal of the American Academy of Child and Adolescent Psychiatry, 27*, 650–654.

McMahon, P. M. (2000). The public health approach to the prevention of sexual violence. *Sexual Abuse: A Journal of Research and Treatment, 12*, 27–36.

McMahon, P. M., & Puett, R. C. (1999). Child sexual abuse as a public health issue: Recommendations of an Expert Panel. *Sexual Abuse: A Journal of Research and Treatment, 11*, 257–266.

Medea, A., & Thompson, K. (1974). *Against rape.* New York: Farrar, Straus & Giroux.

Meehl, P. E., & Rosen, A. (1955). Antecedent probability and the efficiency of psychometric signs, patterns, or cutting scores. *Psychological Bulletin, 52*, 194–216.

Meeks, W. M. (1963). Criminal sexual psychopaths and sexually dangerous persons. *Corrective Psychiatry and Journal of Social Therapy, 9*(1), 22–27.

Megargee, E. I. (1981). Methodological problems in the prediction of violence. In J. Hays, T. Roberts, & K. Solway (Eds.), *Violence and the violent individual* (pp. 179–191). New York: Spectrum.

Mehrabian, A., & Epstein, N. (1972). A measure of emotional empathy. *Journal of Personality, 40*, 525–543.

Melella, J. T., Travin, S., & Cullen, K. (1989). Legal and ethical issues in the use of antiandrogens in treating sex offenders. *Bulletin of the American Academy of Psychiatry and the Law, 17*, 223–231.

Meloy, J. R. (1988). *The psychopathic mind. Origins, dynamics, and treatment.* Northvale, NJ: Aronson.

Melton, G. B., Petrila, J., Poythress, N. G., & Slobogin, C. (1987). *Psychological evaluations for the courts: A handbook for mental health professionals and attorneys.* New York: Guilford Press.

Mercy, J. A. (1999). Having new eyes: Viewing child sexual abuse as a public health problem. *Sexual Abuse: A Journal of Research and Treatment, 11*, 317–325.

Mercy, J. A., & O'Carroll, P. W. (1988). New directions in violence prediction: The public health arena. *Violence and Victims, 3*, 285–301.

Metz, C. E. (1978). Basic principles of ROC analysis. *Seminars in Nuclear Medicine, 8*, 283–298.

Meyer-Bahlburg, H. F. L. (1978). Behavioral effects of estrogen treatment in human males. *Pediatrics, 62*, 1171–1177.

Meyer-Bahlburg, H. F. L., & Ehrhardt, A. A. (1982). Prenatal sex hormones and human aggression: A review, and new data on progestogen effects. *Aggressive Behavior, 8*, 39–62.

Migeon, C. J., & Forest, M. G. (1983). Androgens in biological fluids. In B. Rothfield (Ed.), *Nuclear medicine in vitro* (2nd ed.). Philadelphia: Lippincott.

Miller, D. (1984). *A survey of recidivism research in the United States and Canada* (Publication No. 13709). Massachusetts Department of Correction.

Miller, G. A., Levin, D. N., Kozak, M. J., Cook, E. W., McLean, A., & Lang, P. J. (1987). Individual differences in imagery and the psychophysiology of emotion. *Cognition and Emotion, 1*, 367–390.

Miller, R. D. (1988, January). The *Terry* hearings to determine the release of offenders committed under Wisconsin's sex crimes law. *Wisconsin Bar Bulletin*, 17–71.

Miller, R. D. (1998). Forced administration of sex-drive reducing medications to sex offenders: Treatment or punishment? *Psychology, Public Policy, and Law, 4*, 175–199.

Miner, M. H., Marques, J. K., Day, D. M., & Nelson, C. (1990). Impaact of relapse prevention in treating sex offenders: Preliminary findings. *Annals of Sex Research, 3*, 165–185.

Moeller, T. P., Bachmann, G. A., & Moeller, J. R. (1993). The combined effects of physical, sexual, and emotional abuse during childhood: Long-term health consequences for women. *Child Abuse and Neglect, 17*, 623–640.

Mohr, J. W., Turner, R. E., & Jerry, M. B. (1964). *Pedophilia and exhibitionism.* Toronto: University of Toronto Press.

Monahan, J. (1978). Prediction research and the emergency commitment of dangerous mentally ill persons: A reconsideration. *American Journal of Psychiatry, 135*, 198–201.

Monahan, J. (1981). *Predicting violent behavior: An assessment of clinical techniques.* Newbury Park, CA: Sage.

Monahan, J. (1997). Clinical and actuarial predictions of violence. In D. Faigman, D. Kaye, M. Saks, & J. Sanders (Eds.), *Modern scientific evidence: The law and science of expert testimony* (Vol. 1). St. Paul, MN: West.

Monahan, J., & Steadman, H. J. (1996, September). Violent storms and violent people. *American Psychologist, 51*, 931–938.

Monahan, J., & Wexler, D. (1978). A definite maybe: Proof and probability in civil commitment. *Law and Human Behavior, 2*, 37–42.

Money, J. (1968). Discussion on hormonal inhibition of libido in male sex offenders. In R. P. Michael (Ed.), *Endocrinology and human behavior.* Oxford: Oxford University Press.

Money, J. (1970). Use of an androgen-depleting hormone in the treatment of male sex offenders. *Journal of Sex Research, 6,* 165–172.

Money, J. (1986). *Lovemaps.* New York: Irvington Publishers.

Money, J., & Bennett, R. G. (1981). Postadolescent paraphiliac sex offenders: Antiandrogenic and counseling therapy follow-up. *International Journal of Mental Health, 10,* 122–133.

Money, J., Ehrhardt, A. A., & Masica, D. N. (1968). Fetal feminization induced by androgen insensitivity in the testicular feminizing syndrome: Effect on marriage and maternalism. *Johns Hopkins Medical Journal, 123,* 105–114.

Money, J., Wiedeking, C., Walker, P., Migeon, C., Meyer, W., & Borgaonkar, D. (1975). 47, XYY and 46, XY males with antisocial and/or sex-offending behavior: Antiandrogen therapy plus counseling. *Psychoneuroendocrinology, 1,* 165–178.

Morgan, R. (1980). Theory and practice: Pornography and rape. In L. Lederer & A. Rich, (Eds.), *Take back the night: Women on pornography* (pp. 134–147). New York: Morrow.

Morris, N. (1982). *Madness and the criminal law.* Chicago: University of Chicago Press.

Mosher, D. L., & Anderson, R. D. (1986). Macho personality, sexual aggression, and reactions to guided imagery of realistic rape. *Journal of Research in Personality, 20,* 77–94.

Mosier, W. A., & Altieri, J. J. (1998, March–April). Clinical issues in forensic psychiatry. *The Forensic Examiner,* 19–23.

Mossman, D. (1994a). Further comments on portraying the accuracy of violence predictions. *Law and Human Behavior, 18,* 587–593.

Mossman, D. (1994b). Assessing predictions of violence: Being accurate about accuracy. *Journal of Consulting and Clinical Psychology, 62,* 783–792.

Mould, D. E. (1988). A critical analysis of recent research on violent erotica. *The Journal of Sex Research, 24,* 326–340.

Mugglestone, C. J. (1983). Drug treatment of hypersexuality. In D. Wheatley (Ed.), *Psychopharmacology and sexual disorders* (pp. 165–170). Oxford: Oxford University Press.

Muram, D., Miller, K., & Cutler, A. (1992). Sexual assault of the elderly victim. *Journal of Interpersonal Violence, 7,* 70–77.

Murphy, S. M. (1990). Rape, sexually transmitted diseases and human immunodeficiency virus infection. *International Journal of STD and AIDS, 1,* 79–82.

Murphy, W. D. (1990). Assessment and modification of cognitive distortions in sex offenders. In W. L. Marshall, D. R. Laws, & H. E. Barbaree (Eds.), *Handbook of sexual assault: Issues, theories, and treatment of the offender* (pp. 331–342). New York: Plenum Press.

Murphy, W. D., & Barbaree, H. E. (1994). *Assessments of sexual offenders by measures of erectile response: Psychometric properties and decision making.* Brandon, VT: Safer Society Press.

Murphy, W. J. (1998). Aggressive strategies for plaintiff's counsel—Debunking the "False Memory Syndrome" myth in traumatic memory cases. *Sexual Assault Report, 1,* 35–48.

Murray, M. A. F., Bancroft, J. H. H., Anderson, D. C., Tennent, T. G., & Carr, P. J. (1975). Endocrine changes in male sexual deviants after treatment with anti-androgens, oestrogens or tranquilizers. *Journal of Endocrinology, 67,* 179–188.

Murrin, M. R., & Laws, D. R. (1990). The influence of pornography on sexual crimes. In W. L. Marshall, D. R. Laws, & H. E. Barbaree (Eds.), *Handbook of sexual assault: Issues, theories, and treatment of the offender* (pp. 73–91). New York: Plenum Press.

Nash, M. R., Hulsey, T. L., Sexton, M. C., Harralson, T. L., & Lambert, W. (1993). Long-term sequelae of childhood sexual abuse: Perceived family environment, psychopathology, and dissociation. *Journal of Consulting and Clinical Psychology, 61,* 276–283.

National Conference on Sex Offender Registries. (1998, May). Proceedings of a BJS/SEARCH Conference (NCJ 168965). Washington, DC: U.S. Department of Justice, Bureau of Justice Statistics.

National Criminal Justice Association. (1997, October). *Sex offender community notification. Policy report.* Washington, DC: Author.

National Victim Center & Crime Victims Research and Treatment Center (1992, April 23). *Rape in America. A report to the nation.* Arlington, VA: Author.

Nedoma, K., Mellam, J., & Pondelickova, J. (1971). Sexual behavior and its development in pedophilic men. *Archives of Sexual Behavior, 1,* 267–271.

Neumann, D. A., Houskamp, B. M., Pollock, V. E., & Briere, J. (1996). The long-term sequelae of childhood sexual abuse in women: A meta-analytic review. *Child Maltreatment, 1,* 6–16.

Neumann, F., & Kalmus, J. (1991). *Hormonal treatment of sexual deviations.* Berlin: Diesbach Verlag.

Neumann, F., Von Berswordt-Wallrabe, R., Elger, W., & Steinbeck, H. (1968). Activities of anti-androgens: Experiments in prepuberal and puberal animals and in foetuses. In J. Tamm (Ed.), *Testosterone* (pp. 134–143). Proceedings of the Work Shop Conference, Tremsbuettel. Stuttgart: Thieme Verlag.

Newman, J. P., Schmitt, W. A., & Voss, W. D. (1997). The impact of motivationally neutral cues on psychopathic individuals: Assessing the generality of the Response Modulation Hypothesis. *Journal of Abnormal Psychology, 106,* 563–575.

Nichols, H. R., & Molinder, I. (1984). *Multiphasic Sex Inventory Manual: A test to assess the psychosexual characteristics of the sexual offender* (Research Edition Form A). Tacoma, WA: Nichols & Molinder.

Niezgoda, S., Loftus, P., & Burgess, A. W. (1998, January/February). CODIS-DNA profiling: A new tool against rapists. *Sexual Assault Report, 1,* 33–45.

Nisbett, R. E., & Borgida, E. (1975). Attribution and the psychology of prediction. *Journal of Personality and Social Psychology, 32,* 932–943.

Norris, F. H. (1992). Epidemiology of trauma: Frequency and impact of different potentially traumatic events on different demographic groups. *Journal of Consulting and Counseling Psychology, 60,* 409–418.

O'Brien, S. (1983). *Child pornography.* Dubuque, IA: Kendall/Hunt.

Offender Programs Report. (1999, March, April). Vol 2, No. 6. Kingston, NJ: Civic Research Institute.

Office of Justice Assistance, Research & Statistics. (1979). *How to protect yourself against sexual assault.* Washington, DC: U.S. Government Printing Office.

Ogata, S. N., Silk, K. R., Goodrich, S., Lohr, N. E., Westen, D., & Hill, E. M. (1990). Childhood sexual and physical abuse in adult patients with borderline personality disorder. *American Journal of Psychiatry, 147,* 1008–1013.

Omenn, G. S. (1997a). *Framework for environmental health risk management. Final report.* Vol. 1 of The Presidential/Congressional Commission on Risk Assessment and Risk Management. Available at the Riskworld website: http://www.riskworld.com.

Omenn, G. S. (1997b). *Risk assessment and risk management in regulatory decision-making. Final report.* Vol. 2 of The Presidential/Congressional Commission on Risk Assessment and Risk Management. Available at the Riskworld website: http://www.riskworld.com.

Ortmann, J. (1980). The treatment of sexual offenders. Castration and antihormone therapy. *International Journal of Law and Psychiatry, 3,* 443–451.

Overholser, J. C., & Beck, S. (1986). Multimethod assessment of rapists, child molesters, and three control groups on behavioral and psychological measures. *Journal of Consulting and Clinical Psychology, 54,* 682–687.

Pacht, A. R. (1976). The rapist in treatment: Professional myths and psychological realities. In M. J. Walker & S. L. Brodsky (Eds.), *Sexual assault: The victim of the rapists* (pp. 91–98). Lexington, MA: Lexington Books.

Pacht, A. R., & Cowden, J. E. (1974). An exploratory study of five hundred sex offenders. *Criminal Justice and Behavior, 1,* 13–20.

Pacht, A. R., Halleck, S. L., & Ehrmann, J. C. (1962). Diagnosis and treatment of the sexual offender: A nine year study. *American Journal of Psychiatry, 118,* 802–808.

Paitich, D., Langevin, R., Freeman, R., Mann, K., & Handy, L. (1977). The Clarke SHQ: A clinical sex history questionnaire for males. *Archives of Sexual Behavior, 6,* 421–436.

Pallone, N. (1990). *Rehabilitating criminal sexual psychopaths: Legislative mandates, clinical quandries.* New Brunswick, NJ: Transaction Publishers.

Palmer, R. L., Oppenheimer, R., Dignon, A., Chaloner, D. A., & Howells, K. (1990). Childhood sexual experiences with adults reported by women with eating disorders: An extended series. *British Journal of Psychiatry, 156,* 699–703.

Paone, D., Chavkin, W., Willets, I., Friedman, P., & Des Jarlais, D. (1992). The impact of sexual abuse: Implications for drug treatment. *Journal of Women's Health, 1,* 149–153.

Parke, R. D., & Slaby, R. G. (1983). The development of aggression. In E. M. Hetherington (Ed.), *Manual of child psychology. Socialization, personality, and social development* (Vol. 4, pp. 549–641). New York: Wiley.

Parker, H. (1984). Intrafamilial sexual child abuse: A study of the abusive father. *Dissertation Abstracts International, 45,* 3757A. (University Microfilms No. 85-03,876)

Parker, H., & Parker, S. (1986). Father–daughter sexual abuse: An emerging perspective. *American Journal of Orthopsychiatry, 56,* 531–549.

Patterson, C. M., & Newman, J. P. (1993). Reflectivity and learning from aversive events: Toward a psychological mechanism for the syndromes of disinhibition. *Psychological Review, 100,* 716–736.

Paveza, G. (1987, July). *Risk factors in father–daughter child sexual abuse: Findings from a case–control study.*

Paper presented at the Third National Family Violence Research Conference, Family Research Laboratory, Durham, NH.

Perilstein, R. D., Lipper, S., & Friedman, L. J. (1991). Three cases of paraphilias responsive to fluoxetine treatment. *Journal of Clinical Psychiatry, 52,* 169–170.

Peters, S. D. (1988). Child sexual abuse and later psychological problems. In G. E. Wyatt & G. J. Powell (Eds.), *Lasting effects of child sexual abuse* (pp. 101–117). Newbury Park, CA: Sage.

Pfohl, S. J. (1979). From whom will we be protected? Comparative approaches to the assessment of dangerousness. *International Journal of Law and Psychiatry, 2,* 55–78.

Phillips, D. P. (1974). The influence of suggestion on suicide: Substantive and theoretical implications of the Werther effect. *American Sociological Review, 39,* 340–354.

Phillips, D. P. (1979). Suicide, motor vehicle fatalities, and the mass media: Evidence toward a theory of suggestion. *American Sociological Review, 84,* 139–148.

Pinizzotto, A. J., & Finkel, N. J. (1990). Criminal personality profiling. An outcome and process study. *Law and Human Behavior, 14,* 215–233.

Pithers, W. D. (1990). Relapse prevention with sexual aggressors: A method for maintaining therapeutic gain and enhancing external supervision. In W. L. Marshall, D. R. Laws, & H. E. Barbaree (Eds.), *Handbook of sexual assault: Issues, theories, and treatment of the offender* (pp. 343–361). New York: Plenum Press.

Pithers, W. D. (1993). Treatment of rapists: Reinterpretation of early outcome data and exploratory constructs to enhance therapeutic efficacy. In G. C. N. Hall, R. Hirschman, J. R. Graham, & M. S. Zaragoza (Eds.), *Sexual aggression: Issues in etiology, assessment, and treatment* (pp. 167–196). London: Taylor & Francis.

Pithers, W. D., Gray, A., Busconi, A., & Houchens, P. (1998). Children with sexual behavior problems: Identification of five distinct child types and related treatment considerations. *Child Maltreatment, 3,* 384–406.

Pithers, W. D., & Laws, D. R. (1988). The penile plethysmograph: Uses and abuses in assessment and treatment of sexual aggressors. In *Sex offenders: Issues in treatment.* Washington, DC: National Institute of Corrections.

Plummer, C. (1984). *Preventing sexual abuse: What in-school programs teach children.* Unpublished manuscript.

Polanyi, M. (1964). *Personal knowledge. Towards a post-critical philosophy.* New York: Harper & Row.

Polusny, M. A., & Follette, V. M. (1996). Remembering childhood sexual abuse: A national survey of psychologists' clinical practices, beliefs, and personal experiences. *Professional Psychology. Research Practice, 27,* 41–52.

Popper, K. R. (1975). *The logic of scientific discovery.* London: Hutchinson.

Porch, T. L., & Petretic-Jackson, P. A. (1986, August). *Child sexual assault prevention: Evaluation of parent education workshops.* Paper presented at the meeting of the American Psychological Association, Washington, DC.

Porter, F. S., Blick, L. C., & Sgroi, S. M. (1982). Treatment of the sexually abused child. In S. M. Sgroi (Ed.), *Handbook of clinical intervention in child sexual abuse.* Lexington, MA: Lexington Books.

Prentky, R. A. (1985). The neurochemistry and neuroendocrinology of sexual aggression: Review and metatheory. In D. P. Farrington & J. Gunn (Eds.), *Aggression and dangerousness* (pp. 7–55). New York: Wiley.

Prentky, R. A. (1996). Community notification and constructive risk reduction. *Journal of Interpersonal Violence, 11,* 295–298.

Prentky, R. A. (1997). Arousal reduction in sexual offenders: A review of antiandrogen interventions. *Sexual Abuse: A Journal of Research and Treatment, 9,* 335–347.

Prentky, R. A. (1999). Child sexual molestation. In V. B. Van Hasselt, & M. Hersen (Eds.), *Handbook of psychological approaches with violent offenders: Contemporary strategies and issues* (pp. 267–300). New York: Kluwer Academic/Plenum Publishers.

Prentky, R. A., & Burgess, A. W. (1990). Rehabilitation of child molesters: A cost-benefit analysis. *American Journal of Orthopsychiatry, 60,* 108–117.

Prentky, R. A., & Burgess, A. W. (1991). Hypothetical biological substrates of a fantasy-based drive mechanism for repetitive sexual aggression. In A. W. Burgess (Ed.), *Rape and sexual assault III. A research handbook* (pp. 235–256). New York: Garland Publishing.

Prentky, R. A., & Burgess, A. W. (1992). Rehabilitation of child molesters: A cost–benefit analysis. In A. W. Burgess (Ed.), *Child trauma I: Issues and research* (pp. 417–442). New York: Garland Press.

Prentky, R. A., Burgess, A. W., & Carter, D. L. (1986). Victim responses by rapist type: An empirical and clinical analysis. *Journal of Interpersonal Violence, 1,* 688–695.

Prentky, R. A., Burgess, A. W., Rokous, F., Lee, A., Hartman, C., Ressler, R., & Douglas, J. (1989). Serial vs. solo sexual homicide: The role of fantasy. *American Journal of Psychiatry, 146,* 887–891.

Prentky, R. A., Cohen, M. L., & Seghorn, T. K. (1985). Development of a rational taxonomy for the classification of sexual offenders: Rapists. *Bulletin of the American Academy of Psychiatry and the Law, 13*, 39–70.

Prentky, R. A., & Edmunds, S. B. (1997). *Assessing sexual abuse: A resource guide for practitioners*. Brandon, VT: Safer Society Press.

Prentky, R. A., Harris, B., Frizzell, K., & Righthand, S. (2000). Development and validation of an actuarial instrument for assessing risk among juvenile sex offenders. *Sexual Abuse: A Journal of Research and Treatment, 12*, 71–93.

Prentky, R. A., & Knight, R. A. (1986). Impulsivity in the lifestyle and criminal behavior of sexual offenders. *Criminal Justice and Behavior, 13*, 141–164.

Prentky, R. A., & Knight, R. A. (1991). Identifying critical dimensions for discriminating among rapists. *Journal of Consulting and Clinical Psychology, 59*, 643–661.

Prentky, R. A., & Knight, R. A. (1993). Age of onset of sexual assault: Criminal and life history correlates. In G. C. N. Hall, R. Hirschman, J. R. Graham, & M. S. Zaragoza (Eds.), *Sexual aggression: Issues in etiology, assessment, and treatment* (pp. 43– 62). London: Taylor & Francis.

Prentky, R. A., Knight, R. A., & Lee, A. F. S. (1997). Risk factors associated with recidivism among extrafamilial child molesters. *Journal of Consulting and Clinical Psychology, 65*, 141–149.

Prenkty, R. A., Knight, R., Lee, A. F. S., & Cerce, D. (1995). Predictive validity of lifestyle impulsivity for rapists. *Criminal Justice and Behavior, 22*, 106–128.

Prentky, R. A., Knight, R. A., & Rosenberg, R. (1988). Validation analyses on the MTC Taxonomy for Rapists: Disconfirmation and reconceptualization. In R. A. Prentky & V. Quinsey (Eds.), *Human sexual aggression: Current perspectives* (pp. 21–40). New York: New York Academy of Sciences.

Prentky, R. A., Knight, R. A., Rosenberg, R., & Lee, A. (1989). A path analytic approach to the validation of a taxonomic system for classifying child molesters. *Journal of Quantitative Criminology, 5*, 231–257.

Prentky, R. A., Knight, R. A., Sims-Knight, J. E., Straus, H., Rokous, F., & Cerce, D. (1989). Developmental antecedents of sexual aggression. *Development and Psychopathology, 1*, 153–169.

Prentky, R. A., Lee, A. F. S., Knight, R. A., & Cerce, D. (1997). Recidivism rates among child molesters and rapists: A methodological analysis. *Law and Human Behavior, 21*, 635–659.

Presidential/Congressional Commission on Risk Assessment and Risk Management. (1997a). *Framework for environmental health risk management*. Final Report Volume 1. Washington, DC.

Presidential/Congressional Commission on Risk Assessment and Risk Management. (1997b). *Risk assessment and risk management in regulatory decision-making*. Final Report Volume 2. Washington, DC.

President's Commission on Obscenity and Pornography. (1970). *Technical reports of the Commission on Obscenity and Pornography*. Washington, DC: U.S. Government Printing Office.

Pribor, E. F., & Dinwiddie, S. H. (1992). Psychiatric correlates of incest in childhood. *American Journal of Psychiatry, 1*, 52–56.

Priest, R., & Smith, A. (1992). Counseling adult sex offenders: Unique challenges and treatment paradigms. *Journal of Counseling and Development, 71*, 27–32.

Proulx, J., Pellerin, B., Paradis, Y., McKibben, A., Aubut, J., & Ouimet, M. (1997). *Sexual Abuse: A Journal of Research and Treatment, 9*, 7–27.

Pullen, S. (1996). Using the polygraph Part One: An overview. In K. English, S. Pullen, & L. Jones (Eds.), *Managing adult sex offenders on probation and parole: A containment approach* (pp. 15/3–15/6). Lexington, KY: American Probation and Parole Association/The Council of State Governments.

Pynoos, R. S. (1994). Traumatic stress and developmental psychopathology in children and adolescents. In R. S. Pynoos (Ed.), *Posttraumatic stress disorder: A clinical review* (pp. 65–98). Lutherville, MD: Sidran Press.

Quay, H. C. (1975). Classification in the treatment of delinquency and antisocial behavior. In N. Hobbes (Ed.), *Issues in the classification of children* (Vol. 1). San Francisco: Jossey–Bass.

Queen's Bench Foundation. (1976). *Rape victimization study: Final report*. San Francisco: Author.

Quinn, T. M. (1984). Father–daughter incest: An ecological model. *Dissertation Abstracts International, 45*, 3957B. (University Microfilms No. 84-29,752)

Quinsey, V. (1977). The assessment and treatment of child molesters: A review. *Canadian Psychological Review, 18*, 204–220.

Quinsey, V. L. (1984). Sexual aggression: Studies of offenders against women. In D. Weisstub (Ed.), *Law and mental health: International perspectives* (pp. 84–121). New York: Pergamon Press.

Quinsey, V. L. (1986). Men who have sex with children. In D. Weisstub (Ed.), *Law and mental health: International perspectives* (pp. 140–172). New York: Pergamon Press.

Quinsey, V. L., & Chaplin, T. C. (1988). Preventing faking in phallometric assessments of sexual preference. In R. A. Prentky & V. L. Quinsey (Eds.), *Human sexual aggression: Current perspectives* (pp. 49–58). New York: New York Academy of Sciences.

Quinsey, V. L., Chaplin, T. C., Maguire, A. M., & Upfold, D. (1987). The behavioral treatment of rapists and child molesters. In E. K. Morris & C. J. Braukmann (Eds.), *Behavioral approaches to crime and delinquency: Application, research, and theory* (pp. 363–382). New York: Plenum Press.

Quinsey, V. L., Chaplin, T. C., & Upfold, D. (1984). Sexual arousal to nonsexual violence and sadomasochistic themes among rapists and non-sex-offenders. *Journal of Consulting and Clinical Psychology, 52,* 651–657.

Quinsey, V. L., Chaplin, T. C., & Varney, G. (1981). A comparison of rapists' and non-sex offenders' sexual preferences for mutually consenting sex, rape, and physical abuse of women. *Behavioral Assessment, 3,* 127–135.

Quinsey, V. L., & Earls, C. M. (1990). The modification of sexual preferences. In W. L. Marshall, D. R. Laws, & H. E. Barbaree (Eds.), *Handbook of sexual assault: Issues, theories, and treatment of the offender* (pp. 279–295). New York: Plenum Press.

Quinsey, V. L., Harris, G. T., Rice, M. E., & Cormier, C. A. (1998). *Violent offenders. Appraising and managing risk.* Washington, DC: American Psychological Association.

Quinsey, V. L., Lalumiere, M., Rice, M. E., & Harris, G. T. (1995). Predicting sexual offenses. In J. C. Campbell (Ed.), *Assessing dangerousness: Violence by sexual offenders, batterers, and child abusers* (pp. 114–137). Newbury Park, CA: Sage.

Quinsey, V. L., Rice, M. E., & Harris, G. T. (1995). Actuarial prediction of sexual recidivism. *Journal of Interpersonal Violence, 10,* 85–105.

Rabasca, L. (1999, April). Child-abuse prevention efforts still too few. *American Psychological Association Monitor,* 30.

Rada, R. T. (1976). Alcoholism and the child molester. *Annals of the New York Academy of Sciences, 273,* 492–496.

Rada, R. T. (Ed.). (1978a). *Clinical aspects of the rapist.* New York: Grune & Stratton.

Rada, R. T. (1978b). Classification of the rapist. In R. T. Rada (Ed.), *Clinical aspects of the rapist* (pp. 117–132). New York: Grune & Stratton.

Rada, R. T. (1981). Plasma androgens and the sex offender. *Bulletin of the American Academy of Psychiatry and the Law, 8,* 456–464.

Rada, R. T., Laws, D. R., & Kellner, R. (1976). Plasma testosterone levels in the rapist. *Psychosomatic Medicine, 38,* 257–268.

Rada, R. T., Laws, D. R., Kellner, R., Stivastava, L., & Peake, G. (1983). Plasma androgens in violent and nonviolent sex offenders. *Bulletin of the American Academy of Psychiatry and the Law, 11,* 149–158.

Radzinowicz, L. (1957). *Sexual offenses.* London: Macmillan & Co.

Random House dictionary of the English language. (1967). New York: Random House.

Ransley, M. T. (1980). Repeal of the Wisconsin Sex Crimes Act. *Wisconsin Law Review, 1980*(5), 941–975.

Rapaport, K., & Burkhart, B. R. (1984). Personality and attitudinal characteristics of sexually coercive college males. *Journal of Abnormal Psychology, 93,* 216–221.

Reinisch, J. M. (1981). Prenatal exposure to synthetic progestins increases potential for aggression in humans. *Science, 211,* 1171–1173.

Reinisch, J. M., & Sanders, S. A. (1982). Early barbiturate exposure: The brain, sexually dimorphic behavior and learning. *Neuroscience and Biobehavioral Reviews, 6,* 311–319.

Reiss, A. (1951). The accuracy, efficiency, and validity of a prediction instrument. *American Journal of Sociology, 61,* 552–561.

Reppucci, N. D., & Haugaard, J. J. (1989). Prevention of child sexual abuse. *American Psychologist, 44,* 1266–1275.

Resick, P. A. (1987). Psychological effects of victimizaiton: Implications for the criminal justice system. *Crime and Delinquency, 33,* 468–478.

Resick, P. A. (1990). Victims of sexual assault. In A. J. Lurigo, W. G. Skogan, & R. C. Davis (Eds.), *Victims of crime: Problems, policies, and programs* (pp. 69–85). Newbury Park, CA: Sage.

Resick, P. A. (1993). The psychological impact of rape. *Journal of Interpersonal Violence, 8,* 223–255.

Ressler, R. K., & Burgess, A. W. (1985). Violent crimes. *FBI Law Enforcement Bulletin, 54,* 1–31.

Ressler, R. K., Burgess, A. W., & Douglas, J. E. (1988). *Sexual homicide: Patterns and motives.* New York: Free Press.

Ressler, R. K., Burgess, A. W., Douglas, J. E., Hartman, C. R., & D'Agostino, R. (1986). Sexual killers and their victims: Identifying patterns through crime scene analysis. *Journal of Interpersonal Violence, 1*, 288–308.

Rice, M. E. (1997). Violent offender research and implications for the criminal justice system. *American Psychologist, 52*, 414–423.

Rice, M. E., & Harris, G. T. (1995). Violent recidivism: Assessing predictive validity. *Journal of Consulting and Clinical Psychology, 63*, 737–748.

Rice, M. E., & Harris, G. T. (1997). Cross-validation and extension of the Violence Risk Appraisal Guide for child molesters and rapists. *Law and Human Behavior, 21*, 231–241.

Rice, M. E., Harris, G. T., & Quinsey, V. L. (1990). A follow-up of rapists assessed in a maximum security psychiatric facility. *Journal of Interpersonal Violence, 5*, 435–448.

Rice, M. E., Quinsey, V. L., & Harris, G. T. (1991). Sexual recidivism among child molesters released from a maximum security psychiatric institution. *Journal of Consulting and Clinical Psychology, 59*, 381–386.

Richer, M., & Crismon, M. L. (1993). Pharmacotherapy of sexual offenders. *Annals of Pharmacotherapy, 27*, 316–320.

Riger, S., & Gordon, M. T. (1981). The fear of rape: A study in social control. *Journal of Social Issues, 37*, 71–92.

Rist, K. (1979). Incest: Theoretical and clinical views. *American Journal of Orthopsychiatry, 49*, 680–691.

Rivera, B., & Widom, C. S. (1990). Childhood victimization and violent offending. *Violence and Victims, 5*, 19–35.

Roberts, L. (1991). Fight erupts over DNA fingerprinting. *Science, 254*, 1721–1723.

Roberts, L. (1992). DNA fingerprinting: Academy reports. *Science, 256*, 300–301.

Rocky, S., & Neri, R. O. (1968). Comparative biological properties of SCH 12600: (6-chloro 4,6 pregnadien 16-methylene 17-alpha-ol-3,20-dione-17-acetate) and chlormadinone acetate. *Federation Proceedings, 27*, 624 (Abstract No. 2300).

Roe, K. M., & Schwartz, M. (1996). Characteristics of previously forgotten memories of sexual abuse: A descriptive study. *Journal of Psychiatry and Law, 24*, 189–206.

Roesler, T. A., & Wind, T. W. (1994). Telling the secret: Adult women describe their disclosures of incest. *Journal of Interpersonal Violence, 9*, 327–338.

Rogers, C. M., & Terry, T. (1984). Clinical interventions with boy victims of sexual abuse. In I. Stuart & J. Greer (Eds.), *Victims of sexual aggression* (pp. 91–104). New York: Van Nostrand–Reinhold.

Rogers, R. (1986). *Conducting insanity evaluations.* New York: Van Nostrand–Reinhold.

Rogers, R., Salekin, R. T., & Sewell, K. W. (1999). Validation of the Millon Clinical Multiaxial Inventory for Axis II Disorders: Does it meet the Daubert Standard? *Law and Human Behavior, 23*, 425–443.

Romero, J. J., & Meyer-Williams, L. M. (1985). Recidivism among convicted sex offenders: A ten-year follow-up study. *Federal Probation, 49*, 58–64.

Rose, R. M. (1978). Neuroendocrine correlates of sexual and aggressive behaviour in humans. In M. A. Lipton, A. DiMascio, & K. F. Killam (Eds.), *Psychopharmacology: A generation of progress* (pp. 541–552). New York: Raven Press.

Rosenberg, R. (1981). An empirical determination of sexual offender subtypes. In R. A. Prentky (Chair), *Assessment of subtypes of rapists and pedophiles: Implications for treatment.* Symposium presented at the meeting of the American Psychological Association, Los Angeles.

Rosenberg, R., Knight, R. A., Prentky, R. A., & Lee, A. (1988). Validating the components of a taxonomic system for rapists: A path analytic approach. *Bulletin of the American Academy of Psychiatry and the Law, 16*, 169–185.

Rosenfeld, A. (1977). Sexual misuse and the family. *Victimology: An International Journal, 2*, 226–235.

Rosenfeld, A. A., Nadelson, C. C., Krieger, M., & Backman, J. H. (1977). Incest and sexual abuse of children. *Journal of Child Psychiatry, 16*, 327–339.

Rosenfeld, J. P., Angell, A., Johnson, M., & Qian, J. (1991). An ERP-based, control-question lie detector analog: Algorithms for discriminating effects within individuals' average waveforms. *Psychophysiology, 28*, 319–335.

Rosenfeld, J. P., Cantwell, B., Nasman, V. T., Wojdac, V., Ivanov, S., & Mazzeri, L. (1988). A modified, event-related potential-based guilty knowledge test. *International Journal of Neuroscience, 24*, 157–161.

Rosenfeld, J. P., Nasman, V. T., Whalen, R., Cantwell, B., & Mazzeri, L. (1987). Late vertex positivity in event-related potentials as a guilty knowledge indicator: A new method of lie detection. *International Journal of Neuroscience, 34*, 125–129.

Rosler, A., & Witztum, E. (1998). Treatment of men with paraphilia with a long-acting analogue of gonadotropin-releasing hormone. *New England Journal of Medicine, 338*, 416–422.

Ross, C. A., Anderson, G., Heber, S., & Norton, G. R. (1990). Dissociation and abuse among multiple personality patients, prostitutes, and exotic dancers. *Hospital and Community Psychiatry, 41*, 328–330.

Ross, C. A., Miller, S. D., Reagor, P., Bjornson, L., Fraser, G. A., & Anderson, G. (1991). Abuse histories in 102 cases of multiple personality disorder. *Canadian Journal of Psychiatry, 36*, 97–101.

Ross, C. A., Norton, G. R., & Wozney, K. (1989). Multiple personality disorder: An analysis of 236 cases. *Canadian Journal of Psychiatry, 34*, 413–418.

Ross, K. P., & Hochberg, J. M. (1978, Spring). Constitutional challenges to the commitment and release procedures under Massachusetts General Laws Chapter 123A, the "Sexually Dangerous Persons" Act. *New England Journal on Prison Law, 4*(2), 253–307.

Roth, S., & Lebowitz, L. (1988). The experience of sexual trauma. *Journal of Traumatic Stress, 1*, 79–107.

Rothbaum, B. O., Foa, E. B., Riggs, D. S., Murdock, T., & Walsh, W. (1992). A prospective examination of posttraumatic stress disorder in rape victims. *Journal of Traumatic Stress, 5*, 455–475.

Rousseau, L., Couture, M., Dupont, A., Labrie, F., & Couture, N. (1990). Effect of combined androgen blockade with an LHRH agonist and flutamide in one severe case of male exhibitionism. *Canadian Journal of Psychiatry, 35*, 338–341.

Rowan, A. B., Foy D. W., Rodriguez N., & Ryan, S. (1994). Posttraumatic stress disorder in a clinical sample of adults sexually abused as children. *Child Abuse and Neglect, 18*, 51–61.

Rubey, R., Brady, K. T., & Norris, G. T. (1993). Clomipramine treatment of sexual preoccupation [Letter]. *Journal of Clinical Psychopharmacology, 13*, 158–159.

Rubin, R. T., Mandell, A. J., & Crandall, P. H. (1966). Corticosteroid responses to limbic stimulation in man: Localization of stimulus sites. *Science, 153*, 767–768.

Ruch, L. O., & Chandler, S. M. (1983). Sexual assault trauma during the acute phase: An exploratory model and multivariate analysis. *Journal of Health and Social Behavior, 24*, 174–185.

Ruch, L. O., Gartnell, J. W., Armedeo, S., & Coyne, B. J. (1991). The sexual assault symptom scale: Measuring self-reported sexual assault trauma in the emergency room. *Psychological Assessment, 3*, 3–8.

Ruch, L. O., & Leon, J. J. (1983). Sexual assault trauma and trauma change. *Women and Health, 8*, 5–21.

Rule, B. G., & Ferguson, T. J. (1986). The effects of media violence on attitudes, emotions, and cognitions. *Journal of Social Issues, 42*, 29–50.

Russell, D. E. H. (1975). *The politics of rape: The victim's perspective*. New York: Stein & Day.

Russell, D. E. H. (1980). Pornography and violence: What does the new research say? In L. Lederer & A. Rich (Eds.), *Take back the night: Women on pornography* (pp. 218–238). New York: Morrow.

Russell, D. E. H. (1982). The prevalence and incidence of forcible rape and attempted rape of females. *Victimology, 7*, 81–93.

Russell, D. E. H. (1984). *Sexual exploitation: Rape, child sexual abuse, and workplace harassment*. Newbury Park, CA: Sage.

Russell, D. E. H., & Howell, N. (1983). The prevalence of rape in the United States revisited. *Signs: Journal of Women in Culture and Society, 8*, 688–695.

Russell, D. E. H., & Vandeven, N. (Eds.) (1976). *Crimes against women: Proceedings from the international tribunal*. Millbrae: Les Femmes.

Sadoff, R. L. (1964). Psychiatric views of the sexual psychopath statutes. *Corrective Psychiatry and Journal of Social Therapy, 10*(5), 242–255.

Salekin, R. T., Rogers, R., & Sewell, K. W. (1996). A review and meta-analysis of the Psychopathy Checklist and Psychopathy Checklist-Revised: Predictive validity of dangerousness. *Clinical Psychology: Science and Practice, 3*, 203–215.

Sales, E., Baum, M., & Shore, B. (1984). Victim readjustment following assault. *Journal of Social Issues, 37*, 5–27.

Sanday, P. R. (1981). The socio-cultural context of rape: A cross-cultural study. *Journal of Social Issues, 37*, 5–27.

Sandifer, M. G., Hordern, A., & Green, L. M. (1970). The psychiatric interview: The impact of the first three minutes. *American Journal of Psychiatry, 126*, 968–973.

Sano, K., Sekino, H., & Mayanagi, Y. (1972). Results of stimulation and destruction of the posterior hypothalamus in cases with violent aggressive, or restless behaviors. In E. Hitchcock, L. Laittinen, & K. Vaernet (Eds.), *Psychosurgery* (pp. 57–75). Springfield, IL: Charles C. Thomas.

Sansonnet-Hayden, H., Haley G., Marriage, K., & Fine, S. (1987). Sexual abuse and psychopathology in hospitalized adolescents. *Journal of the American Academy of Child and Adolescent Psychiatry, 26*, 753–757.

SAS/STAT User's Guide, Version 6, Fourth Edition, *v* 2. (1994). Cary, NC, SAS Institute.

Schecter, J. O., Schwartz, H. P., & Greenfield, D. G. (1987). Sexual assault and anorexia nervosa. *International Journal of Eating Disorders, 5*, 313–316.

Schiller, G., & Marques, J. (1998, October). *The California Actuarial Risk Assessment Tables (CARAT) for rapists and child molesters.* Paper presented at the Annual Meeting of the Association for Treatment of Sexual Abusers, Vancouver, Canada.

Schklar, J., & Diamond, S. S. (1999). Juror reactions to DNA evidence: Errors and expectancies. *Law and Human Behavior, 23*(2), 159–184.

Schlank, A. M. (1995). The utility of the MMPI and the MSI for identifying a sexual offender typology. *Sexual Abuse: A Journal of Research and Treatment, 7*, 185–194.

Schlesinger, L. B., & Revitch, E. (1983). *Sexual dynamics of antisocial behavior.* Springfield, IL: Charles C. Thomas.

Schneider, B. (1981). Validation of sex offender subtypes through personality assessment. In R.A. Prentky (Chair), *Assessment of subtypes of rapists and pedophiles: Implications for treatment.* Symposium presented at the meeting of the American Psychological Association, Los Angeles.

Schneider, J. G. (1994, August). Legal issues involving "repressed memory" of childhood sexual abuse. *The Psychologist's Legal Update, 5*, 3–16.

Schopp, R. F. (1998). Civil commitment and sexual predators: Competence and condemnation. *Psychology, Public Policy, and Law, 4*, 323–376.

Schulhofer, S. J. (1998). *Unwanted sex: The culture of intimidation and the failure of law.* Cambridge, MA: Harvard University Press.

Schultz, L. G., & DeSavage, J. (1975). Rape and rape attitudes on a college campus. In L. G. Schultz (Ed.), *Rape victimology* (pp. 77–90). Springfield, IL: Charles C. Thomas.

Schultz, R., Braun, B. G., & Kluft, R. P. (1989). Multiple personality disorder: Phenomenology of selected variables in comparison to major depression. *Dissociation, 2*, 45–51.

Schwartz, B. K. (1988). *A practitioner's handbook for treating the incarcerated male sex offender.* Washington, DC: National Institute of Corrections, Department of Justice.

Schwartz, B. K. (1999, March/April). Limited resources and the treatment of psychopathic (sex) offenders. *Offender Programs Report, 2*, 81–93.

Schwartz, B. K., & Cellini, H. R. (Eds.). (1995). *The sex offender: Correction, treatment, and legal practices.* Kingston, NJ: Civic Research Institute.

Schwartz, B. K., & Cellini, H. R. (Eds.). (1997). *The sex offender: New insights, treatment innovations, and legal developments* (Vol. 2). Kingston, NJ: Civic Research Institute.

Schwartz, M. D., & Clear, T. R. (1978). Feminism and rape law reform. *Bulletin of the American Academy of Psychiatry and the Law, 6*(3), 313–321.

Schwendinger, J. R., & Schwendinger, H. (1974). Rape myths: In legal, theoretical, and everyday practice. *Crime and Social Justice, 1*, 18–26.

Scott, J. E., & Cuvelier, S. J. (1987). Sexual violence in Playboy Magazine: A longitudinal content analysis. *Journal of Sex Research, 23*, 534–539.

Scott, J. E., & Schwalm, L. A. (1988). Rape rates and the circulation rates of adult magazines. *Journal of Sex Research, 24*, 241–250.

Scott, R. L., & Stone, D. A. (1986). MMPI profile constellations in incest families. *Journal of Consulting and Clinical Psychology, 54*, 364–368.

Sechrest, L. (1987). Classification for treatment. In D. M. Gottfredson & M. Tonry (Eds.), *Prediction and classification* (pp. 293–322). Chicago: University of Chicago Press.

Segal, Z. V., & Marshall, W. L. (1985). Heterosexual social skills in a population of rapists and child molesters. *Journal of Consulting and Clinical Psychology, 53*, 55–63.

Segal, Z. V., & Stermac, L. E. (1990). The role of cognition in sexual assault. In W. L. Marshall, D. R. Laws, & H. E. Barbaree (Eds.), *Handbook of sexual assault: Issues, theories, and treatment of the offender* (pp. 161–174). New York: Plenum Press.

Seghorn, T. K., & Cohen, M. (1980). The psychology of the rape assailant. In W. Cerran, A. L. McGarry, & C. Petty (Eds.), *Modern legal medicine, psychiatry, and forensic science* (pp. 533–551). Philadelphia: Davis.

Seghorn, T. K., Prentky, R. A., & Boucher, R. J. (1987). Childhood sexual abuse in the lives of sexually aggressive offenders. *Journal of the American Academy of Child and Adolescent Psychiatry, 26*, 262–267.

Segreaves, R. T. (1989). Effects of psychotropic drugs on human erection and ejaculation. *Archives of General Psychiatry, 46*, 275–284.

Serin, R. C. (1991). Psychopathy and violence in criminals. *Journal of Interpersonal Violence, 6*, 423–431.

Serin, R. C. (1996). Violent recidivism in criminal psychopaths. *Law and Human Behavior, 20*, 207–217.

Serin, R. C., & Amos, N. L. (1995). The role of psychopathy in the assessment of dangerousness. *International Journal of Law and Psychiatry, 18*, 231–238.

Serin, R. C., Barbaree, H. E., Seto, M., Malcolm, B., & Peacock, E. (1997, May). *A model for a clinically-informed risk assessment strategy for sex offenders* (Research Report No. 56). Ottawa: Correctional Service of Canada.

Serin, R. C., Malcolm, P. B., Khanna, A., & Barbaree, H. E. (1994). Psychopathy and deviant sexual arousal in incarcerated sexual offenders. *Journal of Interpersonal Violence, 9*, 3–11.

Serin, R. C., Malcolm, P. B., Khanna, A., & Barbaree, H. E. (1997). *Psychopathy and sexual deviance: Implications for sex offender risk assessment and treatment outcome.* Paper presented at the 16th Annual Research and Treatment Conference of the Association for the Treatment of Sexual Abusers, Arlington, VA.

Seto, M. C., Barbaree, H. E., Serin, R. C., & Malcolm, B. (1997). *Applying a differentiated assessment model to treatment outcome.* Paper presented at the 16th Annual Research and Treatment Conference of the Association for the Treatment of Sexual Abusers, Arlington, VA.

Sgroi, S. M. (1982). *Handbook of clinical intervention in child sexual abuse.* Lexington, MA: Lexington Books.

Shah, S. A. (1981). Dangerousness: Conceptual, prediction and public policy issues. In J. R. Hays, T. K. Roberts, & K. S. Solway (Eds.), *Violence and the violent individual* (pp. 151–178). Jamaica, NY: SP Medical & Scientific Books.

Shapiro, D. L. (1991). *Forensic psychological assessment: An integrative approach.* Boston: Allyn & Bacon.

Shealy, L., Kalichman, S. C., Henderson, M. C., Szymanowski, D., & McKee, G. (1991). MMPI profile subtypes of incarcerated sex offenders against children. *Violence and Victims, 6*, 201–212.

Silberman, C. E. (1978). *Criminal violence, criminal justice.* New York: Random House.

Silbert, M. H., & Pines, A. M. (1981). Sexual child abuse as an antecedent to prostitution. *Child Abuse and Neglect, 5*, 407–411.

Silbert, M. H., & Pines, A. M. (1984). Pornography and sexual abuse of women. *Sex Roles, 10*, 857–868.

Simkins, L., Ward, W., Bowman, S., & Rinck, C. M. (1989). The Multiphasic Sex Inventory: Diagnosis and prediction of treatment response in child sexual abusers. *Annals of Sex Research, 2*, 205–226.

Simon, N. G. (1981). Hormones and human aggression: A comparative perspective. *International Journal of Mental Health, 10*, 60–74.

Singer, J. L. (1966). *Daydreaming.* New York: Random House.

Slovic, P. (1987). Perception of risk. *Science, 236*, 280–285.

Smeaton, G., & Byrne, D. (1987). The effects of R-rated violence and erotica, individual differences, and victim characteristics on acquaintance rape proclivity. *Journal of Research in Personality, 21*, 171–184.

Smith, D. G. (1976). The social content of pornography. *Journal of Communication, 26*, 16–33.

Smith, D., & Over, R. (1987). Male sexual arousal as a function of the content and the vividness of erotic fantasy. *Psychophysiology, 24*, 334–339.

Somoza, E., & Mossman, D. (1990). Introduction to neuro-psychiatric decision-making: Binary diagnostic tests. *Journal of Neuropsychiatry and Clinical Neurosciences, 2*, 297–300.

Soothill, K. L., & Gibbens, T. C. N. (1978). Recidivism of sexual offenders: A re-appraisal. *British Journal of Criminology, 18*, 267–276.

Soothill, K. L., Jack, A., & Gibbens, T. C. N. (1976). Rape: A 22-year cohort study. *Medicine, Science and Law, 16*, 62–69.

Spodak, M. K., Falck, Z. A., & Rappeport, J. R. (1978). The hormonal treatment of paraphiliacs with Depo-Provera. *Criminal Justice and Behavior, 5*, 304–314.

Stahl, F., Gotz, F., Poppe, I., Amendt, P., & Dorner, G. (1978). Pre- and early postnatal testosterone levels in rat and human. In G. Dorner & M. Kawakami (Eds.), *Hormones and brain development* (pp. 99–109). Amsterdam: Elsevier/North-Holland.

Steadman, H. J., & Cocozza, J. (1978). Criminology and psychiatry, dangerousness and the repetitively violent offender. *Journal of Criminal Law and Criminology, 69*, 226–231.

Stein, D. J., Hollander, E., Anthony, D. T., Schneier, F. R., Fallon, M. D., Liebowitz, M. R., & Klein, D. F. (1992). Serotonergic medications for sexual obessions, sexual addictions, and paraphilias. *Journal of Clinical Psychiatry, 53*, 267–271.

Stein, J. A., Golding, J. M., Siegel, J. M., Burnam, M. A., & Sorenson, S. B. (1988). Long-term psychological sequelae of child sexual abuse. In G. E. Wyatt & G. J. Powell (Eds.), *Lasting effects of child sexual abuse* (pp. 135–154). Newbury Park, CA: Sage.

Steinem, G. (1980). Erotica and pornography: A clear and present difference. In L. Lederer & A. Rich (Eds.), *Take back the night: Women on pornography* (pp. 35–39). New York: Morrow.

Sterkmans, P., & Geerts, F. (1966). Is benperidol (RF 504) the specific drug for the treatment of successive and disinhibited sexual behavior? *Acta Neurologica et Psychiatrica Belgica, 66*, 1030–1040.

Stermac, L. E., & Quinsey, V. L. (1986). Social competence among rapists. *Behavioral Assessment, 8*, 171–185.

Stermac, L. E., Segal, Z. V., & Gillis, R. (1990). Social and cultural factors in sexual assault. In W. L. Marshall, D. R. Laws, & H. E. Barbaree (Eds.), *Handbook of sexual assault: Issues, theories, and treatment of the offender* (pp. 143–159). New York: Plenum Press.

Stewart, B. D., Hughes, C., Frank, E., Anderson, B., Kendall, K., & West, D. (1987). The aftermath of rape: Profiles of immediate and delayed treatment seekers. *Journal of Nervous and Mental Disease, 175*, 90–94.

Stille, R. G., Malamuth, N., & Schallow, J. R. (1987, August). *Prediction of rape proclivity by rape myth attitudes, and hostility towards women.* Paper presented at the annual meeting of the American Psychological Association, New York.

Stoleru, S., Gregoire, M.-C., Gerard, D., Decety, J., Lafarge, E., Cinotti, L., Lavenne, F., Le Bars, D., Vernet-Maury, E., Rada, H., Collet, C., Mazoyer, B., Forest, M. G., Magnin, F., Spira, A., & Comar, D. (1999). Neuroanatomical correlates of visually evoked sexual arousal in human males. *Archives of Sexual Behavior, 28*, 1–21.

Stone, M. H. (1990). Incest in the borderline patient. In R. P. Kluft (Ed.), *Incest-related syndromes in adult psychopathology* (pp. 183–204). Washington, DC: American Psychiatric Press.

Struckman-Johnson, C. (1988). Forced sex on dates: It happens to men, too. *Journal of Sex Research, 24*, 234–241.

Sturup, G. K. (1968). Treatment of sexual offenders in Herstedvester, Denmark: The rapists. *Acta Psychiatrica Scandinavica,* Suppl. 204, 44.

Summit, R. C. (1983). The Child Sexual Abuse Accommodation Syndrome. *Child Abuse and Neglect, 7*, 177–193.

Summit, R. C., & Kryso, J. (1978). Sexual abuse of children: A clinical spectrum. *American Journal of Orthopsychiatry, 48*, 237–251.

Sun, M. (1984). Panel says Depo-Provera not proved safe. *Science, 226*, 950–951.

Sutherland, E. H. (1950a). The diffusion of sexual psychopath laws. *American Journal of Sociology, 56*, 142–148.

Sutherland, E. H. (1950b). The sexual psychopath laws. *Journal of Criminal Law and Criminology, 40*, 543–554.

Swanson, D. W. (1971). Who violates children sexually? *Medical Aspects of Human Sexuality, 5*, 184–197.

Swets, J. A. (1992). The science of choosing the right decision threshold in high-stakes diagnostics. *American Psychologist, 47*, 522–532.

Swett, C., & Halpert, M. (1993). Reported history of physical and sexual abuse in relation to dissociation and other symptomatology in women psychiatric inpatients. *Journal of Interpersonal Violence, 8*, 545–555.

Symmers, W. St. C. (1968). Carcinoma of the breast in trans-sexual individuals after surgical and hormonal interference with primary and secondary sex characteristics. *British Medical Journal, 2*, 83–85.

Tanenbaum, S. G. (1973). Toward a less benevolent despotism: The case for abolition of California's MDSO laws. *Santa Clara Lawyer, 13*, 579–612.

Taylor, S. E., & Thompson, S. C. (1982). Stalking the elusive "vividness" effect. *Psychological Review, 89*, 155–181.

Tennent, T. G., Bancroft, J., & Cass, J. (1974). The control of deviant sexual behaviour by drugs: A double-blind controlled study of benperidol, chlorpromazine and placebo. *British Medical Journal, 2*, 261–271.

Terr, L. C. (1988). What happens to early memories to trauma? A study of twenty children under age five at the time of documented traumatic events. *Journal of the American Academy of Child and Adolescent Psychiatry, 27*, 96–104.

Terr, L. C. (1991). Childhood traumas: An outline and overview. *American Journal of Psychiatry, 148*, 10–20.

Terr, L. C. (1994). *Unchained memories: True stories of traumatic memories lost and found.* New York: Harper Collins.

Teten, H., & Turvey, B. (1998). A brief history of criminal profiling. *Knowledge Solutions Library.* Electronic Publication, URL:http://www.corpus-delicti.com/demo/.

Thorne, F. C. (1966). The sex inventory. *Journal of Clinical Psychology, 22*, 367–374.

Thornton, D. (1987). Treatment effects on recidivism: A reappraisal of the "nothing works" doctrine. In B. J. McGurk, D. M. Thornton, & M. Williams (Eds.), *Applying psychology to imprisonment* (pp. 181–189). London: Her Majesty's Stationery Office.

Tingle, D., Barnard, G. W., Robbins, L., Newman, G., & Hutchinson, D. (1986). Childhood and adolescent characteristics of pedophiles and rapists. *International Journal of Law and Psychiatry, 9*, 103–116.

Toch, H. (1970). The care and feeding of typologies and labels. *Federal Probation, 36,* 15–19.

Tracy, F., Donnelly, H., Morgenbesser, L., & MacDonald, D. (1983). Program evaluation: Recidivism research involving sex offenders. In J. G. Greer & I. R. Stuart (Eds.), *The sexual aggressor* (pp. 198–213). New York: Van Nostrand–Reinhold.

Travin, S., Cullen, K., & Melella, J. T. (1988). The use and abuse of erection measurements: A forensic perspective. *Bulletin of the American Academy of Psychiatry and the Law, 16,* 235–250.

Tribe, L. H. (1971, April). Trial by mathematics: Precision and ritual in the legal process. *Harvard Law Review, 84,* 1329–1393.

Trudell, B., & Whatley, M. H. (1988). School sexual abuse prevention: Unintended consequences and dilemmas. *Child Abuse and Neglect, 12,* 103–113.

Truesdell, D. L., McNeil, J. S., & Deschner, J. (1986). The incidence of wife abuse in incestuous families. *Social Work,* March–April, 138–140.

Turvey, B. (1998). The role of criminal profiling in the development of trial strategy. *Forensic Medicine Sourcebook.* Omnigraphics.

Turvey, B. (1999). *Criminal profiling: An introduction to behavior evidence analysis.* London: Academic Press.

Ullman, S. E., & Knight, R. A. (1995). Women's resistance strategies to different rapist types. *Criminal Justice and Behavior, 22,* 263–283.

Usdin, G. L. (1967). Broader aspects of dangerousnes. In J. R. Rappaport (Ed.), *The clinical evaluation of the dangerousness of the mentally ill* (pp. 43–47). Springfield, IL: Charles C. Thomas.

Valzelli, L. (1981). *Psychobiology of aggression and violence.* New York: Raven Press.

van der Kolk, B. A. (Ed.). (1987). *Psychological trauma.* Washington, DC: American Psychiatric Press.

van der Kolk, B. A. (1993). *Biological considerations about emotions, trauma, memory, and the brain.* Unpublished manuscript.

van der Kolk, B. A. (1994). The body keeps score: Memory and evolving psychobiology of posttraumatic stress. *Harvard Review of Psychiatry, 1*(5), 253–265.

van der Kolk, B. A., & Fisler, R. A. (1993). The biologic basis of posttraumatic stress. *Primary Care Clinics of North America, 20,* 417–432.

van der Kolk, B. A., & Fisler, R. A. (1995). Dissociation and the fragmentary nature of traumatic memories: Overview and exploratory study. *Journal of Traumatic Stress, 8,* 505–525.

van der Kolk, B. A., & Greenberg, M. S. (1987). The psychobiology of the trauma response: Hyperarousal, constriction, and addiction to traumatic reexposure. In B. A. van der Kolk (Ed.), *Psychological trauma* (pp. 63–87). Washington, DC: American Psychiatric Press.

van der Kolk, B. A., & Saporta, J. (1991). The biological response to psychic trauma: Mechanisms and treatment of intrusion and numbing. *Anxiety Research, 4,* 199–212.

Venables, P. H. (1974). The recovery limb of skin conductance response in 'high risk' research. In S. A. Mednick, F. Schulsinger, J. Higgins, & B. Bell (Eds.), *Genetics, environment and psychopathology.* Amsterdam: North-Holland.

Vuocolo, A. B. (1969). *The repetitive sex offender.* Roselle, NJ: Quality Printing.

Waigant, A., Wallace, D. L., Phelps, L., & Miller, D. A. (1990). The impact of sexual assault on physical health status. *Journal of Traumatic Stress, 3,* 93–102.

Walker, L. E. (1991). Posttraumatic stress disorder in women: Diagnosis and treatment of battered woman syndrome. *Psychotherapy, 28,* 21–29.

Walker, L. E. (1992). Battered woman syndrome and self-defense. *Notre Dame Journal of Law, Ethics, and Public Policy, 6,* 321–334.

Walsh, E. R., & Cohen, F. (1998). *Sex offender registration and community notification.* Kingston, NJ: Civic Research Institute.

Walsh, E. R., & Flaherty, B. M. (1999a). Civil commitment of sexually violent predators. In B. K. Schwartz (Ed.), *The sex offender: Theoretical advances, treating special populations and legal developments* (pp. 34-1–34-12). Kingston, NJ: Civic Research Institute.

Walsh, E. R., & Flaherty, B. M. (1999b). Update on Megan's Law. In B. K. Schwartz (Ed.), *The sex offender: Theoretical advances, treating special populations and legal developments* (pp. 35-1–35-9). Kingston, NJ: Civic Research Institute.

Walsh, E. R., & Flaherty, B. M. (1999c). Non-*Hendricks*-related constitutional challenges to sexually violent predator statutes. In B. K. Schwartz (Ed.), *The sex offender: Theoretical advances, treating special populations and legal developments* (pp. 36-1–36-8). Kingston, NJ: Civic Research Institute.

Ward, I. L. (1984). The prenatal stress syndrome: Current status. *Psychoneuroendocrinology, 9,* 3–11.

Warr, M. (1985). Fear of rape among urban women. *Social Problems, 32,* 238–250.

Washington State Institute for Public Policy. (1998, August). *Sex offenses in Washington State: 1998 update* (Document No. 98-08-1101). Olympia, WA: WSIPP.

Wason, P. C. (1960). On the failure to eliminate hypotheses in a conceptual task. *Quarterly Journal of Experimental Psychology, 12,* 129–140.

Wason, P., & Johnson-Laird, P. N. (1972). *Psychology of reasoning: Structure and Content.* Cambridge, MA: Harvard University Press.

Webster, C. D., Douglas, K. S., Eaves, D., & Hart, S. D. (1997). *HCR-20. Assessing risk for violence. Version 2.* Vancouver, BC: Mental Health, Law, and Policy Institute and Simon Fraser University.

Webster, C. D., Eaves, D., Douglas, K. S., & Wintrup, A. (1995). *The HCR-20 scheme: The assessment of dangerousness and risk.* Vancouver: Simon Fraser University and British Columbia Forensic Psychiatric Services Commission.

Webster, C.D., Harris, G. T., Rice, M. E., Cormier, C., & Quinsey, V. L. (1994). *The violence prediction scheme: Assessing dangerousness in high risk men.* Toronto: University of Toronto Centre of Criminology.

Weinberg, S. (1955). *Incest behavior.* New York: Citadel Press.

Weiner, B. A. (1985). Legal issues raised in treating sex offenders. *Behavioral Sciences and the Law, 3,* 325–340.

Weiner, I. (1962). Father–daughter incest. *Psychiatric Quarterly, 36,* 607–632.

West, D. J. (1981). Adult sexual interest in children: Implications for social control. In M. Cook & K. Howells (Eds.), *Adult sexual interest in children* (pp. 251–270). New York: Academic Press.

Westen, D., Ludolph, P., Misle, B., Ruffins, S., & Block, J. (1990). Physical and sexual abuse in adolescent girls with borderline personality disorder. *American Journal of Orthopsychiatry, 60,* 55–66.

Whalen, R. E. (1984). Multiple actions of steroids and their antagonists. *Archives of Sexual Behavior, 13,* 497.

Whitcomb, D. (1998). Children and the Internet. *The APSAC Advisor, 11*(4), 1.

Whitman, W. P., & Quinsey, V. L. (1981). Heterosocial skill training for institutionalized rapists and child molesters. *Canadian Journal of Behavioral Science, 13,* 105–114.

Whittaker, L. H. (1959). Oestrogens and psychosexual disorders. *Medical Journal of Australia, 2,* 547–549.

Widom, C. S. (1989). The cycle of violence. *Science, 244,* 160–166.

Widom, C. S., & Ames, A. (1994). Criminal consequences of childhood sexual victimization. *Child Abuse and Neglect, 18,* 303–318.

Williams, J. E., & Holmes, K. A. (1981). *The second assault: Rape and public attitudes.* Westport, CT: Greenwood Press.

Williams, L. M. (1994). Recall of childhood trauma: A prospective study of women's memories of child sexual abuse. *Journal of Consulting and Clinical Psychology, 62,* 1167–1176.

Williams, L. M., & Finkelhor, D. (1990). The characteristics of incestuous fathers: A review of recent studies. In W. L. Marshall, D. R. Laws, & H. E. Barbaree (Eds.), *The handbook of sexual assault: Issues, theories, and treatment of the offender* (pp. 231–255). New York: Plenum Press.

Williams, S. M. (1995). Sex offender assessment guidelines. In T. A. Leis, L. L. Motiuk, & J. R. P. Ogloff (Eds.), *Forensic psychology: Policy and practice in corrections* (pp. 122–131). Ottawa: Correctional Service of Canada.

Winfield, I., George, L. K., Swartz, M., & Blazer, D. G. (1990). Sexual assault and psychiatric disorders among a community sample of women. *American Journal of Psychiatry, 147,* 335–341.

Winick, B. J. (1998). Sex offender law in the 1990's: A therapeutic jurisprudence analysis. *Psychology, Public Policy, and Law, 4,* 505–570.

Wisconsin State Department of Public Welfare. (1965). *Wisconsin's first eleven years of experience with its Sex Crimes Law* (Statistical Bulletin #C 46). Bureau of Research, State Department of Public Welfare.

Witt, P. H., DelRusso, J., Oppenheim, J., & Ferguson, G. (1996, Fall). Sex offender risk assessment and the law. *Journal of Psychiatry and Law,* 343–377.

Wolfe, D. A., Sas, L., & Wekerle, C. (1994). Factors associated with the development of posttraumatic stress disorder among child victims of sexual abuse. *Child Abuse and Neglect, 18,* 37–50.

Wolfgang, M. E. (1988). The medical model versus the just deserts model. *Bulletin of the American Academy of Psychiatry and the Law, 16,* 111–121.

Wolfgang, M. E., & Ferracuti, F. (1967). *The subculture of violence.* London: Tavistock.

Wolfgang, M., Figlio, R. M., & Sellin, T. (1972). *Delinquency in a birth cohort.* Chicago: University of Chicago Press.

Wood, P. L. (1975). The victim in a forcible rape case: A feminist view. In L. G. Schultz (Ed.), *Rape victimology* (pp. 194–217). Springfield, IL: Charles C. Thomas.

Working Group, Sex Offender Treatment Review. (1989). *The management and treatment of sex offenders.* Ottawa: Solicitor General.

Wyatt, G. E. (1992). The sociocultural context of African American and white American women's rape. *Journal of Social Issues, 48,* 77–91.

Yalom, J. D., Green R., & Fisk, N. (1973). Prenatal exposure to female hormones: Effect on psychosexual development in boys. *Archives of General Psychiatry, 28,* 554–561.

Yates, A. (1982). Children eroticized by incest. *American Journal of Psychiatry, 139,* 482–485.

Zillman, D. (1971). Excitation transfer in communication mediated aggressive behavior. *Journal of Experimental Social Psychology, 1,* 419–434.

Index

329